# THE HISTORY
# OF THE ROMANIAN
# PEOPLE

*Coordinating Committee*

**A. OȚETEA**
**I. POPESCU-PUȚURI**
**I. NESTOR**
**M. BERZA**
**V. MACIU**

# THE HISTORY
# OF THE ROMANIAN PEOPLE

*Edited by*

**ANDREI OȚETEA**

*Member of the Academy
of the Socialist Republic of Romania*

**TWAYNE PUBLISHERS, INC.,**
*New York*

**ISTORIA POPORULUI ROMÂN**
published by Editura Ştiinţifică,
Bucharest — Romania, in 1970

TRANSLATED BY EUGENIA FARCA

**ISBN O-8057-5920-4**

THE NATIONAL HISTORIES SERIES
**Sherman D. Spector, General Editor**
Volume 1
**The History of the Romanian People**

# Contents

## A NOTE TO THE READER

A practice common to historians in socialist states is to present divisions of history to reflect Marxist-Leninist historical interpretations. Thus the Romanian historians who produced this volume consider "Ancient History" to treat the era from prehistory to about the tenth century A.D. Medieval History (or "The Middle Ages") encompasses the era from the tenth to the nineteenth centuries because Marxists consider the birth of Modern History to coincide with anti-feudal revolutions (such as herein described as the basis of Tudor Vladimirescu's revolt against the feudal landlords in 1821). And Contemporary History denotes the era since the end of World War I (1918 to the present).

# Foreword

by

SHERMAN DAVID SPECTOR *

AS editor of the National Histories Series, of which this book is the first volume, I am pleased to recommend this work to its American readers. The intent of the Series is to present the historical evolution of a nation as that nation's historians see it. In this way, indigenous historians can present contemporary interpretations of their national history, and American readers may gain new perspectives and insights not generally available in the West. The original work — *Istoria Poporului Român* — was produced for a Romanian audience, and its success has led to its appearance in an English-language translation. An Italian-language edition has also appeared. Now Americans interested in the origins and evolution of the Romanian people will have the privilege of examining the long struggle for national existence, freedom, and social progress which this hardy nation has experienced over the past millennia. Among other themes of this work are the constructing of the national state before and after the First World War, Romania's role in the Second World War and her contribution to the defeat of Nazi Germany, the immense postwar economic and social changes, and the popular urge for peace and friendship with all nations.

This history is especially commended to those dispassionate and objective American readers who wish to acquire an appreciation of the struggles Romanians have endured since they were swept up into the whirlwind of international politics. This book, whether one agrees with its historical interpretations, is testimony to the admirable endurance of the Romanian people.

* Professor of History, Russell Sage College, Troy, New York, Author of *Rumania at the Paris Peace Conference* (Twayne, 1962), and *A History of the Balkan Peoples* (with the late René Ristelhueber) (Twayne, 1972); Fulbright-Hays research professor at University of Bucharest in 1970.

# Introduction

## The Country and the People

AT the time of their greatest expansion to the west and east, the Dacians, the remote ancestors of the Romanians, were dispersed from the mountain areas of present-day Austria and Bohemia to the steppes north of the Black Sea. Their land was hemmed in by two steppes — the Pannonian plain and the plain north of the Black Sea — and its center was in the mountain-ringed citadel of Transylvania. From prehistory to our day, whenever the people of the Carpathians formed a state of their own and made it an organized body, it had Transylvania, of a nearly circular shape, as its nucleus. The Romanian nation itself spread out within the same limits, as can be seen from the territories occupied by these Roman descendants today.

But the symmetrical nature of the territory is caused by a second feature aside from the shape of the Carpathians, which even the ancients compared to a crown: all the streams springing from them ultimately flow into the Danube, even though they at first radiate from the mountain core. Because of this, the Carpathian basin of the Danube, which before reaching Romania has few tributaries on its left bank — and those that it has are at great distances from one another — henceforth molds itself upon the rounded shape of the Transylvanian Carpathians. Consequently, one can see at a glance that the Carpathians, the Danube, and the Black Sea are the geographical coordinates of Romanian territory. It should be stressed, however, that the unitary aspect of mountain and river scenery is not a consequence of a monotonous identity of physical features, but the result of a great variety of complementary geographical elements. Let us examine here the more important of these elements.

To begin with, the ring of mountains in the center of Romania encloses a tableland of no great height (1,200-1,500 ft.) which was formerly a seabed carved out by streams and turned into hills and dales, with a plain to the northeast, and a number of well-sheltered lowlands all around. Mountains seldom exceeding 6,000 ft. border the tableland. Throughout the Carpathians, including the spurs projecting into Maramureş and Bucovina, and those of Oltenia and Banat, there are only twenty peaks exceeding this height, and only five of these rise a little above 7,500 ft. (Moldoveanul, the highest, is 8,347 ft.). Most of these mountains do not form ramparts of sheer rock; their summits are broad, with gentle slopes and wide expanses of flat land, which account for the specific Carpathian toponymy, for a considerable number of terms, such as: Muntele Şes (Plain Mountain), Neteda (The Smooth), Masa (The Table), Podurile (The Bridges), Poiana (The Glade). On these summits it becomes quite warm in summer — hence such names as Şesul Cald (The Warm Plain), Vărateca (The Summery) — and this is the reason why the Carpathians have no glaciers or eternal snows like the Alps but boast a much richer flora than the latter mountains and form one of the most extensive pastoral areas in Europe. Permanent settlements dot the valleys to heights above 3,600 ft. and on the plateaus there are pastoral settlements at 4,800 ft., for which reason the uninhabited heights in the Carpathians account for a little less than 20 percent of the total mountain area. As V. Mihăilescu has said, "The Carpathian highlands are more widely inhabited than is currently believed and affirmed".

The main mountain ring is mostly surrounded by a second one, the Carpathian foothills, separated from the central massif by a succession of lowlands which in many instances look like smooth plains. Further down again are the hills, which in certain areas rise up stepwise and form wide plateaus.

At the foot of the hills are the plains, the greatest of which is the Romanian plain, whose center, the Bărăgan, was built up from detritus of rocks on the bed of a sea. As the bed was filled, a flat plain emerged, containing salt lakes that looked like so many white patches. Judging from its flora and fauna, this shadeless plain is obviously an extension of the great eastern steppe.

Between the Danube and the Black Sea — Romania's sea front — there is a gently rolling expanse which in the north rises to the bare crests of the Măcin, a mountain much older than the Carpathians and eroded very nearly down to its base. To the east it slopes down to the Black Sea, with lagoons all along the coast; these were formerly bays used in the past by Greek sailors, but now choked with alluvium. This coast is truly a lagoon coast and, in geography, it has served as a type in the classification of all similar ones. In the course of time the map of this part of the country, like that of the Danube Delta, has changed incessantly.

The Danube meadowland has an untypical aspect. From the Iron Gates onwards, the Danube has mostly a high, precipitous right-hand bank, while its left bank is low, with ponds and backwaters, widespread willow woods, grasslands, and fields flooded regularly every year. This area is commonly called Balta (Backwaters), and this is the name given in the past (when the river meadow, which is now being drained, was wider) to all the riverside districts of the counties along the Danube in Muntenia.

Beyond Călăraşi, the Danube branches out twice, forming two "internal deltas" between the Ialomiţa and Brăila backwaters, subsequently to divide into three main arms and form the delta proper.

Romania is crossed by the 43rd parallel and the 25th meridian, the latter dividing her territory in two nearly equal parts. The whole area is 91,738 square miles. The country is located in the temperate zone, the climate inclining towards the continental while, with reference to Europe, the country lies in an area of transition between the eastern and the southern climes. In Moldavia, in the Romanian Plain, and in northern Dobrudja, the winters are severe and droughts as well as some of the flora and fauna have been influenced by the proximity of the great Podolian steppes. On the other hand, the milder climate of Oltenia, Banat and southern Dobrudja is due to the remote influence of the Adriatic and the Mediterranean. However, the temperature and rainfall, as also the flora and fauna, show the prevailing influence of the Central European climate.

Naturally, the manland relationship within the territory enclosed by the Carpathians and the Danube has not been the same everywhere and at all times. We refer to the real influence of the physical environment upon man's life and not to so-called "geographical determinism" — a one-sided theory which, we should stress, Romanian geographers (Mehedinţi, Vîlsan) opposed in the early years of this century.

The main environmental conditions that have influenced the early history of this country have been its relative location in Europe, the manner in which the land was formed, and the extensive forests that have covered it all the time.

During a very long period, from the time of the Scythians to the Tartar invasion of the thirteenth century, the Carpathians and the Lower Danube were an obstacle to the nomads pushing westward from Central Asia. The Age of the Great Migrations of populations and of periodic invasions with the object of plunder lasted longer here than in any other part of Europe. West of the Carpathians there was more security, states were built up earlier, and civilization assumed more advanced and more lasting forms. But despite many calamities down through the ages, the territory between the Carpathians and the Danube offered its inhabitants conditions which enabled them to stand their ground and preserve their entity throughout the territory now inhabited by the Romanians.

The importance of the mountains in the life of the Romanian people can be indicated in a number of ways. The Dacians were known to the Romans as a mountain people *(Dacii inhaerent montibus)* and it was natural that their offspring should continue to live primarily in that geographical environment. Those who in the past have studied the life of the Romanian people during the Middle Ages have never doubted that the natives found safety in the mountains during the Age of the Great Migrations, for they had before them examples of the age in which they lived themselves of people withdrawing to the mountains in wartime. Such withdrawals, which were actually an old military strategy — practiced, for example, by Stephen the Great — were measures taken by the administration itself. A foreign traveler, Paul of Aleppo, who himself went into hiding in the mountains in fear of the Turks and the Tartars at the time of Prince Constantin Şerban, records that the Prince sent out horsemen "to let all the country know that the people should leave their homes and withdraw to the mountains". The flight to the Carpathians was so common a thing that the same traveler points out as a specific feature that the mountaineers around Cîmpulung, Argeş, and Cozia had found an important source of income in acting as carters under certain circumstances. "When there is a rumor that the signal for flight has been given, the latter [carters] immediately come to the capital city, load the people's belongings on to wagons and conceal them in safe places known to them alone. These carters are all well known to the tradespeople". It is significant to note that in Romanian the basic mountain terms are of Latin origin: *munte* (mountain), *plai* (flat land), *culme* (summit), *muchie* (ledge), *piatră* (stone), *coastă* (mountainside), *față* (front), *dos* (back), *vale* (valley), *cheie* (gorge) etc. And we will also find that the lowlands within the Carpathian range and around them have been among the areas with the densest population during the periods known to us through historical records. It is impossible, therefore, to believe that they were unpopulated even in the most remote periods. It is within those old nuclei of the Romanians' life, whose names (Maramureș, Făgăraș, Hațeg, Ouaș, Vrancea, Cîmpulung) are mentioned in the records of early times, that the oldest villages are to be found in our day, their inhabitants all displaying a strong feeling of regional entity, which is also reflected in the folklore. When a Făgăraș man crosses the river Olt to go north, he "sets foot in Transylvania". In Vrancea an old custom required that a local man's bride "should not have drunk water from the Milcov river", by which is meant that she should be a native of Vrancea, while a man of Ouaș will proudly say: "Were you to lavish oats on me / I would still keep to my native Ouaș / Were you to lavish rye on me / Ouaș is still my country". This state of mind is to be accounted for by the consciousness of an old autonomy, by the remembrance of a form of para-state organization of their own, to which historical records testify but which is doubtlessly much older than the records. Actually, the first political formations which preceded the feudal states are known to have cropped up in the Carpathian foothills. The name given to the inter- and sub-Carpathian lowlands is also significant. They are called "countries", which means organized territories; the word could not have been, as is sometimes supposed, a term used by feudal chancelleries. Had the latter supposition been true, we would not have found it circulating among the people with this meaning, as in the rhyme of the native of Ouaș quoted above. Both the word "country" and "mountain" occur in the name of the oldest of the free Romanian states, the Moldavians calling Wallachia "Muntenia" or "The Mountain Country". From this it may be inferred that this originally was a Carpathian state, as is shown by its successive capital cities and by the order in which the different parts of the state are named in the title assumed by Mircea the Old and in historical tradition itself.

But what drew the native population to the Carpathians was not only the need of safety from danger but also the economic value of the mountains, this being particularly true in the Middle Ages. For even if we do not lay stress on the two great sources of wealth, especially as far as the medieval world was concerned — gold and salt, which were not to be found in the neighboring countries — we should note that the sun-drenched tablelands of the Carpathians were often tilled up to heights of 3,000 ft. And we should also stress another fact which throws light on what has already been said concerning the lowlands: on the plains closed in by the heights, and in the rivermeadows of the lowlands, farming has been practiced from ancient times, often with some primitive irrigation, as in a number of villages in the Oltenian lowlands; also, the vine and fruit trees have also grown there continuously. The inhabitants of these districts were essentially tillers of the soil and stock breeders, raising especially cattle, goats, and pigs on the village commons. Peasants with fixed abodes, they had always led a life which had been quite different from that of the shepherds who moved from their mountain homes together with their flocks. These were also mountain people, but they accounted for a very small part of the Romanian villagers, inhabiting comparatively few villages and specializing in stock-breeding.

When the first principalities (Voievodate) — whose territories at the beginning spread over both sides of the Carpathians, an example in point being Litovoi's Principality set up in 1247 — began to expand, they first extended over the amphitheater of heights all around, which the people never thought of as different from the mountains; the people living in the hills are called *munteni* (mountain people) by the villagers of Muntenia's plain to this day. The population of the hills, already dense in that period, was thus incorporated into the mountain states that were taking shape. As the political organization of the Romanians south and east of the Carpathians occurred after the penetration of foreign feudal rule in the center of the Romanian territory, several distinct Romanian states came into being.

Next to the mountains, a term which we use in the comprehensive way indicated above, forests played an important role in the life of the Romanian people during the Middle Ages. In the Carpathians and in the hills, the forests, together with the rugged configuration of the territory, made it difficult for outsiders to penetrate. In the old forests (for which the word of Latin origin — *codru* — is used) the population cleared land for fields or enlarged the glades in which villages were huddled. The terms used for forest clearing in mountain and hill areas — *runc* (glade), *arșiță* (forest pasture), *curătură* (clearing), *secătură* (dry forest land) — show that it was essentially the work of the Romanians, for the terms are of Latin origin. On the other hand, this vast clearing of forests pursued from of old and reflected in toponymy is implicit proof that the population consisted of sedentary farmers.

But the forests spread beyond the hills, sometimes very far into the plains. South of the Carpathians they divided the plain in two, making a wide barrier in the Bucharest area and in what was formerly the Vlașca county. A dense forest crossed by small muddy streams that widened out into marshes was to be found here. The specific nature of this forest accounts for the word *pădure* in Romanian — a word derived from the Latin *padulem* (paludem) meaning marshes or backwaters. During the migration period the forest of the Romanian Plain could only be crossed on foot and was impenetrable for the foreigner who did not know the paths. Like the regular armies of a later date, the horsemen of the steppe were compelled to go round it, and this difficulty, which irked them so, is shown by the name the Turanians had for the western part of the forest: Teleorman — Mad Forest. For the natives, however, the forest, like the mountains, was the specific habitat, which is apparent also from the fact that the author of a western cosmography of the sixteenth century knew that the Romanians, descendants of the Romans, "lived in woods and mountains." Consequently, the most densely populated area in the lowlands was the plain between the Bărăgan and the steppe land in the Teleorman county.

The Danube meadow and Delta, like the Siret meadowland, were to a great extent similar to the marshy forest in
the Romanian Plain. The food resources available for men
and beasts and the shelter offered by the woods and thickets
of the backwaters account for the string of sizable villages
existing along the Danube, the uninterrupted life in those
parts being in striking contrast to the scattered and ephemeral
settlements of the steppe. The biggest village whose existence
is recorded in Muntenia in the sixteenth century, was on the
Danube: it is Prundu near the Greaca backwaters. Owing
to the river meadow the Romanians were in closer touch
with the Danube throughout their history than were the
peoples south of the river. On the high southern bank mostly
urban centers were to be found, and their purpose was in
the first place military. In the nearly five hundred years of
Turkish rule the garrisons that were stationed in those towns
kept the villagers away from the water. On our side of the
Danube, on the other hand, the meadow was populated by
farmers, shepherds who had come down from the Carpathians, beekeepers, and fishermen.

Compared with this area where the native population was
permanently settled, the open plain afforded living conditions
that were widely different. Closely bound up with the great
steppe that stretches from north of the Black Sea to the Pacific
Ocean, it was an area where the migratory populations from
Central Asia on their way to Europe passed through and
halted, while in the eighteenth and nineteenth centuries it
was the main arena of anti-Ottoman wars. Grigore Ureche's
observation that Romanian territory was "in the way of hardships" should be understood as referring primarily to this
area. This accounts for the enormous number of villages of
the Romanian Plain that have disappeared and also for the
toponymy of that area where such names as Pribegi (Wan-
derers), Băjenari (Exiles), and Goniți (Expelled), frequently
occur. Other names show that the people had gathered
together as a result of compulsive measures or of privileges:
Adunați (Come Together), Atîrnați (Subjected), Slobozia
(Freed). And yet these facts should not close our eyes to one
no less indubitable truth: that ever since ancient times there
had been an autochthonous population in that plain, as testi-
fied to by written sources and by archeology. This population

lived alongside a nomad population, as it did at the time of Darius's expedition, or alone, as in the days of Alexander the Great and of Lysimachus. Things must have been much the same in the Middle Ages for there is no other explanation possible for certain categories of toponyms to be found in the plain. To begin with, there is the name of Vlaşca, the Romanian forest belt, and the names of several villages, some of which have disappeared. The names had obviously been given to the Romanian districts and settlements by a population of another type living in the neighborhood — in this case, the Slavs. The name of Rumânaţi — the former name of the Romanaţi county — and of some villages in the county of Teleorman were fashioned in the same way and, as Nicolae Iorga remarks, are due to the Cumans. The same situation is reflected by an inverted historical process, when the Romanian population named settlements and places inhabited by strangers after the latter's ethnic names (Comani, Berindei, Tătari, etc.). On the other hand the names given by the Turkic populations of the tenth to the thirteenth centuries in their own language as, for instance, the streams ending in the suffix -*ui*, are also proof of the existence of a native element in those areas; for the names would have disappeared altogether if the Romanians had not accepted and preserved them. Most of those names were strictly local, being known only to the inhabitants of a few villages.

In Wallachia and Moldavia the plain was the main area in which the changes of the modern epoch took place. In this area of immense landed estates belonging to the boyars or the monasteries — an area where the social environment was widely different from that of the uplands, where most of the free villages were to be found — the economic processes through which the peasantry passed after 1829 unfolded with greater intensity. "The iron yoke" of compulsory service, the peasant uprisings, and the successive land distributions were mass phenomena of considerable significance. As a consequence, while the economy of the areas that were mostly populated by free peasants and had enjoyed a privileged situation in the past, stagnated largely through lack of arable land, the plain in less than a century changed greatly owing to the "agrarian revolution" and to the "demographic explosion" which enabled the population to increase many times over large areas.

Other developments, this time exterior ones, in the political and economic geography of the Balkan Peninsula and of Europe generally, brought about a change in the relative importance of certain components of the geographical structure of our territory from one period to the next. This becomes apparent when we consider the importance in the course of time of the Black Sea and of the Danube in the history of this part of the European Continent.

In the hazy dawn of antiquity, the Black Sea first appears as inhospitable to the Greek sailors, but from the eighth century B.C. it became an area of thriving navigation. It was the age when material goods and cultural influences reached Dacia through the Dobrudjan seacoast cities. Here, up to the fifteenth century A.D. sea trade thrived despite the crises caused by wars and invasions. By the close of the fourteenth century the two free Romanian States had their natural boundary along the Black Sea coast, and consequently Mircea the Old and Prince Roman called themselves rulers of the land down to the sea. When the Genoese were compelled to leave these waters, the Black Sea became a Turkish lake and the area went through a dark period. For several centuries the Sultans' war fleets alone sailed here, apart from the ships that supplied Constantinople with products acquired under a monopoly regime. The Black Sea was no longer an international waterway.

In many respects the destiny of the Danube was conditional upon that of the Black Sea. In ancient times the Danube was named Istros by the Greeks and Danubius by the Romans, this showing that there were actually two basins, each with a life of its own, with the Iron Gates dividing them. For the Greek sailors the Lower Danube provided a waterway in continuation of the sea. Little wonder, therefore, that the main Pontic city at the time — Histria — was named after the river. When the Romans reached our part of the Danube, they ruled it by means of a string of fortified towns along the steep bank of Moesia, and also by their fleet and the bridgeheads on the left bank, where the towns and territories were well organized and where Roman influence had been felt long before Dacia's conquest. The same bridgeheads preserved the influence of the Roman Empire north of the Danube after Emperor Aurelian withdrew from that area.

Under the Turkish rule there was no trade on the Danube with countries other than the Ottoman Empire, and consequently an economic recession was brought about. River traffic henceforth brought in no profits to Wallachia and Moldavia and when the Treaty of Adrianople changed the situation, the consequences were of the utmost importance for the Romanian principalities, bringing about new orientations in politics, economy, and culture. A free Danube brought us nearer to Western Europe which thenceforward spoke of Moldavia and Wallachia as the "Danubian Principalities". (This was the time when the most important of our periodicals was *The Danube Star*, which, incidentally, was also printed in French). The demand for Romanian wheat in the Continental markets and also the need to ensure the freedom of this axis of European trade, which could be jeopardized by any one great neighboring power, caused many measures of an international character relating to the modern Romanian State and "the Danube problem" to be taken. The Danube, it should be noted, was the first river in the world for which a commission was set up to watch over the freedom of its outlets to the sea. At the same time the Danube's new importance wrought many transformations in our economy during the period of its renascence.

Consequently, the Danube, the Black Sea, and the Carpathians are the three elements which, together, account for the original features and the unity of the territory on which the Romanian people was formed and developed.

*Part 1*

# ANCIENT HISTORY

# CHAPTER I

# From the Early Inhabitants to the Dacians

ROMANIA'S territory was already inhabited when, physically and spiritually, man was evolving from his animal condition, a phenomenon which occurred throughout the Pleistocene period of the Quaternary geological era. This period began some three million years ago and ended about ten thousand years ago. As regards climate, the Quaternary era witnessed repeated glaciations.

The period between man's appearance in the Carpatho-Danubian area and the beginning of Geto-Dacian political formations is the age when the primitive commune, the socio-economic formation of the longest duration, was formed and developed. The primitive commune was based on common ownership of means of production; as the process of social differentiation intensified, the principle of kinship was replaced by the territorial principle. The progress made by the forces of production, the invention and improvement of farming implements, the working of copper, bronze, and iron, among other factors, induced changes in the social pattern so that the first antagonistic classes in history made their appearance at the close of this period.

## 1. Early Inhabitants. The Stone Age

RECENT finds on Romanian territory and around it show that the Carpatho-Danubian area was long ago integrated in the wide geographical area over which the early stages of the anthropogenic process unfolded.

Primitive chipped stone tools discovered in the lower reaches of the river Olt, for example, in the valley of the river Dîrjov, a left-bank tributary, and at Bugiuleşti on the right bank of the Olt, strongly favor the assumption that early *homo erectus*, who represents the second stage of anthropogenesis, lived also in this country in the course of his peregrinations.

A denser and more permanent population of the Carpatho-Danubian area and of the surrounding territory is found after the next "leap" of anthropogenesis which turned *homo erectus* into the more developed type of man, the Neanderthal type. The cranial capacity inherited from Pithecanthropus develops and Neanderthal man makes fire artificially. Now a tested hunter and food gatherer, with a "kit" of chipped stone tools restricted as to types, but of great efficiency, because they were more skilfully chipped and more intelligently handled; discoverer, as it seems, of the wooden spear (and there are some who think that even the stonehead spear was discovered at the time); in a position to bring down by chase or attack the big animals that roamed the tundras and the steppes and to hunt game in the mountain heights, Neanderthal man settled on this territory, dwelling in caves (for example, at Ohaba-Ponor in Transylvania, Baia de Fier in Oltenia, Cheia and La Adam in Dobrudja) as well as in the open air (for example, at La Izvor, Ripiceni village, on the river Prut). Over most of Romania's territory we find traces of his activities at the beginning of the last glaciation (conventional date: ca. 70,000). Neanderthal men consequently constitutes the first denser human population in Romania.

The presence of so-called *homo sapiens fossilis* (fossil intelligent man) some 35-40,000 years ago is recorded on the European continent. This is the last stage of the long process of man's emergence from his animal condition. From that stage onwards man is fully evolved and will no longer react to the stress and the pressures of nature and of his own society by important transformations of his physical structure, but only by cultural adaptation.

Romania's territory was intermittently traversed and inhabited by such fully evolved men in various stages of cultural development. They were now organized in maternal clans founded on kinship, the first form of crystallized society.

Having reached a high technical level in the working of stone tools by flaking, and of bone, horn, and ivory tools by cutting and polishing, *homo sapiens fossilis* attained an advanced stage of the still primitive hunter and food gatherer's economy. The skull found in the Cioclovina cave in Transylvania is a reliable testimony to the existence of fully evolved man on Romania's territory.

The essential differentiation wrought at the time is the division of mankind over wide geographical areas into three great fundamental races (white, yellow, and black). It should be recalled that Romanian territory has been integrated in the Eurasian area of the Europoid (white or leucodermous) race.

The end of the last glacial (Würm) subcycle is the beginning of the present-day geological period (the Holocene). Seriously affected by the effects of glaciation owing to its northern position, Europe underwent profound transformations in its climate, its physical and geographical aspect, its fauna and flora. In this period, man, now fully evolved and having to live through conditions which made great demands on his inventiveness and powers of adaptation, changed from a creature that took his food from nature's reserves directly (by hunting or food gathering) into a quasi-creator of his food sources, by growing plants and raising the animals he had tamed. Archeologically, he passed from the Paleolithic stage (the Old Stone Age) to the Neolithic (the New Stone Age).

It is questionable whether there has been on Romania's territory at least a partial organic change-over from the old way of life (of the Paleolithic food gatherers and hunters) to the Neolithic producers, or whether this was an area of historical lag in the Paleolithic forms of life. In the Mesolithic period the use of bow and arrow as a main hunting weapon came into general use on Romanian territory too. Important progress was made when the handle axe began to be used, for these tools brought about a revolution in the work and the way of life of the ancient society established on this territory.

The New Stone Age (the Neolithic) on Romanian territory, as elsewhere, was an age when these places were densely and permanently populated, for this was now possible owing to the new forms of a complex productive economy (the growing of plants and the breeding of domesticated animals) which increasingly favored the sedentary way of life. In the fourth millennium B.C. Romania and the surrounding regions seem to have become the homeland of Neolithic tribes which were to remain at this stage until the second millennium B.C.

During that period the early primitive plant growers and animal raisers who inhabited these places developed a material and spiritual culture which was among the most advanced on the continent of Europe. The first flow of Neolithic "settlers" in the area between the Tisa and the eastern Bug reached here from the south by crossing present-day Serbia and Bulgaria. They brought with them a fairly advanced Neolithic culture (named the Criş culture on our territory), with a comparatively well developed pottery, including painted ware characteristic of the evolution of the whole Neolithic period in Romania and, at the same time, proof of its high level. Against this background, the Mediterranean racial type (as a sub-branch of the great Europoid race) prevails in this part of Europe and has preserved its predominance over Romanian territory to this day.

The movement and mixing of tribes and the contacts between cultures continued in the Neolithic period, though over more restricted geographical areas and with more limited effects. On Romania's territory we further find that populations and cultural elements continued to intrude from the south (the Balkan Peninsula) from where cultural innovations unceasingly penetrated, and also from the northwest, with Europe's continental core exerting pressure.

The mixture of tribes and cultures brought about the development of a widespread and mature Neolithic culture on Romanian soil under the continued southern cultural influences that reached this territory through the Danube plain. Neolithic cultures are characteristic of these areas. They are all distinguished through the high level of the technique of painting on burnt-clay vases. In our specialized literature, these cultures are known as Boian-Gumelniţa in the Danube plain and in Dobrudja, Cucuteni-Ariuşd in Moldavia and eastern Transylvania, and Turdaş-Petreşti in Oltenia, Banat, and western Transylvania. Fundamentally, they are closely related to one another, being regional versions of an original Neolithic stock, though they are different from those found in the neighboring regions, whether to the west and northwest of them (the Tisa-Middle Danube area in Slovakia and Moravia), or to the north (beyond the upper reaches of the Dniester), and to the east of them (beyond the Dnieper).

"Seaboard" Mediterranean currents, apparent for a time in Dobrudja (Hamangia culture) were soon assimilated by the Boian-Gumelniţa complex in Muntenia and northeast Bulgaria. Northwest Transylvania — actually the Someş Gates area where the tableland opens wide towards the Tisa plain — is connected in the course of history with the last-named region, as shown by the infiltration of the bearers of the late Tisa culture. This still more cogently indicates that neither the Carpathian ranges, whether western, southern, or eastern, nor the great gap of the Lower Danube constituted impassable frontiers, but, on the contrary, were avenues of life and culture which extended unhindered on both mountainsides and both banks.

The fundamental unity of the variegated aspects of the mature Neolithic culture within the framework of the Carpatho-Balkan regional block showed prolonged stability. The general level of culture then attained relied on the remarkable development of the two main branches of the economy — plant cultivation and stock breeding — as well as on advanced exploitation of other resources available in the territory, from among which the first metals to be worked played the most important role, as will be seen later. The gold nuggets of the gold-bearing deposits of Transylvania, like the gold dust in the sands of the streams, soon drew the attention of the Neolithic population who engaged in fairly remote intertribal exchanges right from the beginning.

Sheep, goats, cattle, and pigs were the animals mostly raised and over the widest areas, while as regards plants the primitive species of millet, wheat, and oats were soon superseded by species improved through cultivation and selection. More rational tilling of the high-quality arable land in these parts *(chernozem)* and more competent selection of the cultivated species account for the prosperity of the tribes that were bearers of the aforementioned Neolithic cultures. The data available on the intensive religious life of the population (idols, shrines, magic practices) show that it was almost exclusively centered on the fertility cult.

## 2. The Copper and Bronze Age

THE working of native copper was of great importance and yielded rich results; in the Late Neolithic period it assumed considerable proportions. Copper was generally the first metal to be used by ancient man, and not only for ornaments, like gold, but also as raw material for tools. In Transylvania, Oltenia, and partly in Dobrudja, there existed and still exist substantial copper ore deposits.

Close to the deposits there were in ancient times lumps of native copper. Owing to the comparatively wide use of native copper even for tools (awls, chisels, picks) the last period of the Carpatho-Danubian Neolithic period might be termed Eneolithic (the age of stone and copper). The idea of using copper and the technology applied for the purpose reached these parts again from the east, where this metal had long been known and used. "Exports" of native copper in the form of finished goods (primarily picks) can be traced far into central, northern, and eastern Europe. However, the metal resources of the Carpatho-Danubian area were to be fully turned to account only much later, when a more advanced technology making possible the use of copper ores (by reduction) on the one hand and the making of bronze (an alloy of copper and tin or other nonferrous metals) on the other hand, became widespread in these regions.

Bronze metallurgy was introduced during the period of transition from the third to the second millennium B.C., consequently around the year 2000. That moment was an important turning point in the history of Europe, for it involved not only the penetration and development in these parts of the first complex metallurgy (bronze metallurgy) but also a profound ethnic and especially linguistic transformation as a result of which the foundations were laid for the formation of the peoples speaking Indo-European languages. In the Carpatho-Balkan area these were the first stages in the formation of the Thracian tribes.

The events which occurred on the territory of present-day Romania at the end of the Neolithic period are among the most reliable indications in support of the view that, on the one hand, the Neolithic populations of these regions did not speak Indo-European languages (as certain theories still contend), and were consequently pre-Indo-European from this point of view, and, on the other hand, that "Indo-Europeanization", or adoption of Indo-European languages, occurred as a consequence of the infiltration of new peoples from the east, in the last resort from a vast Eurasian area that stretched from the Lower Volga across the Aralo-Caspian steppes to the Yenisei in southwest Siberia. According to the latest investigations, it would seem that these regions were "the primitive homeland" of the peoples speaking Indo-European languages and that it is from here that their westward expansion began around 2400—2300 B.C., as approximate but well-grounded calculations have established. They were groups of seminomadic herdsmen with a social structure and a material and spiritual culture that differed from those of the old Neolithic population into whose territories they penetrated. And their anthropological type was also different. The pastoral character of their economy, the patriarchal and stratified structure of their society, as reflected by certain particulars of rite and ritual, evidenced by their graves covered with earthen mounds (tumuli, barrows), with the corpses strewn with red ochre; the use of the domesticated horse and before long of the first four-wheeled vehicles borrowed from the Mesopotamian East (the wheels were of compact wood and spokeless); their warlike aggressiveness heightened by the use of the stone battle axe and of the dagger (made of stone or metal) — are all strikingly different from the way of life of the Neolithic population of the Carpathians and of the Lower Danube. It is at the end of the Neolithic period that the mound-covered graves of this foreign population appear, from the Dnieper to the Danube plain and subsequently as far as eastern Hungary; and such graves have also been found in Dobrudja and in northern Bulgaria.

However, the archeological observations now available prove that the old Neolithic population was not destroyed or totally expelled by the newcomers, but that there was coexistence and intermingling, so that the local substratum was linguistically assimilated, itself assimilating the newcomers' culture in course of time. The process undoubtedly lasted several centuries and was of a complex character, part of the settled Neolithic population being dislodged and mov-

ing with the migration of the mobile groups of herdsmen
over great distances, for considerable hordes of those herdsmen traversed the Carpatho-Danubian territory on their
way to the west, that is, towards Central Europe, and also,
and especially, southwards towards the Balkan Peninsula,
Greece and the Aegean Sea, and generally towards the warm-
er districts of the eastern Mediterranean. The latter groups
established liaison with the areas where the Cretan (Minoan)
civilization had flourished or where the impact of that civilization had spread (in Greece proper and the islands). It was
thus that a cultural "counter current" came into being, elements of a higher culture being transmitted from the more
evolved southern regions to the northern ones, where the
new ethnic, linguistic, and cultural synthesis took place.

Though we are unable to trace the important ethnic process under discussion in its most minute details at the present stage of investigation, it is not to be doubted that a
goodly part of the stationary Neolithic population was
absorbed in the course of the new synthesis and that important
groups of nomads remained here and became sedentary,
before long abandoning their pastoral way of life. The connections established with the advanced centers of population helped to spread bronze metallurgy and primitive,
wooden plough agriculture in the Carpatho-Danubian area,
this being achieved by means that were undoubtedly
varied but are difficult to specify at present. The new
groups of tribes being formed rose to a new stage from
the economic, social, and cultural standpoints when the period
of migration and of comparative turmoil terminated. The
specific features of the Bronze Age were an advanced technology based on bronze metallurgy, the use of the primitive
plough, widespread stock-breeding, and a better organized
structure of a comparatively differentiated society, within
which the tribal leaders, the groups of fighters, and the tribal
mass began to assume the form of developing classes.

At the end of the Neolithic period certain groups retain-
ing a pastoral character spread over wide areas in Oltenia,
Banat, and the Transylvanian plateau, as bearers of the Coţo-
feni culture. Gradually the unification process of the tribes
in the regions outside the Carpathians began to take shape,
so that Muntenia, Oltenia, and southeast Transylvania appeared

to be occupied by the great union of Glina III tribes; Moldavia and Dobrudja were occupied by a kindred union of tribes (Foltești); while on the Transylvanian plateau the group distinguished by their "dotted earthenware" was consolidated. They were all tribal unions, at times of a more marked pastoral character, at other times more agricultural. These unions were made up of various elements that had come into contact during the stage of great dislocations and were each, to a different extent and through various channels, affected by the southern cultural counter-current. Underlying it all were the traditions of the local Neolithic substratum, the ethnic and cultural contributions of the eastern nomads, and the abundant influence of southern cultures. Whatever came into being at that time outside the Carpatho-Balkan area — new syntheses generated by the same events — assumed a different aspect and encroached on this area only partially in the marginal regions. Consequently, it would appear that the regional Carpatho-Balkan bloc resumed its old individuality within the framework of the new world that was coming into being in Europe, its specific features causing it to stand apart from the surrounding regions and defining its proper Indo-European character. Subsequently, no other movement of populations was totally to dislodge the population now settled within this area. Therefore, considering that when the first scanty rays of historical records light up this area, the presence of Thracian tribes is revealed in these parts, we must conclude that during the period under study, around 2000 B.C., the homeland of the Thracians was built up here, and from them Daco-Getian tribes were later formed in the Carpatho-Balkan area.

The different stages of stabilization soon assumed crystallized forms, a number of powerful tribal unions with a high Bronze-Age culture gradually developing in the proto-Thracian area, starting from certain formative areas and relying on an advanced use of natural resources. These were kindred tribes which for a long time developed on the basis of a stable mutual balance. Thus, in the Muntenian plain and in northeast Bulgaria a group of a more marked pastoral character was formed — the *Tei* group — which temporarily penetrated into southeast Transylvania. On the Central Moldavian plateau as far as the Buzău range of the Carpathians, the Monteoru group was formed — a powerful group of farmers and herdsmen. North Moldavia was occupied by the Costişa kindred group while Oltenia sheltered the tribes of the Verbicioara culture, also accepting the offshoots from a "Danubian" group (Gîrla Mare) in the Danube area. Ultimately, the Transylvanian plateau was occupied by people of the Wittenberg culture, the Banat by the Periam-Pecica culture, while Crişana, together with the neighboring districts of northeast Hungary (down to the Tisa) and with eastern Slovakia, were inhabited by a union of tribes showing great power of expansion and characterized by the Otomani culture.

For about four centuries, from the seventeenth to the thirteenth centuries B.C., these tribal unions were constituted and consolidated, developing in conditions of comparative stability and peace by exploiting the gold, copper, salt, pasture land, and fields of the aforementioned areas. From the sixteenth to the fifteenth centuries B.C., they kept up close contact with the early Greek world, which was fully constituted at the time in the Mycenaean civilization; they most probably exported gold and received in return quality weapons and ornaments. As has lately been shown, this was the age when the Balkan Carpathian area was the greatest gold storehouse in Europe and when it also turned its scantier silver resources to good account.

The Thracian communities of the Bronze Age proper, well organized and usually grouped around some elementary fortifications, were in the second millennium a most flourishing European unitary center, with a great variety of regional aspects and close mutual political and economic relations. They continued to use and develop the superior Oriental-type axe for work and battle, an axe made of copper or bronze with vertical blade and handle hole; it was unlike the axes of the rest of Europe, which on account of the scarcity of raw material were flat and later had a longitudinal handle hole (the belt, which required less metal per piece). Subsequently, they adopted, especially in the Transylvanian area, the Mycenaean or north-Italic bronze swords and soon developed original types of swords with metal hilts, as well as other offensive and defensive bronze weapons.

This was a situation that changed as a result of new displacements and new clashes of tribes, initially occurring at the two extremities of the Carpatho-Danubian bloc, the

Western and Eastern extremities, its ethnical and cultural pattern being thereby modified to a bigger or smaller extent, without the bloc being wholly dislocated. It was only when these new protracted upheavals, with the intermingling of tribes they involved, had come to an end that the Geto-Dacian tribes were formed out of the early Thracian mass of the Carpatho-Balkan populations of the Bronze Age.

The developments considered here are the continental-European preliminaries to the so-called "Aegean migration," at the same time including the process of full separation, and of migration to their European settlements, of the great Indo-European peoples of antiquity — the Celts, Italics and Illyrians to the West, the Scythian-Sarmathians to the East, and the Balto-Slavs to the North. Together with them, new waves of continental-European populations were ultimately to make their way towards Greece (the Dorians) and towards Asia Minor (the Phrygians and the Armenians).

On the continent of Europe the "Aegean migration" appears to have begun in the fourteenth century B.C. with a southward and eastward movement of the powerful Central European group, known during the middle period of the Bronze Age as "the tumular grave culture", which penetrated into eastern Hungary and northern Yugoslavia. In connection with our own area, it is interesting to note that the western "proto-Thracian" groups — Otomani in Crişana and Periam-Pecica in Banat — although pressed upon and themselves pressing on towards the east (towards the center of the Transylvania plateau and Oltenia) stood their ground and were even drawn, as important participants, into the process whereby a new cultural synthesis was formed in the basin of the middle Danube and the Tisa — a process which was soon to lead to the birth of the so-called early Hallstatt culture in the twelfth century B.C.

A different process occurred in the eastern area of the Carpatho-Danubian bloc, where a new westward pressure was exerted (similar to that which impelled the first Indo-Europeans into Europe around 2400 B.C.). The pressure was again started in the Middle Volga area, where in the meantime the populations that practiced tumulus burial had developed in the Bronze Age into a group known as "the wooden structure tomb" group *(srubniie* in Russian), those populations almost undoubtedly representing the Iranian Indo-European branch. In their westward drive, this group reached the Dnieper, probably in the fourteenth century B.C., thus contacting the Carpatho-Danubian elements, themselves pushing eastward owing to the aforementioned western pressure. The Monteoru group, the most active in this "encounter", assimilated the eastern elements in a first stage and was dislodged in the following stage (thirteenth-twelfth centuries B.C.) when it again switched over to a predominantly pastoral way of life and changed its culture and partly its ethnical character, by mixing with the new eastern elements.

Archeology makes it clear that about the thirteenth century B.C. a new cultural and ethnic synthesis took place between the Dnieper and the western Carpathians on the basis of the local Bronze Age cultures (mainly the Monteoru, Costişa, and Wittenberg cultures) and of certain eastern elements of the "srubnoi" complex. Archeologists have named that synthesis Noua (on Romanian territory) and Sabatinovka (in the U.S.S.R.). Certain types of eastern bronze metallurgy practiced in the Urals and the Caucasus centers thus penetrated into the Carpatho-Balkan area, primarily in the extra-Carpathian area. It should be emphasized, however, that in its turn the Carpathian metallurgical center was fully expanding eastward, some of its forms (as, for example, the "celt" axe of the Transylvanian type) exerting great influence in the extra-Carpathian zone that stretched down to the Dnieper.

Consequently, it is quite clear that the new Noua-Sabatinovka complex was primarily formed on the basis of local Carpatho-Danubian elements and that contact with the groups that came from the east means that the area down to the Dnieper was connected to the Carpatho-Danubian area rather than vice versa.

The geographical spread of the Noua culture, which extended north of the Carpathians to beyond the upper Dniester and assumed a special regional aspect on the Transylvanian plateau, did not reach the western provinces of Romania — Crişana and Banat — as has already been shown, nor the southern ones: Oltenia, Muntenia, and Dobrudja. In the last-named provinces at the time of the movements which led to the formation of the Early Hallstatt culture in the west and of the Noua-Sabatinovka culture in the center (the Transylvanian plateau) and in the east (Moldavia, and the eastern area down to the Dnieper), there is at first a westward pressure and penetration from Banat into Oltenia and subsequently into Muntenia and possibly further down to Dobrudja, a penetration which superposed and profoundly modified the Verbicioara and Tei cultures through western influences. In the second place, probably as the effect of a southern cultural current due to penetration towards the Aegean Sea (and possibly farther) of certain groups of the Carpatho-Danubian population, a southern group was formed along the two banks of the Muntenian Danube, a group only recently identified (especially at Zimnicea and at Coşlogeni not far from Călăraşi), one which participated in the formation of the Noua-Sabatinovka complex by transmitting western and southern influences. It was thus that a more markedly south-oriented zone took shape in the Danubian sector of this country, with mere Noua-Sabatinovka infiltrations making themselves felt here.

The period considered as the end of the Bronze Age proper, whose features, in as far as they can be determined today, have been shown in the aforementioned paragraphs, is primarily characterized from the economic standpoint by a return to the predominance of the pastoral way of life — though agriculture did not die out altogether — by a marked development of bronze metallurgy (and very likely of salt extraction), and a great mobility and intermingling of tribes speaking kindred languages, though the local Carpatho-Balkan ethnical and cultural setup was not affected. Instability continued in the following centuries but it assumed a significant historical aspect when what was rightly called the counter-offensive of the Carpathian bloc began in the twelfth century B.C. Groups of warlike herdsmen and tillers of the soil living on the western fringes of the Carpatho-Balkan bloc who were making good use of the Carpathian copper ore deposits and who, on the basis of local traditions, had achieved a new society and new cultures of the Early Hallstatt type, then started from their formative area in Slovakia's Carpathians and from the regions between the Western Mountains and the Middle Danube, including northern Yugoslavia, on a powerful eastward drive, leaving their culture on their way to the groups that had formed in the "Final

Bronze Age" (the Noua-Sabatinovka group and the southern Lower Danube group); they achieved a new mobile Carpatho-Balkan unity — the Early Carpatho-Balkan Hallstatt — which showed characteristic traits in material culture and, of course, in their linguistic structure as compared with the early Central European Hallstatt. Subsequent developments show that to the west of the area they occupied there was a zone of Celtic, Italian, and Illyrian populations, and in the east — for a time only beyond the Dnieper — a zone of Iranian peoples, while in the Carpatho-Balkan area material culture and the linguistic (toponymic) and historical data discernible at that time or later suggest once again that it was the Thracian bloc that dwelt here. Proof of it lies in the fact that during the disturbances at the close of the Bronze Age, populations speaking the Thracian language or populations closely related to them (Phrygians, Myssians, and Bithynians) infiltrated into Anatolia.

## 3. *The Iron Age*

IRON Age I (so-called Early Hallstatt) lasted up to the eighth century B.C. Its salient feature was a predominantly pastoral and mobile life, the population moving from their place of settlement in search of good pasture land after each season. The settlements were extensive, mostly fortified in the Carpathian area and open in the plain, and the social structure was strongly differentiated, with chieftains recalling the Greek aristocracy of the Homeric age. The new metal, which once again was to bring about a revolution in European society and culture, was becoming known through imports from the Greek-Aegean area and subsequently through the transmission of technological knowledge from Hittite Anatolia and the Near East. These seem to have been the channels through which iron became known to the Thracian tribes of the Early Hallstatt beginning with the tenth and the ninth centuries B.C. In the Babadag settlement in Dobrudja certain iron objects and slag dating from that time were found, and this proves that the iron ore deposits had begun to be worked locally by reduction. At Cernat in the Covasna county, a store of objects of about the same period (ninth-eighth centuries B.C.) included raw iron bars in the form of blades, an iron knife fairly Central European in type, and two massive iron picks of the Southern Mediterranean type, apart from certain local bronze objects (including a fibula of a Carpathian character). These might have been obtained in southeast Transylvania by locally working the iron ore.

As we have seen, the southeastern region of this country had to a certain extent drawn apart from the rest of the Carpatho-Danubian area as early as the final Bronze Age transition period, forging closer connections with the Balkan area. This points to an accentuated differentiation among the Thracians, if not to the very beginnings of differentiation (which might have come about when the Indo-Europeans first infiltrated here at the close of the third millennium B.C.). The differentiation process, which gradually intensified in course of time, is also evidenced by the fact that in the eleventh century B.C., the Early Hallstatt culture of the Lower Danube (the Babadag type) shows certain differences from the same culture in Transylvania. On the other hand, the Babadag Thracian culture of the Early Hallstatt fairly vigorously set its seal on Moldavia too, and exercised its influence as far as the Dnieper (the Ciorniiless culture). This is a situation which to a certain extent repeats that of the Noua-Sabatinovka complex and raises the much debated problem of the Cimmerians and their connection with the Thracians or rather with their Scythian branch. The Cimmerians, a people akin to but not identical with the Thracians, lived north of the Black Sea. In the last decades of the eighth century B.C. they began to withdraw from those parts and were replaced by the Scythians. By the year 600 B.C. the latter people had settled down along the Dnieper, as shown by archeological evidence.

The Cimmerians seem to have been either a column of the Thracians which had remained in Eastern Europe at the time of the first Indo-European migration, or Thracian groups which had expanded eastward from the Carpatho-Balkan area at an earlier date (fourteenth century B.C.) or more recently (tenth and ninth centuries B.C.).

The Cimmerians were dislodged at the end of the eighth century B.C. by the Scythians, themselves pushed across the Volga from the east by other Iranian peoples. But while it is well attested that the Cimmerians had crossed the Caucasus into Urartu and Asia Minor, their westward penetration into the Carpatho-Danubian area in the eighth century B.C. is still controversial. At this point we should show to what extent an analysis of archeological sources strengthens or refutes Herodotus's contention that the Cimmerian chieftains had died a tragic death on the banks of the Dniester (and this would go to prove that they had extended westward).

It is most characteristic that around the supposed date of the clash between the Cimmerians and the Scythians, a number of complex and significant transformations and phenomena occurred in our Carpatho-Balkan area, though the culture and ethnical features of the Carpatho-Balkan Thracian stock clearly continued unimpaired. So far research has not been able to reveal fully the complexity of those phenomena, and their main features can only be faintly glimpsed.

During the latter half of the eighth century B.C., the Carpatho-Danubian Early Hallstatt culture underwent a number of transformations that entitle us to speak of a new period: the Middle Hallstatt. This was a comparatively short period lasting from ca. 750 to ca. 600 B.C. and ending the age of predominance of the pastoral way of life, which had begun at the close of the Bronze Age with a new expansion of this way of life. Greater mobility of the tribes once again brought about increased cultural unity throughout the Carpatho-Balkan area.

The uniformity of the cultural aspect has become known owing to the recent research of Romanian archeologists, and was named the Basarabi culture after the finds made at Basarabi near Calafat. Obviously this culture is directly developed from a prior local stock and has given rise to all the subsequent groups of the period of full consolidation of the Geto-Dacian tribes.

The tribes so far determined to have belonged to the Basarabi culture, from Banat to the Dniester and from the upper Dniester to the Balkan Mountains, with isolated elements cropping up in West Hungary (Sopron), Carinthia (Frögg) in Upper Austria, Western Serbia (the Drina basin), and South Bulgaria (the Maritza basin) — again raised a livestock, now more intensively and with greater mobility. Indeed, their wide diffusion suggests a vast movement of flocks in search of pasture. They lived mostly in the open regions of the wide river valleys (especially in the plain of the Lower Danube, along the Mureș and the Dniester). The hilly districts were less frequented. It is thus possible that the technique of incision decoration, a feature which has become general in Basarabi ware, distinguishing it from the preceding stages, might have been due to an impulse from the East, ultimately from the Caucasus districts. At this time other "Cimmerian" elements in art, some of a zoomorphic character, though not Scythian, penetrated into the wide Carpathian area. At the same time we should not overlook the fact that now, when the great Thraco-Cimmerian unity (as it was rightly called) had been achieved, the Carpatho-Balkan area assuming a specific aspect within the framework of the Central European Hallstatt, a number of Carpathian cultural elements spread far to the east and also to the Hallstatt area proper in the west. Wide use of horses, this time also as mounts, is a specific feature of the Carpatho-Balkan communities of those times, when various types of metal trappings (bits, guards, belt distributors), were made on the basis of local tradition and of eastern models that reached the Thraco-Cimmerian ethnic and cultural environment by various channels. This feature and also more extensive iron dressing were to be transmitted to the following period and to be intensified.

But the Basarabi period is not only characterized by such relations and by the tribal contacts and intermingling in the east-west and west-east directions. Its culture, as can be inferred from the earthenware and metal objects, was greatly influenced by the south of the Balkan Peninsula, where the Hellenic culture of the geometric and archaic periods had gradually extended northward and begun to infiltrate into the Carpatho-Danubian area. An example of this important phenomenon might be the fact that a fibula of Greek type had reached the Hallstatt (pre-Basarabi) settlement at Brad through imports as early as the ninth century B.C., while another, of the eighth and seventh centuries B.C., was found at Poiana on the river Siret; subsequently the later fibulae of the "Balkan" (now Greek-Thraco-Illyrian) type were to become characteristic of the Basarabi culture. It was thus that, through the intermediary of the southern Thracians and of the Illyrians, the slave-owning Greek civilization then in the making sent its first harbingers to the Carpatho-Danubian area, heralding the arrival of Greek colonists in this region.

During the period characterized in the wide Carpathian area by the local synthesis of Basarabi of great cultural and ethnic uniformity, the Greeks began to settle on the western and northern coasts of the Black Sea.

This is the first time that the age-old connections of the Carpatho-Danubian area with the centers of advanced civilization east of the Mediterranean and in the Aegean — connections which had formerly been established over great distances and through the intermediary of the intervening regions and populations — became direct connections, the Mediterranean civilization in its highest form, the Hellenic, being transplanted to the southeastern maritime border of the Thracian lands.

As early as the mid-seventh century B.C., the second "wave" of the Hellenic colonization movement had dotted the coast of the Mediterranean with Greek towns. This time the wave swept over the western and northern coasts of the "landlocked sea" which the local population had named the Black Sea, this being interpreted by the Greeks as inhospitable (*axeinos*). However, the sea soon became a Greek sea and "hospitable" (*euxeinos*).

The Greek colonists — farmers and traders — reached Histria (at the far end of the Sinoe gulf) and Olbia (in the Bug estuary) in the mid-seventh century B.C., coming from the Ionian Miletus in Asia Minor. Other Ionians from the same metropolis were to settle at Tomis (present-day Constanța) and Tyras (Cetatea Albă), probably in the next century, while at Callatis (Mangalia) Dorian Greeks settled, having come from the Pontic Heraclea on the southern, Anatolian, coast of the Black Sea. In the course of time a string of such colonies developed along these coasts, a phenomenon which is of considerable importance for the history of these districts. The Greek colonies became an integral part of the history of the Carpatho-Balkan area, acting as intermediaries between the mother cities that boasted a highly developed civilization and the "barbarian" world where they took root, at first through economic links and then through their political connections with the natives and their influence on the local Thracian society, which they guided towards higher forms of socio-political organization. On the other hand, the local Thracian environment also set its mark on the historical development of these towns: in the course of time the tribal unions of the native population, as part of which the tribal aristocracy now found new economic possibilities and a suitable political ground for consolidation and development, became "protectors" of the Greek colonies, levying "tribute" on them.

We are thus faced with much more than a sporadic contact between "civilized" people and "barbarians"; a complex and prolonged historical process was under way, during which time the two parties exerted a mutual and durable influence on each other.

Owing to its nature and orientation, Greek colonization was restricted to the narrow strip of coast where they first occupied the land by force of arms or by understanding with the local tribes. Inland, the Greeks penetrated only as traders, which they did to great distances, first as middlemen for the goods brought from their remote homeland with which they had maintained close connection, and later by selling their own artisan production while exporting overseas the surplus of the native production obtained by barter, or the products of their work as fishermen and farmers.

The pressure and expansion of the Scythians after they had crossed the Dnieper in the sixth century B.C., were of an altogether different character. Warlike nomads organized in a tribal union of herdsmen accustomed to keep the stable agricultural population under their dominion and to exploit them, the Scythians proper ("royal" Scythians) now grazed their flocks on the steppes north of the Black Sea, making predatory excursions in order to ensure the safety of their nomadic life and to enlarge their basis of exploitation. They were in the main Iranians, with a possible Mongoloid infiltration into their leading stratum.

Recent archeological research enables us more reliably to reconstitute historical developments in the Carpatho-Balkan area during the period between the sixth and the third centuries B.C. when it came under the pressure and threat of the eastern Scythians. This was not a massive overrunning, an outflow of the Scythians into and over the Carpathian area as far as Central Europe. On the contrary, it has been found that the effects of Scythian pressure were far more restricted and that this period was actually the historic moment when the Geto-Dacian tribes were organized and finally consolidated over a wide Carpatho-Balkan area.

Though the developments that took place from about 600 to 550 B.C. cannot be accurately reconstituted, the fact that there was an Illyrian infiltration into western Oltenia, and that archeology shows a cultural and topographic transformation of the Basarabi culture around 500 B.C., to which should be added the presence of a group of foreign, eastern population, especially in Transylvania, and a Scythian coloring of material culture as regards armament and horse trappings, throughout the Carpatho-Balkan area—all proves that certain disturbances occurred around the Thracian populations, very likely owing to the Scythian raids. However, it should not be overlooked that, as already mentioned, "eastern" elements, including "the zoomorphic style" in art, connected with those on which Scythian culture relies, penetrated into the Carpathian area as early as the eighth and seventh centuries B.C., simultaneously with Cimmerian infiltration.

In the first half of the sixth century B.C. an eastern population infiltrated into the Carpatho-Danubian area. What distinguished it from the local population was, in the first place, its different burial rites (level inhumation or within barrows) with the horse, or part of it, being laid in the grave. Its armament was also more constantly and more completely Scythian. This population, traced only quite sporadically in the rest of the country, settled mainly in the upper Mureșbasin (with the two Tîrnava rivers). This phenomenon is strikingly alluded to by one of the traditions recorded by Herodotus concerning the Agathyrsi, according to which, in his time, that is halfway through the fifth century B.C., the latter lived around the sources of the Mureș, wore gold ornaments, had wives in common, and were very much like the Thracians as regards their other customs. From other passages in Herodotus, as well as from later records, it would appear that the Agathyrsi had formerly lived in Scythia, east of the Carpathians, and somewhere north of the Black Sea. However, there is no inference anywhere that they were actually Scythians; they rather appear to be one of the populations bordering on the Scythians, possibly Cimmerians or Thracians, as their material culture in Transylvania proves to be absolutely Thracian right from the beginning as far as earthenware is concerned. Both Herodotus's text and archeological data prove that by the fifth century B.C. they had been fully assimilated by the local Thracian population (in the first place discarding the inhumation rite and switching over to the local Thracian rite of cremation). The same assimilation process occurred again in the fifth century within the Illyrian group that had penetrated into Oltenia. Both processes are proof of the assimilation power of the native stock.

As a result of this eastern infiltration, of the raids, and of the continuous Scythian threat, the local population, indubitably descendants of the preceding Basarabi culture, judging by their material culture and their burial rites (cremation), was found to be differently distributed geographically around 550 B.C. In the first place, the extra-Carpathian regions of open plains appear to be nearly (but not quite) emptied of population throughout the period under discussion, which is Late Hallstatt (ca. 575—ca. 350 B.C.). It was only along the banks of the Danube that the population was denser. This is definitely proved by archeology, which confirms and explains the information provided by Herodotus and Strabo, according to whom a "Getian wilderness" (this being understood as an uninhabited region belonging to the Getians) was to be found north of the Danube.

On the other hand, in the hilly regions, so far ascertained from Gorj to Buzău (the so-called "Ferigele" group after the cemetery of Ferigele in the Vîlcea county) and also northward in the districts of Moldavia's Carpathian foothills (the closely related "Bîrseşti" group named after the cemetery to be found within the radius of the village of Bîrseşti in Vrancea), as well as in Dobrudja and again south of the Danube, on the pre-Balkan platform in the north of the People's Republic of Bulgaria, cremation cemeteries were mostly to be found throughout the period from ca. 550 to ca. 350 B.C., in the neighborhood of stable settlements of the local population, which continued the tradition of the preceding period, with Scythian additions where armament is concerned. Iron metallurgy now appears to have been fully assimilated and to have developed.

In the extra-Carpathian area of the country, in the central Moldavian plateau and as far as Dochia, on the outskirts of the town of Piatra Neamţ, there are impressive strongholds of earth and stone covering large areas and standing on high ridges. These strongholds built by the local population against the Scythian threat have only recently been identified and have been only partially studied on account of the large areas they occupy (18 acres at Moşna in the Jassy county and 90 acres at Stînceşti in the Botoşani county). From the mid-sixth century to the third century B.C., a chain of strongholds, of which twenty perhaps have been identified so far, made of Moldavia's central plateau an advanced bridgehead of the Geto-Dacian world, which proved to be storm-proof. In times of danger, the population in the open settlements would withdraw into those strongholds, taking their belongings with them. These strongholds were consequently for times of stress, but discoveries show that they also served as places of residence of the tribal aristocracy.

In the west of the country, the Thracian population which had partly mixed with the eastern "Scythian" population, mostly lived in the Tisa plain. In the north, the same Thracian population was to be found in the Sub-Carpathian Ukraine and in east Slovakia.

It is from this Late Hallstatt stock and against its background that the tribal unions known in written historical tradition (Herodotus, Thucydides) as Getian and later as Dacian arose in the Carpatho-Balkan area, with their high culture at the level of Iron Age II (Latène Culture, after the name of the corresponding culture created by the Celts in Western Europe) — a culture which is the effect of assimilation by the autochthonous stock of the influence of Mediterranean civilization transmitted by the Greeks. This was an organic and a fairly slow process beginning in the fifth century and reaching full maturity in the first century B.C., in Burebista's time. During Decebalus's period there is further progress, which brings this culture to a stage approaching civilization (of the slave-owning type).

The simple acquisition and use by the local tribal aristocracy of a number of Greek products, obviously more frequent in the coastal area where there was direct contact between the Geto-Dacians and the Greeks as early as the first part of the sixth century B.C. — this being synchronous with the same process in Central and Western Europe — does not mean a switch-over to a new socio-economic and cultural stage. Luxury craftware (fine earthen-ware, metal weapons, personal adornments) or certain foods, which were also luxuries (oil and wine), imported from the Greeks or, and especially in the period dealt with here, through the intermediary of the Greeks settled along the Black Sea coast, were for a time simply imports, indicative of the social position and the orientation of the local tribal aristocracy, but which did not for the moment bring about important changes in autochthonous society and culture. The latter still preserved their Late Hallstatt features, the only difference being that the local aristocracy was beginning to consume Greek luxuries and some were enriched by trading with the Greeks. The same is true for the infrequent gray vases, common but wheel-made, which sporadically penetrated, especially in the fifth century B.C. throughout the area of the Geto-Dacian groupings mentioned above. Such vases came from shops that have not yet been identified but which were probably Balkan. It is nevertheless remarkable that in the extra-Carpathian zone such Greek imports occurred as early as the first half of the sixth century, as shown by the finds at Artand in Bihor (for example, a beautiful bronze *hydria* most probably Spartan-made), while at Stîncești in Moldavia they occurred in the second half of the sixth century (Chios amphorae). Wine, a specifically Mediterranean product, probably began to be consumed in Europe as early as the end of the Bronze Age owing to the connections established with the Mycenaean world. The Greek colonists along the northern coasts of the Mediterranean were supplying wine to the tribal aristocracies on the continental mainland in the seventh century. During the fourth and third centuries B.C. imports of wine and oil, which came in amphorae from the isle of Thasos or from Sinope (on the southern coast of the Black Sea) as were also imports of some Greek craftware (burnt clay vases, metal objects, personal adornments, and weapons) were intensified both in Moldavia and in the Danube Valley. From the fourth century on, Greek coins began to penetrate into these regions from the Greek settlements along the coast (Olbia and Histria). The Transylvanian plateau, however, proved refractory to the penetration of Greek goods until quite late (third century B.C.).

The transformation process of production relations within Geto-Dacian tribes, which also brought about a switchover to a new, specifically Dacian culture of the Latène type, was gradual and complex, as it was also in the rest of Europe, among the Celts and the Illyrians. It began everywhere in the southern regions, which were nearer to the Greek world. In the Carpatho-Balkan area, it is first attested in the southern Thracian area, south of the Balkan range. When the population of the Danube plain partially withdrew in the sixth to the fourth centuries B.C., as shown earlier, the Geto-Dacians retreating to the hills and the tablelands, and also along the Danube, the Getae on the south Danubian pre-Balkan platform — the Vraţa and Dobrina-Varna groupings — were only for a short time, and not completely, separated from those in the Carpathians. For this reason it is not right to name the former southern Thracians and the latter northern Thracians. Ultimately, it is only the tribes south of the Balkans, where the state of the Odrysi was set up in the first half of the fifth century that should be considered as southern Thracians. The new, specifically Geto-Dacian society and culture were first effectively organized as a result of these contacts on the pre-Balkan platform and in the plain north of the Lower Danube in the latter half of the fourth century B.C. Advanced agriculture was then practiced, wheel pottery and other crafts were separated from agriculture and stock-breeding, and the aristocracy was consolidated, "kings" (*basilei*) standing out from its ranks. The names of these kings are mostly unknown; there was one, however, who encountered Alexander the Great in the Danube plain in 335 B.C., another from whose supposed grave the silver horse trappings in the "Craiova treasure" are assumed to have been obtained, and yet another buried in the Hagighiol barrow in the Tulcea county in the second half of the fourth century B.C.

It is from this background that Dromichaites, who defeated Lysimachus, the Macedonian King, at the turn of the third century B.C. was to rise; it is this world he will represent.

It is clear, therefore, that the decisive role in the rise of Geto-Dacian society to the higher stage of Iron Age II cannot be attributed to the Scythians. The Scythians, warlike nomadic herdsmen, remained at the level of the Late Hallstatt up to the fourth century B.C., importing Greek luxuries but being unable to produce them or improve on them. There is no significance in the fact that as early as the sixth century B.C. the Getae had partially adopted the armament and the battle tactics of the Scythians (and this could have been brought about partly through the intermediary of the Cimmerians).

In the meantime, there had certainly been transient Scythian infiltration into the Getian area, especially in Dobrudja and in the Danube plain, just as Scythian armament and tactics exerted an influence over the Getae. The passage in Thucydides' *Histories* referring to the last decades of the fifth century B.C. once again confirms Herodotus's information concerning an event of the century before (Darius's expedition against the Scythians ca. 514 B.C.) according to which the Getae (who were different from the Thracians) mainly lived north of the Balkans and in Dobrudja, bordering on the Scythians, and used the same weapons as the latter, fighting as mounted archers. But Getian culture as a whole having developed on the basis of different age-old autochthonous traditions over the Carpatho-Balkan area, preserved its original character, just like Getian art.

Nor can it be asserted that the Greeks were sole factors in the advance achieved by the Geto-Dacians in Iron Age II. It is true that the Greeks paved the way by their connections with the Geto-Dacian tribes as early as the sixth to the fifth centuries B.C., and that it is due to their influence and their direct impulse that the southern Thracians advanced to the Latène level (Iron Age II named after La Tène in Switzerland) as early as the fifth century B.C. — a culture which they later gradually transmitted farther north up to the northern Carpathians! This is how ultimately a single culture arose in the vast Carpatho-Balkan area. It was of the Latène type but Thraco-Geto-Dacian in character, a culture parallel and equivalent to the one created in Western Europe by the Celts, though different from it.

These two great peoples of Europe in those days — the Celts (Gauls) and the Geto-Dacians — came into contact, exerted mutual cultural influence but from the latter half of the fourth century B.C. they came to grips. The vast migrations and conquests of the Celts encompassed Pannonia down to the Adriatic but were compelled to give a wide berth to the Dacian bloc in the Carpathians, though not without infiltrating into the peripheral districts of that bloc. The most powerful infiltration was in Crişana, in northwest Dacia, where Celts settled in great numbers as early as the fourth century B.C., overlapping the Dacians and mingling with them. It is from Crişana that Celtic groups penetrated along the valleys of the Someş and Mureş into the Transylvanian

plateau up to the Tîrnave valleys as well as into the neighborhood of the Bîrsa plain, while other groups were to skirt
Dacia in the north and pass through sub-Carpathian Ukraine
and southern Poland in order to reach the valley of the Dniester in stray bands whence they went further to the northern
coast of the Black Sea. Celtic place-names in northern Dobrudja, like Noviodunum (present-day Isaccea) and Arrubium (Măcin), in Bugeac, such as Aliobrix (probably Cartal-Orlovka),
attest their presence at one time even about the mouths of
the Danube. Outside the Transylvanian plateau, where up
to the end of the third century B.C. and in certain places even
later, there seems to have been Celto-Dacian coexistence,
with the Celts being fully assimilated, it is only sporadically
that Celtic elements penetrated within the Geto-Dacian bloc.
In Oltenia the Scordisci Celts of the Sava region infiltrated
in the second and first centuries B.C., mixing with the Dacians
of those parts and being also assimilated. On the same occasion Geto-Dacian culture assimilated a number of elements
of Celtic culture, integrating them into its traditional fund,
which remained essentially unaltered in its originality. The
Dacians' coexistence and intermingling with the Celts is a
process of historic importance.

The fact that northwest Dacia north of the Danube, including the Transylvanian plateau, was so powerfully infiltrated
by the Celts for a comparatively long period — and, as it
seems, also dominated by them from the military and political
points of view — is a reason for the social and cultural evolution of the Dacian people in those parts becoming later synchronous with that of the Geto-Dacians of the southern and southeastern extra-Carpathian regions and still later acting as a
decisive factor in the political and military life of the Geto-
Dacian bloc north of the Danube. This branch of the Geto-
Dacians known by the new name of Dacians (probably after
the name of a leading tribe in the tribal union) exerted their
influence from around the year 200 B.C. But, as asserted by
the Roman historian Trogus Pompeius at the end of the first
century B.C., "Dacii quoque suboles Getarum sunt" (the
Dacians are also descendents of the Getae).

It is from the core of the "Carpathian stronghold" that
the outburst of unifying military, political, and cultural energy
was to arise during Burebista's century.

# CHAPTER II

# The Geto-Dacians

MENTIONED in historical records as early as the sixth century B.C., the Getae along the Lower Danube first organized themselves politically during the subsequent centuries, the most important tribal union being that headed by Dromichaites. During the third century B.C. we find the first indications of a similar union built up by the Dacians living in the mountains. During the first century B.C. an ephemeral union of all Geto-Dacian tribes took place under Burebista's leadership. Later, the tendency of the Roman empire to establish its border along the Lower Danube led to frequent conflicts between the Dacians and the Romans, culminating in two fierce wars waged by Emperor Trajan in Dacia, which resulted in the overthrow of Decebalus's kingdom and the transformation of Dacia into a Roman province.

## 1. Hellenic Cities: Histria, Tomis, Callatis

BEFORE commencing this chapter devoted to the Geto-Dacian native population, we ought to dwell for a moment on the three Greek colonies of Histria, Tomis, and Callatis, which in ancient times flourished on the Getian coast of what is today Romanian Dobrudja. As we have already shown and as we shall mention with further examples in this chapter, these trading cities — parallel with other Pontic cities, like Tyras and Olbia on the coast of the present-day U.S.S.R., and Dionysopolis (Balcic), Odessos (Varna), Mesembria (Nesebar), and Apollonia (Sozopoli) on the coast of present-day Bulgaria — maintained busy economic connections with the Carpatho-Danubian regions, exercising fruitful influence on the development of Geto-Dacian society and speeding up its progress. These are the oldest urban settlements in the neighborhood of the Geto-Dacian lands, and simultaneously direct centers of the high Hellenic civilization, the source of Europe's civilization. Thanks to their economic activities and their cultural impact, the territory of this country was for the first time drawn into the orbit of world history.

Istros or Istria (Histria in Latin), the oldest of them, was set up during the seventh century B.C. (more precisely in 657) by Miletus, the famous Ionic city on the Aegean coast of Asia Minor. The site was south of the mouths of the Danube at the far end of the gulf which, owing to subsequent sand deposits, was to become the present-day Lake Sinoe. Its Greek name was that of the Danube, which Greeks as the Geto-Thracians named Istros. The Milesians set up their colony on that site mainly in order to make good use of the Danube for commercial penetration into the Geto-Dacian lands, and also with a view to profitable fishing in the Delta. Thanks to this economic background, Histria soon became a most flourishing city.

As early as the fifth century B.C. Histria began to mint its own silver coins, and the example it set was later to be followed by the other cities in the vicinity. As a result of its economic development, the city witnessed conflicts during that century between the aristocracy, which by virtue of tradition held a monopoly over political rights, and the numerous traders, sailors, and craftsmen, who were barred from access to the high offices and magistracies, although by their work and often also by their fortune, they played a main role in building up the prosperity of the city. Aristotle quotes the class struggle at Histria as a typical example of the social transformation wrought in many Hellenic cities. And it is also from him that we know that ultimately the privileged class was overthrown, the Histrian rebels enforcing a democratic constitution of the Athenian type. Although it had resulted from local developments, the event is not without connection with the fact that Athens had asserted its hegemony in Pontus Euxinus by a naval demonstration headed by Pericles. The democracy set up in Hellenic cities was an important factor in economic progress and in the development of culture and public works.

The second Greek town in Dobrudja to reach a flourishing condition in a short time was Callatis. This Doric colony which emerged comparatively late on the coast — at the close of the sixth century B.C. — had been founded by farmers from Pontic Heraclea (today Eregli on the coast of Asia Minor), a city which had previously been a colony of Megara in central Greece. The people of Heraclea raised the city of Callatis on the site of present-day Mangalia, where natural defense conditions were nonexistent and where the coast had no economic value apart from its mediocre advantages as a harbor. On the other hand, the steppe around, inhabited by Getian and Scythian herdsmen, had a soil and climate most favorable to the growing of corn. The development of this city relied on its grain trade. The grain was in such demand in the market of southern Greece and grain-growing so profitable that the Scythian herdsmen in the neighborhood gave up their nomadic life and turned ploughmen with an autonomous organization and their own kings, who issued coins minted in the shops of Callatis. The height of the city's prosperity was reached in the fourth and the third centuries B.C., when its wealth and glory exceeded that of all the other Hellenic colonies in the Left Pontus, as the western coast of the Pontus Euxinus was then called. Its cultural development was no less remarkable. From here came the famous geographer Demetrios of Callatis (third Century B.C.), the tragedian Istros Callatianos, the literary historian Satyros Peripatheticus, and the rhetorician Tales whose works were greatly appreciated in ancient times but unfortunately were not preserved.

Although raised as early as the seventh century, possibly simultaneously with Histria, and in any case not later than the early sixth century B.C., the Milesian city of Tomis on the site of present-day Constantza, more exactly on its central promontory, remained obscure for long, being merely a place of call for the sailors who reached the shelter of this unique natural harbor on the monotonous middle portion of the Dobrudjan coast. Apart from the port, there were no economic advantages to be derived from its location, nothing comparable to Histria or Callatis, for there was no river to enable the sailors to reach the interior of the country and no native population numerous enough in its vicinity to ensure trade development. Economically, it was of service as a harbor for the needs of seagoing vessels; it acted as a naval station, this ultimately securing its growth, prosperity, and primacy.

A radical change was brought about by the advance of silt deposits at the mouths of the Danube, which being carried southward by the sea current along the coast, became an obstruction to Histria, forming underwater belts most dangerous to navigation. Many Greek traders who wished to reach the interior of the country by way of the Danube, soon developed a tendency to avoid the Delta and shortened their way by transhipping the goods and taking them across Dobrudja by land. As the shortest and easiest way inland was from Tomis, this none too rich little town became increasingly favored by the sailors who had their goods transhipped here, thus bringing in great profits. Traffic along this route became regular after Lysimachus's Macedonian domination established order in Dobrudja. It was then that the Danube port of Axiopolis (present-day Hinogu near Cernavoda) was created at the far end of the land route.

The city's sudden development earned it the envy of the neighboring towns of Histria and Callatis, which tried to subjugate it around 260 B.C. Tomis was saved through the intervention of Byzantium, the powerful Megarian city on the Bosphorus (on the site of what was to be Constantinople), which had financial interests here and consequently supported free traffic in Tomis. The Byzantine fleet overcame the naval forces of Callatis while Histria had to submit to the curtailment of maritime transit in its waters and be content with the income derived from fishing in the Delta, which was fairly high and where there was no competition. After this critical moment Tomis prospered without hindrance. And when Roman domination began in these parts, Ovid who had been exiled here, found a city which was already the main center of Dobrudja. Subsequently Tomis became "the most flourishing metropolis of the entire Left Pontus," as it was described in inscriptions and on coins.

The three Hellenic cities had specialized, each according to its economic background: fishing at Histria, commercial transhipment at Tomis, large-scale farming at Callatis. They were organized according to the model set for all Greek towns, forming independent states *(poleis)*, with a territory of their own, with defense facilities and an autonomous life. Their political authority consisted of a Council *(boulé)* and the People's Assembly *(demos)*. The council members *(bouleutai)* and the various magistrates (administrative, judicial, financial, military, and religious) were elected by the people annually. The foremost magistrate, the *eponymos* (whose name served to specify the year when he was in office) was the priest of the God Apollo at Histria and Tomis. At Callatis, a Doric city, there was a *basileus*, whose name had no monarchic significance, in spite of his signification as "king". The organization of these cities was that of a slave-owning democracy par excellence.

When they came under the authority of the Roman empire, Histria, Tomis, and Callatis preserved their autonomous institutions, being considered as "allied" cities (*civitates foederatae*) and being entitled to mint their own coins (though only bronze ones), although they were closely dependent on Roman officialdom. Nevertheless, the peace Rome had established proved so favorable to their economy, it secured for them so long a period of prosperity, that their devotion to the Empire was unshakable. Among their religious institutions, particular importance was attached to the imperial cult and their gratitude was also expressed by the erection of temples, by the holding of divine services, and by festivals. A community named Pentapolis, which included the towns of Dionysopolis and Odessos, was formed by the cities along the Left Pontus shore for the practice of this cult in common. Later, with a sixth city, Mesembria, joining the community, it was named Hexapolis. The Pentapolis or Hexapolis was headed by an elected president named *Pontarches*, who resided at Tomis, the main city of the community.

Histria, Tomis and Callatis kept up their economic activities and their connections with the populations on the left of the Danube until the Eastern Roman Empire abandoned Dobrudja in the seventh century A.D., when the repeated attacks of the Avars and Proto-Bulgars finally destroyed them after well over twelve centuries of life during which, assiduously and creatively, they had spread without intermission the values of Greek civilization on the territory of Geto-Dacian homeland.

## 2. *The Early Getae*

WE know from ancient historical records that the territory of present-day Romania mostly coincides with that of Dacia, a country inhabited by Getae and Dacians from remote times. The populations thus named spoke the same language, had the same Thracian origin and the same culture, and shared between them the Carpatho-Danubian area, a large geographic unit.

The only difference between the Getae and the Dacians was the region they occupied, the former living in the plains south and east of the Carpathians, primarily on the two banks of the Lower Danube, while the latter held sway over the mountainous regions of Transylvania. When the ancient Greek writers wished to name all the tribes of Dacia by one name, they preferred to call them Getae, these having been known to them for a longer time than the Dacians, as they were nearer to the Hellenic cities along the coast of Pontus Euxinus. On the other hand, the Romans called them Dacians for they had been in more frequent contact with the latter people owing to their westerly position. During the modern period the double name — Geto-Dacians or Daco-Getians — is generally used as more convenient, for it expresses the fundamental unity of the two populations while taking the regional individuality of each into account.

Herodotus, the Greek historian, said that "the Thracians were the greatest of all peoples after the Indians," and that "had they been under a single leadership and with a unitary consciousness, they would have been invincible and by far the most powerful of all peoples." They were divided into many tribes, which lived independently and seldom formed a powerful political union, and that only in certain parts of their territory.

Among the numerous Thracian tribes, three main groupings are distinguished, which with time showed distinct features according to their evolution under different geographical, economic, historic, and cultural conditions. One group of the three were the Mysians and Phrygians of Asia Minor, the second, the Thracians proper *(Thraces)* of the Balkan Peninsula (thus named in history), and the third, the Geto-

Dacians, to whom should be added the North Thracian tribes of the Carpi, Costobocae, and of other populations of the northern Carpathians. There are differences between the dialects, religious practices, customs, and cultural trends of the three groups.

The oldest records mentioning the Getae belong to the sixth century B.C., while the Dacians are only mentioned in historical sources at the close of the third century B.C.

Dacia's historical records begin with the information transmitted by Herodotus on an important event which took place about 514 B.C., when Darius son of Hystaspes, the Great King of the Persians, undertook his famous expedition against the Scythians with the purpose of bringing all the rich coasts of Pontus Euxinus under his rule. At the head of a great host, this monarch crossed the Bosphorus and Thrace towards the Danube (Istros), while the fleet of the Greeks of Asia Minor, who had been subdued by him, was sailing in the same direction along the western coast of the Pontus, also called the Left Pontus. Along the coast of southern Thrace Darius met only three tribes, who submitted to him. However, when he had crossed the Balkans (Haemus) and entered Dobrudja, he was faced by the Getians on the banks of the Danube, who opposed him. Finally the Getae were defeated and compelled to enter the ranks of the Persian army, but Herodotus nevertheless praises their gallantry and moral discipline, describing them as "the most courageous and fairest of the Thracians." He speaks about their contempt for death, inspired by the belief that the souls of those fallen in battle were immortal. However, their brave opposition to the impressive Persian hosts depended not only on warlike virtues but also on their number. Indeed, they must have been numerous if we admit that even at that time they formed a widespread union of tribes on either bank of the Lower Danube, in the Muntenian plain, northern Bulgaria, Dobrudja, and southern Moldavia, as will appear in the following centuries.

At about the same time, the Agathyrsi in the Carpathians are shown by Herodotus to have broken away from the Scythians and to have taken a neutral stand during Darius's expedition.

At the time referred to by Herodotus, Scythian expansion had reached its maximum westward limit and, after some last thrusts, was beginning to decline, despite the victory they had won over Darius. Actually, that victory was not so much a military success (there is no mention of a battle) as the result of the climate and of the hardships encountered in the great eastern steppes, which decisive factors compelled the Persian monarch to retrace his steps.

A number of elements in Dacia's toponymy (e.g., Naparis, present-day Ialomiţa, Araros, which may have been present-day Buzău, and possibly Dunaris, from which the Romanian name for the Danube — Dunăre — is supposed to have derived); certain elements of the Geto-Dacian language that are not to be found in the language of southern Thracians; the accentuated Iranian character of the Geto-Dacian religion, and even some names of peoples, among them the very names of Getae and Dacians — have been considered as probable reminiscences of Scythian domination. These reminiscences are the most important differences between the Geto-Dacians, the representatives of the northern Thracians, and the Balkan Thracians, who were far less affected by Scythian influence. And yet, the name *Dacian* may well have been derived from an old Thracian word, if we compare it with *daos*, which is the Phrygian term for wolf, as Hesychius explains. In that case, it might be of totemic origin, especially if we recall the wolf's head with a dragon's tail *(draco)* on the Dacian banner.

## 3. *The Getae of the Danube Plain; The Tribal Union Headed by Dromichaites*

EVEN though Darius had failed to reach his goal in the Great Scythia beyond the mouths of the Danube, it seemed probable that he would establish the boundary of his empire along the Lower Danube, for he had been successful against the Thracian and Getian tribes there. However, the withdrawal of the Persian forces pursued by the Scythians and the subsequent defeats of Darius and his successor, Xerxes, in Greece made it impossible for Persian authority to be established for any length of time north of the Straits.

Conquered for a brief spell, the Thracian and Getian tribes recovered their independence as soon as Darius's forces left their land. Shortly after 500 B.C., a state of the Balkan Thracians was founded, a stable union of tribes having been organized under the rule of the kings of the Odrysian tribes, the first of whom was Teres. Teres's son, Sitalces, consolidated the Odrysian state and extended it to the mouths of the Danube, incorporating the Getae north of the Balkans, those in Dobrudja included, as well as the Scythian enclaves close to the Left Pontus. Thus Darius's wish to turn the Danube into a boundary was achieved, though not by him and in favor of his empire, but by the local Geto-Thracians in favor of the Odrysian state. The Getic and Thracian tribes of Dobrudja then became autonomous elements of this state, on the basis of mere association, according to the rules of the tribal unions in the stage of military democracy, which was then the social system of all the populations of the Balkano-Carpatho-Danubian area and of the rest of Europe.

Macedonia's emergence as a great Hellenic power in the Balkan Peninsula under the energetic rule of Philip II was not without considerable effects on these regions. After over a century and a half of existence, the Odrysian kingdom, weakened by domestic strife, was conquered by Philip in 341 B.C. and turned into a Macedonian province *(strategia)*. Following this considerable annexation, the Macedonian king felt the need of extending his authority to the Danube, which he did by force of arms. As reported by the ancient historian Pompeius Trogus, an excerpt of whose history was preserved by Justin, a Scythian power had emerged at that time in Dobrudja under the leadership of Ateas, who seems to have come from the regions north of the Black Sea. Having formed a coalition of the local Scythian enclaves, he had built up an independent state in the northeastern corner of the one-time Odrysian kingdom, taking advantage of its decadence and of its subsequent suppression. The coins of the Scythian king were found only in the region between Callatis and Odessos. Following the collapse of the Thracian kingdom, an alliance was formed between Philip and Ateas, the latter nominally acknowledging Philip's authority over the mouths of the Danube and promising him the succession to his territories in exchange for assistance against a local king. Trogus's text speaks of this king as *Histrianorum rex* (King of the Histrians), without giving his name or any other particulars about him.

But the text makes it clear that this enemy of Ateas was very powerful, so that he could not have been the chieftain of a small group of Hellenized natives *(mixhellenes)* around the city of Histria. "The King of the Histrians" must have been the leader of a great union of Getian tribes living on either side of the Danube, then named Istros (latinized into Hister).

These "Histrians" opposed Ateas's expansion towards the regions along the Danube and, having formed an alliance with the Triballians, threatened him with a devastating war. The Triballians, a Thracian population from the Lower Oescus (Isker), somewhat lower down than present-day Oltenia, had refused to be incorporated into the Thracian kingdom and all attempts made by the Odrysian kings to subdue them proved unavailing. Sitalces himself had fallen in a battle against them in 424 B.C. and now Philip II found it in his interest to encourage Ateas to make war on them.

In the meantime, however, the anonymous *Histrianorum rex* died, and this must have induced a temporary weakening of the Getian union he was heading as well as of his connections with the Triballians. Ateas considered the situation sufficiently favorable to shake off Philip's patronage and denounce the pact he had concluded with him. The Macedonian king, who was then at war with Byzantium, raised the siege of that Greek city on the Bosphorus and led his armies into Dobrudja, demanding that Ateas give him access to the mouths of the Danube through his territory so that he might establish his rule over that furthermost frontier region by dedicating a statue to Heracles. As the Scythian king refused to have his land encroached upon, an armed conflict ensued. During the battle fought somewhere in southern Dobrudja, the Scythian forces, despite their greater numbers, were defeated. Ateas, who was greatly advanced in years, fell in battle. Then Philip, followed by an immense convoy of Scythian prisoners and captured cattle, returned to Macedonia through the lands of the Triballians, where he was unexpectedly attacked. The Macedonian King was wounded in battle and only with great difficulty did he get home with his army, leaving all the spoils of war taken from the Scythians behind.

The results of Philip's action on the banks of the Danube were not far-reaching. It is true that his victory over Ateas consolidated his authority in Dobrudja and that the Pontic cities which had formerly hesitated, finally submitted to his overlordship. On the other hand, the Triballians were still troublesome and, united with the trans-Danubian Getae, fomented unrest in the territories bordering on Macedonia.

Thus, when Philip died in 335 B.C., Alexander, his son and heir, found it necessary to undertake an expedition to the Danube, as a preliminary safety measure before setting out on his prodigious conquests in Asia. Defeated in the first clash on the river Lyginus (probably present-day Panega), a tributary of the Oescus (Isker), the Triballians under their king Syrmos, withdrew to a Danube ait, repelling all Macedonian attacks by water. Realizing that resistance was possible mainly through the aid received from the Getae on the left bank of the river, Alexander decided to make an audacious demonstration against the latter; crossing the Danube one night with improvised facilities, he unexpectedly attacked the Getian forces, which despite their great numbers, were compelled to leave in all speed their poorly fortified citadel on the Danube bank and to withdraw into the steppe. Alexander was cautious enough not to pursue them and to be content with the rich booty of provisions and cattle he had found in the conquered citadel, and with his important moral success. Without Getian support in the offing, the Triballians were compelled to submit to the young Macedonian king. Other populations between the Adriatic and the Danube, among them the Celts, recent arrivals in these regions, sent Alexander messengers with tokens of friendship.

The political success of Alexander's sally is proof of the impressive strength of the Getae, whom he had defied though refusing to fight them and to be inveigled in the meshes of their wily withdrawal. These were no doubt the same Histrian tribes that had opposed Ateas some years previously. From the minute account of Alexander's campaign along the Danube by Ptolemy son of Lagos, as transmitted by Arrian, we learn that the local Getae were fishermen and traders, for which purpose they used numberless one-oar boats, and also successfully practiced farming. On the northern bank of the Danube, the Macedonian foot soldiers had to bend down the high wheat with their long spears *(sarissae)* aslant for the cavalry to pass.

In 326 B.C. nearly a decade later, while Alexander was at the height of his successes in Asia, strategus Zopyrion, governor of Thrace, sought to extend his authority north of the mouths of the Danube, by undertaking an expedition in the Bugeac and beyond the Dniester and attacking the Greek town of Olbia, which was not prepared to submit to Macedonian supremacy. Repelled by that city and forced to withdraw for lack of provisions, Zopyrion shortly found himself unable to cross the Danube on his return because of the rising waters. Taken by surprise by a great army of the union of Getian tribes, he was killed together with most of his troops. Alexander's premature death in 323 cut short his plan of returning to the Danube to smash the power of the Getae.

The plan was, however, followed by Alexander's general and successor, Lysimachus, who had become king of Thrace when the Macedonian conquests were divided. His excessive levies caused the Hellenic cities in Dobrudja to revolt. Though they were supported by the trans-Danubian populations and primarily by the Getae, Lysimachus after prolonged efforts ultimately succeeded in isolating and defeating them. For nearly six years Callatis had put up an heroic resistance. Now master of the sea coast and of the Dobrudjan mainland, the Thracian king, having decided to ensure the safety of his Danube frontier, sent his son Agathocles with an army into the Bărăgan steppe across the river to subdue the union of Getian tribes under the leadership of King Dromichaites, who had refused to resign himself to the loss of his territories along the right bank of the Danube.

The expedition was a failure: Agathocles was defeated and taken prisoner. After he had ransomed his son, Lysimachus crossed the Danube with a great army in 291, but suffered the same fate as his son, persisting, as he did, in his decision to traverse the Bărăgan steppe in pursuit of the Getae who, according to their tactics, withdrew farther and farther into the steppe. Exhausted by hardships, thirst, and a low morale, the Thraco-Macedonian hosts suddenly found themselves surrounded by Getae in large numbers and were forced to lay down their arms. Lysimachus and his followers were taken to the citadel of Helis (so far unidentified) where Dromichaites' political wisdom succeeded in saving them from the massacre the Getae, intoxicated by victory, threatened them with. It is characteristic of the type of military democracy of Getian society in those days that the Getian king, whose authority over his men was far from absolute, had to resort to speeches and artful reasoning in order to repress their fury and convince them that peace with great and lasting advantages was to be preferred to futile vengeance that would bring new wars in its train. Lysimachus being released, a solemn pact was concluded on Dromichaites' terms. The alliance between the two rulers was consolidated by the Getian king's marriage with Lysimachus's daughter.

This dynastic kinship propelled the union of Getian tribes along the Lower Danube into the political sphere of the Hellenistic world, with important consequences for the development of Getian culture. As from third century B.C., archeology attests a new cultural impetus, with marked intensification of Greek influence. First exerted at the time when the Pontic cities were founded in the seventh and the sixth centuries B.C., that influence never ceased to act on the Getae as a consequence of increasingly active trade. A stable grain production and intensive economic traffic on the Danube, ascertained by Alexander's army on the occasion of their expedition in 335, were the results of the demand for grain and other products on the part of Greek traders, who offered in exchange produce specific to their southern orchards, such as wine and oil, and the high quality products of their shops, such as weapons, tools, metal ornaments, luxury ware, and fine fabrics. Local assimilation of the Greek forms and techniques only came about when Hellenic influence, apart from its economic aspect, gained political support and connections between the Getae and the Hellenistic world of Thrace and Macedonia were strengthened. Thrace, which had been under the influence of Greek civilization for a long time — and that was no superficial influence — was now becoming a center radiating that civilization. In the regions north of the Danube, particularly in Muntenia and southern Moldavia, Greek penetration was greatly promoted by Hellenized Thracians, closely related to the Getae. On the other hand, Macedonia helped to spread the elements of Greek civilization by land, to western Dacia, Oltenia, and up to Banat and the central regions of Transylvania.

## 4. First Appearance of the Carpathian Dacians

THE invasion of the Galatians, which profoundly shook the Hellenistic states of Macedonia and Thrace up to Asia Minor, was an outflow of the vast Celtic migration which started in Gaul, over northern Italy and Central Europe, and penetrated into Dacian territory as early as the fourth century B.C. Celtic warriors — the Scordisci, Boii, Teurisci — settled in the vicinity of western Dacia, while other tribes infiltrated within the country as far as eastern Moldavia and Dobrudja. In their expansion, the Celts spread their specific forms of culture, named Latène after La Tène in Switzerland. Their culture was similar to that of the Geto-Dacians and at the same level, and both peoples were influenced by Greek civilization. Celtic artifacts frequently occur over the territory of this country, mostly in Transylvania and Oltenia, where continued finds attest the presence of Celtic warriors, while in Muntenia, Moldavia and Dobrudja the finds are less frequent.

As a consequence of Celtic migrations, groupings of Germanic populations appeared in Eastern Europe towards the close of the third century B.C., and from among them the Bastarnians, coming from the eastern parts of Germany, spread along the North Carpathian foothills and settled in Galicia and North and Central Moldavia; archeology characterizes them by a specific culture — the Oder-Vistula culture — which was first studied at Poieneşti in the Vaslui county in the Socialist Republic of Romania, and at Lukashovka (Orhei) in the Moldavian Soviet Socialist Republic.

The Bastarnians' invasion of Moldavia and their drive towards Transylvania over the Carpathians caused the local Dacian tribes to rise in opposition, this being the first time they are mentioned in historical records. The historian Pompeius Trogus tells of the Dacian king Oroles who, having been defeated by the Bastarnians, regrouped his forces and after reproving them, resumed the fight and repelled the enemy. Yet, this must have occurred only in the Carpathian foothills, for in the rest of Moldavia the Bastarnians dwelt for nearly two more centuries.

The battles fought against the Celts and then against the Bastarnians induced the Dacians of the Carpathians to form a durable union of tribes after the example of the Getian union along the Danube. The organizer of this new political power seems to have been a king called Rubobostes, whom Trogus mentions only briefly and vaguely, and who seems to have lived around the beginning of the second century B.C.

Two inscriptions found at Histria speak of the relations about the same time of the Greek cities in Dobrudja with certain native kings who were most probably Getians. One of the inscriptions, which might date from the third century B.C., mentions that a delegation had been sent to Zalmodegikos to negotiate the return of some Histrian hostages and of various incomes the city had been deprived of. There is no indication whether the name stands for a person or a place, and neither are the whereabouts mentioned, nor the people. It might, however, be inferred that Zalmodegikos was the king of a population far removed from Histria, probably dwelling left of the Danube, in Muntenia or in southern Moldavia. The name seems to be indisputably Getian. The second inscription, dating from the early second century B.C., is more precise. It tells of the difficulties Histria had experienced and of the opposition it had shown the enemy thanks to forces sent by an important king named Remaxos from the left bank of the Danube. The name of the king might well be Getian, too.

While the unions of Dacian tribes were being consolidated in Transylvania and in the Moldavian Carpathians, the old union of Getian tribes on the Lower Danube stood its ground during the troubled times of the invasions of the Celts and Bastarnians, and was as well-knit and strong as ever. Ultimately, a balance was established between the Geto-Dacians and their Celtic and Bastarnian neighbors, and alliances were forged, mainly with a view to joint plundering forays south of the Danube. On the Getian territory in Muntenia and southern Moldavia archeology attests that in those days there was an uninterrupted development of the local culture, with Greek influence.

The most significant historical process in the second century B.C. was Rome's eastward expansion as a consequence of its wars with Macedonia. When the homeland of Philip II and Alexander had become a Roman province in 148 B.C., the Getae and Dacians, singly or cooperating with the Celts and Bastarnians, carried on unceasing attacks against the new power that had been established in the middle of the Balkan Peninsula. Indeed they were its most implacable enemies. The prolonged resistance of the Illyrians, Dardanians, Scordisci, Triballians, and Thracians to the advance of the Romans, always found support in a Geto-Dacian alliance. Nevertheless, the Romans slowly but ineluctably strengthened their domination east of the Adriatic, showing a tendency to establish their boundary along the Danube.

It was in 74 B.C. that their forces first reached the Danube line, when Proconsul Scribonius Curio, having defeated the Dardanians, advanced as far as the Iron Gates. However, he did not dare to cross into Dacia, being, as Florus states, "scared of the dark woods there". Two years later, on the occasion of the war against Mithridates, king of Pontus, who had organized a vast anti-Roman coalition, which included the populations around the Black Sea, another Roman general — M. Licinius Terentius Varro Lucullus — subdued the Greek cities in Dobrudja and advanced up to the mouths of the Danube. But, this first attempt at enforcing Roman authority in Dobrudja did not last long for in 61 B.C. Proconsul C. Antonius Hybrida, bringing about an uprising of the local Greek cities by his pecuniary extortions, was defeated not far from Histria with the assistance of the Getae and Bastarnians.

## 5. Burebista Unites the Geto-Dacian People

THE fruits of this victory were gathered by the Getae who were then organizing a vast union of tribes, which included all the Geto-Dacian tribes under the leadership of Burebista. The latter did not originate in Dacia's Carpathian center: he was the head of the old union of Getian tribes on the Lower Danube. Strabo, who has given the most accurate information on the regional difference between the Getae and the Dacians, though the two belonged to the same people, asserts that Burebista was of Getian origin. Supported by the moral authority of the High Priest, Decaeneus, he succeeded in inculcating a sense of discipline into the Getae, enforcing sobriety, forbidding them to drink too much wine and ordering them to root out the vine, which they were beginning to cultivate assiduously after the methods they had learned from the Greeks and the Thracians of the Balkans. This particular is an additional indication that Burebista had his seat primarily among the Getae of Muntenia and Lower Moldavia, whose climate, unlike that of the Dacian mountains, is most favorable to the vine.

Valuable information on that great Getian king is given in an important Greek inscription that was found at Diony-sopolis (Balcic). It is an honorary decree whereby that Pontic city rewarded one of its citizens, Acornion, for having headed the city's messengers repeatedly and at his own expense, first to Burebista's father, whom he met in his capital, Arge-dava, then to Burebista himself who, in the meantime, had become "the foremost and greatest of Thracian kings," "hold-ing sway over the whole land on both banks of the Danube". Obviously, Burebista's own territory, with the Danube di-viding it and considered by his contemporaries to be part of Thrace, could be no other than that of the union of Getian tribes which had maintained close relations for centuries with the former Odrysian kingdom that stretched to the Danube mouths. Ancient records never consider the Dacians of the mountains as part of Thrace, even though they admit that they were relatives of the Thracians.

Argedava, residence of Burebista and of his predecessors, was probably situated on the river Argeș, if we take into account toponymic similarities for, as Vasile Pârvan soundly argued, the name of the river as pronounced by the Getae must have sounded something like Argesis, the term Ordessos used by Herodotus being only a Greek-Scythian deformation. The valley of the Argeș was at the time a main trade route between the Pontic cities and central Dacia, a continuation of the Danube, and consequently the natural route to be chosen by messengers coming from Dionysopolis. On the other hand, archeological research has revealed a number of stations along this valley, proving a remarkable develop-ment in the second and first centuries B.C. — the epoch of Burebista and of his predecessors. The Getian citadel of Popești on the right bank of the Argeș not far from Bucharest appears to be specific to Getian development and proof of profound assimilation of Hellenistic influence. It undoubtedly had held priority over all other stations in Dacia in those times, and its central position was suitable for the residence of a leader of the united Getian tribes of the Lower Danube plains. Its identification with Argedava, the seat of Burebista's dynasty, is the most probable hypothesis based on our present-day knowledge of this matter.

In the Geto-Dacian world, made anxious by the progress of Roman expansion and realizing the need of closing their ranks to oppose it, the old union of Getian tribes seemed to be the soundest, the most powerful, the best fitted to direct Geto-Dacian tendencies towards solidarity. Thus, before long Burebista who, according to available information, was an outstanding personality, headed an impressive political formation that incorporated immense territories stretching as far as Bohemia and the vicinity of the Austrian Alps, to the Northern Carpathians, to the Southern Bug and the Black Sea, to the vicinity of the Adriatic and to the Balkans. As Strabo states, he could always have at his command a force of 200,000 men.

The Getian king owed his extraordinary power not so much to force of arms as to his power of persuasion. The unification of the Geto-Dacians was stimulated by the imminent Roman threat and was facilitated by the concentration of the innumerable Geto-Dacian tribes into four regional unions, two being those of the Getae of the plains and of the Dacians in Transylvania. No data are available concerning the other two, but it can be supposed they were somewhere in the northern and eastern Carpathians, one in Maramureş and Slovakia north of Dacia, the other in Galicia and Moldavia. Once these unions had coalesced, Burebista could set about solving the problems of each by war, suppressing all the Celtic states of Central Europe, in the first place those of the Scordisci, Taurisci, and Boii in Pannonia, and extending Geto-Dacian rule over all the Danubian lands. He also subordinated to his interests all the rich Greek cities along the western coast of Pontus Euxinus — from Olbia (in the estuary of the Bug and Dnieper) to Apollonia (present-day Sozopoli not far from Burgas). Acornion's inscription, mentioned above, proves that some of these cities, Dionysopolis among them, had been for long under the Getian king's protection, but others came under his authority only when their resistance had been quashed. Olbia, for example, was completely destroyed by the Getians and there are indications that Histria also was devastated, while an inscription found at Mesembria (present-day Nesebar) clearly shows that that city at the Pontic extremity of the Balkan Mountains opposed Burebista's attacks by force of arms.

Acornion's inscription is also revealing as regards the stand taken by the Getian king in the great events that shook the Roman world in his time. While the civil war between Julius Caesar and Pompey was raging, in 48 B.C., soon after Caesar's transient defeat at Dyrrachium, Burebista sent Acornion, now become his diplomatist, to Heraclea Lyncestis in Macedonia, to negotiate an alliance with Pompey who no doubt agreed to recognize the Getian king's immense conquests in return for the military aid the latter offered. However, Caesar's decisive victory at Pharsalus took place before the forces of the Getian king could reach the theater of war. Nevertheless, Rome considered the Getian threat so serious that the Pharsalus victor decided to forestall it by undertaking a great expedition in Dacia. A mighty army had been concentrated in Macedonia for the purpose, and Caesar was all ready for war when he was murdered on the Ides of March in 44 B.C. The expedition was called off.

Soon after, Burebista himself suffered the same fate as his opponent, for he was overthrown and killed by a conspiracy of malcontents. These were most probably heads of the regional unions of tribes who wished to regain their freedom. They were unwilling to accept a permanent coalition in the form of a monarchic centralization incompatible with the spirit of tribal autonomy rooted in the tradition of Geto-Dacian society, especially in view of the fact that after Caesar's death the Roman threat was not serious enough to justify their subordination to a supreme chief. Burebista's death was followed by the parceling out of his huge political entity; it was divided into four parts, one of them (there is no specification as to which) being subsequently divided in two.

Burebista's intention to change the shaky confederation of Geto-Dacian tribal unions — built in haste and rather as a transitory alliance — into a durable, well organized state is evidenced by his deeds. Moreover, it was the Geto-Dacian people's only chance of successfully resisting the immense bloc of Roman power. Once at the head of the great union he had built up, Burebista left his regional residence in the plain, Argedava, to found a new seat at Royal Sarmizegetusa (Grădiştea Muncelului), a stronghold built in a mountain range difficult of access.

Even though centralization, according to Burebista's plan, was unsuccessful, being too far removed from the stage of socio-political development of the Geto-Dacian tribes at the time, that it continued a military democracy, the meteoric passage of such a powerful figure in the history of the Geto-Dacian people had profound consequences. It was Burebista who laid the foundations of the Geto-Dacian state. He forged closer connections between Geto-Dacian tribes and promoted intensive intertribal economic circulation, which led to a swift and uniform spread of the Getian culture of the Lower Danube throughout the Carpatho-Danubian territory under his authority. It was he who established the center of gravity of the Geto-Dacian state in the Dacians' mountains. It might well be that the main part in the conspiracy that removed him was played by the Dacian aristocracy. It is a fact that the regional tribal union which profited most as a result of the removal of the Getian king was that of the Dacians. Installed in the capital city and having taken over the elements of the incipient state which Burebista had created, this union of the Transylvanian mountains was to continue to develop in the following years. They now held the prominent place which the Getians of the Romanian plain had held for centuries.

## 6. *The Danube Getae Fall under Roman Rule*

ALTHOUGH the Geto-Dacians after Burebista's death ceased to be an impressive power, for they were no longer united, their policy towards Rome during the new civil wars which followed Caesar's death was just as active and as much opposed to the representative of the Italic Peninsula. At the battle of Philippi in 42 B.C., Caesar's murderers were aided in their opposition to Octavian and Mark Anthony by a Dacian corps headed by one Coson, whose name is to be found on the gold coins minted by Junius Brutus on that occasion. Such coins have been found in great number in Transylvania. Coson might be identical with the Dacian king Cotison who ruled southwestern Dacia and who was shortly to enter into negotiations with Octavian, but historical sources do not show conclusive proof of the identity. During the Civil War of 31 B.C., which ended with Mark Anthony's defeat at Actium, Octavian had no Geto-Dacian ally on his side. On the other hand, his rival, who represented the East, had been supported by Dicomes, a king of the Lower Danube, who, though prepared to resume Burebista's policy and despite the subsidies he had received, did not take part in the fight. Events were too quick for him, as formerly at Pharsalus, and the war ended before the Getian corps arrived. Actually, it was a naval battle that decided the destinies of the war. The latest observations seem to point to Moldavia's Carpathian foothills as the seat of King Dicomes.

Undisputed leader of the Roman power after Actium, Octavian sought to establish a firm boundary along the whole course of the Danube for the empire he was organizing. The occasion to do so arose sooner than he expected in the territory at the mouths of the river, for he had to face a great migration of the Bastarnians into the Balkan Peninsula. Octavian sent M. Licinius Crassus, Proconsul of Macedonia, against the aggressors. The Proconsul had to wage war for two wearisome years (29-28 B.C.) before he could break the resistance of the Thracian populations, crush the Bastarnians and conquer the whole peninsula up to the Danube. Among the Getians on the right bank of the river, he had a devoted ally in the local king, Roles, who had suffered great losses at the hands of the Bastarnians. On the other hand, in the middle of the present-day territory of Dobrudja, the Roman general came up against the fierce resistance of the Getian tribes headed by Dapyx. After defeating Dapyx, who committed suicide, Crassus attacked the Getian tribe in northern Dobrudja headed by Zyraxes, ending the war with the conquest of the Danubian city of Genucla, where he recovered the trophies taken from the Romans thirty years earlier following the defeat of C. Antonius Hybrida. The Romans entrusted the newly conquered land to the Odrysian kingdom of Thrace, which was revived as a client state. Octavian, who had in the meantime become emperor under the name of Augustus, did not deem these regions to be sufficiently safe to install direct Roman administration there.

Dobrudja and the other territories on the right bank of the Danube were thus incorporated in the sphere of Roman authority. This was a great blow to the old union of Getian tribes which, greatly weakened after Burebista's death, had its territories limited strictly to the Danube border and was squeezed between Thraco-Roman authority on one side and the Sarmatians on the other. The latter were Iranian nomads kindred to the Scythians. Having overrun all the vast steppes north of Pontus Euxinus, they had now reached the mouths of the Danube. In the end, a balance and even a partnership was established between them and the Geto-Dacian populations, who joined them in their plundering raids in the Roman-protected Balkan countries. The fact is that the Getians of Muntenia and Moldavia ceaselessly made such raids, creating an atmosphere of terror in the territories subject to the Thracian kingdom. The poet Ovid, who was exiled by Emperor Augustus to Tomis between 9 and 18 A.D., gives in his works impressive testimonies of the precarious life of the inhabitants of Dobrudja in those days under the constant threat of trans-Danubian attacks. Augustus took a number of energetic measures to put an end to this state of affairs and to consolidate his boundary along the Danube. While a great uprising of the Illyrians in Dalmatia and Pannonia was suppressed after a long war (6-9 A.D.), Consul Cn. Cornelius Lentulus crushed a Getian army which had overrun the territory south of the Lower Danube and enforced a pact on the Sarmatians under which the latter agreed to keep far from the mouths of the Danube. Soon after these successes, from about 9 to 11 A.D., the Roman general Sextus Aelius Catus crossed the Danube into the Muntenian plain and after several bloody battles during which no less than three local kings fell, suppressed the union of Getian tribes and compelled the population to pull down their strongholds and leave the territory. Some 50,000 Getians settled in what was to be the Province of Moesia, as subjects of the Roman Empire. Archeological research carried out in the main Getian strongholds of that area — Zimnicea on the Danube, Popeşti on the Argeş, Piscul Crăsanilor on the Ialomiţa —, where there is no further proof of habitation after the early years of our era, leaves no doubt that the measures taken by Aelius Catus were uncompromising.

This is an event of outstanding importance. The old political formation of the Getians on the Lower Danube, which had been a strong and flourishing body for so many centuries and a source of progress for Geto-Dacian culture, was now totally stamped out. The Getians who had been outside this area, for example at Tinosul further north on the river Prahova on the outskirts of the Carpathian foothills, were not a Getian force, for they were dependent on the goodwill of the Romans. And even the Getians of Moldavia, who were still free, were unable to undertake anything of note on their own. Their offensive against northern Dobrudja in the years 12 and 15 when they conquered the cities of Aegyssus (Tulcea) and Troesmis (Igliţa-Turcoaia) from the Odrysians, had only ephemeral results for, despite their gallantry, they were forced to flee when the Roman army intervened. Thenceforth they made no further attempt to attack the frontier of the Empire.

Following their great success, the Romans continued to consolidate still more intensively their frontier along the Danube. In 46 Emperor Claudius considered the moment ripe to suppress the Odrysian kingdom and to establish there a Roman provincial régime. The territory south of the Balkan Mountains then became the province of Thrace while the territory along the Danube, Ripa Thraciae, comprising also Dobrudja, was incorporated into the province of Moesia. The latter province founded by Emperor Tiberius in 15 A.D., occupied more or less the territory of present-day Serbia and also the lands of the Triballians. Now it was extended all along the Lower Danube down to the sea. The governors of this province made it their concern to defend the river frontier and to promote the economic activities of the autonomous Pontic cities now under imperial patronage. Important data are given in this respect by the elaborate inscription which shows the boundaries *(horothesia)* of the city of Histria. From among the governors mentioned in this document as benefactors of the Greek cities in Dobrudja, Tiberius Plautius Silvanus Aelianus is also known for his many important activities mentioned in his famous epitaph at Tibur (Tivoli), Italy. It is mentioned that under Emperor Nero between the

years 57-67, more precisely around the year 62, he nipped
in the bud a Sarmatian movement north of the mouths of
the Danube, freed the Greek city of Chersonesus (near Sebas-
topol in the Crimea) which was being besieged by local
Scythians, and colonized 100,000 Transdanubians (Bastarnians, Sarmatians, Roxolani, and Dacians from Moldavia
and from north of the Carpathians) who, pressed by the
expansion of the Iazygian Sarmatians, asked the Roman
Empire for asylum. Aelianus assigned to them territories in
Moesia where they settled with their families and their chieftains, tilling the sparsely populated land of the province
and increasing the Empire's revenue by their tribute. The
Iazygians, some of whom had settled in the steppe of west
Dacia between the Pannonian Danube and the Tisa, were
compelled to observe Roman peace and Roman organization.

## 7. *Geto-Dacian Culture*

GETO-DACIAN culture was on the ascendant. Its beginnings had been in the Getian area along the Danube, on the
basis of Geto-Dacian elements but under the impulse of Greek
influence. Later, it assumed its own creative impetus and aspect,
and spread over the entire territory occupied by the Geto-
Dacians when Burebista united them. After the death of the
great Getian king, far from ceasing its progress, it reached
full maturity during the first century A.D., at the time when
the Dacian state at Sarmizegetusa assumed political prominence in the Carpathian territories.

As a result of demographic growth and of economic
development, the Geto-Dacian settlements became very
numerous between the third and the first century B.C. and
also in the first century A.D., as attested by archeological
research. Apart from the purely rural settlements which
occupied convenient places in the valleys, on river terraces
and in forest glades, there were fortified settlements whose
frequency is truly impressive. The latter were densely populated places of the oppidum type — named *dava* by the
local people — genuine economic, political, religious, and
military centers of the tribes: budding towns and actually
performing the functions of towns. Although they did not

resemble the Greek-Roman towns, Greek authors do not hesitate to speak of them as *polis*, a term they also use for the urban localities of the Mediterranean world. Such Geto-Dacian centers had emerged at places important for economic and strategic reasons: crossroads, fords, mountain passes, places where valleys met or where transport means had to be changed. They were situated on dominant heights in isolation, and natural defenses were supplemented by ditches, vallums, and stockades. Beginning in Burebista's time, stone walls of an improved technique reinforced with timber were built in the capital in the Dacian mountains with the assistance of craftsmen enticed from the Roman empire, primarily Greek; walls were also built according to local concepts based on Celtic influence.

In the settlements of the Danube plain, where there were no stone quarries, all structures were made of wood and clay, which were also basic materials for most of the dwellings in the west of Dacia. The houses were usually built above the ground and consisted of one or several rooms. They had an earthen floor and roofing of straw, reeds, or boards. Roofing tiles were currently used in the settlement of Popești on the river Argeș. In this important Getian settlement of Burebista's time, a large conglomeration of houses with many rooms, each designed for a special purpose, has been found. It undoubtedly belonged to the head of a tribe or of a tribal union. It spreads over more than 6,000 sq.ft., and includes a large rectangular structure with sacred hearths inside and an apse along the northwestern part. Places for religious use similarly shaped and oriented were also to be found in the Dacian cities on the tops of the Orăștie mountains.

At Grădiștea Muncelului, on the mountain where Sarmizegetusa Regia was situated and where the main shrine of the Geto-Dacians was to be found, there were stone circles and aligned wooden poles with discoidal stone pedestals, and in the center of the most sacred of those circles there was a structure with an apse as described above. The principal circle had a 90-ft. diameter and consisted of two rows of parallelipipedic andesite blocks placed close to each other, the row towards the inside consisting of thirty groups of six uniform blocks each, followed by a seventh lower and broader block. This order has been interpreted as a symbol for the half-year calendar connected with the sun rite.

For ages the Geto-Dacians had been known to be greatly devoted to their god, Zamolxis, who was worshiped in caves and on the heights. They believed that death in battle secured eternal life. Their religion was Uranian, solar and henotheistic, belief in other deities, apart from the main one, being admitted. The Geto-Dacians were famed for their magic practices and their medical art based on wide knowledge of healing herbs. Generally they attached no great importance to funeral rites. Compared with the number of their settlements, few graves have been found, and those hardly ever grouped in large cemeteries. Burial rites varied according to the region, the tribe, and the epoch. An evolution is observed from frequent inhumation in the fifth to third centuries B.C. to general cremation in the following centuries. There were both flat and tumulus graves. The tumuli were raised over the place of cremation, with burnt bones and fragments of burnt offerings mixed indiscriminately without being deposited in urns. At Poieneşti in Moldavia and at Zimnicea in Muntenia slow cremation is found to have been practiced: the corpses were laid in graves that were actually heated ovens and subsequently covered with earth (fourth to third centuries B.C.).

The Geto-Dacians' main pursuits were agriculture and animal husbandry, whereby they procured their means of subsistence as well as goods sought after by Greek traders who gave in exchange the products of their art and crafts. In the Geto-Dacian settlements explored so far, iron implements (ploughs, shares, hoes, spades, sickles) have frequently been found, as well as primitive quirns or rotary two-piece ones, made of sandstone or volcanic tuff. The grain was usually kept in holes in the ground, but starting from the first century B.C. big burnt-clay storage jars *(pithoi)* were used for the purpose. A large number of these have been found at Popeşti dating from Burebista's time, and in the strongholds in the Orăştie Mountains of a later period. Apart from wheat and rye, the Geto-Dacians ate millet. Their animals were cattle and sheep, pigs and goats and also horses, animals of prime necessity in transport and in battle. Hunting, fishing, and beekeeping were additional pursuits.

Besides their work to procure food, the Geto-Dacians practiced various crafts. Very many iron objects have been found in their settlements for the working of wood and metals. Their tools were of various types, for fairly evolved crafts: smith's work, bronze casting, and the production of personal adornments out of precious metals after Greek models. Beginning in the third century B.C., there is a sign of greater commercial activity: the minting of coins imitating the Macedonian and Thasos types. In the first century A.D. they counterfeited the Roman Republican denarii but the silver title was occasionally higher than that of the original coin. For the purpose they used directly molded dies.

The most representative category of products showing the progress achieved by Geto-Dacian culture is earthenware. Besides the traditional hand-made types, whether porous or burnished, there have been found in Geto-Dacian settlements a considerable number of wheel-made types showing great craftsmanship and an advanced technique. Among the luxury ware made by Getian potters there are in particular cups and bowls decorated in relief with dies in imitation of the Hellenistic model but with elements suggesting local imagination. The main center of manufacture was in the city of Popeşti on the Argeş whose earthenware shops ranked foremost in the Geto-Dacian world not only in the production of common pottery but also of big storage jars and amphorae imitating those of Rhodes. Roofing tiles were also made at Popeşti. In the first century A.D. remarkable progress was made by the shops at Sarmizegetusa (Grădiştea Muncelului) where painted ware showing realistic figures was being produced apart from the other types of ware.

Inside the country trade was carried on by local people, while outside the country the Geto-Dacians traded with the Greeks and Romans. In their settlements Greek, Macedonian, and Roman coins are frequently found, mostly silver coins and occasionally some of gold and bronze. Counterfeit coins are also to be found. There are moreover countless imported goods of various categories: tools, weapons, personal adornments.

The Geto-Dacians dressed in woolen and hempen fabrics, and in winter they also wore furs. The reliefs on Trajan's Column and on the Adamclisi Monument give a correct picture of their dress and physique. Their weapons were spears, straight or curved swords, shields, and arrows. The Getae of the plain, once under Scythian influence, were mounted archers of repute. Spurs and arrowheads have been found in their settlements in large numbers.

Though the Geto-Dacians had made great progress in practical life, they were faithful to their old traditions in their spiritual life. Their religion still called for human sacrifices, a trait common to other European populations at that time. They did not know how to write; the Greek amphorae they imitated from the Greek ones bore a seal but no letters. Neither is there any writing on their coins, which were imitations of Macedonian models. At Grădiştea Muncelului, however, isolated Greek letters are to be found on the walls of the city, possibly written by the craftsmen brought from other countries. It is also at Grădiştea that an enormous religious vase of local make was found bearing a stamp with a Dacian inscription in Latin letters: *Decebalus per Scorilo*, "Decebalus son of Scorilo" — obviously a reference to the last Dacian king.

Most of the Geto-Dacians' artifacts belong to the ornamental category. Without excelling, they gave proof of good craftsmanship as shown by their jewelry and earthenware. Their bone tools are engraved with fine geometrical motifs. The human figure is only represented by primitive bronze or clay semblances for religious or magic purposes (as a defense against evil spirits).

The progress of Geto-Dacian culture was part of their evolution from the tribal stage to the slave-owning system. It was a period of military democracy when constant wars of plunder were waged and the trend towards individualism and social differences appeared. Beginning in Burebista's time, the Geto-Dacians were enjoying all the essential conditions for the organization of a state; the productive forces and goods production had developed (archeological finds are sound proof of the above statement); division of labor, as attested by the development of crafts and trade, had been accentuated; private property had gradually appeared, to begin with ownership of mobile goods, then land ownership; labor was carried out by slaves, who were also an article of trade in great demand in the Greek and Roman markets; social classes, and no doubt the conflicts that go with them, had appeared. The aristocracy — the *pileati*, in Dacian *tarabostes* — are shown in ancient images wearing bonnets *(pileus)* in contradistinction to the common people *(comati)* who wore their hair loose without any headdress. The state, whose centralizing organization was vaguely put together under Burebista, gradually brought under its sway the whole territory of the Dacian mountain tribes, to assume the robust aspect it had in the time of Decebalus when it showed so manifestly its cohesion, power, and aspirations towards a higher stage of civilization, before being suppressed by the Romans.

## 8. *Decebalus's Wars against the Romans*

DEFEATED in all their attempts to oppose encirclement by the Romans and almost wholly isolated after the fall of the Getian power, the Dacians of Transylvania were for a long time on the defensive in their mountainous country following the reign of Augustus. However, the civil war which raged in the Roman Empire from 69 A.D. to 70 A.D., after Nero's death, was an occasion for them and for the Sarmatians to resume their attacks south of the Danube. Even during Nero's reign, in the winter of 67-68 A.D., the Roxolan Sarmatians had crossed the Danube into Dobrudja and, taking two auxiliary Roman cohorts by surprise, had slaughtered them. Encouraged by these easy victories and by the aggravation of domestic affairs in the Empire, they returned to northern Dobrudja in greater numbers the following winter. M. Aponius Saturninus, Governor of Moesia, was prompt to retaliate: his legions fell on the invaders' armored cavalry *(catafractarii)* and completely smashed them as their horses could not move freely on account of a slippery ground. At the close of the year 69 when Aponius had taken his forces to Italy to support Vespasian against Emperor Vitellius, the Dacians also went into action, devastating a number of Moesia's districts. Their advance was only repelled by the unexpected intervention of an eastern legion which was crossing Macedonia on its way to Italy. Soon after, early in 70, when Vespasian had been proclaimed Emperor, the Sarmatians again crossed the Danube into Dobrudja with overwhelming forces. When the new governor of Moesia, C. Fonteius Agrippa, sought to oppose them, he was killed with the greater part of his legions. His successor, Rubrius Gallus, finally succeeded after fierce fighting in putting them to flight.

It was through this legate that Vespasian reestablished Roman order along the Danube. Moesia's boundary was greatly reinforced, the legions in the province were increased to four, and the military fleet on the Danube, which had been active ever since Augustus's time, was reorganized. Following these measures, the Dacians were persuaded to conclude a peace treaty with the Empire, which they observed faithfully for fifteen years. An inducement to this end had been the periodic payment made by the Romans. It was only in 85, under Emperor Domitian, that they tried to take advantage of the difficulties this son of Vespasian was encountering along other frontiers, by claiming that their subsidy should be increased. Their claim was rejected. This is a possible interpretation of a statement reported by Jordanes after Dion Chrysostom, contemporary with these events, to the effect that the Dacians had broken the pact "concluded earlier with other emperors", "because they feared Domitian's stinginess".

Unexpectedly the Dacians overran Moesia, inflicting a disastrous defeat on the Romans. The forces that stood in their way were slaughtered, together with the governor of the province, C. Oppius Sabinus. Domitian was alarmed and hastened to the Danube. Following the measures taken by him, the invaders were driven back across the river. In 86 the province of Moesia, being considered too big to carry out the military duties devolving on it, was divided in two: Moesia Superior, west of the river Ciabrus (Tzibritza), more or less present-day Serbia, and Moesia Inferior in the east, which incorporated the land of the Triballians, the former Ripa Thraciae, most of present-day Bulgaria and the whole of Dobrudja. The two provinces were ruled by a governor that had a consulary rank and was entitled *legatus Augusti pro praetore*. Each governor had an army made up of two legions and of auxiliary forces. Cornelius Fuscus, the praetor's prefect, was put in command of a great army that was to undertake reprisals in Dacia. Sure of victory, Domitian returned to Rome without waiting to see the results of the expedition.

Aware of the danger but considering himself too old to face the Romans, Duras, king of the Dacians (also called Diurpaneus), abdicated in favor of Decebalus, son of Scorilo, who had ruled before him. Decebalus was endowed with exceptional military and political qualities and proved well able to meet the emergency. Cornelius Fuscus crossed the Danube on a pontoon bridge in the summer of 87 and sought to reach the center of Dacia by the shortest route which ran through Banat along the Bistra Valley towards Sarmizegetusa. Being impulsive and venturesome, brave but rash, the exact opposite of his skilled and cautious Dacian opponent, he let himself be drawn into the trap the latter had laid for him, and with his army met his death in a fearful slaughter which may have taken place in the Tapae Pass (the Iron Gates of Transylvania). This was one of the most memorable of the disasters inflicted on the Romans. The banners, war engines, and weapons which had fallen into Dacian hands were taken to one of the strongholds in the mountains around Sarmizegetusa.

Decebalus was in no haste to take advantage of his success by a new invasion of Moesia, where he would have run the risk of compromising the glorious prestige he had won. In his wisdom, he used his prestige to strengthen his authority within the country and to win allies outside it. He realized that the Roman Empire had vast resources and that a new Roman offensive against the Dacians was to be expected. Aware of the superiority of Roman civilization, he sought to entice craftsmen and deserters from the Empire by every possible means so that he might build strongholds and war engines and initiate the Dacians in Roman military tactics.

Domitian reacted promptly and energetically. A new army of impressive proportions was formed and an able and experienced general, Consul Tettius Julianus (who had participated in the victory won by Aponius Saturninus in Dobrudja against the Roxolans in 69) was put in command. Julianus crossed the Danube, possibly at Drobeta, in 88 and taking the straight way through Banat in order to penetrate into Transylvania by way of the Bistra Valley, he defeated Decebalus's forces at Tapae, the same place where Fuscus's disaster had occurred the year before. Vezinas, a Dacian dignitary, second in rank after Decebalus, was only saved from captivity by pretending death and getting away from the battlefield during the night. Following this defeat, Decebalus gave proof of outstanding military ability — more than on the occasion of his former victory, for he succeeded in circumscribing the consequences of defeat and delaying the enemy's advance. What was left of his forces regrouped and withdrew in good order inside the country. Frontinus reports that in order to gain freedom of movement and to check Julianus's advance, even though only for a brief time, the Dacian king ordered that branches should be lopped off some of the forest trees, and clothes and weapons be put on the trunks to give the Romans the impression that a great army had come to replace the vanquished one. For a time his stratagem was successful, but ultimately the Roman forces reached the neighborhood of the mountains clustering about Sarmizegetusa. Decebalus asked for peace.

Domitian's first impulse was to refuse the request and continue the war until all Dacian forces had been crushed, but having been defeated in the meantime by the Quadi and the Marcomanni at the Pannonian Danube, he consented to a compromise peace in 89 A.D., the Dacian king thereby becoming a client of the Roman Empire in exchange for an annual stipend and assistance offered him in the way of craftsmen skilled in the building of cities and of war engines. Decebalus did not pay homage to the Roman emperor, but sent his brother Diegis instead. The latter being heir presumptive (according to the agnatic rule of succession to the throne) was fully entitled to represent the Dacian state. Domitian permitted the substitution and was also content to have merely a symbolic implementation of the stipulation that the Dacians should return the trophies taken from the Romans at the time of Fuscus's disaster.

The peace of 89, being equivocal, aroused deep discontent among the senators in Rome who were in fierce conflict with

1. TOOLS FROM THE PALEOLITHIC AGE

CLAY VESSELS TYPICAL OF THE CUCUTENI CULTURE

3. NEOLITHIC STATUETTES

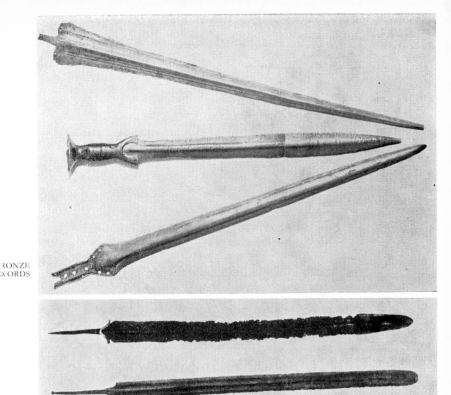

IRON
SWORDS
AND
HELMET
CELTIC
ORIGIN

6. DECEBALUS, IN A SCENE ON TRAJAN'S COLUMN

7. BATTLE SCENES ON TRAJAN'S COLUMN

8. ROMAN COIN FROM TRAJAN'S TIME (OBVERSE AND REVERSE)

9. METOPES OF THE
ADAMCLISI
MONUMENT

10. RUINS OF THE ADAMCLISI MONUMENT AND MODEL OF THE RECONSTITUTED MONUMENT

Domitian. This unfavorable view is the only comment that has come down to us. And yet the peace was not so unfavorable to the Romans. Decebalus had lost much of his independence and was closely bound up with the interests of the Empire to which he was doing good service not only by abstaining from acts of hostility but also by watching the neighboring populations and inducing them to assume a similar pacific stand. It is undeniable that he faithfully observed the pact throughout the rule of Domitian and of Nerva until Trajan's war, which was solely the latter's initiative. The Dacian king's peaceful attitude was not only due to the subsidies that were regularly paid him but also to the fact that the Romans had taken forceful military measures. The authority of the Dacian state had been removed all along the Danube and restricted to the Transylvanian mountains. Banat, Oltenia, Muntenia, and Moldavia had become areas that served as a glacis for the Roman frontier along the river. Archeology attests that important Getian citadels north of the Danube plain, such as Tinosul on the river Prahova and Poiana on the Siret, ceased to exist from that time onwards, though formerly they had been spared.

Even though Decebalus seemed to be docile at the time, the growing prosperity of the Dacian state and the consolidation of its forces filled the Romans with well-founded fears for the future. With the assistance of the craftsmen the Romans had procured, the mountains around Sarmizegetusa had been turned into a formidable system of fortifications whose advanced techniques were designed to make Decebalus unconquerable not only by trans-Danubian neighbors (for in Domitian's pact this was the reason for the subsidy paid him) but also by the Romans. Consequently, as soon as Emperor Trajan ascended the throne in 98, he made it his aim to suppress this highly dangerous center. Trajan was a military man and shared in every particular the views of the Roman senators. Moreover, the conquest of Dacia was to bring substantial economic benefits to the Empire.

After detailed preparations, war was declared by the Romans in the spring of 101 without any provocation from the Dacian king. Unlike Domitian, Trajan enjoyed a most favorable strategic position: he had immense forces which were well

organized and under the command of an outstanding general —
himself; there were no other involvements along the Empire's
frontiers; he had full freedom of action, and had started hostilities at the moment and place chosen by himself; his opponent, however, had restricted possibilities, his forces being
small in number, and he was almost isolated and compelled
to be only on the defensive in his fortified mountains. However long and gallant Decebalus's resistance in the mountains, his downfall was a certainty to the Romans from the
beginning of the campaign. And yet, the Romans won only
after two hard-fought wars carried on over a period of six
years, and the efforts and risks of the Roman army were
immense. Trajan had to face the severe geographic conditions of the theater of war around Sarmizegetusa, the gallantry and discipline of the Dacian people, and especially the
energy and wisdom of their king, Decebalus.

Far from passively awaiting the threat, Decebalus sought
to counterbalance the inferiority of his forces and the difficulties of his position by wise and audacious moves. He
made an alliance with the Dacian, Sarmatian, and Germanic
populations north of the Carpathians, primarily with the
Suevian Buri of Slovakia and Maramureş, whom Tacitus
mentions in his works, and, no longer isolated, built up a
vast plan whereby he meant to take advantage of Trajan's
offensive tactics. When the huge Roman army had penetrated
deep into Transylvania's mountains, Dacia's allies were to
spill into Dobrudja in large numbers — in the regions far-
thermost from the Carpathians — and, taking advantage of
the poor Roman defense in those parts of the *limes*, were to
make speedily for the Balkan provinces in order to intercept
Trajan's communications with the rest of his Empire and
strike at him from behind while Decebalus undertook a coun-
teroffensive. Thus encircled, the Roman army would have
been threatened with unprecedented disaster. The success
of the plan largely depended on perfect coordination of the
moves of heterogeneous forces placed at an enormous distances from one another, as well as on complete secrecy of the
allies' intentions, on cunning, and constant misinforming
of the Roman emperor. It was of the utmost importance
that operations in the Dacian mountains should be prolonged by every possible means until winter, for the hard frosts

of this part of Europe would facilitate the allied invasion along the Lower Danube while locking the Roman fleet at Drobeta which would otherwise have been an excellent instrument for rapid Roman moves inside Dacia. Decebalus and his allies faithfully carried out what had been demanded of them by this grand plan. But skill alone was not enough. The mildness of that winter's frosts was in favor of the Romans and compromised everything.

At the beginning of the war in the summer of 101, the Romans took the initiative. Two armies, coming from Moesia and Pannonia respectively, crossed the Danube by pontoon bridges at both ends of the Cazane defile, one under the command of Laberius Maximus, governor of Moesia Inferior, at Drobeta, the other under Trajan, at Lederata. Skirting the Banat mountains, Trajan advanced along the valleys of the Caraș, Cernovăț, Bîrzava, and Pogăniș, and Laberius along the valleys of the Cerna, Belareca, Domașna, and Timiș, the two armies meeting at Tibiscum not far from present-day Caransebeș, having been offered no resistance. No sooner had Trajan crossed the Danube and started on his expedition through Banat, than a messenger brought him a communication written in Latin letters on a mushroom, asking him to stay his advance and make peace. The message was from the Buri and the other allies of King Decebalus. By thus warning Trajan that the Dacians were not isolated but enjoyed the support of numerous warlike populations, Decebalus hoped to induce the Roman emperor to start negotiations for peace or at least to overhaul his war machinery, which would have enabled the Dacian king to gain time. But Trajan continued his march onwards. Having joined forces at Tibiscum, the two Roman columns advanced along the Bistra Valley towards Sarmizegetusa.

It was at Tapae, the narrow, forested place now called the Iron Gates of Transylvania, that Trajan first met resistance. Having abstained from hostile acts so far, Decebalus decided to give battle thinking that even if the day went against him it would delay the enemy's advance. Topographic conditions here were unfavorable to the deployment of the Romans' superior forces. The clash was fierce but shorter than expected. Only the auxiliary Roman forces fought, for the battle was won before the legionaries had cause to inter-

vene. With a violent storm raging and impressed by the death
of a Dacian chieftain struck by lightning, the Dacians abandoned their positions and withdrew, though in good order.
They had been defeated by the elements and their super-
stitious fears rather than by the superiority of the
Romans.

The Roman army in pursuit of the Dacians occupied the
Hațeg country and penetrated into the Orăștie mountains
by way of Boșorod and Costești. In one of the Dacian citadels,
the Romans recovered the booty taken by Decebalus on the
occasion of Cornelius Fuscus's disastrous expedition. It
should be recalled that after the peace negotiated with Domitian in 89, this booty had not been returned by Decebalus.
Simultaneously a wing of the Roman army under the command
of Laberius Maximus undertook an expedition along the
Luncani Valley southwest of Sarmizegetusa (Grădiștea Muncelului) where he conquered by a surprise attack an important
citadel, possibly on the site of present-day Piatra Roșie; he
also captured Decebalus's sister. The Roman advance over
the mountains was very slow on account of a variety of difficulties and primarily because of the resistance of the Dacians,
who withdrew towards Sarmizegetusa only by slow degrees,
never abandoning a position without fierce fighting and
destroying everything they could not carry away with them.
In order to gain time by tergiversation, Decebalus sent the
emperor a great deputation of his allies headed by Buri foot
soldiers and Sarmatian horsemen, to bring to his notice that
they, too, would go into action if he didn't cease hostilities.
Trajan refused to deal with them but was soon met by another delegation, this time of lower class Dacians, *comati*, who
handed him a request for peace direct from Decebalus. The
Roman emperor again refused the request, which was osten-
sibly insincere as it had not been transmitted by the representatives of a class possessing political responsibilities. However, all this served the dilatory purposes of the Dacian king.
Winter was coming and military operations would cease without any decisive result having been obtained by the Romans.
Nevertheless, they were so near the main target of the war,
Sarmizegetusa, and Decebalus's position seemed so desperate
that they could spend the winter looking forward to the promising prospects of the following spring.

But the Romans' dreams were rudely shattered, for at the height of winter unexpected news reached them that the bulk of Decebalus's allies had crossed into Dobrudja and the remaining territory of Moesia Inferior and were attacking the weak auxiliary Roman garrisons along the Lower Danube. It was only then that Trajan realized how serious had been the threat made by the Buri and their allies. His victorious advance into the Dacian mountains could end by being a dangerous trap if the Dacian plan were carried out. The initiative had passed into the hands of his able opponent without his being aware of it. The emperor had to readjust things without delay in order to meet this unexpected situation. Leaving behind only sufficient forces to keep the positions that had been won, he took the bulk of his army to Drobeta where his fleet was stationed. Fortunately for him, winter was surprisingly mild that year. The reliefs on Trajan's Column — that precious document that gives a full account of the Dacian wars in eloquent scenes — show how on the Daco-Sarmatian coalition crossing the Danube, the crust of ice being thin broke under the weight of some of their cavalry and caused a grievous disaster. Trajan is then shown in the early months of 102 embarking his forces and impedimenta and floating swiftly on the ice-free waters of the Danube. Having disembarked in one of the ports of Moesia Inferior, possibly Novae (Shishtov) or Sexaginta Prista (Ruse), he made for the interior of the province at the head of his cavalry and defeated beyond recovery the Sarmatian horsemen, after which he took all his forces to the Shipka Pass and caught up with an important Dacian army not far from present-day Tirnovo, which he surprised during the night and crushed after savage fighting. Here he ordered that a citadel — Nicopolis ad Istrum, present-day Stari Nikiup — should be immediately built. This victory made communications between his army and the rest of the Empire safe, while Decebalus's plan was dealt its first blow.

Nevertheless, the plan still held good for the counter-offensive of the Dacian king in the Transylvanian mountains after Trajan's departure ended with the defeat of the Roman forces while the main column of Decebalus's allies, the most numerous and strongest, was advancing from northern Dobrudja to the Balkans. Trajan went to meet them with all his forces. The clash that took place on the Adamclisi Plateau in the forested steppe of southwestern Dobrudja was an all-out slaughter. This is the battle that is the most extensively represented on the Column. All the Roman forces took part in it: auxiliaries, legionaries, pretorians, the emperor's personal guard, the Roman war engines; the enemy were slaughtered indiscriminately and for the first and only time wounded Romans belonging to the auxiliary forces as well as to the legions are shown. It was a victory won by the Romans but at the cost of an immense sacrifice. The column shows barbarians in flight or captured in great numbers, and it also shows Trajan delivering a speech to thank his men and handing out rewards.

The mutilated text of Cassius Dio refers to this battle and not to the easy victory won at Tapae. It says: "Trajan saw many wounded among his men and killed many of the enemy, and as bandages were insufficient he is said not to have spared his own clothes, which he tore into strips to bind the wounds; for those who had died in battle he ordered that an altar be raised and services to their memory be officiated every year." The altar was discovered at Adamclisi, where the battle was fought. The foundations and steps form a square with sides of 36 ft. still above ground, while what is left of the wall discovered among the ruins entitles us to conclude that they were about 18 ft. high, all covered with the names of the Roman soldiers fallen in battle, whose number is estimated to total nearly 4,000, an enormous figure for a victorious army. The inscription on the frontispiece of the structure reads: *In Honorem et Memoriam fortissimorum virorum cui pugnantes pro Re Publica morte occubuerunt* (In honor and to the memory of the gallant men who fighting for the state were brought down in death). Heading the list of the fallen was the name of a *praefectus* whose name has not been preserved but who must have been *praefectus castrorum*, a senior officer in charge of army administration and in command of the reserves left behind in the camp and consisting of those recovered from their wounds and of veterans soon to be discharged *(missicii)*. The fallen include such *missicii*, which clearly proves that the reserves had joined in the battle. This only occurred when the situation was desperate and the front was broken, and when the sudden intervention of men of value under the command of an able officer such as a *praefectus castrorum*, for he was chosen from among the best centurions, could alone mend matters. To the memory of this gallant officer, who at the cost of his life turned what was already considered a defeat into a brilliant victory, a round mausoleum was raised, whose remains archeologists have detected below a tumulus on the battlefield.

At Adamclisi, Trajan was on the brink of catastrophe but this made his victory all the more important, since Decebalus's plan was now definitely beyond realization and Trajan was indisputable master of the destinies of war. Decebalus's victory over the forces Trajan had left in the mountains now lost its significance. The Roman emperor commemorated his victory in Dobrudja not only by the altar and the mausoleum mentioned above but also by a monumental trophy inaugurated in 109 A.D. whose impressive ruins — a cylindrical mound of compact concrete nearly 36 ft. high and 90 ft. in diameter — still towers over the Dobrudjan steppe. Originally, a hexagonal pedestal supporting a colossal lime trophy rose above the roofing, which was in the shape of a truncated cone. The cylindrical body, which is all that is left, was plated with lime blocks, some of which form metopes and battlements showing scenes of the battle or figures of barbarian prisoners carved in relief. These are most valuable ethnical documents as well as remarkable works of provincial, rustic art of expressive and dramatic realism. Among the barbarians shown here the northern Dacians are predominant; they are represented fighting with a big curved sword which they hold in both hands after the manner of the Sarmatians, while the Suevian Buri, who are also pictured frequently, are shown with naked torso and with hair plaited on the side of the head, as Tacitus describes them.

Apart from the three monuments raised on the battlefield, there is a fourth commemorative structure at Adamclisi: the citadel in the vicinity founded at the time by the veterans who had fought in the battle and significantly named Tropaeum Trajani. Obviously the destinies of Trajan's wars in Dacia had been decided on the Lower Danube. The campaigns that followed were extremely hazardous and Decebalus's resistance fierce, but after Adamclisi Dacia's final fall had become inevitable.

Immediately after the Adamclisi victory, Trajan reembark-
ed his forces, sailed up the Danube and returned to the
Transylvanian mountains to resume his advance towards
Sarmizegetusa. Operations had to start from scratch as during
his absence the positions occupied the year before had been
lost to Decebalus. After fighting fiercely throughout the
summer to conquer the numerous fortified mountain tops of
the Orăștie range, the Romans finally found themselves in
the vicinity of the Dacian capital. The Moorish prince Lucius
Quietus and his African cavalry having surrounded this almost impregnable citadel by surprise, Decebalus decided to
ask for peace and to accept all the conditions that might be
set by the victor. It was for him the only means of preventing
the extinction of the Dacian state while hoping for more
favorable prospects in the future. On the other hand, Trajan,
too, was obliged for the moment to give up some of the plans
made at the start of war, for he could not demand fresh
efforts of his men, exhausted by two years of uninterrupted
campaigns. At the close of 102 A.D., a solemn peace was
concluded, but the terms were very hard on the Dacian king
who had to hand over all the war engines, all the Roman
craftsmen and deserters in his service, and take upon himself
not to accept others, to dissolve his citadels, his capital included, and to maintain only such foreign relations as Rome
approved of. As a security, a permanent Roman garrison was
left in the Dacian state, namely at a place in the Hațeg country
where later the colony named Ulpia Sarmizegetusa was to
spring up. Trajan returned triumphantly to Rome.

It was a two years' peace. Neither of the opponents could
consider the peace otherwise than as a truce. Trajan made
intensive preparations for a second war. A bridge was built
over the Danube at Drobeta (present-day Turnu Severin) by
the skilled architect Apollodorus of Damascus. On the other
hand, well aware of the catastrophe ahead of him, Decebalus
decided to violate the peace conditions which had been intended to cripple him. He again began to entice craftsmen to
come from the Roman Empire, to rebuild his citadels, and
seek allies. Then, early in 105 he started hostilities by a surprise
attack on the Roman garrisons in the vicinity of his capital,
though without success. This he did to forestall the Romans
and obtain freedom of action. Longinus, commander of the

occupation forces, sought to enter into negotiations in order to gain time for Trajan, now on his way to the Danube with the bulk of the Roman army. Longinus was captured by a cunning trick but his heroic suicide brought to nought Decebalus's plan for exacting easier terms from Trajan in exchange for the release of such a valuable hostage. The Dacian king then resorted to extreme measures, paying for the assassination of Trajan. The emperor had in the meantime reached the banks of the Danube. In this attempt, too, Decebalus failed, for the plot was discovered. Considering Decebalus as lost, his allies of the first war, who had been defeated at Adamclisi, broke with him and concluded a pact of friendship with the Roman Empire. Furthermore, a message the Dacian king had sent to Pachorus, king of the Parthians, proposing that he should attack the Roman Empire in the east, was left unanswered. Seeing no way out of the deadlock, Decebalus decided to fight on alone to the last, his one aim now being to prolong the combat for as long as possible and to give the enemy forces more than they had bargained for.

The events of the second war are not easy to interpret on Trajan's Column, for they are not complemented by written records. It is probable that in order to completely encircle the Dacian forces, the Romans attacked Dacia simultaneously from several directions: through Banat, along the valleys of the rivers Jiu and Olt, and also perhaps through southern Moldavia and eastern Transylvania. The main action, however, was fought in the Orăștie Mountains in the spring and summer of 106. All the citadels on the mountain tops were conquered one after the other with great difficulty, and Sarmizegetusa itself was finally surrounded. Opposing the Roman assaults with epic gallantry, the capital only fell when its water supplies were exhausted and its last defenders had died of thirst. At the last moment, Decebalus and a group of noblemen succeeded in making their way on horseback along secret paths through the Roman ranks in the hope of building up new centers of defense against the invaders in other parts of Dacia. But finally surrounded by the enemy, Decebalus stabbed himself with his curved dagger to avoid being taken prisoner. His head was shown to the Roman troops and then taken to Rome and exhibited on the Gemoniae steps before being thrown into the Tiber so that the people of the Urbs should know that their great adversary was really dead and that the bitter wars against him were at an end.

After the fall of Sarmizegetusa Regia the Romans took every measure to preclude that this sacred place of the Dacians should serve to arouse the people of Dacia in future: they deported the population of the region to other parts of the country, destroyed the religious monuments of the shrine and for a long time kept a garrison in the conquered citadel. In 106, the year of victory, the Dacia Decebalus had ruled was proclaimed a Roman province. Trajan remained for nearly a year after that in what had been the theater of war in order to organize the province. Colonia Ulpia Trajana, subsequently to be called Sarmizegetusa, was to be the main city of the new province. It had been founded in the Hațeg country at the place where Longinus's garrison had formerly been stationed, and was more than thirty-five miles away from Decebalus's Sarmizegetusa Regia in the Orăștie Mountains.

Dacia's conquest by the Romans was a decisive event in the history of this country, for intensive Romanization of the province in the years that followed laid the durable foundations of the Romanian nation, descendants of the worthy Geto-Dacian people and heirs to the inestimable values Rome implanted in the country.

# CHAPTER III

# Roman Dacia and Scythia Minor

TRAJAN'S victory over the Dacians, a hard-won victory, was the crowning of Roman efforts to consolidate their Lower Danube boundary. By conquering Dacia, the Roman Empire had reached the height of its expansion. Situated in the center of the arc formed by the Danube between the Pannonian Plain and the Black Sea, this Carpathian bastion which had been for a long time not only a basis of Dacian power but also the rallying point of the various peoples of Southeast Europe against the Roman Empire, had now become a Roman possession and a means of imposing the strategic superiority of Rome on all the peoples of this entire area. A Romanized Dacia consolidated the Roman element in East Europe and laid the foundations from which emerged the Romanian people.

## 1. Organization of the Province of Dacia under Trajan

THE part Dacia had to play in consolidating Roman domination along the Danube was of such importance that Trajan took great pains to make of the country a durable Roman outpost. Immediately after his final victory in 106, which gave him mastery over the whole of Dacia (*Universa Dacia*), the Roman Emperor began to organize the land he had conquered.

At first *provincia Dacia* was confined to the inter-Carpathian areas of Decebalus's former kingdom, such as it had been after the peace with Domitian in 89 and with Trajan in 102. The lands beyond these confines, which had formerly been part of the great Geto-Dacian homeland, had come under Roman authority before that, as annexes to the provinces of the right bank of the Danube. Banat and West Oltenia (where the Drobeta bridge was to be found) were part of Moesia

Superior, while the rest of Oltenia, together with Muntenia, Lower Moldavia, and part of Southeast Transylvania along the river Olt (from Turnu-Roşu to Oituz) had been occupied by forces from Moesia Inferior. Dobrudja (Scythia Minor) was also part of that province. Soon after 106 part of these territories were to be incorporated in the new province of Dacia. North Transylvania, Crişana, Maramureş, and most of Moldavia were outside the boundaries of Roman domination, the populations of those parts being bound to the interests of the Empire merely by pacts which secured their autonomy.

*Provincia Dacia* of Transylvania was ruled by a governor, *legatus Augusti pro praetore* of consular rank, who had at his command an army made up of several legions: the XIII Gemina, the IV Flavia, and possibly the I Adiutrix. The first governor who participated in the organization of the province in the presence of the emperor was D. Terentius Scaurianus.

The very first year the new province was settled with considerable masses of Romanized elements brought over from all parts of the Empire *(ex toto orbe Romano)*. It is perhaps the only instance in Roman history of such substantial official intervention in a Romanization process. Trajan was anxious to create within the shortest time a Roman country in a territory which had formerly been a great threat to Roman peace. A large part of the native population, now disarmed and disorganized, had remained in regions determined by the victors, to whom they had officially submitted. Having become sparse after the two wars, which had taken a heavy toll of human lives, and after the emigration of the more active political elements to the Northern Carpathians, the Dacian population was below the new Roman colonists in point of civilization as well as socially. The best land and the more important economic positions were given to the new arrivals.

The Roman elements in Dacia developed in close unison with those of the neighboring provinces, primarily those of the two Moesias and of Illyricum. The native population, naturally attracted by the higher standard of life that was rapidly developing in their midst, began to value its advantages and to adopt the forms of Roman civilization. Romanization was being carried out in the same manner in the intermediary regions between Transylvania and the Danube, that is in Banat and Oltenia. Towards the end of Trajan's rule at the earliest, they were entirely withdrawn from the jurisdiction of the two Moesia provinces. The whole of Oltenia, together with a strip of land south of the Transylvanian reaches of the river Olt, was made into a separate province, named Dacia Inferior. The other Dacia, made up of Decebalus's former kingdom enlarged through the incorporation of Banat, was named Dacia Superior. The two Dacias were two successive creations and not the result of the division of the province set up in 106, as it is usually believed. The adjectives Superior and Inferior bore no reference to the geographical features of the provinces (for Dacia Inferior, which spread along the valley of the Olt in Transylvania, possessed the higher mountains); they described the situation of the provinces with reference to the Danube, as had formerly been done when what is now Lower Austria and West Hungary were given the name of Pannonia Superior, Hungary and part of Yugoslavia were named Pannonia Inferior, Serbia — Moesia Superior, and North Bulgaria and Dobrudja — Moesia Inferior.

The two Dacias had a separate organization and were not on an equal footing. There were no legions stationed in Dacia Inferior but only auxiliary forces. Its governor was a *procurator Augusti*, who belonged to the equestrian class and was invested with the right to command the forces of the province (*cum jure gladii*). Dacia Superior, on the other hand, held a priority position from every point of view; it continued to be occupied by legionary forces and to be ruled by a *legatus Augusti pro praetore*, superior in rank to the procurator of Dacia Inferior, even though the latter enjoyed autonomy in asserting his authority.

Trajan did not attempt to incorporate within the Roman Empire all the Geto-Dacian lands, which showed such natural, harmonious unity. Muntenia and Lower Moldavia always remained outside the Roman provincial régime, although their importance in the communications between Dacia and Moesia Inferior, primarily with the cities along the Dobrudjan coast, was evident. This apparent anomaly is to be accounted for by military reasons. The necessity of ensuring the defense of the Empire along the Lower Danube was the essential aim of Roman policy in this part of Europe. While the Danubian *limes* (frontier) was weakened in Banat and Oltenia where the main support was the mountain ranges of Dacia Superior and the Olt Valley, the situation was different in the lower reaches of the Danube, where the river was an impressive and continuous obstacle, invaluable in these regions of flat land. Incorporation of Muntenia and Moldavia in the Dacians' provincial organization would have raised strategic problems impossible to solve on what was one of the frontiers most threatened from the northeast. Consequently, Trajan had to be cautious and preserve the Danube line of military defense while assigning to Muntenia and Lower Moldavia the role of exterior safety areas depending on Moesia Inferior but noncolonized and nonurbanized.

The line along the right bank of the Lower Danube was not abandoned for the sake of an illusive frontier further north ; on the contrary, it was consolidated and the legions stationed in Moesia Inferior were increased to three: Legio I Italica at Novae (Shishtov), XI Claudia at Durostorum (Silistra ), and V Macedonica at Troesmis (Igliţa). It is to be noted that two of the three great army corps were stationed in Dobrudja. In the space between them, numerous units of auxiliary forces were stationed. A powerful military fleet — *Classis Flavia Moesica*, organized in Vespasian's time — plied up and down the river.

Only auxiliary troops were stationed along the *limes* of Dacia Inferior. They were placed at short intervals along the Olt Valley, both south of the Carpathians and in Transylvania up to the Oituz Pass, where the castrum of Angustia (Breţcu) connected the valleys of the Trotuş and the Siret to Dobrudja by means of the ford at Dinogetia guarded by the Roman citadel of Bărboşi on the left bank of the river and by that of Bisericuţa not far from Garvăn on the right bank. Thus surrounded on all sides by the powerful forces on the Danube and the Olt, Muntenia and Lower Moldavia were accessible from the military and commercial standpoints; their inhabitants, who were exclusively rural, were concentrated in the hilly areas, were taxed and recruited into the army like any provincial population, and were constantly in contact with the Roman life of the neighboring provinces. Actually, inside those areas there were small auxiliary Roman garrisons such as the bridgeheads on the left bank of the Danube (for example

the Bărboşi citadel already mentioned) and various castra
facing the sub-Carpathian passes of Jidava, Rucăr, Tîrgşor,
Mălăieşti, Drajna, and others. The Breţcu castrum guarded
the Oituz Pass on the Transylvanian side and also served to
assert Roman rule over Lower Moldavia.

The military, political, and administrative organization of
wide scope imposed by Trajan along the Lower Danube
spread not only over the various regions of Dacia but also
over the provinces along the right bank of the Danube —
the two Moesias and Thrace — where many towns were founded by the same emperor. From among them Oescus (Ghighen)
on the Danube, facing Oltenia, was raised to the rank of a
*colonia*.

It was Dobrudja which profited most by the new Roman
order installed after the conquest of Dacia. Considerably
reinforced by military troops, surrounded only by regions
which in different ways depended on Rome, this area between
the Danube and the Black Sea was to live henceforth through
a long period of peace and thus attain a high standard of
civilization. This was the first time in its eventful history
that peace had come to it. Spontaneously colonized by numerous farmers who had come individually from the center of
the Empire and by the veterans of its many garrisons, Dobrudja
was to become a center of Roman influence and develop
without interruption in close connection with the Roman
elements of Carpathian Dacia, while also attracting the local
Geto-Thracian populations. Many urban centers were to spring
up inside the region and around the castra along the Danube.
At the same time, the old Hellenic cities along the Pontic
shores, such as Histria, Tomis and Callatis, were to rise to
great economic prosperity under Roman protection.

Having made sure that the measures he had taken in Dacia
and in the neighboring provinces were effective, Trajan
returned to Rome in 107 and celebrated his triumph with
great pomp. He bolstered the finances of the Empire with
the immense treasures captured in Dacia, and had the sumptuous Forum that bears his name built in the center of Rome,
with the Trajan Column towering in the middle of it. This
commemorative monument preserved to this day gives the
history of the great Dacian wars carved in relief spiralwise.
The building of the column was started in 113 A.D.

## 2. Consolidation of Roman Rule

AFTER waging another war in the east against the Parthians from 114 to 117 A.D., Emperor Trajan died on August 11, 117, at Selinunt in Cilicia. His successor, Hadrian (P. Aelius Hadrianus), a nephew whom he had adopted at the last moment, proved a worthy continuer of his work. With a lucid, realistic mind, Hadrian realized that the Roman Empire had reached its utmost limits of expansion in relation to its forces and resources, and that an attempt to exceed those limits could only lead to dangerous involvements. Consequently, his first move was to make peace with the Parthians and abandon the new provinces which Trajan had hastened to create in Armenia and Mesopotamia at a time when military conditions were still precarious.

Hadrian was an excellent soldier and gave much attention to the organization of the army. Whenever necessary, he acted energetically in defense of the Empire.

As early as in 117 the Roxolan Sarmatians north of Pontus Euxinus, encouraged by the difficulties the Romans were up against in the Parthian wars and by the absence of part of the Danube garrisons, began to stir, demanding that the subsidies paid them by the Empire should be increased. After Trajan's death, they found the moment ripe for increasing their threat and, as a first move, they prompted their Iazygian kinsmen on the Tisa plain to attack Dacia. Hadrian met the situation with the utmost promptness. He immediately sent back to their garrisons the Dacian and Moesia Inferior forces which had participated in the Parthian war, and then came to the Danube in person. His energetic intervention resulted in a conciliatory attitude towards the financial claims of the Roxolans, and peace was restored in eastern Dacia without the necessity of resorting to arms. The new treaty concluded on this occasion was so satisfactory to both sides that the Roxolans observed it for a long time. As to the Iazygians, their attack on Dacia seemed all the more serious as the consular governor of the province, C. Julius Quadratus Bassus, had just then died. Being obliged to go to Rome to be invested emperor, Hadrian entrusted the campaign against the Iazygians to an able general, Q. Marcius Turbo, who, though belonging merely to the equestrian class, was given the exceptional mission of commanding all the legions in Dacia and in Pannonia Inferior by a juridical fiction. Counterattacked on two sides, the Iazygians were defeated and compelled to submit.

When peace had been reestablished, Hadrian gave his attention to the two Dacias and to Moesia Inferior, now sufficiently consolidated to take upon themselves the reorganization measures suggested by his defensive policy. In Dacia Superior only Legion XIII Gemina remained with a garrison at Apulum (present-day Alba Iulia). Legion IV Flavia was removed to Moesia Superior, more precisely to Singidunum (Belgrade), a point of junction between the two provinces from where it could more efficiently watch the Iazygian populations in the west. With a view to economizing his forces, Hadrian did away with the auxiliary garrisons in Muntenia for there was no point in their remaining now that Provincia Dacia had been consolidated. On the other hand, the *limes Alutanus* was greatly reinforced. Hadrian also directed that the woodwork of Trajan's bridge at Drobeta should be destroyed for the services this grand structure afforded could not compensate for the danger of its falling into enemy hands in the event of a surprise invasion and of its allowing an easy penetration into the Empire.

These military measures were misunderstood by part of the Roman public of his time, since they in their view indicated that Hadrian intended to abandon Dacia, as he had abandoned Trajan's conquests in the east. Eutropius, a later historian, writes to this effect, adding that the emperor's councillors prevented him from carrying out his plan, which would have left considerable numbers of Romans at the mercy of the barbarians. This intimation of the thorough Romanization of Dacia barely a decade after the conquest is worth remembering, though it is unbelievable that such a clearsighted emperor, who had had a long military and administrative experience in the Danubian provinces and had won distinctions in the Dacian wars, could have entertained the thought of giving up a possession of such strategic value.

Misinterpreting Hadrian's defensive policy, modern historians ascribe to the emperor the intention of giving up his possession of Muntenia and Lower Moldavia, which provinces he is supposed to have ceded to the Roxolans when they made their thrust in 177 A.D. Though there is no documen-

tary evidence to this effect, a supposed invasion on the part
of the Roxolans is cited in support of this arbitrary hypothesis.
Hadrian's biography, which mentions the events of 117,
makes it clear that the move of the Roxolans at the time was
a mere agitation *(tumultus)* without any actual action on
their part and that their object had been an increase in subsidies without any claims of territory. The incident ended with
a stable, firm peace made by Hadrian in keeping with the
interests of Rome. It would have been absurd for an emperor
of Hadrian's ability to have permitted, at a moment when
Roman prestige was at its height, rebel Sarmatians to settle
in the very heart of the strategic nucleus on the Lower Danube
— on the plain which the Romans had endeavored to maintain uninhabited for over a century as a safety area for the
garrisons along the Danube. The withdrawal from the castra
in the hilly areas mentioned above is no argument supporting
the abandonment of Muntenia, this being a measure taken
solely for reasons of military organization, one not restricting
the area subject to Roman authority. An indefatigable admi-
nistrator, Hadrian spent most of the twenty-one years of his
principate (117-138) journeying throughout the Roman provinces in order to inspect them. Apart from his military
intervention of the year 118 at the time of the Sarmatian
disturbances, he traveled across Dacia and Dobrudja in 123-
124, his aim being to see that the Roman forces were properly
trained and the administrative bodies were functioning satisfactorily. His visit made a considerable contribution to the
economic development of the provinces, such as the consolidation and maintenance of roads, the building of public works,
and the development of urban centers. It was during his
principate that certain Dacian towns, such as Napoca (present-
day Cluj) and Drobeta (Turnu Severin) were given the title
of *municipium*. In Moesia Inferior the *canabae* (civilian settlements) around the Durostorum castrum assumed such a
remarkable town-like aspect that, though juridically depending
on Legion XI Claudia stationed there, they were given the
quasi-municipal title of *canabae Aeliae*, after Hadrian's gens.

The political and military order established by Hadrian
along the Lower Danube was continued by his successor,
a peaceful emperor and an excellent organizer, T. Aelius
Antoninus Pius (138-161), Hadrian's foster son, under whom

the Roman world reached the culmination point of its stability and progress. It was, however, a time when frequent mild disturbances occurred in the provinces, showing discontent with the strict taxation system of the Romans and foreshadowing a mounting social crisis, despite the economic prosperity and the high living of the well-to-do classes.

Disturbances also occurred in Dacia, the free Dacians beyond the borders of the province harassing and carrying on attacks. Their dependence on the Empire was merely political and, as they enjoyed full liberty of organization in their territories, they could at any time contest it. An attack on the province recorded to have occurred in 143 was easily repelled, but another of greater proportions took place in 156-157 when the provincial army was obliged to wage a systematic war against the offenders. Finally, the free Dacians were driven back beyond the *limes* along the valleys of the Someş rivers.

At the time, as also under the succeeding emperors, there was a new division of Roman Dacia into Dacia Porolissensis, Dacia Apulensis and Dacia Malvensis. The last-named was the former Dacia Inferior while the other two shared between them the area covered by Dacia Superior whose northwestern regions, including the city of Porolissum, formed Dacia Porolissensis governed, like the former Dacia Inferior, by a *procurator Augusti cum jure gladii*, who had a group of auxiliary forces under his command. It was during Hadrian's rule that the province had been divided into three parts, proof of which is a military diploma of the year 133 recently discovered at Gherla and attesting to the existence of Dacia Porolissensis at the time. The names of Dacia Superior and Dacia Inferior continued to be used after that date. It was only under Marcus Aurelius that the names were discarded to be replaced by the adjectives Apulensis and Malvensis derived, like Porolissensis from Porolissum, from the names of cities on their territory, namely Apulum and Malva. The last-named locality, which in the third century is recorded to have been a *colonia*, has not been identified so far. Dacia Apulensis incorporated the greatest part of Dacia Superior, together with the Transylvanian portion of Dacia Inferior along the Olt Valley. It was the most important of the three provinces, with the biggest territory, the most numerous and most prosperous cities, and the most numerous forces, primarily Legio XIII Gemina. Its governor was a *procurator* as in the two other Dacias. According to the new organization, the two provinces, though autonomously administered, were more closely united than they had formerly been, all three depending on a *legatus Augusti pro praetore trium Daciarum*.

The inroads of the free Dacians into Dacia were the only warlike events to occur in the Carpatho-Danubian provinces under Antoninus Pius. At the time Dobrudja, undisturbed by foreign threats, enjoyed a flourishing state, as never before in its history. This region, which was the center of gravity of the whole Moesia Inferior, with the most numerous and most important garrisons and a busy economic life, had become profoundly Roman. The inscriptions and constructions of Dobrudja of Antoninus's time are proof of the prosperity of the cities as well as of the countryside down to the most out-of-the-way places.

Under Antoninus Pius's successor, his foster son Marcus Aurelius Verus, the Roman Empire experienced fearful trials, in contrast with the comparative peace it had formerly enjoyed.

During the first year of his principate, in 161, Marcus Aurelius had to organize an expedition against the Parthians who had attacked the eastern provinces. A great army which also included troops from the Danube regions, namely Legio V Macedonica stationed in Dobrudja, was sent eastward under the command of his foster brother Lucius Aurelius Verus, the co-regent emperor. After five years of struggle, the Parthians were defeated and compelled to make peace. Hardly had that war ended when another of far greater proportions and much more dangerous, broke out in Europe along the higher and middle reaches of the Danube. In 166 all the Germanic populations beyond the river, and primarily the Marcomanni and Quadi, forced their way across the Roman *limes* and, having overrun Pannonia, reached as far as northern Italy. Shortly after, in 167, the free Dacians also overran the province of Dacia, while other populations of the northern Carpathians such as the Bastarnians and the Costobocae, were preparing to take action. The situation was extremely serious, for the attacks were simultaneous and placed the Roman army at a distinct disadvantage. The monolithic force of this army was now for the first time counterbalanced by

an immense coalition of forces which included all the Trans-
Danubian populations, from Vindelicia to the Iazygian steppe
and to the northern Carpathians. This was not due to an understanding among these populations, who had always lived in
discord; it was a spontaneous and uniform effect of the pressure of the Goths who, possibly on account of the growing
severity of the climate, had left their Scandinavian territories,
crossed the Baltic, and were slowly but in great numbers making
their way southward, thus driving the local peoples in the
direction of the Roman Empire.

At the time a frightful plague, which the Roman forces had
brought from the East, was becoming increasingly virulent
in the Empire. Marcus Aurelius controlled the panic in Rome
and took prompt measures to cope with all difficulties. The
main military efforts were concentrated against the Marcomanni and Quadi, troops having been brought from all parts
of the Empire. In 167, the Roman army under the command
of Marcus Aurelius, assisted by his brother, took the offensive. After a year's fighting the provinces which had been
overrun were liberated and the aggressors driven back across
the Danube. At the same time peace was reestablished in
Dacia where the free Dacians in their plundering raids had
reached as far as the gold-bearing areas in the Western Mountains and the neighborhood of Sarmizegetusa. Legio V Macedonica, now back from the East, helped to drive away the
invaders. This legion did not return to its castrum at Troesmis in Dobrudja but was directly transferred to Dacia where,
after order had been restored, it had its garrison at Potaissa
(present-day Turda). The defense forces of the province were
of double strength and the governor of the three Dacias was
again of consular rank.

The victory of 168 did not in any way remove the possibility of further invasions. On his return to Rome, Marcus
Aurelius, arriving alone for Lucius Verus had died on the
way, made preparations for a new offensive, resorting to emergency measures in recruiting soldiers and procuring funds.
The war was resumed in 169 and lasted for five years. It was
waged along the left bank of the Danube, in the mountains
held by the Marcomanni and the Quadi, and in the steppe
of the Iazygian Sarmatians, and was attended by many trials,
Roman successes alternating with defeats. Generals of great

ability lost their lives in disastrous battles, among them being M. Claudius Fronto, Dacia's consular governor, who had participated in the battles fought against the Iazygians as chief of the forces of his own province and of Moesia Superior. Ultimately, the Roman armies, encouraged by the Emperor's perseverance, succeeded in putting down all resistance and the barbarians submitted one after the other: the Marcomanni in 172, the Quadi in 174, and the Iazygian Sarmatians in 175.

In 170 the Costobocae (Dacians of the northern Carpathians) had overrun Dobrudja and penetrated as far as Greece. Finally defeated, they were settled as *dediticii* (unconditional subjects) in various provinces in the center of the Empire.

Despite the great trials the whole of the Empire was experiencing, the Carpatho-Danubian provinces generally maintained the prosperity they had enjoyed under Marcus Aurelius. It was at this time that, owing to their development and to their advanced Romanization, numerous towns were raised to the rank of municipium, among them: Troesmis, Tropaeum Trajani, Durostorum and Novae (Shishtov) in Moesia Inferior. In Dacia, Marcus Aurelius set up a *municipium* at Apulum, which shortly after, possibly under Emperor Commodus, was raised to the rank of *colonia*. It was again Marcus Aurelius who raised the *municipium* of Napoca (Cluj) to the rank of *colonia*. It is also certain that during his principate Romula became a *municipium*.

The peace with the Marcomanni, Quadi, and Iazygians was not of long duration. Around 177 these populations again rose in arms against the Empire. In order to sow discord among them, Marcus Aurelius concluded a new peace with the Iazygians, setting conditions more favorable than the preceding ones, among other things entitling them to maintain relations with their Roxolan kinsmen in the East by crossing the province of Dacia, with the approval of the Roman authorities every time. Having thus solved the Sarmatian problem, Marcus Aurelius concentrated all his forces against the Marcomanni and Quadi, whom he reduced to total capitulation after some resounding victories. The emperor was planning to make a new Roman province of their land and to remove the boundary of the Empire along the line of the northern Carpathians, thus solving a difficult problem for the Empire, when he died on March 17, 180. His successor was L. Aurelius Commodus, his own son, who had been sharing authority with his father since 177. Disorderly and frivolous, without any serious thought for the State, and far from inheriting his father's outstanding talents, Commodus made haste to return to Rome, giving up the idea of a new annexation to the Empire and making a peace such as the defeated barbarians had never dreamed of. However, thanks to the great victory won by Marcus Aurelius, the peace was effective and lasting, definitely putting an end to the long and troublesome wars against the Marcomanni.

Under Commodus's rule a number of conflicts with the Buri and free Dacians were quashed. Hostages and prisoners were taken from the Buri — Decebalus's allies of old bordering on Dacia — and the obligation was laid on them to make a desert area 40 stadia (four and half miles) wide along the Roman *limes*. The same obligation was laid on the Vandals and Iazygians. At the same time thousands of free Dacians were settled, probably within the Dacian province, as *dediticii*. Later, ca. 184 A.D., an army under the command of D. Claudius Albinus and C. Pescennius Niger took the offensive in the north of the province against other free Dacians and neighboring populations, compelling them to observe the peace of the province.

The Danube provinces were within the focus of Emperor Septimius Severus. Under his rule, Dacia and Dobrudja enjoyed a period of peace and prosperity. The *limes Alutanus* of Dacia Malvensis was removed east of the River Olt in Muntenia, a *limes Transalutanus* being built at the time between Flămînda on the Danube and the Bran Pass. In Dacia, Septimius Severus raised a large number of towns to the rank of *municipium*, among them being Porolissum (Moigrad), probably Dierna (Orşova), Tibiscum (Caransebeş) and Ampelum (Zlatna), while Drobeta (Turnu Severin) and possibly Romula (Reşca) were promoted to the rank of *colonia*. The canabae of Legio V Macedonica at Potaissa (Turda) developed into a town in so short a time that Septimius Severus gave them the rank of *municipium* and a few years after of *colonia*. At Apulum (Alba Iulia) not far from the *municipium* instituted by Marcus Aurelius and raised to the rank of *colonia Aurelia*, possibly by his son Commodus, a second town was soon created, and Severus gave it the title of *municipium Septimium* and later of *colonia*. The two neighboring towns are mentioned simultaneously in inscriptions with their different titles.

Inspired by monarchic tendencies, Septimius Severus strengthened his dynasty, which continued his policy after his death. His son, M. Aurelius Antoninus, also named Caracalla (211-217), traveled through Dobrudja and Dacia as far as Porolissum. On that occasion he renewed the Roman pacts with the free Dacians, from whom he took many hostages. His successor, the usurper Macrinus (217-218), was to release those hostages in the hope of winning a more lasting friendship.

It was under Caracalla that the famous Edict named Constitutio Antoniniana was issued, extending the right of Roman citizenship to all the free townsmen of the Empire. Although the Edict was inspired by fiscal reasons, the aim being to levy taxes from which the peregrini (the inhabitants who were not Roman citizens) were exempted, its effects promoted Romanization, for a large number of people became Roman citizens, the consciousness of solidarity with the Roman people thus becoming more widespread and being strengthened, while the Romanization process in the provinces that had already been won over by Latin civilization was speeded up. This was the case of the Danubian provinces, including Dacia and Moesia Inferior. But there was another consequence of the Constitutio Antoniniana: the titles of *colonia* and *municipium* lost their value for, being based on the degree of Romanization of the inhabitants of certain towns in contrast to other settlements where the peregrines prevailed, these titles lost their sense when everywhere there were only equal citizens. Actually, after Caracalla these titles fell into disuse and were given only exceptionally to towns as ornaments, without any practical use.

Under Caracalla's successors — Macrinus, already mentioned, Elagabalus (218-222) and Severus Alexander (222-235) — Dacia, like the other Danubian provinces, enjoyed a period of peace. Severus Alexander showed special solicitude for Dacia. It is to be observed that, particularly under the rule of Elagabalus, an adolescent who was also high priest of the Syrian god Baal, Eastern religious rites spread widely throughout Italy and the Latin provinces of the Empire. Among the soldiers and traders of Eastern origin living in Dacia and Scythia Minor such rites had been practiced for many years.

## 3. Roman Civilization in Dacia

THE last stage in the ascension of the Roman Empire now being under consideration, we should dwell for a moment on the essential aspects of Roman slave-owning civilization as it developed in *provincia Dacia*.

The area and the organization of the lands conquered by Trajan north of the Danube have already been shown, though only briefly. Mention has also been made of the legions which had their garrisons in Dacia, Legio XIII Gemina with its garrison at Apulum being the permanent one, while Legio V Macedonica with its headquarters at Potaissa was added after 167 A.D. As regards the many auxiliary forces in the province (infantry cohorts of 500 or 1,000 men, cavalry alae, and numeri of non-Romanized warriors), their various ethnical names are only significant at the moment when they were set up, for later they also included soldiers recruited in the provinces where they had their garrisons. They can, however, generally give an indication of the peoples of the Empire which helped in the defense of Dacia. Those units mostly came from Dalmatia, Pannonia, Raetia, Gaul, the Rhineland, the Alpine countries, Hispania, and Britannia, all Roman provinces. Those originating in Thrace, in the East, in Greece, Africa, and the North Pontic areas, were less frequent. On coming to Dacia, the legions had about the same ethnical composition, the difference being that their men were at the very beginning perfectly Romanized. The auxiliary forces came from the East, especially from Syria, more precisely from Palmyra, were made up of archers *(sagittarii)*, the bow being alien to Roman military tradition but very necessary on the borders of a province surrounded by populations that used it currently. The forces in Dacia, the legions included, are estimated to have averaged 40,000 men.

While recording the events that occurred from Trajan to Severus Alexander, we have mentioned in the order of their emergence the main towns of Dacia organized as *municipia*. According to the data available at present, there were at least eight towns in Dacia which attained the supreme rank of *colonia*. This was a very high figure in relation to the neighboring provinces: five in Pannonia Inferior, four in Moesia

Superior, one in Moesia Inferior. From among Dacia's *colo-niae*, Ulpia Sarmizegetusa alone received that title directly, as it was inhabited only by Roman citizens from the moment Trajan created it. The others — Napoca, Potaissa, Drobeta, Romula and Malva and the twin towns of Apulum, first went through the stage of a *municipium*, with fewer juridical privileges and a proportion of peregrini in their population. Porolissum, Tibiscum, Ampelum and Dierna were *municipia*, and it is uncertain whether they were ever raised to the rank of *coloniae*. With them the total number of cities with a Roman Constitution in Dacia rises to twelve, and further epigraphic finds might well add to their number. Many other places, Micia, Aquae, Alburnus Major, Salinae, Brucla and Sucidava among them, might well have aspired to a higher urban position as they enjoyed great economic prosperity. Rural settlements attested to have been *pagi* or *vici*, were like towns in many respects. Settlements of an urban character emerged around hot springs famous for their healing properties. Such were Băile Herculane (not far from Roman Admediam), Geoagiu (Germisara), Călan (Aquae). Moreover the civilian *canabae* that were built up around the castra occasionally turned into towns of smaller or greater size.

The coloniae and municipia had an autonomous administration with a management council similar to the Roman Senate, and named *ordo decuriorum* or *curia*. It was made up of *decuriones* recruited from among the richest citizens. It was from among the councillors that the townspeople elected the various magistrates every year. The magistrates were headed by two *duumviri*, recalling the two Consuls in Rome. In the municipia there were sometimes four leaders: the *quattuorviri*. Once in every five years one of the *duumviri* or *quattuorviri* was appointed as *quinquennalis*, with powers similar to those of the Censor in Rome, being entitled to check on the Council of *decuriones* and appoint councillors if required, to make a census of the population and to establish local taxes. Among the other magistrates of Roman provincial cities, the more outstanding were the *aediles* whose task it was to see that the streets, markets, and public buildings were properly cared for and maintained, and that the town was well supplied with necessaries, as well as to organize festive events and to maintain order. The *quaestores* looked after the finances of the city. The officiators of official religious rites are frequently mentioned in inscriptions. They were the *pontifices*, *flamines*, *sacerdotes*, and *augures*. The members of the *Augustales* College had an important part to play. When Dacia had been divided into three parts, an imperial cult was officiated for all the three provinces at Ulpia Sarmizegetusa by a *sacerdos arae Augusti*, also named *coronatus Daciarum trium*. This was done on the occasion of the periodical meeting of a *concilium provinciarum Daciarum trium* made up of delegates from all over Roman Dacia, whose task was to discuss administrative, economic, and religious questions of common interest.

Archeological finds in the Roman cities of Dacia prove that the latter had attained a remarkable level of development. The streets were paved and provided with a drainage system; there were central markets (forums) surrounded by portici and shops, and there were also temples, public buildings for administrative purposes, private homes, shops, warehouses, and large public baths. Close to the city there was often a great amphitheater. Water was brought from springs by means of aqueducts. Around the castra there were baths and sometimes amphitheaters for the use of the soldiers and of the civilian population of the neighboring *canabae*. Outside the towns large and complex country houses *(villae)* have been found. These were isolated on large landed estates. From the great military roads which crossed the province from end to end linking the towns and castra between them, there have been left in places big slabs of hard stone laid over a bed of gravel and sand. The roads were marked with milestones indicating the distance to the nearest locality in thousands of steps (mille passuum = 1348.11 yd.) and at every stage (ca. 12-15 miles) there was a *statio* or a *mansio* with watch and maintenance posts, inns, relay horses, stores of military provisions, etc. Where the cities ended, funeral monuments bordered the roads. They were of lime or marble and carved on them were inscriptions, the portraits of the buried dead, and mythological symbols.

The great development of Dacian cities is to be accounted for by the busy economic activities carried on in Dacia from the very first years of its transformation into a province. The main pursuits in the country were farming, stock-breeding,

and mining. In farming small and medium farms predominated. They were owned by veterans, civilian colonists brought
over from other parts of the Empire, and also by the subjected
Dacians. It was only later, in the third century, as the general
crisis of the Empire was aggravated and the masses were
impoverished, that great landed estates were built up at the
expense of the smaller farmers. There were also large imperial estates consisting of arable land, pastures, and forests
which were leased out. On the large estates both slaves and
free workers did the work, the latter being paid in cash or
in kind from the products of their work. Wheat was given
priority, but orchards were also extensive. Cultivation of
the vine was introduced on a large scale. Extensive pasture
land fed numerous herds of cattle and flocks of sheep while
the vast Carpathian forests offered high quality wood for
building and other purposes. From among the country's
mineral riches, the most important was gold, which was
mined by slaves as well as by free miners, particularly in the
metal-bearing district of the Western Mountains, at Ampelum
(Zlatna), and at Alburnus Major (Roșia) where workers of
Illyrian origin had been colonized, the most numerous being
the Pirustae who in their homeland had become skilled in
this difficult work. The mines were imperial property under
the supervision of a *procurator aurariarum* who, assisted by
many subordinates, collected the precious metal and drew
up statements of the output. Other metals — silver, copper,
lead, and iron — accounted for a much smaller part of Dacia's
economic activities. But the rich salt mines of the country,
of which the main one was Salinae (the Mureș salt mine Ocna
Mureșului), were extensively mined by the lessees of imperial property. There are also indications that stone quarries
were worked, stone being in great demand owing to the development of the cities.

The transport of goods was facilitated by a dense network
of roads and by the use of rafts plying along the rivers, especially the Olt and the Mureș, not to mention the intense sailing
on the Danube. In the towns, commerce and the crafts were
the main economic activities. Many traders came to Dacia
from the East, being drawn thither by the country's wealth.
In their turn Dacian traders took their wares to other provinces
of the Empire. There were banking transactions in Dacia,

with credit companies or individual usurers. The Roman coins in current circulation in the province were of silver and bronze, and exceptionally of gold. In the third century a mint in Ulpia Sarmizegetusa minted imperial coins of bronze with the symbols of the province.

The crafts were of great variety, relying for the most part on local raw materials. Vestiges and indications have been found everywhere attesting to the existence of shops where metals, wood, fabrics, and hides and skins were processed. Ceramic needed for building purposes was being produced in quantities. It included roofing tiles, bricks, pipes as well as pottery, lamps, and figurines. Jewelry was made out of metal and engraved semiprecious stones. From among the craftsmen, inscriptions mention smiths *(fabri)*, stone cutters, builders *(architecti)*, house painters *(pictores)*, leather workers *(coriarii)*, cloth makers *(centonarii)*, raftsmen *(utricularii)*, litter bearers *(lecticarii)*. Both the traders and the craftsmen associated in *collegia*, vocational mutual aid associations organized by decuria under the leadership of a *magister* or *praefectus*. Official quarters laid upon such associations duties foreign to their craft as, for example, fire fighting, repairs to the towns' fortifications, etc. Each *collegium* sought to uphold its interests against possible misuses of authority, by seeking the protection of a rich and influential person, a *patronus*, and also by hiring a juridical defender, *defensor*. There were also religious colleges, arranging funerals and the worship of a certain deity in common.

Taxation, a most oppressive aspect of Roman administration, was the mainspring of abusive practices. There were onerous toll gates *(portoria)*, taxes being levied on goods at every turn: on their entering the province, on being conveyed along the highroads and over bridges, and on their entering the towns. Freedmen and slaves made up the very numerous personnel of the toll gates, serving their patrons and at the same time deriving handsome benefits for themselves. On the other hand, abusive practices were also current in the recruiting of men for work and the requisitioning of tools and provisions, duties which the imperial clerks and the army laid in an arbitrary manner upon the villages lying in the vicinity of the highroads. Despite the measures taken by the imperial authorities, such abusive practices could not be checked, and the crisis the Empire went through in the third century increased them.

Production relations were those specific to a slave-owning society. In Dacia, too, as all over the world in those days, society was divided into antagonistic classes: primarily the slaves and their masters. But there were great social differences within these two main classes. Among the free citizens the great plutocrats emerged from the multitude of poor workers. Moreover, all slaves were not subjected to the same conditions. While those working in the mines and in the fields were cruelly exploited, toiling to exhaustion, those slaves who supervised the former or were assigned various administrative or fiscal duties, enjoyed fairly favorable conditions, which the free paupers often envied. Freedmen *(liberti)* were often appointed to public functions of some responsibility. From among the old classes of Roman society, the senatorial aristocracy was only represented in Dacia by a number of great officials whose missions were of restricted duration; they were provincial governors, commanders of legions, and *tribuni laticlavii* of the legions. The equestrian class included a few of the local people, apart from certain senior officers in the legions, the commanders of auxiliary forces, the procurators of the provinces, and other transient dignitaries. The rest of the population was made up of Roman citizens *(cives Romani)*, who enjoyed certain privileges and immunities and owned most of the landed estates, standing out in marked contrast to the mass of the peregrini. These were mostly paupers but there were a number of traders and rich landowners among them. Furthermore, there were *dediticii*, ploughmen or shepherds with very restricted rights. These were either the descendants of Dacians subjected after fierce resistance during the wars, or barbarians from beyond the boundaries accepted in the province. Caracalla's edict, by generalizing the right to Roman citizenship (which, however, was not granted to the *dediticii* or to the slaves), closed the juridical differences between the privileged colonists and the peregrini. But this was an indication that the slave-owning society was disintegrating and its old social arrangements were tottering. Although slave labor was still to have a determining part to play, it was becoming ever more obvious that it was no longer very profitable and this opened wide the gates for the use of paid, free labor. Slaves were frequently enfranchised. The state of affairs in the Roman Empire promoted great social flexibility, and individual ascent from the very lowest classes to the highest was frequent, especially through military service.

This did not mean social harmony, but an internal crisis of the Empire which, in its struggle against the great contradictions in its structure, had lost the true significance of some traditional values and evolved towards new forms. Wealth, primarily agricultural wealth, was being concentrated in the hands of a minority. The small landowners, when dispossessed, increased the ranks of the poor workers who offered their labor for an insignificant pay. Foreign wars, which were very frequent during Marcus Aurelius's principate and after him, were to aggravate the crisis, increasing taxation excesses, abusive practices, ordeals, and requisitions, and generating discontent, resistance, and uprisings. Although insufficiently attested in Dacia, these were general phenomena which must have existed here as in all the other provinces. Inscriptions have been found in Dacia that spoke of *latrones* (robbers, outlaws) whose frequency in the second and third centuries throughout the Empire is proof of deep-going social unrest. It was only when faced by the invasions from beyond the borders that all the inhabitants of the province became to a certain extent one, for the enemy, being out to plunder and enslave, made no difference between those they met on their way. This was not real social solidarity but simply the result of a temporary identity of all before a common threat. On the other hand, many of the paupers who were beyond the invaders' fury sought to take advantage of the exploiters' difficulties, robbing them or, if they were slaves, making their escape.

It should be remembered, however, that these acute aspects of the social contradictions became characteristic and preponderant only during the great crisis of the mid-third century and that in the preceding period, under the rule of the Emperors of the Antonine and Severan stock, there was sufficient balance to allow the splendid Roman civilization to flourish in Dacia. Apart from rapid economic prosperity, we should note the high level of cultural progress in the province. All the inhabitants, irrespective of their ethnical origin or social status, spoke only Latin among themselves and with the authorities. Education through schools and other means, was widespread. Writing was in general use, as proved by the many inscriptions, of which some 3,000 (all Latin, with the exception of about 35 in Greek) have been discovered so far. The waxed tables preserved in a mine at Roşia (Alburnus Major in Roman times) show that writing was in daily use even among the lower strata of the population whenever deeds, even though insignificant, were required. The verse on funeral monuments shows a prevailing interest in literature and lofty thoughts. A taste for immortalizing thoughts, deeds, and persons in inscriptions and through artistic representations was widespread here as in all provinces. From among the fine arts, sculpture, in particular relief, was mostly practiced. It was par excellence the art of the province and often assumed summary and rustic forms, though always reflecting a robust, realist spirit identical with that of the art of the western Danubian provinces and also having close affinities with the sculptures of Moesia Inferior. Painting found expression on less durable materials and consequently there are no important vestiges of it left. To form some idea of what it was like, we can only make deductions from the polychrome mosaic of those days, of which some remarkable specimens with heroic or mythological representations have been preserved at Ulpia Sarmizegetusa and Apulum. Also worth mentioning are the many finely cut gems and cameos that have been found. Though an important number of them were imports, a not insignificant proportion were the work of local craftsmen. Burnt clay and bronze figurines, mostly representing divinities, were also quite frequent.

The religious beliefs of the province were cosmopolitan, like the origin of the inhabitants who gave expression to them in inscriptions. A great variety of gods were worshiped in Roman Dacia, most of them Italic: Jupiter Optimus Maximus, Juno, Minerva, Mercury, Apollo, Diana, Venus, Mars, Liber-Libera, Silvanus, Hercules, etc. In the order of frequency, next follow the mystic Eastern gods brought over by soldiers and traders from Asia Minor, Syria, and Egypt: Mithra, Cybele, Isis, Serapis, Jupiter Dolichenus, etc. Most widespread was the agrestic cult of Dionysos, an old Hellenic god. With so many cults in vogue, Eastern and Hellenic deities frequently fused with the Roman ones. Inscriptions show that gods specific to the province were also honored, among them Dacia, Terra Dacia, Genius Daciarum, Dii et Deae Daciarum. On the other hand, the old Dacian religious concepts crop up under the name and forms of Roman divinities: Liber, Libera, Diana Augusta, Diana Regina, Silvanus, Nemesis. It is also from ancient local beliefs that the cult of the Danubian Horsemen was derived, marble or bronze sculptures of which are to be found in all the provinces along the Danube, and primarily in Dacia. The Thracian Horseman, a divinity specific to Thrace and Moesia Inferior, is also frequent in the Carpathian province. Christianity, which at the time of Dacia's occupation by the Romans was still in the illegal stage, is not met with north of the Danube before Aurelian. It was only in the fourth century that it penetrated intensively into Dacia. In Dobrudja, however, it is attested earlier and with sufficient force, for on the occasion of the various persecutions there were many martyrs in that region.

This is but a brief survey of the main aspects of Roman civilization in Dacia. It was under the aegis of this civilization that the intensive Romanization process took place, as a prerequisite to the formation of a Romanic people north of the Danube: the Romanian people. The civilian population brought over by Trajan and the army were basic factors in that process.

When discharged after around twenty-five years' service, the legionaries and auxiliaries became veterans, and received Roman citizenship together with considerable juridical and material benefits. Most of them did not return to their place of origin but settled in Dacia where they had spent such a long span of their lives and where they had illegitimate families which were subsequently recognized officially (they often lived with Dacian women) and where they could do well for themselves, especially as landowners and often as outstanding members of town councils. The army thus played an active and fundamental part in Romanizing Dacia, being also the main factor in the social rise of the native population and its participation in the development of Roman civilization in the province. The Dacians did not maintain an obstinately hostile attitude towards the victors but took part in the new life that flourished in their country. From their midst the Romans recruited many auxiliary troops sent to other parts of the Empire, and the Dacians also increasingly provided men for the Roman legions and auxiliary forces in their own province, particularly after the introduction of local recruiting under Hadrian. The populations from beyond Dacia's frontier colonized in the middle of the province after Marcus Aurelius, also provided recruits.

Dacia's population — apart from the native elements who were numerous but who seldom showed prominence in inscriptions — was based to a great extent on the Latin-speaking colonists brought over by Trajan *ex toto orbe Romano*. Most of them came from the neighboring provinces: Moesia Superior, and Moesia Inferior, the two Pannoniae, Dalmatia, Noricum, Raetia, the two Germaniae, Gaul, Hispania, and Africa. The less numerous colonists brought from provinces where Hellenic culture prevailed — Thrace, Macedonia, Asia Minor, Syria, and Egypt — adopted the culture of the rest of the population and also became factors of Romanization once they had settled in these parts. The traders and craftsmen coming here from the East on their own initiative behaved in the same way. They were drawn hither by the profitable business offered them by a rich country. All these diverse elements fused to give rise before long to a unitary Roman life, all speaking Latin. Roman life attested to have been intensive in the second and third centuries, radiated to great distances into the territories of the neighboring populations (free Dacians, Iazygian and Roxolan Sarmatians, and the new arrivals: the Germanic tribes). The hostility of these peoples towards the Roman Empire did not prevent them from being attracted by the higher values of Roman civilization, as had happened among Decebalus's Dacians in former days.

## 4. *Roman Dacia and Scythia Minor During the Military Anarchy*

THE last representative of the Severan dynasty, Severus Alexander, was murdered by his troops, together with his mother, during the war on the Rhine in 235. The same troops, which mostly came from the territories along the Danube, had forced the imperial purple on C. Julius Valerius Maximi-

nus (235-238), prefect of the recruits and most probably
a Getian from Moesia Inferior, who had reached a high rank
in the army owing to his military merits. Known in history
by the name of Maximin the Thracian (*Maximinus Thrax*),
he stoutly defended the boundaries of the Empire and waged
victorious wars in Dacia where he repelled the attacks of the
Iazygians and of the free Dacians. The armies of Dacia and of
the two Moesias were devoted to him for he had come from
their ranks. He was murdered during the civil war of 238
between his Danubian army and the forces of his rivals in
Italy raised to high station by the Senate. Finally the throne
was occupied by young Gordian III whose full name was
M. Antonius Gordianus (238-244).

This war, like the proclamation of Maximin the Thracian
three years before, was the beginning of the great crisis known
as "the military anarchy." It was the old antagonism between
the army and the Senate brought to its height, each claiming
to be entitled to confer the title of Emperor, and it was also
a consequence of the weakening of central authority in the
provinces. The legions had gradually assumed a regional
character after local recruiting had been instituted by Hadrian,
which, together with the repeated pressures on the Roman
frontiers, had created a trend towards independence in the
legions — basic elements of the army —, each legion seeking
to serve the interests of the province where it was stationed
by bringing to the throne an emperor who would thus be
under obligation to them. The result was an endemic civil
war between the different claimants proclaimed in the provinces along the frontier, and between the latter and the emperors recognized by the Senate. This military anarchy lasted
for more than a generation and, being aggravated by fearful
invasions, epidemics, and starvation which brought in their
train depopulation of the provinces, economic misery, and
cultural decadence, it shook the very foundations of the Roman
State.

In 238, taking advantage of the disturbances within the
Empire, the powerful Carpi — free Dacians who had occu-
pied a large part of Moldavia — invaded Moesia Inferior
passing through Dobrudja in agreement with the Goths, a
Germanic people. Ultimately, Menophilus, the governor of
Moesia Inferior, drove them back. This, however, put an

end to the long period of peace in Dobrudja and started a series of uninterrupted trans-Danubian attacks which for more than three decades were to bring great suffering to the region about the mouths of the Danube.

A new invasion of the Carpi in Dobrudja and Thrace was repelled by Gordian in 242. The same people overran Dacia Malvensis in far greater numbers in 245, during the principate of Emperor M. Julius Philippus, also named Philip the Arab, when the castra on the *limes Transalutanus* were besieged. But Philip was prompt and energetic, and beat back the invaders, pursuing them into their own territories in Moldavia. Undertaking a new attack in 247, the Carpi were crushed and compelled to make peace on terms that were far from easy. Nevertheless, it is probable that the Roman emperor who assumed the title of *Carpicus Maximus* after his victory allowed some of the Carpi to settle between the Danube and the Carpathians as allies of the Empire. The *limes* of Dacia Malvensis was then brought back to the line of the river Olt, that is as it was before Septimius Severus. This was an insignificant strategic adjustment but also the first sign that Roman domination north of the Danube was tottering. Two years of bitter war had brought devastation to the province and spread panic throughout Dacia. Possibly it was then that the mother of Emperor Galerius (306-311), a Romanized Dacian, took refuge south of the Danube at Serdica (Sofia). Philip took measures designed to reinforce Dacia's frontiers and to rehabilitate the devastated localities. The walls of Romula (*colonia sua*) were rebuilt from their foundations. It was Philip who gave the province the right of minting bronze coins.

In 248 while Philip's rights were contested and rival Emperors were proclaimed in Cappadocia and Syria, Dobrudja was invaded by a great coalition of Goths, Carpi, Taïphali, Bastarnians, and Hardingi, led by the Gothic kings Argaithus and Guntherichus. The Goths, who had previously been less numerous than the Carpi, had now become the main coordinating power among the trans-Danubian populations. By now they had spread over the vast areas north of the Pontus Euxinus and had subjected the eastern Sarmatians. Consul C. Messius Quintus Trajanus Decius (249-251), a native of Pannonia Inferior, was sent against the invaders. He defeated them, drove them back beyond the Danube, was proclaimed emperor and soon after repelled an attack on Dacia of the free Dacians and of other barbarians. An inscription found at Apulum calls him *restitutor Daciarum*. On the local coins of those days the province called itself Dacia Felix, in token of gratitude, as it was done under Aurelian.

Being elated by Decius's successes, the Danube armies demanded that he should take them to Italy against Philip who, having been defeated at Verona, was killed by his own soldiers. After Decius had been recognized by the Senate, he returned to Moesia Inferior which in 250 was attacked by immense forces of the trans-Danubian coalition under the Gothic king, Kniva, coming from Dobrudja and the Muntenian plain. The Roman army was unable to stop the devastations in Thrace and Eastern Moesia. Decius was killed at Abritus (Razgrad) in 251, desperately trying to defend these provinces. His successor, Trebonianus Gallus (251-253), commander of the Novae (Shishtov) garrison, was compelled to consent to a peace treaty which allowed the invaders to withdraw beyond the Danube with all the spoils of war. It was a great disaster. The Pontic cities no longer issued any coins, the villages were laid waste, the fields were untilled, the plague was raging, and military anarchy was at its height. Muntenia and Lower Moldavia having been occupied by numerous forces of the Carpi and Gotho-Sarmatians, were lost to the Empire.

In 253 a new Gothic coalition invaded Moesia Inferior but was driven back by Aemilianus, governor of the province, whom the army proclaimed emperor. The civil war that ensued was fought in Italy; both Gallus and Aemilianus died and victory went to P. Licinius Valerianus (253-260), proclaimed emperor by the armies on the upper Danube. Threatened by invasions and by the rivalry of many claimants to the throne, who were supported by the forces on the Rhine and in the East, the emperor for the first time divided the Empire, assuming authority over the East while his son, P. Licinius Egnatius Gallienus (253-269), took over the rest. Gallienus repelled an attack on Dacia of the free Dacians, after which the province was peaceful enough not to be mentioned in any records as a theater of war. After Valerianus was taken prisoner by the Persians in 260 A.D. and had died in captivity, military anarchy assumed vast proportions. Gallienus was left only with Italy and the Danube provinces, the rest of the Empire falling into the hands of usurpers. Even in the provinces under his rule, the Roman troops revolted several times, supporting various claimants to the throne whom Gallienus finally defeated. One of the latter, Regalianus, commander of the armies in the two Moesias, was an able general, a native of Dacia, who claimed to be descended from Decebalus. True or not, the very fact that such a rumor had spread, shows a specific evolution in the consciousness of the Romanized provincials, whose devotion to Rome did not preclude their pride in ancient local values.

The battles between Gallienus and the new claimants supported by the provincial armies favored the resumption of the raids of the Goths and Carpi into Dacia. During their invasion by sea in 267, the north Pontic populations led by the Goths, before heading southwards, entered the gulf of Histria (*Histrum ingressi*), conquered it by surprise and laid it waste (*Histriae excidium*). It was only many years later that the city was rebuilt. Continuing their way, the numerous north Pontic ships were met by a Roman military fleet which, however, could not prevent them from entering the Straits and the Aegean Sea. Finally, a new intervention of the Roman fleet destroyed the entire naval forces of the barbarians who had left their ships and were out on a foray. Compelled to return by land, through Thrace, the invaders were defeated by Gallienus who, after inflicting great losses on them in battle and taking hostages, allowed them to withdraw beyond the Danube.

A new attempt to attack the Empire in the same way and along the same route was made in 269, a year after the death of Gallienus. This time the expedition was of immense proportions, a genuine migration. Masses of Goths, Heruli, Gepidae, Bastarnians, and Sarmatians, with their families and cattle, concentrated at Tyras, at the estuary of the Dniester, and moved along the Dobrudjan coast, some on land, some by ship. On their way they attempted the conquest of the city of Tomis (Constantza), attacking it from the water and on land, but the energetic resistance of this metropolis of the Left Pontus forced them to raise the siege. The migratory populations looted Greece and Macedonia and were finally defeated at Naissus (Nish) by the new emperor M. Aurelius

Claudius (268-270), an able general. This brilliant victory earned him the title of *Claudius Gothicus*. It was one of the decisive victories in the history of the Roman Empire.

But calamities continued. The plague wrought havoc in the Empire and the Naissus conqueror himself fell victim to it in 270. His worthy subordinate, L. Domitius Aurelianus (270-275), sprung from a lower class Moesian family, assumed the title of emperor by the will of the army in Illyricum (the forces of Dacia and of the two Moesias were also part of it) — now the most important army in the Empire. The military anarchy was on the decline and the unity of the Empire was generally felt to be a necessity. Aurelian succeeded in building up its unity by again conquering the provinces in the East from Zenobia, Queen of Palmyra, and forcing the Roman armies in the West — abandoned by Tetricus, the emperor they had elected — to resume discipline. He then repelled many invasions and reorganized the boundaries of the Empire.

On his way to the East in 271, while taking his forces to meet Zenobia's armies, Aurelian made a detour to fight the Goths who had attacked Moesia Inferior and Thrace. Having driven them back from these provinces, he pursued them over the Danube and into Muntenia, where he defeated them in a battle where their king, Cannabaudes, was killed. The title of *Dacicus Maximus* was conferred on him by the Senate, apart from the title of *Gothicus Maximus*. The *Dacicus* in his title might bear a reference to forces of the free Dacians who had associated with the Goths.

The next year, on his victorious return from the East, he found Moesia Inferior invaded by the Carpi and defeated them in the vicinity of Sucidava, in Southwest Dobrudja. Aurelian again built up the unity of the Empire, and well deserved the title of *restitutor patriae* found on an inscription at Callatis. He moreover reorganized the defense of the frontiers, attaching great importance to the Danube *limes*. In view of the balance of power at the time, Dacia needed to be evacuated. Its evacuation probably took place in 274-275, when strategy demanded that a shorter boundary be established along the Danube line, as it had been before Trajan. Shortly after, Aurelian was murdered while on his way to the East for an offensive against the Persians.

The throne was vacant for half a year. The most important among the immediate successors of Aurelian was M. Aurelius Probus (276-282), formerly his collaborator and himself a military man of great ability, and also a native of Illyricum. Under his principate, Dobrudja again rose from the suffering inflicted on it by the trans-Danubian invasions. After defeating many peoples along the Danube boundaries, who had renewed their attacks on the Empire, among them being the Iazygian Sarmatians and the populations recently settled in the Muntenian plain, Probus proceeded to a reorganization of the defense of Moesia Inferior, where he colonized a large number of Bastarnians who had demanded asylum as *dediticii* and who were subsequently to prove their great devotion to the Empire and to Roman civilization. This took place in 279-280. Probus's policy, which followed the line of many of his predecessors, consisted in pacifying the barbarians by settling them in the Empire and enrolling them individually into the Roman army. This policy generally yielded good results but also caused unpleasant surprises. Several troops of Gepidae, Greutungi, and Vandals, colonized in Moesia Inferior as farmers, rose in revolt. They took up arms and captured the ships along the Dobrudjan coast, carrying on plundering raids on land and at sea. The emperor suppressed them and forced the survivors to take refuge beyond the Danube.

Later, under Diocletian (284-305), as part of certain fundamental administrative and military reforms, Dobrudja was separated from Moesia Inferior and became a province in its own right under the name of Scythia, with Tomis as its capital city.

## 5. Imperial Administration Abandons Dacia

THE withdrawal of Aurelian from Dacia had important consequences in the formation of the Romanian people, though it was a further sign of the decline of the Romans that the authorities should withdraw from a profoundly Romanized province which for over 165 years had been a powerful outpost *(propugnaculum)* of the Empire and of Roman civilization projecting into the world of the barbarians. The

migrations which during the previous century had filled
the plains around this Carpathian bastion with numerous
warlike populations, had totally changed the balance of power
along the Danube. The Empire, now without internal resources as a result of the crisis it had undergone, had to econo-
mize its forces by cutting down the long perimeter of Trajan's province and resuming the defensive line along the
Danube. Under the new conditions, Dacia was of no use
to the Empire from a military point of view. It was no longer efficient in defending the Danubian *limes*; on the contrary, it jeopardized it, disjointing the boundary and depriving it of important forces required within. The great barbarian forces skirted Dacia fearlessly to attack the provinces
of Illyricum and Moesia. Withdrawal from Dacia did not mean
that the strategic position before Trajan was being revert-
ed to. Even without Roman forces, Dacia, with most of
its population Romanized, did not consider itself as separated from Rome. And the Empire was still powerful enough
not to allow a new enemy force, like that of the Dacians of
old, to overrun the territory of its former province.

Aurelian evacuated Dacia in good order, unhampered by the
barbarians who had been beaten and reduced to a state of peace
all along the Lower Danube. The forces of the province crossed to the right bank of the river: Legio XIII Gemina occupied
the castrum at Ratiaria (Archar) while Legio V Macedonica
returned to its old garrison at Oescus (Ghighen). The administrative officials were withdrawn simultaneously with
the army and were followed by the rich and by a part of the
townspeople, who were settled between the Danube and the
Balkans. On these territories a new province was founded.
It was named *Dacia*, not only as a consolation to Roman
prestige but also because its army, its administrative machinery, and the foremost social elements of the population
were identical with those of the province that had been abandoned. The new Dacia lay along the Danube contiguously
with what had formerly been Dacia Inferior. Probably the
Dacia of Aurelian was already from the beginning divided
in two provinces which were later attested to: Dacia Ripen-
sis along the bank of the Danube, with Ratiaria as its capital
city, and Dacia Mediterranea in the middle of the country, within
the Balkan Peninsula, with Serdica (Sofia) as its capital city.

Ancient records preserved from sources of later date are extremely sparse concerning Dacia's evacuation. Indeed, the event has but a mere mention. However, there is nothing to justify the contention of certain modern researchers that evacuation had meant total depopulation of the Carpathian province and that the Romanian people of today came from south of the Danube during the Middle Ages. This is not proved by even the vaguest record. The existence of the Romanian people exactly on the territory formerly taken up by Dacia is in open contradiction to such views. To deny the continuity of the Romanian people on the territory of their homeland is to fly against the logic of the general realities of human life and the natural course of things. The territory of the Dacia of Aurelian had neither the area nor the resources of Trajan's Dacia, and neither was it, being without a population of its own, to be able to receive all the inhabitants of the trans-Danubian province to the last man. An important increase in population in Aurelian's Dacia would have caused new towns and villages to be created. But there is not the faintest proof of such an increase in the number of localities in the new province between the Balkans and the Danube: archeology, written records, and toponymy give no indication to this effect. The number of people withdrawn from Carpathian Dacia was small enough for them all to find place in the previously existing settlements beside the local population. On the other hand, the land in Aurelian's Dacia, which, we should recall, was the property of the local landowners, could not have satisfied large numbers of new arrivals from north of the Danube either in quantity or quality.

We might therefore conclude that Roman officialdom evacuated only what strictly belonged to them: the army and the officials *(sublato exercitu et provincialibus*, as it is stated in Aurelian's biography in *Historia Augusta*, *provinciales* referring more particularly to administrative officials), and also what they felt in duty bound to protect first and foremost: the great landowners, the traders, and the rich, that is the holders of the main means of production. As to the masses, especially the peasants who felt bound to the land, they were content to remain in their fields and pastures for they had no vital reasons for leaving them. Official protection did not seem to be indispensable to ploughmen and shepherds who, during the various invasions of the past century, had so often been compelled to shift for themselves, as the soldiers and townspeople, besieged in their cities, had been unable to help them. The Daco-Roman peasants had become used to insecurity under barbarian pressure. No greater evil could threaten them when left to themselves. It is through them that Romanism was perpetuated north of the Danube, to become the lasting foundation of the Romanian people.

Being abandoned by official bodies did not amount to being isolated from the rest of the Roman world. On the contrary, economic, spiritual, and even political connections between the Empire and the former province left of the Danube continued. And when Christianity became the privileged religion of the Empire in the fourth century, after three centuries of clandestine proselytism, missionaries were sent to Dacia who effectively helped to consolidate the Roman elements there. All the basic religious terminology in Romanian is of Latin origin. No migratory population exerted any influence liable to compete with that of the Empire on the Daco-Roman population left in Dacia.

Abandoned Dacia had not been ceded to anyone. Officialdom continued to consider it as a territory belonging to the Empire, as had been in former days the unoccupied and uncolonized territories of Muntenia and Lower Moldavia. As long as there was an imperial army along the Danube no foreign people could make of the Carpathians a center of their power. The free Dacians and the Sarmatians, who immediately settled in the abandoned province, maintained their old connections with the Empire — a kind of conditional dependence —, and finally fused with the mass of the local Daco-Roman population. The later barbarian forces, such as the Goths, Huns, Avars, etc., exercised political supremacy over the Daco-Romans, but from a distance, their centers always being outside the Carpathian arc. The Danube, once again a strategic frontier, never separated the people living on its two banks. They were to continue to develop along the same lines even after the final collapse of imperial domination along the Danube in the seventh century.

The survival of the Roman element in Dacia as well as over vast territories on the right bank of the Danube — for instance in Scythia Minor — under most adverse conditions, is the most lasting success of Roman civilization and one of the most vivid examples of the active, decisive part the Roman Empire played in promoting progress in ancient times.

## 6. The Roman Province of Scythia

WHEN Dacia was evacuated, Dobrudja, which had become a separate province under Diocletian, officially named Scythia, remained under imperial rule. The administrative boundary of this province separated it from what was left of the former Moesia Inferior (Moesia Secunda). It coincided with the geographical boundary between the Southern Dobrudjan steppe and the pre-Balkan forests of Deliorman.

After the reforms made by Diocletian, the province was governed by a *praeses*, who had his residence in Tomis. Its army was under the command of a *dux* and consisted of two legions: Legio I Jovia, quartered at Noviodunum (Isaccea) and Legio II Herculia, which had its garrison at Troesmis (Turcoaia), as well as of numerous auxiliary corps—infantry, cavalry, river sailors — in the Danube castra which made up what was called *limes Scythicus*.

The provinces of Scythia and Moesia Secunda were incorporated in the Thrace diocese, and Aurelian's Dacia in the Moesia diocese. Following the new reforms which made state centralization their aim, provincial towns were no longer autonomous. The titles of *colonia* and *municipium*, which had lost their value already in Caracalla's time, now died out altogether and the Hellenic cities along the coast — Histria, Tomis, Callatis — lost their political individuality, becoming mere provincial towns subject to the central administration and on an equal footing with any of the others. Emperor Galerius energetically defended the Danube boundary, repelling the Goths' attacks in 295-297 and undertaking an expedition north of the river which took him as far as Moldavia. As a result, the power of the Carpi and the Bastarnians was brought to nought, these peoples being mostly deported to various provinces of the Empire and definitely going out of the historical picture. It was also Galerius who defeated the Iazygian Sarmatians in a number of battles.

A *Dacia restituta* (reunited) was spoken of at the time. This did not mean, however, that the Romans again occupied the territories north of the Danube but only that imperial authority was consolidated in the regions evacuated by Aurelian, which had never for a moment been considered out of the sphere of Roman authority.

When the capital of the Empire was removed from Rome to Byzantium (Constantinopolis), there was increased interest in defending the Lower Danube which had a direct impact on the new capital. Constantine the Great strengthened the Danube frontier. In Dobrudja the city of Tropaeum (Adamclisi) was rebuilt from its foundations in 316. It was then that the great walls whose ruins can be seen to this day were raised. In 324 Constantine repelled an attack of the Goths and of the eastern Sarmatians whom he pursued across the Danube and into today's Muntenia, defeating them in a battle where the Sarmatian king, Rausimodus, fell. After a new victory north of the Danube in 332, he forced upon the Goths a peace under which the latter agreed to recognize the authority of the Empire and to supply contingents to the Roman army. Constantine moreover established bridgeheads on the left bank of the Danube, from Bărboşi in Lower Moldavia to Dierna (Orşova) in Banat. A vast protection area, which comprised part of Banat and Oltenia and the whole of Muntenia's plain, was created beyond the Danube *limes*. At Sucidava (Celei) a permanent wooden bridge was built over the river and one of the old Roman roads leading to the Carpathians was repaired. These are measures which evidence the Empire's constant care to keep the territories of the former Dacian province within its grasp.

From among Constantine's sons and successors, Constantius II attached great importance to the defense of the province of Scythia which, having been like a gate giving access to trans-Danubian invasions, was turned into a strong bastion of the Empire with many garrisons.

From among the developments worthy of mention that took place in the province of Scythia in the centuries that followed, is the great rebellion of Vitalianus, a local general of Thraco-Roman origin and a native of Zaldapa (Abtaat). Being in command of the forces of the province, he rose against Anastasius, the then Roman emperor of the East, in 513. The immediate reasons of the uprising were religious, Vitalianus, a staunch orthodox, opposing certain sectarian tendencies at the court of Anastasius. Actually, however, the wide participation of the troops and population of the province in his undertaking is to be accounted for by the discontent aroused by the financial levies. Heading an army of 50,000 soldiers and Thraco-Roman peasants and also having at his disposal a fleet with its base at Acres (Cape Caliacra), Vitalianus attacked Constantinople, the capital of the Empire, several times but without success. After seven years of virulent fighting, the conflict was brought to an end by the succeeding emperor, Justinus, who after smoothing out the religious divergences and easing the burden of taxation, enticed the rebel general to Constantinople in 520 where great honors and dignities were conferred on him, after which he mysteriously disappeared. Vitalianus has gone down in history as one of the most remarkable of the men coming from the Roman population of ancient Dobrudja.

Under Justinian (527-565), Justinius's successor, the province of Scythia lived through a period of economic and cultural advance, and had new fortifications built on its territory. At the same time its church was given a powerful impetus. Monumental basilicas were erected in various localities. After his death, however, the defense of the province was tested by the constant attacks of superior forces, especially those of the Avars.

In 584 Dobrudja was laid waste, the Avars conquering and destroying towns such as Tropaeum and Zaldapa in Scythia and Durostorum and Marcianopolis in Moesia.

Ruined and now largely rural, the province of Scythia continued for a time to be listed among the Empire's possessions, there being a few towns left on the coast and a number of imperial garrisons inland, but before the end of the seventh century even these semblances of the urban civilization of former days disappeared under the blows dealt by a new Turanic people, the Proto-Bulgars.

# CHAPTER IV

# The Formation of the Romanian People

ABANDONED by the troops and the administration of the Roman Empire, Dacia was to weather the storms of the peoples' migration, now and again finding support and stimulus in the Empire. Continuing to live on Dacian territory, the Daco-Romans were to survive the Germanic and Turanic rule in these parts, adjusting themselves to circumstances and taking advantage of the varied geographical features of their ancient homeland. The tenacity specific to the tillers of the soil and to stock-breeders enabled them to actively preserve the ethnical imprint due to their descent from the Dacians and the Romans. And even though adverse historical circumstances prevented them from keeping intact the heritage of their early formation, they were able to preserve to the end what was most valuable in it: the Roman strains rooted in a Dacian background.

## 1. Continuity of Daco-Roman Population in Dacia (The Proto-Romanians)

THE circumstances that brought about the evacuation of the province of Dacia by Aurelian and the political and strategic concepts on which it was based, as shown in the preceding chapter, for a long time made for a continuation of relations between the Empire and the population north of the Danube, and the unfolding historical process concluded with the emergence of the Romanian people in the historical arena. After Dacia's abandonment, written records concerning these regions became ever less numerous until they ultimately ceased to exist, the very rare ones found referring solely to situations and developments arising from the clash between the barbarians — migratory peoples — and the Empire. Consequently, for a long time modern research was unable accurately and wholly to understand the historical process of events in ancient Dacia between the close of the third and the tenth centuries A.D. The concept according to which no historical fact can be established without written records and the tendency to exaggerate the importance and the part played by the migratory peoples caused certain historians to evolve a theory according to which for long centuries the territory of ancient Dacia had foreign peoples settled on it; occupying the homeland of the Dacians one after the other, and living in it as masters, they had swept away every vestige of autochthonous life, Dacian or Daco-Roman. More recent research, however, relying mostly on archeological finds, has proved the existence of many facts and historical events unrecorded in texts or misinterpreted by them; and that the importance and role of the migratory peoples had nowhere been great enough to induce total extinction of the native, whether Pre-Roman or Roman, traditions. In the light of recent research, the history of ancient Dacia in the period of the peoples' migration is no longer a succession of inroads by the Germanic and Turanic peoples, but the final period of the Romanian people's formation over the vast area of what was free Dacia in ancient times.

The process whereby the Romanian people and their language were formed, was a long and complex one. Geographically as well as historically, there was in that process, as for all peoples that were formed in Europe at that time, fluctuations which cannot be specified in every detail but whose general line of development is clearly to be perceived and whose results — the presence of the Neo-Latin Romanian people in these parts — is a scientific reality which cannot be ignored. The latest research has invalidated the concept according to which the Romanian people had been formed solely south of the Danube, with an original "hearth" restricted to certain regions, from which they had proliferated. That concept was founded on the close kinship (by no means an identity) between the Romanian dialects wherever they might be spoken, a remarkable fact, undoubtedly, and a very rare phenomenon. But for the Romanians this might be accounted for by their way of life, the elementary level, whether agricultural or pastoral, which historical circumstances and uninterrupted foreign domination had forced on the Proto-Romanians during the period of transition to feudalism. Another explanation might be the close relationship maintained between the various branches of Roman descendants in Eastern Europe. The words of Albanian origin found almost unaltered in the Romanian language have for a long time served to prove that the Romanians' homeland had been in the west of the Balkan Peninsula. The latest scientific investigations, however, prove that most of these words (among which: barză — stork, brad — fir tree, brîu — waist band, brînză — cheese, a bucura — to rejoice, copac — tree, copil — child, groapă — pit, viezure — badger, mal — bank, mînz — foal, mazăre — peas, moş — old man, vatră — hearth) are the heritage of the Dacian language which is thus attested as an influence on the Romanians' language, just as the seventy-odd Celtic words in the French language are proof of the Celtic foundations of the French people.

Thus considered from a strictly ethnical point of view, the Romanian people prove to be descendants of nearly all the Roman-based populations of Eastern Europe (the descendants of the Romans of the eastern part of the Roman Empire), which in their turn incorporated the Romanized Geto-Dacians as basic elements. In the first chapter of this book it was shown that as early as the end of Iron Age I, one and the same Geto-Dacian population was living in the area extending from the Balkan Mountains to the Northern Carpathians. Recent linguistic research has confirmed this conclusion. Apart from which, the Romans repeatedly removed Dacians north of the Danube to Moesia or to South-Danubian Dacia. And it is also known that the Romanization process involved only the provinces spreading southwards down to the Balkans, to the so-called Jirecek Line, named after the scholar who in 1902 established the limit of Romanization, to be later confirmed with certain important changes by recent research.

Thus, it is obvious that the formative process of the Romanian people in its first stage consisted essentially in the Romanization of the Geto-Dacian population. This historical truth means that the foundations of the Romanian people are rooted in Romanization and in the Dacian people, for — we repeat — it is proved that the population subjected to Romanization in this part of Europe, primarily a rural population, which remained after the decline of town life, was in the first place Dacian, both in Dacia and in Moesia. Having been Romanized, the Dacians went out of the historical picture.

Within the Dacian territories, Romanization did not stop when Dacia was abandoned by Aurelian, but continued until the early seventh century A.D. when the Danube ceased to be the Empire's boundary. All this time Romanization intensified, for Latin began to be spoken by the rural masses once Christianity had become the official religion of the Empire and was spreading by means of preaching and religious services held in Latin. The fact that this new stage of the Romanization process (after 274-275 A.D.) made a full impact on the South-Danubian area and was less effective north of the Danube is only of episodic importance for the formative process of the Romanian people, because ethnographically, and for a long time also politically, as will be seen hereafter, the Danube was no real boundary.

It was thus that a Romanic people, mostly of Dacian origin, arose over extensive areas before the early seventh century under definite historical conditions. They were different from those born in other parts of the vast Roman Empire (in Spain, Gaul, etc.) and certain scholars have inclined to consider this people already Romanian, for they gave it that name. The transformation undergone by phonemes in the phrase *torna, torna, fratre* [1] as pronounced by a native south of the Danube in 578 A.D. and preserved by the Byzantine chroniclers Theophylact and Theophanes, shows that even at that time, from the language point of view, we could speak about a Romanic people different from the other Romanic peoples of those days; we will call them Proto-Romanians. We could, therefore, speak about two main stages in the formation of the Romanian people: Romanization, which gave rise to a Romanic people (the Proto-Romanians) and active preservation of Romanization, which also comprised assimilation of the migratory populations and resulted in the completion of the formative process of the Romanian people. Assimilation of the migratory elements by the masses

---

[1] *Fratre* stands for *frater* in classical Latin, so that the phoneme here is already Romanian.

of Romanic population north of the Danube is proof of its demographic and cultural superiority.

The first stage began simultaneously with the Romanization of the Balkan Peninsula. Economic contacts between the territories south and north of the Danube and the constant displacement of the population which preceded Dacia's occupation by the Romans, created favorable conditions for Romanization. Romanian ethno-genesis consequently relies on two fundamental elements: the autochthonous Geto-Dacian population and the Roman and Romanized colonies. Up to the early seventh century, the Roman elements spread over a vast part of the Carpatho-Balkan territories in Eastern Europe, making up a well-knit whole.

When the Danube *limes* fell, a new stage began in their development. Although connections between the territories south and north of the Danube continued, a process of differentiation began between the Romanian population in the Carpatho-Danubian territories and the Romanic populations south of the Danube, the former's language developing its first specific features.

After the Slavs had settled in the Balkan Peninsula, North-Danubian Dacia became the center of gravity of the Roman elements of Eastern Europe.

The Romanic population north of the Danube (Proto-Romanians) was consolidated through additions of Romanic elements from south of the Danube and through the assimilation of the migratory elements who settled on the country's territory. As can be deduced from many archeological, linguistic, and written testimonies, the formative process of the Romanian people and language ended between the ninth and the early tenth centuries A.D.

The first historical problems concerning the developments that followed Dacia's evacuation are the fate of the former province and its population. The view that the entire population had been evacuated, admitted at times despite the impossibility, both in theory and in practice, of such a measure being taken under the conditions prevailing in those days, is closely bound up with the necessary inference that the Visigoths had occupied the abandoned province. Some such inference is certainly to be made, for it is impossible to imagine that a region so rich in natural resources could have remained uninhabited. Nevertheless, a number of well established historical and archeological facts invalidate the aforementioned theory.

The first fact is that a large part of the Romanized Dacians remained where they were.

Many finds — coins, hoards of money, town buildings that continued to be inhabited — attest the continued life of an important part of the old population, which preserved its connections with the Empire during the period immediately following the official evacuation, as proved by the following fact: in the Roman city of Napoca (present-day Cluj) bronze coins bearing the imprint of Aurelian's immediate successors — Emperors Tacitus (275-276), Probus (276-282) and Carinus (283-285) — have been found amidst the ruins of Roman buildings. For a later period, two finds are of outstanding importance. The first are the ruins of the former town of Apulum (Alba Iulia) with a Roman cemetery of an *urban character* dating from the fourth century A.D., where bronze coins of the time of Constantine the Great (306-336) have been found, and also exclusively Roman grave goods and scattered coins from the whole period extending from Diocletian (284-305) to Gratian (375-383 A.D.) We have here a resumption (to say the least) in the fourth century A.D. of forms of urban life with the attendant influx of Roman coins and of craftsmanship bearing the imprint of the Romans. A second find is the *rural* Daco-Roman cremation cemetery of Bratei (Sibiu county) on the bank of the Tîrnava Mare river. This is a cemetery of 400 graves and was used at the close of the fourth century and the early fifth century A.D., consequently during the invasion of the Huns. This means that a century after Roman troops and Roman administration had left Dacia, the provincial population here lived a stable life. The same cemetery also proves, though retrospectively, how real the Romanization of the Dacians was, for apart from a small number of graves that follow the traditional Dacian rituals, all the others show that the Roman provincial rituals were observed.

Archeological excavations consequently attest the existence throughout the Dacian territory, after the withdrawal of Roman authority, of a Daco-Romanian material culture which was to develop without intermission for a millennium. The continuity of material culture is eloquent proof of ethnical continuity.

Another fact of major importance, referred to in the preceding paragraphs, is that groups of free Dacians — and not Visigoths — infiltrated into abandoned Dacia (abandoned and not ceded to a barbarian people). In the third century A.D., those free Dacians were arrayed on the northwestern, northern, eastern and southeastern frontiers of the province of Dacia while in Muntenia and Moldavia they were living under the name of Carpi between the frontier and the territories of the Visigoths, who had settled further east. Historical and archeological data leave no doubt about this and, in the order of things, it is quite natural that the former Roman province of Dacia should have received a new influx of Dacians after being evacuated. Indeed, the first problem the Roman Empire had to tackle after its withdrawal from Dacia is that of the Carp Dacians east of Dacia; they were defeated by the energetic emperors Diocletian and Maximian in a number of battles and removed to Moesia (mainly Dobrudja, especially along the Danube) and to Pannonia, where it was supposed they would be Romanized in time. This occurred from 295 to 297 A.D. Diocletian again reinforced the Danube frontier and the later Roman chronicles mention reassuringly that the *whole* people of the Carpi had been removed within the Empire — which was obviously an exaggeration.

Consequently, on the one hand the free, independent Dacians were left by the Romans or driven by them to enter an area which removed the danger they represented for the Empire; on the other hand, it was only after the power of the Carpi had been brought to nought that the Empire could see its way to an understanding with the Goths, who were considered less dangerous than the Carpi.

## 2. The Goths in Dacia

THE image built up of the Goths being at every moment and at any cost the enemies of the Roman Empire needs to be revised in the light of certain incontestable facts. It is proved that the relations between the Goths and the Romans relied on political realism and involved mutual concessions and aggressions. After 295-297 A.D. the Visigoths penetrated into Moldavia and Muntenia and it is certain that at least after 323 they were considered as *federates* (barbarian allies) of the Roman Empire, which enables us to infer that there was a certain toleration on the part of the Empire when they were allowed to spread to the Eastern and Southern Carpathians and to the Lower Danube. Another fact which confirms this inference and proves at the same time that the Empire had not lost all interest in its former possessions north of the Danube is the Visigoths keeping away from the territories of the former Roman province of Dacia (the Transylvanian plateau, Oltenia, and Banat). And when in 332 A.D. they tried to overrun those territories starting with Oltenia, Emperor Constantine the Great, who had built the stone bridge over the Danube at Sucidava (Celei) in 328, had them attacked from the rear and defeated them. Thus the Visigoths, during most of the time they spent in these territories, kept watch over the Danube boundary of the Empire, defending the provinces of Moesia Inferior and Thrace and ultimately, even the new capital, Constantinople. This they did as mercenaries, thus establishing with the Romans a precarious but durable balance of forces not devoid of mutual fear. Another fact specific to the situation in North-Danubian Dacia after it had been abandoned was the direct intervention of the Empire for some time, which considerably extenuated the effects of Roman withdrawal from Dacia. It is just possible that Aurelian himself may have maintained a number of bridgeheads left of the Danube; however that may be, it is certain that Constantine the Great and his successors saw that the new frontier was well defended, maintaining Roman forces at the bridgeheads at Orșova (Dierna), Turnu Severin (Drobeta), Celei (Sucidava) and possibly at Constantinians Daphne facing Turtucaia, and at Bărboși on the river Siret in Southern Moldavia as well as in other smaller strongholds on the northern bank of the Danube. The Romans took their armies into Banat, Oltenia, and Muntenia whenever the Iazyg Sarmatians in the west and the Goths in the east disturbed the peace along the frontiers of the Empire. The last defeat of the Visigoths in Muntenia was during the campaign of 367-369 under the command of Emperor Valens. The Roman world even spoke about a partial reconquest of Trajan's Dacia by Constantine the Great and it is probable that part of Banat and Oltenia came again under the Empire's authority. It is, however, difficult to admit that the great earthwork surrounded by a ditch and spreading from Hinova near Turnu Severin to Mizil in the hilly region — Novac's Furrow, as it is called — is the work of the Roman Emperors of the fourth century, for such a fortification in no way fits in with the ethnical and strategic situation of those days when the Goths were installed in Moldavia as well as south and north of the Furrow in Muntenia. On the other hand, in the Roman cemetery recently discovered at Celei, Roman graves of the fourth century were identified, with Roman coins and other grave goods that unmistakably establish their date. It is obvious that members of the Roman frontier troops *(limitanei)*, with their families, tilled the land here and formed a center from where Roman civilization radiated into the former Roman province. And the same can be inferred about the other bridgeheads north of the Danube of those days.

Archeological research and the interpretation of written records in the light of archeological finds have proved that the Visigoths lived for a time in Moldavia (mostly in Eastern Moldavia and very little on the central plateau) and in Muntenia, up to Vedea to the west, and that they were to be found in large numbers along the Danube, between Teleorman and Călărași. The Gothic cemeteries at Sînzana on the Mureș, at Tîrgu Mureș and at Palatca not far from Cluj, which were considered as proof of the penetration and settlement of the Visigoths in Transylvania, were ultimately found to belong to the latter half of the fourth century, certain Visigoth "garrisons" having possibly been asked by the Romans to occupy the upper Mureș line and the "Gate of the Someș" against a threat from the northwest (possibly from the Vandals) or an early infiltration of other Goths, the Gepidae, from the northwest through the "Gate of the Someș". The infiltration was stopped on the Mureș river.

## 3. *Early Christianity among the Daco-Romans*

THE aforementioned developments made it possible for Roman civilization to continue its impact on Dacia in the fourth century and this is reflected by the penetration and

wide circulation of Roman coins, including a large number
of small bronze coins; by the considerable imports of Roman
products, including a great deal of common earthenware,
though part of it may possibly have been made in Dacia,
and by the material culture of the  local population and of
the Visigoths, which bears the distinctive imprint of Roman
influence. The specific Germanic elements are few in number
and restricted to personal adornments. In the rural environment of the former Roman province of Dacia, a Daco-Roman
brand of civilization was built up, not devoid of specific
Gothic elements though Dacian tradition prevailed; this
was due to the local Roman shops, of which few had been
left, being unable to meet the requirements of such widespread
regions. In Muntenia and Moldavia many open-air settlements
of those days, most of them outside the areas settled by the
Visigoths, show specific features proving that there was a
local Dacian population and partly a Daco-Roman population, especially along the Danube, upon whom the impact
of Roman civilization continued to make itself felt. Actually
under the conditions created by the Empire north of the
Danube during the fourth century A.D., with the Visigoths
being kept in check in their capacity as federates, the Dacians
and the Daco-Romans could travel without hindrance over
the wide Dacian territories so that the free Dacians were
able to infiltrate into Trajan's Dacia while the Daco-Romans
could cross over from Dacia into Muntenia and Moldavia.
Undoubtedly, it was primarily in Dacia that conditions were
created for a comparatively peaceful development of the
Daco-Romans and Dacians, by the Visigoths being kept back
from the former Roman province, and this also made it possible for Romanization to continue by internal means. Nowhere
has a withdrawal, a concealment of the native population in
places difficult of access, been established as a general phenomenon in those days, though such a thing might have happened
as an isolated event in certain places and for a certain time.
It has been proved that the natives of Muntenia maintained
direct relation with the Visigoths: in the Gothic cemeteries
at Spanțov on the Danube (Ilfov county) and of Tîrgșor not
far from Ploiești, specific Dacian religious vases have been
found. The excavations made during the last years provide
archeological proof of the existence of a material culture of

the autochthonous population. Thus the Bratei-Morești culture has been attested in Transylvania, the Botoșani-Udești culture in Moldavia and the Ipotești-Cîndești culture in Muntenia — Oltenia, all of them dated to the fourth-sixth centuries. The Daco-Roman material culture of this period was an integral part of the Romano-Byzantine culture which spread over vast areas.

The fourth century A.D. is the century when the Christian religion was recognized (by the Milan Edict of 313) and then the faith was forced upon the peoples of the Roman Empire until it finally became a State religion. Though it is not exactly known how Christianity penetrated among the Dacians and Daco-Romans, for there is no definite proof of the existence of missionaries preaching the new religion, it is a fact that Christianity *did* penetrate among them. The only region for which we have direct, authentic records concerning the making of converts to Christianity is the extra-Carpathian area of this country, contemporary texts describing in detail the missionary work (in Greek, Latin, and Gothic) of Gothic Bishop Ulfilas who translated the Bible into Gothic. Also described are the savage persecutions of the Christians perpetrated by some of the Visigoth chieftains headed by Athanarich, and the martyrdom of Saint Sava drowned in the river Buzău and of other less known martyrs. Nevertheless, although hundreds of Visigoth graves have been found in these regions and many settlements have been investigated, not a single Christian object has been found. On the other hand, in the former province of Dacia about which no such records are available, Christian objects of the fourth century are comparatively frequent, the most important being the find at Biertan (Sibiu county): the vestiges of a chandelier from a Christian shrine and bearing the Latin inscription "*ego Zenovius votum possui.*" Biertan lies in a district where there were never any Goths, so that the Christians there must have been natives of the place and Zenovius himself one of the "unofficial" missionaries. This is a paradox which is to be accounted for by the fact that the North-Danubian Visigoths to whom Ulfila preached with little success — indeed he had to flee to the Empire hurriedly — did not turn Christian during their stay in the territory of Dacia. Their so-called Christianity served only political purposes, for the Roman Empire considered it as a means of creating agents of its own among the natives and thus succeeded in enticing a group of Visigoth leaders. However, we should also recall the repeated ferocious persecutions against Christians in "Gothia" as well as the fact that when the "pro-Roman" Visigoths crossed into the Empire in 376 A.D., they did so headed by their pagan priests and carrying their idols with them. The Visigoths only embraced Christianity (the Arian rite of Greek tradition and using the Gothic language) after 378 A.D., during the reign of Emperor Theodosius I. The lack of Christian objects in the territories dominated by the Visigoths is, therefore, easy to explain, for the Christians did not dare to practice their faith openly. On the other hand, in the former Trajanic Dacia, Christianity (non-Arian and Latin) could spread at will, thus accounting for the original Latin fund of basic Christian terminology in the Romanian language (cruce — cross, sînt = sfînt — Saint, Dumnezeu — God, biserică — church, înger — angel, etc.). This is further proof of the fact that the Visigoths never lived or ruled in the former province of Dacia.

## 4. Dacia under the Huns' Domination: The Gepidae

THE conditions described above suddenly came to an end in 376 A.D. The Huns, a mixed Mongolian population of Asian origin and speaking a Turkic language, led by nomadic herdsmen and warlike horsemen, defeated the Goths and set up a reign of terror, but also of order and political stability, in Eastern and Central Europe for approximately eighty years. This is the first time Asian hordes had overrun Europe, beginning the stormy period of the "peoples' migration" on this continent. Although the action and the role of the Huns were merely episodic, they had serious consequences over the years on the political, military, and ethnical setup in which Dacia was involved. The weakening of the Eastern Roman Empire through the hard blow dealt it by the destructive plundering raids of the Huns, the fall of the Western Roman Empire as a more remote consequence of their invasion, and the access given to other similar Asian peoples to the heart of Europe, are events which had a sharp impact on the destinies of Dacia too.

The Huns, who kept to their nomadic way of life throughout, never settled on Dacia's territory for any length of time. Any settlement of theirs was only temporary, as a base for their attacks and for the exploitation of the local population in the plains (Northeast Moldavia, the Danube Plain, the Tisa Plain). Their domination in Dacia depended upon raids carried out mostly through the intermediary of their Germanic allies, primarily the Ostrogoths and the Gepidae. Among the immediate effects of the Huns' invasion was in the first place the emigration in two stages of the Visigoths from Dacia: the pro-Roman group in 376 and the traditionalist "pagan" group of Athanarich in 381, after a short period of settlement in the so-called Caucaland, on either side of the Buzău Mountains. It is from this time that date the hoards of Roman gold ingots found at Crasna and Feldioara and the coins and personal adornments at Valea Strîmbă in the Odorhei county, all situated in Transylvania. The great gold treasure containing pagan cult objects at Pietroasa in Muntenia is also supposed to have the same origin. Another consequence was the winding up of the Roman bridgeheads north of the Danube by 447 A.D. Under the aegis of the Huns, large portions of Dacia continued under Germanic domination (a Gothic domination, specifically Ostrogoth and Gepid). The compromise reached between the Huns and the Eastern Roman Empire, especially under the rule of Attila (434-453 A.D.), with constant negotiations and mutual embassies, created a *modus vivendi* also for Dacia's population, "deserters" and prisoners coming and going either way, and this made it possible for Dacia to survive despite exploitation and precarious living. It is probable that during the worst periods of Hun invasions, the native population took refuge in hiding places — forests and high districts which the Huns, a people of the steppe, usually avoided. But those periods alternated with periods of peace, when the Empire came to an understanding with the Huns, paying them subsidies as federates and allowing them, as the Goths had formerly been allowed, to buy things at the border fairs of the Empire. At Bucureşti-Cringaşi a small native settlement of those days has been discovered; it includes a pottery kiln and has been dated thanks to a Hun arrow which was found in a house, to about 400-408 A.D. Uldin, an ally of the great Roman general Stilicho, was the Hun leader who ruled in the plains of Oltenia and Muntenia.

At Dodești (Galați county), Costișa (Neamț county), and elsewhere in Moldavia life was organized again at much the same level as evidenced by the ruins of fourth-century settlements, abandoned when the Huns first started their attacks. However, Gothic elements are no longer found in the material culture, which was somewhat on the decline from the technical standpoint. In Transylvania it has already been shown that a fairly prosperous Romanic community was living on the bank of the Tîrnava Mare river at Bratei, tilling the land with iron implements of Daco-Roman tradition and practicing intensive stock-breeding. Many places in Transylvania bear witness to such settlements.

The conditions prevailing in the native villages of the territory controlled by the Huns — villages dependent on one or another Hun or Germanic chieftain of the cosmopolitan "Hun" conglomerate — are attested to in writing by an eyewitness: the rhetorician Priskos who took part in one of the Roman embassies to Attila's court in 449 when, as he states, he was able to speak Latin with a "barbarian", and not through the medium of a Roman prisoner or an interpreter.

Immediately after Attila's death, in 454 A.D., when a Germanic coalition headed by a Gepid king, Ardarich, formerly Attila's close collaborator, crushed the armies of Attila's sons, the power of the Huns disintegrated. The Huns then dispersed and history speaks of them little more.

From among the barbarians who benefited by the new situation in the Carpatho-Danubian area were primarily the Eastern Goths (Ostrogoths) and the third, more western Gothic branch known by the name of Gepidae. The latter had appeared north of Dacia about the mid-third century A.D. and after living under Hun domination, became independent and somehow inherited the Huns' domination over Dacia. The facts recorded in the first decades of the sixth century by the chroniclers Cassiodorus and Jordanes concerning their occupation of Trajanic Dacia up to the Eastern Carpathians and to the river Olt, are invalidated by archeological finds and by the other written records. For however obscure the records showing the situation in Dacia, one thing stands out clearly, namely, that up to 471 A.D. the Ostrogoths — settled in the Empire some time before as federates in the provinces of Pannonia, though a number had remained in the present-day territory of the U.S.S.R. when the Huns overran Europe — did not allow the Gepidae to infiltrate into Dacia. This "strategic balance" enabled the native population to remain for a time under Germanic rule, primarily Ostrogoth rule, but generally of a nonspecified character. Restricted groups of Ostrogoths, possibly those who had been for a little longer time in Moldavia (a small cemetery of theirs has been discovered at Botoşani) and were only passing through Transylvania (where only isolated graves or small dispersed groups of Ostrogoth graves are to be found) kept watch over Dacia's territories which they had probably often traversed in their efforts to regroup themselves in Pannonia when arriving from the East. It should be recalled that the Ostrogoths were federates of the Empire all through this period. Theodoric the Great, who was to be their king, had spent ten years as a hostage at Constantinople. It was only after 471 A.D., when the Ostrogoths left Pannonia and most certainly also the Dnieper areas, settling for a time as federates in Moesia which they left for Italy in 488, that the Gepidae were free to act. But it has been found that they were in fact living only in the plain west of mountainous Dacia, their center being left of the Tisa and up to the river Mureş to the south and to the Oradea Mare-Arad line to the east. From this district a group infiltrated towards Sirmium (Mitrovica on the river Save in today's Yugoslavia) and another group into the Transylvanian plateau. The last-named event took place around 480 A.D., as shown by the princely grave at Apahida not far from Cluj — probably the oldest Gepid monument in inter-Carpathian Transylvania. But in this district the Gepidae only effectively occupied the area up to the river Mureş, entering the region through the Someş gate, certain groups being used only as some kind of garrisons. On the left bank of the river Mureş they had only a number of bridgeheads whence they raided the country up to the Tîrnava Mare river. Like the other Gothic peoples Dacia had to deal with, the Gepidae were federates of the Empire, most certainly refractory, though they exerted pressure on the emperors ruling at Constantinople only from their positions in the Sirmium region — the gate to Constantinople in the middle Danube region. Most of Dacia was not affected by their presence during the period under discussion.

Beginning with Emperor Anastasius (491-518 A.D.) and after the departure of the Ostrogoths from the Balkan Peninsula, the Eastern Roman Empire began a drive for restoring the South-Danubian provinces and establishing a firm boundary along the Lower Danube. This drive reached its culmination during the reign of Justinian I (527-565 A.D.).

The Gepidae, subjected to the powerful impact of the civilization of the Eastern Roman Empire, which for another century was to continue to use the Latin language, had this impact transmitted to them partly through the agency of the Daco-Romans in Dacia, which far from having become a Gepid country, as it had not become a Gothic country, was developing its Romanic traditions, these being revived by the new powerful radiation of the civilization of the Eastern Empire. Justinian rebuilt and reoccupied the bridgeheads left of the Danube and organized the Christian church in those districts. At Sucidava, which had been rebuilt and had become a powerful Byzantine center, the oldest Christian church in the North-Danubian area of this country has been discovered. The whole of Dacia's territory was again caught in the meshes of the Empire's expansion policy, military power, and civilization. As in the fourth century A.D., the districts about the Danube were the more strongly affected by this reversal of policy, though Byzantine coins and craftware penetrated a long way to the north. Christian ritual objects (oil lamps, crosses, etc.) again spread over the territory of the former Dacian province but, as will be seen hereafter, not only there.

Many open settlements of those days identified on Transylvanian territory as, for example, at Bratei but also in many other places, as far as Ciumești in the Satu Mare county, show that life was comparatively prosperous and the main pursuits farming and stock-breeding.

Muntenia and Moldavia, which were dealt a heavier blow by the Huns' invasion and exploitation, also revived under the new conditions as early as the end of the fifth century. The population in these parts kept up the traditions of the third and fourth centuries and is known to have lived in fairly large numbers in open settlements, primarily in the Danube plain but also as far as the Carpathian foothills. Archeological investigations have found such settlements everywhere, from Ipătești on the Olt to Dulceanca on the river Vedea, as well as in Bucharest, at Tîrgșor not far from Ploiești and Budureasca close to Mizil and up to Botoșana near Suceava. In many respects this population proves to have been in close touch with the people of the former Dacian province. Muntenia assumed the aspect of a new "Roman country" of those days, which is confirmed by the spread of Christianity as proved by the numerous Christian finds, particularly metal crosses worn round the neck, which were serially cast in these parts, for even the moulds used for the casting have been found.

The political and strategic conditions spoken of above account for the fact that the Carpatho-Danubian regions were generally, though not completely, unaffected, in any case not directly affected, by the storms that broke out at this time in the steppes north of the Black Sea, again threatening the Byzantine Empire as well as Dacia. From what was left of the Huns who had withdrawn from Pannonia, and of other kindred nomadic peoples newly come from Asia, a new nucleus of warlike nomadic herdsmen known by the generic name of Bulgars had been formed. To differentiate between them and the Slav Bulgarians of today, who bear the name, we will call them Proto-Bulgars. The Proto-Bulgars began their plundering raids against the Eastern Empire in 493 A.D., taking along with them Slav groups as from the beginning of the rule of Emperor Justin I (518-527 A.D.). The Slavs may have come from their original homeland lying between the Vistula, the Pripet, and the Middle Dnieper down to the northern and eastern borders of Dacia. The Slavs known as Anti and Sclavini undertook an endless series of plundering raids in the Balkan Peninsula, where the defense of the Empire had been weakened, principally because the Byzantine armies had been concentrated in Italy to win back that part of the Empire from the Ostrogoths. Most of the raids were organized by the Proto-Bulgars and were under their leadership, though in 551 the Gepidae raided as far as today's Serbian reaches of the Danube. However, neither the Proto-Bulgars nor the Slavs settled for any length of time in Dacia and their hordes seemed to have traversed

Dacia only in part while on their way towards the Empire. This was the first time that the extra-Carpathian regions of this country came to know the Slavs, warlike hordes which made it their aim to penetrate into, and plunder, the Empire.

## 5. Avar Domination. The Slavs ˌSettle in Dacia

AS a result of events that took place between 558 and 568 we find a changed situation. A new Asian conglomerate, which has gone down in history under the name of Avars, defeated and subdued the Proto-Bulgars north of the Black Sea and, taking with them part of the Proto-Bulgars, made their appearance along the Empire's boundary at the mouths of the Danube. The Avars had been driven here by the expansion of the western Turks. Overrunning and plundering the country, the Avars at first claimed the right to settle in Dobrudja, which was imperial land. In the meantime the Gepidae were putting up fierce resistance to the Germanic people of the Longobardi who, coming up the Elbe through today's Czechoslovakia, had in 526 A.D. arrived south of the Danube, in the former Roman province of Pannonia. By 546 the Longobardi had mainly occupied Pannonia. Undoubtedly they had come as "federates" of the Empire, in which capacity they were soon in conflict with their neighbors and competitors, the Gepidae. The political and military entanglements west of this country were smoothed out in 567 when the Avars, deprived of all subsidies by Emperor Justin II, immediately after Justinian's death in 565, crossed into Pannonia, forged an alliance with the Longobardi and crushed the Gepidae. The Empire took good care to retrieve the stronghold of Sirmium. In 568 the Longobardi went to Italy and what was left of the Gepidae fell under the domination of the Avars who settled in Pannonia, thus creating a new political and strategic situation over wide expanses from the North Pontic steppes to Central Europe. This put an end to Germanic domination in this part of the world and opened the way to the Slavs towards the Danube and the Save boundary. Complex consequences ensued for Dacia. In the first place heavy and lengthy fighting broke out between the new military power north of the Danube and the Byzantine Empire.

Under the pressure of Avar attacks, combined with those of the Slavs, the Empire's boundaries firmly maintained along the Danube and the Save until now, were breached in 602 A.D. Before that date, however, faced by a more serious danger — for the Avars' domination here was harsh — the Empire had endeavored to hold the frontiers and at the same time to create stable conditions, as far as possible, in the former Roman possessions beyond the borders.

In the second place, the Avars organized the territory they inhabited or dominated according to Asian traditions, so that their nomadic and warlike tribes settled in the plains of the Middle Danube and of the Tisa, lining their central territories with dependent peoples whom they kept in obedience by means of garrisons and punitive raids. There is no contradiction between such domination and at times aggression, and a certain independence of the subordinated peoples, with occasional violent outbursts even, that freed them from subordination. Nor was there anything unnatural about the Avars' alternating subjection — whether in exchange for payment or forced upon them by force of arms — and aggression against the Empire.

Avars never lived on Dacian territory, the western plains of Crişana and Banat excepted. On the Transylvanian plateau a few groups of Gepidae settled — in different places from those they had occupied between 480 and 568 — on the Mureş, where cemeteries dating from that time have been found at Bandul de Cîmpie, Unirea, and Noşlac. This time an outpost advanced along the Tîrnava Mare river, as proved by the Bratei cemetery. These Gepid "garrisons," who used their own weapons, had adopted the armament and horse trappings of the Avars, and were at that time for the most part Christians (of the Arian rite) and in the service of the Avars, most probably held the native Daco-Roman population in subjection and temporarily kept in check the Slavs' expansion to the northwest of Transylvania. In Eastern Transylvania, up to the higher reaches of the Tîrnava Mică river and in Moldavia, the Slavs most probably penetrated again according to the general dictates of the Avars. In Muntenia and Oltenia there seems to have been something of a Slavo-Avar domination, with the natives prevailing from the ethnical standpoint for, in the settlements discovered in those parts, Slav elements are in a minority. In Moldavia and Eastern Transylvania the native population seems also to have been in a majority. It is clear, therefore, that as part of the organization effected by the Avars, the Slavs did not initially colonize the whole of Dacia, nor the uninhabited regions: whenever they settled for any length of time in certain parts of Dacia, they found themselves among the native population who assimilated them.

It is likely that the Slavs who settled in Dacia were fractions of tribes which had broken away from their home organizations and, having settled among the Proto-Romanians, had ultimately to adopt the local traditions of the village communities. No name of any Slav tribe living in Dacia has been preserved, thus proving that they had neither the possibility nor the time to organize themselves into tribes occupying their own territories, as they are known to have done south of the Danube in the seventh century. Much later, an Armenian geography written in the eighth or ninth century A.D. speaks of the "25 Slav tribes" driven from Dacia by the Goths — possibly Gepidae for this is the name given to all Dacia's population of those days. Those Slav tribes are said to have crossed over into the Balkan Peninsula. The names of some of Dacia's "Slav Kings" (leaders) during the last quarter of the sixth century have survived as, for instance, Ardagast, Mussokios, Pyrogost and Dauritas. It is strange that the first three names recall the old Dacian names of the rivers Argeș, Buzău (Musseos) and Prut (Pyretos). Considering the date, the circumstances, and the place of emergence of those Slav leaders, we might give credence to a warlike Slav domination in certain regions from which they took their names, but not to a substantial Slav colonization.

At the time when the Slavs settled in the aforementioned regions, the linguistic differences were not marked enough to justify their division into eastern and southern Slavs. As shown by the Slav elements assimilated by the Romanian language and the old toponymy of this country, the Slavs of Dacia were in time to develop Slavo-Bulgarian (eastern south-Slav) languages and only in the northeast of the country were elements of an eastern Slav (Russo-Ukrainian) language to appear.

The Slav settlement and Avar domination generally, brought about a lowering of the standard of living and of material culture in Dacia, and this is more obvious in the regions where the Slavs were to be found in larger numbers — a phenomenon that was further aggravated after the connections with the Byzantine Empire were severed. The crafts and trades were checked in their progress, and there is a process of return to a rural life and to natural economy.

During the period between the penetration of the Avars and Slavs north of the Danube and the fall of the Empire's boundaries in 602 A.D., a period of frequent plundering of the Empire up to the Adriatic, the Black Sea, and southward into Greece took place, the Avars and Slavs bringing back to their original territories, apart from booty, a number of prisoners. This fact is recorded with even greater emphasis than in Attila's time. It should be said that unavoidable exaggerations and the impossibility of some of the prisoners returning to the Empire should be taken into account. It is also known that there were refugees and deserters from the Empire to the territories north of the Danube. But it is difficult to believe that the basic elements of the Daco-Roman ethnical and linguistic setup should come from prisoners and deserters. Without altogether overlooking the intermingling between the peoples on either side of the Danube as a living factor in the radiation of Byzantine civilization, it is quite clear that the Daco-Roman natives had always been the main bearers of the formative process of the Romanian people north of the Danube.

From 593 to 602 A.D., having ended the Persian war, the Byzantine Empire under the energetic rule of Emperor Mauricius Tiberius endeavored to wipe out the Avaro-Slav threat, by undertaking a number of military campaigns in Muntenia, north of the Danube, against the Slavs, and around Belgrade to beyond the Tisa, against the Avars. Despite the victories won by the imperial armies, no real success was obtained on account of the weakness of Byzantine society. The armies fighting along the Lower Danube against the Slavs rose in rebellion, and Mauricius Tiberius was overthrown and killed, being superseded by Phocas, the rebel officer (602-610 A.D.). In the chaos that ensued, the Danube and Save boundary fell and the Balkan Peninsula stood open to the Slavs who thereafter swept across the Danube and settled in the dioceses of Thrace and Illyricum. Thenceforth Dacia lost contact with the Empire and no more records concerning it appear in the Byzantine chronicle. At the same time numerous Slavs moved from these parts into the Balkans, as confirmed by the Armenian geography mentioned above and by archeological data. Undoubtedly, some of the Slav groups that crossed into the territories south of the Danube came from the more distant regions north and east of Dacia. The Serbo-Croatians came from west of Dacia into the western part of the Balkan Peninsula during the reign of Emperor Heraclius (610-614). It is obvious that such important developments — the breakthrough of the Empire's frontier and the inflow of Slavs into the Balkan Peninsula — increased the share of native elements in Dacia's total population, and this all the more so as at that time there was no fresh inflow of Slavs into the country.

The Balkan Peninsula being overrun by the Slavs who settled there, the Avars helping them by destroying the Byzantine cities after which they would return "home," was of special significance for the Roman population south of the Danube. Records have been preserved that speak about the population moving southwards from the north of the Peninsula for better safety, the most important records being the testimonies of eyewitnesses of the seventh century in the work entitled *Miracles of St. Demeter* of Thessalonike (today's Salonika). This concerns the refugees coming from Serdica (Sofia) and Naissus (Nish). Presumably the refugees were mostly well-to-do townspeople, citizens of the Empire. The Daco-Roman population north of the Balkan mountains (Moesia and Scythia Minor) must have remained in their homeland but now that the Danube was no longer an official boundary they could cross the Danube at will and so the same ethnical situation of Daco-Romans and Slavs arose on both banks of the river. At the time Slav settlements were few and far between in Dobrudja (only those about Silistra are known to us) and generally throughout the region between the Danube and the Balkans.

It is not very clear how the defeat of the Slavo-Avars beneath the walls of Constantinople in 626, the weakening of Avar domination, and the uprising and southward drive of the Serbo-Croatians affected Dacia. It is most probable that this region kept outside the turmoil that prevailed further west and that the Daco-Roman-Slav population throughout Dacia as well as the Gepidae in the pay of the Avars, installed in Northwest Transylvania, continued very much as heretofore.

On the other hand, a new storm was gathering in the east. A group of western Turks from Asia, known under the name of Khazars, threatened the Proto-Bulgars occupying the territories between the Volga and the Don. Finally, despite the diplomatic interventions of the emperors of Constantinople, Asparukh or Isperikh, one of the sons of the great Bulgar Kaghan, Kuvrat (or Kurt), took his armed people westward and penetrated into the northeastern part of Bulgaria in 681, after crossing Dobrudja and defeating the Byzantine armies sent against him. At the same time another group of Avars newly come from Asia, joined those in Pannonia, thus swelling their ranks. "A second Kaghanate" of the Avars was spoken of from that time onwards.

Asparukh's nomadic and warlike Proto-Bulgars founded the so-called "First Bulgarian Empire" in the north of today's Bulgaria, where they came upon the Slavs and Daco-Romans. With the center of their power at Pliska and Preslav in the northeast of the peninsula, the Proto-Bulgars proceeded according to the Asian manner, evacuating and regrouping the population in the country they were occupying. There was coexistence and close cooperation between the Slavs and the Proto-Bulgars, and by the tenth century A.D. the Proto-Bulgars had been assimilated and Slavicized, and the Bulgarian people were thus formed.

There are no definite records concerning the fate of the Daco-Romans between the Balkans and the Danube, but it is probable, as indicated by archeological data, that they had had to move on to different parts. Some must have remained among the Slavs and the Proto-Bulgars, transmitting to them the traditions of an ancient civilization and being ultimately Slavicized, while others had taken refuge in the mountainous districts of the Balkan Peninsula, grazing their flocks in the mountains and preserving their ethnical identity, and yet others may have been driven to the left bank of the Danube where they joined the other Daco-Romans.

The double (Proto-Bulgar and Avar) Turanic invaders also reached some districts in Dacia. Several hoards of Byzantine silver coins, occasionally with personal adornments — no doubt belonging to the local population — were buried in Muntenia and Oltenia around 680 A.D. And it is possible that the great hoard of gold coins and adornments found at Firtuş in the Harghita county in eastern Transylvania was buried about the same time, though it had been amassed from the time of Aurelian on, or more certainly from the reign of Theodosius I (378-395 A.D.). Another hoard of Byzantine silver coins and adornments was buried around that time at Zemiansky Virbovok in Eastern Slovakia.

On the other hand there is nothing to allow us to suppose that the Proto-Bulgars were dominating north of the Danube at this time or had settled there. On the contrary the Carpatho-Danubian area appears to have further remained under the Avars' indirect control, and the Avars to have remained the enemies of the Proto-Bulgars as they had been for a long time, and to have maintained a "sphere of-interests" frontier along the Danube and the Save. At this time the Proto-Bulgars were intent on organizing and consolidating their South-Danubian state and establishing relations, peacefully or otherwise, with the Byzantine Empire which exercised a powerful cultural influence on the new state. Compelled to give up their customary raids into the Empire, now that the Proto-Bulgars separated them from it, the Avars of the Second Kaghanate strengthened their military power and the organization of the districts under their control. The Gepidae in Northwest Transylvania died out altogether, whether removed thence by the Avars or assimilated by the Proto-Romanians, it is not known. Thenceforward they no longer had cemeteries of their own. At their places of occupation at the "Gate of the Someş," perceptibly Avarized Slav groups settled in the eighth century. This is clearly proved by the tumulus graves discovered at Nuşfalău in the Sălaj county and at the important strategic point of ancient Napoca (Cluj, Someşeni) which up to the present is the farthest point in the country where such graves have been found.

Consequently, we again have the phenomenon of close Avaro-Slav cooperation, the leading strata of the Slavs joining the Avar leaders again, though previously they had drifted apart. This has been ascertained at various places on the outskirts of the areas where the nomadic Avars lived in those days. The Slavs in Dacia, though few now, had by this time

settled definitely on the territory and were increasingly becoming the representatives of the Turanic political and military power acting under the Avars' aegis as feudalism became
more and more pronounced. This accounts for the presence
of Slav elements in the country's political superstructure and
in the toponymy.

For more than a century — approximately between 680
and 796/803 A.D. (when Avar domination came to an end) —
there was comparative peace in Dacia, and the country was
able to develop unhindered from the demographic standpoint
under the conditions explained above. Byzantine influence
was now eclipsed, though still faintly exercised through the
medium of the Proto-Bulgar, Slav, and Avar peoples. Hardly
any Byzantine coins now reached the country. The Avars
did not settle in the Transylvanian plateau or in the remainder
of the southern and eastern Dacian territories. Their raids
were isolated, as proved by an almost total lack of archeological vestiges, in strinking contrast with the frequency of
such vestiges west of the Western Carpathians.

## 6. *The Completion of the Formative Process of the Romanian People (seventh to ninth Centuries)*

THE living standard and material culture during the period
now under consideration (680-803) show that a new evolution was in the ascendant as well as a vast unification process
which gradually brought together the area between the Balkan
Mountains and the Northern Carpathians. The fundamental
factors were the Daco-Roman traditions north and south of
the Danube, the participation of Slav elements, and a fresh
impact of Byzantine civilization. The foundations were thus
laid for a specific Balkano-Carpathic material culture, the
Dridu culture, so-called after the great settlement on the
river Ialomiţa. It was in the eighth century that the Dridu
culture developed, based on the evolution of the Bratei, Ipo-
teşti-Cîndeşti, and Botoşana autochthonous cultures. The
constituting elements were mostly of Daco-Roman origin,
and their existence has been attested without interruption
from the period of the Roman rule to the founding of the

Romanian feudal states. Essentially Romanic and autochtho-nous, the Dridu culture, judging only by the finds made so far, covered nearly the entire territory where the Romanians live today as well as certain districts south of the Danube. It was the only local material culture known in the Carpatho-Danubian area from the eighth to the eleventh centuries.

Being the only material culture, its spread over the entire territory of present-day Romania from the eighth to the eleventh centuries, the Dridu culture belongs to the Romanian population, as has now been attested by written records. In this period the first political organizations appeared under the aegis of that culture.

The Proto-Bulgars, who had crossed south of the Danube during the latter half of the seventh century, had been a mino-rity of nomadic, mounted herdsmen superimposed on the Daco-Roman stock and, like the Avars, brought no funda-mental additions to the cultural medium they found in their new homeland, apart from their nomadic ways of organization, their armament, and horse trappings. The Slavs, on the other hand, had come to these parts with an archaic culture which they developed and enriched in the new surroundings through contact with the Romanized population and the Byzantine civilization, though preserving their own structure and tra-ditions in their spiritual culture. Their material culture in the Balkano-Carpathian area assumed a special aspect nowhere else to be found in the Slav world of Europe in those days, and this proves that the decisive factor was the local Proto-Romanian environment.

The stable settlements, whether agricultural or pastoral, like the cemeteries of the North-Danubian population who, following the developments around the year 680, came to be the bearers of the initial phase of the Dridu culture, are frequent throughout Dobrudja, Muntenia, Oltenia, and South-east Transylvania. They are mostly to be found in the plains, and only few of them in the low Sub-Carpathian foothills, representing a local development of the preceding cultural environment. This is not to be accounted for by a substantial and sudden immigration of a new population. Avar domination over the North-Danubian areas and the nonexistence of Proto-Bulgar expansion in this direction in the eighth century, rule out such a hypothesis. Even south of the Danube this culture was formed after the year 680; in Western Transylvania the powerful Proto-Romanian center around the Western Mountains has not yet been sufficiently studied.

In Moldavia evolution takes the same course beginning with the eighth century, the Slav elements of archaic tradition there being assimilated at a swift rate beginning with that period.

The coexistence of Proto-Romanians and Slavs is now attested throughout Dacia's territory as is also the slow process of the Slavs' assimilation. The rate of advance of that process varied from region to region but no rigorous marking out is possible at the present-day stage of research. In the open country of the western part of the Transylvanian plateau, along a line which might go through Sibiu, Agnita, Mediaș, and Bistrița, there is an area characterized by biritual cemeteries, ca. 85 percent cremation and ca. 15 percent inhumation, where Daco-Roman tradition was more powerfully influenced by Avaro-Slav ways and southern cultural innovations appeared only at a later date. Another area which stands out fairly clearly is the Lower Danube plain, where the population was numerous and mostly of native origin, as is proved by the great cemeteries of the eighth century at Izvorul in the Ilfov county where Christian inhumation prevails, accounting for some 90 percent of the total. Once again it is established that although Dacia had never been officially "Christianized," as all the countries around her were to be at a later date, Christianity was a constant phenomenon of a popular character without any names of missionaries going down in history and without the spectacular conversion of feudal leaders. The first Bulgarian Empire founded south of the Danube was to be "officially" Christianized only after 864 A.D. The process started from the feudal leaders, that is from top to bottom.

The change in the political and military situation in the Balkano-Carpathian area at the close of the eighth century following the final defeat of the Avar power at the hands of the Frankish armies of Charlemagne in the years 791-796 A.D., with the remainder of the Avar forces being driven across the Tisa where they were destroyed by the Proto-Bulgars of Tsar Krum about 803 A.D., affected only slightly the life of the Dacian population. Avar domination was superseded by Proto-Bulgar domination, the latter being far more shadowy than the former, for the Bulgarian Empire was fighting the Byzantine Empire in the south and moreover, as feudalism was becoming more firmly established during this period throughout Dacian territory, domination assumed the form of feudal dependence of the local leaders on the Bulgar Tsars. Naturally, it was the Slav leaders who were again mostly connected with the Tsars, as shown also by the feudal titles of *boier* (boyar) and *jupan* (gentleman) which come to us from the Proto-Bulgars through the Slavs. On the other hand, starting about the mid-ninth century, particularly after the Bulgarian Empire had been converted to Christianity, the Bulgars were becoming increasingly Byzantine, irrespective of the fact that Tsar Simeon (893-927 A.D.) strove to take the place of the Constantinople emperor, or perhaps for that very reason.

The fact is that no Proto-Bulgar colonization is attested in Dacia, and neither was there any garrison of the tsars established in these parts. It is difficult to establish convincingly whether this was the time when the religious service in Slavonic was adopted by the Dacian population, as it was adopted by the Slav countries after the mid-ninth century following the translation of the sacred books by Methodius and Cyril. The available data rather point to a continuation of the previous situation, with Christianity maintaining in Dacia its initial character, without a local organization or a local hierarchy. What was strictly necessary (the ordaining of priests, for example) was probably done by the Bishops south of the Danube. Possibly the disciples of Methodius and Cyril in Moravia were active for a time in the northern and western part of the country.

The political situation also bore a different aspect in Central Europe after the Avars' defeat because the Frankish kingdom of Charlemagne, having occupied Pannonia, had spread its domination and influence up to the rivers Tisa and Timoc, and the Moravian principality, founded in present-day Czechoslovakia at the time, eager to draw away from the German threat, initially received Christianity and a civilizing impact from the Byzantine Empire.

Thus in the ninth century, before the arrival of the Hungarians, an unstable balance of forces existed in the regions west of Dacia between the Frankish kingdom, the Moravian principality, and the first Bulgarian Empire. Neither the Frankish kingdom nor the Moravian principality showed any inclination to oppose the Bulgarian Empire on Dacia's territory, though the Bulgars had hastened to take the place of the Avars in the districts south and east of the Tisa plain. The fact that the frontiers of Charlemagne's kingdom had come so near Dacia was, however, felt through the extension in the ninth century of the influence of Western civilization over the western parts of this country up to well within the Transylvanian plateau. Furthermore, a Proto-Bulgar military campaign that reached at least the Dnieper under Tsar Omurtag (ca. 814-831) suggests that there could have been no threat to Dacia's population from those quarters without a suitable rebuff. The armies of the same Tsar Omurtag waged another campaign that took them up to the Tisa. Both campaigns are indubitably proved by contemporary inscriptions in Greek left by Omurtag himself in honor of two of his commanders killed on these occasions on the banks of the Tisa and the Dnieper respectively. It is significant that there is no testimony to any similar Proto-Bulgar action in Dacia. "Bulgaria beyond the Danube," of which mention is made in the first half of the ninth century in connection with prisoners taken south of the Balkans in the Adrianople region and deported there by the Proto-Bulgars in 813, and their return home after 25 years' imprisonment, should be placed east of Dacia.

It is plain that in the ninth century Dacia, guarded east and west by the Bulgarian Empire, the latter being determined to maintain its sphere of interests, continued its domestic development without being actually under another people's rule but being only controlled, as shown above. Its development consisted in a continuation of the process whereby the Slavs were being assimilated (as the Proto-Bulgar conquerors were being assimilated by the Slavs in the south) and in the spread of feudal organization.

The Proto-Romanian and Slav population was being locally organized on the basis of a process of economic and social differentiation. A new, most intensive development of iron metallurgy with use of the poor, but easily accessible, local ores, as well as the development of agriculture and stock-breeding, increased social differences in the communities, as shown by the discoveries made in many settlements and in some of the cemeteries of those days, primarily in that of Obîrşia in the Dolj county, where Christianity is proved to have been practiced by the population in the ninth century. This is also the time when the foundations were being laid for the principalities of which only a few are mentioned in the extant historical records of the following century.

In 896 the Hungarians, a people of Finno-Ugric origin mixed with, and led by, Turkic groups, made their way towards the Hungarian plain of today from the steppes north of the Black Sea, being driven from there by the Pechenegs. For a short time during the ninth century, they resided in the so-called Atelkuz ("between rivers") in the eastern part of Dacia and skirted it to the north, as archeological finds have clearly proved. The Hungarians' military raids in the northwest and west of the Transylvanian plateau during the first half of the tenth century after having wiped out the Moravian principality and the Proto-Bulgar-controlled political organizations in Crişana and Banat, created a new situation in these regions, which was to terminate after 1001 with the gradual conquest of Transylvania and the implanting there of foreign colonies. The Magyars took little time to assimilate the Slavs they had found in the plains of the central part of their new homeland, and the political predominance of the Slavs on the Transylvanian plateau also came to an end at this time. In close connection with this situation is the wide expansion attested in the early years of the century, of the native population, bearers of the Dridu culture: on the Transylvanian plateau this culture reached the Mureş line (Blandiana, Sebeş, etc.). The fact that the oldest material culture of the Maramureş Romanians — archeologically identified at thirteenth century Siliştea Veche in the Romanian village of Sărăsău on the Tisa, and continued in the culture of the fourteenth century princely villages of Dragoş and Bogdan, for example at Cuhea — obviously originated in the Transylvanian culture of the eighth-ninth centuries and in the Dridu culture, confirms the fact that the Romanians had been in Maramureş for ages and the aforementioned cultures were really Romanian.

In the extra-Carpathian regions, the Pechenegs — a new group of nomadic and warlike Asian herdsmen who had come from beyond the Volga and the Urals as a first echelon of a larger group that was to include the Udi and the Cumans — put an end to Proto-Bulgar domination and for the first time created conditions that resulted in the decline of the political power of the Slavs. In the tenth century, as previously on similar occasions, no destruction or expulsion of the native population over wide areas is attested. The demographic expansion of the population in the same century is proved throughout Moldavia. Even the native settlements in the territories east of the river Siret in Moldavia, continued to exist until the first half of the eleventh century, as proved by the Byzantine bronze coins found there. It was only around 1027 A.D. that the Pechenegs were to take their flocks and herds and their warlike horsemen to the plains of our country, on the occasion of their first independent raid into the Byzantine Empire.

In the meantime, however, Dacia had again established direct contact with the Byzantine Empire. The attempt made by Sviatoslav — a Kiev prince, who had been called upon by the Byzantines to assist them against the Bulgars in 968 but who, with the object of settling in the Balkans, had joined hands with the Bulgars and opposed the Byzantines — brought about an energetic reaction on the part of the Empire: in 971 Emperor John Tzimiskes conquered the central region of Bulgar power in the northeast of the Balkan Peninsula, and subsequently, by 1018, the whole of Bulgaria had been conquered by Basil II, the Bulgaroctonus. The Empire again had its boundaries along the Danube, even spreading north of the river in the first stage and setting up garrisons there. The Byzantine fleet once again sailed up and down the Danube and a new naval base was built for it at Păcuiul lui Soare not far from ancient Durostorum (Silistra).

It is not improbable that the Empire endeavored to forestall the Magyar threat here, as suggested by the Byzantine stone strongholds built at Slon in the Buzău Mountains immediately after 971.

Byzantine coins which had again begun to infiltrate north of the Danube and even up to upper Moldavia in the early years of the tenth century, now reached extra-Carpathian Dacia in large numbers, as did also Byzantine craftware and other goods. A rapid development of the settlements of the native population has been ascertained, the emperor having pardoned them for their alleged disloyal behavior on the occasion of Sviatoslav's raid, as recorded by a Byzantine chronicler. These developments and the domestic phenomena accompanying them in Dacia, marked the final stage of the ethnogenetic process, which also showed a tendency towards maximum extension over the territory of ancient Dacia. The mention made of the Vlachs (Romanians) in the Balkans by a Byzantine source of the eleventh century referring to developments in 976 A.D., and the fact that such remarks subsequently increased in number, is of outstanding significance when compared to the mentions made from the eighth to the eleventh centuries on the Romanian population north of the Danube, designated as Blasi in the chronicle of King Bella's Anonymous Notary (early tenth century), Volohi in the Old Russian chronicle (late ninth century), and the country Balak in the Armenian geography (eighth-ninth centuries). Vlach being the generic denomination then given by the Germans and Slavs to the Romanic peoples, the last two mentions cited above cannot be used to establish the moment when Romanian ethnogenesis ended. The final moment of that process might be considered to be the time when the last Slav groups were assimilated. It should be noted that Vlach was the name given to the Romanians by other peoples in the Middle Ages, though the Romanians themselves have always called themselves Romanians.

As the Romanian people was formed, so was the Romanian language built up over the same territories but under conditions differing from those in which the neo-Latin western languages developed.

The Romanian language is directly derived from popular Latin, whose grammatical structure and main vocabulary it has preserved. Apart from a Latin basis, the Romanian language has preserved elements of the Daco-Getian idiom.

While in full process of formation in the seventh and eighth centuries, Romanian incorporated a considerable number of Slav words which have become part of the vocabulary of common use. Its specific features emerge from the seventh to the ninth century, after which the Daco-Moesian Romanic language became the Romanian language.

The Romanian people thus concluded their eventful ethno-genesis under new historical circumstances: the Empire had again spread to the Danube and beyond it, resuming its traditional policy in Dacia, which implies continuity of a culture showing Romanic features. The Byzantine Metropolitan John Mavropous did not exaggerate when, in 1047, in connection with the Pechenegs, he said: "As a matter of fact they had conquered the country they lived in, plundering it after having chased away the old inhabitants who were weak and *for whom the old Emperors had been most solicitous. . .*"

It was under such auspices that in the difficult and complex situation arising from the settlement of the Magyars in the west of the country and the overflow of the Pechenego-Uzo-Cuman wave east of Dacia, the Romanian people were to build up their own forms of feudal life with a Byzantine Danube acting as a safety factor for at least two more centuries.

*Part 2*

# MEDIEVAL HISTORY

# The Emergence of the Romanian States (Tenth to Fourteenth Centuries)

WITH the conclusion of the formative process of the Romanian people, Romanian feudal society began to be built up and the first political bodies emerged. Feudal institutions on the territory inhabited by the Romanians were naturally influenced by those of the neighboring states where feudal relations were more advanced: the Byzantine Empire, the Second Bulgarian Empire (at the close of the twelfth century), and the Hungarian kingdom. The successive waves of Turanian invaders — Pechenegs, Udi, Cumans and Tartars — and the devastation and dislocation of the population they caused, slowed down the evolution of Romanian society; their political domination was like a pall over the people on the banks of the Lower Danube, accounting for the sporadic and sparse information Byzantine and Western records of that period provide about the Romanians. At the close of the thirteenth century and early in the fourteenth, the decline of the Golden Horde, the unrest in the Bulgarian state and the struggle for the Hungarian crown caused the influence of the three states which disputed the supremacy east and south of the Carpathians to ebb away. And then, with the coming to fruition of the domestic process of feudal relationships, the Romanian states emerged in a chain along the Carpathians. The anti-Mongolian struggle and the endeavors to free themselves of the Hungarian king's suzerainty made it easier for such princes as Basarab and Bogdan to unify the country, and ultimately two Romanian states — Wallachia and Moldavia — appeared in the political geography of Southeast Europe, alongside the older Transylvanian principality·

## 1. Social and Economic Prerequisites of the Emergence of Romanian Feudal States

ALTHOUGH written information about the Romanians in the ninth and tenth centuries is sporadic, archeological excavations enable us to form a picture of their way of life and social structure. The Romanians of that period lived in villages or even in groups of villages, the Romano-Byzantine strongholds along the Danube offering the only examples of urban life.

Farming, stock-breeding, and some crafts were their main pursuits, the most widespread of the crafts being pottery-making. The many imported articles found here, the most frequent being Byzantine amphorae, are to be accounted for by trade with the strongholds along the Danube and the more important Byzantine centers in the Balkan Peninsula.

The social structure of the Romanian population relied on a territorial or village community. The members of a community owned a certain area, which was parceled out into holdings, and used the grass land, pasture land, forests, and streams in common. The leading bodies of territorial communities were the general assembly, the council of the aged — "people good and old" — and the military chieftain ( *Jude* or *Cneaz* ) whose authority, at first limited to periods of emergency, became permanent with time.

Taking advantage of their position, the leaders of the communities compelled the common people to work for them in a variety of ways and to give them part of the products of their work. Usurping the titles of ownership of the community, the chieftains gradually became a landed aristocracy and enslaved part of the peasantry under their jurisdiction.

The emergence of feudal states against the background of the territorial communities that spread over the Carpatho-Danubian area was the result of a lengthy process of development of local economic forces, which made it possible for an aristocracy to be fashioned. The aristocracy relied upon the exploitation of the free rural communities at first, and later upon the enslaved peasantry. Although information concerning the economic life in Romanian territory from the tenth to the fourteenth century is but scanty, it reveals a progress in production and trade and points to the decisive part played by economic and demographic factors in the genesis of Romanian feudal society.

The records available on the Lower Danube regions show that in the latter half of the tenth century this was a densely populated area carrying on busy trade. *A Tale of Past Times*, also known as *Nestor's Chronicle*, reports that Sviatoslav,

Prince of Kiev, during his first expedition into the Balkan Peninsula in 968, was amazed at the large number of products traded in at the Danube mouths and wished to move his place of residence to those parts. In a letter to his mother, he wrote: "In Pereiaslavetz (Dobrudja) all the riches are gathered: gold, fine fabrics, wine, and various fruits coming from Greece, silver and horses from Bohemia and Hungary, furs, wax, honey, and slaves from Russia." From the same source we hear of the existence of 80 "gorods" — fortified settlements of farmers, stock-breeders, fishermen, and crafts-men, such as has been revealed by the excavations at Garvăn. A few decades later, *Fragments of the Greek Toparch* speak of the same economic prosperity and dense population, from the ranks of which a section of local chieftains emerged, showing the tendency to shake off the Byzantine rule. During the eleventh century the title of the heads of Paradunavon — the Byzantine district which included Dobrudja — also men-tions the Danube towns, while the chieftains' uprising under the Byzantine Emperor Michael VII Parapinakes, makes it plain that they were a political and military power with a sound economic background.

In the thirteenth and fourteenth centuries the presence of Genoese traders at the Danube mouths around Vicina and Chilia (old-time Lycostomo) is proof of the wealth of the local chieftains, who bought Italian cloth, offering grain, wax, and honey in exchange.

The districts at the foot of the mountains in Oltenia and Muntenia, as described in the diploma of the Knights of St. John in 1247 also appear to have made notable economic progress; many flour mills and natural fish ponds alongside fields and grass-land, point to a mixed economy, including the products of husbandmen and stock-breeders, which pro-vided the incomes of the land-owning class *(majores terrae)* and of the Hungarian crown. In 1330, Basarab I offered King Charles Robert 7,000 marks in payment for peace. This shows the economic power of the country over which the Romanian prince ruled. The considerable monetary funds of the country resulted also from the custom duties paid along the trading routes that crossed the country. There was an intensive move-ment of goods along the "Moldavian Road" which connected the Genoese settlements at Cetatea Albă (then Moncastro),

Chilia, and Vicina to Lvov. And this also accounts for the large number of settlements mentioned in the cartography of the age along this road.

Turanian invasions checked the economic development of the Romanians, but the rise in production and productivity brought about by technical progress and demographic growth, made it possible for the country to overcome its vicissitudes, and intensified social differences in the communities. The heads of the communities strengthened their economic power and political authority and insisted on the privileged position they had reached. The most important means of reaching that goal was the state, and consequently a state was created.

## 2. The First Romanian Political Organizations in Transylvania, Dobrudja, Wallachia, and Moldavia

DURING the ninth and the tenth centuries the native population of Transylvania and Banat practiced agriculture and stock-breeding as well as a number of crafts and mining. Economic development brought about the emergence of an aristocracy *(nobiles)* — landowners possessing large flocks and herds and exercising their authority upon the people living on their domains. It is against this socio-economic background that the first Romanian political formations were organized in this area. The results of the latest archeological research added to written records give a clear image of those political organizations. Between the rivers Someş and Mureş in Crişana, there was the dukedom (Voivodship) of Menumorut, with the citadel of Biharea as its center; another dukedom was to be found between the Mureş and the Danube. The latter was headed by Glad, whose residence seems to have been the citadel of Cuvin between the Timiş and the Danube. On the Transylvanian plateau between the Gates of the Meseş and the sources of the Someş, was the dukedom of Gelu whose residential city was Dobîca, where a strongly fortified citadel has been found with many imported articles and Byzantine coins.

In the first half of the tenth century, these dukedoms strongly opposed the attempts made by the Hungarians in the Pannonian plain to conquer Transylvania. The battles, and the determination shown by the local people in their defense, are described in the chronicle of King Bella's Anonymous Notary — *Gesta Hungarorum* — compiled towards the close of the twelfth century on the basis of written records that have been lost and of oral tradition. Only after thirteen days' fighting was the citadel of Biharea conquered from the Romanian prince Menumorut. On the Transylvanian plateau, after Prince Gelu had fallen in battle the Magyars had to come to an understanding with the heads of the local population, which is proof of the power of this political body.

Apart from the principality mentioned in the chronicle of the Anonymous Notary, archeological research proves conclusively the existence of other political formations with powerful centers, as, for example, the principality in the Middle Mureș district with Țeligrad and Bălgrad as its centers, as well as the political formations in the Bîrsa, Făgăraș *(Terra Blachorum)*, Amlaș, Hațeg, Ouaș, and Maramureș country. These do not appear in the aforementioned chronicle, as Hungarian expansion had not yet made contact with them.

After the first wave of Hungarian penetration into Romanian territory, the political formations here continued to develop and to be consolidated. Gelu's principality, now under the leadership of his successor Gyla (Jula), is described as "a very extensive and very rich country" *(Regnum latissimum et opulentissimum)*. Gyla's refusal to submit to the authority of Stephen, the Hungarian king, and to turn Catholic, brought about an armed conflict, as a result of which Gyla was taken to Hungary in captivity together with his family and his treasure store.

In their struggle for independence during the tenth century the local leaders sought help from foreign powers interested in supporting them in this endeavor. We might conclude from *The Legend of Saint Gerhard* that Ahtum, Glad's successor and ruler of the territory between Orșova and Mureș, maintained connections with Byzantium via Vidin early in the eleventh century. Having a powerful army at his command, Ahtum opposed the Hungarian king in the matter of levying duty on the salt transported by raft on the Mureș to the Pannonian plain.

Political organizations similar to those in Transylvania also existed in other parts of the country in the tenth century. An inscription discovered in the village of Mircea Vodă in Dobrudja attests the existence in 943 of a chieftain, one Jupan Dimitre. During Sviatoslav's second expedition to Bulgaria in 969, the ruling figures left of the Danube joined those in Dobrudja siding with the Kiev prince and continuing to support Sviatoslav even when his army was besieged by the Byzantines at Silistra in 971. In order to compel the citadel to surrender and to cut off all connection between the Muntenian plain and the besieged, the Byzantine Emperor John Tzimiskes sent a fleet to the Danube and raided the district left of the river. As a result some of the rulers went over to Byzantium. Messengers were sent to the emperor by some of the fortresses promising submission.

All these political developments were obliterated by Hungarian expansion and by the new wave of Turanian peoples who invaded Romanian territory in the period from the eleventh to the thirteenth century.

Coming into contact with the Romanian population, some of the Pechenegs, Udi, and Cumans abandoned their nomadic way of life and in the course of time were assimilated. Infiltrating into the ruling class, they contributed to the consolidation of the local political organizations by using their power and their connections among the conquerors. [1]

In Transylvania, despite the victories won by King Stephen I, Hungarian rule over West Transylvania and Banat suffered fluctuations and this was further accentuated by the Pecheneg attacks and the crisis which the Hungarian kingdom underwent. For half a century Romanian political organizations developed outside the authority of the Hungarian crown, and this accounts for the name given to the district: Ultrasilvana, Transilvana, Erdeelu (country beyond the forests).

---

[1] As a result of prolonged coexistence with the native population, the Pechenegs and Cumans left their mark in toponymy and the vocabulary of the Romanian language. Peceneaga, Picineagul, Pecenişca, Beşinău, Beşenova, and other place and river names are derived from the Pechenegs, while of Cuman origin are place names such as Cumani, Comana, Vadul Cumanilor, Comarnic, and Comăneşti, and the names of rivers ending in -ui: Bahlui, Covurlui, Desnăţui, Călmăţui, etc., and the names ending in -abă: Toxabă, Tîncabă, Basarabă, etc. It is also from the Cumans that come a number of words such as: cioban (shepherd), beci (cellar), cătun (hamlet), duşman (enemy), etc.

During the latter half of the twelfth century and the first quarter of the thirteenth the conquest of Transylvania by the Magyar feudal kingdom was complete. The extension of Magyar rule to Transylvania brought about certain changes in the ranks of the ruling class as well as among the peasantry: certain local chiefs entered the ranks of the ruling elite of the conquerors' society and the process of dispossessing and making serfs of the peasant communities was intensified.

The districts along the Lower Danube, where Byzantine influence was stronger than elsewhere in Romanian territory, were of exceptional political and economic importance during the eleventh century despite the adverse conditions created by the invading peoples. Anna Comnena, daughter of Emperor Alexius of Byzantium, when writing about her father's struggle against the Pechenegs in the Danube area, mentioned the existence of small political organizations in Dobrudja, whose established civilization is described with enough clarity to preclude confusion with the nomadic populations. These organizations were sufficiently powerful to try to draw away from Byzantine authority. Their struggle against Byzantium from 1074 to 1088 is part of the domestic unrest that shook the Empire after the Macedonian dynasty had become extinct. Byzantium ultimately defeated them by dint of great efforts, with the assistance of the Cumans. A similar process, though perhaps of lesser amplitude, took place in the Danube plain. There is a strange coincidence to be noted between the disturbances in Dobrudja mentioned above and the moment when written records began to emphasize the political role of the native population north of the Danube. The Getae on the left bank of the Danube, whom Anna Comnena and Michael Psellos speak of as allies of the Sauromats (Pechenegs) against Byzantium, were Romanians, also mentioned by Kinnamos on the occasion of the Byzantine expedition of 1166 against the Hungarians. They are said to be "old colonists from Italy."

In Moldavia also a number of documents of the eleventh century and of a later date illustrate the important role played by Romanian political organizations on certain occasions. For example, the Polish sources on which Dlugosz's Chronicle relies point out that in 1070 the "Wallachians" fought alongside the Ruthenians and the Pechenegs in support of Vyacheslav of Polotsk and against Boleslav, king of Poland.

The policy of expansion of the Hungarian kingdom south and east of the Carpathians was inaugurated by King Andrew II (1205-1235) when he called upon the Teutonic Knights to become the instruments of his policy. The extension of the authority of the Hungarian crown and the attendant Catholic proselytism were a threat to the Romanian political organizations built up in the shadow of Cuman domination or through Romanian-Cuman cooperation. The response of the native population was in line with the reaction of the Orthodox world against the political and religious offensive of the Hungarian kingdom. Thus, an alliance was formed between the Romano-Bulgarian state and the Nicaea Empire. The conflict between the Bulgars and the Magyars in 1230 was along the same line. It ended with the victory of the Hungarian kingdom, following which the Severin Banat was set up on the northwestern border of the Bulgarian Empire. This was assigned the task of guarding the frontier. It included the eastern part of the Timişan Banat, which preserved the name and also transmitted it to the present-day Caraş-Severin county. The Severin Banat also included a strip of Oltenia, which accounts for Oltenia being sometimes called the Severin county.

With the Magyar kingdom and the Bulgarian Empire at rivalry, the Romanian leaders, first those east of the river Olt and subsequently those of Oltenia, acknowledged the suzerainty of the Hungarian king in order to safeguard their privileges.

The process whereby Hungarian suzerainty was being consolidated was interrupted by the great Tartar invasion which was followed by a comparatively long Mongolian rule over a considerable part of our territories (Muntenia and Moldavia). The rate of economic development was thus slowed down but never interrupted altogether.

The diploma whereby Bela IV, king of Hungary, bestowed the Severin county and "the whole of Cumania" upon the Knights of St. John in 1247 is of considerable importance as a measure of the development level reached in the territory between the Carpathians and the Danube in the mid-thirteenth century.

The diploma shows that the main branches of the economy were farming, stock-breeding, and fishing. Large estates had been formed and social differentiation into distinct classes was in process of consolidation. The phrase *majores terrae* describes the dominant class while the term *rustici* is used for the peasantry taxed by the feudal lords and performing labor service for them. The diploma also shows that there were close trade connections between the lands south of the Carpathians, Transylvania and the Balkan Peninsula. Foreign and transit trade as well as inland trade resulted in intensive monetary circulation bringing in great incomes, half of which the king was to reserve for himself, as expressly stated in the diploma. The information about the monetary circulation is confirmed by the discovery of thirteenth-century hoards on Oltenia's territory: coins minted after the model of Viennese dinari at Turnu Severin, a large number of pfennig coins from Frisach, Carinthia, and Cologne found in the vicinity of Craiova, and silver dirhems of the Golden Horde at Calopăru.

Politically, the country was organized into principalities. Along the Olt were the principalities of Ioan and Fărcaş and also Litovoi's principality, which included the Haţeg country, while on the left bank of the Olt Seneslau's principality was to be found. Though they were dependent on the kingdom of Hungary, the principalities enjoyed a certain autonomy which the Knights of St. John were to observe.

Economic connections, facilitated by the development of boroughs and the emergence of a number of towns drawn into the international trade circuit thanks to the trade routes, supported the unification process of Romanian political organizations.

During the latter half of the thirteenth century an inclination to sweep aside Magyar suzerainty became manifest south of the Carpathians, assuming the form of armed struggle. A first attempt was made by Prince Litovoi, most probably in 1279. Litovoi died on the battlefield and his brother, Bărbat, was taken prisoner and ransomed on payment of a large sum of money. The military and economic power of the Romanian principalities, which were not far removed from independence, is proved by the struggle they waged against a powerful state and by the payment of a considerable ransom for a leader.

As early as the thirteenth century, the Hungarian kings endeavored to extend their sway east of the Carpathians. The Cumans' Catholic bishopric set up in southwest Moldavia in 1227 with the aim of converting the Cumans and the Brodniks to Catholicism, was only an outpost for Hungarian expansion eastward. The diplomas issued by the Royal Hungarian Chancellery and by the Papal Chancellery for the Cumans' bishopric provide information about the presence of the Romanians (Wallachs) in the bishopric, about their advanced religious organization, which included bishops, and about their refusal to turn Catholic as well as about the influence exercised by their religious organization on the faithful in the Hungarian kingdom, many of whom were adopting their religion.

Information derived from various sources proves the existence of Romanian political bodies east of the Carpathians at the time of the Tartar domination in those parts: there is a Papal Bull of March 25, 1245, the account given by the Pope's messenger, Giovanni da Pian del Carpini, sent to the Tartar Khan in 1247, and the notes under 1276-1277 in the chronicle of Thomas Tuscus.

The Tartar Empire's critical state at the close of the thirteenth century favored the political leaders on Moldavian territory inasmuch as they were able to stabilize their power. As in the case of the other Romanian principalities, this was a sign that the various political bodies were about to unite.

In order to make better use of Transylvania's natural resources and to strengthen their domination over that principality, the Hungarian kings encouraged the immigration of Magyar, Szekler, and Saxon colonists who were to settle in the principality alongside the native Romanian population. The Saxons came from Flanders, Luxemburg, and Saxony. For a short period, the order of the Teutonic knights was also brought to Transylvania. The settlement of other peoples side by side with Romanians created a certain solidarity among the masses producing material goods, irrespective of their ethnic origin and led to mutual influences and to economic development in Transylvania. A number of strongholds were erected to defend the principality and around the stronghold the counties — administrative units — were built up. The Hungarian kings gave the Saxon colonists economic and administrative privileges so that they were able to carry on a lively political and economic activity and to organize themselves in administrative units of their own, which they called *sedes* (seats).

When Transylvania was reduced to subordination by the Magyar state the process whereby the peasantry was brought into serfdom was intensified. The communities of free peasants were taken over largely by the king and the aristocracy around him, the Catholic clergy, and those natives that had rallied round the royal power. Large landed estates were formed and the obligations of the peasantry towards the landowners increased. With large incomes came political power so that the nobility obtained considerable privileges from the kings, and the privileges were laid down in the Golden Bull of 1222, which was confirmed in 1231. Large-scale grants of immunities, particularly at moments when the central power underwent a crisis, accentuated the process of feudal fragmentation. In order to keep the great nobility within bounds, the kings sought the support of the lesser nobility into whose ranks members of the lower strata were raised. Gradually two categories emerged in the nobility, with different sociojuridical status and different interests: the great nobility termed *potentes* or *iobagiones regis* (a word which in time came to be applied to the peasantry dependent on the landowners) and the gentry: the *servientes* or *familiares*.

Among the peasantry there were three categories in the thirteenth century: the free peasants, the dependent peasants, and the slaves.

The free peasants lived in village communities located mostly in the peripheral districts of Transylvania where no large estates could be formed and where the nobility's attempts to enslave the peasantry met with much resistance. These peasants sought to preserve their freedom by assuming military obligations.

Among the dependent peasantry there were three categories with a different economic and legal status: a) the dependent peasants proper, who came to be called serfs, and who had the use of a plot of land (termed *sesie*) which they tilled, and for which they contributed labor service and money payment; these peasants could bequeath their own homestead; b) the *jeleri*, free landless peasants; c) the servants engaged in work around the landowner's home.

The lowest social category were the slaves, entirely at the mercy of the landowners.

In the thirteenth century the process of separating the crafts from agriculture and the setting up of towns was moderately advanced. The towns of Sibiu, Alba Iulia, Cluj, Oradea, and Rodna are mentioned in the first half of the thirteenth century. They were mostly destroyed by the Tartar invasion; they were rebuilt in the latter half of the thirteenth century and grew in the following century.

Mining went ahead in the thirteenth century. As well as the natives, the colonists — foreign "guests" who enjoyed great privileges — also worked in the metal and salt mines.

The constant tendency of the landowners to extend their estates by taking over the land of the free peasants' communities, and the increased obligations of the peasantry towards the state and the noblemen, and, for the Catholics also towards the Roman Catholic Church, no less than the exactions of officialdom, caused the peasantry to rise in revolt, their revolt often assuming the form of flight and outlawry.

The peasants' struggle to keep their ancient liberty and the deep-rooted traditions of the native organizations, set their seal on the evolution of feudal relationships in Transylvania, which showed a tendency towards a specific form of organization, a *regnum Transylvaniae* distinct from Hungary. Certain leaders of Transylvania such as Stephen, son of King Bela IV, and the princes Roland Borşa and Ladislau Kan, assumed royal prerogatives and endeavored to carry on an independent policy.

## 3. *The Romanian States — Wallachia, Moldavia, and Dobrudja — are organized*

INTERNAL developments and a number of changes in the international situation enabled the Romanian leaders south of the Carpathians to found an independent state at the turn of the thirteenth century. The critical events that the Tartar Empire went through after the death of Nogai Khan and the disturbances that broke out in Hungary with the extinction of the Arpad dynasty, caused the feudal landowners south of the Carpathians to rally round Basarab, a prince of the Argeș district, whom they elected as Grand Voivode and Prince (1317-1352). Under circumstances which are as yet insufficiently known, Basarab unified the territory between the Carpathians and the Danube, thus being the founder of Wallachia, which under him played an important part in Southeast Europe. At the request of Michael Shishman, the Bulgarian tsar, he took part in the battles fought in the Balkan Peninsula when the Byzantine Empire was on the downgrade. In 1323 Basarab assisted the Bulgarian tsar against Byzantium, and in 1325-1328 he won several victories against the Tartars, thereby extending his authority eastward up to the vicinity of Chilia. The district north of the Danube mouths, which Basarab incorporated in Wallachia, kept that prince's name. In 1333 Basarab again supported the Bulgarian tsar, but this time in the latter's struggle against the Serbian prince Stephen Urosh III, with Byzantium as an ally. The allied army was defeated at Velbujd (Küstendil). In an effort to check Magyar expansion over his country, Basarab formed matrimonial and political ties with the Bulgarian and Serbian rulers.

He occupied part of the Severin Banat, which was one of the main directions of Magyar expansion. The campaign undertaken by Hungary in the autumn of 1330 was intended to subordinate Romanian political bodies to Saint Stephen's crown and to suppress their autonomy. The Hungarian king, Charles Robert of Anjou, organized an expedition to Wallachia "in order to recover the confines of the kingdom, which Basarab ruled over without any right." At Posada (November 9-12) Basarab won a brilliant victory against his former suzerain, causing the expedition to fail of its purpose.

Basarab's victory made Wallachia independent and favored its development. The unity and stability of state life were enhanced and Wallachia entered upon a period of prosperity, the population becoming more dense and the trade more active. Favorable socio-economic conditions promoted the development of art. It was during the reign of Basarab that the erection began of the Princely Church at Curtea de Argeș — a splendid monument of Romanian medieval art.

Basarab well deserved to be called "the Great" for he achieved great things: he liberated the territory of Wallachia from Tartar domination, shook off the suzerainty of the Hungarian crown, organized the state, and created a dynasty which was to ensure the stability of this new political order.

Basarab's son and successor, Nicholas Alexander (1352-1364), continued his father's policy and succeeded in strengthening the political position of Wallachia and at the same time his dynasty. He maintained friendly relations with the neighboring rulers and married one of his daughters to Strachimir, the Bulgarian tsar at Vidin, another to Stephen Urosh, the Serbian prince, and yet another to Duke Ladislau of Oppeln, Hungary's Palatine. Fighting alongside Louis of Anjou, the Hungarian king, against the Tartars, he completed the work of his predecessor, liberating new territories from under their sway.

With the approval of the Patriarch of Constantinople, Nicholas Alexander, in 1359, founded the first Metropolitan Church of Wallachia at Curtea de Argeş, thus laying the foundations of church organization in his country. The church became a great supporter of the dynasty. Jachint, former Metropolitan of Vicina, was the first Metropolitan "of all Ungro-Vlachia." Subsequently, the Metropolitan of Wallachia was granted the power of jurisdiction over the Romanians in the Hungarian kingdom with the title of "Exarch of the Highlands."

Nicholas Alexander also continued his father's work in the erection of churches. During his reign the Princely Church at Curtea de Argeş was completed and the old church of the Cîmpulung Monastery was erected. It is there that his grave was found. The inscription on the gravestone calls him: "The great and only ruler, Prince Nicholas Alexander, son of Prince Basarab the Great."

It was Nicholas Alexander who initiated the policy of the Romanian princes of supporting the Orthodox Church in the Balkan Peninsula by means of gifts, particularly landed estates. Nicholas Alexander himself endowed the Cutlumuz Monastery on Mount Athos.

Nicholas Alexander's successor, Vladislav Vlaicu (1364-1377), further organized the country and promoted trade and the cultural life, endeavoring at the same time to curb the centrifugal tendencies of the boyars (the feudal landholding nobility). For the first time Romanian coins — they were of silver — were minted, with a Latin inscription. On January 20, 1368,

MIRCEA THE OLD

12. SEAL OF THE TOWN OF BAIA

13. THE BATTLE OF NIKOPOLIS (1396)

15. IANCU OF
HUNEDOARA

17. THE BATTLE OF →
ZLATIȚA (1443)

18. IANCU OF HUNE- →
DOARA RECEIVING
TURKISH EMISSAR-
IES AT SZEGEDIN
(1444)

19. CHRISTIAN AR- →
MIES ON THE WAY
TO VARNA (1444).

16. THE HUNYAD CASTLE

Ein wunderliche vnd erschröckenliche
hystori von einem großen wütrrich genant
Dracole wayda Der vo so gar vnkristen-
liche marter hat angelegt die menschē als
mit spissen, auch oy leüt zu tod geschyssen rc.

Gedruckt zu bamberg im Lrrrri. iare.

20. VLAD THE IMPALER

21. RUINS OF THE STRONGHOLD
OF POENARI

22.
STEPHEN THE GREAT

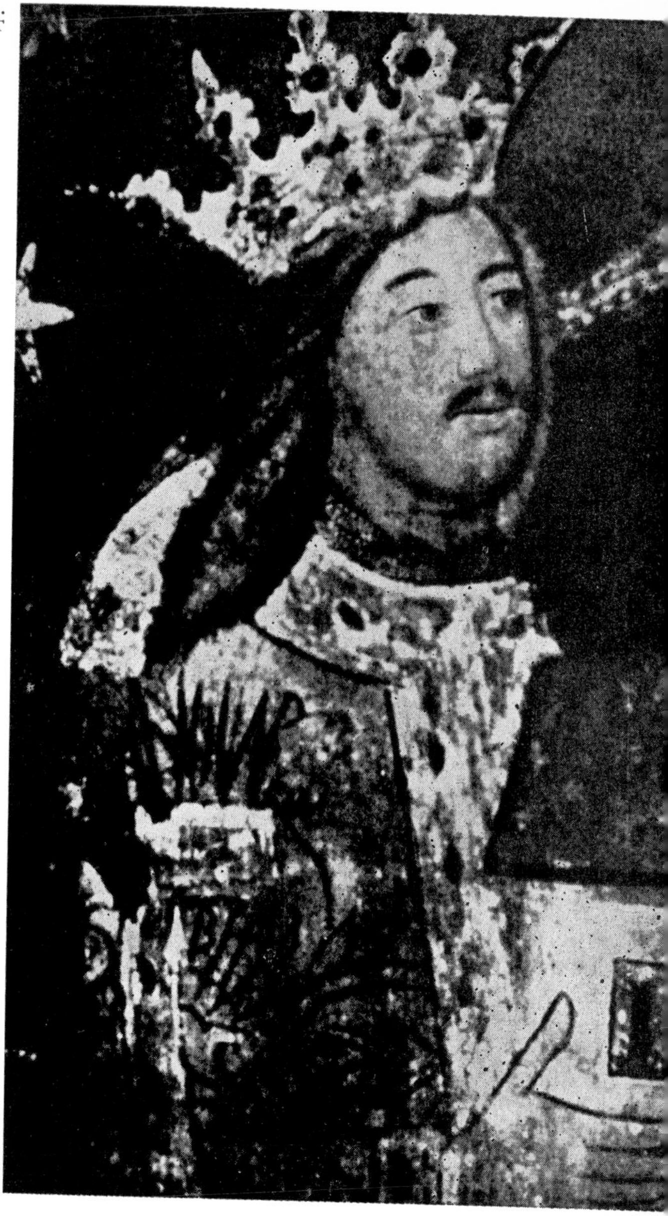

23. THE BATTLE OF BAIA (1467)

24. RUINS OF THE STRONGHOLD OF SOROCA

the prince issued a diploma written in Latin to confirm the ancient trade privileges that the citizens of Braşov had been granted in Wallachia. The prosperity of the country and the increase in population induced him to demand that the Constantinople Patriarchate set up a second Metropolitan Church at Severin (the first was at Argeş). His request was granted by the synodical act of October, 1370. Religious life became more vigorous through the introduction of monasticism by Nicodim, a monk from Serbia, who founded the Vodiţa Monastery. The oldest document extant concerned with internal affairs (1374) is that whereby the prince endowed the monastery. Following the example of his father, Vladislav also endowed the monasteries on Mount Athos. For the Catholics in Wallachia and for those in the territories under his rule on the other side of the Carpathians, a bishopric was founded with its seat at Argeş, where the ruins of an old Catholic Church — Sîn Nicoară — are still to be seen.

During the last years of his reign, Vladislav fought against Hungary and died fighting against that kingdom. His successors, Radu I and Dan I, continued the struggle against Hungary. By tradition Radu is known as Radu the Black and was for long considered as the founder of the country.

The second Romanian independent state, Moldavia, was formed east of the Carpathians by the union of the existing political organizations, as Wallachia had also been formed. An important part was played by the Romanians who came down from Maramureş.

Increased domestic trade favored by the emergence of towns, big and small, as well as intensive transit trade, helped to build up the economic unity of Moldavia. A deed issued by the Papal Chancellery on October 4, 1332, mentions a local leader who had usurped the rights created by the Hungarian kings for what had been the Cumans' bishopric. It stated that "the estates, property and rights of the Milcovia Bishopric" had been taken over by "the powerful people of those parts" (a potentibus illarum partium).

The participation in 1325 of a Romanian army recruited on Moldavia's territory, together with Polish, Ukrainian, and Lithuanian armies, in hostilities against the Margrave of Brandenburg, is another indication that the power of the leaders east of the Carpathians had been strengthened.

The unification of the political bodies on Moldavian territory was brought about by their struggle against foreign invaders, particularly the Tartars. The victories won by Basarab against the Tartars from 1325 to 1328 strengthened the desire of the Romanian leaders in Moldavia to free themselves of Mongol rule. And when in the fifties of the fourteenth century the Hungarian king Louis of Anjou set out on an expedition designed to remove the Mongol pressure from the boundaries of his kingdom, he found full support among the Romanian population.

Following the victories won, a march (a fortified border district) was founded in Moldavia in 1352-1353, which subsequently was to develop into an independent Moldavian state. Dragoş, Voivode of Maramureş, who had distinguished himself in the battles fought against the Tartars, was appointed as head of that state. The ties between Transylvania and Moldavia, and especially between Maramureş and the northwestern part of Moldavia, whose ethnical and cultural unity was of long duration, were thereby strengthened.

The dependence of Dragoş and his successors on the Hungarian crown, much against the local political trends towards independence, caused dissatisfaction among the native rulers, who decided to overthrow both Dragoş's dynasty and Hungarian suzerainty. As in the struggle against the Tartars, the Romanian population of Moldavia was supported by the political leaders of Maramureş who opposed the policy of the Hungarian kings whose aim was to suppress self-governing states and form counties under Hungarian administration. Heading the Maramureş resistance was Voivode Bogdan; he was described as an "infidel" in the Hungarian records of 1343.

Defeated in his attempt to end the subjection of Maramureş to the Hungarian crown, Bogdan joined the movement in Moldavia, and was elected by the Moldavian boyars as leader of the local forces opposed to Hungarian policy. Taking advantage of the fact that Louis of Anjou, king of Hungary, was engaged in a war against Venice and was moreover concerned with the problems raised in the Balkans by the death of tsar Stephen Dushan (1355), Bogdan removed from the Moldavian throne Dragoş's successor, Balc, son of Sas, and in 1359 laid the foundations of an independent Moldavian state.

The Hungarian kings' attempts to reduce to obedience "the Vlach rebels who had diverged from the path of fidelity" were brought to nought by the latter's resistance. King Louis was forced to give up his plan of subjecting Moldavia to the Hungarian crown and to be content with confiscating Bogdan's property in Maramureş, which he bestowed on Voivode Balc who had been driven out of Moldavia.

Under Bogdan, Moldavia extended its territories, incorporating other political orders east of the Carpathians, and the Hungarian kings ultimately accepted the situation.

The independence of Moldavia won under Bogdan as well as its development and unifying process under the princes of his dynasty induced the following generations to ascribe to Bogdan the foundation of the Moldavian state.

It was also in the fourteenth century that Dobrudja became a state playing an important political part in the Balkan Peninsula. The nucleus of the Dobrudjan state was the "Cavarna Country" mentioned in a diploma Tsar Ivan Asen II of Bulgaria granted to the people of Ragusa. Tsar Constantine Tich formed an appanage for Prince Smiltza out of this socio-political unit. Halfway through the fourteenth century the unrest prevailing in Byzantium as a result of the struggle for the throne made it possible for Dobrudja to strengthen its autonomy.

In 1346, Balica, its leader, fought in Byzantium and was awarded the title of Despot. After his death Dobrotich succeeded to the throne of the Cavarna Country, first as a vassal of Byzantium and later as an autonomous ruler recognized by Emperor John V Paleologus against whom he had fought for the territory south of Varna.

Dobrotich extending his authority to the Danube, Dobrudja was drawn into a long war against the Genoese who had created factories at Vicina and Lycostomo and wished to make sure of a trade monopoly in that region. In order to cope with the resistance of the Genoese traders who had the Ottoman Empire for allies, Dobrotich strengthened his political organization which became one of the most important factors in the Balkan Peninsula after 1371.

It is not known under what circumstances the Dobrudjan state passed from Dobrotich to his son Ivanko, mentioned in historical records with the title of Despot, like his father. Ivanko minted his own coins, which were made of copper and inscribed in Greek. This is a sign that he was an independent ruler. In 1386 he made peace with the Ottoman Empire and the following year he concluded at Pera a peace and trade treaty with the Genoese. In 1388 a great Turkish expedition headed by Vizir Ali Pasha threatened to turn the territory between the Danube and the sea into a pashalik. The energetic intervention of Mircea the Old, the Wallachian prince, removed that threat and Dobrudja was united with Wallachia.

Shortly before the Battle of Nicopolis, Dobrudja was subjected to Turkish rule but was again conquered by Mircea the Old in 1404.

There are few historical records available for the period between the tenth and the fourteenth centuries but, nevertheless, it is known that certain political formations played a decisive part in the development of the Romanian people who gradually assumed a historical identity; their political organization developed and they themselves asserted their own identity and originality after having led an anonymous life as a result of the superposition of foreign rule on autochthonous political realities.

# CHAPTER II

# The Romanian Countries in the Fourteenth and Fifteenth Centuries

THE establishment of Wallachia and Moldavia as feudal states was of decisive importance for the Romanian people, who, being organized in independent states, were safe from the danger of incorporation by the neighboring powers or the migratory peoples, and could follow their own path of development, asserting their creative talents. Demographic and economic development as well as social and military organization ensued. The new state organization strengthened internal unity and enabled the two countries to resist the permanent tendencies of the great neighboring states towards expansion. Unlike the south-Danubian states, which collapsed under the Ottoman conquerors, the Romanian countries resisted their offensive and retained their political entity. A number of outstanding figures embodied this resistance and ably coped with the problems of the Romanian people.

## 1. Economic Life

THE economic features characteristic of feudalism were a natural economy, each estate endeavoring to produce everything required, and a low technical level. When the productive forces developed and the social division of labor intensified, the towns assumed ever greater significance as centers for the advancement of the crafts and of trade.

The main resources of the people in the Romanian countries in the fourteenth and fifteenth centuries were derived from agriculture, the growing of the vine, animal husbandry, beekeeping, fishing, forestry, and the wealth of the subsoil. Agriculture, the main production branch, was practiced particularly along the river valleys and on the hillsides, where the population was more dense. The Danube plain, frequently laid waste by the nomadic peoples, was mostly forested and the population sparse. Agricultural implements were primitive and did not allow of widespread crops and a large output. The most important technical progress made at the time was the use of the iron plowshare that turned the furrow, in place of the wooden one, which merely scratched the earth. As most of the country's territory was wooded, the land had constantly to be cleared. Fire was often used for the purpose as were also picks, spades, and plows, to prepare the soil for crops of millet, wheat, rye, and oats. The first crop after the clearing was usually fairly abundant, the crop of the second year medium, while the third-year crop was poor, so that the peasants were compelled to sow the seed on newly-cleared land after the third year.

Apart from this agricultural technique described as "wild fallowing" crop rotation was also practiced, cereals alternating with grass.

A primitive agricultural technique and permanent insecurity resulted in the agricultural output being only sufficient to satisfy domestic consumption, with a small surplus for export. For this reason years of drought and the devastations of war in one region or another caused famine.

Vine-growing had been practiced widely in the country time out of mind. In the fourteenth and fifteenth centuries it brought considerable incomes to the feudal lords and to the administration, and a number of taxes were levied on it, one of which, the *perper*, so-called from the Byzantine coin *hyperperon*, was the first tax in cash known to have been paid in Wallachia. Wine was one of the Romanian products that was being exported in those days.

The breeding of cattle, horses, sheep, and pigs was a main source of income in the Romanian countries. Foreign observers who had the occasion to visit these parts were impressed by the number and quality of the livestock. One of the first trading privileges granted to the towns of Braşov and Lvov by the ruling princes of Wallachia and Moldavia showed livestock to be a main export article.

Bee-keeping, like fishing, which was mostly practiced in the Danube backwaters rich in fish, no less than the forests with the products and game they yielded, were sources of food for the population and brought in considerable incomes. Honey and wax, fish and forest game were important export articles.

The riches of the subsoil were being exploited mostly in Transylvania. Salt, gold, silver, and iron were mined in large quantities. In Wallachia and Moldavia salt mining was practiced on a large scale for home consumption and for export to the whole of the Balkan Peninsula as well as to Poland and the Ukraine. In Wallachia salt was obtained from Ocnele Mari, and copper was mined at Bratilov not far from Baia de Aramă during the reign of Mircea the Old.

The crafts were unequally developed over the Romanian territory during the fourteenth and fifteenth centuries. In Transylvania, less exposed to devastating Turkish and Tartar inroads, the crafts and towns reached a higher level of development than in other parts. In most Transylvanian towns, though not in Wallachia and Moldavia, the craftsmen were already organized in guilds in the fourteenth century. There was a busy trade in craftware which went from Transylvania to the territories east and south of the Carpathians.

During the latter half of the fifteenth century, the number of craftsmen in the towns of Wallachia and Moldavia increased and the administration began to pay attention to the interests of the townspeople, craftsmen as well as traders.

Unlike the towns of Transylvania — Brașov, Bistrița, Cluj, and Sibiu — the towns of Wallachia and Moldavia long preserved the basic elements of a rural economy, being primarily trading centers and not craftware producers.

During the fourteenth century and the first half of the fifteenth century, domestic trade was poorly organized. It had a periodic character, being carried on at weekly or annual fairs.

The towns of Brașov, Sibiu, and Bistrița, three Transylvanian trading and craftware centers along the border, were the places where Transylvania, Wallachia, and Moldavia came in touch commercially. While Sibiu mostly traded with Wallachia, and Bistrița almost exclusively with Moldavia, Brașov, owing to its position, was the trading center of all three Romanian countries.

As town life developed south and east of the Carpathians and the number of local traders increased, the ruling princes of Wallachia and Moldavia realized what advantages could be derived from the prosperity of the towns, which were actually directly subordinated to them. Towards the close of the fifteenth century, the international treaties concluded by Moldavia and Wallachia show that the administration took note of the demands of the townspeople. After 1485 special clauses provided protection for traders.

Owing to their geographical position, the Romanian countries benefited as a result of transit dues. It was through Transylvania and Wallachia that the trade routes linking Western and Central Europe to the Pontic shores and the Balkan Peninsula passes, while the routes linking the Baltic to the Black Sea went through Moldavia. The Romanian territory being now integrated in the circuit of medieval trade, the towns of Chilia and Cetatea Albă played a most important part in the development of Moldavia, Wallachia, and Transylvania.

Traders from the Levant and from Transylvania sold overseas goods and spices south and east of the Carpathians while from Western and Central Europe came cloth, linen, weapons, and farming implements. Foreign traders bought cattle, horses, hides and skins, wax, salt, fish, and other goods from Wallachia and Moldavia.

Like domestic trade, transit traffic was subjected to numerous taxes levied at the border or inside the country. The proceeds went to the ruling princes, to the monasteries or to the boyars.

Monetary circulation was considerable in the Romanian countries during the fourteenth and fifteenth centuries as a result of domestic and foreign trade and of transit traffic. Romanian silver coins *(aspri)* circulated apart from foreign ones: perpers, ducats, florins, groschen and zlotys. Romanian coins were first issued in Wallachia under Vladislav Vlaicu (1364-1377) to be continued up to the time of the rule of Radu the Handsome (1462-1475), while in Moldavia they were minted for the first time under Petru Mușat (1375-1391) to be continued up to the reign of Ștefăniță (1517-1527).

## 2. *Social Structure*

THE salient feature of feudal production relations is the fact that the main means of production — land — belonged to the landowners, whether laymen or churchmen. The peasants only held the lots received from the feudal landowners, tilling them with their own implements; in exchange for the land the peasants worked or paid in cash (labor services, the tithe, and taxes paid in cash).

Feudal society was consequently based on antagonistic classes and therefore the history of feudalism is characterized by a sharp class struggle between landowners and the actual producers.

Documents of the thirteenth century show the hierarchical nature of landownership. On the same estate the dependent peasants exercised their right to use the land, the vassals the right to usufruct, and the landowner the right of ownership. From the fourteenth century on, when the ruling princes made their appearance, the ruling prince was added to the other categories. The ruling prince had a higher title of ownership to the land of the whole country *(dominium eminens)*. This structure which expressed the manner in which the rent was distributed among the ruling classes, offered means of compulsion over the dependent peasants and made up the military hierarchy.

The boyars' landownership, which existed before the independent Romanian states emerged, was termed *ocină* or *baştină*. It could only be confiscated by the ruling prince in the event of betrayal or disinheritance.

When the ruling princes made their appearance, conditional landownership was also created, resulting from the princes' donations for "right and faithful service."

In their turn the great boyars were also entitled to make a gift of lands, thus creating vassals (servants) who made up their military hosts.

The estates of the monasteries originated in the gifts of the ruling princes and were subsequently extended by donations, purchases, and usurpation until the monasteries ranked among the greatest feudal landowners of the country.

It was the landowners' aim to extend their estates and, at the same time, to increase the number of dependent peasants who were to till them. The enserfed peasants owed labor to the landowners as well as payment in produce. In order to compel the peasants to carry out their obligations, the landowners had servants who saw that their tasks were carried out.

The owners of large estates enjoyed the privilege of feudal immunity so that no state bodies could infringe upon their estates. The princes' prerogatives consequently passed on to the landowners, who were entitled to levy taxes, administer justice, and convene their vassals in the event of war. Starting from the latter half of the fifteenth century, the princes' administration sought to restrict immunity privileges.

A feudal estate was made up of three parts: seigniorial land, which belonged to the landowner and which the dependent peasants had to till by performing labor service; the plots tilled by the peasants, in exchange for which they paid a tithe; and the common land (grass land and forests). During the fourteenth and the fifteenth centuries and even later, the peasants' holdings made up the largest part of a feudal estate in Wallachia and Moldavia. The seigniorial land was very small compared with the area taken up by the peasants' holdings.

On the feudal estates there was a considerable number of Gipsy slaves in Wallachia and of Gipsy and Tartar slaves in Moldavia. They were used for different jobs. Many of them were craftsmen, especially smiths, while others were servants working outdoors or indoors. Some were used to enforce the landowners' will. The slaves were an integral part of the estate of the boyars and monasteries. They could be bequeathed like chattels, — they were at the disposal of the landowners who could sell them, make a gift of them, or exchange them.

Landowners derived considerable incomes as they alone were entitled to possess flour mills, wine presses, spinning mills and fulling mills, and they also had a monopoly of spirits and levied customs duties on the territory of their estates.

In the early years after the organization of Romanian feudal states, the dependent peasants were called by names of a general character *(liudi, siraci, siromahi, horani)*, names which were applied to all the unprivileged. Towards the close of the fifteenth century the dependent peasants were being increasingly named *vecini* in Wallachia and later in the sixteenth century *rumâni*. As from the mid-sixteenth century the term *vecin* was used in Moldavia, and in Slav documents also *sused*.

From the fourteenth to the sixteenth century, and possibly also before that period, there was close connection between the dependent peasant and the land he was entitled to use. Provided he fulfilled the obligations incumbent on him, the peasant could not be driven from it. With the passage of time, with the landowners systematically usurping the age-old rights of the peasants, the connection between peasant and land was loosened and personal connection with the landowner was tightened. From the fourteenth to the sixteenth century the dependent peasants still enjoyed the right to leave the estate.

A considerable part of the rural population in Wallachia and Moldavia still lived in free villages, which mostly lay in the Carpathian foothills, though there were also many in the plain. In Transylvania there was a free peasantry, especially on the royal land, where Saxons had been settled, and in the outlying districts: Hațeg, Făgăraș, Maramureș and elsewhere. The existence of a free peasantry and the fact that in Wallachia and Moldavia there was still limited exploitation of the enserfed villages in those days, account for the great victories the Romanian people won over foreign invaders.

The free villages had a collective leadership made up of "good and aged people". And it was these people who decided when farming work was to begin and what crops were to be sown in various parts of the village land. They judged the less important suits arising in the village, decided the taxes each villager had to pay in order to make up the ruling prince's due, and saw to it that the taxes were levied.

The inhabitants of the towns, whether big or small, made up an important social category whose weight in economic and political life increased in Wallachia and Moldavia in the fifteenth century. In Transylvania it had increased even earlier. Most of the townspeople in Wallachia and Moldavia were Romanians. In the Transylvanian towns, however, the Romanians were less numerous for they were held to be socially inferior and interdictions were laid upon them.

The peasants' obligations towards the landowner and the ruling prince consisted in tithes (in Transylvania — *terragium*), statute labor, or services. Occasionally taxes had also to be paid.

Tithes were usually levied on all the products of a peasant homestead, the most frequently recorded being the tithe on grain, sheep, pigs, wine, honey and wax, fruit and fish.

Services included transport and everything needed in transport such as guides, watches, etc., as well as various services around the boyar's or the prince's manor. The general term of *angarii* was also used to designate them. The peasants also had to mow the landowner's hay and to transport it so that fodder would be available in the wintertime. It was also the peasant's obligation to fell trees for the landowner, to fulfill his military obligations and to accommodate the messengers and officials of the prince, who had been entrusted various missions in the district.

The peasants were also obliged to pay taxes and to do military service. Documents frequently speak of taxes *(biruri)*, which the ruling princes hardly ever ceded to the boyars. With the passage of time these became the greatest burden. In the sixteenth century, particularly in the latter half of that century, the word *biruri* was used for all taxes and cash contributions levied by the ruling prince.

## 3. *The Bobîlna Uprising*

IN the Romanian countries the struggle of the peasantry against feudal exploitation assumed various forms: petitions, refusal to work, refusal to pay taxes, flight. In Transylvania, where the peasantry was more cruelly exploited than south and east of the Carpathians, the class struggle also assumed the form of rebellions, which culminated in the Bobîlna uprising.

The main cause was the aggravation of feudal exploitation: increased obligations towards the landowners, increased taxes to be paid to the State and to the Church (the "nona" tax was then introduced), and cancellation of the right to change one's place of habitation. Discontent flared up as a result of Bishop Gheorghe Lepeș's demand that the outstanding taxes should be paid in a new "big and heavy" coin. Hussite ideology penetrating among the rural masses of Transylvania intensified the resistance and offered a program of struggle and the tactics to be used in the struggle.

In the spring of 1437 the peasants, both Romanian and Hungarian — with leaders whose names have gone down in history, among them Mihail Românul, Anton Nagy (Anton the Great), Pavel of Voivodeni, "the standard-bearer of the community of Hungarian and Romanian inhabitants" — won a great victory at Bobîlna over the nobility, whom they compelled to negotiate on their own terms. At Bobîlna an understanding was reached between the peasants in revolt and the noblemen, providing, among other things, the right freely to change one's place of habitation, abolition of the "nona" tax, and annual control of the noblemen's observance of these provisions by the peasantry's representatives. After Bobîlna the nobility consolidated their forces and at Kapolna (not far from Dej) on September 16, 1437, concluded the so-called *Unio trium nationum* with the leading strata of the Saxons and Szeklers. The privileged social classes united against the peasants in order to put down any revolt and to keep peasantry in their existing condition. The Kapolna Union became the basic institution in the constitutional organization of Transylvania. It was in force until the revolution of 1848. Excluded from the Union, the Romanians, who formed the majority of the population, were treated like a "taxable mob," merely tolerated by the others.

The Kapolna Union caused the uprising to flare up again. Although less numerous now, when many had returned to their homes, the peasants battled afresh at Apatiu on October 6, 1437, but the struggle yielded no decisive result. A new understanding between the peasants and the nobility established less favorable conditions for the peasants. The dissatisfied peasants resumed their struggle, being supported by the miners and the townspeople of the lower classes, and succeeded in taking some important towns: Dej, Turda, Aiud, and Cluj. The privileged classes concentrated their forces and with the support of the Hungarian king the uprising was suppressed. The leaders were hanged on the hill facing the town of Turda. Many of the peasants were mutilated.

As in other peasant uprisings, the peasants were defeated at Bobîlna on account of poor organization and lack of leaders. Their defeat once again showed that the peasantry cannot liberate itself by its own forces.

## 4. *Political Organization*

THE structure of feudal society determined the forms of political organization. On the upper rung of the hierarchical ladder was the ruling prince or Grand Voivode in Wallachia and Moldavia and the Voivode in Transylvania, followed by the great boyars or noblemen. Considered as the supreme master of the whole country, the prince possessed all public power: executive, judicial, legislative, and military. He exercised his power through the agency of his officials, who did not yet have any definite attributes, for they also fulfilled judicial, administrative, and fiscal duties.

Succession to the throne of Moldavia and of Wallachia was hereditary, though not in the order of primogeniture, for the boyars could elect any member of the ruling family to succeed the late ruler. The system enabled the boyars to contest the prince's authority and made it possible for foreign powers to interfere in internal affairs.

The prince's power was supported and controlled by the Prince's Council, made up of the great landowners, whether they held any office in the state or not. Gradually, however, the Council came to be made up of state officials only. At first they were recruited from among the *familiares* in the prince's immediate environment, who fulfilled personal functions, as the High Steward and the Cupbearer. All important deeds — the donation of estates and whatever concerned foreign relations — were discussed by the Council and confirmed by the Council members.

In the course of time public offices were defined and domestic duties were separated from the public ones. The number of offices then increased and the attributions were limited. [1]

---

[1] The most important court officials were: the *vornic* (palatinus — Court Marshal), the leading official of the prince's court; the *logofăt* (cancellarius — Chancellor), the most important officer in the prince's chancellery; the *vistier* (thesaurarius — Treasurer), who kept the accounts of the prince's incomes; then followed the *spătar* (gladifer — Swordbearer), bearer of the prince's sword during ceremonies; the *stolnic* (dapifer — High Steward), who had the prince's table and his guests in his care; the *paharnic* or *ceaşnic* (pincerna — Cupbearer), who procured wine for the court; the *comis* (comes stabuli — Equerry), who looked after the prince's stables and equipages; the *postelnic* or *stratornic* (cubicularius — Chamberlain), who had the care of the prince's private apartment. During the first stage of organization of the prince's court, these officials were to be found in the Prince's Council beside the great boyars who held no offices, and side by side with the territorial officials: the *pîrcălab* (castelanus) and the *starost* (capitane). The *ban* was one of the territorial officials of great importance in the history of Wallachia. He is first mentioned as a member of the Prince's Council in the reign of Mircea the Old.

In fifteenth century documents other officials who held various functions at the prince's court are mentioned as members of the Council besides the

For their services the dignitaries received part of the taxes and fines levied by them for the account of the ruling prince.

Transylvania preserved its status as a principality (voivode-ship) even after it had merged with the Hungarian kingdom. A prince (voivode) with supreme administrative, judicial, and military duties was at the head of Transylvania until it fell under Turkish suzerainty in the sixteenth century.

In the course of time the power of the voivode varied according to the ratio of forces between him and the king of Hungary. When the central power underwent a crisis there was a tendency for the Transylvanian princes to free themselves from regal authority and to look towards the creation of a dynasty: from 1344 to 1376, with short intermissions, six members of the Lackfy family held the dignity of voivode and between 1415 and 1437 there were two members of the Csaky family.

Appointed and revoked by the king, the voivode was entitled to choose his subordinates — from the vice-voivode and comites to the notaries — from among the *familiares* in his personal service. From the beginning of the fifteenth century, the voivodes often spent long periods outside the boundaries of Transylvania, mostly residing at the royal court. When this occurred, they left the leadership of the country to the vice-voivodes. Vice-voivode Lorand Lepes ruled Transylvania for over twenty years (1415-1438). From the middle of the fifteenth century on the voivodes entrusted the administration of public affairs to governors during their absence and the latter were entitled to choose vice-governors in their turn.

General assemblies (general congregations) were usually of a juridical nature in Transylvania, and seldom tackled economic or administrative problems. They were usually convened by the voivode, though the king, and occasionally the vice-voi-

---

great officials. Among them was the *clucer*, who held the keys of the provisions storehouse; the *sluger*, who saw that the court was supplied with meat; the *pivnicer*, who supervised the prince's cellars; the *cămăraş*, who was in charge of the mint and later of the personal estate of the prince *(cămara)*; the *medelnicer*, who looked after the prince's table services and laundry.

During the latter half of the fifteenth century, while the central power was being strengthened, the office of *armaş* was set up, the armaş being the executor of punishments decreed by the prince. During Stephen the Great's reign, a most important official was the Suceava Gatekeeper *(portar)*, who headed the army.

vode, were also entitled to convene them. Like all similar assemblies in the Middle Ages, they had a pronounced class character and the enserfed peasantry was never represented. Although the Romanians made up the majority of the population, they generally did not participate in the assembly, for most of them were serfs. And even Romanian gentry and other free men were rarely mentioned at the assemblies of 1291 and 1355.

In Wallachia and Moldavia the ruling princes exercised their control of free villages and of the estates of the lesser boyars through the agency of the county bodies. On becoming administrative units, the counties were headed by *sudeti* or *pîrcălabi* in Wallachia and by *pîrcălabi, starosti,* and *sudeti* in Moldavia.

The towns, whether big or small, were comparatively autonomous, being administrated by elected bodies: the *șoltuz* or *voit* in Moldavia and the *județ* in Wallachia, assisted by a council made up of twelve councillors *(pîrgari)*. A more comprehensive council was the Council of Good and Aged People. The prince's dignitaries — the *vornici*, and in Moldavia the *ureabnici* from the sixteenth century on — imposed their authority on these elected bodies. Free villages were headed by a *cneaz* or a *jude,* also called *vătăman* in Moldavia. These were also assisted by a Council of Good and Aged People in the exercise of their duties.

The enserfed villages were headed by the representative of the landowner, whether boyar or monastery, named *pîrcălab* in Wallachia and *vătăman* in Moldavia.

The territory of Transylvania was divided into counties headed by *comites,* who were at first appointed by the voievode. By the close of the fourteenth century the counties, as also the other administrative centers, such as the Romanian districts and the Szekler and Saxon sedes, were already well organized. Romanian districts were organized according to their age-old laws *(jus Valachicum)* which the Magyar rule was compelled to observe.

In Wallachia and Moldavia the supreme judge was the ruling prince, who was alone entitled to pronounce capital punishment and to decide the suits between landowners. The boyars and monasteries, holding the privilege of immunity, exercised the right of judging labor conflicts. The free peasants

1 *Helmet from the Coţofăneşti Hoard*

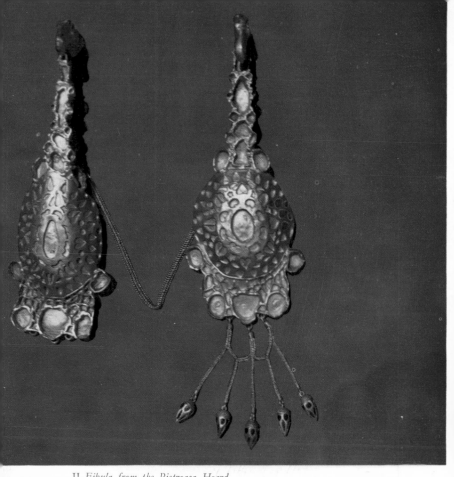

II *Fibula from the Pietroasa Hoard*
III *Vase from the Pietroasa Hoard*

were judged by the representatives of the community or, like the townspeople, by the prince's dignitaries.

As far as penal law was concerned, vestiges of the ancient clan customs were preserved for long: relatives were entitled to avenge a member of the family, and on the other side the head of this one could be ransomed from the relatives.

An old legal practice mentioned in documents was the use of witnesses under oath, especially in peasant suits, such evidence being decisive. As the feudal régime consolidated, the right to bear witness was held only by free people and by landowners.

A suit was judged on the basis of common law termed "the custom of the land". As the Romanian feudal states improved their organization, written laws came to be used apart from the unwritten law. The former were originally made up of the decisions issued by the ruling prince as laid down in the charters issued by the prince's chancellery. In mid-fifteenth century some collections of Byzantine laws were copied at the bidding of the ruling princes for their guidance in legal matters. A *Zakonik* (collection of laws) copied at Tîrgoviște dates from 1451, and in Moldavia the copy of Matei Vlastares' *Syntagma* dates from 1472. The *Syntagma* comprises Byzantine penal and civil laws. In principle the prince's sentence was final for the term of his reign. The case could only be reopened under a new prince. In order to prevent the suits from being reopened, a heavy fee *(zavesca,* later termed *ferîie)* had to be paid. The fee is mentioned in fifteenth century records.

The army was made up of the prince's men and of the men of the great boyars, who recruited them from their estates, as well as of other peasants and of townspeople. The men of the prince and of the boyars formed the bulk of the army.

In Transylvania Romanian gentry and voivodes played a most important part in the battles waged against the Turks at the close of the fourteenth century and in the fifteenth century. The towns had to recruit men for the army, though from the end of the fifteenth century a sum of money could be paid instead.

In the event of a great threat such as Turkish invasions, the "great army" was convened by the prince. This amounted to mass recruitment, a system applied especially by Iancu of Hunedoara, Vlad the Impaler, and Stephen the Great.

The equipment and armament varied with social position. The boyars and great noblemen were equipped like the western knights in mail shirts and armor and carried shields. They fought on horseback with swords and spears. Foot soldiers mostly fought with bows and sometimes with spears and swords; the peasants called upon to enlist fought with scythes and picks. To besiege strongholds catapults were used which discharged stones against walls and their defenders. Halfway through the fifteenth century firearms began to be used: mortars made of castiron or copper with bombs of stone or iron. The Transylvanian towns, especially Braşov and Sibiu, were important producers of mortars.

The defensive system relied to a great extent on strongholds, whether those inside the country (Neamţ, Suceava, Poienari, Unguraşi, Ineu, Cetatea de Baltă, Deva, etc.) or those along the borders (Hotin, Soroca, Chilia, Cetatea Albă, Tighina, Severin, Giurgiu, Turnu, Bran, etc.). The strongholds were built of large stone blocks, with ramparts and bastions.

## 5. Struggle Against Ottoman Expansion

DURING the reign of Mircea the Old (1386-1418) the Ottoman Empire, now including most of the Balkan Peninsula, reached the Danube line, thus threatening Wallachia. Mircea the Old was the first of the Romanian princes who, by their struggle and sacrifices, even in defeat, saved the Romanian countries from sharing the fate of the other Balkan states which the conquerors turned into *pashaliks*. The example set by these princes nurtured the flame of independence which inspired the struggle and policy of the Romanian people through the ages. From the beginning of his reign, Mircea the Old established good relations with Moldavia: he intervened in the struggle for the throne of Moldavia and brought about the ascent of Alexander the Good. The political disturbances in the Hungarian kingdom enabled him to extend his authority in Transylvania, where he enlarged the fiefs of his forerunners. He also incorporated Dobrudja, Wallachia thus reaching its greatest extension ever. In 1404-1406, Mircea titled himself

"I Mircea, Grand Voivode and Prince of all the Ungro-Vlachia Land and of the parts beyond the mountains and towards the Tartar territories, the Almaş and Făgăraş, Duke and Prince of the Severin Banat and on either side over the whole Podunavia and also as far as the Great Sea, and master of the Dîrstor citadel."

Mircea strengthened the power of the state and organized the different high offices, promoted economic development, increased the state's revenue, and minted silver money that enjoyed wide circulation not only inside the country but also in the neighboring countries. He gave the merchants of Poland and Lithuania trade privileges and renewed those his predecessors had given to the people of Braşov. Mircea the Old could thus afford to increase his military power. He fortified the Danube citadels and strengthened "the great army" made up of townspeople and of free and dependent peasants. He also proved a great supporter of the Church. He raised the splendid church at Cozia after the model of the Krusevac Church in Serbia and endowed it generously, as he also did other churches and monasteries.

While organizing the country, he also took good care to form a system of lasting alliances that might enable him to defend the independence of the country. Through the inter-mediary of Petru Muşat, ruling prince of Moldavia, he conclud-ed in 1389 a treaty of alliance with Vladislav Iagello, king of Poland. The treaty was renewed in 1404 and 1410. He main-tained close relations with Sigismund of Luxemburg, the king of Hungary, relying on their common interest in the struggle against Ottoman expansion.

His interventions in support of the Christian peoples south of the Danube who were fighting against the Turks, brought him into conflict with the Ottoman Empire. Mircea the Old was repeatedly victorious in the battles he fought against the Turks: at Rovine on the river Argeş in 1394 and later in 1397 and 1400. He was a master of military tactics and showed great gallantry, which inspired his troops. He can be consi-dered to rank among the great army commanders of his time. As a result of his victories against the Turks, the position of Wallachia was assured and the expansion of the Ottoman Empire in Central Europe was temporarily checked. The German historian Leunclavius described him as "the bravest and ablest of the Christian princes."

The defeat of Sultan Bayazid Ilderim by Timur Lenk (Tamerlane) at Ankara in 1402 opened a period of anarchy in the Ottoman Empire and Mircea took advantage of it to organize together with the Hungarian king, a campaign against the Turks. In 1404 Mircea was thus able to impose his rule on Dobrudja again. He moreover took part in the struggles for the throne of the Ottoman Empire and enabled Musa to ascend that throne. It was at this time that the prince reached the height of his power.

From 1414 to 1417 the Ottoman Empire resumed its attempts to expand north of the Danube. Mircea the Old facing by himself an enemy that possessed forces greatly superior to his own, decided to pay the Ottoman Porte a tribute to regain peace, though without any vassalage.

In the first decades of its existence as a state, Moldavia had to face Hungary's repeated attempts to reestablish her suzerainty over the territories east of the Carpathians. The ruling princes of Moldavia endeavored to parry the threat with Poland's support.

Latcu (1365-1374) succeeded to the throne after Bogdan, the creator of the Moldavian independent state. In 1370 he had to cope with the joint Polish-Hungarian threat as Louis I, king of Hungary, was elected king of Poland as well. In order to weaken the pressure of Hungary, Latcu turned Catholic and came into touch with the Pope. It was a purely political move and consequently the Catholic religion in Moldavia did not survive Latcu's reign. Latcu himself was buried in the Orthodox Church at Rădăuți.

Latcu's successor, Petru Mușat (1374-1391), taking advantage of the deterioration of the Polish-Hungarian union following the death of King Louis in 1382, tried to shake off Hungarian pressure by creating friendly relations with Poland. The Treaty of Lvov concluded with Poland in 1387 offered Moldavia support against the Hungarian threat.

Petru Mușat attached great importance to economic, administrative, and religious organization. He was the first to mint Moldavian silver coins and during his reign the country's revenues increased considerably thanks to domestic trade and transit tolls. In 1388 the Moldavian prince lent the king of Poland 3,000 silver rubles, for which he was given the Halicium territory (Pokuția) as security. He founded the Moldavian

Metropolitan Church and placed his relative Iosif at the head of it. Although it was canonically recognized by the Constantinople Patriarchate only much later, the Moldavian Metropolitan Church helped to strengthen the power of the ruling princes.

The reign of Roman I (1391-1394) and of Stephen I (1394-1399), though of short duration covered two important moments in Moldavia's history. Under Roman I Moldavia's boundaries reached "the sea shore", while under Stephen I Sigismund of Luxemburg, king of Hungary, was defeated at Hindău and his attempts to reduce Moldavia to subjection came to nought.

Brought to the throne with the support of Mircea the Old, Alexander the Good (1400-1432) gave Moldavia a long period of economic prosperity while his feudal state was consolidated and its international prestige enhanced.

From the very first years of his reign, Alexander the Good realized that it was in the interest of the Moldavian state to continue the policy of cooperation with Poland. The Moldavian armies repeatedly fought alongside those of the Polish and the Lithuanian ones against the Teutonic Knights, gaining distinction at Grünewald in 1410 and at Marienburg in 1422.

His economic and military power enabled him to evade the consequences of the Treaty of Lublin concluded by Poland and Hungary in 1412, which stipulated that Moldavia was to be divided if Alexander the Good did not provide the Hungarian king with military assistance against the Turks. Subsequent attempts on the part of Sigismund to reestablish Hungarian suzerainty over Moldavia failed.

Alexander the Good took interest in the political situation of Wallachia and succeeded in helping certain princes to the throne: Prince Aldea, for example, added to his name that of his protector and called himself Alexander Aldea. His policy was followed by all the great Moldavian princes who tried to make of the leaders of Wallachia devoted allies in the struggle against the Turks.

Like Wallachia after Mircea the Old, Moldavia went through a period of internal struggles at the death of Alexander the Good. The country's capacity of resistance was thus weakened and this paved the way for foreign intervention.

When Ottoman pressure increased in the fifties of the fifteenth century, it was Transylvania under the leadership of Iancu of Hunedoara (1441-1456) that played an important part in the struggle of the Romanian countries against the Turks, with a military confederation of the three countries ensuing as a result. In 1438 Iancu of Hunedoara was Ban of Severin; by 1441 he had become Voivode of Transylvania and Comes of Timişoara, as well as a tried fighter against the Turks, whom he had defeated repeatedly. From 1442 on Iancu of Hunedoara intervened in the internal policy of the two Romanian countries, placing princes on their throne in order to ensure that Moldavia and Wallachia would assist him in his anti-Ottoman struggle. In 1448 he was ceded the citadel of Chilia, one of the key positions of the anti-Ottoman front, in exchange for the support he had given Peter II to gain the Moldavian throne. Master of Chilia, Iancu of Hunedoara could control political developments in the territories of Moldavia and Wallachia.

With an eye to the innovations in military tactics and techniques, Iancu of Hunedoara created a fighting system under which the bulk of the army was made up of popular elements; he introduced the Hussite tactics of the camp built up of linked wagons, and created a wide system of alliances with the neighboring countries in the struggle against the Turks.

After having defeated a number of Turkish plundering hordes, Iancu of Hunedoara tried to liberate the Balkan Peninsula from the Ottoman yoke. In 1443 he organized a great expedition against the Turks, the so-called "long campaign," and succeeded in crossing the Balkans and reaching Sofia. The crusade organized the following year (1444) was insufficiently prepared, however, and led to the Varna disaster when the king of Hungary met his death. In 1448, using forces from all the Romanian countries, Iancu of Hunedoara, now governor of Hungary after King Vladislav's death again tried to strike at the Turkish possessions south of the Danube. The decisive battle was fought at Kossovo where the Turks were victorious.

In the years that followed, internal difficulties prevented Iancu of Hunedoara from undertaking new military actions against the Porte. The truce of 1451, which also involved the Romanian countries, was merely a respite during which new campaigns were being prepared, as shown by the negotiations carried on with Byzantium in 1452.

The last great victory of the brilliant Romanian commander was occasioned by Sultan Mohammed II's attempt to overcome the resistance of the Hungarian kingdom at Belgrade. On July 21-22, 1456, the Ottoman army which was besieging the town suffered a great defeat and was compelled to postpone its advance towards Central Europe. Shortly after this victory Iancu of Hunedoara died from the plague. Thanks to his brilliant resistance, Iancu of Hunedoara delayed Ottoman expansion towards Central Europe for more than half a century.

Moldavia had bowed to the Porte, as decided by Petru Aaron, the ruling prince, and the Moldavian boyars at Vaslui (1456), and Iancu of Hunedoara had just been victorious at Belgrade, when Vlad the Impaler (1456-1462) became ruling prince of Wallachia. While the decision made at Vaslui aggravated the situation of Wallachia, the defeat of Sultan Mahommed II under the walls of Belgrade had shown the efficiency of firm and organized resistence to the Ottoman invaders. But after the death of Iancu of Hunedoara, with Serbia being turned into a *pashalik* in 1459, Ottoman pressure increased along the Danube and became a direct threat to Wallachia's independence. In the military duel ahead of him, Vlad decided to take the initiative.

Before declaring war upon the Porte, Vlad the Impaler undertook some bold political measures. In order to strengthen his authority he restricted the political and military power of the great boyars, created a powerful army, and supported the local traders. In order to restrict the competition of Saxon traders, "border fairs" were set up, where foreign traders sold their goods. Vlad moreover took military action against the Saxon traders, plundering the Bîrsa country a number of times.

The conflict between the prince and the great boyars — a consequence of the prince's centralizing policy — assumed violent forms, the prince suppressing a considerable number of his opponents. A permanent army recruited from among the court officials and the peasants and subordinated to the prince's authority superseded the private troops of the great landowners.

In 1459 Vlad refused to pay tribute to the Porte, and in the winter of 1461-1462 he attacked and destroyed the Ottoman garrisons on both banks of the Danube, from Zimnicea to the mouths of the river. An expedition headed by Sultan Mohammed II himself ensued. According to the Byzantine chronicler Laonic Chalcocondil, the Sultan had at this time the most powerful armies the Turkish Empire had been able to muster since the conquest of Constantinople. Vlad used the conventional tactics of the Romanian princes: laying waste the territory before withdrawing, and harassing the enemy. In the night of June 16, 1462, Vlad attacked the Sultan's camp and the success he thus won built up his Europe-wide fame. The Sultan occupied the capital city of the country — Tîrgoviște — which had been abandoned by the Wallachian prince, but without any political and military effect. By June the Ottoman army was withdrawing in disorder under the repeated blows of the Romanian forces.

Vlad the Impaler's victory could only have been effective if supported by a coalition of the forces of the Christian states. In the summer of 1462 the Turks resumed their attempt to subject Wallachia, this time with new tactics: it was no longer the Sultan that headed the forces along the Danube but Vlad's brother, Radu the Handsome, a docile instrument of the Porte who had no intention of striking at the position of the great boyars. The betrayal of the boyars and the hostility of Mathias Corvinus, king of Hungary, brought Vlad's rule to an end. The Romanian prince crossed the Carpathians and was imprisoned at Buda.

Vlad the Impaler had won European fame. His feats of arms, his energy, and the sternness with which he put down all opposition, placed him among the outstanding political figures of his age, although he became the prototype of the bloodthirsty tyrant under the name of "Dracula." It was King Matthias Corvinus who was responsible for blackening his name, for he wished to compromise the Romanian prince whose anti-Ottoman policy showed clearly that the Hungarian king had canceled his plans of an anti-Ottoman crusade. For the Romanian people Vlad the Impaler was a remarkable statesman and leader, who defended the independence of their country.

## 6. The Rule of Stephen the Great (1457-1504)

CHRONICLER Grigore Ureche described Stephen as "a well-balanced man, not in the least slothful, who knew how to cope with his work and could be found where you least expected him to be. Master of the craft of war, he went wherever he was needed so that seeing him his men would not disperse and for that reason there was seldom a war that he did not win. And when others defeated him, he did not lose hope for, when vanquished, he would rise above his vanquishers." Stephen reigned in Moldavia for half a century, strengthening the country politically, defending its independence and making of it one of the main political powers of Eastern Europe.

The fundamental problems Stephen was called upon to solve were: to do away with feudal division, centralize the state, and defend the country's independence. Outstanding political ability, mastery of the military art, and great determination were the grifts that helped Stephen to carry out these aims and brought him success. The political, diplomatic, and military measures taken by the Moldavian prince were part of a unitary system which was grounded in a broad concept of politics.

When he ascended the throne of Moldavia, the country had gone through a quarter of a century of internal struggles during which the great boyars had strengthened their position while Hungary and Poland had found the means of enforcing their suzerainty by installing their protégés on the throne. The boyars fought against Stephen's centralization program for they were used by now to having a nominal ruler on the throne. The opposition of the great boyars induced Stephen to find allies among other categories of Moldavian society: the lesser boyars, the townspeople, and especially the free peasantry. Stephen was thus able to build up a powerful army that enabled him to dispense with the troops of the great landowners and to cope with the threats from abroad. In implementing his centralization policy he had the support of "the brave", men of great worth risen from the people. The policy of the prince was radically changed, as shown by the system of remuneration: it consisted of incomes derived from the fines levied in the capacity of dignitaries of the ruling prince. The central authority now no longer bestowed prerogatives for the benefit of people who were thereby rendered immune. Privileges were granted to those who assisted the progress of the centralization policy. Throughout Stephen's reign, the great boyars systematically opposed the measures he took, for they were a threat to their political and military position. The struggle between the prince and the great boyars either assumed violent forms or was carried on by devious ways. The more important episodes in the opposition of the great landowners were the boyars' betrayal at Baia; the internal crisis of 1485-1486 and Stephen's defeat at Scheia which ensued from it; the boyars' opposition when Stephen named Bogdan as his successor and the energetic reprisals that followed. There was now a contradiction between the development of Moldavian society and feudal division, which had become anachronistic. Stephen's domestic policy provided Moldavia with the means of opposing the expansionist trends of the great neighboring powers and also of asserting itself in the international arena.

Immediately after ascending the throne Stephen started a military action in the outlying regions of Poland. This he did in order to strengthen his power and to avert the danger of new Polish interference for the benefit of the prince that had been removed from the throne. Stephen's inroads caused King Casimir of Poland to give up his plan of bringing Petru Aaron back to the Moldavian throne by armed intervention and simultaneously to abandon his plan of interfering in Moldavia's internal affairs. Though Stephen accepted Polish suzerainty according to the Overchelăuți Treaty of 1459, he gradually restricted it during his reign.

The attempt made by Matthias Corvinus, king of Hungary, to use Petru Aaron, who had left Poland for Transylvania, against Stephen, opened a period of conflicts in Moldo-Hungarian relations which culminated in the Hungarian king's campaign of 1467.

This campaign was not only due to Stephen's repeated inroads in the Szekler districts as reprisals against the support given by the Hungarian king to Petru Aaron. Matthias Corvinus had far more valid reasons: in 1465 the Moldavians had occupied Chilia and in 1466-1467 Stephen had supported the separatist movement in Transylvania. Furthermore, the Hungarian king was determined to impose Magyar suzerainty on Moldavia.

In the second half of November, the Hungarian army entered Moldavia along the banks of the river Trotuş and subsequently occupied and burned down the towns of Bacău, Roman, and Neamţ. Faced by an adversary of superior numerical force and mistrusting his boyars, Stephen withdrew to the north of the country. During the night of December 14, the Moldavian prince attacked the Magyar army by surprise at Baia and compelled Matthias, who had been wounded during the battle, to leave the country in great haste.

The victory at Baia was not exploited because of the treachery of a great number of boyars: a plot with the Great Vornic (Court Marshal) among its leaders was in preparation. Stephen discovered it and the reprisals that followed showed his determination to put an end to boyar anarchy.

Stephen's campaigns in Wallachia were the prelude to a great anti-Ottoman war which he undertook in order to avert the danger of his country being enslaved by the Porte. His hostilities against the Porte began when in 1473 he placed Laiotă Basarab on the throne of Wallachia, entrusting him with the mission of enlarging the anti-Ottoman front and of ensuring Moldo-Wallachian unity of action.

The struggle against the Ottoman threat made of Moldavia a factor in one of the dominant problems of the fifteenth century, giving its activities European significance. This accounts for Stephen's extensive international relations and for the wide response his feats of arms called forth.

Stephen's anti-Ottoman activities began within the comprehensive coalition which included Venice, Hungary — now more friendly to Moldavia — and Uzun Hasan's Turkish State. The coalition acted under the aegis of the Pope. In 1472 Stephen had entered into relations with the Turkic Khan, while in 1474, through the intermediary of Venice, he asked Pope Sixtus IV's support in his anti-Ottoman struggle.

It was also in 1474 that Stephen rejected the demand of Sultan Mohammed II that Chilia and Cetatea Albă should be ceded to him and refused to pay tribute to the Porte, thus openly severing relations with the latter. Early the following year an immense Turkish army under Soliman Hadamb, *beglerbeg* of Rumelia, marched into Moldavia. On the morning of January 10, 1475, Stephen took the Ottoman army by surprise at Podul Înalt, not far from Vaslui, inflicting a serious defeat on it. The widow of Sultan Murad II pointed to the seriousness of the defeat when she asserted that "the Turkish hosts had never suffered a more serious defeat." The victory called forth fervent response throughout Europe. The Pope wrote to the Moldavian prince: "Your feats of arms have made your name so famous that it is on everyone's lips". The Polish chronicler Jan Dlugosz described the Moldavian prince as "the worthiest to be entrusted with the duties of command and leader against the Turks."

But the Ottoman Empire could not accept a defeat which threatened its strategic position in Southeast Europe and in the basin of the Black Sea. Stephen himself warned the European powers that a new military campaign against Moldavia was inevitable and that a common action of the Christian states was necessary.

In the summer of 1475 an Ottoman fleet entered the port of Caffa, an important Genoese colony in southern Crimea, and conquered it. This had serious consequences for Moldavia. Henceforth, and for a long time to come, the Tartars in the Crimea, now dependent on the Porte, became the latter's political and military instruments.

With the Ottoman power installed in the Crimea, Stephen had to face a great threat. This induced him to strengthen his relations with Matthias Corvinus, whose suzerainty he recognized in the summer of 1475, though the act concluded on the occasion was more in the nature of a treaty of alliance.

In May, 1476, Sultan Mohammed II launched an expedition against Moldavia which was one of the greatest the Ottoman Empire had ever undertaken. Stephen withdrew, evading battle in the open field and laying waste the territory. Simultaneously, the Tartars overran the country, which compelled the Moldavian prince to divide his forces. Stephen said at a later date with reference to the Turks' attack: "They found me alone, with all my soldiers scattered about the country to protect their homes." With only his courtiers about him, Stephen tried to oppose the Turks at Valea Albă on July 26, 1476, but was defeated. The Sultan, however, did not succeed in his aim politically for he was forced to leave Moldavia on account of the stubborn resistance of the strongholds as well as because of the plague and famine which were playing havoc with the Ottoman army. Furthermore, he had been informed that an army corps was soon to come from Transylvania. The allied Moldavian and Transylvanian forces then took the offensive, entered Wallachia and placed Vlad the Impaler on the throne. Vlad, however, was soon to be killed by the boyars. In the years that followed Stephen endeavored to control the situation in Wallachia in order to coordinate the two countries in their anti-Ottoman struggle.

International developments after the death of Mohammed II enabled the Ottoman Empire partially to reach its aims in Moldavia: in 1484 the Turks occupied Chilia and Cetatea Albă, important economic and strategic centers, as a result of a surprise attack. In the years that followed Stephen endeavored to win back these two cities with the support of the Polish king, Casimir, who demanded in exchange that Stephen do homage personally and consequently accept rigorous vassalage. In the autumn of 1485 at Kolomea, Stephen took a vassal's oath, which he had evaded doing for a quarter of a century.

Polish support, however, proved insufficient to enable Stephen to win back the two cities. And when Poland made peace with the Turks in 1487, the Moldavian prince was placed before an accomplished fact and in his turn had to pay tribute to the Porte. This was in fact a redemption of peace.

When the rivalry between Poland and Hungary increased, Stephen sided with the Hungarian kingdom. He received from King Matthias Corvinus two important fiefs in Transylvania: Ciceu and Cetatea de Baltă. With the Moldavian princes in possession of these fiefs, the connections between Moldavia and Transylvania grew closer. Faced with the hostility of the Polish king, Stephen strengthened his alliance with Ivan III, grand duke of Moscow, and through the intermediary of the latter, with the Tartar Khan of the Crimea, Mengli-Ghirai. John Albert, Casimir's successor, despite the warnings of his brother Vladislav, now king of Hungary after Matthias Corvinus's death, intended to reduce Moldavia to subordination and even to install one of his brothers, Sigismund, on the throne. Under pretense of an anti-Ottoman campaign, the Polish king marched into Moldavia at the head of a great army, making for Suceava (1497). The stubborn resistance of that stronghold and the fear of being attacked by the superior forces of Stephen's allies caused John Albert to change his plans. On the way back to Poland, the Polish army suffered a serious defeat in the Cosmin woods. Two years later, through the intermediary of the Hungarian king, Stephen concluded a treaty with Poland which ended juridically also the situation created by the homage he had paid at Kolomea. Moldavia's position was now better than it had ever been. The attempts made by three great neighboring powers — Hungary, the Ottoman Empire and Poland — to subjugate it had failed. On July 2, 1504, the man whom contemporaries described as "most subtle and skillful in the craft of war" and who had fought 36 battles in defense of his country, passed away after having written the most splendid page in Moldavia's history. To all his successors, Stephen was a symbol of justice and independence.

# CHAPTER III

# The Beginnings of Ottoman Domination.
# The Epic of Michael the Brave

THE beginnings of Ottoman domination in the first half of the sixteenth century opened a new chapter in the history of the Romanian countries. The vigorous progress of the preceding century was checked by Ottoman expansion, which brought its influence to bear on the life of the Romanian people in all spheres. The great boyars extended and strengthened their power by enserfing free villages and increasing feudal impositions. The trend was for the nobility to seize all political power and to rise above the prince's authority. With Turkish domination assuming ever more oppressive forms, the three Romanian countries reacted by repeatedly participating in anti-Ottoman campaigns. This policy culminated in the epic of Michael the Brave at the end of the century.

## 1. The Peasant War Headed by Doja

MOSTLY owing to its more advanced economic development, Transylvania was in the early years of the sixteenth century the arena of class conflicts of a wider scope than anything Moldavia and Wallachia were witnessing at the time. In Transylvania the serfs' obligations were more oppressive than those in the two other Romanian countries. The development of the towns and intensified trade stimulated the growth of agricultural production and brought in its train increased feudal obligations. The peasantry reacted vigorously against the new conditions and was joined in its struggle by other sections of society impelled by their own interests. Preceded by successive movements of a local character over the space of a quarter of a century, the uprising of 1514 was to involve wide territories in Transylvania. It was a joint struggle of the Romanian and Hungarian peasantry, of the oppressed Szeklers, the poor sections of society in many towns, the workers in the salt and metal mines, and even certain rich townspeople and members of the lesser nobility, against the mighty magnates. The uprising started at Buda in Hungary and the occasion was the recruiting of an army for the crusade against the Turks: the serfs were offered the prospect of freedom if they enrolled in the army. The crusade was proclaimed in April, 1514. At the Rakos camp some 40,000 men, according to contemporary estimates, had gathered under Gheorghe Doja's command. The noblemen opposing the continuation of enrollment, together with the treatment meted out to the families of those that had enrolled, turned the anti-Ottoman campaign into a struggle against feudal domination. While the uprising was extending throughout Hungary and Transylvania, spontaneously or stirred up by Doja's men, the main army of the rebels advanced along the valley of the White Criş and of the Mureş towards Lipova and from there to Timişoara, where powerful forces of the nobility had entrenched themselves. Although the rebels won a number of victories, the more important of which were those of Nădlac and Cenad, and although they had made their way into some big towns such as Arad, Cluj, Sighişoara, and Bistriţa, the town of Timişoara resisted the siege. New forces sent from Buda or brought over by John Zapolya, voivode of Transylvania, came to the rescue of the nobility and on July 15 Doja's army was defeated. Five days later Doja was tortured to death: he was seated naked on a red-hot iron throne while his flesh was torn from his body by tongs. The other leaders of the rebel army were each subjected to various tortures. The peasant resistance, with battles being fought at Cluj and Biharea for example, was defeated throughout Transylvania.

Having inflicted cruel punishments on the participants in the uprising, the dominant class took advantage of the victory to issue regulations to be in force a long time. The Diet that met at Buda decided that the serfs should do labor service for 52 days a year (the convention of 1437 had stipulated only one day a year) and that the right of changing one's place of habitation should be abolished, "full and eternal serfdom" being enforced. This was the last step of enslavement. The Tripartitum Code, also named the Werböczi Code after the person who drew it up, sanctioned these measures. Actually the Code was not applied in Transylvania, where the serfs had a lesser number of days to contribute during the first

IV *Battle fought by Basarab I against Charles Robert in the mountains*
*(1330)*

V *The Bucharest Constitution. Water color by Costache Petrescu showing
a group of revolutionaries*

VI *The National Assembly held on May 3-5 | 15-17,
1848 on the Plain of Freedom in Blaj. Contemporary chromo-lithograph*

half of the sixteenth century, and it was differently carried out in every part of the country. The legislative measures instituted after the failure of the 1514 uprising aggravated the economic and juridical situation of the peasantry. They were part of the process whereby their exploitation was intensified and their servile dependence was tightened — a process characteristic of the districts east of the Elbe. The savage reprisals and the tasks enforced upon the peasantry were to make it impossible for them to cooperate with the ruling classes in the defense of the kingdom against the Ottoman power, at the time in full process of expansion. And the disaster that followed the defeat sustained at Mohacs in 1526 is to be accounted for by the lack of support from the peasantry no less than by the lack of unity and determination of the nobility.

## 2. The Romanian Countries in the New Stage of Ottoman Expansion

THIS was the time when the Ottoman Empire was ascending towards its greatest heights. With the conquest of Eastern Anatolia, Syria, and Egypt under Selim I (1512-1520), the Empire had doubled its territory, which now spread into three continents. Holding hegemony in the Mediterranean and expanding towards Central Europe, the Ottoman Empire came into a centuries-long conflict with the Habsburgs and this brought about a Turkish-French rapprochement. The struggle of the Habsburg and Ottoman Empires for Central Europe gave the Romanian countries the opportunity of renewing their fight for the recovery of independence.

The conquest of Belgrade in 1521, opened to the new Sultan, Suleiman I, the way towards Central Europe. During the first campaign, Suleiman brought the boundaries of his empire to the Danube and the Drave; in 1526 he defeated the Magyar army at Mohacs and three years later, in 1529, he reached the ramparts of Vienna. In Hungary the death of King Louis II, who had fallen at the battle of Mohacs, brought about a fierce struggle for the throne, the nobility being divided into supporters of John Zapolya, voivode of Transylvania, and of Ferdinand of Habsburg, brother of Emperor Charles V. While Ferdinand established his sway over the western and northern districts of the kingdom, John Zapolya, with the support of the Ottoman Porte and paying it tribute, succeeded in keeping the largest part of Hungary and the whole of Transylvania. But as Ferdinand was still bent on ruling the entire kingdom, Transylvania was often the theater of war between the two competitors. The struggle finally ended in 1538 when, in accord with the Treaty of Oradea, the Habsburgs were appointed heirs to Zapolya. When Zapolya died in 1540, the Sultan appointed the latter's son, John Sigismund, to the throne, and a year later, as a result of Ferdinand's attacks, Suleiman annexed the Hungarian territories that had been under Zapolya's sway, creating the Buda *pashalik* in 1541. There were now two Hungaries, one under the Habsburgs and the other under the Turks. John Sigismund, under the suzerainty of the Porte, kept the principality of Transylvania, which included the western districts of Banat and Crişana as well as certain counties of Hungary proper. This was the beginning of a new epoch in the political history of Transylvania, which had become a vassal of the Sultan and had been detached from the kingdom of Hungary, this being in keeping with its ancient tendencies towards autonomy. But Banat was annexed by the Turks in 1552 and organized into a *pashalik*, with Timişoara as its capital city. Part of Crişana was also incorporated in the *pashalik*.

Hungary's defeat at Mohacs and the transformation of Transylvania into a vassal of the Porte weakened the anti-Ottoman resistance system on which the struggle for independence of the Romanian countries had relied in the fifteenth century.

For more than three decades after Stephen the Great's death, Moldavia maintained with the Porte the relationships established through the struggle carried on by that great prince, although the tribute paid to the Turks had been increased under the reign of Bogdan III the One-eyed (1504-1517). The latter's successor, Ştefăniţă (1517-1527), evaded the request of sending his forces to Transylvania to assist the Sultan's troops; he defeated the Tartars in 1518 and even routed a Turkish army that was returning from a plundering foray in Poland (1524). The messengers sent by the Moldavian prince to the Polish king in 1522 voiced Moldavia's wish to be independent. As in the days of Stephen the Great, Moldavia was spurring on other countries to undertake a joint struggle in defense of the solidarity interests of the Christian states.

With Wallachia's growing dependence upon the Ottoman Empire, the threat to Moldavia became more and more serious. Yet efforts were still being made in Wallachia towards an anti-Ottoman orientation with the help of Transylvania and the Hungarian kingdom, and even towards incorporation into a wider international campaign. But these efforts could come to nothing with the presence of the Turks in their strongholds along the Danube, the constant struggle for power among the boyars, the conflicts between the latter and the ruling prince, and the Turkish support given to one or the other faction wishing to place a certain prince on the throne. The years during which Neagoe Basarab (1512-1521) ruled the country, in contrast with the short reigns that preceded and followed him, stand out as a period of internal stability and of important cultural growth, while in the field of foreign relations Wallachia carried out its obligation towards the Porte, accepted the suzerainty of Hungary, to counterbalance Ottoman influence, and established contacts with Poland and even with Venice and the Papacy. Christian solidarity, however, dit not assume the form of an anti-Ottoman struggle. There was only a cultural impact throughout the Orthodox countries of Eastern Europe.

After Neagoe Basarab's death, the Turkish governor of Nicopolis attempted to appoint Turkish dignitaries in Wallachia as a prelude to turning it into a *pashalik*, but the plan met strong opposition headed by Radu ot Afumaţi (1521-1529), who was assisted by the voivode of Transylvania. The many battles fought against the Turks along the Danube from 1522 to 1524 were the last tenacious efforts made against the Turks in Wallachia. In the end Radu himself accepted the princely dignity from the Sultan, though his being recognized by the Porte meant that the Sultan was compelled to accept a situation created by local forces.

Despite the adverse domestic and foreign conditions of the first decades of the sixteenth century, Wallachia made some progress in state organization, in particular during the reigns of Radu the Great and Neagoe Basarab. In Moldavia, Ştefăniţă's coming of age unleashed a conflict between the great boyars, who had ruled after Bogdan's death, and the young prince, who intended to assert his authority. The first stage of that conflict was marked by the beheading of Luca Arbore in April, 1523. In the autumn of the same year the boyars attempted to depose Ştefăniţă by force of arms. The prince, however, defeated the rebels with the aid of the lesser boyars and the free peasantry and secured undisputed sway.

The policy of strengthening central authority, of developing the state machinery and curtailing the privileges of the great boyars was also carried on with remarkable consistency by Ştefăniţă's successor, Petru Rareş (1527-1538). For a decade Moldavia again became a factor of importance in international policy. Petru Rareş's dominant idea was to defend Moldavia's independence, which meant opposition to the Ottoman Empire. But allowing himself to be drawn into the conflict between Ferdinand of Habsburg and John Zapolya in Transylvania, and resuming the struggle against Poland for the possession of Pokuţia, he split up his forces. He first sided with Ferdinand of Habsburg, then, during the campaigns he undertook in 1529, he assisted Zapolya, whose rule was ensured by the victory the Moldavian hosts won at Feldioara. As a result, the old possessions of the Moldavian princes in Transylvania were extended and the influence of Petru Rareş was felt in that province. It is not unlikely that the thought of ruling the whole of Transylvania occurred to him at the time.

The conflict between Petru Rareş and the Ottoman Empire began as a result of the assassination of Suleiman's envoy, Aloisio Gritti, followed by an alliance with Ferdinand in 1535 and by instigations to a general struggle against the Turks. But this son of Stephen the Great had many enemies: both the Moldavian boyars and the Polish king complained about him to the Sultan. The campaign of 1538 pinioned him between three enemies. With prompt moves, Petru Rareş defeated the Tartars at Ştefăneşti, obtained from the Poles the promise that they should withdraw from Hotin, and was preparing to face Suleiman's attack as his father, Stephan the Great, had done. His resistance was, however, ineffectual owing to the betrayal of the great boyars who went over to the Sultan's camp and accepted Ştefan Lăcustă (Stephen the Grasshopper) as ruling prince. This was the first Moldavian prince appointed by the Porte. A Turkish garrison was left with the prince and a district between the rivers Prut and Dniester in the southeast of the country was subjected to the authority of the Turkish governor at Cetatea Albă. The town of Tighina then became a Turkish stronghold and a few years later the town of Brăila in Wallachia was also annexed by the Ottoman Empire.

The defeat of Moldavia in 1538 by the Turks, without any battle being fought, meant an end to her independence. Petru Rareș, when resuming the throne three years later, continued to nurture his plans of freedom though he was unable to carry them out. The fall of Moldavia enabled the Porte to increase its sway over Wallachia. And when Transylvania passed under Turkish suzerainty at about the same time, the three Romanian countries entered a new stage in their history.

## 3. Beginnings of Ottoman Domination

THE beginnings of Ottoman domination over the Romanian countries, for which different forms of dependence in the past had paved the way, but which had been delayed by the struggles waged for a century and a half, was the result of international politics, of the disproportion between the forces of the two contenders, and of the constant struggles between the boyars and the ruling prince, which prevented any joint effort being made and enabled the Turkish Empire to act as arbitrator in domestic conflicts.

In this new stage of relationships with the Ottoman Empire, Moldavia and Wallachia could no longer pursue a foreign policy of their own. Their military forces, which had deteriorated on account of the new situation and of internal sociopolitical transformations, were obliged to participate in the expeditions of the Ottoman Porte under Turkish commanders. The very throne of the ruling prince was in the hands of the Sultan who confirmed the boyars' election of a prince or the succession to the throne, or else chose and appointed a prince, the latter practice tending to come into general use with time. A new prince was usually invested with his dignity at Constantinople and the ceremonial there was designed to emphasize his dependence on the Porte.

Any departure from the fulfillment of his obligations meant dethronement and sometimes the payment of yet more serious penalties. The ruling princes continued to be elected from among the members of the ancient princely families, even though the kinship with former ruling princes was sometimes fictitious. Before long, however, the Sultans began to appoint princes without taking into consideration their origin. Peter the Lame, for example, a descendant of the Wallachian princes, came to rule Moldavia (1574). Prompted by caution, for a long rule opened the possibility of independence, and by interest, for the prince that was appointed to the throne had to pay for the dignity, the Turks frequently changed the princes and this detracted from their authority which was, moreover, undermined by continued conflicts with the boyars. And it was also the boyars who encouraged the tendencies of the Porte to interfere in the domestic problems of the two countries.

The dominant feature in the history of the two Romanian states in the sixteenth century was their autonomy at a time when the Balkan peoples had for long been under the direct rule of the Ottoman authorities, their territories having been turned into *pashaliks*. And yet in the course of time the Sultan tended increasingly to consider the two countries as provinces of the Empire and their ruling princes as his beys. Nevertheless, even the Turks preserved the consciousness that these "provinces" of the Ottoman Empire had a different status. There was no longer any danger of their being turned into Turkish *pashaliks* and this was the consequence of the line the Empire took and of the economic progress of the Romanian countries, which made it clear that it was more profitable to exploit them through the agency of local bodies. The long resistance of the Romanian countries had taken place at a moment when the threat of their being suppressed as states had been most serious.

Consequently the Romanian states continued to preserve their internal system, their laws, a social pattern of their own, without the superimposition of a dominant Ottoman class. The Romanians thus enjoyed better conditions of political and cultural development and were a rallying point of the Christian peoples in the Empire — a center of support.

Transylvania's relations with the Porte were generally similar to those of the other two Romanian countries, with certain differences in favor of Transylvania, which were mostly due to the competition between the Habsburgs and the Ottoman Empire over its territory. Hence there was more freedom in foreign relations, far less Ottoman interference in domestic affairs and in general a political life that the suzerain power did not narrow down much. The prerogative of the diet to elect the prince of Transylvania was mostly observed, though the election had be to confirmed by the Sultan and a representative of the Porte was to be present when the prince was enthroned.

In Moldavia and Wallachia the Turkish ruling circles oscillated between applying conditions specific to the countries "conquered by force of arms" or to those that had submitted to them and had agreed to certain conditions and obligations.

The economic obligations enforced by the Porte on the three countries were generally the same, the difference being only the severity of their enforcement.

The main obligation, which was a sign of dependence of the state, was the payment of the tribute. Established before the period of actual Ottoman domination, like certain other political obligations, the tribute increased gradually, in particular in Wallachia: from 24,000 gold coins in 1542 to around 155,000 in 1593. In Moldavia it rose from 10,000 gold coins during the first reign of Petru Rareș to 35,000 under Bogdan Lăpușneanu (1568-1572), further rising to 65,000 for a brief span in 1593. In Transylvania the tribute was of 10,000 gold coins in 1541 — and had only risen by 50 per cent by the end of the century, the rise taking place in 1575.

Apart from paying tribute and making emergency contributions to meet the Empire's military needs, the ruling princes of the Romanian countries were under the obligation of annually sending gifts *(peshkesh)* to the Sultan and the Turkish high officials. In the latter half of the sixteenth century those gifts equaled the tribute in value.

Important gifts were also sent to Constantinople whenever there were changes among the high dignitaries of the Empire as well as on the occasion of outstanding events in the Sultan's family. The envoys of the Porte to the Romanian countries also received rich gifts.

But the greatest expenditure for Moldavia and Wallachia was occasioned by the appointments to the throne and the struggle of the princes to keep the throne. It was a time when most offices were bought in many parts of Europe and the throne of the Romanian countries became the object of transactions for the benefit of the Sultan and of the grand vizir in the first place but also for the benefit of other influential personages. Between 1581 and 1590 Wallachia paid at least 3,500,000 ducats when Mihnea and Petru Cercel contended for the throne.

Furthermore, annual supplies in kind were made, though these were of comparatively low value, as well as war supplies, either unpaid or paid at prices established by the Porte, and labor contributions: transportation, and workers for the maintenance of Turkish citadels, etc. Finally, the Romanian countries had to supply Constantinople with foodstuffs so that their trade was being increasingly monopolized by the Empire. Turkish and Eastern traders generally were frequent in Transylvania and very frequent in Moldavia and Wallachia, where their transactions were concluded under a privileged regime. Indeed a monopoly regime was gradually established for certain products the exports of which to other countries were forbidden as long as the requirements of the Porte had not been met.

Ever more intensive exploitation, in particular of Moldavia and Wallachia, resulted in a serious check on the development of Romanian society, at a time when the Ottoman Empire was in its decline. Savage taxation, especially of the peasantry, contributed, along with other factors, to arrest economic development and speed up the process of enserfment of the free peasantry. The progress made by Romanian society in the fifteenth century and in the first decades of the sixteenth was checked, the decisive factor in the slowing down of the rate of development being the loss of political and economic independence.

The living conditions of the peasantry deteriorated during the latter half of the sixteenth century. In both Moldavia and Wallachia those peasants who were still free were the butt of the boyars' attack, overburdened as they were with taxes that compelled them to sell their cattle, then the plots of land that were no longer joint property, and finally to become serfs.

The boyars' estates increased considerably, simultaneously with the increase in the number of dependent peasants, whose living conditions were greatly worsened. The serfs had to fulfill their obligations to the state, which were even more oppressive than those to the boyars, even though the taxes paid by the serfs were lower than those levied on the free peasants. As a result, most of the peasant homesteads fell into ruin by the end of the century.

The peasantry, whether free or dependent, strove their utmost to oppose resistance. They opposed the landowners by going to law to shake off serfdom, redeemed themselves whenever it was in their power to do so, made use of the right to change their place of habitation — a right that was gradually restricted by the landowners — and even rose in revolt as they did in Moldavia in 1536-1564, as also in 1581 and in 1591. Flight from the landowner's estate was most frequent, sometimes whole villages breaking away to seek safety in other parts of the country, to become outlaws or to go into exile beyond the country's borders. From Moldavia, they preferred to go over to the Cossack lands, and from Wallachia, across the Danube or into Transylvania.

Continuing their efforts to enslave the peasantry, the dominant class suppressed the right of displacement by tying men to the land for all eternity. This was the last stage of servitude current also in other countries of Eastern Europe as well as in Russia during the sixteenth century. "Michael's tie," the act enforcing this measure, probably dates from the first years of the reign of Michael the Brave. It applies not only to the serfs but also to the free but landless peasants who had settled on the boyars' estates and who were also deprived of the right of leaving the estate they had settled on. A similar decision was issued about the same time in Moldavia, though certain provisions were less hard on the peasants there. By tying the man to the land it became easier to levy the state taxes.

In Transylvania, where the peasantry had been tied to the land after Doja's uprising of 1514, labor service was thereafter greatly increased. This came as a result of the enlargement of the noblemen's allodial estate (the nobleman's reserve), which had to meet the increasing requirements of the main estate with its entire non-productive civil and military population, and also to supply the market.

The economic position of the nobility as a class was strengthened in all the three Romanian countries and this enhanced its preponderance in political life and accounts for the continuation of the feudal system in these countries for a long period.

In Transylvania ten years of frequent Turkish interventions after the Peace of Oradea in 1538 were unable to give any stability to the reign of John Sigismund on whose behalf Isabella, his mother, ruled in the capacity of regent. The only authority that succeeded in imposing itself was that of Bishop George Martinuzzi, appointed governor by the Turks and won over by the Austrians. Habsburg rule, as exercised by General Castaldo (1551-1556), was unable to ensure internal stability and to prevent the establishment of the Timişoara *pashalik* in 1552.

When John Sigismund returned to Transylvania in 1556 with the support of Alexandru Lăpuşneanu, prince of Moldavia, and Pătraşcu the Kind, prince of Wallachia, he was faced by the same unsteady internal situation which he was unable to dominate, and also by conflicts with the Habsburgs, which finally resulted in the loss of the northern "Partium" districts. When he died in 1571, the pro-Ottoman group with the Sultan's support brought Stephen Bathory to the throne. The prince's authority was strengthened after several years' struggle against the imperial forces and their partisans. At the close of 1575 Stephen Bathory was elected king of Poland, again with the support of the Porte. His brother, Christopher, ruled Transylvania with the title of voivode, but the country was actually under the effective leadership of Stephen. The throne was to be inherited by Sigismund, Christopher's son, heir apparent since 1581.

Stephen Bathory's reign was important insofar as Transylvania's autonomy was strengthened. During Bathory's rule in Poland (1575-1586), the principality became a reserve of military forces for Poland's policy in the east as well as of material resources. At the same time Transylvania was then able to assert itself on an international basis.

## 4. The Struggle for the Recovery of Independence

DESPITE Ottoman domination, Moldavia and Wallachia continued within the focus of European diplomacy. The many plans of anti-Ottoman struggle, made especially in the Habsburg camp, took into account the military assistance that might be given by the Romanian countries, for their warlike tradition, as well as their desire to recover their independence, were well known. Furthermore, the power of the Roman Catholics was offset by Protestant proselytism among the peoples of the Orthodox religion. These converging tendencies resulted in the appointment of Iacob Eraclid, also called Prince Despot (1561-1563), to the throne of Moldavia with the support of the Habsburg Empire, the German Protestants, and the Polish noblemen. Although Despot tried to stimulate the boyars by reminding them of the Romanians' Roman origin and of their right to freedom, he came into conflict with them and was unable to rise against the Ottoman Empire. Nor could Petru Cercel (1583-1585) build up a precise political orientation in Wallachia despite his generally admitted desire for independence. This Prince had been trained in Western Europe and had become prince of Wallachia with the support of Henry III, king of France.

It was only Prince John the Terrible (1572-1574) of Moldavia who brought things to a head by appealing to the forces of the entire country. Refusing to accede to the demand of the Porte to increase the tribute twofold, the Moldavian prince made ready to resist and even attacked Peter the Lame at Jiliştea when the latter was approaching the country's border with a Turkish-Wallachian army to oust him from the throne. The Moldavians reached Bucharest, where they enthroned a prince for a few days, then went over to Brăila and burned down that town which was under Turkish suzerainty. Hard blows were also dealt the Turkish forces in the Lăpuşna district, and in the vicinity of Tighina and Cetatea Albă. In early summer the Ottoman armies moved towards Moldavia in force, while the Tartars made their way from the East. At the Danube the Turks were able to cross the river, for Hetman Eremia did not defend the ford, according to the duty assigned to him. And once again the boyars betrayed their trust, for during the night that preceded the battle of Lake Cahul (June 10, 1574) a group of them crossed over to the Turkish camp and when the battle began the cavalry abandoned the prince and went over to the enemy. Prince John was left with the peasantry, the Cossacks who were fighting on his side, and a sound artillery, which was to prove of good use before a torrential rain ruined his ammunition. The Moldavians and Cossacks stood their ground before the successive attacks of enemy forces and even counterattacked successfully. In the end, however, they were forced to retreat, which they did in good order, despite the heavy losses they had sustained. At Roşcani, they fortified their position, digging ditches all round and making a camp of wagons. Surrounded by Turks and Tartars, they resisted without water for three days, when the prince decided to surrender. Although promises had been given on oath, he was brutally killed and his body was tied by the legs to two camels driven in opposite directions and thus quartered. The Tartars overran the country, laying it waste.

The anti-Ottoman struggle did not come to an end on the death of Prince John. A whole series of princes — brothers, sons, or nephews of Prince John, some of them real and some presumed — successively tried their luck during the rule of Peter the Lame. And this with Cossack support, for they put their hopes in the common people who were eager to shake off oppression both within and outside the country. Under the socio-political conditions prevailing at that time, their attempts had no chance of success.

## 5. The Three Romanian Countries Unite under Michael the Brave

MICHAEL the Brave (1593-1601) came to Wallachia's throne at a time when the exactions of the Ottoman Empire and of its representatives were putting the economy of the country in frightful jeopardy; at the same time ever more serious infringements of its autonomy heralded the installation of a new form of Turkish domination, here as in Moldavia. The only way out of the difficulty was to fight, and for a long space of time, with few exceptions, all strata of society rallied to the cause. An anti-Ottoman coalition — The Holy League — set itself the aim of driving the Ottoman Empire out of Europe, and the participants in the League counted on the assistance of the Balkan peoples who had been constantly on the move during the last decade of the century. The forces concentrated by the allies — who included the Pope, Spain, and the Austrian Habsburgs, with support given by the German princes and by certain small Italian states, including Tuscany — were of unequal force and insufficient to reach their objective. A great impulse was given to the war by the Romanian countries joining in the conflict. A new front was thus opened, and the Christian peoples of the Balkan Peninsula now cherished hopes of liberation.

Early in 1594 Sigismund Bathory, Prince of Transylvania, joined the League, and in the summer of the same year an alliance for an offensive was concluded between Michael the Brave on the one side and Sigismund and Prince Aaron of Moldavia on the other. In August, 1594, Prince Aaron also concluded a treaty with Emperor Rudolf II. A joint action of the three Romanian countries could thus be undertaken.

Before the end of the year, on November 13, Turks in Wallachia were killed and war was declared. Similar acts occurred in Moldavia. While the Transylvanian and imperial forces struck at the Ottoman forces in Banat, the two Romanian princes attacked the Turkish citadels along the Danube and carried the war beyond the river into Dobrudja and Bulgaria. The Turkish and Tartar forces coming to appoint new princes faithful to the Sultan were defeated in the battles fought at Putinei, Ştefăneşti, Şerpăteşti, Rushchuk, and Silistra.

Taking advantage of this difficult moment, the boyars concluded a treaty with Sigismund Bathory on May 20, 1595, subordinating Wallachia to the Transylvanian prince. They thus minimized Prince Michael's authority, and took upon themselves the much coveted right of ruling the country. This was to be carried out through the agency of a council of twelve boyars whom Sigismund alone could change, and the latter's agreement was also necessary when death sentences or confiscation of fortune had to be carried out. Between the prince of Transylvania and this Council, Michael had little authority, while the boyars, counting on the fact that the new master was a long way off, believed they had established the boyars' rule and provided a legal basis for it. The treaty included other provisions: Greeks were not allowed to hold any high offices in the country and no foreigners could own landed estates. The boyars thus removed all competition from abroad. At the same time Stefan Răzvan, appointed prince of Moldavia by Sigismund in place of Aaron, signed a similar treaty. Consequently, just before the great Turkish campaign began, Sigismund could call himself prince of Transylvania, Wallachia, and Moldavia. Subsequent developments, Michael the Brave's policy, and the war that followed with the demands and situations it created, prevented that title from becoming an actual fact and also delayed the establishment of the rule of the nobility in Wallachia.

In the summer of 1595 the Porte sent to Wallachia an expedition to re-establish its authority. Heading it was the new grand vizir, Sinan Pasha, for Ferhad Pasha had previously proved unable to cross the Danube. Michael chose to give battle at Călugăreni, where the river Neajlov flowed into Cîlniştea, a place bordered by wooded hills and furrowed by streams and fens. The battleground diminished the disproportion between the two forces. The Romanians fought bravely, the prince himself setting the example of gallantry, so that the Turks were finally compelled to withdraw, having incurred severe losses (13-23 August, 1595). But Michael could not risk a new battle without support from abroad. He withdrew to the mountains in expectation of Sigismund's arrival while Sinan Pasha fortified the cities of Bucharest and Tîrgovişte in preparation for a long rule which seemed to herald the transformation of the country into a Turkish *pashalik*.

Early in October Sigismund came to Wallachia with Transylvanian troops as well as with German soldiers sent over by Archduke Maximilian, and three hundred Tuscan horsemen. Stefan Răzvan, prince of Moldavia, soon joined him with his own forces. Having defeated the Turkish garrison at Tîrgovişte, Stefan Răzvan made for Bucharest while Michael and Sigismund advanced towards Giurgiu where Sinan's army was crossing the Danube. The Turkish rearguard was smashed and the Turks' prisoners, who had been reduced to slavery, were released. The citadel of Giurgiu was conquered after a two-day siege during which the technique of the Italians had proved of great help. The Ottoman expedition was an utter failure.

Wallachia had reconquered her freedom and simultaneously her Danube boundary. On the other hand, in Moldavia Polish armies headed by Chancellor Ian Zamoyski installed Ieremia Movilă as prince at the end of August. The latter was the representative of the great Moldavian boyars faithful to Poland. It was thus that the regime of the nobility was installed in Moldavia under the patronage of Poland, where it had also triumphed. But the juridical statutes of the rule of the nobility were not so well defined in Moldavia as in the treaties concluded by the Wallachian boyars with Sigismund. Having recognized Poland's suzerainty, Ieremia Movilă also asked for his ascendancy to the throne to be confirmed by the Porte. This he did with the consent of the Polish king who did not wish to be at war with the Ottoman Empire. In expectation of better times to come, the Porte was glad to confirm Ieremia Movilă as prince of Moldavia and, consequently, for about two decades Polish intervention restricted Ottoman domination in these parts. The anti-Ottoman front had suffered greatly as a result of Moldavia's defection. The attempt made by Stefan Răzvan in December, 1595, to recover his throne, was defeated.

In continuation of the war against the Ottoman Porte, Michael's forces, together with Serbian and Bulgarian outlaws, fought the Turks south of the Danube as far as the passes of the Balkan Mountains. Romanian resistance prevented the Tartars from crossing Wallachia and thus crowning the Ottoman victory at Keresztes over the Habsburg forces and Sigismund by laying waste the country. Turnu was the last Turkish citadel in Wallachia to be conquered. At the close of 1596 the Porte sent Michael the princely banner he had earned by his military actions, thereby acknowledging its incapacity to oust him from the throne and accepting a situation which had to be regarded as inevitable for the time being. Michael himself was content to cease hostilities against the Turks for a time so as to shake off all subjection to the prince of Transylvania as well as to better his relations with the boyars.

In order to strengthen his position, Michael established direct and lasting relations with Emperor Rudolf II, who in the summer of 1597 contributed to the upkeep of 4,000 mercenaries. On June 9, 1598, a treaty was concluded at Tîrgovişte whereby Michael accepted the emperor's suzerainty without the obligation to pay tribute and without the emperor being entitled to interfere in the country's internal affairs. The emperor also undertook to observe the right of hereditary succession to the Wallachian throne for Michael's family. The Wallachian prince was to receive continued military aid and an important role was assigned to him in the anti-Ottoman war.

Michael was forced to continue in his anti-Ottoman policy in order to strengthen his country's independence and his connections with the Balkan peoples, who awaited liberation. So in the autumn of 1598 Michael sent an army corps to Sigismund — now back in Transylvania after having ceded that province to Rudolf II a few months previously — to defend Oradea, which was besieged by the Turks. But a more important battle was being fought along the Danube where Michael repelled a Turkish inroad into Wallachia, crossed the Danube and during a two-month campaign defeated the Turkish forces at Vidin, Nicopolis, and Cladova and laid waste the territory between the Danube and the Balkans.

Sigismund's new withdrawal from the principality of Transylvania in March, 1599, caused Michael to focus his attention on that province, for the new prince, Cardinal Andreas Bathory, was carrying on a policy designed to bring him nearer to the Ottoman Empire. In this he had Poland's support. Combined Polish and Turkish support was to bring Simeon Movilă, brother of the Moldavian prince, to the throne of Wallachia. Michael was therefore under the necessity of conquering Transylvania to make safe his throne threatened from all sides, and also in order to enable Wallachia and Transylvania to continue their anti-Ottoman policy in the Balkans. Michael turned for support to the emperor, but the latter delayed sending forces, and he decided to undertake the conquest alone.

Well organized, the campaign for the conquest of Transylvania unfolded according to Michael's plans: on October 18/30, 1599, Andreas Bathory was defeated at Selimbăr and on November 1/13 Michael entered Alba Iulia, and hence

25. NEAGOE BASARAB AND HIS FAMILY

27. GRAVESTONE OF RADU OF AFUMAȚI

28. PRINCE JOHN THE TERRIBLE

MICHAEL WAIVODA WALACHIÆ TRANSALPINÆ VTRAQVE FORTVNA INSIGNIS: ET IN VTRAQ. EADEM VIRTVTE. ÆT. XLIII

cum priul. S.Cæ.Mᵗⁱˢ

Tanti facit nomen Christi: Maiestatem Cæsaris: Remp
Christianam, et Ecclesiæ, Sub Pont. Max. Concordiam: Suæ
prodigus, publicæ deuotus Saluti: etiamsi dira omnia,
et dii aduersarentur: Ficta obruens factis

S. Cæ. Mᵗⁱˢ Sculptor Ægi Sadeler ad viuum
delineauit, et D.D. Pragæ. 1601

30. THE BATTLE OF CĂLUGĂRENI (1595)

31. THE BATTLE OF TÎRGOVIȘTE (1595)

32. SINAN PASHA WITHDRAWING ACROSS THE DANUBE AT GIURGIU (1595)

33. THE BATTLE OF GORĂSLĂU WITH THE TROPHIES TAKEN DURING THE BATTLE (1601)

35. MATEI BASARAB

36. VASILE LUPU

forth for eleven months Transylvania was under the rule of the Romanian prince.

In order to build up the old coalition of the three Romanian countries, it was necessary to conquer Moldavia, a pawn in Poland's policy, where Sigismund Bathory, who wished to recover the throne of Transylvania, found shelter. The campaign of May, 1600, took only a few days. The citadel of Suceava surrendered and Ieremia was pursued up to Hotin where he was defeated in a short battle. Subsequently Ieremia withdrew into the citadel of Hotin and then crossed into Poland. Michael was now entitled to call himself "Prince of Wallachia, Transylvania, and Moldavia".

Back in Transylvania, Michael had to face the uprising of the Transylvanian nobility supported by the Saxon patriciate. The rebels moreover obtained the assistance of Georgio Basta, the emperor's general, and succeeded in defeating Michael's armies at Mirăslău (September 18, 1600). Simultaneously Zamoyski marched into Moldavia, re-installed Ieremia Movilă, and in early October continued his way to Wallachia with Simeon Movilă in his train. Michael was defeated by Zamoyski at Bucov on the river Teleajen on October 20. Another victory won on the river Argeș resulted in Simeon ascending the throne of Wallachia. The latter rallied the boyars round him and was confirmed in his office by the Porte.

Michael headed for Vienna and Prague in an effort to obtain the Empire's support. Developments in Transylvania, where Sigismund was re-elected as prince, favored him. Now supported by Basta, Michael set out to re-conquer Transylvania. Together they won a victory at Gorăslău over Sigismund's forces (August 3). In early July, Simeon Movilă had been driven out of Wallachia. Conditions again appeared to be favorable to Michael. But on August 9/19, 1601, he was killed by Basta's men in his camp at Cîmpia Turzii.

During the eight years of his reign Michael had liberated Wallachia from the domination of the Ottoman Porte, had enabled it to play an outstanding part in Southeast Europe and had achieved the political unity of the three Romanian countries. It was grand work with most important consequences.

The Romanian countries had united as a result of their joint struggle for the recovery of their independence. But over and above immediate circumstances, it was the result of historical solidarity built up over the centuries and for this reason it had been attempted in various forms: by Sigismund Bathory before Michael and was to be attempted by others after him. Michael, it is true, relied on the fact that the majority of the population in the three countries spoke the same language and had the consciousness of belonging to the same people. But this could not have been a decisive factor at the time, and Michael, whose political activity included certain measures favoring the Romanians in Transylvania, did not base his rule on it, for this would have required the overthrow of the entire system of political privileges on which the Transylvanian constitution depended, and the inception of a social revolution which Michael, himself the representative of a feudal state, had no means of achieving. For all these reasons, Michael's rule in Transylvania could never have been the rule of the Romanians for the Romanians. If made permanent, it would naturally have assumed an ever more pronounced Romanian character. The same holds true for the unification achieved by Michael. Unification had to take into account the historical realities of the three political bodies that were to be ruled by one supreme leader. Obviously, here again time alone would have allowed the consequences of a unitary rule to mature. But to make it longlasting, it would have had to resist the pressure of the decisive social forces within the three principalities, and these were bound up with the ancient tradical tions of autonomy represented by Sigismund Bathory in Transylvania and by Ieremia Movilă in Moldavia. And the political forces outside them — Poland and the Ottoman Empire — also had to be taken into account. Michael could only have resisted such pressure by his own solidly built up power or by efficient aid received from the Habsburg Empire.

But Wallachia could not offer Michael the necessary power. The boyars' opposition there increased steadily, undermining the authority of the ruling prince, and Wallachia was the main support of his power. The country was exhausted by wars and by the effects of prolonged exploitation by the Porte, and the masses, who had supported the anti-Ottoman struggle, could not wish a system, exclusively in the service of the landowners, to be strengthened. To the very end Wallachia provided Michael with military forces, but the country could not be relied upon to provide sufficient forces to hold the two other principalities in subjection. A permanent army equipped with the war engines used at the time meant not only having a considerable number of men at one's disposal but also great material resources for the men's upkeep and for armament.

Michael received no assistance from the Habsburgs: no military support to supplement his own forces, no moral support such as a great power could have provided. The Habsburg Empire, supposing it had a purpose overruling its constant hesitations, only aimed to extend its rule, and Michael did not intend to act merely as a tool. Consequently, his fall was to be expected, and it was also to be expected that the fruits of the crime Basta had ordered to be perpetrated would not be reaped by the Empire.

On Michael's death a new situation was created in the relations of the Porte with Wallachia and the two other countries. For a century the effects of the united struggle of the Romanian countries, whose main leader had been Michael the Brave, made themselves felt, and all subsequent attempts at resistance were inspired by Michael's feats of arms. And unification, though achieved for such a brief space of time, also left its traces. Secretly it made its way into the people's consciousness and was added to everything that had brought the Romanians together, until it finally became a symbol, heralding the building up of a unitary Romanian state.

# CHAPTER IV

# The Heritage of Michael the Brave

AFTER prolonged efforts, the Porte restored its domination over the Romanian countries at the beginning of the seventeenth century, but the stubborn resistance they opposed compelled it to change its exploitation system and to curtail its demands. Under the new circumstances thus created, the boyars strengthened their authority, increasing the feudal obligations of the peasantry, while boyar factions contended for control over the ruling prince.

The offensive of the Christian powers after Vienna had been relieved altered the international position of the Romanian countries, which now became the object of competition among three great rival powers. At the close of the seventeenth century Transylvania, though part of the Habsburg Empire, passed under the suzerainty of the Porte.

## 1. Restoration of Ottoman Domination

THE tragic death of Michael the Brave brought in its train the restoration of Ottoman domination over the three Romanian countries, though in each one of them this was achieved only by dint of great efforts.

In Transylvania the struggle between the Habsburgs and the Porte continued until 1606 when peace was signed at Zsitvatorok without either side having obtained any real success. The rivalry between the empires favored the struggle between the factions of the nobility. It was only after Gabriel Bethlen (1613-1629) had been brought to the throne with Turkish support that anarchy came to an end. The Ottoman regime was now restored in Transylvania for the next three quarters of a century.

In Wallachia the policy of independence and the fighting spirit were sustained after the death of Michael the Brave. For a brief spell the powerful Buzescu family ruled the country, then Radu Șerban (1601—1602—1611) came to the throne. But his installation was confirmed by the Porte only after he had defeated his rival, Simeon Movilă, ultimately supported by the Tartars, and Radu Mihnea who came with Turkish support, and had gained a brilliant victory over the prince of Transylvania near Brașov. However, neither this victory, nor that of 1611, gained also in the vicinity of Brașov over Gabriel Bathory, led to the installation of Habsburg domination in Transylvania. While Radu Șerban was fighting in Transylvania, the Turks brought Radu Mihnea (1611-1616) to the throne of Wallachia, the latter having justified the confidence of the Porte by the services he had rendered.

The restoration of the Ottoman regime in Moldavia took place in 1611. After the death of Ieremia Movilă in 1606 and the short reign of Simeon Movilă (1606-1607), the throne had been maintained in the Movilă family, despite the fierce rivalry between the descendants of the two princes. But in order to end Polish interference and secure domination over the country, towards the close of 1611 the Porte appointed Ștefan Tomșa to the throne, at the time occupied by Constantine Movilă. Ștefan Tomșa did his best to break the power of the great boyars who had ruled under the Movilă princes, but the Porte ultimately entrusted the throne to Radu Mihnea with the mission of rallying the boyars round him and of making peace in this border country.

The new wave of Ottoman domination that swept over the Romanian countries came under conditions that were altogether different from those prevailing at the close of the sixteenth century. There was no longer any danger of their being turned into *pashaliks*, and although princes were frequently sent from Constantinople without the boyars being consulted, this did not create a permanent system. Representatives of the Porte came more rarely than heretofore to the Romanian countries, and direct interference of the Turks in domestic affairs was less harsh.

The economic obligations of the Romanian countries to the Porte changed to a certain extent. When Radu Șerban of Wallachia resumed relations with the Porte, the tribute amounted to 32,000 ducats, or about 20 per cent of its maximum value at the close of the sixteenth century. The tribute paid by Moldavia was about 30,000 ducats. The annual gifts made to the great dignitaries of the Porte had also decreased in value. At the end of the sixteenth century the heaviest expenditure was incurred by the prince on his accession to the throne. In the first decades of the sixteenth century conditions in this respect were quite different. When Radu Mihnea was ousted from the throne in the spring of 1611, Radu Şerban offered up to 100,000 ducats to be recognized as ruling prince. In 1623 it is estimated that no more than 100,000 gold ducats were paid by Radu Mihnea for his own installation as prince of Moldavia and that of his son, Alexandru Coconul, in Wallachia. A few years later, however, in 1629, Radu Leon paid 200,000 ducats to obtain the throne.

It is obvious therefore that after Michael's mighty struggle for independence, the obligations of the Romanian countries towards the Porte were much less onerous than at the end of the sixteenth century. As for Transylvania, the tribute was again reduced to 10,000 ducats which was the sum paid before 1575. It is true that when Matei Basarab became prince of Wallachia through force of arms, the tribute was doubled and the investiture expenses, which also included the debts incurred by his predecessor, rose to 400,000 ducats according to certain authorities. But this was in payment for a reign that was to last for more than two decades. As in the sphere of political relations, the second half of the century was to bring about an increase in material impositions to the Porte, without ever reaching the level of the days preceding the reign of Michael the Brave, until the eighteenth century.

## 2. Economic and Social Life

LIGHTER obligations towards the Ottoman Empire enabled on the one hand a comparatively fair rebuilding of Romanian economy, which had been on the brink of ruin at the close of the preceding century, and, on the other hand, some progress, though slow as yet, in certain branches of production. Documents mention that land had been cleared, this indicating an increase in the areas under crops, though travelers who came to these countries were amazed to see wide expanses of most fertile land lying fallow. Human settlements increased in number, which is a sign of demographic as well as of economic growth. Winter wheat sown after the land had been ploughed twice, was superseding spring wheat. Vine-growing was also developing. During the latter half of the seventeenth century maize began to be grown and was to become the peasants' staple food. In Transylvania maize had been grown since the beginning of the century. Tobacco was also grown in the Romanian countries at the time.

Sheep, pigs, and cattle were bred for foreign trade and were also a main source of income for both the peasant homestead and the feudal landowners. Preda Brâncoveanu, it is said, sent 1,000 oxen to Constantinople every year.

From the sixties of the century there were indubitable signs of progress in the production of craftware: new branches emerged and the crafts were organized in guilds. As a result, the towns of the Romanian countries developed into traders' and craftsmen's centers, though most of them were still small and relying on agriculture. There were weekly fairs and also large fairs that drew buyers and sellers from distant countries. In the seventeenth century inns were built for the traders, who also had their guilds. The most important towns were Jassy in Moldavia and Bucharest in Wallachia. Under Constantine Brâncoveanu, Bucharest was reported to have had 50,000 inhabitants. With a busy trade and an advanced cultural life as its main features, it was one of the important centers of Southeast Europe.

In the seventeenth century, Transylvania continued to be a land of grain, wine, and cattle. Its craftware production with an organization of older date than in the other Romanian lands was also of greater proportions — a supplier of the home and foreign market. The guilds already had long-standing traditions behind them and constituted powerful bodies, although social contradictions were rife within them and the central power occasionally took measures to curtail their privileges. There was a busy city life in Braşov, Sibiu, Cluj, Bistriţa, and Sighişoara. More advanced forms of production of a manufactory nature were occasionally met with: at Alba Iulia there was a workshop casting big guns and at Porumbacul de Sus a glassware shop. Similar glassware shops were founded in Wallachia by Matei Basarab and Constantine Brâncoveanu.

In Moldavia and Wallachia salt mining was carried on extensively and from the reign of Matei Basarab the ore deposits at Baia de Aramă and Baia de Fier were also mined. Exploitation of the subsoil held a far more important place in the economic life of Transylvania than in the other Romanian countries. Salt was extracted here as well as silver, iron, and gold, the latter being obtained in Moldavia and Wallachia only from the mountain streams. In the second half of the century mercury was also extracted, in particular at Abrud and Zlatna. Trade capital was invested in the mines which used equally serf and paid labor.

Foreign trade in Moldavia, Wallachia as also in Transylvania was carried on mostly with the Ottoman Empire and with each other, though relations were maintained also with other countries, for example Poland, the Habsburg Empire, and Venice. This was the time when in Transylvania trading companies were set up: Greek traders founded a company in Sibiu in 1636, while similar companies were started in other towns. In 1672 the Oriental Company was founded — a powerful concern playing an important part in Transylvanian foreign trade. Such associations included Romanian traders, whose importance was to increase considerably during the following century.

Economic progress in the seventeenth century did not involve a rise in the living conditions of the bulk of the population, which was made up of peasants. In Wallachia the peasants were tied to the land with great strictness, as established by Michael the Brave's deed. In Moldavia a serf who ran away from the boyar's estate could no longer become a free peasant after a number of years, that right having been abolished in the second half of the century. The Code of Laws printed during the reign of Vasile Lupu confirmed the right of the landowners to pursue the runaway peasants.

While the process of enserfing the free peasantry continued and feudal estates grew more extensive (although certain villages succeeded in freeing themselves in the first half of the seventeenth century), serfdom became ever more oppressive. The serfs could be moved from one estate to the other by the landowner, and could even be sold without their holding, being consequently separated from their land and reduced to a condition of sheer slavery. There were cases when serfs recovered their freedom by giving the landowner gypsy slaves, one head for another.

In the second half of the century the cases of serfs being released from serfdom became more frequent, in particular in Wallachia, but the conditions of the men thus freed did not change greatly; a few of them recovered their land also, the remainder being obliged to settle on the boyars' estates and work for them. Initially they were bound to give the landowner only a share of the crops but with time they had also to perform labor services, a practice which came into almost general use towards the end of the century. Consequently, their dependence on the landowners was increased.

In Transylvania also the powerful feudal structure of society was preserved and this prevented a switch over to a more advanced stage of organization of production relations. Part of the peasantry remained free, as in Moldavia and Wallachia. This occurred especially among the Szeklers, and on the lands of the emperor and the king, where the Saxon sedes were located and where there were also many Romanians. Făgăraș, Haţeg, and Zarand were districts where the ancient freedom of the Romanians was preserved.

But even in these districts serfdom made great strides so that the number of free Romanian and Szekler peasants diminished and even the free Saxon peasants on the emperor's lands were becoming increasingly dependent on the dominant class. The right to pursue runaway serfs was laid down in the codes of law drawn up in those days: *Approbatae constitutiones* (1653) and *Compilatae constitutiones* (1669).

The nobility was becoming even less homogeneous than previously as a class, owing to frequent cases of ennoblement in the seventeenth century. Endeavoring to create a social basis that would oppose the tendency of the upper nobility towards domination, and to increase their military power, the princes of Transylvania invested with the rank of nobility people recruited from the free population, whether Hungarian, Szekler, or Romanian, and even those in the higher categories of serfdom. Owing little land, with only a few serfs to work for them or without any servile labor at their disposal, the new nobles were, from the economic and political points of view, in a situation that differed totally from that of the upper nobility. The latter continued to be the social class that contended with the prince for the exercise of state power, for it possessed widespread estates with many serfs, as well as fighting men and sometimes even strongholds. Consequently they dominated the diet. After the disturbances of the first decade of the century, Gabriel Bethlen installed a régime of internal political stability, which was mostly maintained by his successors — George Rakoczy I (1630-1648) and George Rakoczy II (1648-1660). The Transylvanian prince thereby acquired much freedom of action and Transylvania was thus able to play an important international part during the decades that followed.

## 3. *Transylvania During the Thirty Years' War*

MAINTAINING relations with the Porte, to whom he was compelled to cede Lipova and to give support in its military campaigns against Poland, Gabriel Bethlen first put an end to the Habsburgs' attempts to undermine his rule; this he did by concluding the Treaty of Tyrnavia in 1615 and subsequently starting an offensive on the territories of the Habsburg Empire. The outbreak of the Thirty Years' War (1618-1648) was an opportunity for him to carry out his plans of conquering Habsburg Hungary and of weakening the Catholic forces while supporting the Protestants, he himself being a Calvinist, and endeavoring to strengthen that faith in Transylvania. Allied to the Czechs, Bethlen marched to the ramparts of Vienna in the autumn of 1619. Although there was nothing real about the title of king of Hungary bestowed by a diet that autumn, nor about the title of king of Bohemia received from another diet a year later, Gabriel Bethlen succeeded in the annexation of seven counties of the western regions. This was stipulated in the Peace of Mikulov in 1622, which was successively renewed after fresh military interventions, at Vienna in 1624 and at Bratislava in 1626.

Relations with Moldavia and Wallachia played an important part in Gabriel Bethlen's foreign policy. He even worked out a plan — suggested no doubt by the attempts previously made by Sigismund Bathory and Michael the Brave — of building up the kingdom of Dacia, which would include the three Romanian countries, to be placed under his rule with the consent of the Porte.

Gabriel Bethlen's death was followed by the struggle for power waged by the various factions of the nobility, as well as by Habsburg attempts to reconquer Transylvania or at least to recover the seven counties. When George Rakoczy I's throne became more secure, he put an end to these disturbances and Transylvania was able to participate again in the Thirty Years' War. Following negotiations, an alliance was concluded by Transylvania, France, and Sweden in 1643. Supported by the main anti-Habsburg powers an subsequently by forces from Moldavia and Wallachia, George Rakoczy started a campaign early in 1644, Transylvania taking an active part in the war for a year and a half. Intent on getting rid of one adversary, the Habsburgs were glad to conclude peace at Linz in 1645 on terms similar to those of the Treaty of Mikulov. At the close of the war, Transylvania sent delegates who stood alongside those of the other powers, when the Peace of Westphalia was concluded in 1648.

## 4. *The Régime of the Nobility*

WHILE in Transylvania a comparatively powerful central authority was exercised by the prince — Gabriel Bethlen and subsequently the two Rakoczy princes — the régime of the nobility — of the boyars — was installed in Moldavia and Wallachia; the great boyars dominated the political life of those countries through the intermediary of the Prince's Council and by holding the main public offices. It was a régime that relied on accepted practices rather than on definite institutions so that it had no uniformity while it was enforced. The authority of the ruling prince was occasionally enforced more potently, when the internal balance of forces, or the personality of a prince, made this possible.

Installed in Moldavia under the aegis of Poland at the close of the sixteenth century, the boyars' régime began to be patronized by the Porte when Radu Mihnea came to the throne. This prince succeeded in co-operating with the great boyars, the prince thus being allowed a fairly wide margin of power.

This was achieved especially during Radu Mihnea's second principate (1623-1626), when the throne of Wallachia was occupied by his son, Alexandru. In Wallachia, where the efforts of the great boyars to monopolize the power were of long duration, the new political régime acquired greater stability after the restoration of Ottoman domination. In both countries a prince would rule for a brief spell, from a matter of months to several years, for frequent changes suited the interests of the Ottoman Empire and of his dignitaries as well as the régime itself, competition aligning the boyars in rival factions or parties, which in support of another claimant to the throne occasionally offered open battle to the ruling prince. The struggle between the various factions was fanned by the different trends adopted in foreign policy. In Moldavia, for example, there was a group of boyars attached to Poland, in particular under the Movilă princes and their kinsman, Miron Barnovschi Movilă (1626-1629, 1633).

Consolidation of Ottoman domination in Moldavia with the discarding of Polish interference, formed the basis of Turco-Polish conflicts which culminated in the expedition of Sultan Osman in 1621. The latter, however, was unable to advance further than Polish-occupied Hotin, where the Poles supported by the Cossacks offered bitter resistance.

The attempt made by Gaspar Graziani to free Moldavia by force of arms was also part of the Turco-Polish wars. Appointed ruling prince by the Porte in 1619, the Dalmatian Graziani joined the Poles and, despite the opposition of his Council, decided to end Ottoman domination. At Tuțora on the Prut, the Polish-Moldavian forces were surrounded by the Turks and Tartars, and before the Polish army, in a desperate situation and having incurred heavy losses, could retreat, Gaspar Graziani with only a few followers had already left the camp. He was killed by two of his boyars in the vicinity of Jassy in September, 1620.

An internal problem with most serious consequences was the appointing of Greeks to high offices and their coming into possession of landed estates. Plots in great numbers were then hatched and even open battles fought against the ruling prince. The number of Greeks about the prince — kinsmen, creditors, reliable collaborators, clients, etc. — had greatly increased as a result of the restoration of Ottoman domination in the early seventeenth century and the frequent appointment by the Porte of princes who had lived among the Greeks in Constantinople. There was consequently much competition from foreign elements in the exercise of high offices and, moreover, the prince was thus offered instruments that were independent of the great boyars so that the system was a threat to the boyars' régime. To a certain extent, insofar as the throne represented the authority of the Ottoman Empire, it was also a blow dealt at the autonomy of the country.

In Wallachia the movement against the Greeks began when plots were hatched by them against Radu Mihnea and Alexandru Iliaş. When the second plot was revealed the Greeks were bitterly attacked, elements from wide sections of society taking part in the movement, which occasionally assumed the aspect of a peasant uprising against the boyars.

In Moldavia there was a general resistance movement against Alexandru Iliaş, the boyars also calling upon the courtiers and the peasantry to support them. The latter congregated in large numbers under the impulse of fiscal oppression. A number of Greek boyars were killed and the prince was compelled to leave the country (1633). It was Vasile Lupu who was to benefit by this movement for he was appointed by the Porte without any of the boyars being consulted.

Anti-Greek reaction was also shown in the boyar opposition, with a wider popular movement joining in, against Prince Leon Tomşa (1629-1632) in Wallachia. In 1631 under pressure of the anti-Greek current, the prince was compelled to promulgate a law giving satisfaction to the autochthonous boyars. A number of measures were taken against the Greeks: all Greeks, with the exception of those married to Romanian women, were to leave the country and their estates to be confiscated and given over to the prince. Fiscal decisions were made for the benefit of the boyars, of the mercenaries, the prince's chancellors and the priests. Other decisions were made concerning the election of Metropolitans and bishops, the aim being that the Patriarch of Constantinople should not send Greek prelates; Greek monks were to quit the monasteries, and the Romanian monasteries which had been dedicated to religious institutions in other countries were to shake off their dependence.

Apart from fiscal and juridical privileges and the elimination of Greek competition, the boyars, who profited most by the decisions of 1631, also strengthened their title of ownership over the landed estates through extension of the right of bequeathal. Despite these concessions, Matei of Brâncoveni continued the struggle against the prince and finally obtained the throne with the help of internal forces and of the pasha of Silistra. Not far from the monastery of Plumbuita on the outskirts of Bucharest, Matei, subsequently to be called Matei Basarab, defeated an army of Moldavians, Tartars, and Turks who were on their way to install Radu Iliaş, newly appointed by the Porte. The latter recognized the change made on the initiative of domestic factors—which meant recognition of the country's autonomy and of the stand taken against the increasing part played by the Greeks—and granted the banner of the principate to the new ruler.

## 5. *Matei Basarab and Vasile Lupu*

THE reigns of Matei Basarab (1632-1654) and Vasile Lupu (1634-1653) are noted as periods when the prince's authority was increased — though within the limits of the boyar system and of Ottoman domination; when intensive political activities brought about an extension in foreign relations, and when culture and art showed outstanding achievements. These reigns were of long duration, due to a certain stability in the relations between the prince and the political forces of the country as well as to generally favorable international circumstances. Doubtless the resumption in 1635 of the war of the Ottoman Empire against Persia, which ended in 1639, and the Turkish campaigns against Venice for the conquest of Crete, which began in 1645, were favorable to the Romanian countries.

It is important to note that comparatively large military forces were built up in the Romanian countries at this juncture. Thus Matei Basarab had a strong army made up of the lesser gentry with offices at Court, and of horsemen and mercenaries, which included infantrymen called *seimeni*, as permanent forces. To these were added the hosts of the great boyars and the peasants recruited in time of war. The army of Vasile Lupu, when his power was greatest, was not far below that of his neighbor. The economic progress made during the first decades of the century gave the prince the means of keeping up these forces but, nevertheless, the expenditure required for the purpose, the increased obligations towards the Ottoman Empire, the wide constructive activities, and, in Moldavia, the great pomp of the prince's court, greatly increased taxation.

The relations among the three Romanian countries were also one of the factors of stability, though oscillations were not infrequent. Finally, the personality of the two princes, varying greatly but both remarkable, should be taken into account. Matei Basarab must be regarded as the type of the "local prince" with a realist political outlook and relying on tradition. Vasile Lupu, impelled by the will to conquer — with his eyes also on Wallachia — found it suitable to establish close connection with the Greeks at Constantinople, supporting and, at the same time, dominating them. Out for prestige, the rigorous ceremonial of his court savored of the "imperial". Both princes desired their country's independence and were skillful enough to ensure a certain amount of freedom. Both succeeded in asserting the existence of their states in the polity of Central and Eastern Europe. They were great military commanders always at the head of their armies, indefatigable in founding religious institutions, and showing much interest in culture.

Matei Basarab's relations with George Rakoczy I, who had helped him when he was in exile in Transylvania, date from the beginning of his reign. The pact of friendship and mutual assistance that linked the two countries, the Transylvanian prince being recognized as preeminent, was repeatedly renewed, with Matei annually sending gifts to Rakoczy. And the pact proved of good use to the two princes in their relations with the Porte. When the Sultan decided to depose Rakoczy in 1636, Matei proposed that as a preventive action the Transylvanian prince should take the offensive and carry the war beyond the Danube. He offered assistance and pointed to the prospect of a wider coalition with the participation in it of the Holy Roman Empire and of the king of Poland. He even applied to Emperor Ferdinand II to this end but without success for the imperial forces were busy fighting in the Thirty Years' War.

In 1637, when Vasile Lupu made his first attempt to bring Wallachia to subjection on behalf of his son, John, who had received the throne from the Porte, Matei Basarab obtained Transylvanian support. The preparations made by Matei and the Sultan's change of mind reduced the war to a mere clash at Rîbna, after which Vasile Lupu withdrew from the contest. In 1638 the Moldavian prince concluded with George Rakoczy I a pact similar to that previously concluded by Matei Basarab and, consequently, when Vasile Lupu engaged in a new campaign against Wallachia in 1639, there was no Transylvanian support forthcoming to the Wallachian prince. This time Vasile Lupu's son was to remain as prince of Moldavia while Vasile Lupu himself was preparing to become prince of Wallachia, as decided by the Sultan. Vasile Lupu had already taken upon himself the title of prince of the two countries, when the Moldavian armies were defeated at Ojogeni on the river Prahova. Matei Basarab's military success induced the Porte to allow him to keep the throne of Wallachia.

The three Romanian countries continued to foster relations through the bilateral agreements between Transylvania and each of the two other Romanian countries, but the conflicts between Moldavia and Wallachia decreased their efficiency. Wider possibilities arose when the princes of Moldavia and Wallachia made peace in 1644. In 1640 Matei Basarab had again contacted the Habsburg Empire to induce it to begin a war against the Ottoman Empire, but Emperor Ferdinand III refused to act, as his predecessor had done. With the same aim in view, Matei approached Venice as well as Poland.

When George Rakoczy II (1648-1660) became prince of Transylvania, the relations of Moldavia and Wallachia with that province continued. But it 1650 Moldavia was attacked by the Cossacks allied to the Tartars, pressure being thus exercised on Vasile Lupu to draw him away from Poland and into the alliance of Hetman Bohdan Chmielnicki. Ultimately an alliance was concluded and in 1652 Vasile Lupu's daughter, Princess Ruxandra, married Bohdan's son, Timuş. An understanding was also reached between Matei Basarab and the Cossacks. Vasile Lupu was shortly after compelled to take refuge in Poland (1653), for part of the boyars, rallying around Chancellor George Stephen, brought the latter to the throne with the assistance of George Rakoczy II and Matei Basarab.

A few weeks later, however, the new Moldavian prince was driven away by the Cossacks and, resuming the throne, Vasile Lupu with Cossack support marched against Wallachia, also having his eyes on Transylvania. Matei Basarab's hard-fought but crushing victory at Finta again brought George Stephen to Moldavia's throne and Vasile Lupu spent the rest of his life in Constantinople. In 1654 Matei Basarab died after a long rule, and Constantine Şerban (1654-1658), Radu Şerban's illegitimate son, succeeded to the Wallachian throne. The Porte accepted the two princes.

## 6. Uprising of the Seimeni. The Anti-Ottoman Struggle

POLITICAL relations among the three Romanian countries were resumed, with Transylvania as the center; they were used mainly as an instrument of repression to serve class interests. During the last year of Matei Basarab's reign the Doro-banţi foot soldiers and the *seimeni* mercenaries had caused a number of disturbances and the *seimeni* of Moldavia undertook a similar action in 1654. On February 17, 1655, the most violent uprising of the seventeenth century broke out in Wallachia. It was known as the Seimeni's uprising, the latter being its most active elements. The uprising included vast sections of the people, which shows that through feudal and fiscal exploitation social antagonism had reached an acute stage.

Because of Constantine Şerban's decision to abolish the Seimeni corps, the Dorobanţi, in sympathy with the latter, rose in protest although the Seimeni were mercenaries and mostly of Balkan origin while the Dorobanţi were natives of the country. The movement of protest assumed quite early the most violent forms and a considerable number of boyars — the most powerful and richest — were killed and their houses plundered. Other mercenaries and local soldiers, including the numerous cavalry corps, joined in the movement which extended rapidly to various towns — Bucharest, Tîrgo-

vişte, Ploieşti, and Buzău — as well as to the villages. Numerous craftsmen, the poorer population of the towns, and the
dependent peasantry took action alongside the rebel troops,
being prompted by interests of their own, though related to
those of the soldiers. The rich merchants and the boyars in
their country houses were attacked; the rebels refused to carry
out their feudal obligations and destroyed the deeds of ownership; and hostility was also shown against the clergy and the
church. As the state and the dominant class were deprived of
the means of suppressing the rebels, the latter were able to
hold out for more than four months, preventing meanwhile
any action on the part of the prince who, though not deposed,
was kept under close watch. Although of long duration and
enlisting large sections of the population, the uprising did
not become a homogeneous and unitary movement. There
was no unity of command of the military forces participating
in it and the forces did not cooperate to the same extent. The
most active were the Dorobanţi foot soldiers and the Seimeni.

Finally an expeditionary force was sent out to end the
uprising. At the request of the boyars and of Constantine
Şerban, and with the consent of the Porte, a Transylvanian
army under the command of the prince himself and Moldavian
troops commanded by George Stephen, who also had Tartar
support, marched into Wallachia in June and defeated the
rebels at Soplea (June 26, 1655). Centers of resistance continued
their action until the autumn.

After the Soplea battle there seemed to be a stronger link
between the three countries. But Constantine Şerban was
compelled to accept a new treaty with George Rakoczy II,
which recalled the one Sigismund Bathory had forced upon
Michael the Brave rather than the pacts that had linked Matei
Basarab to the two neighboring princes beyond the mountains.
The Transylvanian prince was given the right to control
Wallachia's foreign policy and even to have his say in the
appointment of the prince's dignitaries. George Stephen, on
the other hand, while observing his alliance with Rakoczy,
also sought support in Moscow, concluding a treaty to this
end in 1656.

In 1657, in opposition to the Porte, the princes of Moldavia
and Wallachia assisted George Rakoczy II in his unsuccessful
attempt to take the throne of Poland. In the early months

of the following year, the two Romanian princes were deposed, Mihnea III being appointed by the Porte in Moldavia and Gheorghe Ghica in Wallachia.

In Transylvania where George Rakoczy II — dethroned in the autumn of 1657 to be replaced by Francisc Rhedey — had succeeded in recovering the throne, the Grand Vizir Mehmed Köprülü at the head of an expeditionary force enthroned Acatiu Barcsay the following year and annexed Inău, Lugoj, and Caransebeş to the Timişoara *pashalik*. But George Rakoczy II again recovered the throne and, relying on him, as well as on Venice and the Pope, Mihnea III, who had also taken the name of Michael, now a symbol, on coming to the throne, decided to liberate Wallachia from the authority of the Porte. On his accession to the throne, Mihnea began to act for the benefit of the peasantry, helping the serfs to redeem their freedom and selling the peasants the estates that had been confiscated from the boyars. At the same time he built up his army and made efforts to cooperate with the soldiers. The prelude to the anti-Ottoman struggle, which began in September, 1658, was the assassination of a considerable number of great boyars who might have opposed the struggle. The signal was the slaughtering of the Turks at Tîrgovişte and in other towns. The pasha of Silistra was defeated, Giurgiu and Brăila were conquered, and audacious blows were inflicted on the right bank of the Danube. In October a new treaty was concluded with George Rakoczy II, which did not include the hard terms forced upon Constantine Şerban. Clashes with the Turks continued in the districts along the Danube and a victory was won at Frăţeşti in November. But Constantine Şerban having failed in his attempt to obtain the throne of Moldavia, and George Rakoczy II having been defeated, Mihnea was compelled to withdraw from Giurgiu to Tîrgovişte and make his way to Transylvania.

The anti-Ottoman campaign headed by Mihnea III ended in Wallachia, after a month and a half of heroic efforts which were not aided by sufficient military forces nor by favorable circumstances. In Transylvania George Rakoczy resisted for another six months, but the defeat inflicted on him at Floreşti in May, 1660, and the prince's subsequent death ended the struggle. At the end of August, Oradea, which had continued to resist, being supported by the population of the surrounding districts, surrendered. The town became the center of a new *pashalik* which was to ensure Turkish domination in Transylvania. A new attempt on the part of John Kemeny to shake off Ottoman domination was defeated in January, 1662.

# 7. *Struggle between Boyar Factions.*
# *The Habsburg Regime Is Installed in Transylvania*

THE efforts of the Ottoman Empire to defeat the Romanian countries' attempts at liberation and to curtail the autonomy the latter had enjoyed for two decades, as well as to increase the income it derived from them, were characteristic of the late sixties of the seventeenth century. The ability of the Porte to carry out its policy with success was due primarily to the period of restoration it was going through under the leadership of the grand viziers of the Köprülü family; on the other hand, the Romanian countries' military forces were on the decline after the reigns of Matei Basarab and Vasile Lupu.

Hence, as a result of stronger Ottoman domination, the terms of office of the ruling princes became shorter and their appointment was, with rare exceptions, made directly by the Porte without any previous election in the country; the system of triennial and annual confirmation came into general use (called *mucarer*, which meant the tribute paid the Porte on such occasions); the activities of the princes were closely watched, and there was Turkish interference in domestic affairs. Economic pressure also intensified: extraordinary contributions had to be made, the office of prince had to be bought, and the countries had also to make the Porte gifts of produce and to provide free labor. The total volume of demands was greater in Wallachia but weighed more heavily on Moldavia, the latter's resources being more restricted.

Considerable changes also occurred in Transylvania, the Porte showing a tendency to subject it to the same conditions as the other two countries: economic and political oppression increased, though the situation in that province still differed from that of the other two. The territorial losses incurred by Transylvania weighed heavily on the province.

Increased Ottoman domination decreased the authority of the ruling princes and increased the part played by the nobility in the management of state affairs. Divided into factions, the noblemen contended violently for power. Permanent internal disturbances and frequent appeals to the Porte enabled the latter to increase its authority.

Intensive political struggles were waged in Wallachia for two decades between the parties of the Cantacuzino and the Băleanu families, the former being considered as representatives of the native boyars and the latter of the Greek boyars, although there were also Greeks in the first grouping.

The struggle for supremacy between the different factions assumed a most violent character: in 1663 Court Marshal Constantine Cantacuzino, a confidential counsellor of Matei Basarab and married to Radu Şerban's daughter, was killed on orders from Grigore Ghica (1660-1664). The conflict caused frequent changes of the ruling princes until ultimately the Cantacuzino faction, relying on the vast estates of Constantine Cantacuzino's ten sons and sons-in-law, proved victorious, bringing Şerban Cantacuzino to the throne in 1678.

Similar events were taking place in Moldavia where the great boyars were the leading authority and the ruling prince was often tutored by one or the other of them. Here, too, the various factions showed different political trends, inclining either to Poland or to the Ottoman Empire. Chronicler Miron Costin and his brother Velicico fell victims in 1691 in the struggle between the Costin and Ruset families.

In Transylvania, too, the prince's authority decreased during the reign of Michael Apafi (1661-1690), and the domination of the great noblemen intensified. The noblemen's faction headed by Michael Teleky, after dispersing the anti-Ottoman-minded faction which had supported John Kemeny, finally took the reins of government and defeating all attempts at overthrowing it made by Dionisie Banffy and Paul Beldy, the Szekler commander, enjoyed a long reign.

Socially, the political power of the noblemen favored the extension of feudal estates, many of which merged for the benefit of one owner, and there was also a trend towards more intensive exploitation of the dependent peasantry — those who had settled by agreement on the estates and were now being reduced to serfdom — with new labor obligations being exacted. As has been said, however, there were frequent cases of release from serfdom.

In Wallachia, the economic development of the early years of the century continued at a steady rate, though hampered by socio-political conditions, while in Transylvania it came to a standstill altogether in certain sectors, as, for example, in mining and craftware production. Transylvania's economy was seriously affected by the military campaigns that led to the restoration of Ottoman domination (1657-1662), and later by the prolonged struggle between the Austrians and the Turks as a result of which the domination of the Habsburg Empire was enforced upon that principality.

But it was in Moldavia that the situation was most serious. After the devastation of the territory in 1650 and the developments of the last years of Vasile Lupu's reign, the country became the theater of war between the Ottoman Empire and Poland; this war was brought about by Hetman Doroshenko's acceptance of the Porte's protection in Western Ukraine, which he needed in order to cope with Poland. From 1672 to 1676 five successive campaigns took place and five times the Turkish armies passed through Moldavia on their way to the Ukraine and Podolia. And until 1681 there were further expeditions to the Ukraine against the Cossacks and the Russians, for the Cossacks had asked the Tsar's protection to help free them from Turkish interference. In 1672 the Turks conquered the Kamenetsk citadel which they retained as they also did Podolia, until the Peace of Karlowitz in 1699. Turkish-controlled territories north of Moldavia, with a strong citadel to support them, was a new means of dominating Moldavia and placing an extra burden upon the country, for it was through Moldavia that the Ottoman Empire effected the connection with its new possession.

The Polish-Habsburg victory at Vienna in 1683 and the anti-Ottoman coalition—the Holy League of 1684 — in which the Habsburgs, Poland, Venice, and Malta, and a little later Russia joined, made of Moldavia an everlasting battle ground in the Polish sector. The war broke out in the winter of 1683-1684 when the former prince, Stefan Petriceicu, marched into Moldavia with Polish support. Stefan Petriceicu, however, only held the throne for a few months. In 1684 the Polish campaigns began but made little headway — Hotin being the farthest point reached that year. In 1684 and 1691, under the reign of Constantine Cantemir (1685-1693), Sobieski, the Polish king, and his army marched deep into Moldavia though the two expeditions failed of their purpose. Apart from these royal expeditions, small armies carried on periodic raids and Polish garrisons were established in northwest Moldavia, namely at Suceava, Neamțu, and a number of monasteries and were kept there until the Peace of Karlowitz. The Polish campaigns were the cause of frequent Tartar inroads, which also made their contribution to the ruin of Moldavia. As a result of these long periods of precarious conditions, of plunder and of exhaustive material contributions, Moldavia's economy lagged far behind that of Wallachia, though its material possibilities had been greater in the past. Consequently, it came to be considered more advantageous for a prince to pass from the throne of Moldavia to that of Wallachia.

After the relief of Vienna, the Habsburg armies marched into Hungary and settled there for a number of years, defeating the Ottoman forces and organizing the conquered territories. Buda, the main city of the Turkish *pashalik* for 145 years, and a key stronghold of Ottoman rule, was stormed in September, 1686. A year later, in 1687, the victory won at Mohacs opened a way south of the Danube and the Drave and made possible the liberation of the rest of Hungary. Belgrade, the second fulcrum of Ottoman domination in the Danube area, fell in 1688. In 1691, after the Turkish successes of the preceding year, including the recovery of Belgrade, a crushing defeat was inflicted on the Sublime Porte at Szalankemen.

In the meantime the Habsburg forces had entered Transylvania. Early in 1685 negotiations had begun with a view to the emperor assuming authority in Transylvania, though its ancient privileges were to be maintained. The Făgăraș Diet, under the pressure of the imperial forces, decided on May 13, 1688, to free itself of the vassalage of the Porte and accept the emperor's protection. Leopold's Diploma of December, 1691, recognized the position of Transylvania as distinct from Hungary and its political organization as based on the union of the three privileged nations and on the four accepted religions. The diet was maintained, as was also the administrative and judicial organization and the entire legislation. The last prince of Transylvania, Michael Apafi II, although recognized by the diet, was taken to Vienna on his father's death in 1690, where he ended his life without ever having ruled. Leopold's diploma thus ensured the further existence of the Transylvanian principality while enforcing the class privileges of the leading sections of the population.

For a time operations on the battle front came to a standstill. Subsequently there were some Ottoman successes, but after the Zenta victory on the Tisa in 1697 the destinies of war finally favored the Habsburg Empire. Under the Peace of Karlowitz of 1699 the Ottoman Empire gave up its suzerainty over Transylvania which, except for Banat, passed under the authority of the Habsburg Empire.

The situation created along the northern border of Wallachia and the serious crisis in the Ottoman Empire determined the political trends of Wallachia where Şerban Cantacuzino reigned from 1678, for the Cantacuzinos had finally triumphed. While lavishly serving the interests of those nearest to him and taking rigorous measures against opponents, the new prince wished to be more than the crowned head of a boyar faction. Therefore he made it his aim to raise the principate above the boyars and to take over as much authority as possible. A family alliance with the opposite camp — the Băleanus — was intended to strengthen the throne.

His attempts to recover authority at home went hand in hand with his striving to liberate the country from dependence on the Ottoman Empire. After having participated together with the Moldavian and Transylvanian princes in the siege of Vienna on the Turkish side, Şerban Cantacuzino started negotiations with the Habsburgs while at the same time establishing connections with Poland and Russia. While preparing his army for war, he sought, by means of understandings with the Bulgarians and the Serbs, to rally the Balkans to the campaign he was planning. His negotiations with the Austrians, however, during which he demanded that his authority be fully recognized and his family have the right of succession, were concluded only in 1688; and while the envoys, who were to confirm Wallachia's acceptance of the emperor as its suzerain and the country's decision to shake off its dependence on the Ottoman Empire were still on their way to Vienna, he died.

37. HIGH STEWARD CONSTANTINE CANTACUZINO

38. THE PRINCELY CHURCH AT CURTEA DE ARGEŞ

39. THE THREE HIERARCHS' CHURCH AT JASSY

40. BRÂNCOVEANU'S PALACE AT MOGOŞOAIA

## 8. The Reigns of Constantine Brâncoveanu and Demetrius Cantemir

HIS successor, Constantine Brâncoveanu (1688-1714), his sister's son, enjoyed one of the longest reigns in the history of Wallachia. This was largely due to his immense fortune, to the revenue he derived from the country, to his political ability, and to external circumstances favorable for a considerable time. It was a reign of economic progress and of great cultural and artistic achievements, with the personal initiative of the prince and of the Cantacuzinos as a whole playing an important part. The country won international prestige at the time, in particular in the countries of the Orthodox faith, but its state of dependence continued to bring humiliation upon the crown and country, though the suzerain occasionally showed that he valued his vassal. In his domestic policy Brâncoveanu no longer showed the authoritativeness prevailing during the reign of Şerban Cantacuzino and, surrounded by members of the Cantacuzino family, who shared his responsibilities, he succeeded in obtaining the support of most of the boyars and consequently in ending their opposition.

For a quarter of a century Constantine Brâncoveanu kept the autonomy of Wallachia intact, though three empires were contending for supremacy in Southeast Europe. The treaty with the Habsburgs prepared by Şerban Cantacuzino was accepted by Brâncoveanu, but its execution was delayed. He succeeded in preventing the penetration of Austrian troops into Wallachia in the autumn of 1689 and he himself, together with Turkish and Tartar troops, marched into Transylvania in 1690, showing himself a factor in the defeat of the Habsburg General Heissler, at Zărneşti. But Brâncoveanu resumed relations with the Habsburgs and in 1695 he received the title of Prince of the Empire, though still remaining a subject of the Porte, which in 1699 bestowed on him the office of prince for the rest of his life. Notwithstanding this, in 1703 he was summoned to Adrianople and it was only on payment of large sums of money and by agreeing to pay a much higher tribute that he was able to save his throne and his life. During the last part of Brâncoveanu's reign the economic pressure of the Porte was increased, foreshadowing a new period of maximum exploitation of Wallachia's resources for the benefit of the Ottoman Empire and of its dignitaries.

While maintaining relations with the Porte, Constantine Brâncoveanu and the Cantacuzinos kept in close touch with Moscow with whom a treaty was concluded providing for Peter the Great's assistance in shaking off Ottoman domination. A similar agreement with the Tsar was concluded by Demetrius Cantemir, prince of Moldavia, in the autumn of 1710. The Treaty of Luck concluded in April, 1711, stipulated that Moldavia had agreed to become the Tsar's protectorate, that the country's autonomy was recognized, that the prince was to have full authority in ruling the country and to enjoy the right of succession in his family. Demetrius Cantemir's principles of government, which he had no time fully to put into practice, are set forth in his writings. Essentially his aim was to do away with the political instability specific to the régime of the nobility by ensuring the prince's freedom of government and by the heredity of the throne. For these reasons the main points concerning the country's internal organization were set forth in the Treaty of Luck, similar to those Şerban Cantacuzino demanded when negotiating his treaty with the Habsburgs. In both Romanian countries these provisions met with the opposition of the great boyars who realized that their political privileges were being jeopardized. The attempt to end the boyar régime had no chance of success unless it were undertaken in close connection with the Porte, and primarily for its benefit, or else, against the Porte. The latter solution, which was in keeping with the general interests and with the liberation tendencies manifest in the two countries, was adopted both by Şerban Cantacuzino and by Demetrius Cantemir, who also tried to put it into practice.

Tsar Peter I started his campaign immediately after the conclusion of the Treaty of Luck. The great Moldavian boyars mostly kept out of the war; thus, the army hastily brought together by Demetrius Cantemir included only country gentry, petty dignitaries, craftsmen, and some of the boyars' men. The Tsar's armies came by way of the Prut Valley. Brâncoveanu camped at Urlaţi, not far from Ploieşti, awaiting further developments — not joining the Turkish camp, as he had been requested, and not giving the Russians any assistance, as he was expected to do. Thus the Battle of Stănileşti, fought in July, 1711, was lost by the Russians whose war preparations had proved insufficient. Brâncoveanu's small army could not have changed the situation.

While the long era of Phanariot rule began in Moldavia about this time, Nicholas Mavrocordat being the first of the line, Brâncoveanu succeeded in keeping his throne until 1714, when he was deposed and subsequently beheaded at Constantinople after witnessing the beheading of his four sons with remarkable fortitude. His downfall may be accounted for by the Porte's lack of confidence, and its desire to make a great demonstration of its strength and also put its hands on the prince's great fortune, while at home Brâncoveanu's conflict with the rest of the Cantacuzinos did not ease the situation. His successor, Stephen Cantacuzino, was also executed, together with his father, High Steward Constantine Cantacuzino, in 1716, when the throne of Wallachia was entrusted by the Sultan to Nicholas Mavrocordat, who then abandoned the throne of Moldavia.

## 9. The Habsburg Régime in Transylvania

LEOPOLD'S Diploma, upon which the new régime of Transylvania after its annexation by the Habsburgs was based, made no mention of the Romanians. The reason is that the Diploma was a political instrument designed to win over the privileged classes, and the Romanians were not among the privileged. The Constitution of the principality, which the Habsburgs had maintained, overlooked them and their religion entirely, and the *Approbatae* of 1653 had already declared them to be merely tolerated. A longevous process had created three political "nations": the noblemen, and their allies — the Saxon communities and the privileged Szeklers. The noblemen ultimately came to mean the Hungarian nation, for it was the noblemen of that nation who held the political power. The term "nation of the nobles," which had a social and political significance, thus acquired an ethnical significance, with a tendency to exclude the Romanian nobility of Transylvania, few of whom remained. The religious reform, with the struggles it had brought about, had caused the three religions of most of the leading strata of the population, and also those of the Hungarian, Saxon, and Szekler masses, to be included in the Constitution and to be recognized by the state side by side with Catholicism, which had few supporters. The three religions were Calvinism, Lutheranism, and Unitarianism. The notion of "Romanian nation" had an ethnic significance. The social condition of the bulk of the Romanian population at a time when the consciousness of nationality was growing among the Hungarians as well as among the Romanians, affected their situation as a people. Although the masses continued their joint social struggle as a result of their similar living conditions, the Hungarian nobility came to consider the Romanians, who made up the bulk of the serfs, as a danger to their class privileges. Hence the measures taken repeatedly against them. Ultimately the entire people were declared to be merely tolerated while the aristocratic constitution of Transylvania, based on privileged conditions and orders, became increasingly aristocratic in character.

It was under these circumstances that the idea of the Eastern Orthodox Church of Translyvania joining the Catholics was born. This was part of the far-reaching program of extending the Pope's authority and the Catholic faith in Eastern Europe, and also belonged to the arsenal of the Habsburgs' government system. Metropolitan Teophilus accepted the union in the synod convened at Alba Iulia in February, 1697, express mention being made that the faithful were to preserve the Orthodox rites and that the Romanian priests should enjoy the same privileges as the Catholic priests, while the laymen of this faith should be "recognized sons of the homeland" and no longer merely tolerated. Teophilus's successor, Athanasie Anghel, confirmed the union in two new synods held at Alba Iulia in 1698 and 1700. The Union was put on a legal basis by two imperial diplomas in 1699 and 1701, the latter diploma providing that the faithful who had joined Rome should be considered as equal before the laws to the other citizens. This, an essential provision, remained a dead letter. Supported by the clergy, whose social condition was thus being improved, the union with Rome yet progressed slowly, having aroused much reaction among the masses and causing the ruling princes and the Church in Wallachia as well as the Eastern Orthodox Patriarchs to intervene against it. Catholic control over the Uniate Church was strengthened, a Jesuit theologian assisting the Metropolitan, who was made bishop of the Uniate Romanians.

The union with the Catholic Church, like the whole imperial rule in Transylvania — for the latter was bound up with the union — had for a long time against it a wide anti-Habsburg and social movement that started in the territory of the kingdom of Hungary and swiftly swept over Transylvania. The movement was headed by Francis Rakoczy II from 1703 and rallied Hungarians, Romanians, Slovaks, and Ruthenians, though it never had real unity and was mostly spontaneous in its organizational forms. There was a fundamental contradiction between the aims the participating elements had in view, for their class conditions were different. The nobility wished to shake off Habsburg domination while the mass of the people were against the Habsburgs because of the heavy impositions and because they also wanted liberation from feudal servitudes. In Transylvania the rebels' aims were mostly social and for that reason few of the nobility joined the movement, although Rakoczy was proclaimed prince of Transylvania by the diet of 1704.

The struggle ended in 1711 when the nobility signed the Peace of Satu Mare which re-established Habsburg authority in Transylvania. At this time, when Moldavia and Wallachia came under Phanariot rule, Transylvania witnessed the lasting installation of an Austrian régime after a period of crisis in the rule of the Habsburgs.

# CHAPTER V

# The Phanariot Régime in Moldavia and Wallachia.
# Habsburg Absolutism in Transylvania (1711—1821)

IN the eighteenth century the two empires which competed for domination over Romanian territory — the Ottoman and the Habsburg Empires — consolidated their domination of Moldavia, Wallachia, and Transylvania respectively, restricting their autonomy and subjecting them to increased exploitation.

The reforms of the absolutist régime in Transylvania and of the Phanariot system in Moldavia and Wallachia leading toward centralization gradually gained their objectives. In Transylvania where a great power strove to develop its economic basis and to adjust itself to the progress of the advanced countries of Europe, the reforms were bolder than in Wallachia and Moldavia, where they were also more restricted in character. The economic development of the two latter countries was hampered by the régime of brutal spoliation installed by the Ottoman state which proved unable to make a systematic effort towards internal renewal.

## 1. Salient Features of the Phanariote Régime

THE changes in the political situation of Eastern and Southeastern Europe where the domination of the Porte, previously uncontested, was threatened by the successes of Austria and Russia, gave a strong impetus to the liberation struggle in Moldavia and Wallachia. Having been given a warning in 1711 as to the seriousness of the threat, after Moldavia's desertion and the expectant attitude of Wallachia, the Porte reacted by increasing its domination over the two countries. In order to avoid the serious consequences of their possible rejection of its rule, the Ottoman Empire decided to secure effective control over their political life and consequently installed the Phanariot régime, which was to check the emancipation struggle of the Romanian countries.

The local princes had always proved inclined to join the anti-Ottoman struggle and therefore did not inspire the Turks with confidence. As it was impossible to turn Moldavia and Wallachia into *pashaliks*, a formula which had proved to be inapplicable to the Romanian countries also in the past, the Turks used the Phanariot princes as instruments to reduce them to obedience.

The Phanariot princes were mostly recruited from the top section of Greek society at Constantinople, residents of the Phanar district. Their political ambition depended upon the fortune they had acquired in the preceding centuries from trade and the management of the Porte's incomes. In the latter half of the seventeenth century the Porte saw its territorial expansion checked for good and was compelled to seek support in the Christian states of the West and to take as associated in state leadership the most active of the subjugated peoples — the Greeks. The high offices of Grand Dragoman of the Fleet and Grand Dragoman of the Porte were entrusted exclusively to the Phanariots, and this was the beginning of their political influence which increased as the crisis of the Ottoman Empire became more serious.

The Phanariot régime sensibly restricted the autonomy of Moldavia and Wallachia, for it had been installed to keep these countries under subjection. Appointed directly by the Porte, the ruling princes of the two countries belonged to the Ottoman administrative hierarchy. The interference of the Porte in domestic affairs made itself increasingly felt; repeatedly the Ottoman Empire took the initiative in ordering that certain measures should be applied in social and political organization, though these were matters of the exclusive competence of the local authorities.

Henceforth Moldavia and Wallachia no longer had a foreign policy of their own: the Phanariot princes carried on intensive diplomatic activities to serve the interests of the Porte. Under the circumstances, there was a further decline in the military power of Moldavia and Wallachia, which had already been obvious in the preceding period; the armies of the two countries were gradually being reduced to the prince's guard and to a small number of troops strictly necessary for the keeping of public order and for guarding the frontiers.

The Porte needed faithful tools in Moldavia and Wallachia not only in order to reduce them to obedience but also to exploit their resources more systematically, for this was a time when the upkeep of the large Ottoman army and administration could no longer be met from the spoils of conquest but had to be obtained from the economic and demographic potentialities of the empire's territory which was gradually being restricted by the defeats of the Turkish armies in the wars waged against the European powers. Consequently, during the reigns of the Phanariot princes Moldavia and Wallachia were cruelly exploited. The tribute, the Bairam gifts, the gifts for the annual and triennial renewal of the prince's appointment, the taxes instituted in favor of the Sultan (*geaigea*), amounted to immense sums. The struggle between the claimants to the throne and the rapid succession of princes were among the main means of squeezing the Romanian countries dry, for they assumed the form of actual auctions.

Furthermore, in wartime products and labor service were supplied free of charge, causing the countries immense losses, and certain products were bought by the Porte at its own prices. The Turkish Empire enforced a strict monopoly over certain products and the princes were frequently warned that no exports were to go to other countries; thus Moldavia and Wallachia should fulfill their duty as granaries of the Ottoman Empire.

The mere substitution of Phanariot princes for the local princes was not sufficient to attain the double aim — political and economic — which had determined the Porte to constitute the régime. A program of reforms was also implemented in the social and political institutions of the countries in order to consolidate the central power, now strictly subordinated to the Porte. The reforms were to the detriment of the boyars.

In the eighteenth century the flight of the dependent peasants from the estates they were tied to assumed proportions which completely disorganized the system of taxation and of social exploitation, compelling the authorities to change their government methods. It was the state's main concern to deal with it and consequently the reforms designed to check it topped the list of the reform program.

The many fiscal, social, administrative and judicial reforms whereby the policy of the Phanariot régime was carried out were designed to end the peasants' flight, to eliminate the factors that caused it, and to provide the state with the means of implementing the new program of government.

A product of the crisis of the Ottoman society of the seventeenth and eighteenth centuries, the Phanariot régime experienced all the vicissitudes that attended the decline of the Turkish Empire as well as the struggle of the great powers to take over the might it had wielded.

The crisis originated in the Turkish Empire's incapacity to adjust itself to the economic and technical progress of European society. As its technical lag increased, the Ottoman army proved more and more unable to oppose the armies of the great European states. Henceforth it could no longer take the offensive, and offensive was vital for a state that had arisen through conquests and was being kept up by conquests.

While the political and military power of the great European states depended upon the development of production and trade, the Ottoman Empire confined itself to intensifying the fiscal exploitation of its subjects in order to meet its obligations. But oppression gave rise to increased resistance of the oppressed peoples, and this was a significant aspect of the crisis of the Ottoman Empire in the eighteenth and nineteenth centuries.

Ever on the defensive and incapable of resisting Austrian and especially Russian expansion by its own strength, the Ottoman Empire survived only through the competition and opposing interests of the great European powers.

The wars waged by Austria and Russia against the Ottoman Empire had greatly weakened the latter and helped to create new conditions for the liberation of the Romanian people. Romanian volunteers took part in the anti-Ottoman wars and Romanian boyars submitted memorials at Petersburg and Vienna asking that the autonomy of the two countries and of their fundamental institutions should be respected. In this manner did the Romanian people assert their will to be free from Ottoman domination. On the other hand the Russo-Austro-Turkish wars turned the territories of the two countries into theaters of war and resulted in overall destruction and plunder, and, what is more serious, they were deleterious to the territorial integrity of the Romanian countries.

## 2. Installation of the Phanariot Régime and the First Reforms (1711-1768)

NICHOLAS Mavrocordat, member of one of the most outstanding Phanariot families, who embodied the policy of Turco-Greek cooperation, was chosen by the Porte to reestablish Ottoman domination in Moldavia after the Stănileşti victory and to prevent the desertion of Wallachia on the eve of a new war against Austria. Nicholas Mavrocordat inaugurated the Phanariot régime in Moldavia in 1711 and in Wallachia in 1716.

The unrestricted tasks Wallachia had to carry out after the outbreak of the Austro-Turkish war (1716-1718) and the decisive victories won by the Austrian forces under the command of Eugene of Savoy at Petrovaradin in 1716 and at Belgrade in 1717, gave a vigorous impulse to Wallachian resistance to the newly founded Phanariot régime. Under the threat of the prince's domestic policy and especially of fiscal exploitation, which no longer spared them, the Wallachian boyars pinned their hopes on the Austrians with whom they started negotiations. The memorials submitted during the war by the boyars and the upper clergy to the court in Vienna demanded that the country's autonomy should be recognized within the Habsburg Empire and its institutions should be allowed to govern themselves. This naturally implied that the social and political domination of the great boyars was to be enforced.

Though violently suppressed by Nicholas Mavrocordat, the opposition of the boyars ultimately triumphed, not without some victims, among whom were Metropolitan Antim Ivireanul and a number of great boyars. Answering the call of the boyars, the Austrians, who had previously occupied Oltenia with the support of volunteers recruited from the Romanian peasantry, marched into Bucharest and captured the Phanariot prince by surprise. A simultaneous attempt on the part of the Austrians to take prisoner Michael Racoviţă, the Moldavian prince, with the support of a number of Moldavian boyars, failed (1717).

In order to restore its control over Wallachia, the Porte resorted to John Mavrocordat, Nicholas's brother. Ruling under the title of Caimacan, John repudiated the internal policy of the captive prince, thus succeeding in partially deteating the hostility of the boyars and in consolidating his authority.

The Peace of Passarowitz, concluded in 1718, recognized the territorial gains of the Austrians. Serbia, including Belgrade, the Banat of Timişoara, and Oltenia, then came under Habsburg rule.

During the two decades of Austrian rule in Oltenia (1718-1739) a number of reforms were introduced, which gradually extended over the main fields of social and political life. The fiscal system was reorganized, fiscal assessment was established on strict demographic evidence, the privileges of the boyars were restricted, agrarian relations were established on the basis of definite rules, and reforms were introduced in the administration and in the juridical system, all of which were designed to incorporate Oltenian society into the political system of Habsburg absolutism. The very narrow margin of autonomy initially allowed to the province was suppressed in 1726, when the office of *ban* was abolished and Ban George Cantacuzino, son of the former ruling prince, Sherban Cantacuzino, was ousted from his office.

Again appointed prince of Wallachia after peace had been concluded, Nicholas Mavrocordat (1719-1730) endeavored to create suitable conditions for stabilizing the peasantry, whose constant displacement handicapped the system of fiscal exploitation. Abolishing the numerous taxes levied throughout the year under various names as a result of Turkish demands, the prince instituted one fixed tax levied four times a year. The fiscal reform carried out by Gregory Ghica (1726-1733) in Moldavia relied on the same principle. But these measures shared the fate of most Phanariot reforms, which had scarcely begun to be applied when they were infringed in order to meet the Porte's demands. With the Russo-Austro-Turkish war again turning the territory of the two countries into a theater of war (1736-1739), their implementation was abandoned.

Russia availed herself of the favorable opportunity offered by the war. Having conquered Azov and the Crimea, the Russian forces reached the Dniester in 1739, occupied the citadel of Hotin and marched into Moldavia. Under the convention that the Moldavian boyars concluded with the commander of the Russian forces, the country's autonomy was recognized and its institutions were maintained. After a few initial successes, the Austrians failed to take Vidin and were defeated a number of times. In 1737 they had to abandon the Wallachian counties they had conquered a short time previously, and, at the same time, the hope of subjecting the whole of Wallachia to their rule. At the end of the year they were also compelled to abandon Oltenia, where the Habsburg régime had estranged all sections of the population: boyars, clergy, and peasants. In consequence of the Peace of Belgrade of September, 1739, the Austrians lost Serbia and Oltenia.

Oltenia's reincorporation into Wallachia following the Peace of Belgrade, and the necessity of creating a uniform régime for the two provinces made it imperative to speed up the policy of reforms. It was Constantine Mavrocordat (1735-1741) who was at the helm of the country at the time. During nearly four decades of ruling alternatively Wallachia and Moldavia (1730-1769), Constantine Mavrocordat, the most remarkable personality among the Phanariot princes, reorganized the fiscal, social, administrative, and judicial institutions of the two countries in the same spirit.

Laid waste by the wars of many years, Moldavia and Wallachia required suitable conditions to increase their population, and only fiscal stabilization, as in the past, could create such conditions. The Law of 1740 was primarily designed to meet this necessity. Two years later the French public learned about this law for it was published in the *Mercure de France*.

Under the provisions of the law, the numerous taxes were superseded by a fixed tax levied four times a year; at the same time an attempt was made to suppress the joint and several responsibility of village communities towards the treasury — a feature specific to the medieval fiscal system.

In order to make the fiscal reform effective, it was necessary for all taxpayers to be registered in the treasury books. The lists drawn up for the purpose by Constantine Mavrocordat and later by his successors to the throne made it their aim to keep a strict demographic record, while formerly the number of taxpayers and their assessable capacity were but imperfectly known. In this sphere, however, the centralizing policy of the Phanariot princes came up against the resistance of the great boyars, who derived a great part of their incomes from the peasants who were legally exempted from taxation *(pos-luṣnici* and *scutelnici)* or from those they kept hidden illegally on their estates.

The administrative reorganization carried out by the Law of 1740 was designed to create an executive and control body which the state required if the success of the reforms, and primarily of fiscal reforms, was to be ensured. Constant control of village life that the prince was to exercise henceforth, required a suitable administrative machinery, and consequently county officers *(ispravnic de judeṭ)* were appointed, with administrative, fiscal, and judicial duties. This was the most important and most durable of the administrative reforms of the Phanariot prince, Constantine Mavrocordat. He was the first to introduce paid civil servants in Wallachia, thus trying, though without success, to end the traditional practice whereby officials paid themselves from levies on the inhabitants under their authority.

The comprehensive effort to reorganize state institutions could not leave out the administration of justice. The main aim of the reform in this sphere was to strengthen the administration of justice by the state, by restricting the jurisdiction of the church and of the boyars, and to enforce written procedures to the detriment of the oral ones, as well as to establish a hierarchy of courts of law.

The reforms were first experimented on in Wallachia and subsequently extended to Moldavia when Constantine Mavrocordat was transferred to that country (1741-1743).

The new prince of Wallachia, Michael Racoviṭǎ (1741-1744) infringed the fiscal reform of his predecessor and instituted one of the fiercest fiscal exploitations of the Phanariot period, levying taxes at many different periods of the year. The peasantry reacted promptly: over 15,000 peasants emigrated south of the Danube while many others went into hiding in the country, jeopardizing the incomes of the treasury and of the Porte. The Ottoman Empire was alarmed and again appointed C. Mavrocordat (1744-1748), assigning to him the task of bringing back the runaways and investing him with the authority necessary to break the resistance of the boyars who opposed the application of the reforms. Mavrocordat restored the fiscal régime he had introduced during his previous reign and set about preparing for one of his most important reforms: the abolition of serfdom.

Already during his preceding reign, Constantine Mavrocordat had issued state rules governing the relations between landowners and peasants; in 1744 he established that the peasants were to do twelve days' labor service for the boyars and monasteries. As the law applied only to those peasants who had settled on the estates of the boyars and monasteries by agreement, and not to the serfs whose obligations were at the landowners' discretion, the serfs refused to respond to the prince's call to return to the villages from where they had fled (October 26, 1745). Under pressure of their refusal, Mavrocordat enforced a new rule on March 1, 1746, whereby the serfs who returned to their villages were freed. Instead of putting an end to the peasants' flight, this measure intensified it, for the serfs who had not left their homes now did so in the hope of being freed from serfdom according to the provisions of the law. In order to end this state of affairs, Mavrocordat issued the Charter of August 5, 1746, abolishing serfdom. The serfs were entitled to redeem their freedom for the sum of 10 thalers, if their masters refused to free them free of charge.

Three years later, on April 6, 1749, Mavrocordat also abolished serfdom in Moldavia under pressure of the masses of serfs who had gathered in Jassy. In Moldavia as well as in Wallachia, the struggle of the dependent peasantry and the new policy of the Phanariot princes converged to put an end to the most oppressive form of personal dependence of the peasantry. Economic dependence, however, continued, for it was bound up with land ownership and land continued to be owned by the boyars and monasteries.

The stability which Mavrocordat endeavored to establish in the two Romanian countries could not resist the régime of Ottoman exploitation. Shortly after the prince had restored the fiscal reform, Ottoman demands compelled him to infringe his own rules. The four yearly levies were increased and rose to twenty under the following princes. But as the Porte's requirements could not be met even in this way, the old taxes were enforced. The cow tax aroused the most bitter resistance as it had to be paid by the boyars as well. The consequence could only be a mass flight of the peasantry, and this disorganized exploitation and greatly reduced its efficiency. And then the princes were again compelled to enforce the reform. The Phanariot age was a constant alternation between fiscal oppression without precedent in the history of the Romanian countries, and short respites when the reforms were enforced.

The Russo-Turkish war of 1768-1774 offered the Romanian countries a new occasion to free themselves from the Ottoman rule whose exploitation was so oppressive. Russia's armed intervention in Poland with the aim of consolidating Russian political influence induced the Porte to declare war in 1768. Being poorly equipped and without discipline, the Ottoman forces suffered a number of grievous defeats. In 1769 the Turks were driven out of the Romanian principalities with the assistance of Romanian volunteers. When peace negotiations started at Focşani and Bucharest in 1772, delegations of Wallachian and Moldavian boyars demanded the re-establishment of the two countries' autonomy, with the guarantees of Russia, Prussia, and Austria.

The Peace of Kuchuk Kainarji in 1774 established the preponderant part to be played by Russia in Eastern and Southeastern Europe. Having obtained independence for the Crimean Tartars and freedom of navigation for her merchant vessels in the Black Sea and through the Straits, Russia put an end to the exclusive rule of the Porte in the Black Sea, which thenceforth ceased to be a Turkish lake.

In exchange for her services to Turkey during the war, Austria obtained a considerable part of Moldavian territory — Bukovina — which she had actually occupied before having received the consent of the Porte (May 7, 1775).

## 3. End of Phanariot Rule (1774-1821)

THE Peace of Kuchuk Kainarji restored Ottoman domination in Moldavia and Wallachia and simultaneously the Phanariot régime. Turkish rule continued its oppressive policy, the two countries being ruthlessly exploited, but internal disintegration and the new defeats inflicted in the wars with the Christian powers made it ever more difficult for it to enforce its will.

The transformations wrought in Southeast Europe, where a bourgeoisie was beginning to develop, gave a new impetus and new significance to the national liberation struggle. Swept along with the general current, part of the Phanariot aristocracy joined the anti-Ottoman struggle, supporting the Greek patriots and getting in touch with the countries hostile to the Porte. The Turko-Phanariot symbiosis continued, though with rifts that were to cause deep disruptions in 1821.

Military defeats and Russia's political pressure compelled the Ottoman Empire to change its relations with Moldavia and Wallachia and allow them a new juridical status. A number of documents issued by the Ottoman Chancellery in 1774, 1783, 1791, 1798, and 1802 included concessions to the demands of the two countries, which Russian diplomacy supported with the aim of weakening the power of the Porte. In these documents the Porte agreed to establish a fixed sum for the pecuniary obligations of the principalities and to buy certain products (grain and sheep) at the market price in peacetime, which formerly had been bought at prices fixed at Istanbul. The political domination of the Porte was being restricted simultaneously with its economic exploitation. The ruling princes had greater stability, their removal being enforced only in certain cases, and in 1802 a seven-year term of office was established. This also restricted the possibility of the Porte interfering in the internal affairs of the principalities. Although the provisions of the above documents were far removed from the demands of the representatives of the principalities, and their efficiency was reduced by the Turks' infringements, they established a new juridical status for Moldavia and Wallachia and thus caused a rift in the system of Ottoman domination.

Much the same effect was obtained by the setting up of foreign consulates, an expression of the new balance of power in international affairs, which ended the exclusive domination of the Porte in Southeast Europe. Russian consulates were established in Moldavia and Wallachia in 1782 and Austrian consulates in 1783, while Prussia had her own consulates in the principalities in 1785, France in 1796 and Great Britain in 1803. These consulates showed that the Great Powers were interested in the resources of the Romanian countries and considered their geographical and political position of importance. Russia availed herself of the concessions forced upon the Porte, whereby the Romanian countries obtained some privi-

MICHAEL VAIVODA, VALACHIÆ TRASALPINÆ HÆREDITARIᵘˢ

FIDE ET CON STANTIA

F. Wissman inv. delin. et sculp. 1631.

42. MIHNEA III

Georgius Rakozzi D.G. Princeps Transsilvaniæ Moldaviæ Dux, Comes Palatin. Transsilvaniæ Partium Regni Hungariæ Domi- et Siculorum Comes etc. P.S. excud.

41. GEORGE RAKOCZY II

**43.** CONSTANTINE BRÂNCOVEANU AND HIS FOUR SONS

**Demetrie**  **Kantemir,**
des h. ruſſiſ. Reichs
bey dem ruſſ. Kaiſer
des hohen Senats

und in Moldau Fürſt,
Peter dem Großen
Mitglied und geheimer
Rath.

44. DEMETRIUS CANTEMIR

45. NICHOLAS MAVROCORDAT

46. ALEXANDER YPSILANTI

leges, in order to undermine Ottoman domination in these countries and interfere in their domestic affairs. The consulates she had established in Bucharest and Jassy enabled her to supervise the application of the conventions concluded with the Porte and to exert her influence on the principalities.

Being reinstated in 1774, the Phanariot régime resumed its policy of reforms under the difficult conditions created by the havoc of war. A new effort towards the reorganization of Wallachia was made by Alexander Ypsilanti (1774-1782) who fixed definite dates for the payment of the tribute and gave the country a few years of prosperity. He was the first to try to separate justice from administration, created new courts of law, and gave the country a Code of Laws *(Pravilniceasca Condică)* in 1780, which opened a new stage in the slow process whereby common law was replaced by the written law. A similar policy, though on a more restricted scale, was carried out by Prince Gregory Ghica in Moldavia (1774-1777). It was during his reign that rules were worked out under which civil servants were paid a salary. This was a new effort to do away with corrupt practices, the venality of state officials, and the exploitation of the population by State officials. Gregory Ghica was killed by the Turks, a victim of his conflict with the boyars and of his relations with the Russians.

This time again the peaceful respite offered the two countries was a short one. Breaking its engagements only a few years after the conclusion of peace, the Porte again made excessive demands which undermined the reforms. The new Russo-Austro-Turkish war (1787-1792) proved ruinous to the economy of the two countries. The occupation of the Crimea by Russian troops in 1783 and Russian shipbuilding for navigation in the Black Sea caused the Porte to declare war on Russia in 1787. On the basis of the treaty of alliance concluded in 1782, Austria fought alongside Russia. Having conquered the region between the Bug and the Dniester, the Russian troops marched into the Romanian countries under the command of Suvorov and won the battles of Focşani and Rîmnic in July, 1789. In their turn, the Austrians occupied Wallachia and the counties between the Carpathians and the River Siret in Moldavia. But developments in Western Europe — the insurrection of the Netherlands and the French Revolution — compelled Austria to conclude the Peace of Shishtov in 1791 under which she waived all territorial claims. Russia concluded peace at Jassy in January, 1792, thereby obtaining the territory between the Bug and the Dniester from the Porte.

The French Revolution and the Napoleonic wars which overthrew feudal institutions in Western and Central Europe brought their influence to bear also in East and Southeast Europe. Exposed to the attacks of the French army, Austria was compelled to give up her program of expansion in Southeast Europe, thus leaving room for the play of Russian policy. As France's influence increased in the Ottoman Empire, the effects of her policy made themselves felt also in the Romanian principalities, which now entered the sphere of French interests. Intent on supervising the moves of the Russians and the Austrians, France extorted the Porte's assent to her appointing a consul in Bucharest and a vice-consul in Jassy.

Placing their hopes for a moment in France, the Romanian boyars submitted memorials to Napoleon, demanding the re-establishment of the country's autonomy and the removal of the Phanariot régime. Napoleon, however, looked upon the two principalities as an object of compensation. In 1806, in order to create difficulties for Russia along the Danube, he prompted the Porte to recall Constantine Ypsilanti, prince of Wallachia, and Alexander Moruzi, prince of Moldavia, both of whom favored Russia. Having been won over to Greece and her struggle to shake off the domination of the Porte and restore her own freedom, Constantine Ypsilanti organized an army of Romanians and Balkan people, got in touch with the leaders of the anti-Ottoman uprising which had broken out in Serbia in 1804, and maintained close relations with Russia.

The removal of the two princes by the Porte infringed the provisions of the agreement of 1802, and in 1806 Russia availed herself of the opportunity to occupy the principalities. And when Napoleon concluded peace with the Russians at Tilsit the following year, the Porte remained alone to wage war on Russia (1806-1812).

Romanian participation in the anti-Ottoman war again made a considerable contribution to its victorious end. The Oltenian pandours took part in most of the battles fought by the Russian army in the Wallachian plain and south of the Danube, thus gaining a military experience which was to prove of good use during the Revolution of 1821.

The Russian forces remained in Moldavia and Wallachia until 1812 when, war with France being imminent, Tsar Alexander I concluded peace with the Porte. Following the peace of Bucharest (May 28, 1812), the Romanian principalities were evacuated by Russian troops, with the exception of the territory between the rivers Prut and Dniester (Bessarabia), which was incorporated into tsarist Russia.

The Phanariot régime survived the Russo-Turkish war of 1806-1812. Unable to find another formula for ruling the Romanian countries, the Turks again appointed Phanariot princes, although in recent times they had repeatedly proved disloyal to the Porte.

During the reigns of John Caragea (1812-1818) and Alexander Şuţu (1818-1821) Wallachia was again subjected to fierce fiscal exploitation. Overwhelmed by unbearable taxation and by a fiscal machinery that derived enormous benefits from the offices bought from the princes, whole villages, and occasionally whole districts, were deserted by their populations. The efforts of the executive bodies to check the peasants' flight were of no avail for, though some of the runaways could be brought back to their villages, a movement that had spread throughout the country could not be entirely checked. The reports sent in to the authorities also brought to their attention the emergence of centers of active resistance foreshadowing the events of 1821.

Endeavoring, as so many of his predecessors had done, to decrease the number of inhabitants exempted from taxation, Caragea aroused the hostility of the boyars who now had to pay taxes for those previously exempted. To compensate the boyars, Caragea issued a number of laws — the Caragea Laws of 1818 — whereby the obligations of the dependent peasants were increased.

During the rule of Scarlat Calimah (1812-1819) new laws — the Civil Register of the Principality of Moldavia (1817) — were brought out in Moldavia.

The Phanariot régime was the most oppressive stage of Ottoman domination in Moldavia and Wallachia. Exacting from the two countries through the agency of the Phanariot princes great sums of money and immense quantities of products, the Porte delayed the development of the productive forces and the breaking up of feudal structures. Under the circumstances, the capitalist economy was built up only by slow degrees. The purchase of Romanian agricultural produce by the Porte after 1774 at higher princes than in the past, and increased export possibilities in Transylvania, were a stimulus, but of small proportions, for the landowners. The consequence was an attempt on the part of the landowners to extend their estates by incorporating the land tilled by the peasants. This tendency was first evidenced in Moldavia during the reign of Alexander Moruzi who, by the Charter of January 3, 1805, restricted the peasants' right to use the forests, grass land and pasture land. A more extensive estate required additional labor, which the landowners, who lacked both capital and technical knowledge, found by increasing the obligations of the peasantry. As everywhere in Central and Eastern Europe, in the Romanian countries also, the peasantry's dependence increased when the landowners' estate began to produce for the market. In Moldavia labor service was increased by a document issued in 1766, which established the amount of work to be done per day. The amount of work was far above actual possibilities. In 1777 the landowners obtained that five more days should be added to the twelve established by the preceding act. In Wallachia, *Caragea's Laws* added a day's plowing and additional cartage to the twelve days of work established by the preceding arrangements. At the same time the landowners' tendency to demand that the days of labor should be done during the period of intense agricultural work, was encouraged. But the landowners' efforts to increase the work of the dependent peasants only turned into a movement of wide scope after the Ottoman monopoly was suppressed and Romanian grain entered the circuit of European trade.

The domination of the Porte had adverse consequences on manufacture and production, already greatly hindered by the Capitulations accorded to foreign powers. No protectionist policy could be applied, for the Capitulations gave foreign goods access to the provinces under Ottoman authority in exchange for an infinitesimal customs duty. This accounts for the ephemeral or intermittent nature of most of the manufactories set up at the time. The ones of longer duration were the cloth manufactories of Pociovălişte and Bucharest, the glassware manufactory of Tîrgovişte, the shawl manufactory of Mărcuţa, and the paper mill at Caţichea.

At this stage emancipation from Ottoman domination could alone remove the obstacles barring the way to progress in Moldavia and Wallachia. And this was the aim the revolution of 1821 set out to attain.

## 4. *Transylvania under Habsburg Absolutism*

LIKE Moldavia and Wallachia under the Phanariot princes, Transylvania, now subjected to the Habsburg régime, experienced a new form of government with the same centralizing tendency as its main feature, the difference being that the reorganization program was more far-reaching here and more consistently carried out.

After the Peace of Satu Mare of 1711, the Austrian régime greatly restricted the autonomy of the principality, which was to conform itself increasingly to the pattern of the absolutist state. While the letter of the Leopold Diploma was observed, its provisions were in actual fact being gradually infringed. The institutions embodying the autonomy of the principality were maintained but they were converted into bodies carrying out an absolutist policy. The Diet had an increasing number of representatives appointed by the Court (royalists) and was gradually deprived of its fundamental prerogatives: the right to elect the prince and the other high dignitaries and to make laws. The government *(regium gubernium)* headed by a governor who, with time, came to be directly appointed by the emperor without the Diet being consulted became one of the most efficacious tools of the Habsburg policy. The revenues of the country were forestalled by the Empire and used for its own aims; they were levied, as they had been in the past, through the agency of the Treasury, now reduced to a body carrying out the fiscal policy worked out in Vienna. The activities of the local bodies of power were subordinated to the control of the central ruling bodies: the Aulic Chancellery, the War Council and the Aulic Chamber (the Imperial Treasury).

With time the principality had no longer a military force of its own. First integrated in the imperial army under imperial command, the Transylvanian military force ultimately disappeared altogether. The Austrian forces stationed in the province were the safest guarantee of its loyalty. Imperial commanders frequently interfered in the politics of the principality and were sometimes even appointed as governors. The dominant classes allowed themselves to be dispossessed of part of their political power because the absolutist state allowed the exploitation régime in force to continue. Politically, this meant that the constitutional system established in the preceding centuries was maintained, the only active factors in the principality being considered the "constitutional nations" and the "accepted religions". Socially, it meant continued exploitation, which weighed most heavily on the Romanian serfs.

Banat, conquered by the Habsburg troops and incorporated in the Empire after the Peace of Passarowitz (1718), had a régime different from Transylvania's. No previous pact hindered Austrian policy here as it did in Transylvania. Ruled by military governors and later — in the latter half of the eighteenth century — by civilian presidents, the province was under the double authority of a War Council and of an Aulic Chamber. A colonization policy, the result of the demographic views of the Austrian authorities, brought numerous German, Italian, French, and Bulgarian people into the province. Fiscal exploitation, the removal of the Romanians from their settlements in order to make room for the settlers, the labor required to implement a public works program of wide range, the unfair practices of the administration, and the excesses of the troops stationed in the province, were the causes of a great uprising that broke out during the Austro-Turkish War (1736-1739). It was only during the last year of the war that the imperial army in a large-scale campaign was able to defeat the rebels.

New trends in the Habsburg policy during the latter half of the eighteenth century brought about changes in the compromise that had been reached between the absolutist régime and the privileged estates, a compromise on which the government system of Transylvania was based in the first half of the twentieth century. The Habsburgs revised their method of government and endeavored to introduce a new social and

political pattern. In order to cope with the new realities cropping up in the Empire as a result of the development of a
capitalist economy, the state worked out a new formula for
its government — an enlightened absolutism — which, while
preserving the essential trends of the absolutist policy, now
more comprehensive, more far-reaching, and applied at a
swifter rate — brought to the fore the rationalist ideology
of the eighteenth century, the philosophy of enlightenment,
with the idea of progress at its core.

The concentration of political power in the person of an
absolute monarch and in his governing bodies was now
accompanied by an effort to control effectively all sectors of
social and political life. In order to achieve this aim, the
central authority had to dissolve the power of the nobility
concentrated in manorial, administrative, and judicial institutions established in the preceding centuries, whereby an
important part of social life and of the benefits obtained from
the control exercised over it, were outside the reach of the
state. At this stage absolutism no longer confined itself to
taking over the political power of the nobility, but also began
to undermine some of its social positions. The reforms carried
out by the régime of enlightened absolutism — more timidly
under Maria Theresa (1740-1780) and more systematically
under the impulse of Joseph II, co-regent from 1765 and subsequently emperor (1780-1790) — made it their aim to enlarge
the foundations of absolute power and eliminate the out-of-
date institutions of feudal society in order to enable absolutism
to adjust itself to the new economic and social realities and
thus protect it from revolutionary outbursts.

As a result of the Empire's prolonged military efforts during
the eighteenth century, domestic policy had to make it a main
concern to procure the financial resources required for foreign
wars. The greatest source of funds was taxation, but the state
also endeavored to increase its revenues by implementing a
systematic program of modernizing production and stimulating trade.

A powerful impulse was given to mining, especially in
the second half of the eighteenth century, when the mines of
Transylvania and Banat had to compensate for the resources
of Silesia, lost to the Empire. Derelict mines were again worked
(the gold mines of Baia Mare and Baia Sprie, the lead and

silver mines of Rodna), while other mines were worked to better advantage (the Zlatna and Baia de Arieș gold mines, the Ghelar and Remetea iron mines). The mining resources of Banat were systematically exploited, the Habsburg state setting up four offices for the purpose (at Oravița, Dognecea, Moldova, and Sasca).

The progress of mining techniques enabled the pits to be worked at great depths, and the state opened special miners' schools at Oravița and Zlatna to provide skilled miners. The increasing revenues obtained as a result of such initiatives caused private capital to flow into mining undertakings alongside state capital. Mining companies were then set up, and in the latter half of the eighteenth century also joint stock companies. Transylvanian capital as well as Austrian capital was sunk into such undertakings.

It was also through the initiative of the state that many manufactories were started or re-tooled during this period. The most important were metal works, which developed in step with mining (the iron works at Bocșa, Reșița, and Hunedoara, the copper works at Dognecea). Some of these workshops yielded a large output in the latter half of the eighteenth century. Other manufactories started in considerable numbers at the time produced paper, upholstery, fabrics, glassware, gunpowder, candles, etc. Swept along by the current of state initiative, the nobility began opening manufactories on their estates (glassware, potash and paper mills) though in far smaller numbers. And there were also some manufactories set up with tradesmen's capital (the leather works at Gherla and Timișoara).

In both mines and manufactories paid labor was gradually superseding the servile labor of the serfs carried out as part of their feudal obligations. Feudal enterprises soon became joint enterprises and then capitalist. Extensive mining called for an increasing number of paid workers (over 1,000 men were employed at Săcărîmb and Băița in the latter half of the eighteenth century). Child labor, specific to early capitalism, was widely used.

The ever more exclusive tendencies of craftsmen's guilds restricted the Romanians' participation in production in that sphere. On the other hand, the Romanians made up the bulk of the workers in manufactories and mines.

An important part was played in the Transylvanian economy by domestic crafts, which in certain sectors proved to be dangerous competitors of the production of the guilds.

Agriculture also became the concern of state policy, which supported the extension of the land under crops and the modernization of agricultural techniques. The increase in urban population and the presence of imperial military units raised the demand for agricultural produce and stimulated the landowners' interest in farming. But as the landowners increased their output by extending their lands and not by improving farming techniques, which were still primitive, they lessened the holdings (sessiones) of the serfs, limited the right of their using pasture land and forests, and increased the labor obligations of the dependent peasantry. In 1820 the nobility availed themselves of the favorable opportunity offered by a new conscription (Czirakian conscription) to extend their estates on a large scale to the detriment of the holdings of the serfs.

Intensified agricultural, craftware and manufacturing production was a great stimulus to trade. Trading companies were developing at the time, being supported by the state's mercantilist policy, for they offered the most reliable instrument of penetration in the Ottoman market and facilitated control over trade transactions. The participation of Romanian merchants increased in the Greek companies established at Sibiu and Braşov, but there were also companies of Saxon and Armenian merchants. The Hagi Constantin Pop House of Sibiu (1768-1821) played an important part in promoting economic relations between Transylvania and Wallachia. Despite the restrictions forced upon Transylvania by Austria's policy, trade among the three Romanian countries expanded.

Focusing its attention on the problems raised by material production and trade, whose development was considered as a first condition of raising the fiscal capacity of the bulk of the population, the Habsburg state naturally changed its social outlook. The nobility, having no longer any military duties, were now considered to possess a privilege that was no longer justified: exemption from taxation, which kept immense fortunes out of the imperial treasury. That privilege was first attacked during Maria Theresa's reign, when the nobility was taxed for the first time. Joseph II later introduced the principle of equality of public obligations in the fiscal policy of the Habsburg state, thus continuing and strengthening the measures taken by Maria Theresa. In Transylvania this new fiscal policy proved ineffective.

Enlightened absolutism also took a new stand on the problem of the dependent peasantry, its policy evolving in the eighteenth century from the regulation and restriction of serf obligations under Maria Theresa, to the suppression of some of the fundamental features of serfdom under Joseph II.

The first law on labor service, adopted by the Transylvanian Diet in 1714 at the request of the Court of Vienna, established that the serfs should work four days a week for the landowners, and the sharecroppers three. The nobility evaded the provisions of the law, demanding labor service not only of the head of the family but of the whole family. In 1747 Maria Theresa established that manual workers should contribute four days' work a week and those tending the cattle three days; the sharecroppers were to work one day a week. The law of 1769 maintained these provisions but deducted all other services rendered to the nobles and also the time of journeying to the place of work, from the total of compulsory labor. The nobility, however, found the means of turning the provisions in their favor, especially by concentrating the days of labor service at the period when agricultural work was at its peak.

In its agrarian policy, Habsburg absolutism endeavored to restrict and even to suppress the serfs' personal dependence in order to increase their production capacity and to draw them into the state's sphere of action.

Enlightened absolutism extended its reforms to the administration of justice: "the continuous tables" set up in the counties and sedes administered state justice by means of local courts in session throughout the year. At the same time, offering the dependent peasantry the possibility of appealing against the landowners and against the judicial sentences passed by them, the absolutist state strove to reestablish contact with the bulk of the rural population in this sector, too. Imperial deeds — ordinances, patents, rescripts — all restricted the sphere of application of traditional regulations *(Tripartitum, Approbatae,* and *Compilatae).*

But the nobility found refuge in the ancient autonomy and the ancient institutions of the counties against the attack of absolutist power, and this induced Joseph II to reorganize the administrative system. The principality was divided into eleven counties, no longer autonomous but subordinated to the central power, with its administrative machinery made up of paid officials.

Dismantling the institutions on which the political power of the nobility depended, subjecting the régime of exploitation by the nobility to state regulations, and abolishing religious discrimination, enlightened absolutism paved the way for the disruption of the traditional system of government in Transylvania.

## 5. Struggle of Transylvanian Romanians for Political and Social Emancipation

THE policy of the Habsburgs created a new background for the Romanians' struggle for social and political emancipation. Their first occasion to evade the ruling principles which had kept them outside political life for centuries was the adoption of the Catholic faith encouraged by the imperial authorities. For the Habsburg state Catholicism was an ideological formula designed to give spiritual unity to the many provinces and peoples that made up the Empire. In Transylvania union with the Catholics had a political aim. Having aroused the hostility of the privileged, the absolutist régime needed domestic support to consolidate its rule and sought to find it among the Romanians who formed the bulk of the population. By winning the Romanians over to the Catholic faith, the Habsburg monarchy intended to create a means of exerting pressure on the privileged and, if necessary, a means of undermining their power.

The Uniate rite was an instrument of political domination for the imperial authorities, while for the Romanians, who accepted it, it was a political act: a means of discarding the condition of a tolerated people that the constitution of the principality had imposed upon them. The struggle for political rights, which was the aim of those who had first joined the Catholic faith, became an actual fact under the leadership of the Uniate Bishop Ioan Inochentie Micu-Klein (1728-1751).

The claims which Micu set forth in the many memorials he submitted to the Vienna authorities, and which he supported against the fury of the privileged in the Diet — Micu being a member of the Diet — voiced the aspirations of the whole Romanian population without any social or religious distinctions. In Micu's views the Romanian nation was not identified with a privileged minority but comprised all the people; consequently, his claims were not confined to demanding privileges for the Romanian clergy and gentry but embraced the bulk of the Romanian population, including the serfs, for Micu demanded that the number of days of labor service be reduced and that the serfs should have the right of apprenticing their children to a trade.

Micu not only raised the banner of the Transylvanian Romanians' political struggle and established its program, but also gave it a historical and political foundation. The Roman origin of the Romanians and their continuity on Transylvanian soil, which had been latent in their consciousness since ancient times, now became a political weapon in Transylvania, where the right to political existence was denied this people. The claims of Micu and of the leaders who succeeded him in the Transylvanian Romanians' struggle against national oppression were for fair treatment founded on the Roman origin of the Romanian people, their uninterrupted existence on the territory since ancient times, their number so much larger than that of the other nationalities living there, and their wide participation in public obligations.

But Micu's program exceeded by far the intentions of the Court of Vienna, which wished to exercise strict control over the religious union and to use it only as far as it suited its interests. The gap between the claims of the Romanian bishop and the policy of the Austrian Court was further widened after the outbreak of the war of succession to the Austrian throne (1740-1748). In its struggle for survival, the Habsburg monarchy was saved mostly through the support of the Hungarian magnates, which was obtained by great concessions to them. In order to end the movement created by Micu, which increasingly hindered its policy, the Court summoned him to Vienna. After a short stay in the capital of the Empire, Micu took refuge in Rome where he continued to guide his people until his death.

The failure of the political struggle begun under cover of a religious union and in the hope of radical changes for the Romanians gave rise to a wave of popular reaction against the Uniate faith. Promoted by the Serbian monk Visarion Sarai in 1744 and, on a larger scale and more threateningly for the régime, by monk Sofronie of Cioara in 1759, disturbances arose in South Transylvania which, though first begun as religious reactions, became occasions for making social claims.

A joint movement of the Romanian and Szekler peasantry in 1762-1763 was the result of the setting up of border regiments: two Romanian regiments in Transylvania with their headquarters at Năsăud and Orlat, three Szekler regiments also in Transylvania, and two Romanian regiments in Banat.

At first viewed with hostility by the peasantry, who rose in revolts quelled with much shedding of blood, the Romanian regiments subsequently became factors of social emancipation for the serfs who had enrolled as well as an instrument for the Romanians' political gains. As officers had to be trained, the authorities opened schools in the border districts, whereby the ranks of the Romanian intelligentsia were strengthened in Transylvania.

## 6. Horea's Uprising

THE implementation of the agrarian program of enlightened absolutism created new conditions for the struggle of the serfs. There is no doubt that the attempt made by the absolutist régime to restrict the exploitation of the dependent peasantry by the nobility through well-defined regulations, thus making the peasantry available for exploitation by the state, did not yield the results that had been expected of it. Ignoring the imperial ordinances or evading their provisions, the nobility succeeded in maintaining their positions and even in increasing their exploitation of the peasantry. Oppression became intolerable as a result of increased taxation which, however, did not affect the noblemen's incomes. At the same time, the serfs came to believe that the imperial authorities sided with them in their struggle against the nobility. Their belief was based on the agrarian policy of the state, the succes-

sive attempts to put order in agrarian relations, the interest
shown in the peasantry and the inquiries undertaken by Joseph
II during his journeys to Transylvania. The exasperated peasantry were thus made hopeful, and this state of spirit was
a factor in the great uprising of the Transylvanian serfs of
1784.

The first signs appeared in the Western mountains, which
were to become a centre whence the uprising radiated; at
the Cîmpeni Fair in 1782 the peasants around Zlatna, whose
obligations had been unduly increased through the extension
and modernization of the mines and the rise in taxation, attempted to assert their traditional rights by forcibly opposing one
of the most damaging innovations of the revenue office: the
sale of the right to open taverns. The repression that followed
prevented the incident from spreading, but two years later
a similar uprising swept over most of the country.

The emperor's decision to increase the number of border
regiments as a result of the new stage in the Eastern crisis
foreshadowed by the plans of Empress Catherine II was an
occasion for the serfs to show their feelings. The Romanian
and Szekler regiments set up during Maria Theresa's reign
— the stress of their installation apparently forgotten — now
appeared as a means to freedom, enrolling being the safest
and quickest way of breaking free from serfdom obligations.
Consequently, the peasants enrolled in large numbers, thus
becoming exempt from all obligations to their landlords.

Scared by the proportions of the movement and the refusal
of the serfs to fulfill their obligations, the noblemen demanded
that the government cease their enrolling of them, and were
given satisfaction. The movement was, however, too strong
and the peasants' hopes of liberation too deep-rooted for the
movement to be stopped once under way. On the pretext
of orders from the emperor, Horea, the main leader of the
peasants, encouraged them to resist. Several hundred peasants
marched from Mesteacăn — to where they had been called
by Horea on October 31, 1784 — to Alba Iulia, in order to
enroll. At Curechiu the march turned into an open revolt,
the peasants killing the officials sent by the authorities to
end the movement.

The uprising spread quickly, having behind it a background
of centuries of cruel exploitation. Before long it had swept

over Zarand, the county of Hunedoara, the Abrud mountains, and the Turda county, and hotbeds of revolt also cropped up in the north. In the final stage the whole country was involved. The fury of the rebel serfs razed the noblemen's country houses to the ground and turned the archives showing their debts and the noblemen's deeds of ownership into heaps of ashes. A program was worked out which became ever more radical in its demands. On November 11, the peasants of Zarand sent the noblemen besieged at Deva an ultimatum calling for the abolition of the nobility and the division of the noblemen's estates, and demanding that the noblemen be subjected to taxation. The peasantry demanded not only that their obligations be restricted, but also that feudal relations be suppressed.

Taken aback by the violence and the proportions of the uprising, the government temporized and began negotiating with the rebels, meanwhile awaiting orders from Vienna. Having taken refuge in the towns, the nobles armed themselves and attempted to put up a defense, thus reviving an old institution: the noblemen's insurrection.

In November the imperial authorities began negotiations to end the conflict. A number of conventions agreed upon by the envoys of the authorities and the rebel groups gave satisfaction to the peasantry, granting their main claims. The most important of the conventions — concluded at Tibru on November 12 — admitted the peasants' right to enroll in border regiments and suppressed serfdom. But both the authorities and the nobility carried on negotiations only in order to gain time for reprisals.

Adverse to mass movements, which hastened the course of reforms, Joseph II determined to use force against the rebels. The latter's staunch resistance continued until mid-December when, realizing the hopelessness of their struggle, the peasants spread through the countryside and their leaders took refuge in the mountains. Betrayed to the authorities, Horea and his main collaborators, Cloşca and Crişan, were imprisoned at Alba Iulia and tried. Horea and Cloşca died on the wheel, while Crişan committed suicide.

As a result of the uprising, letters patent abolishing serfdom were issued on August 22, 1785: the peasants' personal dependence was done away with; the dependent peasantry were again allowed to change their quarters, to practice a craft and to marry without the consent of their landlords. The uprising and the measures that followed it were an important stage in the breaking up of feudal relations in Transylvania.

## 7. *Supplex Libellus Valachorum*

THE end of the reign of Joseph II also meant an end to the policy of reforms. The peasants' uprisings in the Habsburg Empire, and subsequently the bourgeois revolution in France, foreshadowed the collapse of the entire régime in which the power of the dominant class was vested. The nobility reacted vigorously and the Empire gave up the enlightenment experiment. Threatened to be swept away, the absolutist power again forged an alliance with the nobility in order to oppose the revolutionary wave. Joseph II himself canceled his reforms, the tolerance edict and the patent on serfdom excepted. After the short reign of his brother Leopold, the reactionary nobles triumphed definitely under Francis I, and a régime was instituted with secret police and censorship as essentials.

Relying on the concepts of enlightenment and invoking the reforms of Joseph II, the spokesmen of the Romanian bourgeoisie in process of formation and mostly made up of small office-holding gentry, intellectuals, and officers in the border regiments, endeavored to oppose the reactionary wave and demanded that the Romanians' political claims be given satisfaction. In March, 1791, a general memorial — *Supplex Libellus Valachorum* — was forwarded to the Court of Vienna. Among those responsible for it were Samuil Micu, Ion Budai-Deleanu, Petru Maior, and Gheorghe Şincai. Resuming Inochentie Micu's arguments—now founded on the historical and philological investigations of the Transylvanian School — *Supplex Libellus* demanded that the Romanians be allowed equality with the other nations. The memorial further asked that the name and condition of tolerated people should be abolished, that the Romanians — clergy, noblemen, townspeople, and peasants — should enjoy rights equal to those of the corresponding estates of the other nations, and that the Romanians should have access to state offices in proportion to their number. The memorial was of outstanding importance, for it proposed to abolish the medieval constitution of the principality and give political promotion to the Romanian nation. Although rejected by the Diet of the principality to which it had been sent by the emperor, *Supplex Libellus* was an important stage in the struggle of the Romanians of Transylvania for emancipation from the régime of national and social oppression to which they had been condemned by the constitution.

# CHAPTER VI

# Romanian Culture in the Middle Ages and Early Modern Times

THE medieval culture of the Romanian people reflects the economic structure that generated it and which it served. From among the many spheres of culture, historiography and art showed achievements which are among the most valuable possessions of Romanian national culture while making a remarkable contribution to the treasure store of European culture. The fundamental ideas set forth and developed by the Romanian scholars were the Roman origin of the Romanian people and their ethnic unity.

Nurtured by constant contact with folk culture and art, Romanian medieval art expressed the creative and artistic power of the Romanian people.

## 1. Culture in the Period of the Centralized Feudal State

THE progress of state centralization, more powerful in Moldavia, is shown in the sphere of culture by the appearance and development of historical literature. The chronicles written on the initiative and under the patronage of the ruling prince were intended to lay down the latter's exploits and to serve his policy. The first — the Anonymous Chronicle of Moldavia, also named the Bistriţa Chronicle; the Putna Chronicle; and the works based on them: the Moldo-German, Moldo-Polish, and Moldo-Russian Chronicles — relate Moldavia's history from its foundation, all starting from a pattern drawn up during the reign of Stephen the Great, and enlarging on that reign. The figure of the Moldavian prince, who fought for the country's independence and held undisputed sway over the country, is glorified by the chronicler who describes the prince as a "victory bearer" — as the Church described the militant Saint George.

The Court Chronicles of the sixteenth century have the same aim: they support the central authority and praise the prince who had commissioned them. The Chronicle of Macarie, Bishop of Roman, written on orders from Petru Rareș, is the history of the years 1504-1551, showing the conflict between the prince and the great boyars from the standpoint of the prince. The historical and literary value of the chronicle is impaired by substantial borrowings from the Slav version of the Chronography written by Constantine Manasses, a Byzantine. Macarie's Chronicle was continued by the Father Superior of the Căpriana Monastery, Eftimie, who narrated Moldavia's history from 1541 to 1554 without borrowing from the Byzantine-Slav model to such an extent. Developments from 1551 to 1574 are laid down in the Chronicle of Azarie, who wrote on orders from Peter the Lame. Being Macarie's disciple, he proceeded very much as his tutor had done, frequently copying from Manasses' Chronograph.

In Wallachia where more frequent and more brutal interference on the part of the Ottoman Porte prevented the consolidation of the throne, historical literature is less significant than in Moldavia. It was only at the close of the sixteenth century that the first chronicles written in Romanian appeared: the Chronicle of the Great Chancellor Theodosie Rudeanu written at Court in 1597 and dedicated to Michael the Brave, and the Chronicle narrating the rule of the same prince written at the suggestion of the Buzescu boyars and comprising praises of the great prince, as well as critical observations on his policy. This is the first boyar chronicle heralding the party chronicles of the following century.

A remarkable work is *Neagoe Basarab's Teachings for His Son Theodosie* ascribed to that Wallachian prince, as the title shows. Relying on religious writings of wide circulation and influenced by similar Byzantine works, the *Teachings* comprises advice on the organization and the wielding of diplomacy, on the waging of wars, etc., and moreover advocates the enforcement of princely authority.

The conditions created for the Transylvanian Romanians by the Hungarian kingdom prevented Romanian historical literature in that principality from developing as on the other side of the Carpathians. The most important work is the final part of the Dubnik Chronicle *(Chronicon Dubnicense)* devoted to the years 1474-1479. Stephen the Great is shown here in a favorable light and Bartholomew Dragfi and Pavel Chinezul are praised, which seems to indicate that the author was a Romanian.

Also worthy of notice are the original works of a religious nature, such as the *Hymns* of Filos, Chancellor during Mircea the Old's reign (Filos assumed the name of Filotei as a monk); *The Praise to Saint Michael of the Sinades*, written by Treasurer Simion Dedulovici at the close of the fifteenth century; and two longer works written by non-Romanians but relating to developments in the Romanian countries: *The Life of Saint John the New of Suceava* by Grigore Ţamblac, a Bulgarian, who was "Primate of the Great Church of Moldo-Vlahia" before becoming Metropolitan of Kiev, and *The Life of Saint Nifon*, written by Gavril, the abbot of the Atonite monasteries, setting forth the views of the Craiovescu boyars and of Neagoe Basarab.

Apocryphal religious writings were very popular. Many of them, under the influence of Bogomil Manicheism, show life in this world as a permanent struggle between the forces of good and evil. Also, the popular romances were relished in all social classes, the most appreciated being *Varlaam and Ioasaph*, a Christian version of Buddha's life, and *Alexandria*, a legendary biography of Alexander of Macedon.

In the early years of the sixteenth century Radu the Great, prince of Wallachia, brought the printing press into the country, the printer being the Serbian monk Macarie, who, after an apprenticeship at Venice, had printed a number of Slavonic books at Cetinje. The first work printed by Macarie was *The missal* in 1508, followed by a *Hymn Book* in 1510 and a *Gospel* in 1512. Macarie's death left a gap in printing, which was resumed in 1545 under the guidance of the Serbian Dimitrie Liubavici. It is to be observed that the Tîrgovişte printing press printed also for Moldavia, which is a confirmation of the close relationship between the two Romanian countries. The first printing press in Transylvania was introduced in 1528, and a *Treatise on the Plague* was printed at Sibiu by the Saxon Luca Trapoldner in 1530. It was also at Sibiu that the first book printed in Romanian was brought out in 1544. This is *The Romanian Cathechism*, printed by Filip the Moldavian to whom the printing of *The Slavo-Romanian Gospel* of 1551-1553 is also ascribed.

The writings in Romanian were of great importance for the development of Romanian culture. The Chancellery and the Church used the Slavonic language in Wallachia and Moldavia and Latin in Transylvania. Though in the past the appearance of the first writings in Romanian was ascribed to the influence of the Hussite doctrine or of the Reformation, it was actually a direct consequence of the transformations wrought within Romanian society, which enabled the lesser Romanian gentry and the townspeople to gain access to culture. These were sections of society that had no knowledge of the ancient Slavonic culture and consequently used the national language and encouraged its use. The first text in Romanian known to have appeared in Wallachia is the letter of a Cîmpulung townsman, Neacşu, to the mayor of Braşov in 1521. In Transylvania and in Maramureş the first writings in Romanian appeared at the end of the fifteenth century and the beginning of the sixteenth: *The Voroneţ Codex*, *The Scheia Psalter*, *The Voroneţ Psalter*, and *The Hurmuzachi Psalter*, all characterized by consistent rhotacism, with intervocalic "n" turned into "r".

As the Reformation spread in Transylvania, its plea for the religious service to be officiated in the language of the faithful, and the proselytism of the followers of the new faith, stimulated the printing of books in Romanian. An important part in spreading Romanian books was played by Deacon Coresi, supported by the Romanian community of the Schei (district in Braşov) and by the ruling princes of Moldavia and Wallachia. The comprehensive use of the printing press by Coresi in Braşov between 1559 — when he printed the first Romanian book — and 1583, helped to build up the Romanian literary language and to shake off Slavonism.

The Reformation was preceded and favored by the spread of humanism, whose illustrious representative was Nicolaus Olahus (1493-1568), who came from a Wallachian family that had taken refuge in Transylvania. Holding high ecclesiastical and lay offices, for he was archbishop and primate as well as regent of Hungary, Nicolaus Olahus kept up close relations with the humanist circles of Europe. Indeed, his correspondence with Erasmus of Rotterdam numbers some forty letters. In his book *Hungaria* (1536), he gives historical and geographic information on the Romanian countries and speaks of the Roman origin of the Romanian people.

The main centers of humanism in Transylvania were the bishoprics of Oradea and Alba Iulia. Interested in science, literature and art, Bishop John Vitez drew many men of letters from other countries to Oradea, where he acted as a Maecenas. The humanists of Alba Iulia under the patronage of Bishop Francis Vardai took interest in the vestiges of Roman rule and civilization in those parts.

From the latter half of the sixteenth century on it is local developments that are more potently reflected in Transylvanian humanism to the detriment of the cosmopolitan spirit, and this also accounts for the large number of writings in the mother tongue. From among the chronicles written in Hungarian, the oldest is that of Gaspar Heltai of Cisnădie (d. 1574), who owes a great deal to Bonfini's works. Written in both Latin and Hungarian, the historical works of Stephen Szamosközy (1565-1612) are the most valuable specimens of humanist historiography in Transylvania and the best written, but the author's hostility towards the Romanians results in an erroneous account of Michael the Brave's exploits, and this detracts from their historical value.

It is the renovating breath of the Reformation that accounts for the progress made in the organization of education. In Transylvania, John Honterus, the reformer of the Saxon Church, established new rules *(Constitutiones Scholae Coronensis)* in 1543, inspired by those of the humanist school of Nuremberg, while in Moldavia Prince Despot founded the ephemeral Latin College at Cotnari (1561-1563), where the German scholar Johann Sommer, a follower of anti-Trinitarianism and the author of Despot's biography, taught. Despot's initiative was continued by Peter the Lame, who brought Jesuits to Moldavia. The school he founded for the boyars' sons functioned at first at Cotnari, then at Jassy where it was preserved with certain interruptions up to the eighteenth century.

## 2. Culture under the Régime the Nobility

IN the seventeenth century Romanian was adopted in the writings of the age even though certain ruling princes, among them Matei Basarab, tried to install new vigor into Slavonic, which had taken refuge in the Church and chancelleries. The ever closer relations among the three Romanian countries, and the express assertion of the Romanian people's Roman origin and unity by the chroniclers of the time as a reflection of the consciousness of the people, invested culture with a national character. Metropolitan Varlaam prefaced his *Homily*, entitled *Romanian Book for Teaching*, by "a word to the whole Romanian nation", while Vasile Lupu called his *Code of Laws*, like Varlaam, *Romanian Book for Teaching*. It was the century when a number of codes and laws were published in Moldavia and Wallachia, these being among the first codes to be published in a national language in Europe. In 1688 a Romanian translation of the Bible was printed, the translation being the work of a team of scholars which included the brothers Şerban and Radu Greceanu.

During this century historiography was again the sphere with the most outstanding achievements to its credit. The preponderance of the great boyars in political life as a consequence of the installation of the régime of the nobility, and the increased access of lay people to culture, which swept away the cultural monopoly of the clergy, accounted for the new type of historiography that emerged at the time. Historical works were no longer written by members of the clergy writing under the patronage, and in the pay of the ruling prince, as had been the case in the preceding century, but by lay people who voiced the political thoughts of the great boyars as a class, or of some boyar factions. Although historical facts were shown and understood according to class interests, Romanian historiography in the seventeenth century can be credited with having sought to prove scientifically the Roman origin of the Romanians and their ethnical unity.

In Moldavia the first historical writing in Romanian was *The Chronicle of the Land of Moldavia* by Court Marshal Grigore Ureche. It was the author's aim to write a history that might serve as a guide, that might "remain to our sons and grandsons, the good in it being a source of teaching and the bad teaching them to avoid it, to ponder over, and only to follow the good". The history of Moldavia is shown here from its foundation to Aaron the Tyrant (1594), in the spirit of the ideology of the great boyars, whose political principles favored a ruling prince devoid of authority and guided by the boyars, like Peter the Lame, whom the chronicler described by a simile borrowed from the Polish historian I. Bielski, as a "queen bee without a sting". Even in the eulogistic portrait made of Stephen the Great, Ureche's admiration for that great prince did not prevent him from remarking upon the stern repression of the boyars' plots, the prince being shown as "hastily shedding innocent blood". But over and above the views of the class to which he belonged are the chronicler's patriotic feelings which impelled him to yearn for a country that was free and strong, worthy of the descendants of Rome. Grigore Ureche was the first Moldavian chronicler to speak of the Roman origin of the Romanian people, adducing as proof the Latin origin of most of the words in the Romanian language. Having stated that the Romanians descended from the Romans, Ureche draws a logical conclusion: the unity of the Romanians everywhere because "they all descend from Rome".

Ureche's work was continued by High Chancellor Miron Costin (1632-1691) who in his *Chronicle of the Moldavian Land from Prince Aaron* on relates the history of Moldavia up to 1661. Relying on a large store of information and endowed with the gift of a great storyteller, Miron Costin produced a work that belongs equally to historiography, political thought, and belles-lettres, abounding in memorable passages. Like his predecessor, Miron Costin was a partisan of the boyar régime and, like him, he wished his homeland to emerge from the difficulties which the vicissitudes of history had heaped upon it. Wishing to enhance the prestige of his nation, Miron Costin devoted a special work, the first of its kind in Romanian historical literature, to the Roman origin of the Romanians. Although the title is *About the Moldavian People*, Miron Costin sets out to show that the Romanians of Moldavia, Wallachia, and Transylvania are "all people arising at the same time," and after giving a number of proofs in support of the Roman origin of the Romanians, he invites the reader to reconsider his condition in the light of this noble descent: "And now, reader, look at yourself as in a mirror to see from where you come . . .".

In Wallachia, the struggles between boyar factions are reflected in historiography by two chronicles: *The History of Wallachia since the Right-Thinking Christians Came to These Parts (The Cantacuzino Chronicle)*, ascribed to Stoica Ludescu, and *The Histories of the Princes of Wallachia*, ascribed to Radu Popescu. The former describes the Cantacuzinos as protected by God and their opponents, the Băleanus, as "possessed by devils" and "enemies of the Romanian people"; the latter, which shows greater understanding and higher historical gifts, attacks the Cantacuzinos and defends the Băleanus. Both works give the history of Wallachia from its foundation to the end of the reign of Şerban Cantacuzino, though a version of the Cantacuzino Chronicle continues up to January, 1690.

But it was only High Steward Constantine Cantacuzino who produced a history which placed Wallachian historiography on the level of the Moldavian chronicles. Having studied at Padua University, Constantine Cantacuzino relied on a large store of information and was able to weigh the value of historical sources. His *History of Wallachia*, which is unfinished, ends with the arrival of the Huns in the Pannonian plain. The fundamental ideas of this work are the Roman origin and the unity of the Romanians. "The Romanians are true Romans and distinguished Romans in their faith and gallantry . . . But by Romanian I do not understand only those in this country [Wallachia] but also those of Transylvania who are still more true-blooded, and the Moldavians, and all those to be found in other parts". It should be observed that the High Steward realized that Roman rule in Dacia did not mean that the autochthonous population had been wiped out, and he was the first Wallachian chronicler to mention the Dacians as an element in the genesis of the Romanian people. It is also to Constantine Cantacuzino that we owe a map of Wallachia printed in Padua in 1700, providing information on the settlements of the country, the monasteries, the administrative divisions, etc. This is one of the most valuable historical maps.

Although compelled to leave Moldavia after his conflicts with Prince Stefăniţă Lupu, who had ordered that his nose should be marked, Sword-bearer Nicolae Milescu has an important place in Romanian culture. His diary from his journey to China (1675-1678) is a remarkable contribution to the geography and ethnography of the Far East while showing a mind and heart open to the beauty of nature and unable to forget his native Moldavia even when traveling along the remote Yenisei.

Belated humanism, which only preserved the cult of antiquity from among all the initial humanistic ideas, might be a description of the translation of the Psalms by Albert Szenczi Molnar (1574-1634), greatly influenced by the French version of Clément Marot and Théodore de Bèze, and of the paraphrases in Romanian, Hungarian, and German of Ovid's maxims by the Saxon poet Valentin Frank von Frankenstein (1649-1697). Other specimens of continued humanism are the memoirs written in Transylvania at the time, the most noteworthy of which are those of Prince John Kemeny and of the Chancellor Nicholas Bethlen.

Cartesian rationalism, a forerunner of the philosophy of enlightenment, found an enthusiastic propagator in John Apaczai Csere (1625-1659), author of a Magyar encyclopaedia, who studied in Holland and taught first at Alba Iulia, from where he was expelled for his advanced views, and subsequently taught at Cluj.

In the sphere of religious literature, we should recall some works of great importance for the development of literary Romanian. Varlaam, Metropolitan of Moldavia, for instance, translated and printed a Homily (the Gospels explained, followed by a number of hagiographic texts) in 1643. The translation is written in a racy, colorful popular language which caused it to be widely popular also in the two other Romanian countries. Influenced by the work of the Polish poet Jan Kochanowski, Metropolitan Dosoftei produced a Romanian translation of the Psalter in verse, this being the first extensive poetical work in Romanian literature. The rhyme and rhythm are often faulty, but the translation becomes melodious when the popular language crops up.

Although of Georgian origin, Metropolitan Antim Ivireanul gave Romanian literature a number of Sermons where social criticism is vigorously and pithily expressed. The principle of the unity of the language is clearly stated by the Transylvanian Metropolitan Simion Stefan, who in his preface to the translation of The New Testament of 1648 shows his concern about finding a means of expression accessible to the Romanians everywhere. A simile of his has become classical. He wrote: "We well know that words must be like coins, and that those coins are good which travel to all countries and so are words good which are understood by all. We therefore sought, as far as we could, to write in such a way as to be understood by all". The endeavor to secure the triumph of the national language, more emphatic in Transylvania, where national oppression was added to social oppression, is also shown by the decision of the Alba Iulia Synod of 1675 to suspend the priests who continued to officiate in Slavonic.

In the seventeenth century a higher stage was also reached in education. With the assistance of Petru Movilă, the Kiev Metropolitan, Vasile Lupu founded a college at Jassy where Latin was studied. The Kiev scholars who taught there, the most remarkable of whom was Sofronie Poceatzki, were followed in the latter half of the century by a galaxy of Greek scholars, one of whom, Ieremia Cacavela, was Demetrius Cantemir's tutor.

In Wallachia humanist education began at Tîrgoviște, where Pantelimon Ligaridis and Ignatie Petriţis organized a college on a par with any of the best similar institutions in the West. But education assumed a new orientation in Wallachia when Constantine Brâncoveanu founded the Saint Sava School (ca. 1695). The school was organized by the disciples of Teophil Corydaleu, foremost of whom was Sevastos Chimenitul, supporters of the neo-Aristotelian philosophy, with many materialist elements. They had been compelled to leave Constantinople as a result of persecution on the part of both church and Ottoman authorities. Under their guidance the Saint Sava School became a center of advanced thought and one of the best educational establishments of Eastern Europe.

The progress made in Romanian education in Transylvania is also worth mentioning though it was less ambitious. Romanian schools of the Calvinist faith continued their activity alongside village and monastic schools, and also increased in number. Gabriel Bethlen's decision to allow the sons of serfs to attend school opened to the latter the gates of the Protestant colleges in the main centers of Transylvania.

After 1603, the only higher educational establishment in seventeenth century Transylvania was the Academic College of Alba Iulia, which was later removed to Aiud and whose activities unfolded under the banner of rationalist philosophy as set forth by Descartes and John Koch (Coccejus). The Synod of 1646 and 1673 of the Reformed Church stigmatized the college for its ideas.

## 3. Culture in the Period of Declining Feudalism

THE installation of the Phanariot régime in Moldavia and Wallachia and the consolidation of Habsburg rule in Transylvania were unable to check the progress of Romanian culture; outstanding achievements were indeed produced by Romanian culture in the Middle Ages and Early Modern Period in certain spheres. Medieval and Early Modern historiography in the Romanian countries reached the greatest heights of scientific investigation in the works of Demetrius Cantemir, and of artistic perfection in the Chronicle of Ioan Neculce. Its rich store of information provided as well as the thorough analysis of historical sources and the outstanding gift of narrative set the works of Demetrius Cantemir, prince of Moldavia, far above the chronicles. It is with them that modern Romanian historiography begins.

Demetrius Cantemir was the first to make a modern synthesis of the history of the Ottoman Empire. His *Historia Incrementorum Atque Decrementorum Aulae Othomanicae* (1715-1716) is a work of wide range relying on Ottoman sources and especially on the author's own conclusions after a long stay at Constantinople. The fundamental idea of Cantemir's work is summed up in the title: after an ascending phase marked by victories and conquests, the Ottoman Empire had entered a phase of decline. The historian's conclusion was a foundation for the prince's attempt in 1711 to free Moldavia from Ottoman domination. Cantemir's *History of the Ottoman Empire* was translated into many European languages and consequently Cantemir became an authority on Eastern problems.

When Cantemir became a member of the Berlin Academy in 1714, he wrote *Descriptio Moldaviae* at the request of that Academy. It is a comprehensive and modern outlook on the geography, social structure, institutions, ethnography, and culture of Moldavia, and it also gives the political concepts of the author: the necessity of fighting the Ottoman Empire and of the ruling prince holding the reins of government.

In investigating the origins of the Romanian people, Cantemir gave proof of a range of information without precedent in Romanian historiography. His *Chronicle of the Ancient Origin of the Romano-Moldo-Vlachs* relies on sounder information than any of those that had previously tackled the problem. In defending the theory of the Romanians' pure Roman descent, the author falls into the exaggeration of Latinizing many words.

While following the line of the chroniclers' tradition, Ion Neculce shows great literary gifts in his Chronicle, which sets forth the history of Moldavia from 1661 to 1743. Less profound than Miron Costin, Neculce is first and foremost a storyteller with a popular strain throughout his work and a moralist at bottom. His history is full of observations and similes recalling a wise and glib-tongued old villager. In this respect, Neculce is a predecessor of Creangă, the great nineteenth century Romanian storyteller.

In Wallachia historiography did not reach the level attained in Moldavia. Radu Greceanu conscientiously, but without any artistic impulse, put down the daily activities of his patron, Constantine Brâncoveanu. The Chronicle of the "Brancovan Anonymous" writer is devoted to the same prince, but the author is a gifted storyteller. Radu Popescu, author of a comprehensive chronicle which takes us as far as 1729, is caught in the meshes of his own passions. While opposing Brâncoveanu and the Cantacuzinos, he becomes most eulogistic when speaking of the reign of Nicolas Mavrocordat, who had raised him to high office.

It was only at the close of the eighteenth century that Wallachian historiography found a remarkable representative in Mihai Cantacuzino, author of *Genealogy of the Cantacuzinos*, which provides valuable information gathered from many historical sources and from personal memories. Cantacuzino also wrote a *History of Wallachia*, an important work on account of the particulars given on the country's institutions and social structure. In his *Chronography*, Dionisie Ecclesiarhul gives the history of Wallachia from 1764 to 1815, mixing up in his narrative — which has the genuine raciness of popular speech — fanciful information on developments in foreign countries as well as passages showing a surprising understanding of certain situations, as, for example, when he speaks about the similarities between the conditions of the French and Wallachian serfs.

The Banat chronicler Nicolae Stoica of Hațeg wrote, among other things, a comprehensive history of Banat whose final part, devoted to the years 1716-1825, includes the author's memoirs, of value through the abundance and novelty of its information.

In Transylvania before the galaxy of historians who were to make up the Transylvanian School and whose works rise above medieval standards, we will only recall here the *History of the Scheia Church of Brașov* by the Protopop Radu Tempea II, who severely condemned the union with Rome; and the Chronicle in verse entitled *Complaint of the Holy Silvaș Monastery of the Hațeg Diocese in Prislop*. This work likewise violently attacked the followers of the union, laying stress on the baneful consequences of religious division among the Romanians.

In religious literature the intensive activity of Damaschin, bishop of Rîmnic, as a translator, secured the triumph of the Romanian language in church, while the *Prayer Book* printed from 1776 to 1780 by Bishop Chesarie of Rîmnic is remarkable for its sermons that gave vent to national feelings. The Romanian prelate tried to divide the national history into periods, showing that an age of wars and an age of monastery building was followed by a period "during which books were translated from Slavonic into Romanian".

Education made good progress following the measures taken by the authorities in the spirit of the Enlightenment. In Moldavia, Hrisant Notaraș, Patriarch of Jerusalem and a scholar who had attended schools in the great centers of culture of the age, supervised the application of Nicolas Mavrocordat's orders concerning the reorganization of education. In 1766 the Academy of Scholarship and Sciences was founded at Jassy, where Romanian was taught as well as Greek, both ancient and modern, and Latin. In Bucharest the Saint Sava School continued in the spirit inaugurated by Theophil Corydaleu. Ypsilanti's reform of 1776 introduced the teaching of history and geography but excluded the sons of peasants from the school. A great stride forward was made in the use of the national language in education when in 1814 an engineering class was introduced at the Princely Academy in Jassy by Gheorghe Asachi, and the Princely School was set up in Bucharest in 1818, with Gheorghe Lazăr, a Transylvanian, as headmaster. Romanian was used by the teachers of that school.

The reform of education in Transylvania under the laws *Ratio educationis* (1777) and *Norma regia* (1781) made education a lay concern, instituted state control and laid greater stress on the natural sciences. Secondary education in Romanian was soon to boast new institutions — the Sibiu seminary, the Beiuş lyceum, etc. — and the competence and devotion of Gh. Şincai, who inspected primary schools, was to provide no less than 300 new schools for the Romanians of Transylvania. Border schools played an important part in the development of primary education.

## 4. Romanian Mediaeval Art

IN Transylvania, occupied by the Hungarian kingdom, the Romanian population, despite adverse political and social conditions, carried on artistic activities according to popular and orthodox tradition and kept up its connections with the sister countries on the other side of the mountains: Wallachia and Moldavia. Up to the fifteenth century the representatives of the lesser local gentry promoted a form of Romanian art which, though unassuming, showed interesting aspects. Craftsmen who were mostly autochthonous built for these gentry stone churches which all showed the same architectural design: a simplified form of a basilica. Such are the churches of the close of the thirteenth century — Sîntă Mărie Orlea, Strei — and those of the fifteenth century: Strei Sîngiorgiu, Criscior, Ribiţa, etc. These churches are impressive by their picturesque quality devoid of ostentation. The frescoes decorating the interior walls are among the oldest extant paintings to have been made by Romanian painters. Against a traditional Byzantine background — paintings such as those of Sîntă Mărie Orlea of a Paleologus pattern dating back to the fourteenth century — local artists, with an unambitious training, combined late Roman and Gothic elements in a spirit that recalls folk art, achieving an interesting and racy art specific to the complex cultural climate in which the Transylvanian Romanians lived at the time (the fourteenth century).

The most precious gems of Romanian art in Transylvania are the wonderful wooden churches of a later date which the peasants built with impressive craftsmanship down the centuries. Combining traditional Eastern Orthodox and Gothic elements, with the image of the peasant house predominating, those anonymous craftsmen of the Romanian villages scattered all over Transylvania, and especially in Maramureş, produced elegant constructions considered by specialists to rank among the most original creations of wooden architecture in Europe.

The ruins of a number of unassuming churches of the tenth to the thirteenth centuries, the ceramics and metal objects found by archeologists in various regions of the country, show that long before they had formed into states the little principalities which were to constitute Wallachia had made the art based on Byzantine traditions their own, attaining a fairly high level of artistic achievement, and a reasonably wide cultural outlook at the turn of the fourteenth century. This accounts for the pomp and richness of court life in Wallachia starting with the very first princes, as also for the grandeur of the monuments they built. Strengthening the traditional connections of the Romanians with the Balkan peoples by means of family relationships with the Bulgarian and Serbian tsars, and having a Greek Metropolitan appointed at Argeş by the Constantinople Patriarchate, the founders of the first Romanian state naturally brought craftsmen from the Byzantine-Slav south to build their first ambitious monuments. The well-known Princely Church at Argeş dating from the mid-fourteenth century is a fine, sober structure of the Byzantine type, with a centralized plan. The rich frescoes that decorate it show many similarities with the so-called "pro-Greek current" of contemporary Serbian painting. This conclusively shows that Wallachia, from its very beginnings, had been within the sphere of the subtle artistic culture of the Constantinople of the Paleologues of the fourteenth century.

A few decades later craftsmen from Serbia brought into the country a new type of structure: the Serbian triconch different from the older triconch adopted in Wallachia, for it had a special way of supporting the tower on four pillars and four recesses around the apses of the nave. A good illustration of the new type of structure is the elegant church of the Cozia Monastery erected in 1389 by one of the most brilliant princes of Wallachia, Mircea the Old (1386-1418). With its rich decoration of hewn stone and ceramics, this church is a perfect architectural achievement of the craftsmen of the Moravian school. This triconch of Serbian origin, later to be adjusted to the local concepts, was to become the fundamental type of medieval architecture in Wallachia. From the standpoint of the history of culture it is worth recalling that the young Romanian state in its development took over the artistic heritage of the contemporary Balkan world, saving from destruction and carrying further the cultural ideals of the peoples south of the Danube who by 1400 had been almost completely brought into subjection by the Turks. While in Transylvania Romanian medieval art had begun under the influence of both East and West, and the original architectural style of Moldavia showed Roman and Gothic influence from the earliest time, as will be shown hereafter, Wallachia was to continue to be the most "Byzantine". In contrast to the pointed roof of the towers of Moldavian churches, the spherical roof of the towers of the old Wallachian churches strikes the eye as a familiar image characteristic of the Balkan landscape.

Turkish interference caused a recession of the economy and of administration, bringing along insecurity and, implicitly, lack of continuity in constructive efforts. This considerably delayed the consolidation and maturity of native art. When, owing to the inevitable development of Romanian society, the artistic vision was fully formed, and Wallachian art reached its utmost development — in the seventeenth century and the first decades of the eighteenth — the prevailing conditions were those of a belated Middle Ages, when the art of the whole Christian East had reached a stage of final decline. This is the reason why Wallachian medieval art, though interesting and showing much variety, could not attain the synthetic outlook and originality of Moldavian art, which had outstripped its classical period at the moment when the Turks halfway through the sixteenth century interfered in Moldavia.

Looking back we have to note that for the reasons shown above, the fifteenth century was an age of restricted artistic activity, the Brădet Church, an unambitious replica of Cozia, being the only monument still extant in good condition. Early in the sixteenth century, during the reigns of Radu the Great (1494-1508) and Neagoe Basarab (1512-1523), of comparative stability and remarkable cultural flowering, a number of larger churches were built. Since they were so different from one another in their architectural design and decoration, it is obvious that no unitary architectural concepts, no specific style, had been formed in Wallachia until then. The most interesting are the church of the Dealul Monastery (1500) and the church of the Argeş Bishopric (1517), because they still belong to local tradition owing to their triconch plan, despite their sumptuous decoration of hewn stone of the Armenian-Georgian type. And there is more in them: both by their luxurious aspect and their unusual shape, these two monuments were to strike the imagination of future generations, who used them as their model in the great edifices of the seventeenth and eighteenth centuries. This is especially true of the Dealul Monastic Church.

However, the unassuming churches built all through the sixteenth century, with their compact structure and friendly, charming aspect, are more interesting than the large ones, for they show the gradual formation of a specific Romanian outlook. Apart from their triconch plan which is adopted by all these churches, their main feature is the specific vividness of the façades. Made according to the traditional Byzantine principle, with alternating strips of brick and plaster, the façades often show blind arcades in relief, these becoming the specific element of Wallachian churches until just before the modern age. They were inspired by the prototype of the church of the Argeş Bishopric but were made in brick instead of stone and divided towards the end of the century by a strip going all round the church in two superimposed registers. One of the most remarkable examples is the Mihai Vodă Church in Bucharest built by Michael the Brave in 1600.

In the first half of the seventeenth century and in particular during the great building activity in the reign of Matei Basarab (1632-1654), there was to be an interesting diversity in the façades. Some churches adopted the forms of the Dealul Church while others, among them the impressive Metropolitan Church of Bucharest (1658), imitated the Argeş church. Churches of a rectangular shape appeared alongside those of the triconch type, and sometimes the former had a bell tower over the pronaos. But the most characteristic element of those times is the handsome open porch with strong brick pillars at the western side of the church. This recalls the veranda specific to peasant and boyar houses in Wallachia and its general use in church architecture is reminiscent of the folk art, for this was an age when the native Romanian art increasingly asserted itself.

In the latter half of the seventeenth century, Wallachian architecture continued faithfully in the style of the preceding age, without any innovations in design. There was, however, a main change in decoration. The fashion for all-plastered façades became general, the latter thus losing their variegated aspect. But similarly, a new decorative concept evolved which surpassed the older one in beauty. Carved stone appeared around the windows and on the decorative strip of the façades, as well as abundantly in the porch, decorating the door leading into the church, the balustrade, the basis, capitals, and sometimes also the shafts of the elegant columns which had superseded the thick brick pillars. Unlike the old geometrical sculpture of the Argeş church, this is floral and vegetal, and the technique is more advanced, with strong reliefs and substantially influenced by Renaissance and Baroque art, with their Corinthian and Neo-Corinthian capitals, with acanthus and fern leaves and anthropomorphic and zoomorphic motifs. This exuberant and eclectic style which gives a specific character to the churches of those days (Colţea, Sinaia, Hurez, Doiceşti, etc.), setting off the beauty of the porch, has been named the Brancovan style because it was most extensively used during the reign of Constantine Brâncoveanu (1688-1714) with its great cultural and artistic achievements. The first decades of the eighteenth century were to adopt the same architectural vision, the last emphatic example being the imposing church of the Văcăreşti Monastery (1722) and the small Stavropoleos Church of Bucharest (1730), a genuine gem of Wallachian art. Thereafter, up to the beginning of the nineteenth century, that is up to the eve of the modern age, religious architecture declined in Wallachia.

Parallel with church architecture, civil architecture, now mostly in ruins, also showed a remarkable development in the seventeenth and eighteenth centuries. The so-called *cule*, fortified boyar houses of two or three storeys, are most original. They are of Balkan origin but an open veranda such as is seen in peasant houses was added to them and their general aspect is completely Romanian, as can be seen in those of Măldărești, Cartiu, etc., of the eighteenth century. The palaces of the great boyars and of the ruling princes show the wealth and refined luxury of the life of the Wallachian upper classes of those days. In their architecture there is a combination of Turkish and Italian influence and of traditional Romanian elements. The interior had vaulted ceilings of great variety, and walls sumptuously decorated with stucco after the Oriental fashion. The most significant examples are the palaces of Potlogi and Mogoșoaia built by Constantine Brânco-veanu.

A distinctive Romanian architectural outlook began to make itself felt in Wallachia during the sixteenth century, while in painting this became apparent only later. Wallachian painting of the sixteenth century is an art of fair craftsmanship, sometimes showing some virtuosity, in its elegance, but cold and old-looking — a specific feature of the decline of contemporary painting in the Balkan countries. The painters were mostly foreign. As the seventeenth century wore on, the number of commissions increased considerably as did also the number of native craftsmen, and consequently specific Romanian concepts are seen in the painters' work. Murals became more decorative, with a large number of ornamental floral and vegetal motifs; folklore elements also emerged: local dress, popular work tools, musical instruments, folk dances, etc. In the boyar churches at Mărgineni, Măgureni, Bordești, Filipeștii de Pădure, and elsewhere, Pîrvu Mutul, the most renowned Wallachian painter of the latter half of the seventeenth century, showed his vigorous gift of portraiture in the portraits he painted of the founders' families and in his own portrait. He gave rise to another generation of Romanian painters, some of whom were responsible for the important ensembles of the Princely Monastery of Hurez (ca. 1700) — the most representative piece of work showing the trends of the age, and the point of departure of the following century's painting.

Though interesting in themselves as cultural phenomena, no innovations could rejuvenate at such a late date medieval painting whose esthetic principles went counter to the growing trends towards a realist outlook. Indeed, painting had become a formal exercise, empty of any significance. For this reason the paintings of the eighteenth and the early nineteenth centuries adorning the small but very numerous village churches, in particular those in Oltenia, are far more interesting. The painters were peasants, unambitious and without any special training, but able to create a spontaneous and vital art despite their compositional naïveté and the faults in their drawing. The murals with greatly restricted religious themes — simplified, rusticated, and circumscribed by vigorous vegetal ornaments — became an impressive line of portraits of peasant founders in national dress completely dominating the walls (in the churches at Bălţişoara, Cîmpofeni, Somăneşti, Schela Horezu, Baia de Aramă, Baia de Fier, etc.). This dissolution of Byzantine esthetics into folklore is perhaps the most original trait of medieval painting in Wallachia.

Having developed from a nucleus in the northeast part of present-day Romania, the Moldavian state was from the earliest years of its existence closely connected with the Western world, through Maramureş, and less with the Balkan world. Consequently, the first brick church erected by the first Moldavian prince — the Rădăuţi Church where the princes were buried — is a Western-type structure, more precisely a Romanesque basilica with three naves and a cylindrical vault but divided into nave and fore-nave according to the Orthodox custom. Later the Moldavian state grew receptive to the artistic forms of the Balkan world. This was achieved through the agency of Wallachia. This is how the triconch of Serbian origin, adopted in Wallachia, as shown above, penetrated into Moldavia where the Saint Trinity Church of Siret was built by Petru Muşat (1375-1391) in that style. But whereas the Cozia Church was faithful in every detail to the traditions of the Moravian school, the Siret Church diverges from them in certain respects, for it has no recesses or pillars of support in the nave, whose shape is more simple and unitary.

Towards the close of the fourteenth century, when Petru Muşat started what we might call a drive of military and church building, and later during the reign of Alexander the Good (1400-1432), Moldavia went through an age of considerable progress in its economy and in culture. The ruins of some churches showing a number of creditable experiments and quests, beautiful manuscripts, with and without miniatures, made by Gavril Uric, and some remarkable pieces of embroidery, make it manifest that this was an age when Moldavian art in full formative process had begun to instill its own concepts of beauty into all the arts, thus laying the foundations of the most original cultural phenomenon of the Romanian people in the Middle Ages.

Moldavian art was to reach its culminating point in the age of Stephen the Great (1457-1504), an age of maximum economic and political, as well as cultural, progress of the Moldavian state. The resounding victories won by the Romanian armies under the leadership of the great strategist in the struggle against the Turks, the Tartars, and the Poles, spread Moldavia's military fame far and wide in Europe, turning the small but heroic state into a powerful bastion of the Christian world, standing after the fall of Constantinople in the way of Ottoman aggression. And the military genius of Stephen the Great was coupled to a great gift for promoting the artistic and cultural development of the country which, under his long reign, was filled with citadels, palaces and churches.

The second great age of progress in Moldavian art was that of Petru Rareș, son of Stephen the Great and audacious continuer of his work (1527-1538; 1541-1546). But when the armies of Petru Rareș were defeated in 1538 by the giant Ottoman offensive led by Suleiman the Magnificent, the Turks began to interfere also in Moldavia. Somewhat restricted during the first decades of the century, Turkish interference intensified towards the close of the sixteenth and in the seventeenth and eighteenth centuries, seriously impairing the independence of the Moldavian state and bringing about a political and economic decline.

As already stated, two types of churches were built in Moldavia at first — the Romanesque church of Rădăuți and the Siret Church of triconch design — and it was along these two lines that Moldavian religious architecture was to develop. The triconch type with cupola was to become the fundamental type, the overwhelming majority of town, village and court churches being built in that style during the fifteenth and the sixteenth centuries. Nevertheless, the rectangular type of church after the Rădăuți model but with one nave, with side arcades and pillars in the northern and southern walls, also continued to be built. Owing to the prestige of the tradition left by Bogdan I, the founder of the state, the rectangular type was to be preserved until the first decades of the sixteenth century in the burial churches. The oldest example of this type of church is to be found at Dolheşti (1470-1480). It might be interesting to note that in bulding the Hîrlău Church (1492), the local craftsmen created the most perfect exemplary of the Moldavian triconch, and thenceforth they were to transfer their creative efforts on the rectangular type of church with the aim of adjusting it to their own vision. The Borzeşti (1493), Războieni (1496), and Piatra Neamţ (1498) churches furnish proof of that contention.

But the craftsmen of Stephen the Great went still further when they built the church of the Neamţ Monastery in 1497, for this famous structure of impressive dimensions is a complex form of the triconch type. This church, the most outstanding example of fifteenth century architecture, was to become the prototype of the great structures of the following century.

But the synthesis achieved by the builders of Stephen the Great between the architecture of the West and of the East did not confine itself to structural problems. It also affected the decoration of the monuments. From the Gothic churches raised by the Catholics in Moldavia at the end of the fourteenth and the early fifteenth centuries, the Moldavian craftsmen adopted a number of specific Gothic elements which they gradually incorporated into their architecture, namely the buttresses and the frames of doors, windows, and portals. With their shape and dimensions adjusted to suit the new churches that were built, they became specific to the Moldavian style in the reign of Stephen the Great, enhacing the beauty of the façades.

But the creative imagination of fifteenth-century builders is shown not only in the composition spoken of above, but also in the new, indeed unique, systems of construction devised by them and not met with elsewhere, either in the East or the West. The most impressive example is the so-called Moldavian vault. Instead of raising the tower of the churches of triconch design on the ring obtained from the four usual pendentives of an Eastern Orthodox church, the Moldavian craftsmen encased in that ring a second row of smaller diagonal pendentives over which they raised a much slimmer tower than the traditional Byzantine type. This type of vault, which came into general use in Moldavia, changed the exterior outline of the tower. Laid on two superimposed, star-shaped bases, corresponding to the two rows of pendentives, and terminating in a pointed roof which dominates the roofs of the three apses, also pointed, and of the western part of the church, this elegant tower enhances the delicate outline of the monuments. Height and slimness are indeed specific to Moldavian churches, especially to those of triconch design, in contrast with the lower and more compact outline of the churches of the Balkan area. Another characteristic of these churches is the irreproachable proportioning of their component parts. To this should be added the manner of decorating the façade, with the long recesses of the apses, the rows of niches all round the edifice below the eaves, the sumptuous polychrome bricks and the broad strip of enameled disks in contrast with the sternness of the rough stone walls recalling those of a stronghold — all of which builds up the image of an architectural style that specialists consider to be among the most original achievements of Christian architecture in the East.

In the sixteenth century Moldavian architecture was to evolve along the traditional line of the preceding century, the difference being that in some of the more important churches, which include a burial crypt with porch after the example of the Neamţ Church, the porch recalls a portico supported on big brickwork pillars, which gives the façade a new, unexpected touch (Humor, Moldoviţa). Halfway through the sixteenth century, churches of the mixed type were built, with a tower above the nave (Zăhăreşti — 1542, Slatina — 1568). This was the prototype of most of the large churches to be built in the following centuries: Dragomirna (ca. 1609), Solca (1615), Golia in the town of Jassy (1650-1660), Caşin (1655), Saint Spiridon in Jassy (1804), Frumoasa (1836).

However, towards the end of the sixteenth century, the unity of the Moldavian style of the classical period was disrupted by outside influences which were to introduce structural changes as well as new principles in the decoration of the façades. The church of the Galata Monastery (1582) shows the influence of Wallachian architecture. The churches of this type have two towers instead of one and their façades are decorated with two registers of blind arcades. In the first half of the seventeenth century a new influence of Oriental origin was to add a sumptuous covering of hewn stone, with interlaced geometrical motifs, on the tower — at Dragomirna, for example — and later on all the walls — for example, at the Three Hierarchs' Church in Jassy. During the latter half of the century the impressive church of the Golia Monastery in Jassy was to introduce transitional Baroque elements: neo-Corinthian pillars to decorate the façades. The eclectic aspect was emphasized in the eighteenth century, as the churches of Saint George (1716) and Saint Teodori (1761) in Jassy show. Finally, with a powerful neo-classical current reaching Moldavia, especially from Poland, Moldavian religious architecture broke away from its old traditions to assume a new aspect specific to the nineteenth century.

Unlike its architecture, where Western elements played an important part, Moldavian painting was faithful to the Byzantine tradition. Slav and Byzantine elements, to which a creative impulse was added by the brilliant local craftsmen, inspired the first great period in the early years of the fifteenth century, though nothing much has been left of the churches thus decorated, except the lovely miniatures made by Gavril Uric. During the reign of Stephen the Great, Moldavian painting appears as the work of a fully crystallized national school with the same principles applied in iconography and decoration. Recently the signature was discovered of the most remarkable painter of those days — Gavril, the Monk of Bălinești (1493) — which proves that the craftsmen were Romanian. A distinguishing feature of Moldavian painting is the perfect harmony between it and the lines and volume of the building; moreover, the proportions of the composition and of the personages, in accordance with the dimensions of the space allotted them, brings the painting in full focus of the viewer's eye. The small number of personages, the clear outline of their figures, the subtle yet robust lines of the compact design, the grave simplicity of gesture and attitude, without a trace of rhetoric, the extreme sobriety of dress and superficial ornaments, expressiveness and calm concentration of portraiture — are all features reflecting the moral climate of sobriety and controlled power of the age of Stephen the Great, as shown by the best paintings of the Voroneţ, Saint Eliah, Pătrăuţi, and Popăuţi churches. The elegant frescoes of Bălineşti add a touch of sumptuousness and subtle poetry.

The painting of the following century is less expressive and shows a tendency towards formal effects and decoration for its own sake. The saints have a military attitude and, with their sumptuous dress and graceful poise, look almost like court pages, a reflection of the brilliant court life of the reign of Petru Rareş. The painters undoubtedly tried to introduce lay freedom into the severe ethics of the medieval esthetic outlook. It is significant that, in this age when towns and crafts were developing apace, the greatest artists were no longer members of the clergy, as in the fifteenth century, but laymen, like the painters Toma of Homor (1535) and Dragoş Coman of Arbure (1541). It was the age when the most original specimen of Romanian medieval art made its appearance: the exterior frescoes — unique in the world — on the walls of Moldavian churches.

While the paintings inside the churches were dedicated to a religious purpose, as everywhere throughout the Middle Ages, their main aim being to save the souls of the faithful, exterior painting was something like a prayer designed to inspire the people in the struggle for the independence of their country, for it appeared at the dramatic moment when the Ottoman threat was most serious.

Imbued with the spirit of folklore, Moldavian exterior paintings are distinguished by elegant outlines generously distributed against the blue background of the apses, as well as by the unequaled brilliance of their coloring inspired by Romanian folk art, by the green fir woods surrounding the monuments, the grass-covered hills, the many-colored flowers in the meadows and the blue Moldavian sky. This makes of the paintings an integral part of the landscape around the churches.

When the Moldavian state declined, mural painting became noncommittal, the heroic subjects of old being superseded by abstract theological subjects. There is a distinct mannerism about them. A brilliant example of such painting is the church of the Suceviţa Monastery, which Ieremia Movilă (1595-1606) commissioned to be painted both inside and out. It is with good reason that Paul Henri described it as "the Testament of Moldavian classical art". The seventeenth and eighteenth centuries witnessed the decline of Moldavian medieval painting, which was more emphatic and more rapid than in Wallachia. At a time when the major art of the age — the chroniclers' art — originating in direct observation of reality, shows the inexorable tendency towards placing man in the center of the world, as does modern art, medieval esthetics based on spiritualism and a symbolism that made the deity the center, had had its day and was lagging irrevocably behind the course of history.

*Part 3*

# MODERN HISTORY

# CHAPTER I

# The Revolution of 1821.
# The Rule of Native Princes
# is Re-established

THE revolution of 1821 meant a great stride forward in the development of the Romanian people. It was a movement essentially different from the spontaneous, unorganized peasant uprisings of the Middle Ages: its program demanded national independence, personal freedom, equality before the law, and removal of all impediments to the free exercise of industry and trade; its motive power was the liberal boyars, the bourgeoisie — at the time in its formative process — and the free peasants, whom Karl Marx considered as belonging to the middle class; it aligned itself within a European revolutionary movement; and its organization and leadership as well as the wide response it called forth in all the countries inhabited by Romanians also made it different from the peasant uprisings of former times.

The abolition of the Phanariot régime and the restoration of the rule of the native princes after Tudor Vladimirescu's revolution did not amount to a mere change of figureheads but was a genuine national revolution. The immense resources that had gone to the maintenance of the ruling princes and the Phanariot court surrounding them were now left in the country and served to modernize Romanian institutions. In 1829, by the Treaty of Adrianople, the Romanians obtained freedom to trade and the right to open factories and mines; they recovered the citadels along the Danube and thenceforth the frontier between the Principalities and Turkey was the Danube. All this was achieved as a result of Tudor Vladimirescu's movement and in conformity with the demands of the boyars. Even though Tudor's comprehensive program was not implemented, the more restricted program set forth in the boyars' memorials was carried out in part immediately after the movement had been defeated and the other part between 1821 and 1831. Like any other national liberation movement, the revolution of 1821 caused all classes of Romanian society to join forces in the struggle against Ottoman domination. And this genuine social and national liberation movement opened a new age in Romanian history: the modern age.

In the period between Tudor Vladimirescu's revolution and the revolution of 1848, the crisis of feudalism was aggravated, the social background of a national policy became more comprehensive, and the intellectuals trained in the schools of the country or abroad worked out a political program and adopted the ideas of the Transylvanian School, turning them into a ready weapon. To begin with, Greek culture supported by the great boyars, the high clergy and the educational system, lost its prestige. After 1821 Greek schools were closed and replaced by Romanian ones, many teachers coming from Transylvania.

In the second place, the abolition of the Ottoman trading monopoly gave a powerful impulse to the national economy while the *Règlement Organique*, putting some order into political life, gave it greater stability and created favorable conditions for the development of capitalism and for the movement towards independence and unification. On the other hand, with the preponderance of the great boyars in state affairs, the *Règlement Organique* aggravated the antagonism between the main classes of society as well as the crisis of feudalism. In all three Romanian countries the crisis was punctuated by a number of revolts which ultimately led to the revolution of 1848.

## 1. Causes of the Revolution of 1821

FROM the latter half of the eighteenth century, the independence movement of the Christian peoples in European Turkey, being favored by the military defeats of the Turks and the revolutionary agitation fomented by France, had made unceasing progress and, as a result of the growth of economic and social forces, assumed revolutionary proportions in the early years of the nineteenth century. The Serbians rose in revolt in 1804 and, after ten years' fighting, achieved their autonomy in 1815. With the Romanian people's national consciousness strengthened, their struggle for the preservation of the autonomy of the Principalities was given a new impetus. Upon the Bulgarians, Paisy's writings (1762) had the effect of setting them at variance with Greek culture and awakened their national feelings. But despite these tendencies to be free from Ottoman rule, their objective could not be attained as their efforts were sporadic and disconnected.

A secret society — *Etaireia* — founded at Odessa in 1814 by three Greek merchants, resolved to unite all the Christian peoples in European Turkey in a joint struggle for their independence. The society gained popularity in all the Mediterranean and Black Sea ports, where Greek colonies were to be found, as well as in the main towns of European Turkey. In Bucharest, Jassy, and Galatz, branches of the society were set up which were joined not only by Greeks but also by a number of Romanian boyars, merchants, and prelates.

*Etaireia* propaganda was favored by the revolutionary movement under way in all South and Central European countries against the reactionary rule which had been restored after the fall of Napoleon. The Carbonari societies were at this time making attempts upon the lives of the reactionary leaders in the Italian states and against their tools. In Spain, Italy, and Portugal revolutions broke out which only the military intervention of the Holy Alliance was able to put down.

The revolutionary movement of 1821, which started in Oltenia, spread throughout the Romanian Principalities, and, though suppressed in the Principalities, continued in Greece, was no local, spontaneous uprising as the feudal rebellions had been. By its causes, aims, and results it was part of the wider movement which threatened the reactionary régimes of Central and Southern Europe.

In the Romanian Principalities the first two decades of the nineteenth century saw the oppression and exploitation of the people ruthlessly practiced and the awakening of national consciousness. The war of 1806-1812 had exhausted the two countries, but they quickly recovered after peace had been concluded. Years of abundant rainfall caused farming output to rise. But although the balance of trade was favorable, the balance of payments showed a deficit that increased with every passing year: gold flowed out of the countries to the Porte and to build up a stock for the ruling princes abroad.

The financial crisis further emphasized the drawbacks of the Turko-Phanariot and feudal régimes. Both producers and merchants complained that customs duties, home taxation, and export licenses, which were sold by the ruling princes, absorbed nearly all their profits. The dependent peasants had additional feudal burdens to bear and, moreover, there were boyar and monastery monopolies, and fiscal extortion, which had become all the more oppressive as the total of tax-payers had been reduced to half the previous figure owing to the increase in the number of those exempted from taxa-tion: peasants, who paid dues to the landowner, and merchants newly risen to the rank of boyar.

The free peasants, who made up one-third of the rural population, complained that though the exports of pigs, wool, and wine were permitted, obstacles were raised in the way of prohibitive taxes. The *pandours*, who were recruited from among the free peasantry, had been exempted from taxation as a reward for their military services. But Prince Caragea canceled their exemption and consequently they became receptive to revolutionary propaganda and joined Tudor Vladimirescu's army.

There was also discontent among the merchants and tradesmen. The régime of the Capitulations made them unable to face the competition of foreign merchants, who were exempted from the taxation the native merchants had to pay. The domestic market could not be protected by a tariff without the Capitulations being abolished, consequently without the overthrow of Ottoman rule.

Even the great boyars, who realized that they could increase the incomes they derived from their lands now that limits had been set to the supplies to the Porte, became partisans of free trade which could not be achieved without the suppression of Ottoman monopoly. In the various me-morials they submitted to the imperial cabinets in St. Peters-burg and Vienna, they demanded that the citadels on the Danube be restored to Wallachia, the tribute to the Porte be cut, trade should become free, and right to open factories and mines be guaranteed.

This was a program whose implementation was likely to open wide prospects for the capitalist system, and all classes of society were ready to rise against Ottoman rule in order to see it carried out. But whereas the boyars had no wish to give up their feudal privileges, the peasants, tradesmen and shopkeepers were eager to overthrow the whole feudal organization, together with the Phanariot régime.

The union of the various sections of society in the struggle for freedom from foreign domination became possible only after a national consciousness had been formed. And this national consciousness was built up by the movement of the intelligentsia known by the name of the Transylvanian School which came into being at the close of the eighteenth century as an expression of the struggle of the Romanian people of Transylvania to have themselves recognized as a fourth political nation. Samuil Micu-Klein, Gheorghe Șincai, and Petru Maior, the most outstanding representatives of this school, gave historical and philological proof of the Roman origin of the Romanian people and language, and consequently of their being the first inhabitants of Transylvania.

They used the heroic name of Dacia as a sum total of the aspirations of all Romanians towards political and cultural unity, and it was on it that they based their reasons for nurturing such aspirations. As part of the community of Latin peoples, the Romanians could defy the so-called superiority of the other political nations and religions as well as the Greek culture in the two Principalities. The word Dacia became a manifesto in the historical and literary publications of the three Romanian countries.

The second generation of the Transylvanian intelligentsia, represented by Timoteiu Cipariu, Simion Bărnuțiu, and George Barițiu, no longer claimed equality with the privileged social categories, but based their claim on the numerical superiority of the Romanians and their great contribution to the state's finances, and thus demanded political preponderance.

The Transylvanian scholars and professors, foremost of whom was Gheorghe Lazăr, spread the ideas of the Transylvanian School also in the two Principalities, turning them into weapons in the struggle for unification and national independence. The educational system introduced by Gheorghe Lazăr at the Saint Sava school was national because the teaching was in the language of the nation and the ideas it advocated were "national". Gheorghe Lazăr's system was continued by Eliade Rădulescu.

Shortly before the insurrection of 1821 all sections of society had been prepared to rise against the Turks. Such was the background against which the *Etaireia* propaganda worked, and as the propagandists, who were mainly Greeks working in the Russian Consulates, had been given assurance of support from Russia, many people joined the *Etaireia*, among them the high clergy, the great boyars with Grigore Brânco-veanu at their head, as well as shopkeepers and artisans. Tudor Vladimirescu, who was to give the signal of a general insurrection, had been initiated into the *Etaireia* shortly before the outbreak of the revolution.

## 2. Tudor Vladimirescu's Movement

BORN into a family of free peasants in the village of Vla-dimiri in the Gorj county around 1780, Tudor Vladimirescu, through education, trade, and the offices he filled, rose above the condition of his parents and became part of those new men whom a memorial of the boyars of Oltenia described as a permanent revolutionary ferment.

In 1806 he was appointed sheriff (*vătaf de plaiu*) at Cloșani in the Gorj county, an office which he held until the revolution. During the war of 1806-1812 he fought at the head of a corps of pandours and was awarded St. Vladimir's Order for gallantry and his services in the field, and was subsequently promoted to the rank of lieutenant and placed under Russian protection.

On January 15, 1821, when Prince Alecu Suțu had just died or was about to die, a Protection Committee was made up of the highest boyars, all affiliated with the *Etaireia*.

The same day the most outstanding among them — Grigore Brâncoveanu, Grigore Ghica (the ruling prince to be), and Barbu Văcărescu — concluded an agreement with Tudor Vla-dimirescu under which the latter assumed the obligation of "raising the people to arms" while the boyars undertook to supply the necessary means for war. Tudor Vladimirescu's action was to be the signal for a general insurrection, when a diversion would be created along the Danube in order to draw the Turkish forces there and thus make it easier for Alexander Ypsilanti to reach Greece.

During the night of January 18-19, 1821, Tudor began a march upon Oltenia in the course of which, at the head of a group of mercenaries, he called to arms all the counties in that part of the country, promising justice and freedom. Within a few days he had accomplished his aim. From the Tismana Monastery he issued a manifesto which ran: "Brothers living in Wallachia, whatever your nationality, no law prevents a man to meet evil with evil...... How long shall we suffer the dragons that swallow us alive, those above us, both clergy and politicians, to suck our blood? How long shall we be enslaved?..... Neither God nor the Sultan approves of such treatment of their faithful. Therefore, brothers, come all of you and deal out evil to bring evil to an end, that we might fare well... And you should come to wheresoever you will hear that the Assembly convened for the good and the benefit of the country is to be found, and whatsoever the leaders of the Assembly advise you to do, do it faithfully and wheresoever they will summon you to come, there you should come!"

The proclamation claimed a legal basis for the uprising — the right to oppose an oppressive government; the army was the "Assembly of Release" organizing a movement for the good and benefit of the community. In conclusion, there was a warning that no one should touch "even a grain" of another's property except for "the ill-gotten property and wealth of the tyrant boyars, which were to be destroyed". For tactical reasons the boyars who joined the movement were to be exceptions, "as promised".

The peasants, however, did not make distinctions. For them all boyars were tyrants and their fortunes ill-gotten, and so all boyar and monastery property was to be destroyed. Possessed by "the spirit of revenge" they "sped blindly" under Tudor's banners. In a few days the uprising had spread over the whole of Oltenia and "the entire Principality began to totter". Wherever he went, Tudor was greeted like "a protective god". The people called him "Prince Tudor".

From Oltenia the uprising extended over the whole of Wallachia and also called forth a powerful response in Transylvania, where the Romanians were sure that the noblemen would soon be exterminated, that Tudor would be coming to mete out justice and rid them of the nobility. In Moldavia there were only local, isolated incidents. There the mass of the people were less stirred because no one had promised to rid them of Ottoman rule and the boyars' exploitation.

Tudor's proclamation was made known throughout Wallachia as well as in Transylvania; it was like a declaration of war addressed to the boyars and to the whole feudal system. The Moldavian Court Marshal, Iacovache Rizo Merulos, wrote to Ypsilanti: "Tudor Vladimirescu had raised all the counties beyond the Olt by the day before yesterday, proclaiming liberty and equality and the abolition of boyar privileges, avenging those unfairly treated and returning the plunder. His proclamations call upon all to take up arms".

Throughout Oltenia the revolutionary spirit turned the formerly "kindly and submissive population" into ruthless avengers of oppression and extortion. The villagers attacked the estates of the boyars and monasteries, broke into the barns and divided the stores among themselves. But the fury of destruction struck especially at the center of the landowners' power, the country houses, where, apart from the fruit of the serfs' labor, the books with the unjust accounts were kept. The books were burned by the rebels. These outbursts against long stored-up injustice threatened to turn the movement into a "blind" uprising and to compromise everything. Tudor consequently severely punished the acts of plunder committed by some of the men in his army. He maintained strict discipline and his *pandours*, who made up most of his army, occupied the fortified monasteries in Oltenia: Tismana, Strehaia, and Motru. These he filled with provisions, leaving garrisons able to resist Turkish attacks. At the same time he took a number of measures for the financial and administrative organization of the country. He changed the prefects (*ispravnici*) and appointed to the posts "husbandmen" risen from the ranks of shopkeepers, whom he invested with administrative and military duties. But his attempt to replace the old boyar administration by a popular one was unsuccessful. Under pressure of the boyars, Tudor had to revoke it. However, his move significantly showed the revolutionary character of the uprising.

In order to lull the vigilance of the Turks and forestall their military intervention, Tudor sent the Porte a statement to the effect that he was faithful to the Ottoman rule and that his movement was against the Phanariot princes who, jointly with the boyars, "robbed and flayed us so that we are left only with our souls". Simultaneously, however, he gave the emperors of Russia and Austria the reasons that had caused the people to rise against their oppressors and "he made bold to demand the support and intervention of the two emperors".

For as long as it was possible, the Protection Committee kept Tudor's uprising and his proclamations secret from the Porte and, when they had to send a report, they minimized the events, describing them as if they had all been a plundering undertaking for the suppression of which the internal military forces sufficed. But the forces the Committee sent to Oltenia to bring the rebels back to "their holy duty of obedience" merely strengthened Tudor's camp. The heads of the mercenaries were members of the *Etaireia*. Having left sufficient defense forces at Craiova, Tudor took the bulk of his army — 5,000 Oltenia foot soldiers, among them many Transylvanian deserters, and 1500 Albanian mercenaries — to Bucharest. Marching through mud and slush at the rate of 25 kilometers a day, an excellent performance for the best organized armies in those days, he reached Bolintinul din Vale near Bucharest on March 16.

Here he learned that the Tsar had condemned the events in Wallachia, threatening to join forces with his allies to put down the revolution and declaring Tudor Vladimirescu to have forfeited the title of Knight of the Order of St. Vladimir and his position as a Russian protégé. This shattered the hopes of success of the *Etaireia*. The principal members of the Protection Committee took refuge in Transylvania.

Although Bimbasha Sava, commander of the Bucharest garrison, tried to prevent Tudor from entering Bucharest before Ypsilanti's arrival, Tudor entered "his capital" where he was received with great enthusiasm by the population. From Bolintinul din Vale, he launched a call to all those inhabitants of Bucharest who had not forgotten that they were "part of the same nation" and had not allowed "the holy love of the homeland" to die in their hearts, asking them to join him in order to restore "our rights". He asked that two delegates be sent him by every guild. Each guild sent ten delegates.

The Tsar's disapproval and the flight of the boyars who had made Tudor join the *Etaireia* movement left him without any "legal justification" and compelled him to conclude with the boyars an agreement whereby he acknowledged "the temporary rule of the country", while the boyars admitted that his movement was "useful and redeeming, and advantageous to the people". The boyars also vindicted Tudor's movement in a report sent to the Porte. Actually they were waiting for Ypsilanti's arrival before taking a stand.

### 3. Alexander Ypsilanti's Intervention

IN the evening of February 22/March 6, Ypsilanti crossed the river Prut and, escorted by 200 mercenaries of the prince's guard who had come to meet him, entered Jassy as a master and took the reins of public administration and the command of the military forces. The Russian consul, Andrea Pisani, did not even make a pretense of arresting him or of protesting against his incursion, and this strengthened the general conviction that he would be followed by a great Russian army. Provisions were prepared for that army; the Metropolitan of Moldavia girded Ypsilanti with a sword during a ceremony officiated at the Three Hierarchs' Church, and the great boyars and the bankers supplied him with money, men and weapons. During the night the Turkish merchants in Jassy as those of Galatz had been killed. The next day Ypsilanti issued two proclamations: one to the Greeks calling them to arms for the liberation of the homeland, another to the Moldavians to set their minds at rest, assuring them that "should the Turks dare to penetrate into Moldavia, an all-powerful force was ready to punish them for their audacity".

These "fatal acts of rashness" overthrew the plans of the Imperial Cabinet, turning Russia into the instigator and organizer of the movement. Tsar Alexander I was consequently compelled to repudiate Ypsilanti.

Ypsilanti was unable to understand that the Tsar, in his capacity as head of the Holy Alliance, could not head a revolutionary movement. An autocrat like the Tsar could only interfere in Turkish territory as a restorer of public order when, as Capodistria stated, an imperious and irresistible

Musas Augusti colit æmulus ille volentes
Per Populos dat jura, viam que affectat Olympo.

47. CONSTANTINE MAVROCORDAT

NIK. URSZ ALIAS HORA TUMULTUS
RUSTICANI VALACHORUM IN TRAN
SILVANIA Æ 1784 EXCITATI AUTHOR

VARG. IUON ALIAS KLOSKA
IUON HOR. Æ PRIMARIUS
CAPITANEUS.

KRISSAN GURIS EX KERPENYES
TUS IN TRANSILVIN Æ 1784 EXCITAT
PRÆCUS TERTIUS.

50. FAIR IN TRANSYLVANIA AROUND 1819

51. TUDOR VLADIMIRESCU

55. THE PAVEMENT FACTORY IN JASSY.

56. STREET IN BUCHAREST IN 1840

necessity had proved that the Ottoman government was unable by its own means to re-establish "a state of affairs compatible with the maintenance of peace". It was the task of the *Etaireia* to create such a state of affairs without compromising Russia so that the Laibach Congress should authorize Russia to re-establish order, or even entrust her with doing so as it had entrusted Austria with the suppression of the Neapolitan revolution. But in that case Russia ought to have been a total stranger to the disturbances in the two Principalities.

With the forces and the funds collected in Jassy, Ypsilanti marched slowly towards Bucharest, as if to permit the Russian army to overtake him. He reached Colentina only on April 6 /18 at the head of a mob of some 5,000 men, of whom barely a hundred were in uniform. The Metropolitan and the boyars hastened to pay their respects to him. But Tudor could be persuaded to visit him only a week later.

The interview yielded no results. Ypsilanti could not persuade Tudor to accept the facts that he "obeyed higher orders" and that a Russian army would soon arrive. Nevertheless, Tudor Vladimirescu did not break with him for fear of "thwarting the plans of a greater power". He promised to procure the provisions necessary for the *Etaireia* army against payment. The agreement, however, did not last. Tudor complained that Ypsilanti was trying to hire his troops and that the *Etaireia* army was plundering a country which Ypsilanti had promised to cross only on his way to the homeland he meant to liberate.

It was a state of tension. This was the moment when a letter arrived from the Tsar condemning Ypsilanti's movement and authorizing Turkey to send troops to the two Principalities. Threatened by a Turkish attack, and in danger of being abandoned by his partisans, Ypsilanti removed his camp to Tîrgovişte, near the Transylvanian frontier, in the hope that Turkey would make a serious mistake and thus justify Russia's military intervention in the Principalities. He had to gain time. When Ypsilanti had left Bucharest, Tudor occupied the monasteries of Mihai-Vodă and Radu-Vodă and the Metropolitan church, which dominated the town, and arrested the Protection Committee, which was making ready to go to Tîrgovişte; he imprisoned them at Belvedere

Dinicu Golescu's country house. For a month and a half, he was master of Bucharest and of the greatest part of Wallachia.

The flight of the boyars who had involved Tudor in the *Etaireia* movement, and Russia's disavowal of the entire movement, gave Tudor freedom of action. Relying exclusively on the masses of the people, he fully endorsed their claims and took measures and issued orders, both within and outside the country, like a sovereign. The people called him openly "Prince Tudor". He promised to cut down the taxes and to defend the peasantry from boyar oppression, and this gained him the support of the masses and enabled him to strengthen his army.

Although the people's "Assembly" was the only organized force capable of defending the country from a disastrous Turkish occupation, Tudor did not proclaim himself as ruling prince, but sought to gain the cooperation of the high clergy and of the boyars in order to conclude an agreement with the Turks. Through the intemediary of the government, Tudor got in touch with the pashas of Vidin, Silistra, and Brăila assuring them, as he had done in his previous reports, that he had risen only against the Phanariot princes and had not departed one inch from his submission and faithfulness to the Porte. Before treating with him, the pashas demanded that he should lay down his arms for "no request of privileges and justice can be made with armed hands".

Realizing that the country could not be saved without the use of arms, Tudor prepared to resist. He made it a general rule that each fiscal grouping should provide two armed men, as the prefect of Olt had done. This was tantamount to a mass levy. After this he surrounded the Cotroceni camp with fortifications and trenches and trained his army.

Tudor furthermore tried to win over Sava, who commanded a corps of Albanian mercenaries. Sava, however, whom Ypsilanti had appointed generalissimo of the *Etaireia* army along the Danube, as he had also appointed Iordache the Olympiot, came to an agreement with the Turks and contributed to the suppression of the followers of the *Etaireia*. When the Turks approached Bucharest, Tudor withdrew towards Pitești in order to spare the capital from fire. It was his intention to reach the fortified monasteries in Oltenia. At the bridge over the river Argeș he came up against Ior-

dache, who obliged him to stop at Golești where he took
Tudor from the midst of his army and surrendered him
to Ypsilanti at Tîrgoviște. The latter put Tudor to death
without a trial. Tudor's arrest could only have been achieved
with the assistance of Hagi Prodan and Dimitrie Macedonschi,
and of a number of pandour captains dissatisfied with Tudor
having put to death nine pandours who were guilty of rob-
bery. Part of Tudor's army dispersed and part of it joined
the *Etaireia* followers and fought at the battle of Drăgășani
where the best of the *Etaireia* army was slaughtered by the
Turks. What was left of Tudor's army withdrew to the
Oltenian monasteries where they resisted the Turkish attacks
for more than a month. The Albanian mercenaries who escaped slaughter crossed over into Transylvania to where
Alexander Ypsilanti also fled, or, pursued by the Turks, withdrew to Bucovina and Bessarabia, skirting the mountains.
Sava and his men were slaughtered by the Turks in Bucharest,
after they had helped to clear the country of *Etaireia* followers.
This was the end of the *Etaireia* insurrection in Wallachia
and Moldavia.

## 4. Consequences of the Revolution

THE two Principalities were occupied by the Turks and
the repression and plunder they were subjected to for the
next sixteen months ruined and depopulated them. Most of
the boyars and merchants emigrated to the neighboring countries and only returned long after the Turks' departure. The
peasants took refuge in the woods, at least as many of them
as could do so, and when they returned they had to pay their
dues to the landowners.

After the extermination of the *Etaireia* followers, the
reorganization of the two Principalities became actual.

Under the pressure of England and Austria, the Porte gave
up the idea of turning them into *pashaliks* and ruling them
through the intermediary of military commissars (*muhafizes*),
so as not to give Russia cause to interfere. Having decided
to appoint native princes, the Turks summoned a delegation
of seven Moldavian and seven Wallachian boyars to Constantinople. The Wallachian boyars brought with them a me-

morial drawn up in Bucharest and comprising 24 points stating the essential grievances that had been included in the memorials addressed to the Russian and Austrian emperors during the revolution.

The Porte took no account of the memorials and demanded that the two delegations should give them written proposals. The demands of the two delegations were almost identical: native princes, a native guard instead of the Albanian mercenaries, a ban on the purchase of real estate by foreign subjects, the removal of Greek monks, the right of holding high office to be reserved exclusively for the natives of the country, and freedom to complain to the Porte.

The Porte only admitted part of these demands and on July 1, 1822, appointed Ioniţă Sandu Sturdza as prince of Moldavia and Grigore Ghica as prince of Wallachia, according to the delegates' demand. The other claims in the boyars' program — freedom of trade, industry, and mining, and reforms concentrating all political power into the hands of the great boyars — were postponed until the conclusion of the Treaty of Adrianople.

The re-establishment of the native princes' rule did not only mean a change of persons. It amounted to the overthrow of a régime — the Phanariot régime — and with it went all the burdens laid upon the country for enriching the Phanariot princes' relatives in Constantinople.

As many of the boyars had taken refuge in Transylvania to return only in 1826, the reprisals against the participants in the revolution were not so severe as was usual after peasant uprisings. The villages were disarmed and had to give guarantees for those who had taken up arms. The pandours and their captains were treated more harshly. The boyars sought to make good their losses and exacted from the peasants the work of the days that had been lost during the revolution. Suits regarding such cases lasted to 1835, this being proof of the peasants' resistance and of the boyars' inability to force them to submit. Karl Marx states that the period between 1821 and 1828 was the best for the peasants.

Farming produce having become more profitable, the boyars asked that the number of work days should be increased from 12 to 14. Their demand was, however, ineffective on account of the peasants' opposition, who refused to work even the usual number of days, and of the scarcity of labor. The public debt increased during the revolution and the Turkish occupation, and payment was exacted now not only from the usual taxpayers but also from the sections of society exempted from taxes, thus diminishing the boyars' income and instituting a precedent that threatened their privileges.

The claims of the lesser gentry were set forth in a memorial drawn up at a secret conference by Ioniță Tăutu in April, 1822. The memorial proclaimed equality of rights for all boyars, observance of the titles to property — and consequently abolition of feudal servitude, and removal of all obstacles to freedom of industry and trade. The memorial demanded that guarantees should be given ensuring personal freedom and inviolability, equality before the law, abolition of the sale of offices, and this not in order to modernize the administration by appointing meritorious people, but in order to enable the boyars to fill public offices in succession and thus benefit by the incomes that went with them. The gentry invoked the principles of the French Revolution but it was not in order to abolish the privileges of the nobility but to benefit by them on a par with the higher boyars. Feudal rights and the boyars' monopolies were not mentioned. However, by advocating freedom for the economy, the secularization of monastic estates, and the setting up of schools in the towns, the memorial "of the Carbonari", as they sometimes called themselves, favored the development of capitalistic methods of production.

The great boyars gave a prompt and stern answer. Those who had emigrated wrote: "The very word 'Constitution' is tantamount to an attempt to do away with authority". In a complaint to the Porte, the great boyars objected to their taxation and that of the clergy, and to the merchants being raised to the status of boyars in large numbers. The prince admonished the authors in public and exiled some of them. Throughout the reign of Ioniță Sandu Sturdza there was political and social unrest in Moldavia, a sign of internal contradictions resulting from the emergence of capitalistic methods of production.

In Wallachia the ruling prince was attacked by some of the great boyars who wished to take his place and who sent reports to the Porte criticizing his financial administration. However, such intrigues were easily terminated by the prince.

The Wallachian gentry claimed the same rights as the great boyars but there were among them some that foreshadowed future events. Thus Eufrosin Poteca proposed that a bourgeois republic should be proclaimed and all citizens be equally taxed.

The intervention of the Russian consuls ended such plans for reform and the Porte was compelled to sign the Akkerman Convention on October 7, 1826, whereby the rule of a prince was to last for a term of seven years and certain rules were to be made to improve economic conditions in the Principalities.

In the meantime the Turks were about to put down the uprising in Greece, which had lasted since 1821. European public opinion, however, forced France and England to intervene. The Turkish fleet was sunk at Navarino, and the Russian armies crossed the river Prut and after a number of brilliant victories forced the Porte to capitulate.

The Peace Treaty signed at Adrianople (September 2/14, 1829) gave Russia the Caucasus area of the Black Sea coastline and the Danube mouths up to where the Prut flows into the Danube; declared navigation to be free on the Danube, in the Black Sea and in the Straits; and confirmed the autonomy of Greece and Serbia.

A separate act, which was an integral part of the treaty, returned to Wallachia the citadels on the left bank of the Danube and established Wallachia's frontier with the "Ottoman States" along the river. The inhabitants of the two Principalities were exempted from providing the supplies that had previously been sent to the Porte and were given full freedom of trading in all the products of the land and of their work. The princes were to be elected for the term of their lives and were to administer the country freely together with a "Divan". The Porte agreed to confirm the *Règlement Organique* which was to be worked out during Russia's occupation of the Principalities. The occupation was to last until all war reparations amounting to 11,500,000 ducats had been fully paid.

The stipulations of the Treaty of Adrianople, which concluded the struggle started by the *Etaireia*, gave the Romanian

Principalities nearly everything the boyars had claimed in their memorials during the revolution of 1821: freedom of trade, once considered by the Turks as the greatest threat to the Empire, the opening of the Danube ports, and the restriction of the Ottoman government's right to interfere in the internal affairs of the Principalities. The suzerainty of the Porte was thus reduced to payment of a tribute and the confirmation of the appointment of the ruling princes.

Considering its consequences, the insurrection of 1821 was a genuine national revolution for Moldavia and Wallachia.

# CHAPTER II

# The Age of the Règlement Organique

THE *Règlement Organique* passed by the Public Assemblies in 1831 was actually a constitution which gave the Romanian Principalities institutions liable to favor the development of capitalism. However, on account of its revolutionary connotations the term "constitution" was replaced by the word *Règlement*.

The régime created by the *Règlement Organique* concentrated all power in the hands of the great boyars; they thereupon instituted what the villagers called "the slavery of compulsory service". Freedom of trade and the fact that offices were no longer sold confined the boyars' sources of income to the exploitation of their estates. The boyars consequently sought to extort as much as possible from the work of the dependent peasants on their estate and to tie them to the land. But with the general resistance of the villagers, the landowners were able to apply the points of the law on compulsory service only partially until 1848. The growth of grain exports in the age of the *Règlement Organique* was not due to the output of the manorial reserve but to the produce taken from the villagers. Almost up to the end of the period the main source of income of the two Principalities was animal husbandry.

Having abolished the monopoly of the guilds, the *Règlement Organique* favored the development of industry, which was also stimulated by the greater profits brought in by agricultural production. A number of industries reached the stage of manufactories in the two Principalities, while steam engines became widespread in Transylvania. Paid labor was used to an increasing extent. In pace with economic progress, the Romanian bourgeoisie increased in number. More and more young people were being sent for higher education to establishments in the West, especially in France. On their return, they headed the renewal movement under way in the country, organizing secret societies and drawing up programs of struggle for social and political emancipation. Despite the repression of all forms of liberalism by the Protecting State, the national movement made decisive progress during that period, paving the way for the solidarity of the three Romanian countries in the revolutionary struggle of 1848.

## 1. The Règlement Organique

UPON the conclusion of peace, the Romanian Principalities were to be occupied by Russia until all war reparations had been paid. General Kiselev was appointed President Plenipotentiary of the Divans of the two Principalities, an office which he held from November 12, 1829, to April, 1834, when the Russian forces left the Principalities. In the exercise of the extraordinary powers with which he had been invested for the reorganization of the Principalities, he used tact and moderation.

The Principalities were in a desperate state. The population, partly decimated by the war, was threatened by plague and starvation. Kiselev organized a sanitary cordon along the Danube as well as a medical service to control the plague. By the close of 1829 the epidemic had been stamped out. In order to fend off starvation, grain was imported from Odessa, and after 1830 granaries were built and corn was stored to prevent the recurrence of such calamities.

The campaign Kiselev organized against the plague and starvation, visiting the hotbeds of disease in person, revealed to him the vices of the administration, which he remedied even before the Règlement Organique had been worked out. He issued decrees whereby justice was separated from the administration, abolished the exemption of dependent peasants from taxes to the state, whereby 40,000 families were at the service of the boyars, built up a national army, and established definite taxes which were brought to the knowledge of the taxpayers. All these measures were to be incorporated in the Règlement Organique.

The Règlement Organique, which did duty for a constitution until 1859, was drawn up by two committees, each made up of four Moldavian and four Wallachian boyars, with the Russian Consul General, Mintchiaky, as chairman.

The text was amended by Kiselev, after which it was examined by the Imperial Cabinet and subsequently submitted to the Divans, who discussed it without having the power to change it. The *Règlement* was promulgated in July, 1831, for Wallachia and in January, 1832, for Moldavia.

State organization relied on the principle of the separation of powers. The executive power was the prerogative of the ruling prince who was elected for the term of his life from among the great boyars by an Extraordinary Public Assembly. In the exercise of the executive power, the prince was assisted by six ministers. In the event of a conflict with the Assembly, the prince had no right to dissolve it but only to prorogue it. Legislative power was vested in the Public Assembly, made up of 42 deputies in Wallachia: the Metropolitan, who was also Chairman of the Assembly, the three Wallachian Bishops, twenty great boyars chosen by seventy boyars of the same rank, and eighteen deputies elected by the boyars of the second and the third rank. The Moldavian Assembly was made up of 35 deputies elected according to the same rules. The judicial power was exercised by tribunals, of which there was one in every county. The courts of appeal were two (Judicial Divans) in Wallachia, one in Bucharest, and another in Craiova, and one in Jassy. They were independent of the ruling prince and the Assembly. "Courts of conciliation" were set up for the settlement of local conflicts in the villages, mostly cases of damages caused by stray cattle. The magistrates and civil servants were to be appointed for a term of three years and could be confirmed in their posts every three years. The *Règlement* did not lay down the principle of the irremovability of judges. Controlling the Assembly and the tribunals, the great boyars could solve all questions referring to agrarian relations to suit their class interest. N. Bălcescu wrote the following concerning the *Règlement Organique* : "Not content to disinherit a whole people and to organize a boyars' state, though recognizing the peasants' ownership over the land they had tilled from all eternity, the *Règlement* increased the landowners' rights immeasurably, and actually made of man a slave to the land, and of property the monopoly of the boyars. Never had oligarchy been better strengthened: inside the country by the *Règlement Organique*, outside it by Russia's powerful support".

Despite the narrow class spirit that had inspired it, the *Règlement Organique* meant a great progress in the modernization of the Principalities. N. Bălcescu himself admitted that "despite all their evils, the *Règlement* enacted some useful principles and became an instrument of progress". Separating justice from the administration and investing judicial sentences with authority, they introduced order and abolished the right of the plaintiff who had lost his case under one prince to re-open it under the following prince. Property and economic transactions were thus consolidated.

The innovating nature of the *Règlement Organique* was apparent especially in fiscal matters which had not been solved by the Phanariot reforms, frequent as they were. To begin with, the *Règlement* reduced the chaotic diversity of taxes to one — capitation — which became a fixed one. For the first time all the people were taxed, for all exemptions had been done away with and a strict record of the population was kept, the registers being far more accurate than in the past and reducing the number of inhabitants whose existence the boyars concealed from the authorities. With the Porte no longer making repeated and unexpected demands, the fiscal régime showed a stability which was reflected in the stability of the population. The *Règlement* abolished indirect taxation, the supplies to the Porte, requisitioning and domestic custom duties, and adopted the modern principle of a state budget based on balanced revenues and expenditure. The budget was debated by the Public Assembly and audited by a special body. But the *Règlement* exempted the boyars and the clergy from taxation.

Furthermore the *Règlement Organique* set up civil registry offices and state archives as well as colleges in Bucharest and Jassy for the training of civil servants. To guard the frontiers, a militia was created which was to constitute the embryo of the national army.

With a view to the unification of Moldavia and Wallachia, the *Règlement* incorporated almost identical provisions in the two countries. More than that: articles 317 in Wallachia and 429 in Moldavia proclaimed that by virtue of their common language, religion, customs, and interests, "the inseparable unification" of the inhabitants of the two Principalities was a "redeeming" necessity.

The *Règlement Organique* wrought radical changes in the structure of landed estates and of agrarian relations. The boyars took advantage of the protection of the Russian army to force upon the peasants the conditions required to produce grain for the market. The feudal estate, on which the peasants enjoyed various rights — the right to cultivate fallow land, to gather firewood and building timber, to use pasture land for their needs — now tended to be turned into an absolute property of the bourgeois type.

In the second place, the peasants were deprived of land whose possession they had enjoyed before the *Règlement* came into force. On the basis of a so-called reciprocity of rights and uses, the land was not distributed according to the needs of a family and the hereditary right over the land, but according to the labor expended for the landowners. Under this system there were three categories of people: the frontrankers, who owned four oxen and a milch cow, or ten sheep, the middle peasants, who owned two oxen, and the last category, who only possessed their arms to work with. The frontrankers received nine acres of land for at most five head of cattle, and the two other categories less. They all got only half of the land, or even a third of what they possessed before the *Règlement* came into force. The remainder of the estate constituted the landowner's reserve over which he had an absolute right of ownership.

Restricting to a maximum five head the cattle for which the landowner was obliged to give land, the *Règlement* struck a blow at animal husbandry which was still the peasants' main source of income. For apart from draft cattle, the villagers kept up to forty head of cattle. Consequently, the dependent peasant who wanted to keep more cattle or to till more land than the *Règlement* admitted had to come to terms with the landowner. "Willing agreements" were to be a terrible instrument of enslavement in the hands of the landowners and their main means of exploiting the villagers.

In exchange for the land, the *Règlement* demanded that the people contribute twelve days' work a year, which were counted according to the work done per day as established by the *Réglement*: so many square yards plowed a day, so many square yards hoed, so many mown, etc. The established day's work could only be effected in two or three days. According to Bălcescu, the number of days' work was actually 56 in Wallachia and 84 in Moldavia per annum.

Such measures strengthened the boyars' economic and political position and, paradoxically, ensured the evolution of society towards capitalism, though on the basis of what were mostly feudal relations. Having in their hands all the political power as well as the means of compulsion of a modernized state machinery, the boyars increased the exploitation of the peasants on their estates, thus creating conditions which the peasants described as "the slavery of labor service".

There was general opposition among the peasants to the Labor Service Law. Having been accustomed to use as much land as they needed, the peasants could not accept the enslaving conditions created by the *Règlement Organique* without opposition and if the discontent did not turn into a general uprising, it was due to the fact that General Kiselev transformed it into a petitionary movement. On most estates, the people prevented the measuring of the land and instead of working on the landowner's reserve preferred to pay cash for labor service. For this reason the land tilled for the benefit of the landowner amounted to an insignificant portion of the estate throughout the time the *Règlement* was in force. Throughout the Brăila county in Wallachia it amounted to 94 acres at most. The landowner derived his income from animal husbandry, the produce paid by the dependent peasantry, the money received in exchange for labor service and especially from the spirits monopoly. In the plain, the peasants continued to use the whole estate, paying dues established by common agreement.

In Moldavia the agitation assumed such serious proportions that Cossack squadrons had to be brought into action in order to put it down. The main reason for dissatisfaction was the recruiting carried out for the army newly created by the *Règlement Organique*. But the law on labor service gave almost equal dissatisfaction to the peasants, proof of which is the fact that after the suppression of the uprising, the struggle continued — the reason now being that "the small holdings assigned them were insufficient for subsistence". The villagers on the bank of the Prut emigrated to Bessarabia, upon which the government was forced to enact a new law suspending the application of the labor service law in the border districts until 1848.

## 2. Economic Life

THE increase in marketable agricultural production was hampered by feudal privileges and the slow development of transport and communication routes and of the home market. Although feudal relations dominated the economy, a number of innovations heralded the growth of capitalism. Plowing and threshing machines began to be imported and later to be manufactured in the country. Selected seed was now used and new plants were being cultivated extensively. Pedigree cattle were imported in order to improve the native breeds. Art and trade schools were opened in Jassy and Bucharest. In Transylvania fodder and industrial plants were introduced and vineyards and orchards were extended.

Despite the economic restrictions of feudal relations, which still predominated, the output of marketable agricultural products increased in the Romanian countries. In Transylvania crop rotation and irrigation were introduced as a contribution to the modernization of farming.

The profits that could be made on marketable agricultural products gave a spurt to industry. The government supported industrial expansion by awarding "stimulating bounties"; it further set up technical schools and did much towards the spread of the technical press and literature. The *Règlement Organique* abolished the monopoly held by the guilds.

Artisan production was slow in changing into capitalist production on account of the predominance of trade and usurers' capital, of the régime of Capitulations which left the national industry unprotected from foreign competition, the low purchasing power of the masses, and the persistence of cottage industry. The dominant form of production continued to be artisan production.

And yet industry was incontestably progressing. After 1838 steam engines increased in number in Transylvania: there were three of them at the Reşiţa works. The commercial manufactories of Sibiu, Braşov, and Sighişoara consolidated their position through exports south of the Carpathians.

In Moldavia and Wallachia the manufactory stage was reached in the food industry (pastes, edible oil, sugar, cured meats) for which there were low-priced raw materials in quantities. The shipyards at Galatz and Giurgiu, the brick yards and breweries, the distilleries, candle factories, paper mills and tanneries, the tobacco and glass plants employed a large number of workers, some of them brought from other countries. The manufactories producing earthenware, textile fabrics, and rope found it more difficult to meet foreign competition. There was an increasing number of paid workers but they often continued their farming, for work was intermittent in the manufactories and these establishments often closed down.

The most developed industry was mining, while one of the most important exports was salt from all three Romanian countries. Oil was beginning to be exploited on an ever larger scale. It was in Transylvania's mninig industry that the capitalist way of production reached its highest development level, mining becoming the most important source of capitalist accumulation. In the gold mines, which had been worked from ancient times, techniques were improved. In 1838 a steam engine was already working at Zlatna and the Baia Mare mines soon followed suit. Joint stock companies were set up in order to obtain the capital required for great depth mining.

Farm production was stimulated by the opening of the Danube ports and the access to world markets, while the abolition of various feudal dues and the development of communication routes enlarged the home market. The customs union of 1846-1848 was a further step forward.

Most of the local traders were concerned with retail trade. Grain and cattle exports were in the hands of a small number of merchants who kept up connections with international firms.

With the development of the means of transportation and trade routes, the home market grew steadily. In 1846 the construction of roads linking Bucharest with Orşova, Focşani, Brăila, Sibiu, and Braşov was begun. This was done by means of the labor services of the dependent peasants and of budget appropriations.

As river navigation would inevitably be an improvement on transport by means of ox-drawn carts, work was begun in order to make the main rivers of Wallachia and Moldavia navigable. The cost, however, proved to be beyond the means of the two Principalities and the venture was abandoned. Sea navigation, on the other hand, progressed steadily. It was during this period that a national fleet of merchant ships began to be built up. In 1834 the first ship flying the Romanian flag unloaded 100 tons of wheat at Constantinople, while another carried oak staves to Marseilles. In 1839 the Galatz shipyards launched seven ships and in 1840 ten. Integration into international trade, though on a small scale as yet, would have been impossible before the Treaty of Adrianople.

Freedom of trade gave a powerful impulse to the fairs, where traders purchased goods for export and for town supplies. The main exports of the two Principalities were cattle, horses, sheep, grain, and building timber. Now that Romanian exports went to a larger number of countries, there was a tendency for England and France to replace Turkey and Austria as the main customers of the Principalities. A favorable balance of trade clearly showed that trade had expanded. From 1835 to 1844 Wallachia's exports increased threefold, from 21,500,000 lei to 64,400,000 lei, while Moldavia's exports rose from 26 million lei to 52 million from 1843 to 1847. After 1840 grain exports rose above cattle exports in value.

The bulk of Moldavian and Wallachian exports was carried on via Galatz and Brăila. In 1837 449 vessels entered the port of Brăila and in 1847 their number rose to 1,383, of which 418 were English. The port of Galatz developed along the same lines, with 236 vessels calling in 1833 and 1,064 in 1847. In 1833 the Porte had acknowledged the right of the Principalities to fly a national flag on their ships.

The trading houses and companies of Sibiu and Braşov played a considerable part in trade expansion. The Romanian commercial company of Braşov with a membership of one hundred handled nearly the entire trade of Braşov. Out of a total number of 139 Braşov traders, 118 were Romanian. The firm Radu Orghidan and Co., and the houses of trade Ioan Iuga and Ioan George also contributed to the expansion of Romanian trade.

## 3. Political Life

THE first princes to ascend the throne during the implementation of the *Règlement Organique* were Alexandru Ghica and Mihai Sturdza. They were not elected as the *Règlement*

laid down, but were appointed by the suzerain and the protecting courts on the basis of the Petersburg understanding
of January 17, 1834. Alexandru Ghica, Prince of Wallachia
(1834-1842), was the brother of the former Prince Grigore
Ghica, during whose reign he had held the highest offices
as he had also done during Kiselev's administration. He was
reputed to be a well-informed man, of outstanding integrity,
and a great patriot.

Mihai Sturdza was prince of Moldavia until 1849. With
a penetrating mind and well-informed, he was also an excellent
organizer and a skilled diplomat able to parry all the blows
dealt by internal opposition and by the suzerain and the protecting courts. These qualities were, however, overshadowed
by his insatiable greed, as well as by excessive pride and an
imperious will, which impelled him to arbitrariness.

Both princes were from the first faced by great financial
difficulties, the result of the deficit left by Count Kiselev's
administration, the tribute which the Treaty of Adrianople
had fixed at three million piastres which had not been paid
during the Russian occupation, and the expenditures required
by the prince's investiture at Constantinople. The Bucharest
and the Jassy assemblies voted for an increase in the Civil
List from 1,200,000 to 1,600,000 piastres and for a contribution of 1,200,000 piastres to cover the expenses incurred at
Constantinople. The 1835 budget could not be balanced. In
order to cover the deficit, the poll tax was increased by thirty
per cent.

A misunderstanding arose between the Assembly and
Ghica over the so-called additional article. During the negotiations carried on at Constantinople for the ratification of
the *Règlement Organique* by the Ottoman government, the
Russian ambassador had introduced certain amendments and
had added on the last page an article stipulating that no law
passed by the Assembly and sanctioned by the prince could
be promulgated unless it had been approved by the suzerain
and the protecting courts. Baron Rückman, Russia's Consul
General, demanded that the article "which had been omitted
by mistake" should be passed by the Assembly. In 1835 Sturdza
had the article passed. In Wallachia, however, the problem
envenomed the relations between the Assembly and the prince
for three years. Ghica would have liked the article passed

without public debates. The opposition, however, contested the authenticity of the article and refused to pass it. Rückman went to Constantinople and returned with a decree *(firman)* compelling the Assembly to introduce the article in the *Règlement*. Both the prince and the Assembly did so in May, 1838. The legislative right belonged to the Assembly only within the limits fixed by the protecting court.

The misunderstandings between the Assembly and the throne were to paralyze both parties and to subordinate them to the protecting court. It was against this state of affairs that a national opposition was built up which obtained the majority in the election of 1837. The opposition was supported by the liberal youth who had been studying abroad from where they returned with a program of liberal reforms. The manifesto of the opposition — The Act of Union and Independence — drawn up on November 1/13, 1838, declared the appointment of Alexandru Ghica as well as the *Règlement Organique* to be illegal and proposed that all Romanians should unite and pass a draft constitution: The Special Act for the Appointment of the Sovereign of the Romanians drawn up on November 5/17. The act proposed that Ion Câmpineanu, head of the National Party, should be appointed as hereditary prince. The great boyars, however, did not support Câmpineanu, preferring Mihai Sturdza whose election would have united the two Principalities. Sturdza, being approached, refused though he was all for unification. Câmpineanu tried to obtain England's support but his attempt only compromised him before the suzerain and the protecting courts.

A far more radical movement was subsequently organized by Mitică Filipescu, who, relying on the radical elements of the bourgeoisie at the time in process of formation, made it his aim to overthrow the entire social order. A secret society was formed to which Bălcescu also belonged. The society counted on the aggravation of the Eastern Question in 1840 and the disruption of the Ottoman Empire, which would have allowed the Romanian Principalities to obtain their independence and to abolish the feudal régime. The conspirators' plans were overthrown when the latent conflict between England and France was smoothed out, and the treachery of some of the members of the society delivered the leaders to the authorities.

The suppression of the revolutionary movement of 1840 did not strengthen Ghica's position. The election of 1841 showed the great boyars to be most powerful and the latter started a ruthless campaign against the prince whom they reproached with the measures taken in favor of the peasantry, especially with the intention of changing the stipulations of the *Règlement Organique* referring to the peasants' freedom to change their place of habitation and to the right to graze their cattle.

The boyars used against Ghica the two attempts made by some Bulgarian immigrants in Wallachia and Bessarabia, to return to Bulgaria in order to stir up revolt against the Ottoman rule. Denounced to the suzerain and the protecting courts, Ghica was deposed on October 7, 1842, after a biased inquiry.

His successor, Gheorghe Bibescu (1842-1848), who had studied law in Paris, was a scholarly man and one of the richest boyars of the country. He was the first prince to be elected in keeping with the stipulations of the *Règlement* by an Extraordinary Public Assembly in which the masses of town and village were not represented. Bibescu owed his election to the campaign he had set afoot, together with his brother, Barbu Ştirbey, against Alexandru Ghica.

The agreement between the Assembly and the prince was of short duration. In 1834 national opposition was built up again in the form of a secret society — *Brotherhood* — headed by Ion Ghica, Christian Tell, and Nicolae Bălcescu, who was just out of prison. The opposition fought not only for the bourgeoisie and the liberal boyars, but also for the lesser bourgeoisie, the workers and the peasants. The conflict between the Assembly and the prince broke out over the concession given to the Russian engineer Trandafilov to explore and exploit the metal mines of the country. Instead of making an unbiased inquiry, the Assembly showed the whole affair to be a form of foreign exploitation and demanded that the concession be canceled. With the assistance of the Russian ambassador, Bibescu obtained a decree from the court entitling him to prorogue the Assembly for the rest of its mandate and to govern for two years by means of decrees. The Assembly elected in 1846 was made up of Bibescu's partisans so that "the age of perfect union between the administration and the Public Assembly" would have lasted for five years if the revolutions of 1848 had not ended Bibescu's reign.

Bibescu's attempt to solve the problem of the monasteries under Greek patronage and administered by Greek monks, who derived an income equal to a fifth of the state's revenue, was unsuccessful on account of the opposition of the Russian ambassador, who defended the monasteries. The most important event of Bibescu's reign was the customs union of 1848 between Moldavia and Wallachia, which made of the territory of the two Principalities an economic unit as a prelude to political union.

Mihai Sturdza, the Moldavian prince, retained his throne from 1834 to 1849, although he met with the same difficulties as the two princes of Wallachia. His reforms prepared Moldavia for the great struggle for the union of the two Principalities. Under his rule Moldavia enjoyed fifteen years of stability which were decisive in the modernization of the country. The modern roads and bridges built at the time with the serfs' unpaid labor as also through appropriations from the state budget enabled northern Moldavia's wheat to reach the Galatz market and linked the most isolated districts with the national market. He organized an efficient postal service, created the first modern hospitals, and improved the prison régime. In 1834 he declared Galatz a free port, thus advancing the town's demographic and economic development. Traffic in the port increased, enabling the local merchants to improve the port, raise a dike to protect it against floods, and rebuild the town in stone.

Sturdza paid great attention to administration and education. With the educational system developing and large numbers of young people being sent to study abroad, the prince was able to provide better informed and more energetic prefects and mayors for the different districts and towns of the country. In 1828 he had helped to found the Three Hierarchs' School and in 1835 he set up the Mihăileana Academy with courses in law, mathematics, chemistry, architecture, and history. Mihail Kogălniceanu was assigned to the history course, which he inaugurated on November 24, 1843. The response that Kogălniceanu's opening speech called forth alarmed both internal and external reactionary circles and the government had to suspend the course. The text of the speech was printed and distributed widely, causing the national spirit to soar.

Throughout his reign Mihai Sturdza had three parties opposing him. The great boyars, who considered themselves his equals and consequently entitled to supersede him, hatched intrigues in the Assembly and in drawing rooms and sent complaints to the suzerain and the protecting courts. Sturdza parried by dispatching counter-demands and taking disciplinary measures.

The little and middle boyars, among whom were many merchants whom Ioniță Sandu Sturdza had raised to the rank of boyar, now clamored for full equality with the great boyars and for their privileges, their claims based on the principles of the French Revolution.

The malcontents under the leadership of Comis Radu Leonte plotted to create an aristocratic state headed by a hereditary prince, subject to the Porte and governed by the boyars, who were alone to hold political rights. They advocated the creation of a tariff-protected national industry, the opening of mines, the setting up of a state bank, the founding of a university, freedom of thought and press, freedom for the gypsy slaves, and free access to all public offices. The plan reflects the structure of Moldavian society where liberal claims stood beside feudal institutions. When Radu Leonte was banished, the plot disintegrated.

The intelligentsia opposed Mihai Sturdza's reactionary régime by every possible means: the press, literature, and meetings. A systematic movement for the union of the two Principalities and for democracy was set afoot by M. Kogălniceanu, C. Negruzzi, Alecu Russo, Vasile Alecsandri, Anastasie Panu, V. Mălinescu, C. Negri, and others. Sturdza fought them by suppressing their publications and exiling the authors to monasteries or, more efficiently, by partly carrying out their program.

Opposition was also forthcoming from the secret society styled the Patriotic Association, which counted Theodor Rășcanu, V. Mălinescu, Alexandru Ion Cuza, Ion Lambrior, and Gr. Carp among its members. The program of the Association was to overthrow Sturdza's régime, set free the boyars' gypsy slaves, obtain juridical equality, and introduce taxation of landed estates — that is, suppress the boyars' exemption from taxes. The Association was influenced by the powerful peasant upsurge of the winter of 1845-1848. Ultimately the Association was discovered and its members arrested or compelled to emigrate.

## 4. Transylvania during the "Age of Reforms"

THE age of the *Règlement Organique* was an "age of reforms" during which the changes wrought during the eighteenth century, as set forth in the preceding chapters, continued. During the first half of the nineteenth century, Vienna was bent on strengthening its economic and political domination over Transylvania. Supported by the Hungarian aristocracy, the imperial cabinet governed here through the agency of central bodies — the Vienna chancellery, the governor of Transylvania and the high officials appointed by the emperor direct — which established the taxes to be paid and the military contingents to be made available and defended public opinion from the contamination of subversive ideas by means of censorship. The Diet was not convened from 1811 to 1834 — a span of twenty-three years. The lesser nobility backed the system, for it had preserved its administrative and juridical monopoly.

Subjected to a double exploitation — social and national — the Romanian people had much to suffer from the system. The process of economic and social emancipation was checked by the fact that Romanians were not entitled to settle in towns, practice certain trades or attend schools; and this also heightened the antagonism between Romanian serfs and the Magyar nobility. The Romanians' revolutionary trends and their desire for political union found efficient support in the activities of the Polish revolutionaries who had taken refuge in Transylvania. It was under the impulse of the Pole Adolf David that propaganda was begun in 1834 for "a republic of the united Romanians".

Even the liberal Magyar nobility admitted the need for reforms and the Vienna Court was thus compelled to convene the Diet. Although being in the majority, the liberal noblemen split into groups showing various tendencies, especially as regards cadastral arrangements, so that their action was mostly ineffective.

The bourgeoisie, which had risen to some importance in economic life, was also eager to gain political power. Though they acted jointly when the aim was to remove the barriers that prevented the free development of industry and trade, they split into factions when it came to sacrificing their own privileges. With national conflicts intensifying, some of the Magyars supported the idea of Transylvania being incorporated within Hungary, while the Romanian bourgeoisie and intelligentsia joined issue with the Romanian serfs in order to defend Transylvania's autonomy.

The serfs were also active. The parceling-out of the peasant holdings, the seizure of the cleared land by the nobility, the oppressive labor service that had to be performed, and the confiscation of pasture land and forests were the causes of strong movements of protest, with the miners joining in, for they also were fighting for social and national emancipation.

The Diet of 1846-1847 considered that putting agrarian relationships in order would end the discontent of the peasant masses. But this was a belated concession. The peasants now wanted full ownership of the land they used. The majority in the Diet passed a draft law which gave the serfs the land they had declared at the census. The draft relied on Cziraky's conscription of 1819-1820. But the peasants, fearing that their taxes would be raised, had then declared areas smaller than those they actually used. The draft was passed by the Diet and sanctioned by the emperor but was never applied. It was the main task of the revolution of 1848 to make order in the relations between serfs and landowners.

## 5. A National Ideology Is Evolved

IN the Romanian Principalities the defeat of the revolution of 1821 did not weaken the national movement; quite the reverse, the movement was strengthened and came to be more closely connected to international developments. The constitutional projects made during the reign of native princes aimed at emancipation from Ottoman rule. During the

Russo-Turkish war of 1828-1829 Iordache Catargi and Mihai
Sturdza "dared to think of restoring a Dacian monarchy"
under a foreign prince that did not belong to a dynasty reign-
ing in the neighboring countries. When it became known
what immense war reparations Turkey had to pay under the
Treaty of Adrianople (11,500,000 ducats) — reparations deliberately calculated to justify a ten-years occupation of the
Principalities — the partisans of the union offered to pay the
sum provided the country was given full independence guaranteed by the Great Powers. By organizing the two Principalities almost identically, the *Règlement Organique* furthered
the national movement and justified its bringing to the fore
the identity of the language, the people's national consciousness, and the common economic interests of the population
in the two Principalities.

The French and English consuls constantly drew their
governments' attention to the importance of the economic
resources and geographical position of the Principalities and
pleaded for their union. "The wish for independence", the
French Consul in Bucharest wrote, "increases with every
passing day. The enlightened Romanians do not doubt that
a great change will occur in their situation". The Moldavians
thought of a confederation made up of Moldavia, Wallachia,
and Serbia under the guarantee of the Great Powers, and the
Wallachians supported the plan. About 1839-1840 the desire
for independence had become general. "More than ever boyars
and peasants cherish their homeland as they see in this state
of affairs, which is new for them, promises for the future;
and the Prince leaves nothing undone to inspire the Moldavians with a feeling of nationality". The words are those of
the French consul in Jassy.

When Prince Albert of Prussia stopped in Bucharest for
a few days on his return journey from Constantinople, he
was thought to have the intention of getting to know the
city where he was to rule "as King of restored Dacia", according to the will of the Great Powers.

Dacia was like a magic word summing up all the aspirations for freedom, union and independence of the new generation in the two Principalities. Petru Maior wrote his *History
of the Romanians' Origin in Dacia* (1812), M. Kogălniceanu
followed suit with his *Literary Dacia* (1840) and A. Treboniu

57. REVOLUTIONARY LEADERS OF 1848 IN WALLACHIA

58. NICOLAE BĂLCESCU

59. MIHAIL KOGĂLNICEANU

60. RELEASE OF POLITICAL DETAINEES, JUNE 1848

61. THE BATTLE OF DEALUL SPIREI

BATALIA POMPIERILOR CU OSTIREA OTTOMANA LA ANUL 1848 SEPT: 13. ÎN DEALU SPIREI.

Laurian and N. Bălcescu with *Historic Magazine for Dacia*
(1845). The word passed from the sphere of science and literature into the political language. And another word which
assumed the same significance at the time was Romania:
Aron Florian published *România*, M. Kogălniceanu, *Romanian
Archives*, and there was also Romania's Literary Association.
Later the phrase Daco-Romania came to be used by the national
movement and also the word Romanianism. Romanians and
other nations alike spoke of the Kingdom of Dacia and of the
Romanian people's constant wish for independence and of
turning the two Principalities into a buffer state such as Belgium, but making a connection between West and East. The
French diplomat Bois le Comte, who visited the Principalities
in 1834, thought that the idea of creating a Grand Duchy of
Dacia made up of the two Principalities, expressed the most
general desire of the Romanian people. Nicolae Roznovanu
who had joined *Etaireia* in 1821 endeavored in 1826, when
the Great Powers were preparing for war against Turkey,
to win over Russia by pointing out to her the advantage
of always finding 200,000 soldiers available in the kingdom of Dacia, provided the country's independence was
recognized.

During the fourth and fifth decades of the nineteenth century, there were profound changes also in the concepts of
the Romanians of Transylvania. The conspiratorial program
of the people of Banat in 1839 included the setting up of
"a united Romanian Republic" made up of Moldavia, Wallachia, and Transylvania. The part played by the Romanians
of Transylvania in promoting the idea of the unification of
all Romanians was also revealed by people of other nations.
An envoy of Prince Czartoryski, namely Woronicz, who
found himself in Bucharest in December, 1839, noted that
the idea of unity was "vigorously upheld by the Romanians
of Transylvania".

With cultural ties with the West becoming closer and the
number of young people studying abroad increasing, these
tendencies were strengthened. Indeed so alarming did the
Russian cabinet find them that Nesselrode drew Bibescu's
attention to "the liberal and subversive tendencies of the
Romanian youth educated in other countries". Such was the
degree of development reached on the eve of the revolution

of 1848 by the Romanian people under the impulse of capitalism and of intellectual development.

In the main towns of Transylvania — Braşov, Sibiu, and Cluj — the intelligentsia within the budding bourgeoisie stiffened its backbone and assumed leadership of the national movement formerly in the hands of the clergy, investing it with a militant political character. While starting from the ideas of the first generation of the Transylvanian School — Roman origin of the Romanians and their continuity on the territory of ancient Dacia — the leaders of the new generation, Timoteiu Cipariu, Simion Bărnuţiu, and George Bariţiu, based their arguments on the demographic preponderance of the Romanians and the great extent to which they fulfilled their fiscal and military obligations. They drew the masses into the struggle, arousing in them the consciousness of a common cultural heritage and of their national rights. The language itself assumed a new significance; it was not only considered as proof of the Romanians' Roman origin but also as an original creation of the Romanian people, and as the closest tie between the people speaking it. It was the duty of the writers to enrich and polish it so that it might express the loftiest ideas and the deepest feelings. The Latin character of the Romanian language was no longer contested. Another important feature of this period was the toning down of religious controversies between the Romanians of the Orthodox faith and the Uniates, and the co-operation of the heads of the two faiths for the promotion of the national movement.

The political orientation of the national struggle now required a press organ to rally and unite the forces, this time not with the aim of winning recognition as a fourth nation, but in order to obtain political preponderance to which demographic superiority entitled the Romanians. The purpose was served by *Gazeta de Transilvania (Transylvania's Gazette)* founded in 1838 by George Bariţiu with the assistance of the Braşov merchants.

A third means of furthering the national struggle in Transylvania was the educational system. In order to raise the cultural level of Romanian priests, the Orthodox and the Uniate bishops founded seminaries with a two-year and later a four-year curriculum. The curriculum of the Blaj Lycée, where the first representatives of the Transylvanian School began their education, was greatly enlarged. It included the study of national and world history and of the exact sciences. Some of the graduates of the Lycée continued their studies in Cluj, Vienna and Rome, and thus proficient people were trained for the Romanian educational system and press in Transylvania. Faithful to the principles advocated by the movement of enlightenment concerning the role of culture in the emancipation of the masses, the Romanian leaders attached much importance to elementary education. Bishop Moga recommended to the archpriests in his diocese to do their utmost to open schools in all the parishes. This initiative was only partially and only gradually put into practice because of lack of funds. However, it was characteristic of the early representatives of the Transylvanian school to make it their aim to draw the masses into the movement for national freedom. The second generation of the Transylvanian School went further, considering the peasantry as an integral part of the nation. Consequently, they demanded that serfdom be abolished, revealing the important part that was to be played by the peasantry in the movement for social and national emancipation.

During the period of the *Règlement Organique* all the main points of the program of the union had already crystallized. They included the idea of Romania acting as a buffer state to soften the clashes between the three empires — the Russian, Austrian, and Turkish — (thus making of the union of the two Principalities a European problem); the principle of nationality; and a constitutional régime under a foreign prince with the joint guarantee of the Great Powers. It was left for the generation that followed to build up these ideas into one concept and to make them triumph.

# CHAPTER III

## *The Revolution of 1848 in the Romanian Countries*

THE revolution of 1848 came as a result of the transformations wrought in Romanian society after the revolution of 1821. Its program, which was more complex and more radical than that of 1821, made it its aim to promote the new capitalist structure of Romanian society, to strengthen its unity, and to prepare it for the struggle for independence. The experience stored during this period and the influence of the revolutionary ideas crystallized into a program of bourgeois-democratic reforms, which was further developed and made specific during the revolution. The revolutions of 1848 in Paris, Vienna, Berlin and Budapest undoubtedly brought their influence to bear on the outbreak and unfolding of the revolution in the Romanian countries. But, as N. Bălcescu said, the European revolutions were only "the occasion and not the cause of the Romanian revolution". The fact that the revolution broke out almost at the same time in all the three Romanian countries was in itself proof of the unity and solidarity of the Romanian people everywhere.

## 1. The Revolution

WHILE continuing the revolution of 1821, the revolution of 1848 in the Romanian countries forms an integral part of the great effort of revolutionary renewal which swept over Europe in the late forties of the last century. When pointing to the historical roots of the revolutionary events of 1848 in Moldavia, Wallachia, and Transylvania, N. Bălcescu observed that the Romanian revolution was no "ephemeral phenomenon, without a past and a future, and without other causes than the fortuitous wish of a minority, and the general European movement... It originated in the past centuries and was hatched by eighteen centuries of toil, suffering, and communion of the Romanian people with themselves".

On the eve of 1848 Romanian society was in a state of acute effervescence as a result of the unrest of the masses and of the young bourgeoisie who claimed that feudal privileges be abolished, that the peasants be given land and that conditions be ensured for a free development of capitalism.

In March, 1848, the revolutionary ferment in the two Principalities caused Nesselrode, the Russian chancellor, to bring to the attention of the ruling princes that the Tsar would not permit anarchy to worm its way into "the Ottoman states under his protection". And before long considerable armed forces had been concentrated on the left bank of the Prut. At Jassy an appeal was made calling for the overthrow of Sturdza and the election of a liberal prince. In Wallachia attempts were made to cause "disorders", as Gheorghe Bibescu reported to Pavel Kiselev, and a revolutionary program entitled *What Are Artisans?* was distributed. The program called for the abolition of boyar privileges, equality of rights, and land for the peasants. The Romanians in Transylvania experienced much anxiety when the Hungarian Diet decided to annex the Principality. Encouraged by the victory of the revolution in Vienna, Simion Bărnuțiu issued a proclamation demanding that a national congress be convened in order to defend Transylvania's autonomy, obtain equality of rights for the Romanians with the other nationalities, and demand that serfdom be abolished. Bărnuțiu's program reflected the deep unrest of the peasantry who threatened to revolt.

Made anxious by the many meetings held in private houses in Jassy and which consequently could not be controlled, Sturdza allowed the partisans of freedom, among whom was V. Alecsandri, Al. I. Cuza, and Zaharia Moldovanu, to meet at the Petersburg Hotel in the evening of March 27/April 8. Some thousand people were present, most of them townspeople from various sections of society, but also many liberal boyars and a number of conservative boyars hostile to Sturdza. After some vehement speeches during which the prince's abusive rule was attacked and freedom was eulogized, a committee was elected to draw up a petition to be submitted to the prince for approval and subsequently to be distributed to the people by way of a proclamation.

The petition comprised thirty-five articles, the first being "religious observance of the Règlement" — this in order to give the movement a semblance of legality. Most of the claims were moderate: personal freedom, the organization of the educational system on a national basis in order to spread culture among all the people, ministerial responsibility, irremovability of civil servants, the setting up of a national bank, and public hearings at the tribunals. Although the peasants had not been invited to the Assembly, it was laid down that their condition should be improved speedily, in their relations with the landowners as well as with the administration. It was not specified, however, whether their improved condition also meant their emancipation and the granting of land. The petition also included more radical claims: that political prisoners, civilian or military, should be released; that the Public Assembly should be dissolved and a new Chamber be formed "without the administration influencing the electorate, so that the chamber should really represent the nation"; that the censorship of home news should be abolished and civil guards formed in all towns. The guards were to be "made up of Romanians as well as of foreigners possessing an estate." The realization of these claims would have resulted in the overthrow of the prince. The general moderation shown in the petition is to be accounted for by the fear of the leaders of the revolutionary movement lest Tsarist Russia should find it a pretext to occupy the country.

The petition was signed by several hundred people, among them the Metropolitan and a number of ministers who had resigned. In the afternoon of March 29/April 10 it was submitted to the prince for approval. Sturdza declared that he could not accept the dissolution of the Public Assembly and civic guards being set up, and when asked whether he could accept the petition as it was, he refused to answer, took refuge in the barracks and ordered the army to put down the rising. The leaders of the movement called upon the people to join in the fight and to raise barricades, but it was too late. Over 300 persons were arrested, some of the boyars were exiled to their country estates or to monasteries and thirteen of the leaders were sent to Galatz under escort to be exiled to Turkey. From among the thirteen, six escaped at Brăila and crossed to Transylvania. Other leaders, among whom was V. Alecsandri, sought refuge in Bucovina and Transylvania. Sturdza prevented Costache Negri, V. Mălinescu, and other young people who were returning from Paris in order to join the revolutionary movement, from entering the country. Although the movement was suppressed, it was the first step in the Romanian revolution of 1848. In Moldavia, as well as in Transylvania and Bucovina, the Moldavian revolutionaries supported by the Romanians of Transylvania, Bucovina, and Wallachia, continued their struggle for the overthrow of the feudal system and of Sturdza as well as for the unity of the Romanian countries into a single state.

Although there was great unrest in Wallachia, Ion Ghica and C. A. Rosetti, who had organized the revolt, waited for the return to the country of N. Bălcescu, I. C. Brătianu, and other Wallachians who had participated in the February Revolution in Paris. On their arrival, a revolutionary committee was formed, and Bălcescu proposed that the insurrection should begin on April 11 /23. Most of the committee, however, opposed the plan, hoping for assistance from the French revolutionary government and from the Romanians of Transylvania. Some weeks later, the brothers Stefan and Nicolae Golescu and I. Eliade Rădulescu, with great influence among the rich sections of the bourgeoisie and the liberal boyars, joined the revolutionary committee. A number of officers and of high administrative officials were also members of the conspiracy.

## 2. *The National Assembly at Blaj*

AFTER Simion Bărnuțiu had issued his proclamation, Aron Pumnul, a Blaj teacher, in conjunction with Avram Iancu and other young intellectuals, called a meeting of the Transylvanian Romanians at Blaj to claim national and social rights. Despite the opposition of the governor, Teleky, 4,000 peasants assembled at Blaj on April 18 /30 under the leadership of Avram Iancu, Simion Bărnuțiu, Ioan Buteanu, A. Papiu-Ilarian, and other young intellectuals called "tribunes". In his speech Bărnuțiu said that the time had come for serfdom to be abolished and for the Romanians to enjoy all rights. He called for larger numbers to be present at the National Assembly convened in the meantime at Blaj for May 3 /15. The first Blaj Assembly had paved the way for the revolution in

Transylvania. In preparation for the National Assembly, a conference was held at Sibiu on April 26 /May 8 with Timotei Cipariu and August Treboniu Laurian, who had come from Bucharest for the purpose, taking part. The conference approved Simion Bărnuțiu's plan of issuing a proclamation to the Romanian nation exacting a national oath and protesting against union with Hungary.

Some 40,000 people participated in the National Assembly at Blaj, the overwhelming majority being peasants though there were also many intellectuals, members of the clergy and bourgeoisie as well as some of the gentry. Also present were some Saxon serfs from the villages between the two Tîrnava rivers with the Saxon scholar Stephan Ludwig Roth at their head. Among the Moldavian refugees were Alecu Russo, Al. I. Cuza, Gheorghe Sion, Lascăr Rosetti, N. Ionescu, and others. Bălcescu was not permitted to come. D. Brătianu came as the representative of the revolutionary committee in Bucharest and Transylvanians residing in Wallachia also turned up. The representative of Banat, Eftimie Murgu, who had been invited to preside over the Assembly, was unable to do so but other intellectuals from Banat and Crișana were present.

On the eve of the appointed date, Sunday May 2/14, a conference was held in Blaj cathedral after the service in order to fix the program of the Assembly. The three currents that had been formed among the Romanians were: loyalists, who proposed that negotiations be carried on with the Vienna Court — among them the bishops Andrei Șaguna and Ioan Lemeni; democratic liberals under the guidance of Timotei Cipariu and George Barițiu; the revolutionary democrats headed by Simion Bărnuțiu, Avram Iancu, and A. Papiu Ilarian. Simion Bărnuțiu's speech was decisive for the orientation of the conference. While welcoming the news of the abolition of serfdom in Hungary, he declared himself against the union of the Principality of Transylvania with the kingdom of Hungary and proposed that the Romanian nation should be recognized in an autonomous Transylvania.

The next day, May 3/15, the National Assembly opened in the Blaj plain, thereafter named the "Field of Freedom". The two bishops — the Orthodox and the Uniate — were proclaimed presidents while Simion Bărnuțiu and George

Barițiu were vice-presidents. On Bărnuțiu's initiative, a motion was passed declaring the Romanian nation "an independent nation" and "an integral part of Transylvania, based on equal freedom." An oath of loyalty to the emperor was taken, as also for the recognition of the Romanian nation and for liberty, equality, and fraternity. Included in the oath was a declaration that they should all "cooperate according to their possibilities, to obtain the abolition of serfdom, freedom for industry and trade, and safeguarding of justice . . .".

The next day A. T. Laurian submitted to the Assembly for approval a petition of rights — the National Petition — comprising sixteen articles, the most important of which were: independence for the Romanian nation with the right to be represented in the Diet of the country and in public offices proportionate to their number, and with the right to use the Romanian language in legislation; independence for the Romanian Church; abolition of serfdom without the serfs making any payment; freedom of industry and trade and abolition of guilds; freedom of speech, writing, and printing; personal freedom and freedom to meet; the setting up of courts of judge and jury; arms for the people and the establishment of a national guard; salaries for the Romanian clergy; a Romanian educational system of all grades, including a Romanian university; taxation proportionate to one's means and the abolition of privileges; the convening of a Constituent Assembly; postponement of the union with Hungary until an assembly had been convened, where the Romanians should be represented according to their number and the importance of their contribution to public obligations. The Assembly approved the National Petition enthusiastically, it being in keeping with the aspirations of the Romanian people.

A delegation headed by Bishop Andrei Șaguna and the Romanian nobleman Alexe Noptsa (Nopcea) was entrusted with the task of pleading for the national petition before the emperor; and the Uniate Bishop Ioan Lemeni, the only Romanian in the Diet, was entrusted with the task of demanding that the Cluj Diet postpone the question of Transylvania's union with Hungary until a Diet had been convened in which the Romanians should be represented proportionately to their importance. A permanent Romanian National Committee was formed at Sibiu. On the third day a protocol was passed and the first Romanian national guard was set up.

The Blaj National Assembly established the program of the Romanian revolution in Transylvania. It rejected the union with Hungary and, as Bălcescu reported, the people clamored: "We want to unite with the country", that is with Wallachia, for the Romanians had always called Wallachia the Romanian Country (*Țara Românească*). Carol Szasz, the commissar of the Hungarian government, showed in his report that the Transylvanian Romanians were anxious to unite with Wallachia and Moldavia.

The delegation headed by Andrei Șaguna did not obtain the sanction of the National Petition from Emperor Ferdinand, for the latter had approved the April Laws which included the union of Transylvania with Hungary. Nor could Lemeni prevent the Transylvanian Diet from passing the union so that in early June Transylvania was considered by the imperial authorities as part of the kingdom of Hungary. The April Laws, which provided for the abolition of serfdom, were also being applied on the territory of what had been the Principality of Transylvania, despite the resistance of the Magyar nobility. This brought about armed conflicts of a social as well as of a national nature, for most peasants were Romanians while the overwhelming majority of the landowners were Hungarian. The Romanians did not recognize Transylvania's union with Hungary for it had been voted by a Diet where they had a single representative, Ioan Lemeni. On May 27/June 8, 1848, the *Transylvanian Gazette* wrote: "The fate of the Romanian nation will be decided in Bucharest and in Jassy, and not in Cluj, Blaj, or Buda". Counting on the united struggle of the entire Romanian people, Laurian proposed on June 20/July 2, 1848, to Bălcescu that a "General Congress of all Romanians" should be convened.

The Romanians in Banat as well as those in Crișana and Maramureș — outlying districts of the Transylvanian Principality, so-called Partium Districts depending on the kingdom of Hungary — fought for the national freedom as demanded by the Blaj Assembly. The Lugoj Assembly of June 15/27 decided that the people should immediately be armed and Eftimie Murgu be apointed as great captain of the people's army of Banat. Elected deputy in the Caraş County, Eftimie Murgu upheld this decision in the Budapest Diet, but Kossuth rejected it vehemently.

## 3. The Moldavian Revolutionaries Evolve a New Program

AFTER the defeat of the March movement, the National Party in Moldavia continued its struggle by means of memorials and lampoons, with the aim of overthrowing the Sturdza administration. At Jassy a secret committee was formed which acted in close connection with the revolutionary leaders who had taken refuge in Transylvania and had removed to Cernăuţi in Bucovina in June.

On May 12/24 a group of Moldavian revolutionaries drew up at Braşov a program more radical than the one adopted in March. It was called "Our Principles for Reforming the Homeland", and provided for the abolition of feudal servitudes: land to the peasants without payment; abolition of boyar privileges and equality before the law; the union of Moldavia and Wallachia "into a single independent Romanian State". The program was influenced by the National Petition which had been passed by the Blaj National Assembly. When the revolution broke out in Wallachia the Moldavian exiles, who had formed a Moldavian Revolutionary Committee at Cernăuţi, contacted the Wallachian revolutionaries through the agency of I. Alecsandri, brother of the poet of the same name, and elected an Executive Committee to which Costache Negri and A. I. Cuza also belonged. Under the influence of revolutionary propaganda, the peasant upsurge in Moldavia intensified and might have turned into a revolution if the Russian army had not occupied Jassy on June 28/July 10.

Being shadowed by the administration, M. Kogălniceanu crossed the frontier into Bucovina where he drew up a draft constitution and at the end of August published a new revolutionary program: "Wishes of the National Party of Moldavia". He had been entrusted with the task by the Moldavian Revolutionary Committee. The program demanded full autonomy for the country, equality in civic and political rights, a public assembly made up of the representatives of all estates, a prince elected by all the estates, responsibility exacted from the ministers and civil servants, freedom of the press, all meetings of the Public Assembly and of the tribunals to be held in public, the country's representatives at Constantinople to be Romanians, individual freedom and inviolability of the home, equal access to education for all Romanians, with schools free of charge, civil guards in town and countryside, courts of judge and jury for issues of the press and for political and criminal cases, abolition of the death penalty and of corporal punishment, irremovability of judges, religious freedom, political rights for all citizens irrespective of race and religion, secularization of the estates of the monasteries dedicated to religious institutions in other countries, councils controlling the administration in the provinces, towns and villages, abolition of ranks and privileges, general contribution to public obligations, abolition of slavery, abolition of the peasants' feudal obligations, land to be given to all peasants against payment. And over and above these reforms — the union of Moldavia and Wallachia, considered as the "keystone, failing which the whole national edifice would have collapsed".

## 4. The Islaz Proclamation.
## The Progress of the Revolution

IN May, 1848, the Revolutionary Committee in Bucharest worked out a program and a proclamation to the people and elected an Executive Committee made up of N. Bălcescu, I. Ghica, and A. G. Golescu. Later, Ghica having been sent to Constantinople to convince the Porte that the revolution was not directed against it, C.A. Rosetti was elected to replace him. As decided by the Committee, the revolution broke out at Islaz in the Romanați county on June 9/21. Eliade Rădulescu, Golescu, and Tell launched a call, and a numerous assembly, mostly made up of peasants, heard the revolutionary program and the proclamation to the people. The program called for equal taxation, an assembly with all classes of society represented, a prince responsible before the law and elected for a term of five years (actually a president of a republic), ministerial responsibility before the law, freedom of the press, the right for every county to elect its administrators, a national guard, secularization of the monasteries dedicated to religious institutions abroad, emancipation of the dependent peasants and the granting of land to them against payment (article 13, considered as the main claim of the revolution by Bălcescu), freedom for the gypsy slaves, free access to education, abolition of the ranks without any offices attached to them, abolition of corporal punishment and of the death sentence, rights for the Jews and political rights for all citizens without discrimination in regard to race and faith. Without demanding the country's independence, the Islaz Program laid down that it was to enjoy full administrative and legislative autonomy. The program rejected the Russian protectorate and the interference of "any foreign power in internal affairs", and demanded that the country's representative at Constantinople should be a Romanian. The last article announced that an extraordinary general assembly was to be convened, made up of the representatives of all classes, in order to work out a constitution based on the 21 articles "decreed by the Romanian People". When the program had been approved, a provisional government was formed consisting of I. Eliade Rădulescu, St. Golescu, Chr. Tell, N. Pleşoianu, and Radu Şapcă. Escorted by a company under the command of Pleşoianu and by numerous peasants, the government went to Caracal, the capital city of the Romanaţi county, where they were met by Gh. Magheru and by townspeople. From there, together with Magheru, they went to Craiova where they were enthusiastically received by the townspeople on June 13/25. The whole of Oltenia was now under the leadership of the revolutionaries.

In Bucharest the insurrection was fixed for June 10/22 at dawn but did not take place owing to the arrest in the afternoon of the preceding day of many revolutionary leaders following an unsuccessful attempt upon the life of Gh. Bibescu. The following day, under the pressure of thousands of townspeople and of peasants from the neighboring villages, Gh. Bibescu sanctioned the program of the revolution and accepted the ministerial cabinet forced upon him, with the exception of Chr. Tell as head of the army, the latter being replaced by colonel Ion Odobescu.

After two days' reign on the terms forced upon him by the revolution, intimidated by the protest of Kotzebue, the Russian consul, Gh. Bibescu abdicated and left for Braşov. The Wallachian revolutionaries organized a provisional government on June 14 /26 with the following membership: I. Eliade Rădulescu, St. Golescu, Chr. Tell, Gh. Magheru, and Gh. Scurtu. The Metropolitan, Neofit, chosen to placate the Porte and the Protective Court was chairman of the government. Bălcescu, A. G. Golescu, C. A. Rosetti, and I. C. Brătianu were secretaries of the government. Colonel Ion Odobescu held the office of head of the army.

On June 15 /27 the government and a great crowd took the oath of loyalty to the Revolutionary Program, in the Filaret plain, thenceforward named the *Plain of Freedom*.

Dissension arose within the government when the program came to be implemented. Dissatisfied with the prominent part played by I. Eliade Rădulescu and Chr. Tell, the radical liberals C. A. Rosetti and I. C. Brătianu resigned. On the other hand, Bălcescu and A. G. Golescu were disconcerted by the delay of the peasantry's liberation and their coming into possession of land. The landowners, with the co-operation of colonels Ion Odobescu and Ion Solomon organized a counter-revolutionary *coup d'état* on June 19 /July 1. Most of the government members were arrested at their offices on the Mogoşoaia Road, but a forceful gathering of the people released them, arresting the two traitor colonels and Major Locusteanu, their accomplice.

A few days later a rumor spread that a Russian army had crossed the Prut and was making for Bucharest. In the evening of June 28 /July 10, the government decided to withdraw northward to Rucăr to oppose the invaders with the support of the Transylvanians. Metropolitan Neofit remained in Bucharest and together with boyars Teodor Văcărescu and Emanoil Băleanu formed a government and re-established the régime of the *Règlement Organique*. The arrested officers were released and resorted to their posts. Because of the protest of the other European powers Russia withdrew her troops to the other side of the Prut and Brătianu aroused the people of Bucharest, overthrew the boyar government, and called back the revolutionary government from Rucăr.

On June 14/26 with the program of the revolution already beginning to be put into effect, the death penalty and corporal punishment were abolished, as also the boyar ranks and the censorship, the political detainees were released, and new administrators were appointed in five counties of Oltenia and later in other counties.

On June 12/24 the newspaper *Pruncul român* (*The Romanian Offspring*) made its appearance in Bucharest, with Rosetti and Enric Winterhalter as editors, and on June 19/July 1, *Poporul suveran* (*The Sovereign People*) under the guidance of Bălcescu, was brought out. These two papers militated for the implementation of the revolutionary program, for the union of the two Principalities into a single state, for land to be given the peasants, and for the country's defense against invading foreign armies.

On June 14/26 the government decreed that the country's flag should be blue, yellow, and red and bear the device: "Justice — Fraternity". Needing a large armed force, the government set up a national guard and subsequently organized troops of volunteer foot soldiers and pandours under the command of Gh. Magheru, appointed General Captain and Inspector of all the country's guards. In early August Magheru went to Oltenia and began organizing what was termed "Trajan's Field" at Râureni near Rîmnicu Vîlcea. Here he concentrated volunteer foot soliders, pandours, and numerous peasants. The Polish immigrants sent Colonel Zablocki to help train the Romanian armed forces in the hope they might serve to extend the revolution in Poland.

On June 26/July 8 the government issued a decision proclaiming the gypsy slaves free and set up a committee to see that this decision was enforced. In order to make fundamental reforms a constituent assembly had to be convened. The assembly was not convened owing to the divergences that arose concerning the representation of the various classes as well as to the foreign threat.

In May, 1848, when Talaat Efendi stopped in Bucharest on his way to Jassy, the moderate liberals handed him a memorial with a number of proposals, among which was the wish of the Moldavians and Wallachians to merge into a single state. In support of this idea, *Pruncul Român* launched an appeal "To Our Brothers in Moldavia", and *Poporul Suveran* published the article "Moldavia's Union with Wallachia", which described the union of Moldavia with Wallachia as "one of the main problems." Agents were sent to Moldavia to rouse the people to revolt and to demand union with Wallachia.

On June 24/July 6, the revolutionary government decreed that commissars recruited from among the radical intelligentsia would be sent about the country to explain the revolutionary program and to incite the peasantry to support the cause of the revolution. Many of the commissars were Transylvanians who considered the revolution in Wallachia as part of the general Romanian revolution.

Freedom and land to the peasants were the main problems and also the apple of discord among the leaders of the revolution. Consequently, the provisional government, where the moderates predominated, lost no time in proposing that its settlement should be postponed and demanded that the villagers fulfill their obligations to the landowners and the lessees that year. The peasants, however, refused to do labor service and pay the tithe on their produce, and in certain places they even attacked the landowners' country houses.

On July 9/21 the government, fearing lest the peasantry should rise *en masse*, instituted a committee made up of a peasant deputy and a landowner for each of the seventeen counties of the country. The committee was to work out a draft law on the implementation of art. 13 of the revolutionary program, which was to be submitted to the constituent assembly for approval. On August 9/21 C.A. Rosetti, on behalf of the regency that had been instituted after the first intervention of the Ottoman army, opened the proceedings of the committee. Chairman of the committee was the liberal boyar Alecu Racoviță, but the proceedings were conducted by the vice-chairman, the Moldavian agronomist Ion Ionescu, who had studied in France and was a fervent partisan of the emancipation of the peasants.

The deputies declared that work was "sacred"; the landowners' representatives demanded that land ownership should be declared sacred, and that it should be ownership of the whole estate. The peasant deputies vehemently protested, declaring that the peasants would consider landownership sacred on becoming owners of the land. At the sixth meeting, the landowners among the deputies accepted in principle that the peasants should be given land but did not agree to the amount proposed. On August 19/31, when the peasant deputies and the majority of the landowners had reached an agreement on the area to be given to the peasants, I. Eliade Rădulescu entered the auditorium and read the decree of the regency whereby the proceedings were to be adjourned. The application of art. 13 of the revolutionary program was thus postponed *sine die.*

In order to strengthen the revolutionary movement, the provisional government contacted the Porte and the revolutionary governments in the other European countries. Before the outbreak of the revolution, Ion Ghica had been sent to Constantinople to win the support of the Porte for the revolutionary program. He sought to persuade the Porte that it was in its own interest to strengthen the economic and political power of the Principalities. Dimitrie Brătianu was sent to establish cooperation between the Hungarian and the Romanian revolutionary movements but failed of his purpose. Later A. G. Golescu went to Transylvania with full powers to represent the revolution in Central as well as in Western Europe, and was subsequently appointed diplomatic agent to the French government. I. Maiorescu was sent to the German parliament in Frankfurt as representative of the two Principalities. Thus did the Romanian diplomatic agents bring the Romanian revolution and the cause of the Romanian people generally to the attention of the main European states.

## 5. *The Revolution Fails in Wallachia*

THE Wallachian revolution had carried the day inside the country. The counter-revolutionary boyars, however, demanded support from the Porte and Russia. But the Porte had been persuaded by Ion Ghica, supported by the Polish emigrants and the British and French ambassadors, not to regard the Wallachian revolution with hostility. On the other hand, a Tsarist army marched into Moldavia and prepared to occupy Wallachia. In order to check the advance of the Russian armies, the Porte sent Suleiman Pasha to Wallachia with an army to re-establish order. After prolonged negotiations, the provisional government on July 28/August 9 agreed to be superseded by a triumvirate committee given the name of "Regency". Made up of I. Eliade Rădulescu, Chr. Tell, and N. Golescu, all three moderate liberals, the Regency declared that it would submit all the changes made from June 11/23 on to the Sultan for approval. Suleiman Pasha declared himself satisfied, recognized the Regency and came to Bucharest on a short visit. The consuls of the European states resumed their official relations with Wallachia, which had been interrupted since the inception of the revolution. In order to consolidate the present state of affairs, a delegation, which included Bălcescu, was sent to Constantinople to submit the reforms to the Sultan for approval.

The Tsarist government protested and demanded that another commissar be sent to Bucharest. The Sultan did not receive the Wallachian delegation and ordered Fuad Efendi to take an army to Bucharest and reinstate the *Règlement Organique*. Thereupon the revolutionaries burnt the *Règlement Organique* plus the *Almanac* of the nobility in Bucharest and in other towns. The Regency invested Magheru with extraordinary powers and sent a large part of the army to Rîureni to put up armed resistance in Oltenia in the event of Fuad Efendi occupying Bucharest.

On September 13/25, 1848, the Ottoman army reached the outskirts of Bucharest. Fuad Efendi summoned 200 leaders of the country to Cotroceni and read a proclamation branding the revolution as a "rebellion" sprung from the spirit of "communism" and informing them that the *Règlement* had been re-established. Bălcescu protested that the rights of the country had been infringed upon, and the revolutionaries cried: "Death rather than the *Règlement*". Fuad Efendi ordered the arrest of the protesters, some of whom were eventually exiled. The leaders of the revolution, sent up the Danube beyond Orșova, succeeded in making their escape and reaching Banat.

On September 13/25 the Ottoman army entered Bucharest. One of its columns advancing up the Spirea Hill came up against a firefighting company strengthened by an army detachment. In the clash that followed there were many casualties on either side. Eliade Rădulescu and Chr. Tell fled to Transylvania where they were followed by numerous revolutionaries. The Russian commissar, Duhamel, who had joined Fuad Efendi, ordered the Russian army to march into Wallachia. With the co-operation of the occupants and of the reactionary boyars, Constantine Cantacuzino re-established the régime of the *Règlement*.

In Oltenia Magheru, having determined to oppose the invading armies, maintained the revolutionary régime for another fortnight, but Eliade Rădulescu and Chr. Tell, who had reached Sibiu by that time, sent word not to oppose the two foreign armies far superior in number. The English consul in Bucharest, R. Colquhoun, gave advice to the same effect. Magheru accepted their decision, dissolved the camp in Trajan's Field on September 28 /October 10, 1848, and withdrew to Transylvania with a number of officers, thus ending the revolutionary struggle which had begun on June 9 /21, 1848 in Wallachia. The new régime set up by the foreign armies, as well as the orders issued by Constantine Cantacuzino, came up against the staunch resistance of the peasants who refused to perform labor service.

## 6. *The Revolution in Transylvania Continues*

AFTER Transylvania was incorporated within Hungary, feudal servitude was abolished in both Hungary and Transylvania. The administration, however, continued to be in the hands of the Magyar and Saxon nobility, and the Romanians who did not recognize Transylvania's union with Hungary were subjected to a reign of terror. In August, A. T. Laurian and N. Bălășescu, both on the Romanian National Committee, were arrested by the Magyar authorities. Simion Bărnuțiu could only escape their fate by seeking the protection of the First Frontier Guards' Regiment. Soon after, the First and Second Frontier Guards' Regiments, made up of Romanians, refused to take orders from the War Ministry in Budapest. The Romanian National Committee convened a new assembly at Blaj, which was in session for ten days, from September 3 /15 to 13 /25, 1848. This time the Romanians who came to the assembly were armed with lances and hayforks and some of them with guns. There were over 20,000, mostly peasants, and their leaders — Avram Iancu, Axente Sever, and Iovian Brad — formed them into a military unit. Simion Bărnuțiu, August Treboniu Laurian, and A. Papiu Ilarian joined the Assembly on the last day. A new resolution was passed protesting against Transylvania's union with Hungary and demanding that a diet and a provisional government should be elected, with Romanians represented proportionately to their number. It was also demanded that an end be put to the pressure exercised upon the peasants to force them to do farm labor for the benefit of the nobility. A memorial was sent to the liberal parliament in Vienna seeking support for the Romanians' claims and for the Principalities. In October began the armed struggle for the removal of Magyar administration in Transylvania: fifteen Romanian legions had been formed, each under the command of a prefect and viceprefect. When war broke out between Hungary and Austria the Romanians demanded arms and officers of General Puchner, the imperial military commander in Transylvania, but their claims were only partly met. Nevertheless, the Romanian legions — an army of peasants supported by the Frontier Guards' Regiments — defeated the Magyar National Guards who were sustained and influenced by the Transylvanian nobility. Saxon peasants from the district between the Tîrnava rivers fought alongside the Romanians under the leadership of Stephan Ludwig Roth. In October the Szeklers held a meeting at Lutiţa, following which they took up arms against the imperial forces. The most powerful resistance was organized by Aron Gabor in the Trei Scaune district, which remained under Szekler administration. In the Romanian districts that had been liberated a Romanian administration was established. The Romanian National Committee in Sibiu was considered to be the real government of the country. Late in December, the Romanians followed Bălcescu's prompting and a meeting in Sibiu proposed that a Romanian principality should be created out of all the Romanian districts in the Habsburg Empire, including Bucovina.

When General Puchner occupied Cluj he ordered the return of all the guns he had distributed, threatening to use his cannons against the Romanian legions if his order was not obeyed. It was obvious that not only the Magyar nobility but also the House of Habsburg was against the Romanians in their desire for national and social freedom. In the meantime the Magyar revolutionary government had sent an army to Transylvania under the command of the Polish general Josep Bem. The latter had come to Hungary with other Polis emigrants hoping to subdue Transylvania and then go to poland to liberate his own country. Having defeated the poorly equipped Romanian legions and the few imperial troops at Ciucea on December 13/25, Bem conquered Cluj, where he advised the Romanians and Saxons to accept the Magyar authority, and he gave an amnesty. He obtained new recruits for his army, especially Szeklers, and by March, 1849, had occupied the greatest part of Transylvania. Alba Iulia and the district of the Western Mountains remained under the Romanians' rule with Avram Iancu as leader. When the town of Sibiu had been conquered, the Romanian National Committee and many other Romanian revolutionaries took refuge in Wallachia where eighty of them, including Simion Bărnuțiu and later also George Barițiu, were under arrest for a few weeks. A delegation of Romanians from Transylvania, the Banat and Bucovina under Andrei Șaguna went to Olmütz in Moravia to submit to Emperor Francis Joseph a memorial proposing that all Romanian districts in the Habsburg Empire be united into a single autonomous principality. Francis Joseph promised to keep count of the Romanians' claims, but the constitution of February 20/March 4, 1849 only recognized the Romanians' national existence without creating a state for them.

Bem's amnesty was not observed. As the Magyar army advanced southwards, punitive expeditions were organized and "blood tribunals" were set up.

## 7. Romanian Revolutionary Resistance in the Western Mountains

IN April, 1849, Bem took his forces to Banat where a mass uprising of the Romanian peasants had dislodged the Magyar local authorities from August to October, 1848. He conquered the towns of Caransebeș and Lugoj and later Mehadia but could not take Timișoara. In the Western Mountains, where many Central Transylvanian peasants had taken refuge, the Romanians continued to resist successfully under Avram Iancu's command against the numerous Magyar detachments which had encircled them.

As the imperial armies were advancing, the Magyar parliament and government removed to Debreczen, where on April 2/14 the Habsburgs were proclaimed dethroned and Hungary to be independent. Kossuth was appointed governor of the Hungarian kingdom. Intent on concentrating all his forces against the Austrian armies, Kossuth determined to sweep away the Romanian resistance in the Western Mountains. He delegated the Romanian deputy Ioan Dragoş to persuade the Romanians to lay down their arms, but the latter would only accept a truce and refused to allow the Hungarian soldiers within their mountain stronghold.

While negotiations with Dragoş were in progress, the Magyar commander Hatvani attacked the Romanians by surprise and occupied Abrud in the evening of April 24/May 6. In the days that followed he was compelled to withdraw, suffering great losses. A week later Hatvani again attacked the Romanians and occupied Abrud but two days later was again defeated. The two attacks cost the Hungarians some 5,000 men. In May and June heavy fighting continued in the Western Mountains, but neither Colonel Kemeny's forces nor those of Paul Vasvari succeeded in defeating the resistance of Avram Iancu's men (the Moţi, residing in the Western Mountains).

The divergence between the Magyar and the Romanian revolutions in Transylvania, fostered by the mistakes of the Magyar revolutionary government who refused to recognize the Romanians' right to self-determination, as well as by the partly well-founded suspicions of some of the Romanian leaders and by the manueuvers of the Vienna Court, caused considerable harm to both revolutionary movements. The Romanian revolutionaries of Transylvania, as well as the Wallachians Bălcescu, Ghica and Cezar Bolliac, endeavored to cooperate with the Hungarian revolutionaries. Bălcescu went to Debreczen and discussed with Kossuth the problem of the relations between the Romanian and the Hungarian revolutionaries, but it was only on July 12, 1849, that Kossuth agreed to sign at Szegedin the *Pacification Project* and the treaty whereby a Romanian legion was formed. On July 16/28, 1849, the Magyar Lower Chamber passed a bill recognizing the national rights of the Romanians and Slavs in Hungary. On Bălcescu's advice, Avram Iancu agreed not to attack the Magyar army as long as the latter was fighting the counter-revolutionary forces of Austria and Russia. In his turn, Kossuth issued a decree whereby the Magyar army was to cease fighting the Romanians. But it came too late. Some days later, on August 1 /13, 1849, General Görgei, commander of the Magyar forces, surrendered to the Habsburg and Tsarist armies at Șiria. The Romanians in the Western Mountains were compelled to lay down their arms when the imperial forces penetrated into Transylvania. The revolution had come to an end in Transylvania.

Although the revolution had been suppressed, it induced the House of Habsburg and the Magyar government to recognize the national existence of the Romanians in Transylvania.

## 8. *Importance of the Romanian Revolution of 1848*

ON the whole, the Romanian revolution of 1848-1849 was a bourgeois revolution for its program tended to consolidate capitalist relationships in the three Romanian Principalities. The program included radical claims of interest to the masses, especially the granting of land to the peasants and a wider franchise. Such claims, as also the participation of the masses of townspeople and peasants in the revolutionary struggle, invested the revolution with a democratic character.

From the national point of view, the Romanian revolution of 1848-1849 made it its aim to unite Moldavia and Wallachia into an independent state, to have the Romanians of Transylvania recognized as a nation and thereafter to unite all the Romanian districts in the Habsburg Empire into an autonomous principality. A more far-reaching aim was the creation of one Romanian state.

The revolutionary forces had achieved a stage of maturity great enough to defeat the counter-revolutionary resistance inside the country but they were unable to repel the armed intervention of the three reactionary empires of Europe.

In historical perspective, the Romanian revolution was the most advanced eastern outpost of the European revolution of 1848, and part of that revolution. It helped to spread the principles of the bourgeois revolution in Southeast Europe.

# CHAPTER IV

## The Union of the Two Principalities

DESPITE the military occupation of nearly three years' duration, the Principalities made great strides in all fields of activity after the revolution of 1848. The national movement advocating union of the Principalities was strengthened. The bourgeoisie increased in number and gave decisive support to the struggle for a national state. Apart from their militant activities inside the country, the revolutionary emigrants spread their propaganda in the capital cities of Europe, succeeding in winning the sympathy of the liberal circles and making the cause of the union of the Principalities an integral part of the European movement for the emancipation of the oppressed peoples. During the Crimean War the union of the Principalities became a factor in the European balance of power. The Treaty of Paris, under which the Russian protectorate was superseded by the joint guarantee of the Great Powers, did not bring about the union of the Principalities, which was left for the Romanians to do. When in 1859 A. I. Cuza was elected as prince of the two Principalities, the Romanian people achieved their unity, which was consolidated by 1862. The representatives of the Romanian people then created the institutions of a modern state, while the land reform of 1864 turned all dependent peasants into free citizens. Cuza's deposition was partly due to the boyars expropriated under the land reform.

In Transylvania the laws of 1853 and 1854 made of the dependent peasants free owners of the holdings they used. Under the "Liberal Empire" which recognized the autonomy of its provinces, the election of 1863 gave the Romanians of Transylvania a relative majority of the mandates so that reforms favoring their development were made. Nevertheless, faced with the obstructions of the Magyar nobility and affected by its defeat, the Imperial Cabinet abandoned the cause of the Romanians and left it to the mercy of Hungary.

## 1. Development of the Romanian Countries After the Revolution of 1848

AFTER the revolution of 1848 was put down, the economy of the three Romanian countries expanded at a more lively tempo owing to the development of capitalist methods of production.

Though serfdom was abolished in Hungary and Transylvania by the laws of April, 1848, the problem of giving land to the former serfs was left in abeyance and was only solved by the patents of 1853 and 1854, when the rulers were compelled to apply the laws of 1848 and to give the peasants titles of property to their holdings.

New relationships between peasants and landowners were enforced in the two Romanian Principalities by the Porte and the Tsarist government under the Convention of Balta Liman of April 19/May 1, 1849, the aim being to forestall a new uprising of the peasantry. The land laws worked out by the committees that revised the *Règlement Organique* were approved in 1851 and applied in 1852. Under them the peasants were comsidered as free tenants while the boyars were owners of the land. The peasants' right to change their place of habitation was still restricted. Venal officials were removed from office in Wallachia and the tithe in kind was abolished in Moldavia; labor service was defined and the peasants were given access to new pasture grounds for their cattle.

Farming made notable strides, some of the landowners and big lessees even using machinery. As a result of the increase in manpower, cattle, and improved implements and machines, the agricultural output, particularly wheat, rose considerably. Wallachia's exports, which consisted mainly of wheat, went up from 76,310.38 lei in 1850 to 164,135.10 lei in 1852, further to rise to 177,010,800.20 lei by 1855.

The increase in farm products stimulated the growth of industry, more vigorously in Transylvania where there was an old industrial tradition, and more slowly in the two Principalities. Although the competition of the more developed regions of the Empire hindered an intensive expansion of Transylvanian industry, the mining industry excepted, Transylvania nevertheless progressed owing to the markets the two Romanian Principalities offered. The metalworking and the mining industries advanced, particularly in Banat. Mining output increased in the Western Mountains and around the town of Baia Mare, and the production of salt also went up. In Braşov, Sibiu and Cisnădie the manufacture of textiles became a thriving industry. The food industry developed at a comparatively speedy rate both in Transylvania and in the Principalities, in particular flour mills sprang up. In the Principalities the number of small industrial enterprises went up, and large enterprises were started in the textile and food industries. Salt was mined at Ocnele Mari, Slănic and Tîrgu Ocna. Crude oil extraction increased when the first oil refineries were set up and kerosene came to be used for lighting purposes. Foreign capital was drawn to this sector of industry. Economic expansion made it necessary to extend the network of roads, to build steel bridges over the bigger rivers and to lay down railway tracks. The first railway lines were built in Banat and Crişana. The Danube was used for exports, especially by the Principalities; ships of ever greater tonnage plied up and down the river. The telegraph was introduced in the Principalities in 1853-1854.

Economic expansion extended the home market, which brought about an increase in town population. In 1860 Bucharest, the most important town in the territory inhabited by the Romanian people, had a population of 121,734, Jassy had 65,745 inhabitants, and the less important towns under 30,000. The foreign trade of the Principalities increased steadily. The balance of trade being favorable, the process of capital accumulation began. Transylvania derived considerable profit from its commercial relations with the two Principalities, while its relations with the western provinces of the Empire were less profitable.

In the Romanian provinces under Habsburg rule Austrian coinage was used while in the Principalities some seventy different coins were in use. This was very confusing and caused great losses to the producers. The attempt made by Al. I. Cuza to create a national coinage was unsuccessful as the Turks considered the minting of money as an attribute of sovereignty. The National Bank of the Habsburg Empire opened a branch in Braşov in 1854 and another in Timişoara in 1855. In 1857 the National Bank of Moldavia was opened with Prussian capital, but it was short-lived.

In order to prevent fresh disturbances in the Principalities, the suzerain and the protecting courts concluded the Convention of Balta Liman on April 19/May 1, 1849. The princes were no longer to be appointed for life but only for a term of seven years. The appointment was to be made by the Sultan after having reached an understanding with the Tsar. The Ordinary and the Extraordinary Public Assemblies were to be superseded by Divans *adhoc* made up of boyars and members of the high clergy appointed by the ruling prince. The *Règlement* was to be revised. The Ottoman and the Russian armies remained in the Principalities until 1851. Grigore Al. Ghica was appointed Prince of Moldavia and Barbu Ştirbei of Wallachia. Both princes made it their aim to improve public administration, the communication system, the educational system, and the army.

After the revolution, the principality of Transylvania once again became a distinct administrative unit, depending directly on the imperial government in Vienna. Banat was united with the Serbian Voevodina to form a province whose capital city was Timişoara. Crişana remained part of Hungary, while Bucovina became a Grand Duchy depending on Vienna direct. The project of the national committee to unite all the Romanian territories of the Empire into one single principality was never realized.

The constitution issued by Francis Joseph on February 20/March 4, 1849, was abrogated in 1851, when a so-called neo-absolutist régime was installed. The administration was controlled by the Vienna government which carried on a policy of centralization and Germanization.

The national claims of the Romanians of Transylvania were not satisfied, and neither were some of their socio-economic claims, such as the claims of the peasants of the Western Mountains to the forests and pasture land. These claims had been upheld by Avram Iancu. Censorship compelled George Bariţiu to withdraw from the editorial staff of the paper *Gazeta Transilvaniei (The Transylvanian Gazette)*. The Uniate Bishopric of Blaj was raised to the rank of a Metropolitanate with two bishoprics, at Lugoj and Gherla. The first Uniate Metropolitan was Alexandru Sterca Suluţiu, a man of courage.

The revolutionary leaders continued their struggle for the implementation of the programme worked out in 1848. Exiled or having emigrated, most of then had gathered in Paris, Brussa, and Vienna where they carried on rewarding and intensive activities in favor of the reforms for which they had fought in 1848, with emphasis on the union of the Romanian countries. From November, 1849, Bălcescu led their activities in Paris although he had not been officially committed to this end. Reorganized into a Propaganda Committee, the Paris exiles, who did their utmost to induce the Western press to favor the cause of the Romanians, published the review *România Viitoare (Romania of the Future)* in the autumn of 1850. On the editorial staff were Bălcescu, C. A. Rosetti, and V. Mălinescu. It was in this paper that Bălcescu published his article *"Progress of the Revolution in the History of the Romanians"*, a genuine program of the revolutionary struggle of the Romanian people. As the peasants' emancipation and the land reform were the main elements of the revolution, Bălcescu published anonymously in Paris *Questions économiques des Principautés danubiennes*. This was in the spring of 1850. The next year, in May and June, the review *Junimea Română (The Romanian Youth)* appeared under his aegis.

The group of exiles around C. A. Rosetti organized the Romanian Revolutionary Committee in Paris in 1851 and delegated D. Brătianu to represent it on the European Democratic Central Committee in London headed by the Italian democratic revolutionary Giuseppe Mazzini. Rosetti and his collaborators published the review *Republica Română (The Romanian Republic)* which militated for the unification of the Romanian people into an independent "democratic and social" republic through revolution. The review was issued in Paris in November, 1851, and in Brussels in 1853.

## 2. *Struggle for the Union During the Crimean War*

IN the summer of 1853 Moldavia and Wallachia were occupied by the Russian armies. France and England formed an alliance with Turkey and declared war on Russia. The Crimean War was to make of the union of the Principalities a problem on which the balance of power in Europe depended. In the autumn of 1853 and up to the spring of the following year the Russians and Turks fought each other along the Danube. The Romanian exiles taking advantage of this state of war sought to stir the people to revolt in Oltenia.

Following the Turco-Austrian Convention of June 2/14, 1854, the Principalities were evacuated by Russia and occupied by the Austrians who remained in occupation until March, 1857, during which time their investments in these countries show that they regarded the territory as their own. In October, 1854, Barbu Ştirbei and Grigore Al. Ghica were re-instated on the thrones of Wallachia and Moldavia, where they reigned under the occupation of the Austrian armies until the end of their seven-year term of office.

The partisans of the union and of progress, stimulated by the favorable turn of events, intensified their activities. In Bucharest they published the gazette *Timpul (The Time)* from December, 1854, to January, 1855, and *Patria (The Homeland)* from February to October, 1855, while in Jassy they issued *România Literară (The Literary Romania,* 1855) and *Steaua Dunării (The Danube Star)*, which was edited by M. Kogălniceanu from October 1, 1855. Most of the Moldavian exiles had returned in 1849 and 1850 with the prince's consent. In Wallachia Barbu Ştirbei, more conservative than the prince of Moldavia, prevented the exiles from returning to the country on account of their radical program of action. However, he was a partisan of the union like Grigore Ghica, though he stood for the preservation of the big landed estates.

Believing that the European revolution on which they had pinned their hopes of union was not possible in the near future, the Romanian exiles in the summer of 1854 approached Napoleon III, Emperor of France, the English government and Cavour, Prime Minister of Sardinia, asking them to declare that Moldavia and Wallachia should be united into a single state under a foreign prince, which to them meant independence. Their demand was upheld by many progressive personalities in Europe, who considered that a Romanian national state would be a factor of progress in Southeast Europe.

At the Congress of Paris, which ended the Crimean War, Count Walewski, foreign minister of France, proposed that the Principalities should be united under a foreign prince, and he was supported by England, Prussia, Russia, and Sardinia. The strong opposition of Austria and the Porte compelled the Congress to propose that the population of the two Principalities should first be consulted on the subject of union and that special assemblies should be constituted for the purpose. A European commission was formed to find out what the population desired. The Congress also decided that Russia's protectorate should be superseded by the joint guarantee of the great powers, that South Bessarabia should be joined to Moldavia, a commission of the Danube riparian states should be set up, in addition to a commission for the dredging of the Danube from Isaccea to where the Sulina arm joins the sea so that high tonnage vessels could navigate the river.

In order to encourage the movement favoring the union, Grigore Ghica enacted a liberal press law and appointed partisans of the union to the main state offices. The movement favoring the union was openly organized. At Socola not far from Jassy a Union Society was set up on May 25/June 6, 1856, with a membership of bourgeois, liberal boyars, and moderate conservative boyars. The purpose of the society was to coordinate the action for the union of the Principalities under a foreign prince. A few days after, a union committee was set up in Jassy which sent delegates to the capital cities of the various districts in order to make up similar union committees. The delegates were welcomed enthusiastically everywhere so that the union movement assumed a mass character.

Austria and Turkey, soon joined by England, bent their efforts at Constantinople on preventing the inclusion of the union problem in the edict *(firman)* convening the *Ad Hoc* Assemblies. Their efforts were of no avail owing to France's opposition. They used the complicity of Toderiță Balș and Nicolae Vogoride, the *Caimacams (Prince Lieutenants)*, to forge the election lists so as to ensure the victory of the antiunion party. At the same time the pro-union press was suspended and a fierce persecution of the pro-union people began.

In Wallachia, the Porte appointed as Caimacam *(Prince Lieutenant)* the former prince who reigned while the *Règlement Organique* was in force: Alexandru Ghica. The latter sought the support of the richest section of the bourgeoisie, supported the pro-union movement, and allowed the moderate emigrants to return to the country. The pro-union party again brought out the review *Timpul* and the exiles in Paris issued the gazette *Concordia* in Bucharest on February 6/18, 1857. The gazette called upon all social classes to co-operate in order to achieve the union of the Principalities and advocated moderate bourgeois reforms. The editor of the review was C. A. Crețulescu. On March 3/15, 1857, the Central Union Committee was set up in Bucharest. In the capital cities of all the counties pro-union committees were formed which carried out intensive propaganda among the masses of townspeople and peasants, and connections were established with the Union Committee in Jassy.

## 3. The Ad Hoc Assemblies

IN the first half of March, 1857, after the Austrian troops had withdraw from the Principalities, the European Commission arrived in Bucharest.

Vogoride continued his persecution of the pro-unionists, arresting them and resorting to terror, deleting the names of those who were declared, or suspected, unionists from the election lists, and preventing them from sitting for public office and from casting their vote. The National Party protested to the European Commission and made pro-union demonstrations when the Commissioners came from Jassy to investigate. Al. I. Cuza, prefect of Galatz, refused to carry out the order to rig the election, and resigned his office, thus creating a sensation. The pro-unionists published in the West compromising correspondence between the Caimacam and his relations and the Vizir and decided to boycott the election.

Vogoride, ignoring the protests, carried through the election, which having been manipulated resulted in an anti-union majority. The powers supporting the union — France, Russia, Sardinia, and Prussia — demanded that the Porte should cancel the election but the latter, supported by Austria and England, refused. As a result, on July 24/August 5, the pro-union powers severed diplomatic relations with the Porte. In order to avert the danger of a European war, and perhaps of a revolution, Napoleon III accompanied by Walewski met Queen Victoria, Lord Palmerston, the British Prime Minister, and Lord Clarendon, the Foreign Secretary, at Osborne House on July 25/August 6. A compromise was reached after three days' talks. Great Britain agreed to convince the Porte to cancel the election and to revise the election lists, and France agreed to give up the plan of a union of the Principalities under a foreign prince.

Pressed by the British government, the Porte canceled the election. The election was then carried out with untampered election lists and gave a complete victory to the National Party. All the leaders of the pro-union movement were returned, among them M. Kogălniceanu, V. Mălinescu, Costache Negri, A. I. Cuza, and Anastase Panu. In Wallachia it was the most important of the exiles who were returned: C. A. Rosetti, I. C. Brătianu, St. and N. Golescu, and Chr. Tell, who were allowed to enter the country late in June, 1857, and also Gh. Magheru and A. G. Golescu.

At the *Ad Hoc* Assembly in Moldavia, Kogălniceanu, as spokesman of the National Party, submitted a proposal in which it was pointed out that "the first, the greatest, most general and most national wishes of the country" were: 1. autonomy; 2. union of the Principalities in a state bearing the name of Romania; 3. a foreign hereditary prince; 4. neutrality of the territory of the Principalities; 5. a public assembly "where all the interests of the nation should be represented." Only two of the 83 deputies declared against the union of the two countries. The other 81 voted enthusiastically for Kogălniceanu's proposal.

In Wallachia the *Ad Hoc* Assembly unanimously passed a proposal which included all the points of the Moldavian resolution, this being proof of the perfect unity of views of the pro-unionists in the two Principalities.

As regards internal organization, the *Ad Hoc* Assembly in Wallachia considered that the problem should be postponed until after union had been effected. The deputies of the peasantry demanded that the peasants should be represented in the future legislative assembly. The Moldavian *Ad Hoc* Assembly debated upon the more important problems of internal organization, which if liberal reforms had been made, would have modernized the whole structure of the state. The solutions advocated were: assurance of personal freedom, equality before the laws and in regard to taxation, abolition of consular jurisdiction, re-organization of the army, freedom of religion, and independence of the Romanian Orthodox Church.

The deputies of the peasantry, considering the program of reforms incomplete, submitted a proposal to the assembly in which, after pointing out that the peasants bore most of the public burden and were oppressed, demanded rights equal to those of the other citizens, abolition of corporal punishment, of the labor service for the administration, and of capitation, the right to elect village officials, abolition of the farming work due to the boyars for which they agreed to pay, the granting of land "up to two-thirds of the estate," and representation in the public assembly. The overwhelming majority of the *Ad Hoc* Assembly rejected the claims of the peasantry.

At the end of 1857 the Guaranteeing Powers agreed that the Porte should close the *Ad Hoc* Assemblies. The European Commission drew up a report to the Conference of the Guaranteeing Powers which included the conclusions drawn from the proceedings of the Assemblies and from other information, proposing the re-organization of the Principalities on a bourgeois basis and making known the vote of the *Ad Hoc* Assemblies in favor of the union.

## 4. The Convention of Paris

THE report of the European Commission was discussed by the Paris Conference in accordance with the directions of the treaty of 1856 (10/22 May-7/19 August 1858). Based on that report, the Conference passed a convention on the international and internal status of the Principalities.

The demand for the union of the two Principalities into one state was not satisfied. It was decided that they should be united under the name of the United Principalities of Moldavia and Wallachia. Full autonomy of the Principalities was, however, recognized under the joint guarantee of the seven signatory powers. The Sultan's suzerainty was maintained but the Porte was not entitled to send armed forces to the Principalities unless "disturbances" arose, and this could be done only with the agreement of the signatory powers. But the treaties the Ottoman Empire concluded with other states also bound the Principalities "in everything which did not infringe their immunities." Each Principality was to be ruled by an elected prince and by an elective assembly. At Focşani a Central Commission was to be set up for the purpose of working out the draft laws of common interest, which, however, only became laws after they had been approved by the two elective assemblies. Each elected a prince for life, whose father was to be Moldavian or Wallachian and who must have an income of three thousand gold ducats from his estate. With the exception of the laws of local interest, all the legislation was to be common to both Principalities, which were to have one single Court of Justice and of Cassation. The armies of the two countries were each to have a flag with a blue stripe in token of unity. The Moldavians and Wallachians were equal before the law and could be admitted to public functions in either Principality. This made it possible for the Principalities to elect the same prince. Privileges, exemptions, and monopolies were abolished and the law that regulated agrarian relations was to be revised. In order to ensure political preponderance to the landowners and the upper bourgeoisie, the electoral law annexed to the convention restricted the number of electors to a few thousand rich people. Nevertheless, the Paris Convention meant progress, for it strengthened the legal basis of the capitalist system. The difference between citizens was no longer based on privileges but on wealth. Although it was not decided that the two Principalities should be united into a single state, the Paris Convention made it possible for the Romanian people to achieve it with the support of the favorable powers.

In accordance with the decisions of the Paris Conference, at the end of October, 1858, three Caimacams were appointed in each Principality: Stefan Catargiu, Vasile Sturdza, and Anastase Panu in Moldavia, and Emanoil Băleanu, Ioan Manu, and I. Al. Filipescu in Wallachia.

## 5. *Election of Alexandru Ioan Cuza in the Two Principalities*

THE three Moldavian Caimacams were in favor of the union, but Ştefan Catargiu was bent on becoming prince at any cost. The ministries were entrusted to pro-unionists: V. Alecsandri became Secretary of State, I. A. Cantacuzino, head of the Finance Department, and Colonel Al. I. Cuza, head of the army. A conflict soon broke out between the conservative Ștefan Catargiu, who was also Home Minister, and the other two Caimacams, who were liberals. The press law, which had been suspended by Toderiță Balș in September, 1856, came into force again against the will of Ștefan Catargiu and the separatist prefects, some of them near relations of Ștefan Catargiu, were replaced by unionists. Relying on the support of the Porte, Ștefan Catargiu sabotaged the work of the Caimacam Administration but the liberal Caimacams, taking advantage of the majority they could count on in the administration, ruled without taking him into consideration. Iordache Pruncul, a separatist, was dismissed, and the liberal A. Teriachiu was appointed as director of the Home Department, being installed by means of the armed forces with the support of Al. I. Cuza. Ștefan Catargiu, having refused to participate in the activities of the administration, was replaced by I. A. Cantacuzino, no account being taken of the protests of the Porte.

The election for the Elective Assembly took place in December. The National Party, fully supported by the masses, was also backed in its election campaign by the papers *Steaua Dunării (The Danube Star)*, brought out by M. Kogălniceanu, *Zimbrul și Vulturul (The Bison and the Eagle)*, and by a new publication — *Romania* — issued by a young historian, B. P. Hașdeu. The moderate conservative party headed by Grigore Sturdza issued a gazette, *Constituționariul (the Constitutionalist)*, while the party of the great boyars rallying around M. Sturdza, who had returned from Paris in order to run for prince, brought out the gazette *Patria (The Homeland)* whose editor was N. Istrati, one of the supporters of Balș and Vogoride.

Six of the sixty deputies who had been elected were invalidated and one — Costache Negri — resigned as he could not agree with the moderate conservatives in the National Party. Together with the Metropolitan, who was deputy by right, there were now 54 deputies, 31 of them belonging to the National Party and the others supporting the group of Grigore Sturdza or of his father, Mihail Sturdza. The success of the National Party appeared to be certain but at least five unionists stood for the dignity of prince without having asked the approval of the Party. Among the five were Lascăr Catargiu, M. Kogălniceanu, and Costache Negri, upheld by friends to oppose Lascăr Catargiu. During the night of January 3/15—4/16, 1859, the deputies of the National Party met in the Natural Sciences Museum in order to establish who the one candidate should be. It was considered that he should be either M. Kogălniceanu or Lascăr Catargiu. The former was not accepted by the moderate conservatives on account of his democratic views, the latter was rejected by the democratic and the radical liberals, as he was known to oppose liberalism and the giving of land to the peasants. When Kogălniceanu left, the unionists finally declared Colonel Al. I. Cuza, the commander of the army, as sole candidate of the National Party. Cuza was not present and nobody had thought of him until then. A firm revolutionary in 1848, and a devoted partisan of the union from 1857 to 1859, Cuza was accepted also by the moderate conservatives for he was considered a moderate liberal. The next day an independent increased the ranks of the 31 deputies of the National Party so that the success of Cuza was ensured by an overwhelming majority. In the morning of January 5/17, 1859, before proceeding to elect the prince, the Assembly passed a resolution showing that the candidate elected to the throne was to remain in office only until the Guaranteeing Powers consented to the complete union of the Principalities and the election of a foreign prince.

The main item on the agenda was then discussed: the election of Cuza, candidate of the National Party, who was on all the 48 voting papers. At 12 o'clock Alexandru Ioan I was proclaimed elected Prince of Moldavia and immediately took the oath. Kogălniceanu made a brief speech on behalf of he Assembly: "By electing you," he said, "the country wantted a new man for new laws," and then advised him to be "the man of the age . . ." to see the lot of the peasantry bettered. "Be kind, be good-hearted, be kind especially to those whom the princes of the past dealt unkindly with or ignored."

The election of Al. I. Cuza aroused great enthusiasm among the crowds awaiting the result of the vote, for the newly elected prince voiced the people's will to freedom and progress. The news quickly spread by telegraph throughout Moldavia and Wallachia. The next day, January 6/18, the paper *Românul (The Romanian)*, of Bucharest joyfully greeted the election, significantly describing Cuza as "the elect of the Romanians." As soon as he was elected, Cuza entrusted Vasile Sturdza with the task of forming the cabinet, which was made up only of unionists, with Vasile Alecsandri as Foreign Minister.

From among the Wallachian Caimacams, Emanoil Băleanu and Ioan Manu were conservatives and supported Gh. Bibescu; the third, I. Al. Filipescu, was a moderate conservative. During the first weeks, the Caimacams worked in full agreement, deciding to forbid all meetings until the election lists had been made. This was to the detriment of the National Party. Despite the objections of censorship, the paper *Românul* brought out by C. A. Rosetti, spokesman of the radical-liberal party, the *Dâmbovița* edited by D. Bolintineanu, one of the Wallachian democratic liberals, and the *Naționalul (The National)* of V. Boerescu, a liberal, firmly upheld the cause of the union and of progress. The conservative groups did not have any paper of their own. Strongly supported by the two Caimacams who opposed the National Party, the Conservatives spread a rumor among the landowners to the effect that the radical-liberals, their most powerful opponents, were socialists and bent on taking their estates to divide among the peasants.

When the election lists were made up, the conservative Caimacams deleted some of the members of the National Party in order to minimize its chances of success in the election. Rosetti and Boerescu were crossed out because they did not have an income of 400 ducats a year as election stipulations demanded of those entitled to be elected in Bucharest; I. C. Brătianu was crossed off the Pitești lists on the ground that he had been sentenced to prison during his exile in France, although the sentence had been given for political reasons. As head of the Department of Justice, Caimacan I. Al. Filipescu, who sympathized with the National Party though he was a moderate conservative, ordered that the Ilfov and Argeș tribunals should put down the names of the above-named in the election lists. The administration, however, carried on a persevering campaign throughout the country to falsify the election to the detriment of the National Party, crossing out its partisans from the election lists, intimidating the electors, and making false reports on the election.

According to the calculations of Béclard, the French Consul in Bucharest, out of the 68 deputies who were elected, 29 were progressive and 39 conservative and moderate. Moreover, three of the four church dignitaries who were deputies by right were also moderates. The conservatives consequently had an incontestable majority in the Wallachian Elective Assembly. Dissatisfied with the election returns, the radical liberals demanded that they should be canceled, and intended to launch a call to the people, which meant causing an insurrection. The moderate conservatives, who cooperated with them as part of the National Party, opposed this measure in fear of the masses. While renouncing the call to the people, the radical liberals nevertheless sent the young intellectuals — contributors to the review *Românul* whom they called "tribunes" and who had been trained in the "red" clubs founded in Bucharest when the exiles had returned from Paris — to rouse the masses of townspeople and peasants.

On the first day several thousand men assaulted the building of the Election Assembly and entered the auditorium, intimidating the conservative deputies. The next morning, "crowds of people from all sections of society and of every age," as N. T. Orăşanu, one of the tribunes, put it, "forced their way into the yard of the Assembly building". Béclard observed that there were "hundreds of peasants whom he could recognize by their dress."

A battalion of foot soldiers sent to scatter the crowd had to be withdrawn under the people's pressure; the people rushed threateningly into the Assembly building. Béclard reported: "Terrible fear overwhelmed a number of the deputies." In the afternoon the people, encouraged by the withdrawal of the army, increased their pressure on the conservatives and the reactionary Caimacams. The peasants arrested at the Colentina barrier to prevent them from participating in the demonstrations were released forcibly and the soldiers who had arrested them were disarmed. The crowd demonstrated angrily before the residence of Caimacam Emanoil Băleanu. Panic seized the conservative deputies, who felt safe neither in the streets nor in their homes. Eder, the Austrian consul, suggested that the Assembly should be removed

to a provincial town where they could proceed to e-
lect the prince without any danger of being attacked by the
crowd.

In the night of January 23/February 4 the leaders of the
National Party assembled at the Concordia Hotel agreed to
conclude a truce with the conservatives through the agency
of the army command, both camps undertaking to withdraw
their candidates. The National Party had decided to support
Alexandru Ioan Cuza, prince of Moldavia.

The next day, January 24/February 5, 1859, the crowd
withdrew from the neighborhood of the Assembly, and the
army was confined to the barracks. Several thousand people
were, however, to be found in the neighboring gardens and
on Filaret hill. A tribune, E. G. Valentineanu, wrote that the
people in the gardens near the Assembly building were prepared "to rush in and compel the Assembly to proclaim the
elect of the Moldavian Assembly."

With the meeting opened, a secret conference was held
during which V. Boerescu proposed that Cuza, prince of
Moldavia, should be elected prince of Wallachia. The majority of the conservatives accepted Boerescu's proposal.

After the mandates had been checked, the 64 all cast their
votes for Cuza as their Moldavian colleagues had done. Cuza
was proclaimed prince amid great enthusiasm. The decisive
step whereby the two Principalities had been united was
celebrated by the people until far into the night, demonstrations being made throughout Bucharest. The news was transmitted by telegraph to Jassy and to all the towns of the two
Principalities and caused immeasurable joy among the people.
As Al. Papiu Ilarian said, Cuza's election in both Principalities caused even greater joy in Transylvania, for the Romanians there hoped that Romania would help them to free themselves from foreign subjection. The courage of the Moldavians and Wallachians was approved by progressive public
opinion all over Europe. The Russian revolutionary democrat
N. Chernyshevsky said that Transylvania should have been
joined to the two Principalities.

Having accepted also the throne of Wallachia, Cuza entrusted
the formation of the cabinet to I. Al. Filipescu. The cabinet
included representatives of all political groups, both conservative and liberal. The election of the same prince in both

Principalities was a great victory in the Romanian people's struggle for an independent national state and for social progress.

## 6. *The Union of Moldavia and Wallachia Is Confirmed*

AFTER his election as prince of Wallachia, Cuza intended to proclaim in Bucharest the complete union of the Principalities but refrained on account of the cautious attitude of France and the reserved attitude of Russia. The Porte considered that the election had gone against the provisions of the Paris Convention and in this was supported by Austria. In order to get the election recognized, Cuza sent the Moldavian Foreign Minister, V. Alecsandri, to seek the backing of Napoleon III, the British government and Cavour, Sardinia's Premier. Napoleon III and Cavour, whose good will was known to the Romanians, promised to help and the British Foreign Secretary was won over by Cuza's cautious and moderate policy after the election. At the conference of the representatives of the Guaranteeing Powers held in Paris on March 26/April 7 and April 2/14, 1859, the representatives of France, Britain, Russia, Sardinia, and Prussia declared for the recognition of the election, while the representatives of the Porte and of Vienna opposed it. Having been defeated by France and Sardinia in the war in Italy, Austria no longer opposed the election when the Conference opened again on August 25/September 6 of the same year, and the Porte, now isolated, gave in, too.

When Cuza's election in the two Principalities had been recognized, the Romanians made it their aim to complete the union and build up a single state. Already in 1859 the telegraph offices had their center in Bucharest and in the summer of the same year, at the time of the war in Italy, the armies of the two Principalities assembled at the Florești camp with the aim of defending the union and possibly of marching into Transylvania. A single general staff was organized for both armies under the prince's command. The following year, 1860, the course of the national currency, the *leu*, was unified, a single War Ministry was set up, the capitation tax was levied also on the privileged, and corporal punishment was abolished in both Principalities. The Central Commission at Focşani, which had begun functioning on May 10/22, 1859, drew up a draft constitution, as well as a draft land reform law in 1860 emancipating the peasants, though without giving them land, and a draft electoral law in 1861, which gave the franchise to the majority of the citizens who were of age.

In December, 1860, Cuza sent the Guaranteeing Powers an appeal asking that the union of the Principalities under one single cabinet be completed and a new electoral law be approved. Since the Porte postponed its answer to these requests, the Elective Assemblies asked the prince that they should be convened in April, 1861, to debate the draft land reform law of the Central Commission at Focşani. The real aim, however, was to proclaim the complete union of the Principalities. Prompted by Costache Negri, the diplomatic agent of the United Principalities at Constantinople, Cuza threatened the Porte by saying he would achieve the union by way of revolution.

The Guaranteeing Powers, concerned by the prospect, were prepared to satisfy the requests of the Principalities and for this purpose a conference of their representatives was convened at Constantinople. As the conference debates were protracted, in November Cuza apprised the Porte that he would call both Elective Assemblies and proclaim the union complete unless his requests were approved. On November 23/December 5 the Porte issued an edict (*firman*) approving the unification of the two Principalities' administrations but only for Cuza's lifetime. On December 11/23 Cuza announced that the union had been completed, and the two Elective Assemblies decided to meet in Bucharest on January 24/ February 5, 1862, thus forming one single National Assembly.

Romania's government — for the United Principalities were now being given that name — was formed on January 22/ February 3, 1862, with Barbu Catargiu, spokesman of the conservative majority in the Assembly, as Prime Minister. The cabinet included representatives of the conservative groups, both Moldavian and Wallachian. On January 24/ February 5, Alexandru Ioan I read a message to the National

Assembly and the cabinet announcing the complete and final union of the two Romanian Principalities. About the union he said: "As I have said, it will be such as Romania wishes it, such as she feels it should be." He pointed out that a new age was opening up for the country and demanded that the union should be strenghthened by "the progressive development of institutions." The Romanian national state was thus formed, although it did not comprise all the territory inhabited by Romanians. However, the conservatives forming the cabinet were a source of anxiety for the masses of townspeople and peasants, as also for the progressive groups which three years before had imposed the election of Cuza in both Principalities. After the solemn meeting, the crowds cheered the prince and the progressive deputies and booed the conservative cabinet members and deputies. The peasant movement headed by Mircea Mălăieru, who sought to overthrow the conservative cabinet with the help of the masses in Bucharest and to compel the country to form a liberal radical government, had been put down the day before with the assistance of the Bucharest regiments.

## 7. *Bourgeois Reforms.*
### *Alexandru Ioan Cuza Is Deposed*

THE conservatives intending to consolidate the capitalist system had meant to do so by dispossessing the peasants of the holdings they used and maintaining the political preponderance of the landowners. On March 25 /April 6, 1862, the conservative cabinet submitted to the Assembly the draft land reform law worked out by the Central Commission of Focșani under which the peasants were released from feudal obligations but lost the holdings they used. M. Kogălniceanu opposed the bill with numerous arguments drawn from history, both that of Romania and of other European countries, and denouncing it as an obstacle to the consolidation of the Romanian nation and to progress. The conservative majority, however, passed it with a few amendments on June 11 /23. The amendment proposed by Kogălniceanu and endorsed by 22 progressive deputies, including Ion Ghica, N. Golescu, Al. C. Golescu, and George Adrian, had been rejected. It provided for the peasants to be given their freedom and the holdings they used upon some payment made to the land-owners as compensation for the labor services and the tithe which had been abolished.

On June 8/20 Barbu Catargiu was shot. The assassin was never discovered. Catargiu had left the Assembly in the carriage of N. Bibescu, Chief Commissioner of the Bucharest Police, after declaring his opposition to the convening of a committee to arrange a meeting, the people nevertheless met on June 11/23 to celebrate the anniversary of the revolution of 1848. The conservative majority was baffled both on account of the death of their former leader and because the prince had not sanctioned the bill passed by them.

Shortly after, Cuza entrusted the formation of the cabinet to N. Crețulescu, a moderate liberal and a partisan of bour-geois reforms effected by "a middle way" that would eschew internal difficulties and external complications. After an unsuccessful press campaign against Cuza, the radical liberals, through the agency of Ion Ghica, came to an understanding with the conservative groups and formed "the monstrous coalition" against the prince's tendency to rule with authority.

Unable to stand its ground against the opposition and to proceed to carry out the land and the electoral reforms, the cabinet presided over by Crețulescu was superseded by a cabinet with Kogălniceanu as premier in October, 1863. On December 13/25, 1863, the estates of the monasteries were secularized, including those of the monasteries dedicated to institutions abroad. More than a quarter of the country's territory thus became state property. The law for the orga-nization of the armed forces was also approved by the radical liberals after Kogălniceanu had accepted the introduction of an amendment providing for the setting up of a civic guard. This strengthened the position of the government and weak-ened the cooperation between radical-liberals and conser-vatives. Cuza, however, opposed the bill and refused to sanc-tion it. Kogălniceanu took advantage of the situation and on March 16/28, 1864, submitted to the Elective Assembly a land-reform bill against which on April 13/25 the majority of the Assembly gave a vote of censure. The radical-liberals had not voted against the government but I. C. Brătianu had submitted a land-reform bill which differed, though not greatly, from the Government's. Cuza did not accept Kogălniceanu's resignation on May 2/14, 1864, and made a coup d'état dissolving the conservative-controlled Assembly.

A plebiscite approved the new constitution which was called "Statute Enlarging on the Paris Convention." The prince's prerogatives were greatly increased, he alone being able to put forward bills, which were to be drawn up by a State Council whose members were appointed, though their appointment could be revoked. The prince was entitled to appoint the Chairman of the Elective Assembly. Under the law there were to be two categories of electors: direct and primary. The direct electors elected deputies by secret ballot while the primary electors elected one delegate for every 100 electors; the delegates assembled in the capital city of the county to vote like the direct electors. The peasants and lower bourgeoisie were politically inferior to the landowners and the upper and middle bourgeoisie, and the rural and urban proletariat enjoyed no franchise. The Elective Assembly, whose deputies were not entitled to interpellate, debated the bills and passed or rejected them. A second assembly, the Moderating Corps, was set up. It was made up of Metropolitans and Bishops, the President of the Court of Cassation, the oldest general and 64 senators designated by the prince. The new legislative body approved or rejected the bills passed by the Assembly.

Cuza went to Constantinople to have the new constitution sanctioned. The representatives of the Guaranteeing Powers and also the Porte approved the constitution, and Cuza also obtained recognition of the right of the United Principalities to amend their laws without the consent of the Powers. On August 14/26, 1864, Cuza promulgated a land law based on Kogălniceanu's bill of March of the same year. The peasants were thereby freed from feudal obligations and put in possession of the holdings they had used, supplemented, if necessary, to reach the number of hectares fixed for the various regions of the country. In fixing the area of the holdings given to the peasants, the number of their cattle was taken into account. The peasants who had been given land were to pay the landowners, through the intermediary of the state, a sum of money which was considerable, but which turned them into owners of the land in the bourgeois meaning of the word. The payment was to be spread over fifteen years. The peasants with-

out cattle received small holdings insufficient for their existence and they were thus compelled to sell their labor power.
Over 48,000 peasant families (newly married couples, peasants
living on "narrow" estates) who were to receive land from
the state received it only in 1878. In many villages, with the
complicity of the state machinery, the peasants were allotted
the poorest land: marshland, sandy soil, and land in precipitous places. The landowners together with the state held about
66 per cent of the country's land while the peasants, including
the free peasants of old, owned only a little over 33 per cent.
Making the peasants independent of the landowners' estates,
the land reform concluded the process of abolishing the feudal
system and paved the way for the swift-paced development
of capitalism in the United Principalities while contributing
to the strengthening of "the nation," as Kogălniceanu had
said.

Bourgeois institutions, first set up in 1859, continued to
spring up. A law was enacted for the organization of the
educational system which made elementary education compulsory, general and free of charge, and developed secondary
and higher education. In 1864 the University of Bucharest
was established, after the University of Jassy in 1860. On
May 1/13, 1865, the Penal Code and the Penal Proceedings
Code were enforced, though they had been elaborated earlier,
whereby foreign consular jurisdiction which had caused so
much prejudice to the economy of the country and to national
dignity was abolished. The consuls of the Guaranteeing Powers
came to the palace *en bloc* to protest against the application of
these laws but without being given satisfaction. A law on
juridical organization and on civil proceedings was promulgated. On December 1/13, 1865 the law on the enforcement
of the Civil Code, which protected bourgeois property and
the bourgeois family, was passed — a most important step
in the organization of Romanian capitalist society.

By the close of 1865 the capitalist system had triumphed
in the main sectors of the United Principalities and a modern
national state had been built up.

Kogălniceanu was unable to see the enforcement of the
land law through as he was compelled to resign in January,
1865. C. Bosianu then headed a cabinet for several months,
after which Cuza again entrusted the reins of government to

the moderate liberal N. Crețulescu. Encouraged by Kogălniceanu's removal from office and the critical financial situation,
the radical liberals and the conservatives came to an understanding and decided to work for the overthrow of Cuza,
who was to be replaced by a foreign prince. The conservatives
opposed Cuza because he had carried through the land reform
and had widened the franchise; and the radical liberals opposed
him because of the authoritarian régime he had installed in
1864. On August 3/15, 1865, while Cuza was on holiday at
Ems in Prussia, the radical liberals incited the shopkeepers
of Bucharest to revolt. Though easily defeated by the army,
the uprising created a climate of distrust in Cuza both at
home and abroad. When he wrote to Napoleon III listing
his achievements and declaring himself ready to give up the
throne, the answer was discouraging. Feeling isolated, he
made it clear in a message he read on December 4/16, 1865,
when the session of the legislative bodies opened, that he
intended to abdicate. An atmosphere had been created and
on February 11/23, 1866, his opponents, with the assistance
of a number of officers, obliged him to do so. Cuza's reign,
though short, was among the richest in achievements in the
history of the Romanian people.


## 8. *Transylvania from 1859 to 1865*

THE peoples of the Habsburg Empire being dissatisfied with
the neo-absolutist policy, which included Germanization,
took advantage of the defeat of the imperial armies in Italy
in 1859 to show their desire for freedom. In fear of a new
revolution, Emperor Francis Joseph dissolved the government in August, 1859, and convened a reinforced Imperial
Council in March, 1860, with representatives of the various
peoples participating in the proceedings. The Romanians of
Transylvania were represented by the Eastern Orthodox
Bishop Andrei Șaguna, those of Banat by Andrei Mocioni,
and those of Bucovina by Nicolae Petrino. After several
months' talks, the Vienna Court, fearing lest the principle of
nationality should dismember the monarchy, decided to set
up again the autonomous states such as they had been prior
to the revolution but on the basis of liberal bourgeois institut-

ions. On October 8/20, 1860, Francis Joseph issued the October Diploma whereby the principality of Transylvania became again an autonomous state, and the old feudal constitution was abolished. A liberal constitution was to be drawn up on the basis of equality of all the people before the law, for which purpose a representative assembly of the nations and confessions was to be convened. In order to draw up an electoral law, a government headed by the Magyar Count Miko Imre was then formed and the comitats and sedes were re-established.

In November, 1860, the Romanians in Banat held a congress at Timişoara demanding autonomy for Banat as a captainship or its incorporation into the principality of Transylvania. Andrei Mocioni submitted a Memorial to this effect to the emperor, but the demands of the Romanians in Banat were not satisfied and the emperor ordered that the province should be incorporated within Hungary.

In January, 1861, the Romanians of Transylvania under the leadership of Metropolitan Alexandru Sterca Şuluţiu and of Bishop Andrei Şaguna, held a national congress at Sibiu. The Congress demanded that the Romanian nation should be recognized and the electoral census be reduced, and it appointed a permanent commission of four to represent the Romanians.

The conference of the representatives of the various nationalities of Transylvania, who were to draw up the electoral law, was held at Alba Iulia on January 30/February 11, 1861, with the Magyar Catholic Bishop, Haynald, in the chair. It was made up of 124 Hungarians, 8 Saxons, and 5 Romanians. Three Romanians refused to come. Instead of drawing up the electoral law, the Magyar majority headed by Haynald proclaimed Transylvania's union with Hungary and closed the conference. The Vienna Court did not approve the decision and maintained the autonomy of the principality.

To replace Count Miko Imre, Folliot de Crenneville was appointed as Premier, with two Vice-Presidents, one of whom was a Romanian: Vasile Pop. The convening of a Transylvanian diet was postponed.

The Romanians demanded the right to call an advisory assembly with a view to setting up "the Transylvanian Association for Romanian Literature and the Education of the

Romanian People" (A.S.T.R.A.), which was to "enhance the education of the people and promote literature with united powers." The assembly was held at Sibiu in March, 1861, when draft statutes were drawn up. The statutes were then approved and the new society was inaugurated at Sibiu on October 23/November 4, 1861. Andrei Şaguna was elected President, Timotei Cipariu Vice-President, and George Bariţiu Secretary. Transylvanian Romanians inhabiting the United Principalities were also elected as members, among them Aron Florian, Simion Bărnuţiu, Ioan Maiorescu, and Al. Papiu Ilarian. Timotei Cipariu described the association as the "staff of nationality." It was decided that a review — *Transylvania* — should be issued for the publication of historical documents. A year later Romanians of the United Principalities were also elected: C. A. Rosetti, Al. Odobescu, G. Sion, and later M. Kogălniceanu. A.S.T.R.A. carried on comprehensive cultural and national activities.

When the great Polish uprising of 1863 broke out, the partisans of Kossuth planned to stir up an insurrection in Hungary, and General Türr came to Bucharest to effect an understanding with Cuza. As a result, the Vienna Court sought to give satisfaction to the Romanians in Transylvania in order to win them over. In April, 1863, the Romanians were allowed to hold a congress in Sibiu. Under the influence of the government the congress accepted an electoral law based on a census of 8 florins at least. Based on the same law, elections for the diet were made and 46 Romanians were elected as compared with 42 Magyars and 32 Saxons. When the diet opened its proceedings at Sibiu in July, the Magyar deputies refused to participate on the ground that they considered Transylvania to be part of Hungary. Romanian predominantly, the Sibiu diet passed bills providing for equal rights to the Romanian nation and its religion and the right to use equally the three languages spoken in the country: Romanian, Hungarian, and German. The two bills were not sanctioned by the emperor who, being paralyzed by Magyar obstruction, had effected a rapprochement with the Magyar aristocracy who demanded Transylvania's incorporation within Hungary. On August 20/September 1, 1865, Francis Joseph decreed that the Sibiu diet should be closed and a new diet be convened on the basis of the electoral law of 1791 which had been slightly changed to enable the bourgeoisie to vote. The result of the elections was naturally unfavorable to the Romanians although they formed an absolute majority in the province. The diet, now dominated by the Hungarian nobility, opened in Cluj in November and hastened to proclaim Transylvania's annexation to Hungary. The nexth month, the emperor ordered the Transylvanian government to send the diet deputies to the Hungarian diet and canceled the bills passed by the Sibiu diet. But in order to give the Romanians some satisfaction, on December 12/24, 1864, he raised the Orthodox Bishopric of Sibiu to the rank of an independent Metropolitanate with two bishoprics: at Arad and Caransebeș, and with Andrei Șaguna as Metropolitan.

As the revolution of 1848 had not been successful, the union of the Romanian people into a single democratic and independent State was delayed, but social and economic development and the Romanians' perseverance in their struggle laid the foundations for a modern national state through the union of Moldavia and Wallachia. The revolutionary aspirations of 1848 were thus partially achieved.

The Land Law of 1864 did not completely do away with feudalism in agriculture. In Romanian economy as a whole, however, the fact that capitalist production tipped the balance created favorable prerequisites for economic, social, and political progress, though the landowners remained politically preponderant.

In the period which followed Cuza's fall the landowners — still a considerable economic force on account of their vast landed estates — held strong positions also in politics and consequently sought to enforce conservative views in accordance with their class interests.

Simultaneously, the extension of capitalistic methods of production increased the part played by the bourgeoisie in social and political life. Intent on developing industry and transport and using science and technique in production, the bourgeoisie within certain limits furthered the progress of society. Considering the special line followed by capitalist development in the country, the bourgeoisie accepted that the large landed estates should be maintained and to a certain extent also feudal relations, and this had unfavorable consequences for the economic development and the social and political evolution of the country. The compromise reached during the last years of Cuza's reign between the landowners and the bourgeoisie was consolidated by the installation of the Hohenzollern dynasty and formed the foundations of the political régime installed in 1866. Despite the changes wrought in the ratio of forces within this coalition, the régime continued until the Romanian national state was set up. But the compromise on which the political régime of the years after 1866 was built did not rule out contradictions and diverging interests among the participating forces.

The evolution of the ratio of social and political forces found expression in the Constitution of 1866, which was subsequently modified.

# CHAPTER V

# The United Principalities Achieve Their Independence

AFTER Moldavia and Wallachia had united to form one state based on bourgeois institutions and with an international status which gave it full autonomy, the Romanian people still had to achieve Romania's independence and complete political unity in pursuance of the general program of the revolution of 1848. From 1866 to 1878, owing to internal and external conditions, they were able to achieve only their country's independence. The situation of the Romanians of Transylvania was aggravated when the Austro-Hungarian monarchy was created by the Compromise of 1867, for it raised new obstacles to their struggle for national freedom. A complex process of economic, social, cultural, and political factors, however, enabled them to gain their independence.

## 1. Economic Development

THE economic development of Romania and of the Romanian territories in the Habsburg Empire helped to strengthen the capitalist system. At the same time Romania's economic development enabled her to free herself from her dependence on the Ottoman Empire. As most dependent peasants had been freed and given land, capitalist relations in Romania's agriculture made headway and the labor force needed for industry, transport, and trade increased. Part of the funds received by the landowners from the emancipated peasants were invested in farming implements and machinery or went to pay the workers, whether seasonal or day workers. A law on agricultural arrangements came into force on March 1, 1866, under which village administrative bodies were obliged to ensure that the farm work they had engaged to carry out was effectively done. The law had been issued in order to compel the workers to perform farming work. On the other hand, the landowners and great lessees did not possess sufficient capital, implements and machines, and neither were they used to capitalist exploitation of the land, so that they came to pass on to the peasants part of their estates in exchange for a tithe on the produce and a number of days' work. Apart from this system, there was another which consisted in dividing the estate into holdings, some of which were tilled for the benefit of the landowners or lessees and others for providing the pay for the peasants' work on those holdings. In 1872 the law on farming arrangements was modified and it then became possible to use soldiers to compel the peasants to carry out their obligations. These were practices supposed to be founded on free contracts, but actually they ensured the intervention of state bodies for the benefit of the landowners. Such practices and the improvement of farming techniques doubled farming output from 1866 to 1878 and helped capital accumulation in the country through steadily increasing grain exports. The peasants of Transylvania and Bucovina, freed from feudal impositions earlier, had reached a more advanced stage of social differentiation though the number of landless peasants and of peasants with very small holdings far surpassed those in better circumstances. In Banat and Crişana paid labor and machines were used to a greater extent than on the Transylvanian plateau and in Bucovina.

The peasants' struggle against the landowners continued, often assuming most violent forms. The rebellion of the frontier guards in May, 1866, the disturbances caused by the peasants who had not been given land, the suits for the marking off of the holdings, often accompanied by revolts and cruel repression, the unfair practices and illegality in the enforcement of the law on agricultural arrangements, especially after 1872, constituted landmarks during this period of unrest.

From 1866 to 1878 the number of industrial enterprises increased two and a half times, but small shops and manufactories predominated. The food industry took pride of place, followed by the textile industry — with four cloth factories — and by the timber industry. There was a considerable rise in salt extraction and the output of crude oil rose nearly threefold from 1866 to 1878. Simultaneously, refineries were set up, of which there were twenty in 1878. Industrial expansion was checked by the competition of foreign commodities and the trade treaties of the Ottoman

Empire, which Romania was obliged to observe. After the opening of railway lines, the competition of foreign commodities was still greater. The industrialists asked the government for a protectionist policy. They were upheld by the theories popularized by Haşdeu and Xenopol and later by P. S. Aurelian. Protectionism implied removal of what was left of Ottoman suzerainty.

In Transylvania industry was more advanced than in Romania. During this period it made further progress but at a slow tempo, being checked by the industrial products of the western provinces of the Habsburg Empire. The most important was the mining industry which mainly belonged to foreign capitalists. Next came the food and the textile industries. After the construction of the main railway lines, the timber industry went ahead rapidly in both Transylvania and Bucovina.

In order to meet requirements, and also to enhance the unity of the state and for strategic purposes, nearly 1,000 miles of railway lines were constructed from 1867 to 1879. The first was the Bucharest—Giurgiu line opened in 1869. Except for the Jassy-Ungheni line and part of the Ploieşti-Predeal line, all the railway trackage was were laid by foreign capitalists — British, Austrian, or Prussian — at prices higher than in Central and Western Europe. Most of the railway network was owned by foreign firms intent on making high profits and not on improvements. However, despite the difficulties encountered in constructing them, the railways proved of good use in the economy and in the struggle for the achievement of Romania's independence.

In April, 1867, a law was enacted creating *a new monetary system and providing for the minting of national coinage*. The nominal *leu* circulating at the time was superseded by a real coin which was also named *leu* and was guaranteed by a gold reserve. However, it was only after the country had become independent that a national bank could be created with the right to issue money. In 1871 the Albina Bank was set up at Sibiu and Romania's Financial Society in Bucharest. The Bucharest Bank was established in 1875. In 1873 the landowners, with state assistance, opened the Rural Land Credit Bank which enabled them to obtain cheap credit. The following year the Bucharest Company emerged and two years later the "România" Insurance Company. Before that time insurance had generally been effected by foreign companies. In order to modernize the state and especially to construct railways, loans were resorted to, the funds being provided by home or foreign sources, so that by 1876 the public debt had risen to 581,800,000 lei in gold. The cyclic crisis of capitalist economy which broke out in 1873 was not without its impact on Romanian economy. The price of grain fell and the farmers had difficulty in paying their taxes. In 1876 there was a serious financial crisis, which was aggravated in Romania by the trade convention with Austria-Hungary of 1875. The convention provided Romanian grain with an outlet in the Empire but allowed free access into the country of Austro-Hungarian industrial products and this increased Austro-Hungarian economic influence in Romania. But the convention also ensured Austro-Hungarian support in Romania's struggle for the recognition of her independence.

## 2. *The Bourgeois Regime Is Strengthened*

ON Cuza's abdication a regency was formed on the morning of February 11/23, 1866. It consisted of N. Golescu, a radical-liberal, Lascăr Catargiu, a conservative, and Colonel N. Haralambie. The Premier was Ion Ghica, a moderate liberal, the Minister of the Interior Dimitrie Ghica, a conservative, the Minister of Public Education and Cults — C. A. Rosetti, a liberal, and the Minister of War — Major D. Lecca. The legislative bodies met to proclaim Count Philip of Flanders, brother of the Belgian King, as prince. The latter, however, did not accept the throne. A conference of the representatives of the Guaranteeing Powers met in Paris and declared against the election of a foreign prince and eventually for the separation of the Principalities. With the tacit consent of Napoleon III with whom he was related, Prince Charles of Hohenzollern Sigmaringen was proclaimed prince of Romania. The separatist movement at Jassy was easily defeated by the army. Faithful to Cuza's memory, the peasants opposed the election of the new prince.

The Elective Assembly was dissolved after the law on farming arrangements and that on the organization of the civic guard had been passed. The Moderating Body also went out of session. The new Assembly proclaimed Charles I as prince on May 10/22, after which it became a constituent assembly and passed the new constitution.

The new constitution which gave the country the name of "Romania" and did not mention her dependence on the Ottoman Empire was liberal in character. It protected personal property and the means of production and ensured individual freedom. Courts of judge and jury were set up for cases dealing with the press, for crimes and other suits. The head of the state was the prince. His dignity was hereditary and he was to reign in accordance with the provisions of the constitution. The government was appointed by him but had to enjoy the confidence of the Assembly of Deputies and of the Senate. The government and the legislative bodies made the laws. The prince had the right of absolute veto for he could refuse to sanction a bill passed by the legislative bodies. He was supreme commander of the army. A complicated electoral system ensured political domination of the bourgeoisie and landowners in the state.

After the constituent assembly was dissolved a new cabinet presided over by Ion Ghica was formed. The cabinet was made up of moderate liberals and moderate conservatives. In October, after protracted negotiations and with France's diplomatic support, the Porte recognized Charles I as hereditary prince.

## 3. Political Life in Romania from 1866 to 1877

THE cabinet presided over by Ion Ghica, having been unable to obtain the necessary majority in the parliamentary election of the autumn of 1866, was compelled to resign and make way on March 1/13, 1867, for a cabinet of a liberal coalition with C. A. Crețulescu as Premier but actually led by I. C. Brătianu, the Minister of the Interior. Counting on the outbreak of a new war between the Habsburg Empire and Prussia and on a general insurrection of the Balkan peoples, the new Romanian government interrupted the negotiations which Ion Ghica had started with Austria-Hungary and replaced the French military mission brought over during Cuza's reign by a Prussian military mission. This caused Napoleon III to assume a hostile attitude.

The Romanian cabinet allowed groups of Bulgarian revolutionaries to organize themselves this side of the Danube and carried on vigorous propaganda among the Romanians in Transylvania, supporting their press and political and cultural organizations. Under the law on the organization of the army of 1868, efforts were made to increase to the utmost the country's military strength. When Napoleon III proposed an alliance with Francis Joseph against Prussia, Andrassy, the Hungarian Prime Minister, opposed it, desiring an understanding between Austria-Hungary and Prussia in the hope that the latter would force Romania to cease her revolutionary propaganda in Transylvania. Charles and the Conservatives were dissatisfied with the massive arming that was going on and the strengthening of the civic guard, and this resulted in the dismissal of Colonel George Adrian from the War Ministry. And when the Legislative Bodies had passed the law entitling a Prussian consortium headed by Strousberg to construct and exploit the railways, Bismarck demanded that Charles dismiss the radical-liberal government, which the Romanian prince hastened to do on November 16/28, 1868.

The new government with Dimitrie Ghica as Premier and Kogălniceanu as Minister of the Interior effected a rapprochement with Austria-Hungary who agreed to Romania's sending a semi-official diplomatic agent to Vienna. Seeing the failure of their plans, the radical-liberals started an ever more violent campaign for the removal of Charles. The Strousberg affair had strengthened the current opposing Prince Charles. The outbreak of the Franco-Prussian War in July, 1870, encouraged the radical-liberals, who believed that France would be victorious, to organize a conspiracy to depose Charles. The insurrection that followed was premature and insufficiently prepared and was consequently a failure. The anti-dynastic current assumed a republican character, particularly after a republic was proclaimed in Paris. Being brought to court, the 41 leaders of the Ploieşti insurrection were acquitted by the court of justice and jury of Tîrgovişte, and on December 14/26 the Assembly of Deputies gave a vote of censure to the government and showed hostility towards

62. EFTIMIE MURGU

63. AVRAM IANCU

LES DÉFENSEURS DE LA NATIONALITÉ ROMAINE
EN
TRANSILVANIE
1848-49.

J. BUTTEANU †    P. DOBRA †    AV. JANCO.    S. BALINT    N. SOLOMON

← 64. REVOLUTIONARY LEADERS OF THE TRANSYLVANIAN ROMANIANS (1848—1849)

66. GENERAL GHEORGHE MAGHERU

67. SIMION BĂRNUŢIU

← 65. THE RÈGLEMENT ORGANIQUE AND THE ALMANAC OF THE NOBILITY ARE HANGED

68. REVOLUTIONARY ROMANIA. ALLEGORICAL PAINTING BY
CONSTANTIN DANIEL ROSENTHAL.

69. DEPUTIES TO THE AD-HOC ASSEMBLY IN MOLDAVIA

70. SOLEMN OPENING OF AD-HOC ASSEMBLY IN WALLACHIA

71. ALEXANDRU IOAN CUZA

**72.** PRINCE CUZA OPENING THE ASSEMBLY OF DEPUTIES (FEBRUARY 29/MARCH 12, 1860)

73' CUZA'S PROCLAMATION TO CROP-SHARERS ON THE PUBLICATION OF THE LAND
LAW (AUGUST 14/26, 1864)

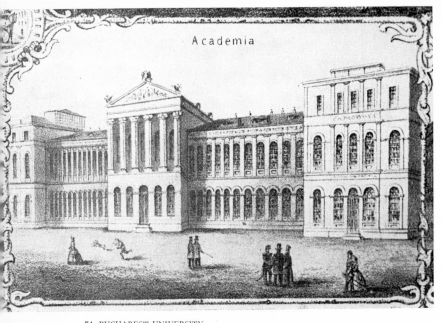

**74.** BUCHAREST UNIVERSITY

**75.** INAUGURATION OF THE ROMANIAN ACADEMIC SOCIETY (AUGUST 1/13, 1867)

6. ROMANIAN DEPUTIES TO THE HUNGARIAN DIET (1861)

77. CONQUEST OF THE GRIVIŢA REDOUBT (AUGUST 30/SEPTEMBER 11, 1877)

79. DEMONSTRATION OF THE BUCHAREST STUDENTS FOR THE SIGNATORIES OF THE TRANSYLVANIAN MEMORIALS (1892).

80. TANTALUS: THE
WORKERS ARE SET
FREE (1895).

81. NICOLAE VERMONT:
"ION, ION! WHY DID
YOU ASK FOR LAND?"

82. CORNELIU MEDREA: 1907

83. THE MĂRĂȘEȘTI MAUSOLEUM

84. TRANSYLVANIAN VOLUNTEERS IN UNION SQUARE IN JASSY, JUNE 9, 1917

85. THE NATIONAL ASSEMBLY OF ALBA IULIA (DECEMBER, 1918)

Charles. Appointed Prime Minister again, Ion Ghica, in agreement with the liberal groups, refused to pay the dividends on the bonds issued by Strousberg as he had not kept his engagements towards the Romanian state.

After threatening to abdicate in a letter published in the *Augsburger Allgemeine Zeitung*, Prince Charles took advantage of the republican demonstrations on the evening of March 10/22, 1871 against the banquet given in honor of William I, recently proclaimed emperor of Germany at Versailles, to dismiss Ion Ghica's cabinet and to appoint a conservative cabinet under Lascăr Catargiu. Fear of the disturbances that a change of prince would cause, and also Prussia's victory over France, tempered the opposition of the radical-liberals for a few years, so that in 1877 the conservatives were able to change the law on agricultural arrangements and the law on the organization of the armed forces. The changes in the former law favored the landowners. Friction between the conservative groups — old right wing, young right wing, and center — was aggravated in 1875-1876. It was only fear of the liberal coalition organized in the spring of 1875 that still rallied the conservatives around Lascăr Catargiu. The economic crisis of 1873-1877 further weakened the position of the conservative government.

Throughout this period Romania's foreign policy was still focused on obtaining her independence. When in November, 1870, Charles tried to persuade the Guaranteeing Powers to consent to the proclamation of Romania's independence, he met with opposition on the part of Chancellor Bismarck. In June, 1873, when visiting the Universal Exhibition in Vienna, Charles demanded Andrassy's support in exchange for a trade treaty favorable to the Habsburg Empire. Andrassy accepted the offer and a trade convention was concluded with Austria-Hungary in 1875. When Gorchakov, the Russian foreign minister, was asked for his consent to the proclamation of Romania's independence in 1873, he refused to give it. But in March, 1876, Russia concluded a commercial and customs convention with Romania, wishing to cancel all the remaining provisions of the Treaty of Paris of 1856 and of the Paris Convention of 1858.

The peasant uprising in Herzegovina and Bosnia in July, 1875, re-opened the Eastern Question. The Romanian people sympathized with the struggle of the rebels, but the conservative government, the moderate liberal group headed by Ion Ghica, and the independent liberal fraction under N. Ionescu were afraid that the Russian armies might march through Romania to attack the Ottoman Empire. The government decided upon neutrality but began to make military preparations. On January 4/16, 1876, Lascăr Catargiu sent the Romanian diplomatic agent a note to the effect that Romania was not part of the Ottoman Empire and would oppose occupation by a foreign army by force of arms. At the same time he expressed his regrets that under the Treaty of Paris of 1856 Romania had not become "a powerful, fully independent state."

## 4. Transylvania from 1866 to 1876

DEFEATED in the Austro-Prusso-Italian War of 1866, Emperor Francis Joseph, eager to take his revenge, hastened to end the talks with the leaders of the Magyar nobility who demanded among other things that Transylvania should be incorporated within Hungary. The Romanians protested in a memorial drawn up on the initiative of George Barițiu and Ioan Rațiu in October, 1866, and signed by 1,493 intellectuals. Francis Joseph, however, did not take the Romanians' opposition into account and on February 5/17, 1867, when the first government of the kingdom of Hungary was appointed, with Julius Andrassy as Premier, Transylvania was incorporated within Hungary. On May 27/June 8, 1867, Francis Joseph was crowned king of Hungary and on that occasion sanctioned the law whereby Transylvania was united with Hungary.

Since 1865 there had been two camps among the Transylvanian Romanians: the active and the passive. The active party headed by Metropolitan Andrei Şaguna thought that the Romanians should participate in political life as they had no state machinery of their own nor a constitutional basis for their demands as the Hungarians had — for the latter could invoke the decisions of the Diet of 1848 sanctioned by the emperor before the Vienna Court. The passive party under George Barițiu and Ioan Rațiu refused to participate in the election and to run for the Budapest parliament. On May 3/15, 1868, after celebrating the anniversary of the national assembly of 1848 in Blaj, the passive party drew up a document — *The Blaj Pronouncement* — protesting, as they had done in 1848, against Transylvania's incorporation within Hungary against the will of the Romanians, demanding that autonomy be maintained, the laws passed by the Sibiu Diet of 1863-1864 be enforced, and a democratic diet be elected so that it should really represent the population of Transylvania. The *Pronouncement* was widely publicized and caused deep unrest among the Transylvanian Romanians. Its authors were brought to trial, but the case was quashed some time after for fear that the Romanians might revolt. In December, 1868, the Hungarian Parliament passed the law of nationalities which laid down that there was a single nation — the Hungarian nation — throughout Hungary and that the "nationalities" were part of it. It was also in 1868 that the law on education was passed under which Hungarian, the official state language, had to be studied in all the schools.

The Romanians of Banat and Crișana started organizing their ranks with a view to resistance against the denationalization policy. At the conference held in Timișoara in January, 1869, a national party of the Romanians in Banat and Hungary was formed, with Alexandru Mocioni as president. In February, 1869, the passive party of the Transylvanian Romanians, meeting at the conference held in Miercurea, set up the Romanian National Party with I. E. Măcelariu as president. The Party demanded autonomy for Transylvania and adopted passive tactics. Though the Royal Hungarian Commissioner dissolved the party, it continued to function underground. Andrei Șaguna was authorized to convene a congress made up of 60 laymen and 30 clerics at Sibiu in September, 1868, where the Organic Statutes of the Romanian Ortodox Church in the Kingdom of Hungary were drawn up. All church bodies were to be elected by an annual congress which also controlled church activities; the Metropolitan himself was to be elected by an extraordinary congress.

Despite a severe law of the press, *Gazeta Transilvaniei (The Transylvanian Gazette)*, under the influence of George Barițiu, and *Telegraful Român* edited by Andrei Șaguna continued to appear and to uphold the cause of the Romanians. The former was issued in Braşov, the latter in Sibiu. In 1868 the paper *Federaţiunea (The Federation)* was published at Budapest, with Alexandru Roman, and later Iosif Hodoş as editors. The paper advocated a federal empire on an ethnic basis. The paper *Albina*, with Vincenţiu Babeş, a Banat Romanian, as editor, came out in Vienna for two years (1866-1868) and then removed to Budapest. The paper expressed the views of the National Party of the Romanians of Banat and Hungary. The paper *Orientul Latin (The Eastern Latin World)*, edited by A. Densuşianu, appeared in Braşov in 1874 and 1875. The spread of democratic ideas was greatly fostered by the review *Familia (The Family)* issued by Iosif Vulcan, first at Budapest, then at Oradea. M. Eminescu published his first poem in this review.

In order to cut down the number of Romanian deputies, the electoral law of 1874 established an electoral census which was higher in Transylvania than in Hungary. The Saxons, who had decided to take part in the election for Parliament in 1872, created the Saxon People's Party in 1876.

## 5. The Beginnings of the Working Class and Socialist Movement

WITH industry developing steadily, the number of workers increased and so did their resistance to the employers' exploitation. The working class movement assumed the form of spontaneous strikes for vocational claims, among others the strike of September, 1868, of the stevedores in the port of Brăila for higher wages and the strike of 1872 of the workers of the tobacco monopoly administration in Bucharest against wage cuts. The workers' movement assumed violent forms, as was the case in March, 1873, when the carters of the port of Giurgiu clashed with the army and there was a great deal of bloodshed. In pursuance of previous efforts, the workers formed associations. In 1858 the Printers' Mutual Benefit Fund was founded in Bucharest, and in 1865 the printers' vocational organization issued the first working class paper: *Tipograful Român (The Romanian Printer)*. In 1867 and 1869 associations of craftsmen, journeymen, and apprentices were founded at Sibiu and Braşov and later in other Transylvanian towns. In 1868 the *General Association of Timişoara Workers* was founded. Its program of action included social and political claims, which meant progress in the workers' class-consciousness. The association was to join the First International created and headed by Marx and Engels and a First International Section thus arose at Timişoara under the leadership of Carol Farcaş and Gheorghe Ungureanu. Four years later the section was wound up by the Budapest Government which was afraid of its democratic policy. Socialist ideas were popular in the homeland many decades ago. Teodor Diamant, a proponent of Fourier's theories, created the first phalanstery at Scăieni near Ploieşti in 1835. Later many of the works of Marx and Engels were spread in the country, among them being *The Condition of the Working Class in England, Manifesto of the Communist Party*, and *Capital*. In 1872 the printers' association was reorganized under C. A. Rosetti's stimulus and was named *Mutual Benefit General Society of the Gutenberg Printers*. The same year the *All-Romania Workers' General Association* was founded in Bucharest, whose press organ — *Lucrătorul Român (The Romanian Worker)*—was published in 1872-1873. A year later the Conservative government headed by Lascăr Catargiu framed a plot against the state and wound up the association.

The socialist movement had its beginning in 1875. A student, Eugen Lupu, set up the first socialist nucleus at Jassy, drawing in a fellow student, Ioan Nădejde. About the same time the *Society of Culture and Solidarity between Students* was founded in Bucharest, an important part in the society being played by C. I. Istrati and N. Codreanu, both medical students. Codreanu was a Romanian refugee from Russia. On May 26/June 7, 1876, *Socialistul (The Socialist)*, the first socialist gazette to be printed in Romanian, appeared in Bucharest.

## 6. *The War of Independence*

A coalition of the liberal political groups against the conservative government compelled Charles on April 27/May 9, 1876, to form a liberal government with Em. Costache Epureanu as Premier, M. Kogălniceanu as Foreign Minister, and I. C. Brătianu as Finance Minister. The liberals were returned in the election for the Assembly of Deputies.

After the defeat of the Bulgarian uprising in April, 1876, the crisis of the Ottoman Empire was intensified owing to disturbances caused by the Young Turks, partisans of bourgeois liberalism, which culminated in the overthrow and assassination of Sultan Abdul Aziz. Thinking that the Porte would be more liberal under the circumstances, Kogălniceanu sent a note to the Romanian diplomatic agents together with a memorial demanding recognition of Romania's independence under the joint guarantee of the Great Powers. The Porte did not answer Kogălniceanu's note. Following Serbia's military action against the Ottoman Empire, Tsar Alexander II met Emperor Francis Joseph at Reichstadt in Bohemia on June 26/July 8 with the aim of reaching an agreement on the Balkan problems. Fearing lest Romania's territory might be encroached upon under the Reichstadt arrangements, Kogălniceanu sent the Porte a new note demanding peremptorily that the country's independence be recognized. But the Ottoman armies gained a victory over Serbia and the European powers were divided in two camps owing to the alliance between the three emperors brought about by Bismarck.

The liberal coalition government was not homogeneous and since the proposal to indict the former conservative government, headed by Lascăr Catargiu, accentuated the divergences within it, Epureanu resigned his office. On July 24, 1876, Charles asked I. C. Brătianu, one of the spokesmen of the radical liberals, to form a cabinet, with N. Ionescu to replace Kogălniceanu. The new cabinet continued to prepare the way for the proclamation of independence. During the last ten days of August a government delegation headed by Brătianu went to Sibiu to pay a "courtesy visit" to Emperor Francis Joseph, thus making known Romania's good neighborly feelings. A month later another Romanian government delegation, again headed by Brătianu, was received by Tsar Alexander II and Gorchakov at Livadia in the Crimea to discuss the conditions under which the Russian army might march through Romania against the Ottoman Empire. The Romanian delegation demanded that a convention be first signed to ensure Romania's territorial integrity.

In the second half of September Romania, made anxious by the victories of the Ottoman armies in Serbia, mobilized her army which was made up of four permanent divisions and their reserves, with a brigade at Calafat to prevent a possible Ottoman attack. Simultaneously, the auxiliary army of foot soldiers composed of sixteen regiments was organized into four territorial divisions. The army did not have sufficient guns, rifles, equipment, and officers, and the finances of the state grievously felt the effects of the economic crisis.

In November, 1876, a Russian diplomat, Nelidov, escorted by Colonel Mihail Cantacuzino, came to Bucharest to draft a Romano-Russian convention. The convention was drawn up but was never signed, Russia having decided to postpone the war until the spring of the following year.

In October a Turco-Serbian truce was made. A conference of the 1856 Paris Treaty signatory powers was convened at Constantinople in December to re-establish peace in the Balkans. The Romanian government sent a delegate to the conference to obtain Romania's independence under the formula of absolute neutrality, with a special guarantee in the event of a war between the Ottoman Empire and one of the neighboring states. The conference refused to discuss Romania's demand and was unable to convince the Porte to make Bosnia, Herzegovina, and Bulgaria autonomous. On December 11/23, 1876, the Sultan promulgated a liberal constitution which made mention of the right of investiture of "the heads of the privileged provinces", meaning Romania, Serbia, Montenegro, and Egypt. The Romanian government protested energetically against this provision of the Ottoman constitution. The current favoring the securing of the country's independence by force of arms was greatly strengthened thereby, despite the opposition of the moderate liberals headed by Ion Ghica, and of the independent liberals to a possible cooperation with Russia.

The Porte rejected the protocol concluded in London on March 19/31, 1877, by the representatives of the European Powers, demanding that the Porte accept the proposals of the Constantinople Conference. After concluding a secret convention with Austria-Hungary, under which the latter promised neutrality in exchange for the annexation of Bosnia and Herzegovina, Russia decided to declare war. On March 31/April 12, 1877, Baron D. Stuart, Russia's Consul General in Bucharest, demanded that Romania sign the convention whereby the Russian armies were permitted to cross her territory.

With the prospect of grave developments ahead, the Foreign Ministry was entrusted to Kogălniceanu who, in accordance with the decision of an enlarged Council presided over by Charles, signed the convention with Russia on April 4/16, 1877. The Russian armies were to be allowed to pass through Romania, paying for all they required, whether for services or materials. The Russian Government agreed to maintain and observe "the political rights of the Romanian state resulting from the domestic laws and the existing treaties, and to maintain and defend Romania's present integrity". A special convention defined the relations between the Russian army and the Romanian authorities.

On April 6/18 the permanent army as well as the territorial army with their reserves were mobilized and it was decided that, if necessary, a militia and civic guards would be raised for the defense of the towns. The third and the fourth divisions were massed south of Bucharest between Oltenița and Giurgiu, while the first and the second divisions were stationed at Calafat and in the neighborhood of that town to prevent the Turks from crossing the Danube.

Russia declared war on the Ottoman Empire on April 12/24 and her forces crossed into Romania, making for the Danube. Convened in an extraordinary session on April 14/26, the Legislative Bodies approved the Romano-Russian Convention. Britain and France opposed the Convention. The Porte attacked the left bank of the Danube, the town of Brăila was bombed on April 26/May 8. The Romanian artillery bombed Vidin on April 26/May 8. Turkey and Romania were in a state of war. As a result of great demonstrations of national solidarity and for independence, on April 29/May 11, 1877, a group of radical-liberal deputies proposed that a motion should be passed for severing the country's dependence on the Porte and for declaring a state of war. After long debates another motion was passed which declared that a state of war had been created with the Ottoman Empire and demanded that the Cabinet obtain recognition of Romania's independence from the Great Powers at the next peace conference. A similar motion was passed by the Senate the next day. On May 9/21 Kogălniceanu, on behalf of the government, declared that Romania was "an independent nation". The Assembly of Deputies, like the Senate, voted for "Romania's absolute independence" with an overwhelming majority. The people had gathered around the building of the Assembly of Deputies and in the neighboring streets to cheer enthusiastically. It was a historic decision the Legislative Bodies had taken, showing that the destinies of the Romanian people were being decided by themselves.

When mobilization had been completed, on April 26 / May 8 the Romanian army numbered 58,700 men with 190 big guns, apart from the frontier guards, the militia, and the civic guards. In June the field forces were organized into four permanent army divisions and reserve divisions. After having covered the advance of the Russian armies towards the Danube, the third and fourth division made for southern Oltenia to ensure the defense of the Danube from the mouth of the Olt to Gruia. In the first days of the war the Romanian navy had helped to put torpedoes along the Danube and to destroy two Turkish monitors in the neighborhood of Brăila.

Grand Duke Nicholas, commander of the Russian armies along the Danube, proposed that the Romanian army should cooperate south of the Danube though without specifying the conditions of cooperation. On May 7/19, the Romanian government asked to have its own base of operation, with the left wing of the army along the Isker. A note from Gorchakov warned Romania that, should she intervene in the war, she was to do it "at her own expense, risks, and perils".

In order to mislead the Ottoman command, a Russian army corps crossed the Danube between Brăila and Galatz on June 10 /22. It was a mere diversionary tactic. The bulk of the army crossed the Danube only four days later from Zimnicea to Shishtov, whence General Gurko marched south and crossed the Balkans at Shipka, reaching Stara Zagora in southeast Bulgaria on July 14 /26. Another army advancing eastward was stopped on the river Lom. A third army attacked Nikopol facing the mouth of the Olt, and occupied it on July 4 /16, being supported by the Romanian artillery and infantry on the left bank of the Danube. On July 8 /20 the Russian army acting in the west attacked Plevna where Osman Pasha had recently installed a numerous army. Being inferior in numbers, the Russians were repelled. With a view to a new attack on Plevna, the Russian commander demanded that the Fourth Romanian Division should cross the Danube and occupy Nikopol and its surroundings. Although no convention had as yet been signed, the Romanian government answered in the affirmative and occupied Nikopol. A new Russian attack on Plevna was repelled with heavy losses. At the same time Gurko was driven back to Shipka, which he was able to hold. There was a danger of the front advancing north of the Danube and of the war being protracted. Grand Duke Nicholas wired Charles to the effect that the Romanian army should demonstrate against the Turks on the Danube and if possible cross the river. The Romanian cabinet ordered the remainder of the Fourth Division to cross the Danube, after which, following a verbal understanding with Tsar Alexander, they sent another two divisions, altogether about 38,000 men. During an interview with Tsar Alexander, it was decided that the Romano-Russian armies which were to attempt a third attack on Plevna should be placed under the command of Charles, assisted by Russian General Zotov in the capacity of Chief of Staff, and by the Romanian General Al. Cernat, commander of the Romanian corps.

The Tsar insisted that the third attack on Plevna should be launched on August 30/September 11. Osman Pasha had brought fresh troops and had built strong redoubts on the hills north, east, and south of the town. The redoubts Grivitza I and Grivitza II, the strongest, were in the sector of the Romanian forces.

The general attack was launched at 3 P.M. It was only at nighftall and after the fourth attack that the Romanians, helped by the Russians, succeeded in conquering Grivitza I. It was the only victory of a day of many casualties. It proved impossible to conquer Grivitza II. Two attacks launched by the Romanians on September 6/18 and October 7/19 were repelled with heavy losses. The Russian command brought in new troops, including the Imperial Guard. It was decided to encircle the redoubt until the Turks in the citadel ran short of food and ammunition.

In order to prevent a Turkish attack from the north, a Romanian detachment of 5,000 men and a Romano-Russian one of 1,200 men attacked Rahova on the Danube on November 7/19 and conquered it after two days with the assistance of some Romanian battalions which crossed the river from the north.

Intending to break through the encirclement and withdraw towards Sofia, on November 28/December 10, 1877, Osman Pasha attacked the Russian forces from the southwest and left a large number of troops along the Opanez to defend his right flank, where Romanians were to be found, as well as other forces at Crishin, where the Russians were stationed. The Turkish attack had chances of success in the early hours of the morning, but the Romanians conquered the redoubts along the Opanez, taking 7,000 Turkish prisoners and entering Plevna where they made Osman Pasha himself prisoner. Osman Pasha ordered his troops to surrender. The main battle of the war against the Ottoman armies had been won.

While the Russian armies were advancing towards Sofia and Philippopolis and crossing the Balkans at Shipka, the Romanian units started an offensive against the Turkish fortresses in western Bulgaria, their main targets being Vidin and Belogragic, both of which were soon surrounded. On January 12/24, 1878, the outside fortifications of Vidin were attacked, the fiercest fighting taking place for the conquest of Smîrdan which was protected by three redoubts. On January 19/31, 1878, when Vidin was about to surrender, an armistice was concluded between the Russians and the Turks, and the fighting ended in consequence also at Vidin and Belogragic. Romania's war of independence had ended.

On February 19/March 3, 1878, the peace of San Stefano was concluded between Russia and the Ottoman Empire: the independence of Romania, Serbia, and Montenegro was recognized, the autonomous principality of Bulgaria was created, and an autonomous administration was introduced in Bosnia and Herzegovina. Dissatisfied with the provisions of the peace, which considerably enhanced Russia's prestige and position in Southeast Europe, the other great powers convened a congress to regulate the status of southeastern Europe. Russia could not oppose the plan and consequently renounced the Treaty of San Stefano and accepted to participate in the Berlin Congress convened and presided over by Bismarck. On June 19/July 1, Brătianu and Kogălniceanu defended Romania's rights at the Congress, basing their contentions on the Romano-Russian Convention of April 4/16. The Treaty of Berlin of July 1/13, 1878, recognized Romania's independence, the country also incorporating the Danube

Delta, Snake Island, and Dobrogea from east of Silistra to south of Mangalia. The Congress allotted Southwest Bessarabia to Russia. Romania was forced to grant civic rights to the non-Christian inhabitants in her territory.

Romania had achieved her independence at the cost of a heavy toll of life on the battlefield and great material sacrifices. The overwhelming majority of the people had enthusiastically backed the war of independence. The intelligentsia had written a great deal in support of the war. In April, 1878, the poet V. Alecsandri published a volume of poems — *Our Soldiers* — singing the gallantry of the Romanian soldiers in the battles for the liberation of the homeland. The painter N. Grigorescu, who had witnessed the heroic feats of arms of the Romanians on the battlefield, made numerous sketches of war scenes and subsequently painted an impressive canvas: *Attack on Smîrdan.*

The Romanians living in territories under Habsburg rule were overjoyed at Romania's successes and supported the war effort by every means at their disposal. An important part was played by Captain Moise Grozea, who fought at Grivitza, by George Barițiu, Judita Măcelariu, and Iosif Vulcan and also by the Arboroasa society of Bucovina.

Having won her independence, Romania, now a sovereign state, was equal in rights with the other independent states. Henceforward she could set customs tarriffs to protect her economy and thus encourage the development of a big industry necessary for a modern economy. The number of the proletariat increased with the growth of big industry. The armed forces necessary for the defense of Romania's territory and the liberation of the Romanian districts still under foreign rule were increased. The country sent diplomatic representatives abroad to protect its interests. Romanian culture was given a great impetus, for the Romanian people had gained confidence after securing their independence by their own sacrifices. The political régime slowly evolved along the path of liberalism towards a bourgeois democracy. On the whole, Romania's independence was the result of the progress achieved and at the same time a basis for her development along the path of capitalism.

# CHAPTER VI

# *The Romanian National State Makes Great Strides*

THE period between the achievement of independence and the outbreak of World War I was marked by a great development of the Romanian state in all spheres. In the economic field the foundations were laid for a great mechanical industry, and the oil industry went ahead: agricultural output was increased through capital, but the manner of exploiting the land caused deep discontent which resulted in widespread rebellions such as those of 1888 and 1907. Foreign trade expanded steadily, providing the necessary resources for intensified modernization of institutions, and the strengthening of the army led to industrial development. The changes wrought in the economy and in the class pattern of society at the end of the nineteenth and the beginning of the twentieth centuries affected the ratio of forces between the two governing parties. While the Conservative Party primarily expressed the landowners' interests, the National-Liberal Party represented mainly the interests of the bourgeoisie, though this delimitation was not absolute. With the country making steady headway along the capitalist path, the National-Liberal Party gained more ground in politics, to be accounted for by the fact that the bourgeoisie, in full process of ascension, still had a part to play in Romania's economic and social life. We should also note the tendency towards diversification in political life, the creation of dissident liberal and conservative groups, which did not bring about essential changes, yet had a certain part to play in political developments.

During this period the advanced forces of Romanian society held an important place. It was the first time in this country that the proletariat, with its vocational and political organizations, asserted itself. The peasantry continued its struggles against the landowners' exploitation and the oppression and unfair practices of the state machinery. Other sections of Romanian society — the progressive intelligentsia, the craftsmen, and traders — worked side by side with these main social forces.

The progressive forces — in the first place the working class and socialist movement — made it their aim to solve democratically the fundamental problems facing the Romanian people. Going beyond the stage of workers' clubs, these forces set up a political party of the working class: the Social Democratic Party of the Workers of Romania.

Once Romania's independence had been recognized and the country proclaimed a kingdom, she played an important part in the policy of Southeast Europe. This was a period when the national culture flourished, with some representatives of the Romanians in the oppressed provinces contributing also. The potent national liberation movement of this period paved the way for the union of all Romanians into a national state.

## 1. Economic Growth

POLITICAL independence enabled Romania to adopt a policy protecting the national industry. The spokesmen of this policy — M. Kogălniceanu, P. S. Aurelian, and A. D. Xenopol — were against free trade, they were supported by the economists siding with the landowners and demanded that the state subsidize the industries of the country. P. S. Aurelian declared that a national industry was "a vital condition for our state". The laws for the promotion of the paper industry (1888) and of the sugar industry (1882) favored the development of industry in these branches, in particular after the customs tariff law of 1886 extended protectionism to the industrial enterprises that used local raw material. When the trade convention of 1875 expired in 1886, Austria-Hungary refused to agree to a new convention based on a protectionist tariff and began a customs war against Romania. On the other hand other countries — France, Russia, the Ottoman Empire — agreed to the customs conventions based on the new tariff, which were concluded between 1886 and 1891. Persevering in the creation of a big industry, the National-Liberal Government promulgated the law of 1887: General Measures for the Promotion of the National Industry. The industrial enterprises that made use of machinery and had a capital of at least 50,000 lei or employed at least 25 workers were exempted from direct taxation, customs duties on imports of machinery and raw materials and in part from the transport costs for such machines and raw material going by rail. Consequently, industry zoomed even after the Conservatives had reduced the customs duty on imports of industrial products in 1891 and 1893. The protectionist system was further strengthened by the new customs tariff of 1904 and the law for the promotion of industry of 1912. The food industry still took pride of place followed by the mining industry, oil refining, and the timber industry. Next came the textile, leather, paper, and building materials industries. After 1900 metal works became of increasing importance.

Transylvanian industry was developed at a still higher rate owing especially to its exports to Romania. The customs war, however, slowed down its tempo of development after 1886 owing to the narrowing down of the Romanian market. The mining industry, especially coal mining in the Jiu pits, held the first place, followed by the food, timber, metal-working, textile, and building materials industries. Capital accumulation progressing at a slow rate, and most of the enterprises being small or only of medium size, the rate of growth was also slow, and on the whole the economy did not exceed the first stage of capitalist expansion.

Romanian agriculture progressed owing to the increase in manpower, to the use of improved implements and of machinery, and to the credit allowed it. In 1878 48,342 newly married couples were allotted 228,328.9 hectares, and under the law of April 6, 1889, 106,714 peasant families received 549,593 hectares. Nevertheless, in the early years of the twentieth century there existed an agricultural proletariat of over 300,000 families, and 1,015,302 peasants with 10 hectares at most, making up a total of 3,319,695 hectares. On the other hand, some 6,552 landowners owned 3,000,437 hectares, and the village bourgeoisie, made up of 36,318 families, owned 695,958 hectares. Consequently, a considerable part of agricultural land continued to be the property of the big landowners, most of whom still preserved semi-feudal production relations. Some 60 per cent of the landed estates were leased and some of the big lessees in Northern Moldavia made up genuine trusts after 1900.

In Transylvania, where part of the land passed into the hands of the well-to-do peasants through the agency of the banks, a number of landless peasants were forced to become factory workers or miners while others took up domestic service, worked by the day on the landowners' estates, or emigrated to America or to Romania.

The expansion of the economy made it necessary to extend the telegraph, road, and railway network and to use river and sea navigation to a greater extent. From 1887 to 1895 a bridge was built over the Danube at Cernavodă by engineer Anghel Saligny, Bucharest being thus linked to Constantza by rail. In 1890 Romanian River Navigation, a state enterprise, was set up, and 1895 saw the establishment of the Romanian Maritime Service whose vessels plied between Constantza and Western ports. The port of Constantza was modernized at the turn of the century.

In 1880 the National Bank of Romania was established as a discount and currency circulation institution, with two-thirds of its capital private and one third provided by the state. The National Bank promoted the expansion of industry and trade and lent the state funds at a reasonable rate of interest. Considerably increasing its reserves of precious metals and capital, it became the greatest credit institution in the country. The shareholders of the National Bank, mostly liberal-minded bourgeoisie, were able to influence political life by means of the Bank. During the last decade of the nineteenth century and the first decade of the twentieth, quite a number of banks were founded, some of them with foreign capital. The Romanian Bank, whose shares belonged mostly to liberals, was opened in 1911 and became the most important credit institution.

In Transylvania there were subsidiaries of Vienna and Budapest banks, and also local banks, such as Albina, which flourished remarkably after 1878. It gave credit to the Romanian bourgeoisie in Transylvania, in particular to the village bourgeoisie, and supplied the Romanian National Party and A.S.T.R.A. with funds.

Romania's foreign trade grew steadily. After 1900 the balance of trade was favourable again, owing especially to growing exports of oil and oil products and of grain and timber.

## 2. *Continued Liberal Rule*

INDEPENDENCE and a policy designed to promote economic expansion strengthened the position of the National-Liberal Party which ruled the country until 1888.

Fulfillment of the conditions laid down by the Congress of Berlin — the granting of full civic rights to Jews and the redemption of the Railway Company bonds — resulted in the recognition of the country's independence and of the Kingdom of Romania. On March 14/26, 1881, the Legislative Bodies passed a law which was also approved by the spokesmen of the Conservative Party, whereby Romania was proclaimed a kingdom and its sovereign a king.

Dissidence and defection in the National-Liberal Party induced I. C. Brătianu to rely on the radical wing of the Party and to give the Ministry of Home Affairs to C. A. Rosetti, who advocated reforms in favor of the peasantry and of the democratization of the country (1881). Rosetti brought before the Legislative Bodies a new bill amending the agricultural arrangements law and another bill stipulating how magistrates were to be appointed. The opposition he met, secretly encouraged by Brătianu, compelled him to resign in 1882. The bill on agricultural arrangements was, however, passed after being slightly modified. Enforced execution of agricultural contracts was abolished, the solidarity of those hired for the performance of work was no longer demanded, and two days a week — Friday and Saturday — were left the peasants for work on their own holdings.

The Treaty of Berlin of 1878 had extended the authority of the European Danube Commission up to Galatz and decided that the Commission, assisted by delegates of the riparian states, should work out the rules governing navigation, policing, and supervision along that portion of the river. In 1879 Austria-Hungary demanded that a joint commission under her leadership should take over these tasks but the proposal came up against Romania's opposition. In June, 1882, Austria-Hungary accepted France's proposal which provided for the setting up of a joint commission of the lower Danube riparian countries plus Austria-Hungary, with the participation of a delegate of the European Commission and presided over by the Austro-

Hungarian delegate. Romania alone opposed his proposal, demanding that Austria-Hungary, which was not a riparian country in the reaches of the Danube over which the joint commission was to exercise its authority, be excluded. In order to solve the problem, the powers that had signed the Treaty of Berlin held a conference in London in March, 1883, to which Romania was not admitted. A treaty was concluded, the Conference deciding to extend the authority of the European Commission up to Brăila. The Commission was to function for another 21 years and the rules governing navigation, river policing, and supervision worked out by the European Commission in June, 1882, were to be applied to the Danube between the Iron Gates and Brăila. Romania opposed this treaty.

P. P. Carp, Romania's Minister in Vienna, who favored a rapprochement with the powers of Central Europe, realized that the Danube question was settled in accordance with Romania's interests and then carried on talks for Romania's joining the Triple Alliance. I. C. Brătianu at Gastein met Bismarck and Kalnoky, the Austro-Hungarian Minister of Foreign Affairs, in Vienna, and on October 18/30, 1883, the Romanian Minister of Foreign Affairs, D. A. Sturdza, signed together with Kalnoky at Vienna, a secret treaty of mutual assistance in the event of an unprovoked attack, for a term of five years to be extended for another three years if not denounced in due time. The treaty was joined by Germany and was repeatedly extended, the last time being January, 1913. Romania thus had a firm position in the international relations of Southeast Europe, which were occasionally strained. The radicals and the conservatives attacked the treaty when they knew about it, the radicals in fear that it might prevent the liberation movement of the Romanians of Transylvania and the conservatives out of sheer opportunism.

The day after Sturdza's appointment as Foreign Minister, which was August 1/13, 1882, C. A. Rosetti threatened to withdraw from politics. This induced I. C. Brătianu to accept the modification of the Constitution according to the demands of the radicals.

The election of 1883 for the Revision Chambers returned a great majority of deputies of the National-Liberal Party. Nevertheless, the revision of the Constitution was postponed and the session of the Chambers was closed on account of the divergences of views between Rosetti and Brătianu, the former advocating one electoral college, the latter wishing to reduce the four colleges to three, as the bourgeoisie would thus be ensured predominance. Also dissatisfied on account of the alliance with Austria-Hungary, Rosetti resigned his office as President of the Assembly of Deputies and drifted apart from Brătianu. Two weeks later, in response to an interpellation, Brătianu confirmed that Romania had joined the League of Peace, which meant the Triple Alliance.

On March 26/April 7, 1884, the government revealed a report on the revision of the Constitution — a surprise move. The new electoral regulations were passed, as Brătianu wanted them, Rosetti's followers not being allowed to speak. Protesting against such a violation of the right to speak, Rosetti withdrew from the Assembly, accompanied by his followers. The break between Rosetti and Brătianu was final. By May 29/ June 10, 1884, the Constitution had been amended. The four electoral colleges of the Assembly of Deputies were reduced to three in each county. The amendment of the electoral regulations laid down in the Constitution weakened the landowners' political power considerably and gave priority to the bourgeoisie. According to the amendments, press offenses against the person of the king, the royal family, and the sovereigns of other countries were to be judged by the courts in keeping with the Penal Code.

In order to strengthen his position, Brătianu had a bill passed in June, 1884, whereby a Crown Estate was created, consisting of twelve extensive landed estates belonging to the state (118,286 hectares, of which 67,198 hectares were forest land). The estate was exempted from taxation and the income derived from it went to the king. The bill came up against much opposition from the Parliament as well as from public opinion. Another bill was passed under which fortifications were to be built around Bucharest and along a line going from Galatz to Nămoloasa and Focșani. This was required by Romania's alliance with Austria-Hungary.

The election held in November, 1884, in accordance with the new electoral law gave Brătianu a great majority which increased his irreconcilable attitude. To oppose his dictatorial proceedings, a United Opposition was formed in November,

1885, being made up of Conservatives and of Liberal dissidents who made it their aim to overthrow the Brătianu cabinet. Having a well-disciplined majority at his disposal, Brătianu enacted laws that satisfied the claims of the bourgeoisie concerning customs protection and the promotion of the national industries, and allowed his followers to enrich themselves by every possible means, including the defrauding of the state. In 1887 the Radical Party formed that year by one of Rosetti's followers, G. Panu, took action against the liberal government alongside the United Opposition. In its program the Radical Party included among other claims universal suffrage and new grants of land to the peasants. Having violently attacked the government and the king in his paper, *Lupta* (*The Struggle*), Panu was sentenced to two years' imprisonment and a fine of 5,000 lei for having abused the sovereign. Panu, however, fled abroad, thus losing the prestige he enjoyed as an advanced democrat. At the close of January, 1888, Brătianu organized a new Parliament election and, by means of pressure and bribery, obtained an overwhelming majority. The United Opposition, now also supported by the Junimea followers, went in for a campaign of daily meetings, press attacks, and street demonstrations against the government. A number of incidents compelled the king to ask for Brătianu's resignation. The latter resigned on March 19 /31, 1888, after being in office for nearly twelve years during which the bourgeoisie had strengthened its priority in the politics of the country and had made considerable advances.

## 3. The Working Class and the Socialist Movement in the Last Decades of the Nineteenth Century. The Peasant Uprising of 1888

THE strides made in industry, transport facilities, and trade brought about an increase in the number of workers, and a corresponding rise in the number of strikes, owing to hard living conditions. After 1879 new vocational organizations were created in various branches of production and it is on them that the Romanian trade union movement was to rely during the last decade of the nineteenth century. The socialist movement, now legal, asserted itself vigorously. The socialist circle of Jassy issued the review *Contemporanul (The Contemporary)* from 1881 to 1891 with Ioan Nădejde as editor, then the *Revista Socială (The Social Review)* from 1884 to 1887. These reviews spread socialist ideas as well as the works of Marx and Engels. In 1885 and 1886, Dobrogeanu-Gherea published in the *Revista Socială* a comprehensive study — *What Romanian Socialists Want* — where he clearly set forth the principles of scientific socialism, for the first time analyzing the social, economic, and political realities of modern Romania in the light of historical materialism and at the same time giving an outline of the program of the socialist movement in Romania. When Engels learned of the activities of Romanian socialists, he wrote to Ioan Nădejde on January 4, 1888, showing his satisfaction that the Romanian socialists had based their program on the fundamental principles of Marxism. In February and December, 1885, the socialist circle of Bucharest brought out *Drepturile Omului (The Rights of Man)*, a political-social paper which spoke to the intelligentsia and the peasants and fought for democratic reforms, while from December 12, 1887, to April 9, 1888, the gazette *Dezrobirea (The Emancipation)*, describing itself as "the organ of the Workers' Party," came out, edited by Anton C. Bacalbașa. In the election of January, 1888, the second college in the county of Roman returned the first socialist deputy, D. Gh. Morțun, who edited the gazette *Muncitorul (The Worker)* in Jassy. In 1887 workers' circles were organized in Bucharest and Jassy, these political organizations helping towards the adoption of scientific socialism by the working class movement and thus raising the movement of the Romanian proletariat to a higher stage. The propaganda some of the Bucharest socialists made in the villages in March and April, 1888, intensified the militant spirit of the peasantry.

After the granting of land to the newly married couples in 1878, many peasants had petitioned the government and the Legislative Bodies for land, but in vain. And with the drought that had played havoc in almost the entire country in 1887, the villagers were faced with starvation. The government distributed maize on credit but the quantities provided were insufficient, while the oppressive methods practiced by the landowners and the great lessees were aided and abetted

by the village and county authorities. The peasants' exaspe-
ration grew. The socialists as well as the United Opposition
made propaganda in the countryside against the government.
A revolt broke out at Urziceni and in a matter of days had spread
to the villages in the neighborhood. The peasants entered
the town of Călăraşi. Before a week was over the uprising had
spread throughout the counties of Ilfov, Dîmboviţa, and
Vlaşca and later to many other counties, especially in Moldavia.
In order to put it down, the Cabinet of Theodor Rosetti,
formed on March 22 /April 3, 1888, from members of the
Junimea movement, sent the army against the peasants, many
of whom were killed, injured, or arrested. By April 11 /23
the uprising had been quelled in the counties around Bucharest, but the peasants resisted in other counties for another
month. The *Dezrobirea*, socialist gazette in Bucharest spoke
in defense of the rebels, but the *Muncitorul* of Jassy advised
the peasants to remain calm and to join the socialist movement, for they might then have their claims granted.

The growth of the working class movement from 1888 to
1899 is evidenced by two great strikes: the strike of the workers
employed at the Central Raillway Shop of Bucharest and
the strike of the printers (1888). The socialist movement
also developed, in particular after Ioan Nădejde and D. Gh.
Morţun were returned in the election of 1888. The next
year five Romanian socialists, including C. Mille, Dr. D.
Voinov, and Emil Racoviţă, participated in the congress
held in Paris which instituted the Second International. In
1890 the Bucharest Workers' Circle became the Workers'
Club with a press organ of its own — *Munca* (*The Labor*).
Other workers' clubs were set up in other towns and some of
them had their own papers. With the working class movement developing, the first class party of the Romanian proletariat — the Social Democratic Party of the Workers of Romania — was formed in March, 1893. Its program made
known that its historic mission was to organize the proletariat with a view to the creation of a socialist society. Regarding
Parliament as a means of gaining power, in the following
years the Workers' Party started a political struggle, sometimes
alongside the dissident liberal groups, striving to obtain universal suffrage. In order to extend their activities to the ranks
of the peasants, the Party created many socialist clubs in the

villages in 1898 and 1899, but these were soon wound up by Sturdza's liberal government. From 1894 to 1900 the Romanian socialists brought out in Bucharest the paper *Lumea Nouă* (*The New World*), which propagated socialism, industrialization, and the country's democratization. Romanian socialists took part in the Brussels Congress of the Second International in 1891 and in the Zürich Congress in 1893, where the Romanian delegation — made up among others of C. Dobrogeanu-Gherea, a Marxist socialist thinker of international repute, and C. Mille — submitted for discussion the problem of land and of the peasantry. Failing to widen their activities among the peasants and the lower bourgeoisie, and keeping to parliamentary tactics, the intellectuals among the leaders of the Party, including Ioan Nădejde, Morțun, Diamandi and Radovici, also described as "the generous ones," disbanded the Party in 1899 and then joined the National-Liberal Party. The consistent militants, headed by Al. Ionescu and Iosif Nădejde, however, continued to fight for socialism in the Workers' Club of Bucharest. From 1890 on, local social democratic organizations were formed in Transylvania with a membership of Romanian, Hungarian, and German workers. With the number of workers increasing, workers' trade unions were started in Transylvania, but a law of the Magyar Parliament forbade railway workers and miners to join them. In the last decade of the nineteenth century the influence of the socialists increased in the ranks of agricultural laborers in Transylvania, who were being exploited by the landowners and the big lessees.

## 4. The Conservative Cabinets

IN order to prevent the indictment of the former cabinet under I. C. Brătianu and the denunciation of the alliance with Austria-Hungary, which the United Opposition had threatened to do, the king entrusted the Junimea group with the formation of the cabinet although this group had no electoral backing. The Premier, Theodor Rosetti, was also Minister of Home Affairs, P. P. Carp, the real leader of the Junimea group, was Minister of Foreign Affairs, Titu Maiorescu was Minister of Public Education and Cults, and Al. Marghiloman, a former liberal who had joined the Junimea, was Minister of Justice. The Cabinet was accepted by the Liberal majority in the Legislative Bodies and continued the building of fortifications and the alliance with Austria-Hungary. In October there was a new election which returned a majority of members of the Liberal-Conservative Party headed by Lascăr Catargiu and Gh. Vernescu. Theodor Rosetti had to reshuffle his cabinet and bring in a number of Conservative-Liberals. The government redeemed the railways from the Austrian Offenheim, who had obtained the concession of them in 1868, and passed a law whereby all the landed estates held by the state could be sold in lots of 5, 10, and 25 hectares, except forest land extending over more than 25 hectares. In March, 1889, Liberal-Conservative cabinets got in, with Lascăr Catargiu and later General Gh. Manu and General I. Em. Florescu as Premiers. On May 17/29, 1890, the stock of silver held by the National Bank was sold for gold, which became the only standard of the national currency. On December 18/30, 1891, Lascăr Catargiu formed what Titu Maiorescu described as "the real and final Conservative cabinet", which also included Junimea members headed by P. P. Carp. The Cabinet was in office until October 3/15, 1895. It strengthened the economic and political position of the landowners; built up a stronger repressive machinery in the villages by means of a special law passed in 1892, whereby the prefects and sub-prefects were entitled to repress any movement that undermined the public order and public safety; in 1892 a rural gendarmerie was set up for the same purpose and a new law on agricultural arrangements was passed. The last important measure taken under the "great Conservative cabinet," as it was described, was the Law on Mines promulgated in April, 1895, on the initiative of P.P. Carp. The law created advantages for foreign, especially German, capitalists, and with the aim of weakening the workers' movement, provided for the creation of assistance and pension funds for the workers. Having become President of the National-Liberal Party in 1892, D. A. Sturdza took advantage of the public opinion in Romania in favour of the national movement in Transylvania and set afoot great street demonstrations against the Conservative government. After the Law on Mines had been passed, the Liberals accused the Conservative government of having created advantages for foreign capitalists. In October, 1895, the cabinet of Lascăr Catargiu resigned under pressure of the demonstrations organized by the Liberals.

## 5. The National Movement of the Transylvanian Romanians

IN Transylvania the Magyar government carried on a policy designed to denationalize the other nationalities living there. A law passed in 1879 enforced the use of the Hungarian language in all schools in town and village. The few Romanian deputies to the Budapest Parliament and the two Romanian Metropolitans of Blaj and Sibiu protested to the emperor against this law. A conference held in Sibiu in May, 1881, with the participation of 153 delegates — both Transylvanian and Banat delegates — decided that the two Romanian parties should merge into one single party and be called the Romanian National Party. It was on the program of the party to raise a number of claims: autonomy for Transylvania, the use of the Romanian language in administration throughout the territories inhabited by Romanians, amendments to the Law of Nationalities, the appointment of state officials who knew Romanian in the territories inhabited by Romanians, a wider franchise, and the abolition of the measures resulting in national oppression. Since the divergences between those advocating an active and those declaring for a passive policy persisted, it was impossible to establish a single policy. However, both sides agreed that a Memorial should be drawn up to show at length the unfair conditions created for the Romanians in Hungary. In 1882, in pursuance of the decision of the Sibiu Conference, G. Barițiu published at Sibiu a Memorial in Romanian, Hungarian, French, and German, which was given a warm reception by the press organs and the progressive political circles of Europe.

In 1883 a cultural association — the Romanian School — was founded at Suceava.

The national movement of the Transylvanian Romanians was also upheld from April 14, 1884, by the paper *Tribuna* (*The Forum*) published at Sibiu from 1884 to 1903, with Ion

Slavici as editor until November, 1886. Slavici had come back to Transylvania from Bucharest for the purpose. The *Tribuna* helped bring forth a new generation of fighters defending the interests of the Romanian people. The paper was written in a literary language that avoided the excesses of the Latinist currents and its standard was very high: Gh. Coşbuc began his career as a writer on its editorial staff.

The damaging consequences for the Transylvanian economy of the customs war waged by Austria-Hungary against Romania in 1886 increased the resistance of the Transylvanian Romanians against the oppression of the Magyar government. A conference of the Romanian National Party held at Sibiu in 1887 decided that a new Memorial should be drawn up to protest against the persecution of the Romanians. The Memorial was to be handed to Emperor Francis Joseph and was also to be published. A favorable climate for launching the Memorial was the creation in Bucharest of the League for the Cultural Unity of all Romanians as well as the *Memorial of the Bucharest Students* printed in French and the *Answer* written by Aurel C. Popovici. The Memorial of the Transylvanian Romanians was published in Romanian, German, and Hungarian showing at length and with definite examples the injustice and oppression to which the Romanians were subjected by the Magyar government and its officials. It was signed by Ioan Raţiu, President of the Romanian National Party, Gh. Pop de Băseşti, and Eugen Brote, Vice-Presidents of the Party, Vasile Lucaciu, Secretary General, Septimiu Albini, Secretary, and Iuliu Coroian, reviewer. A delegation of 300 Romanians led by Ioan Raţiu and made up of representatives of all social strata went to Vienna to hand the Memorial to the Emperor. On May 28, 1892 Francis Joseph, at the request of the Hungarian government, refused to receive the delegation. The delegation filed the Memorial with the Imperial Chancellery, but the emperor sent it to the Hungarian Minister attached to the Imperial Court, without reading it. The Budapest government ordered that the Memorial should be sent to the Prefecture of the county of Turda to be returned to Ioan Raţiu and that the signatories should be indicted. In May, 1894, the Cluj Tribunal judged the case for 18 days and sentenced the signatories of the Memorial to imprisonment. Ten thousand Romanians, most of them peasants, demonstrated in sympathy with the accused. The national movement of the Transylvanian Romanians had gained much prestige; it was supported by the entire Romanian people and called forth a powerful response both in Europe and in America.

## 6. Conservatives and Liberals Rule the Country in Turn

DESPITE the Liberals' violent demonstrations against the Conservative government, the two "historical " parties had come to a tacit agreement in accordance with which they were each in turn to form a cabinet. The system was upheld by King Charles and was applied until 1914 but, with the Conservative Party gradually falling apart, it functioned in favor of the Liberals. It was often described as the "Governmental Merry Go-Round."

The first cabinet to get in was Liberal, with D. A. Sturdza as Premier, and was formed on October 4/16, 1895. When the cabinet ousted from his office the Metropolitan Ghenadie Petrescu, Sturdza had to retire for a time and give way to a Democratic-Liberal cabinet with P. S. Aurelian as Premier. When the conflict with Ghenadie Petrescu was smoothed over, Sturdza took the reins of government again with the support of the group headed by Eugeniu Carada and described as "the Occult." Aurelian and his followers, among whom were Emil Costinescu and Vasile Lascăr, formed a dissident group named the Flag Bearers. When the Law on Mines, which had been suspended in 1895, was reinstated with some amendments, the Liberal government was obliged to resign in April, 1899. It had been considerably weakened by the Flag Bearers' dissidence.

After the collapse of the Sturdza cabinet, Gh. Gr. Cantacuzino took over, the latter being Lascăr Catargiu's successor at the head of the Conservative Party. The following year there was a P. P. Carp cabinet. In February, 1901, the Assembly of Deputies gave the Carp cabinet a vote of censure, thus forcing it to resign. The cyclical economic crisis which broke out in 1899, no less than the peasant uprisings, shattered the two Conservative governments.

## 7. *The Arrangement between Liberals and Conservatives Continues to Work*

THE National-Liberal Party having been strengthened by the "generous ones" joining its ranks, as C. Stere, spokesman for the Populist Movement, had done a few years previously, got in again with D. A. Sturdza as Premier in February, 1901. The Flag Bearers were no longer dissidents and so had a number of members in the Cabinet, and I. C. Brătianu and Spiru C. Haret also held ministries. The "generous ones" and C. Stere, who favored democratic reforms, kept apart. The economic crisis abating, the state was able to balance its budget, partly by cutting the civil servants' salaries. The Trades Law passed in 1902 gave rules and regulations establishing the mode of work in small workshops and created corporations which both employers and workers were obliged to join. As the corporations had been created to prevent the workers from forming trade unions based on the class struggle, the workers began to fight against them as well as for the abolition of the Trades Law. In 1903 a Law on Popular Banks and a Central Fund was passed in order to strengthen the influence of the bourgeoisie on the well-to-do and middle peasants. In 1904 a law on the management of agricultural communities was sanctioned under which the representative of such a community was able to obtain loans on mortgage from the Rural Land Credit Fund. Misunderstandings arising between various groups, brought about the resignation of Sturdza's cabinet in December, 1904. A Conservative cabinet then came in, with Gh. Gr. Cantacuzino as Premier but without any members of the Junimea movement, the latter having formed a party of their own. The main part in the cabinet was played by Take Ionescu, Minister of Finance, who was upheld by a bourgeois wing of the Conservative Party. In order to strengthen its relations with the king, the Conservative government celebrated a Forty Years' Jubilee of Charles' reign in May, 1906, with much pomp and at great expense. The Liberals refused to participate and a socialist circle — "Working Romania" — published the anti-dynastic pamphlet: *Forty Years of Poverty, Slavery, and Shame.* Nearly two months before, on March 13 /26, 1906, a great street demonstration of the students had taken place in Bucharest at N. Iorga's prompting, which was joined by the townspeople. The demonstration was against the cosmopolitanism of the Conservative landowners whom Iorga also criticized in his gazette, *Neamul Românesc* (*The Romanian People*). In order to increase their influence on the intelligentsia of lower bourgeois and peasant origin, the left-wing liberals, with C. Stere and the "generous ones" among them, and with the help of Spiru Haret, published the review *Viaţa Românească* (*The Romanian Life*), which showed a trend towards populism. The review first came out at Jassy in March, 1906, with C. Stere and Paul Bujor as directors and G. Ibrăileanu as editor-in-chief. The withdrawal of the Conservatives from the cabinet on March 12/25, 1907, was the immediate political effect of the great uprising of that year.

## 8. *National Movement of the Transylvanian Romanians from 1894 to 1914*

IN Transylvania the Romanian National Party continued its activities although its leaders were in prison and the party had been dissolved. In November, 1894, a conference held at Sibiu protested against the ordinance whereby the party had been dissolved. The Romanian National Party continued its activities, participating in a Congress of Nationalities made up of Romanians, Serbs, and Slovaks, which was held in Budapest in 1895 and where a program was drawn up to oppose the policy of Magyarization. Upon Raţiu's death in 1902, Gh. Pop de Băseşti, one of the leaders of the Transylvanian movement, was elected president of the Romanian National Party. In 1903 the paper *Tribuna* ceased to appear, having been repeatedly fined, sued, and condemned. In January, 1905, a National Conference was held, which decided that the passive policy be abandoned and an active one of a more comprehensive character be taken up, and demanding that the peasants on state-owned estates should be given land, and universal suffrage be allowed. In the Parliamentary election of 1906, 14 Romanian candidates were returned. In Budapest the Romanian deputies, together with the Serbian and

Slovak formed a group with Teodor Mihali, a Romanian, as president, and Milan Hodza, a Slovak, as secretary. There were two trends in the Romanian National Party: national-radical under the leadership of Ioan Russu-Şirianu, and moder-rate-national headed by Teodor Mihali and Al. Vaida Voevod. When the monarchy came to be discussed, various forms of federalization were proposed to solve the problem of the nationalities which was creating increasing difficulties. In 1906 Aurel C. Popovici published *Die Vereinigten Staaten von Gross-Österreich (The United States of Greater Austria)* proposing that the Habsburg Empire should be turned into a federation of the various nationalities.

The Budapest government, realizing that this would minimize Hungary's position in the monarchy, responded by the Apponyi Law which stipulated that all denominational and private elementary schools should be closed. The schools, in which all subjects were taught in Romanian, were denominational. And the reason given by Apponyi for their closing was that the schoolchildren did not master the Hungarian language satisfactorily. A large meeting of Romanians was held at Sibiu to protest against this law, and their protest caused a number of famous writers to attack the Apponyi Law. Among these writers were Leo Tolstoy and Björnsterne Björnson.

## 9. The Socialist Movement in the Early Years of the Twentieth Century. The Peasant Uprising of 1907

AFTER the Workers' Social Democratic Party was disbanded in 1899, the socialist movement went through a transient period of stagnation until 1902, when a new stage in the development of the working class movement began in Romania simultaneously with the issue of the gazette *România Muncitoare (The Working Romania)*. Before 1907 the main objective of the movement was the struggle against corporations and for the setting up of trade unions. In 1906 a General Trade Union Commission was created as a nucleus for the Romanian trade union movement, with the participation of delegates from all territories inhabited by Romanians, including those under foreign rule.

In 1905 the *România Muncitoare* was published again after having been banned for some time, and this gave a new impetus to the working class movement. Strikes were called, in particular in Bucharest, Galatz, and Turnu Severin, where the strike movement was led by the local socialist circles and the trade unions. In Jassy the Social study Circle, with M. Gh. Bujor, Max Wechsler, and Doctor L. Ghelerter as forceful members, carried on its activity among the intelligentsia and the workers. When the bourgeois democratic revolution broke out in Russia in 1905, the Romanian workers showed their sympathy for the revolutionary struggle of the Russian proletariat and peasants against the autocratic Tsarist government by holding a mass meeting in Bucharest and issuing a gazette *Jos Despotismul (Down with Despotism)*. The Romanian socialist movement gave material and moral support to the 700 sailors on the Russian cruiser *Prince Potemkin*, which had landed at Constantza and asked political asylum from the Romanian government.

In Transylvania a Romanian section of the Social-Democratic Party of Hungary was formed in 1903, the Romanian socialist movement thus assuming a national form. The first Romanian socialist gazette, *Votul Poporului (The People's Vote)* appeared in Timişoara in 1903. The same year *Adevărul — Glasul Poporului (The Truth — The People's Voice)* was issued in Budapest, with Aurel Cristea as editor-in-chief, this being the paper of the Romanian socialist section. In December, 1905, an independent congress of the section was held at Lugoj. After the Romanian socialist section had been set up, the ties between the Romanian socialists on both sides of the Carpathians became closer. Socialist literature was printed in Bucharest and sent to Transylvania, and the socialist press in Romania attacked the national oppression to which the Transylvanian Romanians were subjected. In one of its issues, the paper of the Romanian section of the Social-Democratic Party of Hungary wrote: "The Romanians in this country are the most oppressed; they are deprived of the most elementary rights."

The peasant movement developed in Transylvania at the close of the nineteenth century as a result of the proletarianization of an important part of the peasantry and of socialist propaganda among agricultural laborers. In Crişana and Banat there was an increasing number of strikes at harvesting time. Prompted by the workers of Oradea, the peasants of Aleşd and the neighboring villages rose in 1904 against the authorities who favored the landowners. The gendarmes fired at them and killed 33 peasants and wounded many others, most of them Romanians. In token of solidarity, the workers of Oradea went on strike. In their anxiety, the Magyar landowners caused the Daranyi bill to be passed in April, 1907, establishing the relations between landowners and agricultural laborers: agricultural strikes were banned and the agricultural laborers who opposed the landowners and big lessees were severely punished.

In Romania a great uprising broke out in February, 1907, as a result of intensified exploitation of the various strata of peasants. This was a genuine peasant war, which started at Flămînzi in the county of Botoşani against Mochi Fischer, a lessee who had created a great land trust in northern Moldavia.

On March 4/17-6/19, 1907, masses of peasants devastated the houses of certain lessees in the town of Botoşani. The army went into action and a considerable number of peasants were killed and injured. The uprising spread over the counties of Dorohoi and Jassy. The peasants demanded that the rent for the land they held from the big lessees should be reduced. Before long the rebellion had swept over the southern part of Moldavia and then on March 9/22 it flared up in the counties of Rîmnicu Sărat and Buzău and a little later extended to the county of Teleorman, where it rose to its greatest height. In the days that followed, the villages of the counties of Vlaşca, Olt, and Romanaţi were in arms to be followed by the counties of Dolj and Mehedinţi. The peasants set fire to the landowners' country houses and divided the grain, cattle, and land among themselves. In the towns of Vaslui, Galatz, Rîmnicu Sărat and Buzău, they sought out the landowners, the big lessees and the prefects of the counties. The ruling classes, especially the landowners, were panic-stricken. On March 12/25, 1907, the Conservative cabinet presided over by Gh. Gr. Cantacuzino, unable to put down the revolt, resigned. A Liberal cabinet was then formed with D. A.

Sturdza as Premier, I. C. Brătianu as Minister of Home Affairs, and General Averescu as Minister of War. The next day the two historical parties — the Liberals and the Conservatives — pledged in Parliament to support each other until the revolt had been put down. Brutal repression followed. Many peasants were killed or taken into custody and maltreated, and some of them were tried and sentenced. By the 20th of March, 1907, the uprising had been quelled.

The workers of Paşcani, Galatz, Bucharest, the Prahova Valley, and other parts of the country supported the rebel peasants. On March 11/24, 1907, a large meeting of the Bucharest workers protested against the exploitation of the peasantry and the oppression of the administrative bodies. The young socialist M. Gh. Bujor published a call in the *România Muncitoare*: "To the Conscripted Soldiers and Those in the Reserve," directing the soldiers not to fire at the peasants but to side with them. Many intellectuals spoke or wrote in defense of the peasants. As a result, V. M. Kogălniceanu was arrested as an instigator, and N. Iorga was threatened by the big lessees and the landowners. A. D. Xenopol, Dr. Ion Cantacuzino, Al. Vlahuţă, and I. L. Caragiale also had their say in support of the peasants. Caragiale virulently attacked the ruling classes in an article: "1907 — From Spring to Autumn", which appeared in the Viennese paper *Die Zeit*. In May, Al. Vlahuţă published the poem *"1907"* in the *Viaţa Românească*, unequivocally· accusing the king. Gh. Coşbuc, the poet of the peasantry, as C. Dobrogeanu-Gherea described him, had written his poem *"We Want Land"* more than a decade before, and the poem was used by the peasants as a stimulus in their struggle. The historian Radu Rosetti, who had been studying the history of agrarian relationships in Romania, published *Why Have the Peasants Revolted?* and Dobrogeanu-Gherea, deeply moved by the uprising, brought out *New Serfdom* in 1910, a survey of the agrarian problem in Romania. The uprising of 1907 called forth wide response in Transylvania, in the ranks of the intelligentsia as well as in those of the workers and peasants, and was not without an impact on various countries in Europe. Lenin compared its consequences with those of the bourgeois-democratic revolution in Russia. At the Congress of the Second International, held in Stuttgart in the summer of 1907, the Romanian delegates introduced into the discussion the reasons for the peasant revolt and the manner in which it had been repressed.

After the uprising had been put down, the Liberal cabinet went in for Parliamentary elections and submitted to the legislative bodies bills which, in their view, would solve the land problem. In December, 1907, a law on agricultural arrangements was passed establishing the minimum wages of agricultural laborers and the maximum rent that could be asked of the peasants who rented land. The Rural Fund Law, passed in 1908, provided for the creation of a bank that was assigned the task to purchase landed estates to be sold to the peasants in small holdings. It was also in 1908 that a law was passed forbidding anyone to rent more than 8,000 acres. The next year another law was passed under which the stateowned estates and those which were church, county, or village property or belonged to charitable and cultural institutions, were to be leased to peasant associations. All these measures reduced the landowners' exploitation of the peasants but did not solve the land problem.

D. A. Sturdza having resigned for reasons of health, Ionel Brătianu was elected president of the National-Liberal Party and was asked to form a cabinet in 1908. With the number of strikes increasing and the Workers' Party being reorganized, the Liberal government, in its anxiety, passed a law — the Orleanu Law — in 1909 forbidding state employees to join trade unions.

## 10. The Social-Democratic Party of Romania Is Reorganized

THE Socialist Conference held at Galatz in June, 1907, created the Socialist Union of Romania as the center of the socialist circles and sent four delegates to the Congress of the Second International at Stuttgart. The statutes of the Union were sanctioned by a new conference held in Bucharest in January, 1908, when a draft program was also discussed. With the socialist movement developing at a swift tempo it became necessary to reorganize the Social-Democratic Party, which was done at the Congress of January 31 /February 13 — February 2 /15, 1910. The aim of the Party was "to do away with labor exploitation of any kind and to replace exploitation by the socialization of the means of production." In regard to the agrarian problem, the program confined its aim to "compulsory redemption of as large a part of the big estates, as will be necessary." Other aims were universal suffrage, a lay educational system, and in the national problem "solidarity with the Romanian proletariat of Transylvania." In 1911 C. Dobrogeanu-Gherea published *On Socialism in the Backward Countries*, where it was pointed out that Romanian industry and agriculture were evolving along the capitalist path, and the historic tasks of the working class party were listed. The working class movement was considerably strengthened by the reorganization of the Social-Democratic Party. In 1912 and 1913 there were numerous strikes led by trade-union and Party organizations. In the spring of 1913 the Brăila stevedores went on strike and the Galatz and Sulina Workers followed suit. With the threat of the first Balkan war, Ştefan Gheorghiu in September, 1912, launched a manifesto headed: *Make War on War*. Ştefan Gheorghiu acted on behalf of the Trade Union Propaganda Circle of Ploieşti.

In 1912 and 1913 the Social-Democratic Party fought against Romania's participation in the Balkan Wars, supporting the decisions made by the Congress of the Second International held at Basel in November, 1912. In January, 1914, a Trade Union Congress was held in Bucharest. The Romanian Socialists demanded universal suffrage and also that the state purchase the big landed estates and rent them to the peasants. A general strike was announced for the summer of 1914 with the aim of compelling the Revision Chambers to make the democratic reforms demanded by the socialists. Subsequently the strike was postponed until autumn but never took place on account of the war.

## 11. Romania on the Eve of and during the Balkan Wars. World War I in the Offing

AT the close of the year 1910 the Conservatives were in office again with P. P. Carp as Premier, the latter having been elected President of the Conservative Party in 1907. In 1908 the group headed by Take Ionescu had formed a separate party — The

Democratic-Conservative Party — whose program voiced
especially the interests of the middle bourgeoisie. The new
Parliament elected in 1911 passed a new Trades Law which
determined the hours of work for women and children. Apart
from the obligation imposed on all employers and workers
to join the guilds and consequently the corporations, workers'
insurance funds were created for cases of illness and disability
as well as a fund for old age pensions. In 1912 a new law was
promulgated encouraging the industries that used agricultural
produce, native oil, or minerals as raw materials. When the
government wished to close up the streetcar company in Bucharest, they came into violent conflict with the Liberals
who held most of the shares, and P. P. Carp was compelled
to resign in April, 1912. The new cabinet was formed with
the participation of the Democratic-Conservative Party, with
Titu Maiorescu as Premier.

On September 26/October 9, 1912, the First Balkan War
broke out between Bulgaria, Serbia, Greece, and Montenegro
on the one side, and the Ottoman Empire on the other.
Romania declared her neutrality. In June, 1913, Bulgaria
attacked Serbia and Greece. On June 27/July 10, Romania
declared war on Bulgaria, and, without encountering any
serious resistance, her army reached the outskirts of Sofia
and the Bulgarian government sued for peace. Peace was
concluded on July 28/August 10, 1913, between Romania,
Serbia, and Greece on the one side, and Bulgaria on the other.
Romania annexed Southern Dobrudja down to a line linking
Turtucaia to Ekrene. As peace had been concluded without
the participation of Austria-Hungary, the latter's prestige in
Southeast Europe dwindled.

Undermined by the misunderstandings between the two
Conservative Parties whose alliance had been achieved forcibly
by the king, the government presided over by Titu Maiorescu
resigned in January, 1914. Ionel Brătianu who some six months
previously had announced his program of democratic reforms,
with more land for the peasants and a unique electoral college,
then formed a Liberal cabinet. The Liberals' success in the
Parliamentary election was ensured to a great extent by the
democratic reforms previously announced. After the new
Legislative Bodies had voted for the Constitution to be revised
in April, 1914, they were dissolved and new elections were

made for the Revision Chambers though the revision of the Constitution was postponed on account of the war having broken out in the summer.

The period between 1878 and 1914 was a comparatively quiet one in foreign affairs, but it was shaken by two big peasant uprisings in 1888 and 1907 in Romania, and by the National Movement activities from 1892 to 1894 in Transylvania. It was, moreover, a period of considerable capitalist development of Romanian society, in particular in the economy and in culture. Romania's independence was strengthened and conditions were created for the union of all Romanians into a national state.

# CHAPTER VII

# *Romania in the First World War*

DURING the period 1859-1862 Moldavia and Wallachia united to form a single state that in 1862 was named Romania, and was recognized by the powers which had signed the Treaty of Paris. In 1878 the new Romanian state won its independence and in the decades that followed modern institutions strengthened the state. The First World War and the great October, 1917, Socialist Revolution — which paved the way for the general crisis of capitalism and for great changes in social and international relations — created objective conditions for the union of all Romanians into a national State.

## 1. Romania Remains Neutral (1914—1916)

WHEN the war for a new division of the world among the great powers broke out, Romania, which had concluded a treaty of alliance with Austria-Hungary, was forced to make a decision. On July 21 /August 3, 1914, a Crown Council was called together at Sinaia under the chairmanship of King Charles with the participation of the cabinet and of the heir apparent, Prince Ferdinand, as well as the President of the Assembly of Deputies, former Premiers and the Presidents of the various parties. The king, supported by P. P. Carp, was in favour of Romania joining Germany and Austria-Hungary, to which she was bound by a treaty of alliance which had been extended not long before. Theodor Rosetti declared for neutrality while Al. Marghiloman and Take Ionescu proposed an armed neutrality, a point of view subscribed to by Brătianu, Chairman of the Council of Ministers, who had previously come to an understanding with them and was also upheld by Ion Lahovari, M. Pherekyde, and others. When a telegram announced Italy's decision to remain neutral, Italy also being an ally of Austria-Hungary and Germany,

Charles I accepted armed neutrality, having to submit to the will of the majority in his capacity as constitutional king. Both Italy and Romania felt bound by the treaty of alliance only in the event of an unprovoked attack, but now it had been Austria-Hungary who had opened hostilities.

The defeat of the Austro-Hungarian armies in Galicia and of the German armies on the Marne strengthened the current in favor of the Entente, and hopes were raised of liberating the Romanian territories under Habsburg oppression. The Liberal government secretly acted to this end. With the king's knowledge, Brătianu obtained an agreement that Russia, in exchange for Romania's benevolent neutrality, "should oppose any change of the territorial status quo of the present frontiers" of the Romanian state and should acknowledge her right "to annex the regions of the Austro-Hungarian monarchy inhabited by Romanians." In September, 1914, a secret convention was concluded with Italy under which the two countries agreed not to abandon neutrality without advising each other. In ill health and having experienced great spiritual anxiety, with the thought of abdicating always uppermost, Charles I died on September 27/October 10, 1914. His successor, Ferdinand, whose wife, Marie, was closely related to the English and the Russian dynasties and did not hide her inclination towards the Entente, declared for war in order to liberate Transylvania.

The Romanian National Party in Transylvania suspended its activities when the war broke out. Following the advice given by King Charles and by Brătianu, its leaders did not oppose the war started by Austria-Hungary, some of them even declaring their loyalty. Aurel C. Popovici gave up his idea of the Habsburg Empire becoming a federation of the various nationalities and shortly after took refuge in Switzerland where he stopped the publication of his work in French, being certain that Austria-Hungary's defeat would make possible the union of Transylvania with Romania. Although the German government advised Hungary to make concessions to Romania in order to induce her to enter the war, the Hungarian Prime Minister, Istvan Tisza, only proposed that some territories not belonging to the Hungarian kingdom, should be ceded to Romania.

Having signed the agreement with Russia, the Liberal Cabinet decided to prolong the country's neutrality until the military situation would enable Romania to make a decisive contribution entitling her to incorporate the Romanian territories of Austria-Hungary. In the meantime Romania was to acquire war materials and the Entente to organize an expedition to the Balkan Peninsula and to create a favorable situation on the Eastern Front.

In order to endow the country with sufficient quantities of modern armament, orders were placed in Italy, Britain, and France, credit being allowed by the suppliers. In November, 1915, a General Board was created in the War Ministry to arrange that 30 per cent of the ammunition necessary should be produced within the country, the remainder to be imported. As the fortifications around Bucharest and along the Focşani-Nămoloasa-Galatz line were out of date, on account of the firing range of the artillery, 250 heavy cannons were taken from the forts to build up a heavy artillery. The armament and ammunition that had been ordered arrived in the country only at the close of 1916, so that when Romania entered the war her army was poorly equipped with modern armament.

Although conscription reduced the manpower available for agriculture, the farming output was maintained at the level of the previous years. When Turkey entered the war in October, 1914, and closed the Bosphorus and the Dardanelles, Romania could no longer export grain, oil products, and timber to the Western countries and was compelled to accept the terms of the Central Powers whose share in Romanian exports increased greatly. The government took measures against excessive exports by organizing in October, 1915, a central commission for the sale and exports of grain and grain by-products, and a commission for wine exports. In order to prevent the Central Powers from getting grain supplies from Romania, Britain opened a British Bureau in Bucharest in January, 1916, which bought 800,000 tons of grain, though the grain could not be taken out of the country. Owing to the rise in the price of farm produce, the landowners and grain brokers made considerable profits.

Take Ionescu and N. Filipescu declared openly for Romania entering the war on the side of the Entente, and created the organization named National Action which arranged large street demonstrations. Simultaneously, the *League for the Cultural Unity of all Romanians,* under the leadership of N. Iorga since 1906, was acting in unison. On December 14/27, 1914, the Cultural League, as it was called for short, was reorganized and renamed The League for the Political Unity of all Romanians, with a new governing board made up of the Transylvanian Vasile Lucaciu, Chairman, and of N. Filipescu, Take Ionescu, N. Iorga, Dr. C. I. Istrati, Barbu Delavrancea, Simion Mândrescu, and Octavian Goga. The two organizations co-operated, drawing the people into the struggle for the liberation of Transylvania and Banat. The following year two more organizations were formed which militated for Romania joining the war against Austria-Hungary: the *Unionist Federation* presided over by N. Filipescu, and the *Patriotic Action,* with C. I. Istrati as president.

Divergences between Marghiloman, the president of the Conservative Party, and some front-rank Conservatives such as N. Filipescu and Ion Lahovari, on the question of Romania's participation in the war, caused a break in June, 1915, the Party dividing into Conservatives favoring the Central Powers, and Conservatives siding with the Entente. The latter elected Ion Lahovari as President, and on Lahovari's death chose N. Filipescu. The latter subsequently joined the Democratic Conservative Party and formed a new political body: the Nationalist Conservative Party. In the National Liberal Party also, there was a group that opposed an alliance with the Entente. It consisted of friends of C. Stere and D. A. Sturdza, but neither Stere nor the Sturdza followers dared to overrule the discipline of the Party.

While keeping up appearances of neutrality, Brătianu continued his negotiations for an alliance with all the Entente powers, which Italy had joined in May, 1915, without informing Romania, as she had engaged to do. In the autumn of 1915 there was an increased clamor for Romania to enter the war against Austria-Hungary, though there was also some press propaganda in favor of co-operation with the Central Powers, led by Carp, Marghiloman, and their followers. On December 16/29 and 17/30, 1915, Take Ionescu in a speech to the Assembly of Deputies demanded that the cabinet carry on "a policy of national instinct" and declare war on Austria-Hungary. Brătianu answered briefly saying that he had assumed responsibility for the political situation of the country but refused to go into details. Carp alone violently attacked Take Ionescu's arguments.

## 2. The Socialist and Working Class Movement during Neutrality

FAITHFUL to the decisions made by the Stuttgart and Basel congresses of the Second International, the Romanian Social-Democrats declared against Romania joining in the war. An extraordinary Congress of the Social-Democratic Party and of the trade union movement held in Bucharest on August 10/23, 1914, declared for absolute neutrality and for defending the territorial integrity of the country.

After the extraordinary Congress of August, 1914, there were numerous workers' meetings which debated the decisions that had been made and pointed to the baneful consequences of the armament drive on the workers' living conditions. At the meeting held in Bucharest on November 16/29, 1914, when the session of the Legislative Bodies opened, the Socialists launched the slogan: "Make war on war." In May, 1915, a demonstration against the war took place in Bucharest and in July of the same year the Social-Democratic Party held an Inter-Balkan Socialist Conference in Bucharest with the participation of Romanian Socialists, and of delegates of the left-wing Bulgarian Socialists and of Greek Socialists. The Conference pointed to the imperialist nature of the war between the Central Powers and the Entente and condemned the voting for war credits by the leaders of the Socialist parties in the belligerent countries. In September, 1915, the Social-Democratic Party, in the capacity of initiators, participated in the Zimmerwald Conference (Switzerland) of the Socialist parties and groups opposing war, and endorsed the resolution passed at Kienthal in the spring of 1915. The strike movement became more active, particularly in the Danube ports where unemployment was rife. The Congress of October, 1915, of the Social-Democratic Party approved the main report submitted by Dr. Otoi Călin entitled *Social Democracy and War*, and founded on the documents approved by the Zimmerwald Conference. With Romania's entry into the war in the offing, the workers' demonstrations against war increased in number. The most important took place under the leadership of the Social-Democratic Party at Galatz on June 13/26, 1916, on which occasion nine demonstrators were killed, among them Spiridon Vrânceanu and Pascal Zaharia. Decrying the Galatz slaughter, the workers of the main towns of the country demonstrated anew against war in the following days. The Social-Democratic Party considered that the union of all Romanians into a national state was to be achieved through the victory of socialism and not through joining in the war between two imperialist camps. However, as the course of history proved, conditions for a socialist revolution were not yet ripe in Central and Southeast Europe. The demands of the bourgeois-democratic revolution, started in 1848 and later suppressed, had not all been met. National liberation of the subjected peoples and the union of all the people of the same nationality was a historic necessity. The leaders of the Socialist parties in Austria-Hungary had been compromised by the support they had given to the imperialist war, and the socialist parties in the countries of Southeast Europe were too weak to attempt to seize political power.

## 3. Romania Joins the War

BY August, 1916, neither the armies of the Central Powers, which had been joined by Bulgaria in October, 1915, nor those of the Entente had succeeded in obtaining a decisive victory in the war. Serbia had been defeated and her government had been compelled to withdraw to the island of Corfu with what was left of her army. The great German offensive which began at Verdun in February, 1916, ended after six months of heavy fighting without the victory that had been expected. The French armies had not been defeated, but in August, 1916, they were very weak and needed a long respite in order to renew their forces. On the Eastern Front the great Russian offensive of the spring of 1916 was prolonged into the summer, but was checked in mid-August. The Entente countries, finding themselves in a situation which threatened to become dangerous, for the Central Powers could resume their offensive at Verdun or start a counter-offensive on the

Eastern Front, forced Romania to enter the war, threatening her that she would not be accepted as an ally unless she decided then and there. Russia was the first to order Romania to attack Austria-Hungary in June, 1916, and France followed suit in early July. Hard-pressed, the Romanian government gave in although the country's military preparations had not been completed. On August 4/17, 1916, Romania signed a treaty of alliance and a military convention with the Entente Powers. She was admitted as an ally with rights equal to those of the other allied powers and was given the right to obtain the Romanian territories in Austria-Hungary. Russia engaged to support Romania in Dobrudja by sending one cavalry and two infantry divisions. An offensive was to be undertaken in Galicia and at Salonika in order to help Romania in her military operations against Austria-Hungary. It was decided that Romania was to enter the war on August 15/28, 1916. When the two documents had been signed, Stürmer, Russia's new Foreign Minister, demanded that the great allied powers should revise their treaty with Romania at the end of the war.

A Crown Council held in the Cotroceni Palace on the evening of August 15/28, 1916, decided that Romania was to join in the war against Austria-Hungary. That night the Romanian armies marched into Transylvania. Concurrently, Romania's representative in Vienna submitted his country's declaration of war to the Austro-Hungarian government. Romania went to war for the liberation of Transylvania and of the other territories whose majority population was indisputably Romanian. The war Romania undertook against Austria-Hungary in 1916, like the war of independence of 1877-1878, was welcomed by the Romanian population in Transylvania.

## 4. *The First Phase in Romania's War:* *August — December, 1916*

ON declaring war on Austria-Hungary, the Romanian government mobilized 833,601 men, 522, 890 of them in the fighting units, which consisted of 23 infantry divisions and two cavalry divisions, apart from other units. The army did not possess sufficient modern armament. The time of her entry into the war was unfavorable as there were no great battles being waged on the Western or the Eastern Fronts and the offensives promised by the Entente in Galicia and at Salonika did not take place. The Central Powers were able to withdraw a sufficient number of well-trained divisions from the Western, the Eastern, and the Salonika fronts to send them against Romania.

The government had decided that the troops should advance into Transylvania but General Averescu and other senior officers, as well as the French command, thought it preferable to keep on the defensive along the Carpathians and to march into Bulgaria in order to join the Allied armies at Salonika from where modern armament and ammunition could easily be brought. The view-point of the government, who considered it necessary immediately to liberate the territories inhabited by Romanians, prevailed. During the first days the 1st, 2nd and 3rd Romanian armies liberated Orşova, Braşov, Sf. Gheorghe, Gheorghieni, and Miercurea Ciucului, crossing the Perşani mountains in the northeastern part of the county of Făgăraş, as well as the Volcanic Mountains towards the town of Tîrgu-Mureş. On August 21/September 3, 1916, an army made up of Bulgarian, German, and Turkish units under Field Marshal Mackensen attacked Romania along the Dobrudja front, took Turtucaia after three days' fighting and advanced northward without meeting any opposition, conquering Silistra on its way. The Romanian armies suffered heavy casualties and by the end of September they had been forced to withdraw along the Carpathian line. The German and Austro-Hungarian troops took the way of the Oituz Valley in order to encircle most of the Romanian army in Oltenia and Muntenia, and possibly to capture the government. Their attacks were, however, repelled. Similar attacks were repelled at Predeal and along the Olt Valley. At the end of October, after an unsuccessful attempt, seven German divisions under General Kühne's command started an offensive along the Jiu Valley against a single Romanian division and forced it to withdraw southeast; the Germans then took Craiova and crossed the Olt. In his turn, Mackensen conquered Constantza and Cernavodă late in October and advanced the front to North Dobrudja. On November 11/24 another five German, Bulgarian, and Turkish divisions crossed the Danube at Zimnicea advancing towards Bucharest while the Germans south of Sibiu entered the Olt defile making for Piteşti and Bucharest. In early October, a French military mission under the command of General Berthelot had arrived in the country to help the Romanian units. Advised by General Berthelot, the Romanian general staff had started a counter-offensive along the rivers Argeş and Neajlov, but the Romanian units were attacked by the Germans from the west and were forced to withdraw eastward. On November 23/December 6, Bucharest was occupied only a short time after the king and the government had left for Jassy. Despite her losses, Romania was not out of the fight. Coping with an enemy superior in number, and with better armament and more military experience, the Romanian armies had, nevertheless, inflicted heavy losses on the Central Powers. Romania's sacrifices in men and territory enabled the allied armies, especially the French, to rebuild their forces. General Ludendorff wrote in his *War Memoirs*: "We defeated the Romanian army, but were unable to destroy it. Despite our victory over the Romanian army we were weaker than we had been."

While the front was being maintained, the government was reorganized, Take Ionescu as a minister without portofolio and some of his followers coming in on December 11/24, 1916. When the Parliamentary session opened in Jassy, the Message of the Crown again pointed to the necessity of a land reform and of a wider franchise. This was done in order to raise the morale of the soldiers.

In the territories that had been occupied — Oltenia, Muntenia, and most of Dobrudja — the Germans imposed a state of military occupation the aim of which was to collect as many agricultural and industrial products as possible to sustain the war of the Central Powers. There were requisitions of grain, cattle, wine, oil products, industrial installations, machines, and various materials. The Romanian General Bank, with German capital, was authorized to issue paper money. By the time the Peace of Bucharest was concluded, the bank had flooded the market with 2,172 million lei, more than half for the German occupation armies and the remainder for the Austro-Hungarian, Bulgarian, and Turkish armies. It was with this money that the occupants paid for part of the agricultural and industrial products taken from the population.

A Romanian administration was organized under the leadership of the Conservative Kostaki Lupu, a follower of P. P. Carp. The latter, together with Maiorescu, Marghiloman, and Stere, had remained in the occupied territory. In the summer of 1917 Stere published *Lumina (The Light)*, a paper which decried Romania's entry in the war beside the Entente. The occupation forces issued a paper in Bucharest: *Gazeta Bucureştilor (The Bucharest Gazette)*, with an edition in German: *Bukarester Tageblatt*. Part of the population, especially townspeople, had withdrawn to Moldavia.

## 5. Military and Political Developments in the First Half of 1917

A balance of forces was created when the Romanian front was along the lower reaches of the river Siret and the Eastern Carpathians. In the winter of 1916-1917 the fighting continued on the Western and Russian fronts without any decisive results, though Germany had started a great submarine war in order to force Britain and France to their knees. The Russian revolution of February, 1917, which removed Tsarism and installed a republic weakened the Eastern Front of the Entente. The U.S. armies came into the war on the Western Front only in the summer of 1918. The Central Powers availed themselves of the lull in the fighting to try to put Romania and Russia out of action, then Italy and finally France, and thus obtain a decisive victory.

Living conditions were very difficult in Moldavia, where the government had withdrawn with a large part of the state machinery, the army, part of the organization for waging war, and part of the population of the occupied territory, and where numerous Russian military units were also to be found. There was a shortage of housing, fuel, and food, particularly in the winter of 1917, which was unusually long and severe. The agglomeration, malnutrition, and insufficiency of hospitals as well as lack of medicines caused an epidemic of typhus which took a toll of tens of thousands of people, especially soldiers and children. In the spring massive requisitioning of cattle and the mobilization of the peasantry brought about farming difficulties, so that it was thought necessary to extend the requisitioning law to agricultural laborers and women. Food supplies eventually improved owing to the Russian government's consent to the Romanian state's organizing storehouses administered by its own officials east of the Prut. From October, 1916, to May, 1918, the state borrowed large sums from the National Bank of Romania and obtained a credit of 40 million pound sterling from the Bank of England in order to meet war requirements. As the National Bank had issued large quantities of bank notes, the Romanian currency began to fall. Afraid that Jassy, too, might be taken by the enemy, the government sent the treasury of the National Bank, to the value of over 300 million lei in gold plus other state and private valuables, to Moscow for safekeeping. This was done on the basis of agreements concluded with the Russian government.

The outbreak of the bourgeois-democratic revolution in Russia on February 25/March 10, 1917, called forth a response also in Romania, where numerous Russian troops, whose commander was under King Ferdinand's nominal authority, were also to be found. The left wing of the National Liberal Party, though with only a small membership, founded a new party in April — the Labor Party — which numbered among its members the former socialist G. Diamandi, Dr. N. Lupu, Gr. Trancu-Iași, Professor M. Carp, and others. The new party pledged itself to militate for the granting of a sufficiency of land to the peasants before long, for workers' legislation reducing the hours of work, for universal suffrage and the country's democratization. With the consent of the government and in pursuance of N. Iorga's advice, King Ferdinand issued a proclamation on March 23/April 5 promising the peasants land and universal suffrage. The proclamation, whose aim was to forestall revolt in the ranks of the peasants serving in the army, was repeated on April 23/May 6, 1917. The king's solemn promises were welcomed by the soldiers and helped to raise their morale. In June the Constituent Assembly passed the amendments to the Constitution whereby the land reform and universal suffrage came into force. On July 10/23 the cabinet was reshuffled, Take Ionescu becoming Vice-Chairman of the Council of Ministers. During the winter and later, many deputies and intellectuals, on the advice of the Chairman of the Council of Ministers, had gone to Odessa and Kherson and even to the United States and France in order to defend the interests of the country.

After Romania joined the war, the Social-Democratic Party was banned for all practical purposes. On September 5/18, 1916, its central paper — *Lupta (The Struggle)* — was suppressed. Dumitru Marinescu, Secretary General of the Party, died at the front. Following the outbreak of the Russian bourgeois-democratic revolution, soviets were organized among the soldiers of the Russian army at the Romanian front. In March and April, conferences were held between the Romanian Social-Democrats and the soviets of Russian soldiers in Jassy and in other towns not occupied by the Germans. Fearing lest an insurrection supported by the Russian soviets might break out, King Ferdinand went to the front on April 18/May 1, and gave another proclamation promising reforms. Numerous Romanian workers took part in the May Day demonstration organized by the soviets of Russian soldiers in Jassy. The demonstrators went to the house where C. Rakovski was under house arrest and freed him. The demonstration assumed a stormy character, the demonstrators clamoring for peace, democratic reforms, and the proclamation of a republic. The Social-Democratic leaders, however, hesitated and the government remained master of the situation. Rakovski and Bujor took refuge at Odessa where they issued anew *Lupta*, which they introduced into the country illegally.

When the front had been fixed, the Romanian government proceeded to reorganize the army, now made up of two instead of three army corps, with fifteen infantry divisions, two cavalry divisions, and a number of independent units. They were equipped with the modern armament that had been bought from France, Britain, and Italy two years previously but which had only reached the country in the winter of 1917. During the winter and spring soldiers and officers were trained to use the new armament and to master the new fighting techniques. The experience gained during the war had raised the military standards of the soldiers and officers, and of the commanding officers of large units. The self-seeking commanders were replaced by officers who had given proof of ability, courage, and patriotism. The French military mission was of great help in the reorganization of the army. The general staff came under the command of General C. Presan, former commander of the third army, while General C. Christescu was appointed commander of the first army though he was subsequently replaced by General Eremia Grigorescu. General Al. Averescu remained in command of the second army.

In the spring, summer, and autumn of 1917 Romanian volunteers from the Austro-Hungarian monarchy who had become prisoners in Russia increased the ranks of the army. On April 13/26, 1917, the organization of Romanian prisoners with its headquarters in Kiev (Darnitza) launched an appeal calling on all Romanian prisoners in Russia to fight for Romania, to enable her to bring about the union of the provinces under Habsburg rule with the mother country. The first batch of 1,500 volunteers, both soldiers and officers, reached Jassy on May 27/June 9, 1917, where they were given an enthusiastic welcome by the population and officialdom. Brătianu, Octavian Goga and Professor I. Nistor spoke at the demonstration in their honor in Union Square. During the following months more battalions of such Romanian volunteers joined the Romanian forces. This encouraged the population who saw in them the heralds of a complete national union.

## 6. *The Romanian Front in the Summer of 1917*

THE Allies having demanded that an offensive should be launched in June on the Romanian and Russian fronts, the First Army occupied an area along the lower reaches of the Siret between the Fourth and the Sixth Russian Armies, ready for an offensive at Nămoloasa, with the help of the Fourth Russian Army, to liberate Eastern Muntenia. The German command had also planned an offensive at Nămoloasa with the intent of encircling the Romanian and Russian armies in Moldavia after having broken the front with the assistance of the German-Austro-Hungarian troops in Galicia and Bucovina who were to start an offensive towards Cernăuți-Hotin-Chișinău at much the same time. When numerous Russian units were withdrawn from the Romanian front to be sent to Bucovina and Galicia to check the German-Austro-Hungarian drive, the First Army changed from the offensive to the defensive in the Nămoloasa area. The Second Army under General Averescu's command went into action at Mărăşti, together with the Fourth Russian Army, on July 11/24, 1917. The enemy lines were broken through along 30 miles to a depth of 20 miles, and the Romanians reached the river Putna. Compelled as they had been to give up their offensive at Nămoloasa when their front northwest of Focşani was threatened, the armies of the Central Powers attacked vigorously in the Mărăşeşti and Oituz area on July 24/August 6, 1917, in order to encircle and wipe out the Second Romanian Army. For a fortnight the Germans attacked the Romanian-Russian positions but were repelled at every attack, counter-attacked and forced to retire. By September there was peace on the Romanian front.

The victories won at Mărăşti, Mărăşeşti, and Oituz inflicted heavy losses in men and materials on the Central Powers and enabled the Romanians to keep Moldavia.


# 7. Armistice with the Central Powers. The Treaty of Bucharest

THE Great October Revolution changed the situation in Eastern and Southeastern Europe. On November 8/21, the Soviet Government issued a decree ordering that hostilities on all fronts should cease immediately and peace be concluded without any annexations or war reparations. On November 13/26, 1917, Soviet Russia proposed to the Central Powers that negotiations for a truce be started. The talks began at Brest-Litovsk on November 20/December 3, 1917, and a truce agreement was signed on December 2/15, 1917, followed by the signing of the peace treaty on February 18/March 3, 1918, between the Central Powers and Soviet Russia. General Scherbachev, Commander of the Russian armies on the Romanian front, did not observe the cease-fire order given by the Soviets but lacked the necessary authority to carry out the plans of the Russian armies on the Romanian front. On November 28/December 11, 1917, the Romanian government concluded a provisional armistice. The Brătianu cabinet resigned and was superseded by an Averescu cabinet on January 26 /February 8, 1918, in preparation for the negotiations with the Central Powers. The main purpose was to gain time in the hope that the Allies would soon defeat the Central Powers. A Romanian delegation sent to Bucharest for talks demanded that the armistice be extended for at least another twenty days. Mackensen, Commander of the Forces of the Central Powers on the Romanian front, would hear of no extension and demanded that the delegations for the conclusion of peace should meet on February 7 /20, 1918. Carp and Stere maneuvered with a view to replacing the dynasty with another which would be satisfactory to the Central Powers, so as to obtain better conditions.

General Averescu met Mackensen at Buftea, where he was informed of the terms of peace. Romania was required to demobilize her army but no territorial concessions to Bulgaria and Austria-Hungary were demanded.

On February 20 /March 5, 1918, the preliminaries of peace were signed at Buftea. The Central Powers annexed Dobrudja to the banks of the Danube leaving to Romania a commercial way of access to the Black Sea through the port of Constantza. The frontier was changed in favor of Austria-Hungary and economic concessions were made to her. Eight divisions were to be demobilized immediately. The foreign military missions were to be repatriated as soon as possible. The French mission left for France by way of Russia.

The terms set by the Central Powers at Buftea were onerous, and General Averescu being unlikely to obtain better ones even if the negotiations were prolonged, a new cabinet under Marghiloman was formed on March 5 /18, the latter being in favour with the Berlin and Vienna governments. After protracted negotiations, Marghiloman and von Kühlman-Burian, the new Foreign Affairs Minister of Austria-Hungary, jointly with the Bulgarian and Turkish delegates, signed the Treaty of Bucharest on April 24 /May 7, 1918. Bulgaria was to have southern Dobrudja up to the Cernavodă-Constantza railway line, with the rest of Dobrudja becoming a condominium of the four conquering powers until Bulgaria and Turkey came to an understanding; Austria-Hungary was to have a large number of villages in the county of Suceava together with the Carpathian slopes up to the summits; the Romanian army was to be reduced to 8 divisions of peace-time strength; the two infantry divisions and the two cavalry divisions in Bessarabia were to keep their complete wartime strength; the country's exports of grain, cattle, and other foodstuffs were to be the monopoly of a German-Austro-Hungarian company soon to be set up; the shipyards at Turnu Severin were to go to Austria-Hungary; petroleum was to become the monopoly of a German enterprise for thirty years; navigation on the Danube and woodworking were to become a German and Austrian monopoly; the National Bank and public finances were to be under the control of German commissars; the Central Powers were to keep six divisions in the occupied territories as well as "the bodies required for economic exploitation," until the peace had been ratified. The Romanian government at Jassy would exercise its authority over Muntenia and Oltenia under German control when the treaty had been signed. In short, the Treaty of Bucharest was turning Romania into a German colony.

## 8. *Romania Joins in the War again*

HAVING signed a peace with Soviet Russia, Germany started a new offensive on the Western Front in the hope of defeating France before the American armies went into action. Her early victories raised the confidence of the supporters of the Marghiloman Conservative cabinet. The Parliament, now incomplete, as many deputies, including Take Ionescu, had left for Western countries, was dissolved, and in May new elections were organized on the basis of the election lists of 1916, after the Peace Treaty of Bucharest. The Liberals not wishing to oppose the Conservative government, the latter were returned. The Radical-Socialist Party recently formed by Stere obtained a number of mandates; its press organ in Jassy — *Momentul (The Moment)* — was fighting for the land reform, universal suffrage and other democratic reforms. General Averescu, who on April 1/14 had founded *the People's League*, together with Argetoianu, Matei Cantacuzino, and Duiliu Zamfirescu, also obtained a number of mandates. This new political organization demanded in its paper

— *Îndreptarea (Straightening Out)* — that those guilty of Romania's defeat should be tried, that the land reform law passed in 1917 should come into force, and also universal suffrage and administrative decentralization. Averescu was very popular and was elected deputy in several constituencies. The Labor Party, undermined by the Radical Socialist Party and the People's League, had much fewer mandates.

The new Parliament had a number of bills to debate but its main task was to ratify the Treaty of Bucharest, which was finally done after long discussions. The king, however, had systematically put off the ratification of the treaty. Amendments to the Constitution were to be made by a Constituent Assembly after the termination of war. In May the government had enforced the law of obligatory agricultural labor and the planting of certain crops, so that all agricultural land should be cultivated and a large output be obtained. The number of gendarmes was doubled, for the government feared peasant uprisings and strikes, which were becoming ever more frequent. In October a newly passed law stipulating that some of the landowners' land must be leased to the peasants, was enforced. Although peace had been concluded, the German and Austro-Hungarian occupiers did not approve of the refugees and the demobilized returning to the occupied territories. On the other hand, the population, especially the people of Bucharest, often received ex-service men as heroes. The shortage of food — for grain and cattle had been sent to Germany and Austria-Hungary in large quantities — made life very hard for the population and caused them to agitate against the occupiers. The working class movement intensified, especially in Bucharest and Ploieşti. In order to make up somewhat for the shortage of food, the German command ordered the Romanian government to send supplies from Moldavia.

The counter-offensive of the Entente on the Western Front, which had begun in July with continuous victories created an atmosphere unfavorable to the Marghiloman government. The Central Powers reproached Marghiloman with postponing the indictment of the Brătianu cabinet ministers, who were considered guilty of having declared war on Austria-Hungary. The matter was debated in Parliament and Al. Constantinescu, former Minister of Home Affairs, was taken in custody but was released after a few weeks. The command of the occupation forces moreover reproached the Romanian cabinet with postponing the ratification of the Peace Treaty of Bucharest. When Bulgaria succumbed after her defeats on the Salonika front in September, 1918, Mackensen changed his stand and was prepared to alter the Treaty of Bucharest in Romania's favor.

On August 15/28, 1918, Marghiloman submitted his resignation to the king, who did not accept it. But the minister understood that defeat was awaiting the Central Powers and that he had played his part in politics. With the military collapse of Austria-Hungary and Germany imminent, the king demanded the resignation of the Marghiloman cabinet on October 24/November 6, 1918, upon which General Coandă, supported by the Liberals, formed the new cabinet. On October 28/November 10, 1918, military units on their way from Salonika crossed the Danube at Zimnicea under General Berthelot's command and were welcomed by the population as liberators. On the same day, the Romanian cabinet mobilized the army which again crossed the Carpathians, now to submit a Memorial to the ministers of the Entente at Jassy, asserting that Romania "was entitled to make good her claims" and demanding that the Treaty of Bucharest be canceled. At the same time the memorial declared that the Romanian state was resuming operations with the Allies. Concurrently, a declaration of war on Germany was sent to Mackensen who was asked to evacuate the country immediately. The following day Germany and the Allies concluded an armistice and World War I came to an end. Mackensen began his retreat on October 30/November 12, 1918. Three envoys of the Romanian National Party of Transylvania arrived in Jassy to inform the Romanian cabinet how matters stood in Transylvania and ask for their support and the help of the army. The Romanian National Committee also sent a delegation to Jassy with the same purpose in view. The Parliament that had been elected in May and the laws it had promulgated were canceled.

The political representatives of the Romanian population in the provinces under Austria-Hungary had fought for liberty as had done the other nationalities, basing their claims on the principle of the right of self-determination.

## 9. Romanian Propaganda Abroad

ALREADY in 1917 a propaganda campaign had been started in the West to inform public opinion in the Entente countries about Romania's territorial claims and the justice of those claims. With the support of the Romanian population in the United States, the brothers Gogu and Paul Negulescu brought out in Chicago the review *România (Romania)* in both English and Romanian, upholding Romania's right to Transylvania and the other territories in the Austro-Hungarian Empire inhabited by Romanians. On June 22/July 5, 1918, Doctor C. Angelescu, assisted by Vasile Stoica, created the Romanian National League in the United States, within the framework of which Professor L. Mrazek and Doctor N. Lupu also worked. The League established contact with Th. G. Masaryk, head of the Czech liberation movement, and also with the representatives of the Serbs and Poles. A large delegation of Romanian refugees under the leadership of Simion Mîndrescu and G. G. Mironescu, took part in the Congress of Oppressed Nationalities of Austria-Hungary held in Rome on March 26/April 8, 1918. Some three months later, on June 5/18, Simion Mîndrescu set up in Italy the Action Committee of the Romanians of Transylvania, Banat, and Bucovina, the purpose being to organize the Romanian prisoners in the Austro-Hungarian army into legions to fight on the Italian front. But the most vigorous propaganda was made in France in 1917 and 1918 by Romanian university professors, M. P.s and publicists, among whom were Take Ionescu, Octavian Goga, Vasile Lucaciu, and N. Titulescu. The inventor Traian Vuia, who had lived in France for years, brought out the review *La Transylvanie* and a committee, which included C. Mille, issued the paper *La Roumanie* in Paris from January 4/17, 1918, on. *The National Council of Romanian Unity*, recognized by the French government as the spokesman of the Romanian people, was formed in Paris on August 27/September 6, 1918. A month later Take Ionescu was elected Chairman of the Council, with Vasile Lucaciu, Octavian Goga, Doctor C. Angelescu, and Jean Th. Florescu, as Vice-Chairmen. The Romanian press and propaganda bureau in Stockholm headed by Gh. Derussi, Romania's former Minister in Sweden, also made a valuable contribution to supporting the cause of Romania's unity.

## 10. Transylvania Unites with Romania

THROUGHOUT the duration of the imperialist war the measures taken by the Hungarian government in Transylvania caused much hardship for the working masses of all nationalities. With men being mobilized by the hundreds of thousands there was soon a shortage of manpower in both industry and agriculture. The right to strike was denied the workers and the hours of work were increased. Agricultural as well as industrial production decreased so that starvation was rife in the towns in 1917. The terrorizing of the working masses, and of the population generally, became worse after Romania's entry into the war, many Romanians being taken to concentration camps in Western Hungary, at Sopron, and even as far as Styria. Some were accused of treason. The review *Luceafărul (The Morning Star)* of Sibiu and the paper *Românul (The Romanian)* in Arad were both suspended. On July 20/August 2, 1917, the Hungarian government implemented a number of measures designed to Magyarize the denominational Romanian schools in the vicinity of the Hungarian frontier. The overwhelming majority of Romanian intellectuals, including Iuliu Maniu, St. Ciceo-Pop and Vasile Goldiş, refused to sign the declaration of loyalty demanded by the Tisza cabinet in December, 1916. The threat of famine, the cruel exploitation and police measures, to which should be added the encouragement given by the Russian revolution of February and especially by the October Socialist Revolution, impelled the workers and peasants to take a stronger stand against the dominant classes in the winter of 1917. There were many strikes, although they had been banned, organized by the trade unions, which had become active again. In October the paper of the Romanian section of the Social-Democratic Party of Hungary — *Adevărul (The Truth)* — came out anew speaking in support of the workers and for the cause of the Romanians. Peace demonstrations took place in various towns towards the close of 1917 and there were many deserters from the army. "The Declaration of the Rights of the Peoples of Russia" published by *Adevărul* and by some bourgeois papers, including *Românul,* the central organ of the Romanian National Party, called forth a wide response among the Romanian population in Transylvania. The peace treaty that was concluded in March, 1918, with Soviet Russia and the Ukraine, and in May with Romania, did not shake the confidence of the masses in the forthcoming collapse of the Austro-Hungarian monarchy. Two general strikes caused the very foundations of Austria-Hungary to totter. In their turn the peasants agitated for land from the big estates. On January 19/February 1, 1918, there was mutiny on the warships in the port of Cattaro; the sailors demanded that peace talks should begin and the right to self-determination of the peoples in the Austro-Hungarian monarchy be recognized. Though the mutiny was repressed, the climate in the navy and the army was ominous. Many Romanians participated in the mutiny. Workers' parades were held at Oradea and Reşiţa to celebrate April 18 /May 1, 1918. Under the influence of the movement of the nationalities for self-determination, Oskar Jaszi, leader of the Radical Party of Hungary, published in the spring of 1918 *The Future of the Monarchy*, condemning "the stupid assimilation policy" carried out by the Magyar and German dominant classes and recommending cooperation with the oppressed peoples. About the same time the Austrian Socialist Karl Renner published his work on self-determination of the nations in Austria-Hungary. In order to save his throne, on October 3 /16, 1918, while the German-Austro-Hungarian fronts were collapsing, Charles I, the Austrian emperor, issued a manifesto *"To My Faithful Peoples"*, declaring for the federative re-organization of Austria-Hungary into six independent kingdoms: Austrian, Hungarian, Czech, Yugoslav, Polish and Ukrainian, with Transylvania to continue as a part of Hungary. The Magyar government informed the emperor that they opposed the idea of federalization, which would have brought about Hungary's dismemberment. The Social-Democratic Party of Hungary also declared for Hungary's integrity. However, in October the revolutionary movement of the oppressed nations suddenly flared up: Romanian, Czech, Slovak, Croatian, Serbian, and Ukrainian soldiers were deserting from the front. On October 5 /18, 1918, President Wilson recognized the right of the peoples of Austria-Hungary to national self-determination and less than a fortnight later — on October 15 /28 — Prague was in revolt and the Czechoslovak Republic was proclaimed. Refusing to fire at the Czech demonstrators and, handing over to them their armament stores, the Romanian military units helped towards the victory of the revolution. The next day revolution broke out in Vienna and shortly after, on October 18/31, the autonomous state of the Serbs, Croatians, and Slovenes was created; revolution flared up in Budapest while on the Italian front the Austro-Hungarian armies were being routed. The revolutionary movement had given rise to a bourgeois-democratic revolution in Transylvania as well, where the local authorities were ousted from office and the measures the Budapest government had previously enforced were ignored. Workers' Councils were organized at Timișoara, Oradea and Petroșani. The soldiers released their imprisoned comrades and the villagers forced the Austro-Hungarian authorities to flee. Everywhere national guards were formed, replacing the Habsburg military units. In many rural districts the peasants rose against the landowners and lessees. In November the membership of the Romanian socialist section amounted to 100,000. The Romanian Socialist Central Committee — its paper *Adevărul (The Truth)* — fought for the national and social liberation of the Romanian people, and early in October joined forces with the leaders of the Romanian National Party. On September 29/October 12, the Executive Committee of the Romanian National Party met at Oradea and passed a resolution pointing out that it was the natural right of every nation to decide its own destiny freely and that the Romanian nation in Austria-Hungary had to determine "without any foreign influence its place among the free nations". It also demanded recognition as the only provisional leadership body in Transylvania. A week later, on October 5/18, 1918, Vaida Voevod read the resolution in the Hungarian Parliament.

On October 16/29 the Romanian Socialist Central Committee and the leaders of the Romanian National Party agreed to form a Romanian National Central Council to represent all the Romanians of Transylvania. Two weeks later the Romanian National Central Council was set up. It consisted of six Social-Democrats, Tiron Albani, Ion Flueraș, and Iosif Jumanca among them, and six members of the Romanian National Party, including Theodor Mihali, Ciceo Pop, Vasile Goldiș, Vaida Voevod, Aurel Vlad, and Iuliu Maniu. The Romanian National Central Council moved from Budapest to Arad to assume leadership of the national liberation struggle of the Transylvanian Romanians. County, town, and village national

councils were officially constituted and the old Magyar authorities were ousted from office. As the talks carried on at Arad
with the new cabinet of Count Mihaly Karolyi failed of their
purpose, a manifesto *To the Peoples of the World* was launched
on behalf of the "Great Council of the Romanian nation" on
November 5/18, 1918. The manifesto pointed out that the
Magyar government having refused the right to self-determination to the Romanians, the Romanian nation "will no longer
have any state connections with Hungary". Furthermore,
support was asked of all the Romanian people, "with whom
we shall henceforth be for all eternity", in order to obtain
freedom and unity. Two days later another manifesto called
together the Grand National Assembly at Alba Iulia for
November 18/December 1, 1918, and the regulations for the
election of deputies were published. Every electoral constituency was to elect five delegates by universal suffrage, apart
from which the clergy of the two Romanian denominations,
the cultural associations, and all public organizations, as well
as the two Romanian parties — the Romanian National Party
and the Social-Democratic Party — were also entitled to send
delegates. The people were requested to come in numbers to
Alba Iulia.

The participants in the Grand National Assembly held in
the building of the Alba Iulia Casino on November 18/Decem-
ber 1, 1918, amounted to 1,228 delegates elected by the electoral
constituencies, and the other organizations of the Romanians of Transylvania, Banat, Crişana, and Maramureş. There
were three presidents: Gh. Pop de Băseşti, President of the
Romanian National Party, and the Bishops Ioan I. Pap and
Demetriu Radu, with Theodor Mihail, St. Ciceo-Pop, and
I. Flueraş acting as Vice-Presidents, and eight secretaries,
among whom were Silviu Dragomir and Gheorghe Crişan.
The Social-Democratic Party was represented by 150 delegates,
including Ion Mihuţ, Tiron Albani, Iosif Jumanca, Emil
Isac, and Dr. Valeriu Roman. The delegates of the Romanian
National Party were more numerous. While the meeting of
the Great National Council was being held in the Casino, 14
mass meetings took place in various parts of the town, with
the participation of some 100,000 people from all over Transylvania, Banat, Crişana, and Maramureş. There were also a
number of representatives from Romania. The Romanian

army was still a long way from Alba Iulia although it had crossed the Carpathians nearly three weeks before.

Vasile Goldiş submitted a political report at the session of the Great National Council as well as a draft declaration to be approved by the Council. The first article of the declaration stated: "The National Assembly of all the Romanians of Transylvania, Banat, and the Hungarian country, whose rightful representatives were assembled at Alba Iulia on November 18/December 1,1918, decree that those Romanians and all the territories inhabited by them should unite with Romania". Article 2 stated that these territories were to be autonomous only until the Constituent Assembly elected by universal suffrage should meet. Furthermore the Declaration promised that all the peoples living together in the area would enjoy national liberty, all religious denominations be equal and autonomous, and universal suffrage, freedom of the press, a radical land reform, and an advanced labor legislation would be ensured. Article 9 created a Great National Council to designate Transylvania's representatives to the Peace Conference. Iuliu Maniu on behalf of the Romanian National Party, and Iosif Jumanca, on behalf of the Social-Democratic Party, made declarations demanding that Transylvania should unite with Romania. In his declaration, Iosif Jumanca stated: ". . . We are here today, as the true representatives of the Romanian workers of Transylvania and Banat, to declare before you, before the Socialist International and before the whole world that we want all Romanians to be united". After these speeches the Declaration was passed unanimously by the Great National Council whose enthusiasm knew no bounds. The fourteen meetings held in the town approved the union with Romania, cheering joyfully. Many representatives of the Romanian National Party and of the Social-Democratic Party spoke at those meetings.

Before winding up its proceedings, the Great National Council elected 150 deputies, who were to make up the new Great National Council, and also a Directing Council, which was to rule Transylvania until the Constituent Assembly had been convened. Shortly after, a meeting of the Saxons at Mediaş also demanded that Transylvania should be united to Romania.

The decision made by the National Assembly at Alba Iulia terminated the process of the national union of the Romanian people into a single independent state. This momentous union had been achieved by the entire Romanian people through a national ideology, through the organization and strengthening of the modern Romanian state, through the activities of the statesmen and leaders of the liberation movement, of the scientists, men of letters and artists, by the sacrifices of the revolutionary years 1848-1849 throughout Transylvania, and the sacrifices made in the war for Romania's independence at Plevna and Vidin and in the years 1916-1918 throughout the country.

In their struggle for unity and national independence, the Romanian people had been urged forward by the progressive elements of modern Europe. The flame of the revolution lit in Europe in 1848 constantly upheld the Romanian people in their efforts and finally loosened the cruel reins which checked their natural development.

# CHAPTER VIII

# Culture in the Modern Age

AFTER Tudor Vladimirescu's revolution, culture developed considerably, helping towards social progress and the movement for a national union and independence. The creation of a national state through the union of Moldavia and Wallachia gave a great impetus to cultural life and to scientific progress. Literature and the fine arts tackled the subjects favored by the various European currents and gave them expression in original works of great value. The Romanian Academy founded in 1866 rallied the writers, artists, and scholars of all the provinces inhabited by Romanians, thus ensuring unity in cultural life and favoring the development of a national culture.

## 1. Education

THE revolution of 1821 and the return of native princes promoted a sound education in the Romanian language. In Wallachia, after Gheorghe Lazăr's death in 1823, his school, which continued to function until 1828, found an energetic guide in Eufrosin Poteca; in Moldavia, Asachi's school continued its courses, with Romanian used for the first time in the teaching of all the subjects. The era of the *Règlement Organique* itself considered the use of the national language in teaching as "the strongest tie in the preservation and improvement of the race and the instilling of love for the homeland".

The age of the *Règlement Organique* started a new stage in the development of education. The regulations of 1833 concerning public schools determined the pattern of teaching institutions, establishing four cycles; schools were proclaimed to be state institutions and Romanian became the only language used in the schools of all grades.

In 1835 the Academy of Higher Studies, also known as the Mihăileană Academy, was created at Jassy, the professors being outstanding personalities of the three Romanian countries, among them Mihail Kogălniceanu, Ion Ghica, Ion Ionescu de la Brad, and Eftimie Murgu.

Significant progress was also made during the period of the *Règlement Organique* in the organization of education in the towns, every capital city of a county having a state school.

Though prevailing conditions were far more oppressive in Transylvania owing to foreign domination, the national language came to be used in its educational system. Here the credit is due to Simion Bărnuţiu and Timotei Cipariu.

When the national state was founded, the educational system underwent great changes. As well trained people were needed in every sphere, the number of schools was increased, and higher education was raised on new foundations. For both primary and secondary education many new schools were built and also schoolmasters were trained. In 1864 a law was passed making four years of primary education compulsory and free of charge, and establishing the period of seven years for secondary education and three years for the university. However, the small number of schools and teachers made it impossible to enforce the law as regards compulsory education. The possibilities of higher education were enhanced after the University of Jassy was founded in 1860 and Bucharest University in 1864. In Bucharest in 1881 an old technical school was reorganized and turned into the Higher School of Civil Engineering. In 1879 the second Medical School in Romania was founded as part of the University of Jassy. In 1913 the Academy of Higher Commercial and Industrial Studies was added to the other higher educational establishments existing in Bucharest.

In 1896 primary education was reorganized by Petru Poni, a Liberal minister, who enforced the same curriculum upon all primary schools — five-year schools — in the villages, and four-year primary schools in the towns. Kindergartens and courses for adults were also started at the time. The same minister founded School House, an institution designed to build primary schools. In 1893 Spiru Haret, another Liberal minister of public education and cults, reorganized secondary education, which was divided into a four-class lower course and a four-class higher course, the latter having scientific, modern and classical sections. The next year, the same minister had a law passed on vocational education.

In Transylvania the decision of the Cluj Diet of 1842 had made Hungarian the language of all elementary schools. The bill never having been sanctioned by the emperor, the decision was not enforced. After Dualism came into force, Romanian was used only in the denominational Orthodox or Uniate schools, which, however, gradually decreased in number owing to the Magyarization policy, particularly after the Apponyi Law of 1906. In Transylvania there were only a few secondary schools where the teaching language was Romanian.

## 2. Science

THE second half of the last century was a pioneering period in modern Romanian science. Under the new conditions created as a result of the formation of the national state and the achievement of independence, the first scientific societies were founded and investigations were carried out with outstanding results. The Romanian Academic Society, created in 1866, became the Romanian Academy in 1879. In 1872 a scientific section with a publication of its own had been added to the Romanian Academic Society. In 1890 the Physical Sciences Society was founded, named the "Romanian Scientific Society" after 1902.

The reorganization of the public health services in line with modern concepts called for a considerable increase in the medical profession. In 1869 Carol Davila (1828-1884) founded a Medical Faculty in Bucharest, with professors such as Victor Babeș (1854-1926), founder of the Bacteriology Institute and author of the first bacteriological treatise in the world, and Gheorghe Marinescu (1863-1938), founder of the Romanian Neurological School. The natural sciences, organized at an earlier date than medical schools—in 1883 the Society of Doctors and Naturalists had been founded in Jassy — also made notable progress. D. Brîndză (1846-1895) created the Botanical Gardens of Bucharest, and Gr. Cobăl-cescu (1831-1892) published in 1862 the first Romanian Geological Treatise on the tertiary deposits in Romania. Geological research grew larger in scope, for interest had been aroused in the capitalization of the wealth of the subsoil. The names to be noted in this connection are Grigore Ștefănescu (1838-

1911) and Sabba Ştefănescu (1857-1931), Gh. Munteanu-Murgoci (1872-1925), who studied the Getian seams in the Southern Carpathians, and L. Mrazek (1867-1944), who made outstanding contributions to the investigation of oil deposits in Romania. The development of the economy also aroused increased interest in chemistry. A Romanian school of chemistry appeared with Petru Poni (1841-1925) and C. I. Istrati (1850-1918) as founders. The former made the chemical analysis of Romanian crude oil, while the latter created the organic chemistry laboratory in Bucharest, where he undertook many investigations and trained a large number of specialists.

Mathematics and astronomy began on a small scale, but with E. Bacaloglu (1830-1891) as an outstanding researcher it subsequently assumed a remarkable impetus reflected in the issue of the *Mathematical Gazette* in 1895, which published important studies and investigations by Spiru Haret (1851-1912), David Emanuel (1854-1941), N. Coculescu (1866-1952), founder of the Bucharest Astronomic Observatory, and Traian Lalescu (1882-1929), author of the first book in the world on integral equations. Linguistics was given much attention: indeed, one of the objectives of the Academy was the publication of a dictionary of the Romanian language. Among the illustrious scholars who brought out works of note were B. P. Haşdeu (1838-1907), who began the monumental dictionary *Etymologicum Magnum Romaniae;* Alexandru Cihac (1825-1887), who published the first scientific etymological dictionary of the Romanian language *Dictionnaire d'Etymologie daco-romane;* H. Tiktin (1850-1936), who compiled a *Romanian-German Dictionary;* Lazăr Şăineanu (1859-1934) and M. Gaster (1856—1939), who made valuable contributions to philology.

As a result of thorough investigations, Romanian scientists made a number of discoveries and inventions which attracted the attention of the scientific world. N. Teclu (1839-1916) invented the burner with adjustment of air and gas currents; D. Hurmuzescu (1865-1954) discovered the ionizing effect of X-rays, and built an electroscope that bears his name and was later to be used by the two Curies in their researches. G. Constantinescu (1881-1965) was the creator of sonicity; in aeronautics Traian Vuia (1872-1953) for the first time flew a self-propelled plane, H. Coandă (1886-1972) was the inventor of the jet plane (December 14, 1910) and Aurel Vlaicu (1882—1913) designed the first metal-built plane.

Romanian philosophic thought was expressed in writings of various kinds — historical, geographical, linguistic, etc. — before evolving into an independent subject. Social militants bent on reforms or initiators and participants in revolutionary movements wrote for the press as well as comprehensive studies issued in pamphlet form or as volumes, their works being based on well-grounded principles. Worthy of being noted here are Theodor Diamant, N. Bălcescu, Cezar Bolliac, D. Bolintineanu, Stephan Ludwig Roth, Eftimie Murgu, Simion Bărnuțiu, G. Barițiu, Timotei Cipariu, C. A. Rosetti, Dr. Russel, Panait Mușoiu, and C. Stere. Among the outstanding political thinkers was also Mihail Eminescu, a great opponent of the liberal bourgeoisie and of capitalism and a defender of the interests "of the old, positive classes" (peasants, artisans) threatened by capitalism. His newspaper articles are one of the sources of the Semănătorul (The Sower) doctrine, and his ideas have points in common with those of the Junimea movement. Most scientists in their works brought forward general ideas, whether deliberately or spontaneously, so that the exact sciences effectively contributed to the development of materialist scientific concepts of the world. In their studies, treatises and courses, scholars like Vincențiu Babeș, Grigore Ștefănescu, Ștefan C. Mihăilescu, and Victor Babeș made notable contributions to this end.

Vasile Conta (1845-1882), the most illustrious spokesman of mechanistic materialism in Romanian culture and thought, was the first to bring forth a well-knit philosophic system in Romania. Guided by the concepts of integral determinism, Conta evolved a "theory of fatalism" according to which social life, like psychic life, was the result of laws similar to those governing the physical world. For Conta, life was an eternal and complex undulatory movement, in process of unceasing change (Theory of World Undulations, 1876-1877). An early death prevented the Romanian thinker from finishing a number of works — First Constitutive Principles of the World, The Basis of Metaphysics — which dealt with basic philosophical questions such as time, space, matter, movement, necessity, etc. In politics, Conta was the spokesman of bourgeois liberalism and occasionally advocated narrow nationalistic views.

At the close of the nineteenth century Marxism began to spread in Romania, an essential role being played by C. Dobrogeanu-Gherea (1855-1920). He was the main writer for the socialist movement, publishing articles in all socialist publications and being the author of the program of 1886 *(What Romanian Socialists Want)*; furthermore, he published works popularizing dialectical and historical materialism, criticizing bourgeois ideology and anarchism, and evolving a scientific basis for aesthetics and for literary criticism. Gherea blazed the trail of materialist thought in Romania though he adopted some positivist concepts in his literary studies, and in his social analisys study, *Neo-Serfdom*.

In their works, the historians of the generation of 1848 — N. Bălcescu, M. Kogălniceanu, G. Barițiu, and S. Bărnuțiu — set forth the fundamental problems of Romanian society of the mid-nineteenth century: the desire for unification, national independence, and social emancipation. Historiographic investigation no longer confined itself to internal sources but resorted to numberless others. N. Bălcescu and August Treboniu Laurian (1810-1881) published *Historical Review for Dacia* (5 vols. 1845-1847) and Al. Papiu-Ilarian (1828-1878) *Thesaurus of Historic Moments for Romania*, which included valuable internal and external documents, travelogues, etc. M. Kogălniceanu collected the *Moldavian Chronicles*. Basing their works on wide information, these historians gave a new orientation to Romanian history, focusing their attention on problems of social history. N. Bălcescu's works—*On the Social Status of Ploughmen in the Romanian Principalities Throughout the Ages* (1846) and *Question Economique des Principautés Danubiennes* (1850) — are well-grounded surveys on social and economic patterns in Wallachia and Moldavia during the transition period from feudalism to capitalism.

After the union of the two Principalities, Romanian historiography entered into a prolific period illustrated by such great figures as B. P. Hașdeu, a writer of wide information, a penetrating historian, who associated philology with history *(A Critical History of the Romanians in the Two Dacias)* and who published historical documents *(Romania's Historical Archives)*; N. Densușianu (1846-1911), who studied ancient inscriptions and published a well-grounded history of Horia's Uprising; A. D. Xenopol (1847-1920), author of a monumental history of the Romanians, who devoted much attention to economic and social factors, thus making a genuine synthesis of Romanian national history; in his work *Les principes fondamentaux de l'histoire*, Xenopol gave his own concepts on history which he regarded as a science; according to him, history, being a science which studies a succession of facts, cannot formulate laws, but can only keep track of the "series" of events and bring out the determining causes; the development of human society, according to Xenopol, is determined by various factors, among which are the great personalities, the preservation instinct, chance, etc.

The early medieval history of this country was studied by D. Onciul (1856-1923), who used a rigorous technique in the examination and interpretation of historical documents. The works he devoted to the founding of the Romanian Principalities gave a new basis for research and opened up new perspectives in the approach to the history of the twelfth to the fourteenth centuries.

Ioan Bogdan (1865-1919) was inspired by the same spirit of critical erudition. He inaugurated the modern study of Slavistics in Romania. C. Giurescu (1875-1919) was the author of some remarkable studies on the patterns of medieval society. Both Bogdan and Giurescu edited historical documents which to this day are noteworthy examples of the scientific publication of such documents.

Ever since the close of the nineteenth century Romanian historiography had been dominated by the personality of N. Iorga (1871-1940). With a prodigious memory and unparalleled erudition, Iorga was the most prolific Romanian historian. His study of foreign archives enabled him to set the country's history on new documentary foundations and to publish numerous volumes or collections of documents. Iorga made important contributions to the study of such aspects of national and world history as the Third Crusade and the history of Byzantium and of the Ottoman Empire. *Geschichte des Rumänischen Volkes* is a synthesis of national history in which Iorga gives a new outlook, for it treats the history of the Romanian people as a whole, brings out the part played by collective creation and integrates Romanian history into European history.

## 3. *Literature*

AS a result of the conditions created after the revolution of 1821 led by Tudor Vladimirescu and of the developments that were to lead to the bourgeois-democratic revolution of 1848, literature went through a decisive phase which integrated it into European culture. Modern Romanian literature began in the latter half of the eighteenth century and was the product and the expression of the Age of Enlightenment. To the Transylvanian School, of great importance in the formation of a national consciousness, we owe historical, philological, and philosophic writings and also an outstanding literary work: *Gypsy Epic* by Ion Budai-Deleanu (1760-1820), the first and most valuable Romanian epic and a poetic monument on the classical pattern. In the last decades of the eighteenth century, the Wallachian boyar Ienăchiţă Văcărescu (ca. 1740-1797) published the first modern Romanian lyrics. His sons, Alecu and Nicolaie, and his nephew, Iancu Văcărescu (1792-1863), followed his example, their poetry making a notable contribution to the "growth of the Romanian language and the praise of the homeland", and thus carrying out the sacred order in their foreruner's *Testament*. In Moldavia, Costache Conachi (1777-1849) played much the same part.

The first periodical publications of some duration — *Curierul Românesc (The Romanian Courier)* edited by Ion Eliade Rădulescu (1802-1872), and *Albina Românească (The Romanian Bee)* edited by Gheorghe Asachi (1788-1869) both coming out in 1829 in Bucharest and Jassy, respectively — were of unbounded importance in the promotion of Romanian literature, for the two editors were the main animators of modern Romanian culture. It is to them that we owe all the great initiatives, all the cultural institutions that were created or were consolidated during the third and the fourth decades of the nineteenth century: the press, education, the theater, the philharmonic orchestra, the societies with a patriotic bent. Ion Eliade Rădulescu wrote a great deal of poetry and prose; his *"Hobgoblin"* is a meritorious poem. Gheorghe Asachi wrote poems on the classical pattern and historical short stories. Vasile Cârlova (1809-1831) was a poet of promise who died in his early youth. He sang about the ruins of

Tîrgoviște, formerly Wallachia's capital, and the young Romanian army. Another outstanding personality was Anton Pann
(ca. 1794-1854) — "as astute as a proverb," as Eminescu
described him. The millenary wisdom of the Romanian people
is set forth in his racy works.

The publication of *Dacia Literară* (*The Literary Dacia*)
was a crucial moment in the evolution of Romanian culture.
The programme of this review, as formulated by Mihail Kogălniceanu (1817-1891), the editor-in-chief, set forth guiding principles which defined not only the review's position but also
indicated far-reaching literary trends that led Romanian literature throughout the nineteenth century and were also effective in the twentieth. Unlike the publications that had appeared
before it, the *Dacia Literară* was to a fair extent a reflection of
the spiritual life of the entire country and not only of a region;
it was open to works "from any part of Dacia, if of a high
standard"; indeed it described itself as "a general repertory
of writers from Moldavia, Wallachia, Transylvania, Banat,
and Bucovina, each with his ideas, his language, and his type".
Making it its aim to imbue all cultural events with the "national
spirit", the review promoted a literature mirroring Romanian
realities and rising out of tradition and folklore. The *Dacia
Literară* devoted great attention to the artistic quality of whatever it published, and discarded spurious values. Consequently, it built up the critical spirit in Romanian culture.
The review was stopped after its third issue, but its work
was continued by *Propășirea* (*The Progress*), 1844, *România
Literară* (*The Literary Romania*), 1855, and by later periodicals
in the two Romanian Principalities.

These publications promoted a national and popular current
which was part of an active, progressive European romanticism. A national literature did not mean a tendency towards
isolation but signified a link with Western literature, first made
manifest by the Transylvanian School. The main principles of
Romanian literature during the period of the review *Dacia
Literară* were also characteristic of Romanticism in general.
They included the use of the national history as a source of
inspiration, comparison of the past with the present, evalua-
tion of folk art, description of the customs in the countryside, and of the beauty spots of the country, local color, por-
trayal of the virtues of the plain man, emphasis on the beauty

of his speech, and a pathetic tone throughout. The feature that set Romanian romanticism apart from European romanticism was the fact that it did not come as a reaction against classicism, which never existed in these parts, but, on the contrary, assumed of the tendencies of classicism such as they were in the literature that developed under normal conditions. Consequently, there will be found during this period of romanticism also some forms of literature which are classical *par excellence*, such as the fable and the epistle. On the other hand, there are also glimpses of realism, obvious attempts to discard romanticism in the first novels, which make it plain that Balzac was known here, for they include social observation — what was described as the "physiology" of society.

This was an effervescent period when literature had not clearly emerged from the more comprehensive phenomenon which is culture. Indeed, literature was at the time less intent on its own aims, being engaged in the struggle for a vital cause: to set a new pattern for society and to achieve national unity and independence. It was what was described as the "heroic age" of the national culture during which men of letters served a variety of purposes and writers were at the same time historians, linguists, philologists, philosophers, journalists, and social militants. A politician and a statesman, as well as the initiator and inspirer of all the activities of national assertion and social renewal, Mihail Kogălniceanu — historian, editor of chronicles, founder of reviews — also asserted himself in fiction, for he wrote one of the first Romanian novels — *The Secrets of the Heart* — as well as short stories and plays. Nicolae Bălcescu wrote history of high literary value, as, for example, *The Romanians under Prince Michael the Brave*. Alecu Russo (1819-1859), a great lover of folk poetry, left us literary and linguistic studies and also a romantic poem in prose: *Song to Romania*. Vasile Alecsandri (1821-1890) was a complex personality who produced outstanding works in all literary genres and also played an important part in politics before the revolution of 1848, during the revolution and in the following period of the union of the Romanian Principalities. Mihail Eminescu described him as a "king of poetry". He sang of the scenery of his homeland, evoked its heroic past, voiced the people's aspiration after national unity, exposed a number of social vices, and made poetry truly Romanian, as a contemporary pointed out, by his orientation towards the people, their oral creations, and their living, melodious language as used in the folk songs and folk ballads. His collection of folk poetry, which appeared in 1852-1853, set its seal on the evolution of Romanian literature and of the Romanian literary language. The poet Grigore Alexandrescu (1810—1885) wrote odes, epistles, satires, fables and elegies; D. Bolintineanu (1819-1872) — authored ballads, historical legends, pastorals, lyrics *(Bosporus Flowers)*, and travel impressions. The prose writer Costache Negruzzi (1808-1868) published a historical short story — *Alexandru Lăpușneanu* — whose charm, like that of his letters, has been preserved intact after more than a century. All these writers have made an impressive contribution to the enrichment of the Romanian language and literature.

The period that followed the union of the Principalities in 1859 was also romantic, but far more quiet, more balanced and marked by achievements that tend towards the monumental. The writers were of an encyclopedic cast, for example, Alexandru Odobescu (1834-1895), who wrote historical short stories and "Pseudokynegetikos", a witty essay, and especially Bogdan Petriceicu Hașdeu, who started a new stage in Romanian history, archeology and linguistics, as well as in paleography and the study of folklore, and who moreover published poetry, prose, and a historical drama, *Răzvan and Vidra*. Odobescu furthermore brought out *Revista Română (The Romanian Review*, 1861) and Hașdeu: *Traian (Trajan*, 1869), *Columna lui Traian (Trajan's Column*, 1870), *Revista Nouă (The New Review*, 1887) as well as other papers and reviews. It was in the *Revista Română* that Nicolae Filimon (1819-1865) published the first great Romanian novel, *Upstarts, Old and New*. Ion Ghica (1816-1897) contributed economic studies to the periodicals of the Union period and gave proof of a vigorous talent in his letters to V. Alecsandri of a later date.

From the late seventies until well after the first years of the eighties, the Junimea society with its review *Convorbiri Literare (The Literary Talks*, 1876) to which nearly all the great writers of the time contributed, was the center of Romanian literature. It was owing to the Junimea society and in particular to Titu Maiorescu (1840-1917), the founder of Romanian literary criticism, that literature was rigorously set apart from culture as a whole and, at the same time, rose to the level of world literature, thanks to such writers as Eminescu, Creangă, Caragiale, Slavici, and Coşbuc. Though partially tainted by philosophic and socio-political concepts that run counter to progressive scientific thought, Maiorescu's ideas brought about a remarkable transformation in various spheres of culture, disparaging all forms that had no content, as well as imposture, and installing the predominance of good sense and truth. The critic made of aesthetic achievement the only criterion in the appreciation of literature, establishing a definite boundary between literary value and non-value. His contribution to the creation of style in criticism was also decisive. The Junimea period has been described as the classical age of Romanian literature for the first truly great writers who created works of lasting value made a name for themselves at the time.

The poet of love and death, and of great emotion before the secrets of the universe, a brilliant mind tortured by the eternal problems of existence, a heart seething with emotion, with an intense feeling for the transient glory of the world, and an ardent, overwhelming love for the country, Mihail Eminescu (1850-1889) invested the Romanian language with an unsuspected splendor and expressiveness. Eminescu reached the highest rung of literary value — a rung which no other Romanian poet has reached so far, in his love poems, satires, the poem *"Evening Star"* and a number of great unfinished poems — "Memento Mori", "Mureşeanu", etc. — as well as in his prose that has mostly a fantastic quality about it.

In his prose — stories, fairy-tales, recollections from childhood — Ion Creangă (1837-1889) portrayed a patriarchal world where reality and myth are inextricably linked and where the people's heart shows an archaic quality.

Ion Luca Caragiale (1852—1912) best known as a playwright — *A Stormy Night, The Lost Letter, Leonida Versus Reaction*, etc. — also wrote short stories and sketches, depicting contemporary society and its evils, but at the same time creating deathless characters of universal value. Ion Slavici (1848-1925) wrote short stories — *Father Tanda, The Mill of Luck and Plenty*, etc. — and novels, *Mara* among others. He was a great and substantial creator, a kind of Balzac of the Transylvanian countryside. In Duiliu Zamfirescu (1858-1922) the

world of great landowners and in no small part of the Wallachian peasantry found a painter of great sensitiveness who was
also endowed with a sharp critical spirit, which, however,
was channeled unilaterally against the big lessees, the old boyar
class being absolved of every fault and even idealized: *Life
in the Country*, *Tănase Scatiu*, etc. George Coşbuc (1866—1918)
revealed an Arcadian Transylvania, with young men as strong
as the oak and girls lithe as ears of corn: *Ballads and Idylls*,
*Spun Yarn*, etc. It was also under the auspices of the Junimea
society that Barbu Delavrancea (1858-1918) entered the world
of literature, though ultimately he opposed the movement.
He was a prose writer and playwright who gave us *The
Setting Sun*, a remarkable historical drama depicting the greatest age of Moldavia's history, and thus contributing to
the patriotic education of wide circles of readers and specta-
tors.

The leaders of the Junimea movement, whose principles
were contested from the first years of its existence, were the
butt of uninterrupted attacks towards the end of the century.
Promoting classical and romantic values and not very receptive to new ideas, to renovating tendencies, the movement
gradually lost its influence during the new, most eventful
historical period when social contradictions were becoming
ever more acute and art was feverishly seeking a new language.
The literary orientation of *Convorbiri Literare* was criticized by
the review *Literatorul (The Literate*, 1880), edited by Al. Macedonski (1854-1920), while the theoretical, ideological, and
aesthetic positions of the Junimea movement were combated
by C. Dobrogeanu-Gherea in the *Contemporanul (The Contemporary*, 1881).

Accusing the *Convorbiri Literare*, without reason, of having
given literature a regional, Moldavian bent, and of having
impelled it towards the influence of German culture, the
*Literatorul* tended to install the supremacy of the *Wallachian*
spirit, resuming Eliade Rădulescu's ideas, and of placing
Romanian culture within the sphere of Latin, mainly French,
spirituality, whose art was then undergoing most interesting
metamorphoses. Macedonski considered symbolism, particularly the symbolist version described as instrumentalism, as the
ultimate expression of the human mind and consequently endeavored to propagate symbolist ideas in Romanian poetry.

His efforts were not without some effect, though he himself, despite his endeavors, did not succeed in becoming a genuine symbolist poet but remained a great romantic in his lasting works: *Excelsior, Sacred Flowers, The Poem of Rondels*. Actually the pioneers of symbolism were Ştefan Petică (1877-1904) with his ethereal, seraphic vision, and Dimitrie Anghel (1872-1914), the poet of flowers, of the sea, of remembrances.

The spokesmen of symbolism in Romania considered symbolism as the only genuine poetry, the only art which could link up the most divergent poetical formulae. Consequently, Romanian symbolism was not a homogeneous current, its unity relying only upon the desire to be different from the poetry of former days. When it had fully crystallized, that is approximately between 1905 and 1916, its main representatives were Ion Minulescu (1881-1944) and George Bacovia (1881-1957), poets of a widely different nature, the former a demonstrative extrovert yearning for great spaces *(Romances for a Later Date, Talking to Myself, I Am not what I Seem to Be)*, the latter far more profound, searching into the abysmal depths of the spirit, one of the damned with a morbid sensitivity, haunted and yearning for "another world" *(Lead, Yellow Sparks)*. Romanian lyrical poetry enriched its register through symbolism, and also increased and perfected its means of expression while the whole structure was changed in pace with modern European poetry.

The review of the Socialist movement in full process of expansion — *Contemporanul (The Contemporary)* — set forth a materialist aesthetic conception rooted in Taine, in the Russian revolutionary democrats, and in historical materialism, in opposition to the aesthetics of the Junimea movement which was inspired by German idealist philosophy: Schopenhauer, Hegel, Vischer, and Hartmann. Considering a work of art as a "product", C. Dobrogeanu-Gherea contended that in order to understand and to place it, it was necessary to study the causes that had given rise to it, to establish what influence it exercised on society and only after that to analyze its artistic structure. In 1886 Gherea engaged in polemics with Titu Maiorescu that made a considerable impact on the problem of personality and of morality in art — problems which during the last decade of the past century and later, well after 1900, were again taken up by writers, critics, and publicists in such periodicals as *Viața (The Life)*, *Adevărul (The Truth)*, *Lumea Nouă (The New World)*, *Evenimentul Literar (The Literary Event)*. While opposing views were confronted, the discussion embraced the very nature of art and its relation to social life, the Junimea spokesmen pleading in favor of "art for art's sake" and the socialist publications steadily defending the theory of "tendentious art". Gherea was the first in Romania to have practiced analytical criticism, thus inaugurating a method which was to be adopted not only by his followers but also by the continuers of Maiorescu, though the latter made substantial correctives to it. The ideas propagated by the *Contemporanul* exercised a vast influence on the writers who were perfecting their skill at the time, and not only on those who, like D. Th. Neculuță, remained faithful to the ideals of their youth their whole life through, or who preserved the memory of those ideals to the end, as Ibrăileanu did, but even on those who did not believe in socialist concepts or who only did so at the beginning of their career and subsequently abandoned them.

In the early years of the twentieth century the process where by literature was integrated into social life continued with increased intensity, though partly tainted by confusion, especially after the socialist party was dissolved in 1899. Currents arose at the time tending to impel literature towards aims of a more general nature — social or ethical aims —, and attaching less importance to its specific structure and evolutive tendencies. There were also currents which tended to put literature into the service of interests contrary to social progress. Reviews such as *Semănătorul (The Sower*, 1901) and *Viața Românească (The Romanian Life*, 1906) brought together writers who had common political ideas rather than artistic affinities. Founded by Al. Vlahuță (1858-1919) and G. Coșbuc, with the support of Spiru Haret, Minister of Public Education, but actually guided by N. Iorga from its second year of existence to 1906, the *Semănătorul* advocated a type of literature that should be rooted in things essentially Romanian — the village, the peasant, a patriarchal world. The *Semănătorul* refused to accept outside influences and wanted literature to be a factor of moral chastisement, of "improvement", with all the forces of the nation drawn into it. Though indisputably sound, the ideas advocated by *Semănătorul* were tainted by a narrow nationalist, retrograde bent. Iorga with the prestige of his fascinating personality, succeeded in rallying round him gifted writers — Mihail Sadoveanu, St. O. Iosif, Panait Cerna, Ion Agârbiceanu — whose works do not wholly reflect the ideology of the review; indeed, they occasionally went against what was retrograde in that ideology. It was only certain obscure writers who expressed those retrograde aspects in writings that were bound to fall into oblivion. Through the collaboration of the great writers mentioned above, the *Semănătorul* was able to publish creditable works continuing the traditions of the literature inspired by the living realities of the homeland and imbued with a popular spirit, like *Dacia Literară* of old. *Viaţa Românească* made it its aim to create literature with a pronounced popular and national character, though it oriented the writers towards problems of great present-day interest and not towards idealization of life in the countryside, towards remembrances of the past. This review pointed to the social aspects of peasant life, but its deficiency consisted in neglecting the town, the proletariat, and the contradictions between workers and capitalists. While *Semănătorul* advocated romanticism looking back to the past, *Viaţa Românească*, within certain limits, stimulated realism. The mistake made by the doctrinaires of this review, who were prominent personalities of Romanian culture (Stere and Ibrăileanu), was a consequence of their endorsement of populism, an ideological current which considered the peasantry as the motive force of social transformation, and underestimated the working class. Like the followers of the *Semănătorul* movement, Stere and Ibrăileanu considered that literature had to express the specific shade of Romanian spiritual life, which for them was predominantly rural in its spirit, rura life also being a source of inspiration, while the town was tol them "part and parcel of cosmopolis". While propagating political and ideological concepts that have been invalidated by social and historical evolution, concepts derived from small bourgeois illusions — *Viaţa Românească* at the same time gave Romanian society valuable, long-lasting literature; it was a wide forum for the broadcasting of advanced democratic and progressive ideas with a beneficial influence on the development of culture. Most of the outstanding writers of the first two decades of our century contributed to it, among them being Calistrat Hogaş, Al. I. Brătescu-Voineşti, Mihail Sadoveanu, Gala Galaction, Ion Agârbiceanu, Tudor Arghezi, and Gheorghe Topîrceanu.

The Transylvanian review *Luceafărul (The Evening Star)*, which appeared in Budapest in 1902 and was transferred to Sibiu a few years after, showed an orientation similar to that of *Viaţa Românească*. *Luceafărul* was a factor of cultural promotion in Transylvania, at the same time cementing the spiritual unity of the Romanian people, for writers from the other Romanian territories published articles in it. The translations published in *Luceafărul* brought to the attention of the Romanian public outstanding Hungarian and world writers of distinction.

In the early years of the century the tendency shown by the *Semănătorul* and the populist movements to isolate Romanian literature from Europe's artistic movement was opposed with growing staunchness by the symbolist poetry which fully triumphed around 1910 and was later to generate the so-called modernist currents.

## 4. The Arts

AT the close of the eighteenth century and during the first decades of the nineteenth profound transformations occurred in the evolution of the fine arts as a result of a more accentuated trend in Romanian society towards a modern culture of European type. In architecture the neo-classical style predominated as an expression of the new tendencies. The traditional forms of religious architecture were combined with classical elements, especially in the ornamentation of monuments. Occasionally even the plan of the buildings was imbued with the classical spirit, examples in point being the "Round" Church of Leţcani in Jassy which dates from around 1795 and the "Teiul Doamnei" Church of 1833. Civil architecture was considerably developed. The Palace of Treasurer Ion Cantacuzino of Jassy, which was to become the residence of the ruling Prince Alexandru Callimachi (1795-1799), the monumental palace erected in Jassy during the reign of Alexandru Moruzi (1806), Dinicu Golescu's house in Bucharest (1815), the palace of Ghica-Tei (1822), are all specific of the architectural framework within which the boyars of those days lived. The best-known architects of the first half of the nineteenth century were Johann Freywald, who had come from Vienna and worked both in Jassy and in Bucharest, Alexandru Costinescu, professor at the Jassy Academy after 1838, and Jacob Melic. The National Theater of Bucharest, designed by the Viennese Joseph Heft and inaugurated in 1852, also belonged to the neo-classical style.

The most representative of the Romanian classical architects was Alexandru Orăscu (1817-1894), graduate of the Munich Academy (1847), who built the old University Palace of Bucharest from 1857 to 1869. With the Romantic taste for the Middle Ages, the neo-Gothic style spread also in the Principalities. Substituting a fanciful Gothic for the old autochthonous traditions, architect Johann Schlatter rebuilt the Bistritza and Tismana monasteries after 1844. Liebrecht House, today University House, was also built in neo-Gothic style roundabout 1860. Side by side with neo-classical and neo-Gothic buildings, the less ambitious townspeople built in a style specific to the towns of old, reminiscent of their peasant traditions, with a veranda closed in with glass.

During the last decades of the nineteenth century, with cultural and social life developing steadily, impressive buildings were erected in Bucharest, mostly in French style. This gave a certain unity to the evolution of urban architecture at that moment. The more remarkable of those buildings are the Romanian Atheneum (1888) by architect Albert Galleron, the Palace of Justice (1895) built by A. Ballu in the style of the French Renaissance, the Ministry of Agriculture (1896) and the Faculty of Medicine (1902) by Louis Blanc, the Savings Bank (1900) by Paul Gottereau, and the General Post Office (1900) by Alexandru Săvulescu.

Ion Mincu (1851-1912) devoted his life to the creation of a modern Romanian style in this country's architecture by an interpretation of old Romanian architectural forms, going thus against the eclecticism of his contemporaries. His aesthetic program was shown by his first buildings: Lahovari House (1886) and the "Bufet" restaurant in the Kiselef Road in Bucharest. But his most important achievement was the Central Girls' School in Bucharest (1890). Following in Mincu's way, the architects of the next generation were to make their contribution to the creation of the so-called neo-Romanian style which was a cultural phenomenon of incontestable vitality though it rarely led to great artistic achievements.

Sculpture had for a long time played a secondary part, being confined to the decoration of the residences of the ruling princes and of the boyars or of the funeral monuments with allegorical figures carved by native craftsmen. As an example we might cite Grigore Sturdza's monument at the Frumoasa monastery in Jassy (1842). The revolution of 1848 was decisive in the history of Romanian sculpture as it gave rise to an art with loftier cultural and aesthetic aims. After 1846 funds were collected in Bucharest for a statue of Gheorghe Lazăr to be made by Ion Costande, an artist of Sibiu trained in Vienna. On Cezar Bolliac's initiative, the revolutionary government of 1848 later decided to erect the statues of Michael the Brave, Tudor Vladimirescu, and Gheorghe Lazăr. These were projects which only came to be realized later. However, immediately after Bibescu's overthrow, a statue of Liberty was erected in Bucharest by an adherent of the revolutionary movement.

The first Bucharest sculptor to create works of notable artistic interest was Karl Storck (1826-1887), who was also the first sculpture professor at the Bucharest School of Fine Arts. One of his pupils, Ion Georgescu (1856-1898), continued his studies in Paris from 1879 to 1882. Well-balanced and sensitive, Georgescu was a delicate modeller with a remarkable intuition in portraiture. He is the most celebrated Romanian sculptor of the nineteenth century. His works include a bust of *Mihail Pascaly* (1882), a statue of *Gheorghe Lazăr*, both in Bucharest (1886), and one of *Gheorghe Asachi* in Jassy (1890). His contemporary, Ştefan Ionescu-Valbudea (1856-1918), highly temperamental, left a small number of works greatly appreciated: *Michael the Madman* (1885) and *The Sleep*.

Dimitrie Paciurea (1875-1932) gave a full measure of his great talent from the very beginning of his career when he carved his *Giant* (1906), a piece of work showing a grandiose romantic impetuosity. In his *Assumption of the Virgin* (Stolojan Chapel in the Bellu cemetery), the artist undertook an interesting attempt to find in sculpture an equivalent for the stylizing of Byzantine painting. Paciurea's busts show exceptional sensitiveness for the luminous vibration of matter as

well as for the minute shades of spiritual life, and to a certain
extent recall Rodin's impressionist art. Withdrawn from
society towards the end of his life, the artist created fantastic
figures which he invested with a symbolism sometimes abs-
truse: *The God of War, The Chimera of Space*. On the other
hand, Fritz Storck (1872-1942) was a classic both by training
and temperament. His works are of great variety, the portraits
being perhaps the most durable: *The Artist's Wife* (1909),
the poet *Alexandru Macedonski* (1917).

In painting as in architecture, the decisive moment for
modern Romanian art was that of the contact with neo-classicism. It was in Moldavia that religious painting first entered
upon a period of neo-classicism, illustrated especially by the
works of Eustatie Altini (ca. 1772-1815). A pupil of the
Vienna Academy, Altini painted from 1802 to 1814 a number
of altar screens, the most remarkable being in Saint Spiridon
Church in Jassy (1813). Altini took up and developed the
traditions of the easel portrait which were spread in the Romanian countries in the eighteenth century. It is also to him that
we owe a great composition in the pre-romantic spirit: *The
Ordaining of Veniamin Costache* (1813). The pre-romantic touch
is also specific to the works of Mihail Töpler, who painted
the portraits of Bucharest society people under Constantine
Ypsilanti and Ion Caragea. From 1820 to 1840 religious
painting was practiced in Wallachia by Nicolae Polcov-
nicul, who was also a meritorious portraitist, having painted
the portraits of Mihail Manu's family in the Leordeni
Church (1825).

In 1812 Gheorghe Asachi returned from Italy and subsequently he was to make a considerable contribution to Romanian
culture. While in Rome from 1808 to 1812 he was admitted
in Canova's studio and came in close touch with some of
the main Italian painters of the time. His artistic training is
shown by his drawing at the library of the Romanian Academy.
After 1830 Asachi played an important part in guiding artistic activities in Moldavia and moreover published historical
studies which helped to rouse the national consciousness
(*Stephen the Great's Mother*, 1833). Painter, lithographer,
and publicist, Constantin Lecca (1807-1887), a Transylvanian
who settled in Craiova and later in Bucharest, spread the taste
for historical themes during the period of the revolution of

1848 and of the Union *(Michael the Brave's Death,* 1845, *Michael the Brave's Entry in Alba Iulia,* 1857). Despite Asachi's efforts, no painter of historical compositions came to the fore from among the pupils of the painting class of the Jassy Academy. Gheorghe Lemeni (1813-1847) and Gheorghe Panaiteanu (1816-1900), who were sent to study abroad, were portrait painters. Portrait painting was indeed the main genre in Romanian painting during the first half of the nineteenth century. Romanian society came to be keen on portraits, a taste which was satisfied by Anton Chladek (1794-1882) in Bucharest and Niccoló Livaditti (1804-1857) in Jassy.

The three painters who participated in the revolutionary movement in Wallachia — Ion Negulici (1812-1851), C. D. Rosenthal (1820-1851) and Barbu Iscovescu (1814-1854) were also mainly portraitists: Rosenthal is well-known for two canvases dedicated to the revolution, *Romania Breaking Her Shackles on Liberty Field* and *Revolutionary Romania.* Iscovescu painted a valuable series of portraits of the leaders of the Romanian revolution in Transylvania, including *Avram Iancu.* Portrait painting, owing to these three revolutionary painters, was invested with a representative and symbolic function. Devoted to the cause to the end, Negulici and Iscovescu died in exile and Rosenthal in an Austrian prison.

Gheorghe Tattarescu (1818-1894) was for a number of years the best known artist in the country after his return from Italy in 1852. With him, neo-classical religious painting was finally crystallized, even dropping into stereotyped methods. His revolutionary ideas found expression in his canvas *Romania Awakes* and in Nicolae Bălcescu's portrait, which he painted in Paris in 1851 where the great historian was in exile. In water color, Carol Popp de Szathmari (1812-1888) produced works of great variety, rich in spontaneous touches, for several decades after 1831 when he first appeared in Bucharest. An indefatigable traveler interested in Romanian scenery, and also in the exotic landscape of the Near East, Szathmari gave proof of a remarkable gift in revealing the charm of contemporary life.

When he exhibited a self-portrait at the Paris Salon of 1853, Theodor Aman (1831-1891), who was to remain in the

French capital until 1858, won a reputation afterwards brilliantly confirmed. In the years that preceded the Union he sent to Bucharest canvases such as *The Last Night of Michael the Great* (1852) and *The Union of the Principalities* (1857), which also brought him well-deserved fame. After the Union Aman and Tattarescu obtained from the authorities the establishment of a school of fine arts in Bucharest (1864). In Jassy a similar institution had been created in 1860, with G. Panaiteanu as director. Portraitist as well as painter of historical scenes, domestic scenes and landscapes, Aman left us works of unequal value but real achievements in all branches of the art. His great composition which he left unfinished — *The Boyars' Feast Surprised by Vlad the Impaler's Soldiers* — is remarkable owing to its fresh colors and the dynamism of its interpretation. The Bucharest society found in Aman an attentive observer well able to give to his canvases the significant details which define a specific environment. His etchings, with the same themes as his paintings, form an essential chapter in the history of Romanian engraving.

The first exhibitions of living artists organized in Bucharest (1865-1868) were given but an indifferent reception, the critics confining themselves to conventional comments. In 1870, however, when Nicolae Grigorescu (1838-1907), exhibited here for the first time, things were altogether different. Heated discussions were aroused by the work of the young painter, similar to those which Manet and his friends, the impressionists, gave rise to in France. Two concepts then assumed distinct forms in Romanian art and were to face each other for several decades: those of Aman and the followers of Academic painting, and those of Grigorescu under whose influence the most gifted pupils of the School of Fine Arts were to develop. Grigorescu was reproached for his pictorial form neglecting the exigencies of a sterile Academism. After an early career as a painter of religious themes, during which time the artist had occasionally risen above the formulae of a belated neo-classicism, he spent long years of study in France (1861-1869). The museums, the romantic art, Courbet, Corot, the Barbizon painters had widened his outlook, as the Paris School of Fine Arts attended by him for some time, had been unable to do. Some of his major works — *The Chailly Guard, Rocky Landscape at Fontainebleau* — date from those years.

After 1870 Grigorescu traveled about his own country as well as abroad — in Italy in 1873 and 1874, in France in 1876 and 1877 — and new experiences gave rise to a long succession of masterpieces: *The Hearth at Rucăr*, 1870; *The Gipsy of Ghergani*, 1872; *Cloaked Jew*, 1874; his first series of studies from Vitré, 1876. In 1877 he returned home for the War of Independence. Hundreds of drawings and studies of outstanding merit date from this war, showing soldiers in camp and in the trenches, officers' portraits, and convoys of Turkish prisoners. After 1878 Grigorescu resumed his journeys to France and lived there from 1882 to 1884. This was the period of full maturity during which he produced studies set in Brittany: *Old Woman Sewing, Fisherwoman of Grandville*. In 1887 he returned to his country and lived at Posada and later at Cîmpina, dedicating the last two decades of his life to the Romanian village which found in Grigorescu its most profound poet: *The Inn at Orăţii*, 1887; *Joyful Peasant Girl*, 1894; *Hills and Dales*, 1896.

Grigorescu's canvases exhibited in Bucharest aroused the vocation for painting in Ion Andreescu (1850-1882). He began painting in 1873 and his artistic skill, especially in landscape painting, won him a place among the European masters of his generation. After an initial period spent in Buzău, where he painted some of his most memorable canvases — *The Drăgaica Fair, Winter in the Woods* — he spent some time in France in 1879 and again in 1882, where he came to know the great art of his age and especially impressionism. Though he showed affinities with Sisley and especially with Pissarro, his profoundly original vision remained unimpaired as shown by his canvases *Beech Forest* and *Winter at Barbizon*. While Grigorescu's works are characterized by a comprehensive register dominated by a serene harmony, Andreescu's world is the creation of a solitary spirit possessed by a melancholy that found no surcease and which the genius of the painter also transmitted to the world of plants, depicting leafless trees and roses that seem to vibrate with a presentiment of extinction.

A pupil of Aman, who later studied in Paris, Sava Henţia (1848-1904) can also be said to have some real achievements to his credit — figures studies and still lifes — influenced by Grigorescu. G. Demetrescu-Mirea (1854-1934) had a similar training but, more audacious in his aspirations, he took up historical and allegorical compositions as, *Michael the Brave Looking at Andreas Bathory's Head* and *The Lonely Peak*. Ultimately he allowed himself to fall into the temptation of painting fashionable portraits in the manner of Carolus Durand. More genuine in his narrow provincial circle, was the painter C. D. Stahi (1844-1920), pupil of G. Panaiteanu, and like him, trained at the Munich Academy. His still lifes sometimes have an aura of poetry about them,

Ştefan Luchian (1868-1916) is generally considered to have blazed the path of twentieth century Romanian painting. After studying at the Academies in Bucharest and Munich, he found in Paris in 1891-1892 an environment that proved to be most favorable to his development: impressionism on its way to being finally accepted by the public, in particular Manet's art, Degas's pastels, and the symbolist primitivism of Gauguin. It was here that he discovered his own personal path, far removed from the routine of the Salon, and definitely modern: *The Last Autumn Race* (1892). Actually Grigorescu's example had already guided him towards independence and back home he continued to consider Grigorescu as his forerunner and master. Luchian played a most important part in organizing the first exhibition of Romanian independent artists in 1896 and in the setting up of the *Ileana Society* in 1897. After 1902 he participated in the exhibitions of the society "Artistic Youth", indeed he was one of the founders of that society. Serious financial difficulties and poor health deepened the artist's sensitivity, without depriving him of his love of humanity and of nature. His sympathy with the humble and the wronged found expression in such works as *Old Nicolae the Cobza Player* and *When Maize Is Shared Out* (1905). Some of his works were inspired by the peasant uprising *(The End,* 1907). In his pathetic self-portraits, the landscape of *Brebu* (1908) and *Moineşti* (1909), in the flowers he painted, especially during the last period of his career, his exquisite draftsmanship and the expressiveness of his colors, built up a spiritual message of uncommon elevation.

The impact of Grigorescu, Andreescu, and Luchian, as well as of Petraşcu, on the later generation, contributed considerably to defining the specific features of the Romanian School of Painting. Echoes of Grigorescu however in a sentimental and idyllic form are to be found in artists of lesser significance such as Ipolit Strîmbu (1871-1934) and Arthur Verona (1868-1946). Belonging to the same generation, Nicolae Vermont (1866-1932) gave proof of more personality in genre painting and engraving.

Octav Băncilă (1872—1944), a Jassy artist trained at Munich, painted significant canvases dedicated to the peasant uprisings of 1907 and to the life and claims of the proletariat: *1907*, *Peace*. Militant draftsmanship developed creditably during this period. Reviews such as *Adevărul (The Truth)*, *Furnica (The Ant)*, *Viaţa Socială (The Social Life)*, *Facla (The Torch)*, *Cronica (The Chronicle)* published satirical drawings showing vigorous social criticism, particularly on the occasion of the uprisings of 1907. The nineteenth century press also published such drawings but it was only with Ary Murnu (b. 1881), Francisc Şirato (1877-1953), and especially Iosif Iser (1881-1958) that they entered the sphere of art. The art of engraving reached a high technical and aesthetic level during this period, owing especially to Gabriel Popescu (1866-1937). Dedicating himself mostly to interpretation engraving, Gabriel Popescu has left masterpieces such as *The Battle of Anghiari* (1914).

The changes which occured in social life in the early nineteenth century, brought about the emergence of a musical art which was national and no longer only religious. The interpretative art as well as composition both made great strides. Ever closer contact with Western Europe caused music to shed its oriental reminiscence, transformed public taste and consequently a new musical life and new musical works emerged to meet the exigencies of a new public.

The foundations of an artistic education were laid by the *School of the Philharmonic Society* which opened in 1834 under the leadership of Ion Eliade Rădulescu (to be transformed into the School of Vocal and Instrumental Music (1835-1837), with Ion Andrei Wachmann as Headmaster) and by the Philharmonic and Dramatic Conservatory (1836-1838) founded by Gheorghe Asachi. When the Music and the Declamation Conservatories were founded in Jassy in 1860 and in Bucharest in 1864, Romanian musical training evolved systematically and continuously and no longer haphazardly.

The objectives were shortly reached in full. In 1866 the first symphony concerts were held and in 1868 a permanent orchestra, conducted by Eduard Wachmann, was inaugurated in Bucharest under the name of *Romanian Philharmonic Society*. The orchestra performed with fair regularity up to the War of Independence and then resumed its activities in 1881.

Musical life developed promisingly in various sectors: choirs were formed, the most important of which was the *Carmen Society* (1901) founded and conducted by D. G. Kiriac (1866-1928), as well as the first chamber music orchestra (Constantin Dimitrescu's string quartet, 1880, and Dimitrie Dinicu's quartet, 1897), while the first musical revues were staged and the first Romanian opera company was built up on the initiative of George Stephănescu (1843-1925). The company played for several seasons after 1885. Thus the foundations of a Romanian opera had been laid. Most of the singers were graduates of the Bucharest Conservatory and some of them gained European recognition, among them Hariclea Hartulari-Darclée (1860-1939), Elena Teodorini (1857-1926), Dimitrie Popovici-Bayreuth (1860-1927), Giovanni Dumitrescu (ca. 1860-1907), etc.

In the Romanian territories under Habsburg rule Romanian songs were cultivated, and national ideas and aspirations were propagated by the singers' reunions and the choir societies conducted by outstanding personalities such as Gheorghe Dima (1847-1925), Iacob Mureșianu (1857-1917), Ion Vidu (1863-1931), Ciprian Porumbescu (1853-1883), Isidor Vorobchievici (1836-1903), and others.

The development of musical life brought a flourishing original creation in its train. The first composers were Alexandru Flechtenmacher (1823-1898), who composed the first Romanian operetta *The Old Witch* —, I. A. Wachmann (1807-1863), Carol Miculi (1821-1897), Ludovic Wiest (1819-1889), and Eduard Caudella (1841-1924), composer of the first

Romanian opera: *Petru Rareş*. It is to the merit of these composers to have combined popular melodies with a classical harmonic system, thus achieving a synthesis which was to prove its viability towards the close of the century when the choirs of Gavril Muzicescu (1847-1903) inspired by the peasant folklore gave the first adequate interpretation of the modal particularities of folk songs and paved the way for a specific musical language.

# Part 4

# CONTEMPORARY  HISTORY

# CHAPTER I

# Romania Between the Two World Wars (1918—1939)

AFTER the Romanian national state had been recognized by the treaties of peace, a process of comparative consolidation took place in Romania through economic rehabilitation, agrarian reform, and unification of the legislative system.

In the years following World War I new political parties and groupings came into being. The working class, the revolutionary and progressive movement in the country, took a growing part in politics. An important event was the creation in May, 1921, of the Romanian Communist Party which was to lead the great political actions of the proletariat, culminating in the fightings at Lupeni, Grivița, and in the Prahova Valley. After the crisis of the years 1929 to 1933 the national economy recovered, and in 1938 some industries attained the highest production level ever known.

In February, 1938, when a royal dictatorship was established, the functions of Parliament were greatly narrowed while at the same time a number of laws restricted civil rights and liberty.

In foreign policy Romania pursued the general line promoted by the League of Nations which guaranteed the territorial status quo and proclaimed the principles of international law guaranteeing self-determination and equality of rights between countries — principles which the Romanian state has always endorsed.

## 1. Romania from 1919 to 1929

THE Romanian national state, in whose creation the entire people had taken part, was recognized by the Peace Conference in Paris which opened on January 18, 1919, to settle the many economic, financial, and territorial problems which the nations of Europe now had to face, and especially the political organization of postwar Europe. All Romanian provinces were now united, and a national, socio-economic and political framework had been created for the more rapid development of the productive forces, for the stimulation of the energy and creative capacities of the people.

The dominant position of the Allied Powers at the peace conference made them in effect an international caucus dictating their views to the whole world. They imposed onerous conditions upon the defeated states, and even the smaller allied countries were deprived of rights previously enjoyed. This was also the case of Romania. Under the pretext that the Romanian government had concluded a separate peace with the enemy in 1918 and the United States had not signed the secret treaty with Romania in 1916, the great powers allowed her only the status of a country with "special interests" at the peace conference.

The sort of treatment meted out to Romania at the peace conference is clearly shown in the memorial which the Romanian governmental delegation submitted to the Supreme Allied Council on July 21, 1919:" . . . From the first Romania's representatives to the peace conference were surprised to see that, without any valid reason, the number of delegates allowed to Romania was inferior to that of other allied states such as Belgium and Serbia. The Romanian delegation, however, abstained from objecting to a decision which might seem merely formal at that moment. But they were still more surprised to find that the frontiers recognized in the treaty concluded with France, Great Britain and Italy in 1916 were now disputed."

N. Titulescu who had studied "all the correspondence and talks between France, Britain, the United States and Italy" at the peace conference and had quoted from the "famous talks between the Four — Clemenceau, Wilson, Lloyd George and Orlando — taken down in shorthand by Mantoux," telegraphed King Carol II: "To begin with I was affected to see how little space Romanian problems were allowed among so many other much less important ones. In the second place I must confess that Romania's position in the light of these documents is exasperating."

During the peace conference problems of the greatest concern to Romania were discussed and settled without the participation of her delegates. Only after repeated protests from the Romanian delegation were they allowed to participate in the conference working committees. The delegation was first headed by I. I. C. Brătianu, then by Nicolae Mişu, General Coandă, Al. Vaida Voevod, and Nicolae Titulescu. The Romanian protest was supported by the French delegation from political and economic motives.

The Peace Treaties of Versailles (June 28, 1919), Saint-Germain (December 9, 1919), Neuilly (November 27, 1919), Trianon (June 4, 1920), and Sèvres (August 10, 1920) were of the utmost importance to Romania's international position. Although on the whole those treaties imposed the domination of the victorious great powers over the capitalist world, they recognized the creation of a number of national states and the rounding-off of others (such as Romania, Yugoslavia, and Czechoslovakia) in Central and South-East Europe. These profound transformations in the life of the European peoples were the result of the struggle of those peoples against the old retrograde empires of the Habsburgs and the Tsars.

The great powers recognized Romania's northern and western frontiers, but their policies often infringed the independence and sovereignty of the country by interference in its internal affairs.

Romania was obliged to assume financial obligations amounting to over 5,000 million francs in gold on the grounds that the Romanian state was liable for part of the debts of the Austro-Hungarian state, or as a "liberation" contribution. Important advantages, mainly of an economic nature, had to be conceded to the great western powers.

Bessarabia's incorporation into the Romanian state was sanctioned on October 28, 1920, by the treaty concluded by Britain, France, Italy, and Japan on the one side, and Romania on the other.

The provisions of the treaties, and also the policy of concessions promoted by the representatives of the Romanian exploiting classes, caused Romania to be dependent on the great western imperialist powers.

This also accounts for the affirmative answer given by the Romanian rulers to the leaders of the Entente, who asked them to provide armed forces in order to help put down the Hungarian proletarian revolution in March, 1919. Alarmed at the possibility of the spreading of revolutionary ideas and of the growing struggle of the working class, as a result of which the revolutionary movement might be victorious in Central and South-East Europe, the Allied Powers overthrew the power of the Hungarian proletariat, drawing the armies of the neighboring bourgeois states — the Romanian, Czechoslovak, and Yugoslav states — into interventionist action and supporting the counter-revolutionaries in Hungary.

Romanian reaction consequently responded to the call of the Hungarian reactionaries and helped them to put down the proletarian revolution, although Bela Kun, in his capacity as foreign affairs commissar in the Hungarian revolutionary government, in a proclamation to the Czechoslovak, Yugoslav, and Romanian governments declared "repeatedly and solemnly that we do not uphold the principle of territorial integrity and now bring to your knowledge that we recognize unreservedly all your national territorial claims." On August 4, 1919 the Romanian royal army entered Budapest and remained there until the spring of the following year.

The Romanian proletariat, the revolutionary movement of Romania, opposed this intervention with determination, firmly denouncing it and supporting the Hungarian councils. The international activities of the Romanian working masses took place under conditions of revolutionary upsurge, the result of the aggravation of internal contradictions during the years of the First World War and of the victory of the Great October Socialist Revolution. They went hand in hand with the defense of Soviet Russia, and with a fearless struggle against the native bourgeoisie and for economic and political rights.

Romania's main problems after World War I were economic recovery and the internal consolidation of the state, primarily by the unification of legislation throughout the country. In foreign affairs the country's territorial integrity had to be defended and the status quo maintained.

A serious economic crisis with deep-lying social and political implications arose from the loss of men and materials, the destruction and disorganization of production and transport, the occupation of the greater part of the country by the central powers, and not least from war expenditure.

The prices of principal foodstuffs had increased from four to six times compared with prewar, and some of them had gone up to twenty times what they were in the first year of the war. Inflation and expenditure in support of the counter-revolutionary intervention in Hungary made everything dearer still. The condition of the working class grew worse following the declaration of a state of emergency and the militarization of industries.

The revolutionary upsurge grew in intensity, and strikes were frequent in various branches of industry and in different areas, culminating in the country-wide general strike of 1920 during which over 400,000 workers went out.

One of the important problems to be settled was that of the peasants. Under pressure of the masses, in particular of the villagers, the rulers were compelled to take certain measures. The land reform was partially enacted in December, 1918, when a decree was issued expropriating a considerable part of the great landed estates. Land had been promised to the peasants at the front in the spring of 1917 and the land reform had been laid down in the Constitution in the summer of that same year, though without practical effect. The law was finally passed in 1921. Out of the 12,240,000 acres expropriated, with compensation, during the period following the passing of the land reform law, 6,928,000 acres were divided between nearly 1,500,000 million families, and the remainder of over 4 million acres of grass land and forest became village property to be used by the peasants on payment of a tax.

The land reform momentarily improved the condition of the peasant masses, restricting the power of the big landowners. It was an important step forward, ensuring as it did the development of the country. Nevertheless, social progress was checked by the fact that considerable areas still remained in the hands of the big landowners, by limitations in the law itself, and by the fact that it was not properly enforced.

In the same year an old claim of the masses for which the most advanced forces headed by the proletariat had agitated for many decades was met. The turnover tax was introduced, this being the main indirect tax.

Another important bourgeois democratic reform concerned the electoral system. In November, 1918, the census system was abolished and "universal suffrage by equal, direct, compulsory and secret ballot" was introduced, with provision for the representation of the minorities in every constituency. The election reform considerably enlarged the right of the masses to act in political life.

The statutes of co-existing nationalities were passed, equality in rights of all citizens, irrespective of nationality, being thus recognized in Romania.

Other measures which helped to strengthen the state and to palliate the material condition of the masses were the unification of the currency — the four coinages circulating in the country without cover were converted into lei — and the reorganization of railway transport through centralization and unification of railway administration.

These reforms and measures dealt a blow at the economic and political power of the most retrograde forces in the country and met some of the claims of the working masses; and they were actually achieved as a result of the action of the masses. A process of democratization was thus under way in various fields of political and economic life. Naturally the régime being based on the exploitation of man by man, the claims were met only partially, and the position of the dominant classes was maintained and strengthened. Furthermore the bourgeois-landlord authorities adopted a number of measures that struck at the revolutionary movement of the Romanian proletariat. The right to strike of the workers in state or private enterprises considered to be of public interest was limited, and the Trancu-Iași Law of September 5, 1920, banned the organization of workers in trade unions overtly directed by a political party.

On March 29, 1923, radical amendments were made to the Constitution, with a number of new articles and paragraphs introduced so that the Constitution could rightly be considered a new one. The four parts and 138 articles of the new Constitution, on the whole, voiced the views of the dominant classes, namely the bourgeoisie and landowners. At the same time it laid down a number of important claims put forward by the masses: the land reform, the electoral system, freedom of speech and assembly, freedom of the press, and equal rights for all citizens irrespective of nationality. There were, however, no real guarantees that the provisions of the Constitution would be put into effect.

A new period began in Romania after 1922: industry and the economy as a whole developed more rapidly, and there was comparative political stability.

Throughout the period of economic recovery, and in the years that followed it, a great struggle took place for the dominant positions in the national economy between Romanian capital — the National-Liberal Party — and the monopoly capital of the great western powers. The Romanian state endeavored to limit the penetration of foreign capital but was unable to resist the economic force and the means of political pressure of the big monopolies. Although the economic positions of the Romanian bourgeoisie were generally strengthened, Romania continued to be dependent on foreign capital.

Under the slogan of "by our own efforts", the Liberal government promoted a policy designed to develop the country's banking and industrial capital by giving priority to the Romanian upper bourgeoisie in the exploitation of the wealth of the country. Foreign capital invested in Romania had to surrender a large part of the shares issued to Romanian capitalists, or at least a part equal to that owned by foreign capitalists. Consequently, part of the profits made by the enterprises thus set up went to the Romanian capitalists.

The Mine Law passed by the Romanian Parliament in 1924 was a result of the "by our own efforts" policy. The Romanian bourgeoisie, who mostly supported the National-Liberal Party, did not sufficiently resist the pressure of the foreign monopolies so that shortly after the law had been passed the Romanian state was making important concessions to foreign capitalists.

From 1923 to 1928 Romanian industry was considerably advanced and diversified, although the consumer goods and the extractive industries still predominated. The share of industry in the social product and in the national revenue increased as a result of increased capital investments and of better equipment on the factory floor. By 1928 industrial output had gone up 56 per cent as against 1919.

The growth of the economic potentialities of the country is best shown by the figures referring to the extractive industries. In 1930 extracted crude oil amounted to 5,792,311 tons as against 968,611 tons in 1918, Romania taking the sixth place in the world. In 1927 lignite extraction amounted to 2,850,011 tons compared with 1,594,719 tons in 1921. In the same year output of natural gas reached nearly 217 million cu.m., and was to rise to 1,200 million cu.m. in 1930, compared with 144,242,051 cu.m. in 1921.

The state allotted subsidies to the industrial undertakings using at least 20 hp or employing at least ten workers. In 1919 there were 2,747 big enterprises in Romania whose aggregate capital totalled 2,834 million lei and which employed 157,424 hands; in 1928 there were 3,966 big enterprises aggregating a capital of 39,770 million lei and employing 206,547 people.

The process whereby production and capital were concentrated and centralized was speeded up after World War I. From 1924 to 1928 the total of socio-industrial capital rose from 18,800 million lei to 46,100 million lei — an increase of nearly 250 per cent. The number of companies with a capital of over 100 million lei also went up, accounting for 7.5 per cent of the total number of companies in 1928 and for over 73 per cent of the overall capital available in the country.

The rise in industrial production brought about a considerable increase in the numbers of the working class. During the three years from 1922 to 1926 the number of people employed in the extractive and the processing industries grew from 234,000 to 306,500, further rising to 450,000 in 1930.

Despite her industrial growth Romania continued to rank among the poorly developed industrial countries. Medium, small, and artisan enterprises still accounted for a considerable share of industrial production.

Although Romania's industrial potentialities increased perceptibly, her economy continued to be predominantly agricultural, with a low development level of productive forces.

Agriculture still accounted for the greatest share of the national economy. Grain production increased with every passing year, from 7,127,700 tons in 1921 to 12,083,900 tons in 1926 and 13,670,900 tons in 1929.

Romania's livestock amounted to a considerable figure: in 1922 there were in the country 5,700,000 head of cattle, and in 1924 there were 13 million sheep. Romania thus held fifth place in the world after the U.S.A., the U.S.S.R., Britain and Spain.

Although Romania's agricultural production had developed considerably during the interwar period, the material and social conditions of the working masses were most precarious. The land reform carried out by the bourgeoisie accentuated social differences in the countryside, increased the number of poor peasants and of the agricultural proletariat while strengthening the ranks of the kulaks. There were large numbers of landless peasants who continued to have a hard time working for the landowners, while those peasants who had been given land on the implementation of the land reform got into debt in order to pay for the land received, and this further aggravated their situation.

The enslaving loans granted by the great international monopolies, no less than Romania's public debt incurred during World War I, resulted in a considerable increase in taxation, a great burden for the working masses. On the other hand, intensified exploitation by the capitalists lowered the already low living standard of the workers. The main forms of increased exploitation were the prolongation of the work day, the tendency constantly to reduce wages, and the employment of unskilled labor, which was far more poorly paid than skilled labor.

Romania's political regime during the period between the two World Wars became involved in the tightening of the domination of the big industrial and financial bourgeoisie, and this gave a reactionary character to the power of the state.

Unable to adopt constructive, democratic ways of solving the great problems facing the country, some of the bourgeois parties were nevertheless compelled to consider Romania's new situation and the revolutionary struggles of the masses, and to include a number of democratic provisions in their programs. The political situation in interwar Romania can best be gauged by the widening front of the struggling masses dissatisfied with their socio-economic and political conditions, and by the intensive struggle carried on by the masses headed by the communists against the exploiting classes and the leaders of the country.

Carrying on their activities against the background of a general crisis of capitalism, the bourgeois and landowner parties of that period made anti-communism a main feature of their policy.

Significant changes were made in Romania's political configuration in those days following the adoption of the general suffrage, which brought the masses into the political arena and caused the regrouping of political forces.

The land reform which weakened the economic basis of the Conservative Party and of the kindred groups — the Progressive Conservative Party, the Democratic Conservative Party — soon caused these parties to go out of the picture.

The National-Liberal Party, headed by Ionel Brătianu, president of the party, Vintilă and Dinu Brătianu, M. Pherekyde, Al. Constantinescu, C. Angelescu, and I. G. Duca, was the greatest political force of the bourgeoisie actively participating in all the political and social reforms made during the first years of the postwar period. However, the reactionary character of the National-Liberal Party was to be brought out ever more strongly as the socio-economic and political positions of the Romanian bourgeoisie, particularly of the big bourgeoisie, were strengthened.

The Romanian National Party, relying on the leaders and the masses of Transylvania, held an important place in political life. Headed by I. Maniu, Al. Vaida Voevod, V. Goldiș, Ștefan Ciceo Pop, and M. Popovici, this party included nearly all those who had struggled for Transylvania's union with Romania. Now that new conditions prevailed, these militants still considered their party as a force that would carry out the radical democratic changes listed in the Declaration of Alba Iulia of December 1, 1918. The leaders of the Romanian National Party, and in the first place Iuliu Maniu and Al. Vaida Voevod, advocated that those reforms were to be made in a conservative spirit.

The National Party of Transylvania, which had a regional character, merged in February, 1923, with what was left of the Conservative parties now grouped under Take Ionescu's leadership; in 1925, with the Democratic National Group led by N. Iorga; and in October, 1926, with the Peasant Party headed by I. Mihalache. The National Peasant Party sprang up as a consequence of the merger. It was a powerful party which inspired broad masses with confidence for it carried on propaganda against the Liberal government and flaunted bourgeois-democratic slogans, some of them fairly advanced.

In time a number of groups seceded from the party which was heterogeneous from the social and ideological stand-point and within which there were ceaseless conflicts in connection with tactics and occasionally with political inte-rests in the election of the leaders. Thus, shortly after the Party had been formed, Iorga's group separated to form the Democratic National Party, and in February, 1927, a consi-derable number of members of the former Peasant Party created a new Peasant Party under the leadership of Dr.N. Lupu.

The active presence of the Romanian people as a whole in political life, the great revolutionary effervescence which followed World War I, the assertion of democratic, progressive currents, as also the contradictions in the ranks of the old parties of the Romanian bourgeoisie and landowners, all contributed to the creation of new political parties and groups.

Founded in December, 1918, the Peasant Party was made up of heterogeneous groups. The social basis of the party consisted of part of the peasantry and of the lower town bourgeoisie, while among the leaders there were bourgeois democratic elements, mostly coming from the Liberal Party, such as C. Stere, Pavel Bujor, and Gr. Iunian. Other leaders, among them Simion Mehedinți, had belonged to the Con-servative Party. There were few new personages, among them I. Mihalache and V. Madgearu. The Peasant Party's aim was to turn Romania into a democratic country, to satisfy a number of fundamental claims of the working peasantry; among other things the expropriation of landed estates (half of the compensation to be paid by the state), graduated in-come tax, abolition of the gendarmerie, and, for the workers, the right to organize themselves and to have a press of their own. The party also intended to give a democratic character to the state machinery and to nationalize the National Bank, thus asserting itself as a democratic, progressive party. Along the line of the peasant-favoring concepts prevailing in Roma-nia since the close of the nineteenth century, the theoreticians of the Peasant Party, in particular Mihalache and Madgearu, upheld the notion of a "peasant state," contending, despite evidence to the contrary, that the peasantry should play the main part in the state. Although they spoke about the com-munity of interests between workers and peasants, they oppos-ed the idea that the working class party might defend the interests of the peasantry and considered that the peasants should form an independent class party.

In 1918 the People's League was founded under General Al. Averescu's leadership. In April, 1920, it changed its name to the People's Party, becoming a bourgeois political formation which created a diversion and at a certain moment gained exceptional popularity owing to its vague promises of carrying out a number of democratic reforms. During the battles of the summer of 1917 General Averescu had become widely popular among Romanian soldiers and among the peasantry generally, promising the soldiers in the 20's to struggle for two fundamental reforms: agrarian and electoral.

Among the leaders of the People's Party there were also landowners such as C. Argetoianu and Matei Cantacuzino, who had seceded from the Conservative Party, and some generals, among whom were Gr. Crăciuneanu and C. Văleanu.

These men were reactionary figures but the party also included some outstanding personalities of Romanian political and cultural life with democratic, progressive views, such as Vasile Kogălniceanu, M. Sadoveanu, Petru Groza, and Victor Babeş, all eager to help improve the condition of the peasants and make of Romania a genuinely democratic country.

In March, 1920, Averescu formed the cabinet, when it was seen that he had made skillful use of his popularity and authority in order to strengthen the precarious socio-political position of the exploiting classes. The democrats in the ranks of the People's Party, disappointed with the political trends supported by Averescu and Argetoianu, left the party, causing its prestige and popularity to suffer greatly.

Other bourgeois parties in existence at the time were of lesser importance. For instance, the National Democratic Party headed by Nicolae Iorga, the Labor Party under Trancu-Iaşi's leadership, and the Magyar and German Parties, which represented the interests of the exploiting classes in the ranks of the co-inhabiting nationalities. This was the time when certain extreme right-wing organizations came into being: the National Christian Defense League with Al. Cuza as president, and Archangel Michael's Legion, a fascist-type organization which was later to assume the name of the "Iron

AMINTIRE DIN TIMPUL GREVEI GEN. LA C.F.R. 1920

86. A GROUP OF WORKER PARTICIPANTS IN THE GENERAL STRIKE OF OCTOBER, 1920

87. CREATION OF THE ROMANIAN COMMUNIST PARTY. FACSIMILE FROM "SOCIALISMUL" ON THE DEBATES OF THE FIRST CONGRESS

## Congresul General al Partidului Socialist din România

### Ziua V

Ședința de dimineață — Joi 12 Mai

88. OILFIELD AT MORENI

89. THE MALAXA WORKS

90. THE REȘIȚA WORKS

91. WORKERS IN THE COURTYARD OF THE GRIVIȚA SHOPS DURING THE STRIKE OF
FEBRUARY 15—16, 1933

92. POSTCARD PUBLISHED IN FRANCE BY THE FRENCH SECTION OF THE INTERNA-
TIONAL RED AID AND WIDELY DISTRIBUTED IN MANY COUNTRIES OF THE WORLD
BY WORKERS' ORGANIZATIONS IN SYMPATHY WITH THE STRUGGLE OF THE ROMA-
NIAN PROLETARIAT.

SECOURS ROUGE INTERNATIONAL ——— SECTION FRANÇAISE
12, Avenue Mathurin-Moreau – PARIS (19ᵉ)

## SOLIDARITÉ POUR LA LIBÉRATION
## DES INCULPÉS DU PROCÈS
## DES CHEMINOTS
## DE ROUMANIE

CONSTANTIN DONCEA

Ouvrier tour-
eur de Grivița.
ondamné pour
rève aux tra-
aux forcés à
vie

CHIVU STOICA

hivu Stoica fut condamné à
5 ans de travaux forcés

heorghe Petrescu — commu-
iste condamné aux travaux
forcés à perpetuité
(pour grève)

0f.50

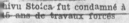

GHEORGHE PETRESCU   DUMITRU POPA

GH. GHEORGHIU-DEI

Membre du Co-
mité Central
d'Action des
cheminots : 15
ans de tra-
vaux forcés.

GHITAAL
VASILIGHIEI

Ghitaal Vasilighiei — com-
muniste : 20 ans de travaux
forcés

Dimitru Popa forgeron tué
par la police au cours des
luttes de février à Bucarest.

Guard". These last two political organizations exerted little influence on Romanian public opinion.

Unlike all the other political parties and groups, from the most reactionary to the most democratic and progressive — all of which intended to maintain the existing system — the Romanian Communist Party played a new and most important part in Romanian political life. Continuing the ideals of social and national liberation of the workers of town and countryside, of the genuine democratization of the country and of its socialist transformation, the Workers' Party, which assumed the name of Socialist Party in 1918 to show its opposition to the reformist social-democracy of the Second International which had proved a failure, organized demonstrations and strikes in various enterprises and branches of production as well as the general strike of 1920 which involved the whole Romanian proletariat. The party carried on intensive political and ideological activities, exposing the exploitation and oppression of the masses of town and country. The Workers' Party struggled for certain aims of the masses to be satisfied immediately and for radical changes in the country.

In the heat of the workers' great struggles of 1918, 1919 and 1920, years of intensive revolutionary action, the working class movement in Romania reached a speedy ideological maturity, with the reorganization of the Socialist Party on a revolutionary basis as its main concern.

The creation in May, 1921, of the Romanian Communist Party based on Marxist-Leninist ideas, as an avant-garde detachment of the working class, was a historic turning point in the development of the working-class movement and a most important moment in the history of the Romanian people. From its very first steps in the political arena, the Communist Party, led by Gh. Cristescu, Secretary General, Alexandru Dobrogeanu-Gherea, D. Fabian, E. Köblös, and others came up against numerous difficulties but asserted itself as an influential political force. During the period between the two World Wars the political arena of the country was greatly influenced by the revolutionary movement of the proletariat, which, headed by the Communist Party, fought fearlessly for democratic rights and liberties and against the exploiting regime and for the satisfaction of the working people's aspirations.

The Romanian Communist Party stated its policy on all the major problems of Romanian society and advocated a number of changes designed to bring about the country's advance, an improvement in the living conditions of the masses, the abolition of the landowners' estates and the defense of democratic liberties.

The Communist Party showed the people that there were good prospects of overthrowing the exploiters, of achieving a transformation of society by revolution, and of building a better and happier life for the working people. The Party succeeded in rallying around its banner and political program of struggle the great masses of workers in Romania — the progressive forces of the nation.

When the Socialist Party became the Communist Party in May, 1921, part of the right-wing social-democratic leaders — I. Jumanca, Gh. Grigorovici, I. Flueraş, E. Gherman, and I. Pistiner, who had withdrawn from the Socialist Party early in 1921 — formed regional social-democratic parties in Muntenia and Moldavia, in Transylvania and Bucovina. In June 1921 these Social-Democratic groups formed the Federation of Socialist Parties of Romania, which, however, lacked mass support. Consequently, its leaders tried to exert an influence on the Trade Unions and this broke up the unity of the Trade Union movement of Romania in 1923.

In May, 1927, the Federation of the Socialist Parties of Romania was dissolved and the Social-Democratic Party was created with a leadership which included Ilie Moscovici, C. Titel-Petrescu, Ion Flueraş, Iosif Jumanca, L. Iordache, Lothar Rădăceanu etc.

In June, 1928, a group of Romanian Socialists among whom were L. Ghelerter, Ştefan Voitec, Constantin Mănescu and Zaharia Tănase, disapproving of the tactics of the Social-Democratic Party in a number of problems, withdrew from the Party and created a new Workers' Party, the Socialist Party of the Workers of Romania.

All through these years the Romanian Communist Party asserted itself strongly in Romania's political arena. After the imprisonment of the delegates who had voted for the creation of the Marxist-Leninist Revolutionary Party in 1921, the Romanian Communist Party carried on intensive political work among the masses with the aim of reorganizing the local sections and of rallying the working masses in its struggle for the recognition of its organizations and of the Party itself, and for the defense of the Communists and of the other revolutionaries who had been imprisoned.

Although working under most unfavorable conditions, the Romanian Communist Party decided to stand for the Parliamentary election to be held early in 1922. To this end the Party organized many popular meetings and submitted its lists of candidates in several counties.

The Dealul Spirei Trial of May 23 to June 4, 1922, of 271 revolutionary militants, many of whom had been delegates to the First Congress of the Party, was a political event of prime importance focussing as it did the attention of the working class and of the progressive political circles upon the Communist Party. The trial was proof of the strength and vitality of the young Communist Party and also showed that it was deeply rooted in the Romanian working class and the Romanian people as a whole.

In the struggle for unity in the working class movement and for building the masses into a homogeneous whole, the Romanian Communist Party created, used, and ran the Red Aid, the Romanian Workers' aid, from 1921 to 1924, alongside the unitary Trade Unions and other working class organizations such as the Socialist Youth Union (1922-1924), which in April, 1924, was named the Communist Youth Union. In August, 1923, the League of the Rights of Man was created for the defense of democratic liberties and of the rights of the working people. Outstanding figures upholding democratic views were part of the League, among them C. Costaforu, C I. Parhon, Zamfir C. Arbore, and St. Voitec.

On July 27, 1924, the Romanian Communist Party, the Communist Youth Union, and the revolutionary mass organizations were dissolved and their offices closed, their archives were confiscated, and their leaders arrested. With the Romanian Communist Party outlawed, the leaders of the Party were faced with very complex tasks. The Party had no experience in organizing underground activities for a long period ahead.

Despite the persistence of Social-Democratic concepts in the ranks of the Romanian Communist Party and the directives of the Comintern, which did not keep count of realities in Romania, the Communist Party generally succeeded in organizing and guiding the struggle of the people for better living conditions and the defense of democratic rights. Various methods were used to forge ties between the Party and the broad masses.

In the autumn of 1925 the Peasants' and Workers' Bloc was created following a decision made by the Central Committee of the Romanian Communist Party. The Bloc was conceived of as a legal political organization guided by the Romanian Communist Party with a membership of comunists, socialists, social-democrats, and left-wing members of the Peasant Party. Its aim was to fight for civic rights and the freedom of organization, assembly, and speech. Apart from the aforementioned claims, the program of the Peasants' and Workers' Bloc included expropriation without payment of the landowners, who were to be left only 100 acres, and the granting of land to the peasants.

A realistic program and flexible tactics worked out by experienced revolutionary militants enabled the Bloc to achieve important successes: it concluded an understanding in the elections of 1925 and 1928 with the Socialist Party, the Social-Democratic Party, and the Peasant Party, thus exerting its influence in the ranks of the working class and of other categories of working people, and participated with success in the village and parliamentary elections.

Greater economic power in the hands of the big banking and industrial bourgeoisie enabled the latter to strengthen their political domination for a time.

In January, 1922, the Liberal Party, as spokesman for the most powerful groups of the dominant class, took the reins of government and kept them with a short interruption (March, 1926 to June, 1927) up to the end of 1928.

As the exploiting classes strengthened their positions, they found ways and means of eluding the democratic liberties laid down in the Constitution. A new electoral law was passed on March 27, 1926, introducing an "electoral premium" and thereby ensuring the overwhelming majority of the mandates for the Government and thus seriously violating democratic principles.

In order to remain in office the Liberal Party resorted to all kinds of arbitrary practices, creating terror through the gendarmerie, enforcing states of emergency, and holding electoral campaigns during which blood was shed and ballot boxes were stolen. The Liberal administration earned the odium of the popular masses in town and village.

The reactionary policy carried on by the Liberal government aroused dissatisfaction in all sections of society, and this further strengthened the alliance between the opposition parties.

Under pressure of the masses roused by its profoundly anti-popular policy, the Liberal Party in March, 1926, had to hand over the reins of government to the People's Party led by General Averescu. In June, 1927, a transition cabinet was formed with B. Ştirbei as Premier but, less than three weeks later, on June 22, 1927, a new Liberal government was formed under the leadership of I. I. C. Brătianu who continued to exert a decisive influence in politics.

With King Ferdinand's health deteriorating, the Liberal Party considered it necessary to take a number of measures designed to defend and maintain its political domination. With the assistance of Queen Marie and Prince Ştirbei, the Liberals in December, 1925, forced Prince Carol to give up his claims to the throne. This course of action was facilitated by Prince Carol's adventurous and immoral life.

When King Ferdinand died in 1927, a regency was formed. The Regents were Prince Nicholas, Miron Cristea, Patriarch of Romania, and G. Buzdugan, President of the Court of Cassation, who supported the Liberal government.

The opposition parties intensified their activities. In the press and by their spoken statements, the leaders of the National Peasant Party revealed the unfair practices of the Liberal administration. Concurrently, the deputies of the National Peasant Party, in order to obstruct the policy of the Liberal cabinet, did not appear in Parliament. On the initiative of the National Peasant Party, a great public meeting was held at Alba Iulia on May 6, 1928, to demand the resignation of the Liberal government. The meeting was an occasion for the Communist Party to rally great numbers of workers and peasants and force the National Peasant Party to enlarge its program of struggle along democratic lines. The impressive demonstration of a hundred thousand people upholding the slogan of "a march on Bucharest" forced the National-Liberal

Party to hand over the reins of government to the National Peasant Party in November, 1928.

Romania's foreign policy after World War I bore the seal of the interests of the Romanian bourgeoisie and landowners. The ruling circles forged a system of international relations and agreements designed to ensure the class domination of the bourgeoisie and landowners inside the country and at the same time to guarantee its territorial integrity which had been achieved by virtue of the international principle of the right of the peoples to self-determination. The ruling circles consequently turned toward France and Britain, whom they considered as likely to defend Romania's interests. The Romanian state moreover strengthened its relations with the neighboring countries — Czechoslovakia, Poland, and Yugoslavia — which were formed, or whose territories were rounded off, after disintegration of the Habsburg and the Tsarist Empires. Romania also fought the policy tending towards a revision of the peace treaties. The stand taken by bourgeois Romania in her foreign relations was also influenced by the fact that the country was a borderland between the capitalist world and the Soviet Union, and difficulties in Romania's foreign policy were also created by the policy of concessions of the great western powers toward Germany. The anti-popular stand of the exploiting classes inside the country was of no small importance in weakening the country's resistance capacity when faced with the great problems looming ahead.

When Romania signed the peace treaties, which also included the League of Nations Covenant, she became a member of that international organization. Romania's representatives at the League of Nations made their contribution to the defense of the principles upheld by this international organization created after World War I. The League debated and defended important issues, such as the settlement of all disputes between states by peaceful means, the exclusion of war as a means of settling differences, disarmament, and a definition of an aggressor.

In 1921 the "Final Statutes of the Danube" came into force. Britain, France, and Italy, although having no frontier along the Danube, became members of the bodies entrusted with regulating navigation along the great European river.

Although Romania never took part in any of the actions of certain western powers against Soviet Russia, the relations between the two countries were strained. Nevertheless, the strain in Romano-Soviet relations eased after 1920. On January, 15 of that year, the Soviet government proposed that talks should be held in order to settle the differences between the two states, but the conference that took place in Vienna between March 27 and 29, 1924, during which the differences between the two countries were discussed, was a failure.

In order to counteract the revanchist intentions of the defeated countries, Romania, Czechoslovakia, and Yugoslavia concluded bilateral treaties in 1920 and 1921, thus laying the foundations of an alliance known as the Little Entente. The Romanian politician Take Ionescu tried without success to enlarge the Little Entente by drawing in Poland and Greece. Take Ionescu's plans failed because of the contradictions existing between Poland and Czechoslovakia on the one hand and Yugoslavia and Greece on the other. In spite of this a treaty of alliance was concluded between Romania and Poland in 1921 with the aim of ensuring the defense of the frontiers of the two states. The treaty was extended in March, 1926.

Romania endeavored to establish good relations with Hungary and Bulgaria despite the fact that the Hungarian reactionary circles kept up an atmosphere of agitation over the new frontiers of the neighboring countries. Under the influence of the policy of domination carried on by the Austro-Hungarian monarchy, the leaders of Horthy's Hungary hoped to build up again St. Stephen's kingdom by including some foreign territories.

Nevertheless, agreements of local interest and trade conventions were concluded between Romania and Hungary during that period, and the problem of the Hungarians choosing to move to Hungarian territory was settled amicably.

Romania was one of the fourteen states which signed the Geneva Protocol of October 2, 1924, unanimously adopted by the League of Nations Assembly and recommending the peaceful settlement of international disputes.

At Locarno on October 12, 1925, Britain, France, Italy, Belgium, Czechoslovakia, and Poland signed arbitration and conciliation treaties with Germany. The same countries minus Czechoslovakia and Poland concluded the multilateral guarantee pact — the Rhineland Pact. This was among the first moves in the Anglo-French policy of concessions to German imperialism, a policy designed to ensure the security of Western Europe. Romania showed hostility toward the Locarno agreement for it gave Germany a free hand to expand eastward.

In June, 1926, Romania signed a treaty of alliance with France together with a military convention, and on September 16, 1926, a treaty of friendship and co-operation with Italy which provided mutual assistance for the defense of the frontiers of the two countries in accordance with the treaties concluded after World War I.

The signing of the Paris Pact better known as the Kellogg-Briand Pact, on August 27, 1928, was an important moment in international affairs. The fifty states which had joined the pact bounded themselves to settle all differences by peaceful means. Romania joined the pact and voiced her wish for its speedy enforcement. This is also shown in the Moscow Protocol of February 9, 1929, concluded by the governments of the Soviet Union, Romania, Poland, Estonia, and Latvia. The Protocol laid down the decision of the signatory states "to contribute to the safeguarding of peace between their countries and to put into force without delay between the peoples of these countries the Treaty of Paris concluded on August 27, 1928, whereby war ceased to be an instrument of the national policy". The Romanian Parliament unanimously ratified the Moscow Protocol with the assent of all political parties and groups.

## 2. Romania during the 1929—1933 Economic Crisis

THE effects of the world economic crisis, whose symptoms from 1928 were felt in Romania on a wide scale, owed their intensity to some specific factors, among which were the preponderance of backward agriculture in the economy, with vestiges of a semi-feudal production, a considerable foreign debt, the taking over of important enterprises by foreign capital, and a sharp reduction in the prices of products designed for export concurrently with the high prices of imported goods.

The various production branches were unequally affected as regards intensity and duration. The oil industry, for example, was even able to increase its output, and the textile and leather industries also produced more goods. Nevertheless, the total volume of industrial production decreased by nearly 50 per cent during the crisis. Coal and the processing industries in particular registered a substantial decrease in output. In 1933 production capacities were left idle to the extent of 73 per cent for pig iron, 43 per cent for steel, and 77 per cent in the timber industry.

The crisis also affected agriculture, the value of foodstuffs produced decreasing from 15,300 million lei in 1928 to 8,500 million lei in 1933.

Hundreds of banks, including two of the biggest — Marmorosch Blank & Co, and the Bercovici Bank — failed, robbing a large number of small depositors of their savings while at the same time making money scarce.

In order to ward off an economic disaster, the National Peasant government of those days promoted a policy of "opening wide the gates" to foreign capital and contracted a number of loans from the west on usurious terms (stabilization, issue and other loans). The result was an increase in the public debt and control of the imperialist powers over the country's policy and economy, as well as deterioration of the living conditions of the working masses in town and village.

In agreement with the foreign monopolists, who had their own experts and supervisors in the country, the Romanian bourgeoisie and landowners tried to remedy the crisis by substantially reducing wages, cutting down the number of the staff ("sacrifice curves" was the term used for this), and by increasing taxation.

A hard life and poor working conditions, unemployment, and the terrorist methods adopted by the administrative machinery increased the dissatisfaction of the exploited population and deepened the contradictions under which the bourgeois regime was laboring.

During the economic crisis the workers of Romania went in for labor disputes, strikes, and revolutionary action against the exploiting classes and their political regime in the hope of putting an end to the crisis by these means.

From 1929 to 1932 there were 377 strikes in 1,054 enterprises, with nearly 830,000 work days lost, while in more than 4,000 enterprises there were some 840 latent labor disputes. The first great class battle during this period was the strike of the Lupeni workers in August, 1929.

With the revolutionary wave sweeping the country, the Fifth Congress of the Romanian Communist Party held at the end of 1931 was an important moment in the life of the Party and the working class movement. The Communist Party was becoming a revolutionary political force capable of organizing and leading the class struggle with a view to serving the vital interests of the working class and of the Romanian people generally.

The government headed by Vaida Voevod signed the Geneva agreement of January, 1933, under the auspices of the League of Nations, which guaranteed loans at exhorbitant interest to the foreign monopolists; while in the country wages were being cut (this being the third sacrifice curve), 30 per cent of factory and office workers were dismissed and consumption taxes were increased. It was then that the Romanian Communist Party called upon the working people to start the greatest class struggle in interwar Romania: the battles of the railway and oil workers of January-February 1933, which added a glorious page to the history of the Romanian people. It was a stirring demonstration of the spirit of struggle, self-denial, and sacrifice of the Romanian workers. Although much blood was shed on their being quelled, these great social battles were an important political victory of the Romanian working class through their immediate results and vital consequences for the political and social life of the next period. These battles of the Romanian proletariat were fought immediately after Hitler's dictatorship had been installed in Germany (1933) and were consequently of great international significance, being as they were among the first large-scale activities to be undertaken by the proletariat against Nazism.

It was as a result of the workers' battles that the government had to give up applying the Geneva agreement and cutting wages. The working class had asserted itself as the most advanced force of Romanian society, as an outpost in the struggle of the people against the fascist danger and for economic and political rights, and for democracy.

The economic crisis also brought about political instability: the cabinets were repeatedly changed or reshuffled, and the political parties of the dominant classes, in particular the two great so-called "historical" parties — the National Liberal Party and the National Peasant Party — were wearied by internal dissensions. As a consequence, new political groups were formed and the old parties were greatly weakened. In 1929 a Liberal Democratic Party was made up under the leadership of I. Th. Florescu. In 1930 a National Liberal Party was headed by Gh. I. Brătianu and a Peasant Democratic Party was headed by C. Stere. In 1932 a Radical Peasant Party was formed under the leadership of Gr. Iunian. During the same period, the group headed by Octavian Goga seceded from the People's Party to form the National Agrarian Party.

The Iron Guard and the Christian National Defense League — fascist organizations — were strengthened with the support of the reactionary members of the dominant classes, the aim being to oppose the workers' activities.

Taking advantage of the people's dissatisfaction with the Liberals' policy, the National Peasant Party was returned in November, 1928. Its home policy was, however, as reactionary and antagonistic to the people as that of the Liberal governments, all promises made while the party was in opposition being forgotten. In order to strengthen its position against the Liberal Party, the National Peasant Party, together with other political groups, helped to bring Prince Carol back, and he was proclaimed king on June 8, 1930. A clique made up of men without scruples, who were eager to get rich quickly and rise to important positions and who held reactionary views, was formed around the king. It included Puiu Dumitrescu, the king's private secretary, Aristide Blank, the banker, N. Malaxa, an industrialist, and some reactionary politicians, such as C. Argetoianu and Nae Ionescu.

From the early day of his accession to the throne, King Carol appeared anxious to install "an authoritarian regime," which meant a personal dictatorship.

After a National Peasant cabinet headed by G. G. Mironescu, a Iorga-Argetoianu cabinet followed on April 17, 1931. The latter cabinet began to put into practice the king's projects: it passed a law on the suspension of compulsory enforcement of judgments concerning landed property (December 18, 1931) and a law on the reduction of agricultural debts (April 19, 1932) — measures which favored the well-to-do peasants and the big landowners. Nevertheless, the government was unable to pay the salaries of its employees and was obliged to resign on May 31, 1932, and give way to a National Peasant cabinet headed by Vaida Voevod.

During the years of the economic crisis the National Peasant cabinets presided over by Iuliu Maniu, G. G. Mironescu, and Vaida Voevod increased Romania's economic dependence on the big foreign monopolies, helped to aggravate the political crisis, and favored the activities of fascist and pro-fascist organizations.

## 3. *Romania Faces the Fascist Peril (1933—1939)*

AFTER the economic crisis of 1929-1933, there was a change for the better in the Romanian economy: industrial and agricultural production rose steadily reaching in 1938 the highest level ever to have been known in capitalist Romania. The level reached at the time is an eloquent illustration of Romania's creative capacities: having united all the Romanian-inhabited provinces within its boundaries, the country made of them an economic whole with high indicators in its development within the limits of the capitalist regime. During this period the process of the concentration of capital and production was accentuated as was also the formation of monopolies, which began to play a dominant part in the country's economic and political life.

A salient feature of the Romanian economy after the economic crisis was the development of industry as a whole, and primarily of the heavy and metalworking industries, which resulted in a number of economic and political phenomena. It should be mentioned that the policy of capitalist industrialization was not part of a general plan for the expansion of the national economy but was dictated by the desire to obtain big profits. During this period the governments of the dominant classes continued their policy of protecting the country's industry. Over and above the customs tariffs of 1929 and 1936, and especially of April, 1928 (Manoilescu), the state took other measures to protect industry. In June, 1933, quota duties were introduced, in December, 1935, a 12 per cent additional ad valorem duty, and in August, 1936, a law was issued for the foundation of enterprises producing new types of goods. The industrial bourgeoisie benefited by the support of the state, and this helped not only to strengthen its economic position but also to intensify the process of capitalist industrialization in the country.

From 1932 to 1937 the value of Romania's industrial production increased by 100 per cent, from 32,400 million to 64,500 million lei.

The expansion of heavy industry in interwar Romania was also illustrated by the increase in iron ore from 6,000 tons in 1928 to 122,000 tons in 1938, while imports of metallurgical semi-fabs decreased from 189,000 tons in 1929 to 23,000 tons in 1937 and the imports of rolled metal from 87,000 tons to 12,000 tons. Capital investments in the metalworking industry went up from 2,100 million lei in 1927 to 5,700 million lei in 1938.

The country's industrial development during the period that followed the economic crisis may also be observed from the following data: electric power output rose from 410 million kw in 1926 to 1,077 million kw in 1936 and to 1,148 million kw in 1938; the value of food production went up from 14,959 million lei in 1926 to 15,577 million lei in 1938, while the value of metalworking production rose from 7,058 million lei to 11,363 million lei, the value of textile production from 6,656 million lei to 14,692 million lei, and of electrical engineering production from 114 million lei to 675 million lei.

Mining output also increased considerably during the period that followed the economic crisis: the crude oil output, which amounted to nearly 5 million tons in 1929, had risen to 8,703 million tons by 1936.

The capital required for the expansion of Romanian industry was mainly supplied by the state in the form of substantial advances, anticipated payment for the orders placed, and bounties from the budget. Nor should the funds provided by the foreign capitalists, whether private capitalists or monopolists, be underestimated.

King Carol II had a personal interest in the expansion of the heavy industry for he held 30 to 35 per cent of the shares of the Malaxa works, about the same amount of shares of the I.A.R. Plant (Romanian Aeronautical Industry) and Astra-Vagoane Works, and a smaller amount in the Reşiţa and Auschnit plants. The king also had an interest in a number of sugar factories, in breweries, in the Mica gold mines, the Buhuşi and Scherg textile mills, and the telephone company.

The country's economic dependence on the imperialist powers increased during that period. It was estimated that on the eve of the Second World War, foreign capital held 38 per cent of the capital of the joint-stock industrial companies.

Economic and, in particular, industrial expansion resulted in a considerable increase in the number of the proletariat, which rose from 450,000 in 1930 to over 800,000 in 1938.

Although agricultural production also developed after the economic crisis of 1929-1933, Romanian agriculture as a whole was still lagging behind. In 1935 the number of tractors used was only 7 per cent more than in 1927.

Economic expansion during that period did not perceptibly improve the lot of the masses. The living and working conditions of the working masses of town and country lagged far behind the progress of capitalist economy and caused numerous conflicts. A few conclusive facts will illustrate the poor conditions under which the working people were laboring: the workers' general wage indicator decreased from 2,760 in 1929 to 1,705 in 1937; from 1934 to 1937 the cost of living increased by 27 per cent, while income tax rose by 23 per cent, and wages went up by only 6 per cent.

Nor were conditions any better for the peasants during that period. They had not sufficient land, the overwhelming majority of the peasantry labored under increasing exploitation, both direct and indirecr, and chronic diseases spread at a tremendous rate as a result of the lack of the necessities of life and of medical assistance. In 1938 the National Agro-technical Institute ascertained that out of about 3,000,000 peasant homesteads, two million had not a single cow, 1,7 million had not a single pig, and a quarter of a million not a single chicken.

In 1929 the Ministry of Public Health ascertained that nearly 70 per cent of the village cottages were built of logs plastered over with clay. The floors were of beaten earth and dung, and the roofs were covered with shingles or thatch.

The conditions of the poor generated great discontent which resulted in local movements and rebellions among the Romanian peasants and those of other nationalities, as for example the revolt in the Ghimeş Valley in 1934 and the strikes and demonstrations of the workers in a number of industrial branches.

Political life was in ferment — the result of economic and social processes, of the increasingly radical trends of the working masses, and of the international situation. This situation was reflected in the antagonism and the struggles between the working masses and the exploiting classes and in the unceasing conflicts between the bourgeois-landlord parties and political groups.

The divergences between the political parties and groups of the exploiting classes were fanned by Carol II, whose maneuvers and backstage combinations were aimed at dis-organizing the political parties and installing a royal dicta-torship.

The Liberal cabinet formed in November, 1933, with I. G. Duca as premier banned the Iron Guard. Duca was a representative of the "old Liberals" who wanted to maintain the bourgeois parliamentary forms of government and the Franco-English, anti-Nazi trend in the country's foreign policy. In answer to the ban, a group of legionaires assassinat-ed the prime-minister on December 29, 1933, on the plat-form of the Sinaia railway station.

On December 30, 1933, Carol II designated C. Anghelescu as premier but replaced him on January 2, 1934, by Gh. Tătă-răscu, leader of the "young Liberals" who held the helm of the country supporting the king and being supported by him.

In his four years' administration Tătărăscu increasingly used decrees as a method of government, thus restricting parliamentary activities. In April, 1934, the Parliament passed a law on "the defense of order within the state" which enabled the government to dissolve any political group that jeopardized the political and social order. This had been done in order to check and suppress all revolutionary and democratic movements.

While special laws were being passed against the revolutionary movement, King Carol and his main collaborators tolerated and even supported terrorist and fascist organizations, such as the Iron Guard, with the aim of using them for their own purposes. It is significant to note in this respect that those who had made the attempt on Duca's life were treated leniently and the legionaires were able to organize congresses and fascist demonstrations.

With a growing internal and external tension, all the political forces in the country gave their views on the policy to be adopted. The fascist organizations, and primarily the Iron Guard which was supported by Nazi Germany, were exposed and branded as obscurantists, mystical organizations jeopardizing the very existence of the Romanian state.

The right-wing political groups and circles led by Vaida Voevod, Gh. Brătianu, and C. Argetoianu, on the other hand, supported and encouraged the fascist organizations, thus undermining the country's resistance against the fascist peril.

The working masses headed by the Romanian Communist Party rose against fascist organizations and their supporters inside the country, as did also the other workers' parties, the Social-Democratic, the United Socialists, and wide circles of the lower bourgeoisie and the intelligentsia, and indeed all outstanding democratic political personages, who showed anxiety at the activities of the legionaires and the increasing danger of the country being dismembered and enslaved by Nazi Germany. From among them we will recall Nicolae Titulescu, Nicolae Iorga, Gr. Iunian, Virgil Madgearu, Victor Iamandi, Armand Călinescu, and Dem. Dobrescu.

But it was the Romanian Communist Party which proved the most consistent political force of all those that rose against the expansion of Nazi Germany, Horthy's revisionism, and the fascist terrorist organizations in the country. The Communist Party proposed that all parties, groups, and figures of note should unite to oppose the fascist peril and defend the country's democratic liberties and national independence and sovereignty. To this end the Romanian Communist Party took the initiative of organizing numerous activities, together with the United Socialist Party and the Socialist group headed by Constantin Popovici. In 1935 and 1936 many underground Communist organizations concluded agreements, binding themselves to uphold the workers' claims and fight in defense of democratic liberties and against fascism. At a number of regional conferences numerous delegates of the Social-Democratic Party openly declared for unity of action with the Communists.

As a result of the intensive activities carried on by the Romanian Communist Party, the Trade Union movement formed into a united whole in 1936, and for the first time since the Romanian Communist Party had been created, May Day demonstrations were held under the banner of the Workers' United Front.

In order to bar the way to fascism and war, the Romanian Communists took the initiative of creating a national anti-fascist committee, with the aim of uniting all those who worked "with hands and brain" so that together they might stave off "the triumph of the current bearing the germ of destruction of everything from which labor and thought spring."

The Romanian Communist Party efficiently combined underground activities with semi-legal and legal work and made large-scale use of all the possibilities offered by civic liberties — even at the time when the latter were restricted — to extend its ties within the most varied parties and political, cultural, and vocational organizations, wherever masses and personalities were to be found who could be rallied to struggle in defense of democracy and national independence.

An important place in the anti-fascist struggle of the Romanian people was held by the Ploughmen's Front, a democratic organization set up in 1933 under Petru Groza's leadership. Tens of thousands of peasants of the Hunedoara, Cluj, and Timiş-Torontal counties had joined the Ploughmen's Front, whose leaders were people who had risen from the peasants.

The anti-fascist struggle was also vigorously carried on by a number of mass organizations, such as the Democratic Students' Front, the Bloc for the Defense of Democratic Liberties, the Democratic Union, the League of Labor, and the Friends of the U.S.S.R.

Dissatisfied with the reactionary policy of the leaders of the Magyar Party in Transylvania — a bourgeois party dominated by counts and capitalists — the democratic elements in the same party created the Hungarian Working People's Union in 1934 (MADOSZ). This was an organization opposed to the fascist peril and Horthy's revisionism and chauvinist instigators, and fighting for a democratic regime, for the promotion of unity of action of all working people irrespective of nationality.

The first important success in the rallying of all democratic forces against fascism was achieved on December 6, 1935, when a solemn covenant was concluded at Țebea under Horea's legendary holm oak, between the Democratic Bloc, the Ploughmen's Front, MADOSZ, and the Socialist Group headed by C. Popovici. The Țebea covenant called forth a wide response throughout the country and promoted a great movement among all those who were hostile to fascism and reaction.

It was along the line of achieving anti-Nazi unity, as advocated by the Communist Party, that the Democratic Front was created in February, 1936, on the occasion of the local parliamentary election in the counties of Mehedinți and Hunedoara. The local organizations of the National Peasant Party in those counties then rallied to the joint front made up of the Democratic Front, the Ploughmen's Front, MADOSZ, and the Socialist group. Election returns were a victory of the People's Front and a defeat for the right-wing parties and organizations.

In August, 1936, the Central Committee of the Romanian Communist Party drew up a program for the people's anti-fascist front which provided for the dissolution and banning of all fascist organizations in the country, the defense of the constitutional régime and of all democratic institutions, the conclusion of a mutual assistance pact with the Soviet Union, and closer relations with France and with the countries of the Little Entente and the Balkan Entente.

The Communist Party also declared it was prepared to have talks with any party and organization with a view to organizing a joint struggle against Nazi and Horthy revisionists. "Should Nazi Germany when unleashing war in Europe and against the U.S.S.R., attack Romania with the assistance of Horthy's Hungary," it was stated in the protocol, "the Communists will consider it necessary to defend every inch of the country's soil." In April and July, 1937, on the occasion of village and county elections, new local agreements of the People's Front were concluded: in Bucharest, between the local organizations of the Democratic Bloc and those of the National Peasant Party and of the Conservative Party headed by Grigore Filipescu; in Jassy, the Radical Peasant Organization rallied to the People's Front. Agreements were also concluded in Ploieşti and elsewhere.

Starting from the idea that the main object of the democratic struggle was to overthrow the Tătărăscu government, and, from the consideration that the National Peasant Party was bent on overthrowing that government, the leaders of the Communist Party called upon the masses to vote for the candidates of the National Peasant Party in the parliamentary election of December, 1937, so that the party might be the representative of all democratic forces. However, Iuliu Maniu, President of the National Peasant Party, together with the Liberal group headed by Gheorghe Brătianu, concluded the so-called "non-aggression pact" with the Iron Guard. Under the circumstances, with the democratic forces unable to form a coalition, the savage campaign carried on by the Iron Guard in the election could not but seriously affect the election returns. For the first time in the political history of the country, the election did not result in a stable parliamentary majority for any of the political parties to enable it to form a cabinet.

In order to gain time before installing a personal dictatorship, Carol II called upon the National Christian ultranationalist Party, headed by Octavian Goga and A. C. Cuza, who had had a small number of votes, to form the cabinet. Also were included some bourgeois of note, such as Armand Călinescu, who voted for a foreign policy opposed to the expansion of Nazi Germany.

The installation of Nazism in Germany on January 30, 1933, had the most serious consequences for the destinies of many peoples in the world. Germany withdrew from the League of Nations on October 14, 1933, made military service compulsory in March, 1935, and openly declared for a revisionist and revanchist policy, demanding that the German colonial empire should be built up again. This meant that Germany's relations with other states were deteriorating, Germany was becoming an immediate danger to the national independence of many countries, including Romania, while jeopardizing human culture and civilization.

The ascension and consolidation of the Nazi régime in Germany, of fascism in Italy and Hungary, and of Japanese militarism, all of which helped to increase the danger of war, no less than the policy of the great western powers — Britain and France — who tolerated aggression and made concessions to the revanchist-revisionist forces, made it necessary for Romania to evolve an independent foreign policy. In that period, too, Romania promoted peace in this part of Europe and acted with determination within international bodies in defense of the European status quo, and for an understanding among nations, for disarmament and collective security in Europe.

The Romanian cabinets of that period carried on a policy of friendship and cooperation with France and Britain who, despite their inconsistency, declared in defense of the status quo, though they gave way before aggression. This they did in order to maintain world domination. Romania belonged to the group of anti-revisionist countries and to the system of political and military alliances based on the participation of the great western powers. For years Romania made a considerable contribution to the international conferences which debated the problems of disarmament, of the safeguarding of peace in Europe and throughout the world. The Romanian representative at the Geneva Disarmament Conference, Nicolae Titulescu, accepted and backed the proposal of the Soviet Union that aggression should be defined, as submitted by Litvinov on February 6, 1933, considering it to be "the clearest document in the course of the lengthy discussions within the Security Committee."

Besides the Little Entente member-countries, the representatives of France, Spain, and China declared in favor of the definition of the notion of aggression. Anthony Eden, the British delegate, considered the Soviet proposal "as too rigid", while the delegates of Mussolini's Italy and Horthy's Hungary rejected the definition considering it as "doubtful" and "unrealizable." The Disarmament Conference reached no decision for the Great Western powers adopted a hesitating attitude. When the various points of view were somewhat reconciled, the first convention defining the aggressor was signed in London on July 3, 1933, by the U.S.S.R., Romania, Poland, Estonia, Latvia, Turkey, Iran, and Afghanistan. An identical convention was signed on July 4, 1933, by the representatives of the Soviet Union, of the members of the Little Entente, and of Turkey.

The London Convention was an event of outstanding importance as it continued the Kellog-Briand Pact. It was a guarantee of the territorial integrity of the signatory countries, opening new prospects in international life in the safeguarding of peace in this part of the world.

Together with the other countries of the Little Entente, Romania rose with determination against the draft Quadripartite Pact inspired by Mussolini — to which Britain, France, Italy, and Germany were to belong. The pact was an infringement of the principle of equal rights for all states in international relations, and implied an amendment to the statutes of the League of Nations and the revision of peace treaties, being consequently against the interests and rights of small- and medium-sized European countries. The four Great Western powers were to constitute a directorate which would decide the destinies of Europe. It was a gross infringement of the League of Nations Charter and a direct encouragement of the revanchist policy of Nazi Germany and her allies.

Nicolae Titulescu, in his capacity as Romania's Minister of Foreign Affairs, tabled a protest of the Little Entente against the agreement, which he described as a plot against peace and a danger to the independence of small countries. He definitely demanded that the clauses referring to the revision of existing treaties should be cancelled. The firm stand taken by the Little Entente and the divergences among the four powers prevented the ratification of the pact.

With the stand of the U.S.S.R. and of the Little Entente member-countries being very much the same with regard to the increasing danger of Nazi Germany, and also considering the rapprochement between the U.S.S.R. and France, the Romanian, Yugoslav, and Czechoslovak governments showed a wish to bring their diplomatic relations with the Soviet Union back to normal.

After talks held at Geneva, Warsaw, and Ankara, the U.S.S.R. resumed diplomatic relations with Romania in 1934. The Romanian-Soviet rapprochement created a climate propitious to the negotiations of a mutual assistance pact between the two countries.

Foreign Affairs Minister Nicolae Titulescu was empowered by the Romanian government to proceed with the conclusion of a mutual assistance pact with the U.S.S.R. At Montreux in Switzerland in July, 1936, Titulescu and Litvinov drew up a Romanian-Soviet protocol which included the main provisions of a mutual assistance treaty between Romania and the Soviet Union based on mutual observance of national independence and sovereignty.

Litvinov, however, suggested that the signing of the mutual assistance pact should be postponed. The talks were not resumed and the two countries continued only to maintain good neighborly relations.

This was also the period when the Romanian government concluded and strengthened regional pacts designed to consolidate peace in Eastern and South-Eastern Europe. Despite the opposition of the revisionist powers, a Balkan understanding — the Balkan Pact — was signed at Athens on February 9, 1934, by Romania, Greece, Yugoslavia, and Turkey, the signatory powers "mutually guaranteeing the security of the Balkan frontiers" and "engaging not to undertake any political action towards another non-signatory Balkan state without the mutual advice of the other signatories, and not to assume any political obligation to any other Balkan State without bringing it to the knowledge of the other parties." The Balkan understanding was a means of fighting against the plots of the revisionist states in this part of Europe and an important step in safeguarding peace and security among the peoples.

Through the efforts of her representative, Nicolae Titulescu, Romania made her contribution within the two organizations as well as at the League of Nations, by asserting the point of view of small and medium countries, defending their independence and national sovereignty, and thus safeguarding peace.

Romania's representatives rose against the aggressive activities of the fascist and revisionist states as well as against the policy of encouraging the militarization of Nazi Germany. Romania protested against the Anglo-German naval agreement of July 18, 1935, under which Nazi Germany was permitted to build up her navy. Romania, like other small and medium countries, was greatly worried by the re-militarization of the Rhineland in March, 1936, and France's passive stand when the Treaty of Versailles was thus infringed. Romania's stand which branded fascist Italy's aggression against Abyssinia and demanded that the sanctions listed in the League of Nations' Pact be applied called forth a powerful response.

In August, 1936, Titulescu made a statement whereby Romania joined the Committee of non-interference in Spain. The Romanian government specified that should a legal republican government seek its support, it reserved for itself the right to decide. During that period Romania maintained economic and diplomatic relations with Republican Spain and allowed weapons and ammunition designed for the Spanish Republican government to pass through Romanian ports. On October 22, 1937, Romania signed the Nyon Pact on the joint measures to be taken to fight the piratical activities of the submarines of the fascist states in the Mediterranean at the time of the Italo-German interference in Spanish affairs. Nevertheless, the Tătărăscu government checked the activities of communist, anti-fascist organizations which struggled in support of Republican Spain and tolerated pro-fascist demonstrations.

Although influenced by bourgeois concepts, Titulescu adopted an advanced foreign policy. Aware of the danger of Nazism to world peace, he rose in defense of the principle of equal rights and of state sovereignty and against the tendencies of the Great western powers to disregard the rights and interests of the other nations. Carrying on intensive work, Titulescu made a considerable contribution to the Romanian people's struggle in defense of their independence and national sovereignty and for safeguarding peace in the world.

In August, 1936, Titulescu withdrew from the cabinet as a consequence of the attacks and intrigues of international reactionary forces and of the right-wing forces within the country. Titulescu's withdrawal weakened the influence of the political circles which opposed the revisionist plans of Nazi Germany and Horthy's Hungary, and also disrupted the unity of the Little Entente.

The Goga-Cuza cabinet called together by King Carol II in preparation of a royal dictatorship was short-lived, lasting only 44 days. On February 10, 1938, King Carol II became a dictator. The cabinet was headed by Patriarch Miron Cristea. It was made up of many reactionaries and of a number of notable members of the old bourgeois parties who were anti-Nazi and considered the royal dictatorship as a means of checking the ascension to power of the Iron Guard.

The royal dictatorship put an end to democratic parliamentary life. It narrowed down the existing bourgeois democratic liberties and banned the activities of the political parties. Leadership was concentrated in the hands of the king.

The new Constitution of February 24, 1938, suppressed all the provisions of the 1923 Constitution which had a general democratic character and vested power entirely in the hands of King Carol II. Parliament had only a formal part to play.

In October, 1938 a decree was issued whereby the workers' trade unions were dissolved and guilds were created, which were considered as vocational bodies subordinate to the aims of the royal dictatorship.

In order to give the impression that the country was governed in the name of the nation, the National Renaissance Front led by members of the royal clique was created in December, 1938. In June, 1940, the National Renaissance Front was named the Nation's Party and was the only legal party in the country.

During King Carol's dictatorship the country was ruled by special decrees. The state intervened more energetically in economic life, favoring a protectionist customs tariff, which further strengthened the positions of the bankers and financiers around Carol II, from among whom we will mention Nicolae Malaxa, Max Auschnit, and Dumitru Mociorniţa.

During the period of royal dictatorship the economic situation of the working class worsened. Strikes took place among the workers, and there was general unrest among the peasantry throughout the country.

The leaders of the National Peasant and the National Liberal Parties, I. Maniu and D. Brătianu, took no definite measures to prevent the installation of King Carol's dictatorship, but merely confined themselves to protest while carrying on their activities within a more limited framework, in spite of the fact that all parties had been banned.

The Romanian Communist Party considered King Carol's dictatorship as a profoundly anti-popular régime and the expression of Romanian reactionary circles. The Party documents, however, pointed out that Carol's dictatorship should not be taken for a fascist dictatorship and that the main enemy was the Iron Guard.

Starting from this premise, the Communist Party established in June, 1938, a program of action which included a number of economic, social, and political measures designed to re-establish the political picture of 1936 and unite all the patriotic forces in order to strengthen the resistance capacity of the Romanian people against the danger of a joint Nazi-Horthy aggression.

When Austria was annexed by Nazi Germany in March, 1938, the gates were opened for Germany's penetration into Southeast Europe. This was an event that had a direct impact on Romania, which was valued by Nazi Germany as a source of raw materials. In order to gain new positions in Romania, the Nazi government sought to take advantage of the difficulties Romania was having in her trade with Great Britain and France, in particular in the spring and summer of 1938. Furthermore, by incorporating Austria, Nazi Germany had gained control of the communications between Eastern and Western Europe.

Under these circumstances the Romanian government did its utmost to maintain and consolidate its regional alliances. After lengthy consultations, the states which had joined the Balkan Entente concluded an agreement with Bulgaria at Salonika on July 31, 1938, under which disputes among the Balkan states were to be settled without force.

Intensified economic pressure on Romania by Nazi Germany caused friction among the Romanian dominant classes. Important financial and industrial circles, to which some of the leaders of the main bourgeois parties also belonged, opposed Germany in her efforts to strengthen her position in the country. The Iron Guard and other pro-Nazi groups as well as some important monopolist reactionary leaders (N. Malaxa and I. Gigurtu) sought to tighten Romania's relations with Germany.

During the Czechoslovak crisis of March-September, 1938, which created favorable conditions for Polish and Hungarian revisionist claims, the Romanian government consistently supported its ally Czechoslovakia.

Romania refused to consider Hungary's offer of a bilateral understanding as long as the Horthy government was not prepared to come to an understanding with Czechoslovakia as well. At the session the Little Entente held at Sinaia in May, 1938, the Romanian Minister of Foreign Affairs stated once again that the clauses of the Romanian-Czechoslovak Treaty would immediately be applied if the Hungarian ruling circles resorted to force.

Continuing along the line of compromising with Germany, Britain and France sacrificed Czechoslovakia. The Munich agreements of September, 1938, opened the way for Nazi Germany towards the countries of Eastern and Southern Europe. Romania's foreign situation was thus aggravated. She had lost an ally in Czechoslovakia, which was also one of her main armament suppliers. The Little Entente actually ceased to exist when Czechoslovakia was occupied.

The Romanian people were warm in their sympathy and solidarity with the Austrian and Czechoslovak peoples who had been the victims of Nazi and Horthy aggression. At meetings and demonstrations, at public conferences and in protests, various political organizations and personages condemned fascist aggression.

In a stern indictment of all dictators who believed in the "old theory that small states had no right to independence" as they were included in the vital areas of the big states and were only named on the maps "in order to show to which of the big States they fell", the historian Nicolae Iorga wrote: "All those who believe that the small States have been done away with are mistaken; they will die and the nations will survive; and it is they who observe their independence and not the madmen who think they can rise against the will of the centuries and do away with them, that are wise . . .".

The Nazi government increased its pressure on Romania. At the same time, the royal dictatorship government, faced with economic difficulties and the pressure of pro-Nazi circles inside the country, received no effective assistance from Britain and France and began to make economic concessions to the Reich during the last months of 1938, demanding in exchange that the leading German circles should guarantee that they would not support the claims of Horthy's Hungary to Romanian territories. The German economic delegation led by Clodius carried on negotiations in Bucharest in November and December, 1938, but made such excessive demands that Romania's representatives were forced to reject them.

Hoping to obtain effective support, King Carol went to France and Britain in November, 1938. Not obtaining the support he expected in Britain, he passed through Germany on his return. Hitler refused any guarantee against a change of frontiers.

Germany's occupation of Czechoslovakia in March, 1939, created great tension between Romania on the one hand and Germany and Hungary on the other. There were plans for a joint German-Hungarian invasion of Romania.

The conciliating attitude of Britain and France and their treachery towards their smaller allies — for they gave free rein to Germany to invade Czechoslovakia and extend its domination in Central and South-East Europe, and this actually meant that Romania was isolated — induced the Călinescu government to conclude an economic agreement with Germany on March 23, 1939, in the hope of thus avoiding a conflict. The agreement came into force during the last months of 1940 and was followed by other onerous treaties which subordinated Romania's economy and policy to the aggressive interests of Germany.

Many progressive political forces, and primarily the Communists, voiced their ardent patriotism, attacking the Romanian-German agreement of March, 1939, and proving to be active defenders of the country's interests. A document of the Romanian Communist Party stated: "The Communists will fight in the first ranks. Unite in a single powerful front against Hitler and his revisionist allies!".

The patriotism of the masses was proved beyond a doubt by their attitude during the great anti-Nazi demonstration held on May Day 1938 when workers and craftsmen marched through Bucharest chanting the slogans: "For a free and independent Romania!" "Down with Fascism!" "Let the Romanian-German economic pact be abrogated!" "Down with the Nazi aggressors!"

Such demonstrations were held in all the more important towns and industrial centers of the country, showing that the Romanian people had rallied to the anti-Nazi movement and that it was their will to fight against the aggressor and against fascism.

Romania's position was becoming increasingly critical owing to Nazi and revisionist pressure, which continued in the spring and summer of 1939; to the reactionary policy promoted inside the country by the exploiting classes; and to the oscillations and even the mistakes made by the ruling political circles in foreign affairs. Under such circumstances, in order to ward off foreign dangers, Prime Minister Armand Călinescu and other ministers hostile to Nazi Germany sought to consolidate Romania's systems of alliances and create fulcrums against the country's political and economic encirclement by the fascist states. In April, 1939, the Romanian government, together with Poland and Greece, accepted the guarantees of Britain and France on the assumption that Anglo-Franco-Soviet negotiations, which were being carried on in Moscow with a view to the conclusion of a mutual assistance pact, would change the international ratio of forces to the detriment of the Nazi aggressors. Furthermore, the Romanian government sought to strengthen its ties with the countries of the Balkan Entente, especially with Greece and Turkey, which seemed ready to resist Nazi aggression in Southeast Europe.

No understanding was reached between the Western Powers and the U.S.S.R., and this had a baneful influence not only upon Romania's situation but also upon the whole of Europe, and even the whole world. On August 23, 1939, an economic convention and a non-aggression pact were concluded between the U.S.S.R. and Germany.

Romania's situation further deteriorated when the Second World War broke out, bringing in its train ruinous consequences for the country, for many peoples of Europe and, indeed, the entire globe.

CHAPTER II

# Culture in the Interwar Period

AFTER 1918 culture was promoted over the entire territory of the country, being enriched by the contribution of the newly incorporated provinces and contributing to the consolidation of the state. The struggle between the progressive and retrograde forces went forward also in the sphere of culture. A number of scientific, literary, and artistic personalities came to the fore, producing works whose value was beyond the standards of a national culture.

## 1. Education

THE enlargement of the country and the great number of civil servants needed, no less than the democratic trends in public life, made it necessary to unify educational laws, to modernize education, and to make schools of every grade accessible to all. In 1924 primary education was organized according to a uniform pattern without any differences being made between town and village schools, while secondary education was organized to meet the requirements of modern life.

The number of primary school teachers increased from 13,600 in the 1918-1919 school year to 47,914 in 1937-1938, while the number of secondary schools, which included theoretical and technical ones, went up from 186 in 1919 to 825 in 1938.

Higher education developed steadily. After World War I the Academy of Law of Oradea, the Polytechnic of Bucharest, and the Academy of Architecture and Polytechnic of Timișoara were added to the Bucharest, Jassy, and Cluj Universities. The number of undergraduates was around 12,000 in the first postwar years and 36,000 in 1933. There were 20 undergraduates to every 10,000 inhabitants.

In general, education of every grade developed considerably during this period. Nevertheless, young people without material means found it difficult to go on to higher education.

During the interwar period the revolutionary movement headed by the Communist Party fought consistently for the democratization of the educational system in order to enable all working people's children to attend schools of every grade. Simultaneously the Romanian Communist Party and the mass organizations strove to give a scientific content to textbooks and to the educational process generally so that the younger generation should possess a well-grounded knowledge of the world and society.

## 2. *Science*

SCIENTIFIC life now entered upon a higher phase. Romanian scholars made considerable contributions to the development of science, and some of them gained world recognition.

There was a galaxy of mathematicians, a number of whom opened up new prospects in the domain. Thus Gh. Țițeica (1873-1939), one of the creators of centro-affine differential geometry, left his name to a class of curves and to a class of surfaces he studied. At Jassy, research on differential geometry made remarkable progress under the guidance of Al. Myller, who was also the author of the notion of concurrent directions. S. Stoilov (1887-1961) was the first mathematician to have given a topological characterization of the functions of a complex variable, introducing the notion of "interior transformation" for the purpose.

A new generation of mathematicians raised the international prestige of the Romanian mathematical school. Al. Pantazi made remarkable contributions to the study of projective differential geometry, O. Onicescu and Gh. Mihoc to the theory of probabilities and to mathematical statistics, Gr. C. Moisil to the analytical mechanics of continuous systems and of modal logic, M. Nicolescu to the study of polyharmonic functions, N. Teodorescu to the theory of equations with partial derivatives, and of non-holonomic spaces, and Gh. Vrânceanu, creator of the school of global differential geometry of Bucharest.

Romanian physicists, although working in laboratories that were but poorly equipped (they were often compelled to work in foreign laboratories for that reason), made discoveries of note. H. Hulubei became an authority on X-rays and was elected corresponding member of the Paris Academy of Science. Other physicists who made their mark were E. Bădărău, who studied the properties of ionized gases, and Şt. Procopiu, who discovered the longitudinal settlement of colloidal solutions and crystalline solutions, a phenomenon named after him, apart from other magnetic phenomena. Remarkable results were obtained in quantic mechanics by Al. Proca (1897-1955), who discovered theoretically the existence of mezones, independently from the Japanese Yukawa. In aerodynamics, H. Coandă discovered the possibility of deviation of a fluid jet flowing into another fluid (the Coandă effect), and E. Carafoli became well known for his studies on aerodynamic profiles.

Research into organic chemistry was undertaken by C. D. Nenițescu, who obtained outstanding results, while Gh. Spacu and R.Ripan studied complex inorganic and analytical combinations.

Intensified geological prospecting during the interwar period helped to extend geological study over the whole territory of the country, as a consequence of which fundamental geological works, which included maps as well as surveys, were written. During this period Gh. Munteanu-Murgoci and L. Mrazek continued to study the soil and subsoil of the country, obtaining marked results. Other meritorious researchers in this field are I. Popescu-Voitești (1876-1944), who studied the genesis of oil and salt deposits and the geological and paleogeographical evolution of Romanian territory, Gh. Macovei (1880-1969) made important contributions to the study of the Cretaceous period in Romania and also of the geology of oil deposits.

In geography S. Mehedinți (1869-1926) promoted an original outlook according to which the earth is considered as a unitary whole made up of planetary covers. Gh. Vîlsan devoted his work to regional research, producing a comprehensive monograph on the Romanian plain, while V. Mihăilescu was the first to give a synthetical survey of the physical geography of the country.

Biological research was carried on by Gr. Antipa (1864-1944), founder of the Natural History Museum of Bucharest and author of some remarkable hydro-biological studies, by

E. Racoviță (1868-1947), the creator of bio-speleology, a new branch of biology, and D. Voinov, an ardent supporter of Darwinism and the head of the Romanian school of cytology.

Botanical studies progressed especially through the activities of I. Prodan, who wrote a thoroughly sound book on plant life in Romania, and Tr. Săvulescu, founder of the Romanian school of phyto-pathology. The preponderantly agrarian character of the economy stimulated interest in agronomy and an Agronomical Research Institute was founded by Gh. Ionescu-Sisești, author of comprehensive studies on wheat- and maize-growing.

The medical sciences benefited by the contributions of scholars of prestige, among them Fr. Rainer, supporter of a dynamic functional orientation in anatomy, C. I. Parhon, one of the founders of endocrinology and the discoverer of the syndrome named for him, C. Levaditti, who made a valuable discovery in the field of infra-microbiology, St. S. Nicolau, founder of the Romanian school of infra-microbiology, D. Danielopolu, who first used the viscerographic method, and Mina Minovici, head of the Romanian school of forensic medicine.

Romanian researchers made a number of technical inventions and discoveries, some of which are applied the world over. T. Vuia devised a steam generator, Gh. Constantinescu a mechanical sonic converter, A. Persu an aerodynamic car without differential, and T. Negrescu made a quantitative spectrographic analysis of alloys.

Philosophy was the object of comprehensive studies. In metaphysics, sociology, political economy, ethics and psychology, as well as in various spheres of the exact sciences and of humanism, there was a general drift of divergent tendencies. Apart from the scientists who gave only incidental considerations of a theoretical nature to their special study, some philosophers and sociologists made their contribution to the progress of rationalistic thought, with general concepts parallel to Marxism or influenced by Marxism. Such were D. D. Roșca, Mihai Ralea, P. P. Negulescu, Mircea Florian, H. Sanielevici, Petre Andrei, and Petre Pandrea. From among the aestheticians and literary critics, we will cite M. Dragomirescu, E. Lovinescu, Tudor Vianu, and G. Călinescu. Lucrețiu Pătrășcanu considered philosophy from the Marxist standpoint in his study *Currents and Trends in Romanian Philosophy*, and gave deep consideration to various aspects of Romanian society in *A Century of Social Developments, Under Three Dictatorships*, and *Romania's Basic Problems*. Athanase Joja made his mark among the Marxist thinkers.

Advanced scientific views, though undermined by ideas that are tributary to bourgeois ideology and to retrograde idealist currents, are to be found in the works of C. Rădulescu-Motru, the theoretician of "energetic personalism", and of Ion Petrovici, D. Gusti, and Eugeniu Speranția. An ideologist of neo-liberalism, Ștefan Zeletin based his arguments on certain theses of historical materialism. Virgil Madgearu, the theoretician of the "peasant state", opposed fascism and this cost him his life.

Romanian culture between the two world wars suffered the baneful influence of some anti-rationalist, right-wing doctrines propagated among others by Nae Ionescu, Traian Brăileanu, and Nichifor Crainic. In his *Trilogies — The Trilogy of Knowledge, The Trilogy of Culture, The Trilogy of Values —* Lucian Blaga (1895-1961) evolved an original philosophic system. Blaga's philosophy is tributary to irrationalism and leads to agnostic conclusions but shows aspects that are incontestably of value, in particular in his original interpretation of culture. His views are most interesting and his observations acute, when dealing with style and metaphor, and the specific nature of various cultures, especially Romanian culture. Throughout his works man and his creative virtues are honored. In the years of fascism Blaga denounced racist concepts and gave public denial to some of the ideas he had previously held and which were at the time misrepresented by the reactionary, obscurantist press.

During the interwar period the immense personality of N. Iorga continued to dominate Romanian historiography, though the great historian had few followers. In the ten volumes of his *History of the Romanians*, a monumental work relying on extensive documentation, Iorga gave priority to the political and cultural life of the Romanian people and devoted much eloquence to the outstanding personages of national history. Believing that the history of a people can only be understood if it is correlated with the history of the neighboring peoples and with world history in general, he showed the part played by the Romanian people in history in his work: *La Place des Roumains dans l'histoire universelle.*

Iorga's historical concepts are idealistic. The great personalities, and the superstructure phenomena generally, are considered to be decisive factors in the development of history, which is regarded as "a manifestation of man's thought, feelings and will". Beyond the rapid succession of events are what he called the permanent historical factors, the land, the race, and the idea, which give a unitary and organic character to history, and enable the historian to rebuild the past by the method of parallelism, similitude, and historical repetitions. Iorga intended to write a comprehensive history of the world — *Man's Historiology* — based on these concepts, when he was assassinated by members of the Iron Guard in 1940.

The monumental work of Vasile Pârvan (1882-1927), *Getica,* makes a most valuable contribution to the study of Geto-Dacian history. Relying on written sources, both narrative and epigraphic, and adding to them the results of his archeological research, Pârvan put the study of ancient history on a sound basis and created the Romanian school of archeology.

The historians of the National History Institute in Cluj, C. Daicoviciu, D. Prodan, I. Lupaş, and Silviu Dragomir among others, studied such problems as Daco-Roman continuity on Romanian territory, the foundation of Romanian medieval states, and the struggle for national emancipation of the Transylvanian Romanians.

In 1931 new trends emerged in Romanian historiography when *Revista Istorică Română (Romanian Historical Review)* was published. The historians P. P. Panaitescu, Gh. Brătianu, and C. C. Giurescu — contributing to that review — laid stress on the necessity of studying the problems of social, economic, and cultural history, and the relations between the culture of the Romanians and of other peoples.

Panaitescu and Brătianu showed a trend toward economic materialism, though not without some hesitation. In his monographs on the great men of Romanian medieval history, Michael the Brave and Mircea the Old, Panaitescu gave a comprehensive survey of the social forces and economic reasons for their actions, while at the same time showing the course of events within the framework of European history. Brătianu studied the social and economic history of Byzantium and the origins of the Romanian people, bringing new arguments in support of the continuity of the Daco-Roman population north of the Danube; moreover, he sought to re-establish the value of the tradition of the chroniclers in the study of the origin of the Romanian feudal states. In his *History of the Romanians* Giurescu devoted much space to economic life and to social and political institutions, but the various spheres of social life are shown parallel with each other without an analysis of historical determination.

Marxist historiography asserted itself during the interwar period in the studies published by A. Oțetea and P. Constantinescu-Iași. Oțetea endorsed the historical materialist concepts in an article published in the review *Însemnări Ieșene (Jassy Notes)* in 1937; while in *Renaissance and Reformation* (1941) he analyzed superstructural aspects in close connection with the economic basis of society. Constantinescu-Iași was the first to divide Romanian history into periods based on the criterion of the succession and evolution of socio-economic formations. This he did in his study: *A History of the Romanians: Main Features and Periods — A New Outlook* (1926).

Romanian historians made valuable contributions to the study of Byzantium (N. Bănescu), of the Later Crusade (F. Páll), Western medieval society (M. Berza), and South-East Europe (V. Papacostea).

Philological and linguistic research yielded noteworthy results in the works of Sextil Pușcariu, initiator of the *Romanian Linguistic Atlas*, O. Densușianu, I. Iordan, and Al. Rosetti.


## 3. Literature


LITERATURE made great strides. *Viața Românească (Romanian Life)*, a review of great prestige which after World War I changed its orientation by abandoning populism, was a forum of radical bourgeois democratism until 1940, when it was suppressed by Nazi censorship. Most of the great figures of Romanian culture, nearly all Romanian writers, contributed to the review. Mihail Sadoveanu (1880-1961) continued to publish his works in this review. He was one of the greatest

Romanian prose writers, giving an unparalleled picture of Romania's past history and showing great insight into the heart of the common people and a thorough knowledge of the language he used.

Other collaborators of the *Viaţa Românească* review during the interwar period were the prose writers Al. Teodoreanu, Ionel Teodoreanu, Cezar Petrescu and Damian Stănoiu among others. The poets G. Topârceanu, a refined humorist, Al. Philipide, an impassioned romantic rising against a prosaic and arid century, Demostene Botez with an elegiac trend, and Otilia Cazimir, who wrote touching lyrical poetry were also contributors. After 1930 Mihai Ralea became director of *Viaţa Românească*, and this great intellectual with a wide outlook published brilliant literary and philosophic essays in the review. G. Călinescu (1899-1965), for a time editor-in-chief of *Viaţa Românească*, was one of the most complex men of letters in the history of Romanian culture. Călinescu was an unrivalled critic, author of some substantial monographs on Romanian literature and of a stupendous history of Romanian literature from its inception to 1940, a most vigorous novelist *(Otilia's Enigma)*, a playwright, a poet, and a journalist. Tudor Vianu, aesthetician and philosopher of culture as well as an eminent professor, was a notable contributor to the review.

All sectors of literature went through a period of unusual creative effervescence during the span between the two World Wars. Modernism, incorporating the currents derived from symbolism, dominated lyrical poetry. The theoretician here was the critic E. Lovinescu (1881-1943) whose review *Sburătorul (The Goblin)*, 1919, together with his literary club, which was given the same name, was the center of a renovating literary movement. In his ample studies, Lovinescu stated the theory of synchronism, of differentiation and of the mutation of aesthetic values, militating for the integration of Romanian literature into the European artistic movement of the time. A supporter of the idea that an aesthetician must be autonomous, as Maiorescu had wished him to be, Lovinescu courageously denounced the attempts made during the period of fascist dictatorship to subordinate literature to the political interests of the regime. Advocating integral aestheticism, Mihail

Dragomirescu, a critic trained by the Junimea movement, created a personal aesthetic system which was appreciated by a number of outstanding Western theoreticians.

The orientation which assumed the name of modernism rather improperly was represented by some of the greatest writers. Greeted as a new Eminescu on the publication of his first volume, *Words That Fit —*, Tudor Arghezi (1880-1967) made unprecedented transformations in poetical syntax and in the language generally, thus making a capital contribution toward a modern refining of the lyrical language. He was a poet, prose writer and publicist. From among his books of poetry we will cite *Mould Flowers, Evening Verse, A Song to Man*, and from among his prose works, *Tablets from Kuti Land* and the *Annunciation Cemetery*. In his works, which are numerous, Arghezi debated all the problems of his day at the same time tackling the eternal problems of man and meditating upon the meaning of existence. Ion Barbu is of an altogether different structure: he wrote compact poetry intellectualized to the point of hermitism and tending towards "aerial purity." The prose writers and playwrights of the first magnitude collaborating with *Sburătorul* were Liviu Rebreanu (1885-1944), founder of the modern Romanian novel *(Ion, The Forest of the Hanged, The Uprising)*, creator of memorable situations and undying characters, and a master of epic construction; Hortensia Papadat-Bengescu (1876-1955), founder of the urban psychological novel in Romanian literature *(A Bach Concert)*; Camil Petrescu (1894-1957), novelist *(The Last Night of Love, The First Night of War)* and playwright *(The Dance of the Bad Fairies, Venetian Act*, and *Danton)*, novels and plays that center on people who "have seen ideas", intellectuals eager to know the essential and aspiring toward fulfillment in the absolute.

An active galaxy of critics came to the fore during the interwar period in a modernist climate. They include Perpessicius, Pompiliu Constantinescu, Şerban Cioculescu, Vladimir Streinu, and Mihail Sebastian who, following Maiorescu's tradition but using modern, analytical methods, ensured continuity in aesthetic orientation. Paul Zarifopol, editor-in-chief of *Revista Fundaţiilor Regale (Royal Foundation Review)*, 1934, a monthly issue of great distinction, was a critic showing much subtlety and sagacity.

Though in principle opposing modernism and advocating "traditionalism", *Gândirea (Thought)*, 1921, practically belonged to modernism, for most of what was fine and durable in it comes under that heading. The doctrine advocated by *Gândirea* is rooted in the philosophy of Oswald Spengler and Keyserling and is fostered by the philosophy of contemporary theoreticians of orthodoxy (Berdyaev, Bulgakov) and by patristic writings (Dionysius the Areopagite). It is a reflection of the anti-rationalism and obscurantism typical of part of bourgeois philosophy in the imperialist age, and consequently exercised a noxious influence and was one of the theoretical springs of the fascist movement in Romania. *Gândirea*, however, had only a superficial effect on the high standard literature it offered. It was in this review that were published most of the poems and philosophical studies of Lucian Blaga, the poet of "metaphysical sorrow" and creator of visions that are unique in their revelatory power and dramatic tension. His volumes of poems *Poems of Light, The Steps of the Prophet, The Watershed*, and *Praise to Sleep*, are of great moment in the history of Romanian lyricism. Blaga was an expresionist, and his poetry and plays, *Zamolxis, The Waters Are Troubled, Master Mason Manole, The Children's Crusade*, and *Avram Iancu*, give a major expression of the national spirit, fitting perfectly into what the writer calls "the stylistic matrix" of Romanian culture. Though modern, and even ultra-modern in their means of expression, Ion Pillat and Adrian Maniu belong to "traditionalism", for they favor the native landscape, the countryside, and the historical past of the country. Vasile Voiculescu and Nichifor Crainic were faithful to the traditional language. Among the prose writers contributing to *Gândirea* were Mateiu I. Caragiale, who wrote that strange and fascinating novel *Old-Time Libertines*, Gib. I. Mihăescu, the novelist of obsession *(The Russian Woman, Dona Alba)*, and Cezar Petrescu, author of more than 40 novels — "a Romanian twentieth century chronicle".

In the literary world of the age a place apart was held by the avant-garde reviews: *Contemporanul (The Contemporary)*, 1921, *Integral (Integrally)*, 1925, *Unu (One)*, 1928, *Urmuz*, 1928, *Alge (Sea Weeds)*, 1931. Among the poets and prosewriters contributing to these reviews were Tristan Tzara, Ion Vinea, B. Fundoianu (B. Fondane), Ilarie Voronca, Ion Călugăru,

Geo Bogza, Saşa Pană, Aurel Baranga, Gelu Naum, and Virgil Teodorescu. In their works such currents as dadaism, constructivism, and super-realism mix and mingle, and though their literary efforts were not exceptional, they left their mark on Romanian writing, stimulating the modernization of expression and maintaining Romanian literature within the evolutive trends of world literature. In the 1940's the writers showing an extreme modernist trend mostly joined the revolutionary movement headed by the Communist Party. Urmuz (Demetru Demetrescu-Buzău, 1883-1923), creator of a brand of absurd humor which foreshadowed Eugen Ionescu, was a forerunner of the avant-garde movement not only in Romanian but also in world literature.

The newspaper *Cuvântul (The Word)*, 1924, the review *Criterion*, 1934, and a number of other less important papers with contributors who were essayists with a philosophical rather than a literary bent showed an obviously obscurantist and retrograde tendency unbalancing to the youth. Some of them subsequently changed their bearings and produced substantial works written in Romanian or in another language and gained world fame. Mircea Eliade, a well-known historian of religions, was a remarkable prosewriter whose fantastic and exotic narratives, *Miss Christina, The Serpent, Doctor Honigberger's Secret*, and *Maitreyi*, are among the notable achievements of Romanian epic literature of the first half of the twentieth century.

Working under circumstances of the greatest difficulty, the Romanian Communist Party did not confine itself to carrying on secret activities but sought to make itself heard legally, through the intermediary of the press, for example. It was under the guidance of the Party that certain publications appeared during the interwar period, among them: *Cultura Proletară (Proletarian Culture)*, 1936, *Bluze Albastre (Blue Overalls)*, 1932, *Reporter (The Reporter)*, 1933, *Cadran (The Dial)*, 1934, *Era Nouă (The New Era)*, 1936. All these were printed in Romanian, but other publications appeared at the time in the languages of the co-inhabitating nationalities: *Szemle, Tomegkultura, Irjatok, Die Welt, Die Woche*. The ideological level of these reviews was above that of the socialist periodicals of the early years of the century: *Facla (The Torch)*, *Viaţa Socială (Social Life)*, and *Viitorul Social (The Social Fu-*

*ture).* The Party also had a word to say in other periodicals of the working class movement, such as *Şantier (The Building Site),* the review of the Social-Democrats, and in publications showing a progressive democratic trend as, for example, *Viaţa Românească (Romanian Life), Cuvântul Liber (Free Speech),* 1933, *Manifest (Manifesto),* 1934, *Insemnări Ieşene (Jassy Notes),* 1936, *Ţara Nouă (New Country),* 1939, and *Korunk* (1928). Among the contributors to these reviews were N. D. Cocea, Alexandru Sahia, Mihai Beniuc, Geo Bogza, Zaharia Stancu, Eugen Jebeleanu, M. R. Paraschivescu, Ion Călugăru, and G. Ivaşcu. With the exception of Sahia, who died in the prime of life, these writers formed the nucleus of the writers of the people's revolution after 1944.

## 4. Art

THE fine arts went through a period of remarkable achievements, assimilating various influences, assuming new forms, becoming greatly diversified, but preserving intact the tradition of harmony, balance and love for the concrete which is typical of Romanian art. Among the outstanding, dominating artists was Camil Ressu (1880-1962), an excellent portrait painter but also a landscapist and painter of grave, true-to-life pictures of the peasant. J. Al. Steriadi (1881-1957) who, coming under the influence of impressionism and showing himself a racy draftsman, entered the sphere of art in the early years of the century with compositions inspired by the life of the ordinary people. He was a painter remarkable for the warm, emotional quality of his colors. Iosif Iser (1881-1958) evolved from rather harsh representations of peasant figures and landscapes to original compositions with intense, velvety colors as a dominant element. Ştefan Dimitrescu (1886-1933) depicted village life, and working peasants in sober, concentrated, moving scenes. N. N. Tonitza (1886-1940) was an artist who put as much fervor into his militant drawings as into his painting and art criticism. His feeling for the expressive and decorative resources of color is revealed in his portraits of children, his still lifes with flowers, his Dobrudjan landscapes, and his nudes.

This was the time, too, when the great painter G. Petraşcu (1872-1949) attained fulfilment. His landscapes, interiors, still lifes, and portraits show poetical plenitude, a brilliant color scheme, and exceptional richness. During the same period other names graced Romanian art. Th. Pallady (1871-1956) produced landscapes both of Romania and France, nudes, and still lifes, with lucidity and flawless refinement as their main features, and an exceptional feeling for the decorative touch and for delicate color harmonies. Francisc Şirato (1877. 1953) achieved a synthesis between light, form, and color-Ştefan Popescu (1872-1948) was a sensitive landscape painter and a draftsman of great talent. Lucian Grigorescu (1894-1965) painting especially landscapes in the impressionist way, with great brilliance and with a fine sense of color scheme. N. Dărăscu (1883-1939) also a landscape painter, excellent in water colors. M. Bunescu (1881—1971) was painter of town sights and seascapes which were remarkable for their color scheme and composition. D. Ghiaţă (1880-1972) created works in whose simple and direct pictorial language and muted colors, not devoid of a sumptuous touch, lie a profound knowledge and understanding of the heart of the peasant and of the rustic landscape. H. Catargi (b. 1894) whose landscapes and still lifes give proof of a rare knowledge of composition and of a palette that is mellow and most expressive. I. Ţuculescu (1910-1962) exhibited a restless artistic temperament, and his works which started from a realistic vision imbued with great poetical feeling evolved toward expressionism and symbolic forms. Among these gifted artists should be included Alexandru Ciucurencu (b. 1903), a brilliant colorist, I. Theodorescu-Sion (1882-1939), Al. Phoebus (1899-1954), and M. H. Maxy (1895-1971), and the Transylvanians A. Ciupe (b. 1900), Catul Bogdan (b. 1897), Al. Ziffer (1880-1962), Aurel Popp (1879-1960), Mattis Teutsch (1884-1968), and Corneliu Mihăilescu (1887-1965).

Decorative painting of the monumental type has also some remarkable achievements to its credit, the most outstanding being *History of Romanian Trade*, in the Auditorium of the Academy of Economic Studies in Bucharest, painted by Cecilia Cuţescu-Storck (1879-1969), the frescoes of Olga Greceanu (b. 1890) in the Institute of Architecture and the N. Iorga History Institute, and the mosaics of Nora Steriadi (1884-1948).

Foremost among the representatives of Romanian sculpture and of modern world sculpture generally is Constantin Brâncuși (1876-1957). Already in 1907 when he produced his *Prayer*, Brâncuși had departed from traditional sculpture, endeavoring to produce archetypes, to reach primordial forms. His art is a constant progress toward the essence—the ultimate symbols of the living forms of nature achieved by a maximum effort in the chiseling and ennobling of materials. Brâncuși gained world fame by such works as *Eve* (1921), *Girl's Torso* (1922), *Socrates* (1923), the many versions of *Miss Pogany's Bust* and of the *Wonder Bird*, and *The Cock* (1941). Form in all these works is ever more rigorously concentrated, and in such works as the *Wonder Bird* and *The Cock* there are profound echoes of Romanian folk art, which become still more obvious, nearly programmatic, in the sculptural ensemble of Tîrgu Jiu (1938): *The Infinite Column, Gate of the Kiss, Table of Silence*.

It was during the period between the two World Wars that many of the Romanian sculptors who still do credit to the country began their activity. To Ion Jalea (b. 1887), who produced such works as *Hercules Killing the Centaur*, *The Archer*, and *Centaur Bending His Bow*, all praise is given. In Ion Jalea the sense of balance and a yearning for serenity instilled by a substantial classicism are undisputed.

The sculptural compositions of Cornel Medrea (1889-1964), among which are the monument to V. Lucaciu and numerous busts, show dramatic tension and moral and intellectual energy. In other works — *Nude, The Thorn* — the artist depicts everyday, nearly elementary life with robust vitality.

Oscar Han (b. 1891), who sculptured the *Mihail Kogălniceanu Statue* in Bucharest and the large bust of the poet Mihail Eminescu, shows a trend toward the monumental, towards a simplification of form and a comprehensive synthesis laden with symbolic meanings.

Other sculptors of note are Romulus Ladea (1901-1971), the son of a Banat peasant and pupil of Paciurea and Brâncuși, Ion Irimescu (b. 1903), Gheorghe Anghel (1904-1966), Boris Caragea (b. 1906), Mac Constantinescu (b. 1900), Constantin Baraschi (1902-1965) and Milița Petrașcu (b. 1892).

The left-wing reviews of the period gave space to a vast number of drawings depicting the struggle against exploitation and fascism. Using a modern, expressive language in their art, the Romanian draftsmen of the time showed themselves to be on a par with the contemporary militant draftsmen of Europe. Among them were Nicolae Cristea (1908-1936), Nina Arbore (1889-1941), Aurel Jiquidi (1896-1962), V. Kazar (b. 1913) and V. Dobrian (b. 1912), to whom should be added the valuable cartoonists I. Ross (b. 1899), M. Gion (b. 1912) and Ion Anestin (1900-1963).

The cartoons of Jiquidi, who chastised the ways of the bourgeoisie with rare gusto, deserve special mention. His illustrations of Caragiale's works are remarkable.

In architecture there were several trends. Some architects continued Ion Mincu's line, seeking modern solutions in order to integrate architecture into the specific national landscape. Others favored French Renaissance architecture, while others again adopted functionalism. The urban landscape consequently became eclectic and hybrid. Among the public and private edifices that strike the eye by their elegance and clear concepts are the Council of Ministers building and the Academy Library by Duiliu Marcu (1885-1966), the Bucharest People's Council by Petre Antonescu (1873-1965), the Republica Works of Bucharest and the Carpați Hotel in Brașov by Horia Creangă (1892-1943).

Between the two World Wars the history of arts found valuable representatives in Professors G. Oprescu, Al. Busuioceanu, and Tudor Vianu. Studies of the old Romanian art were made by Nicolae Iorga, G. Balș, N. Ghika-Budești, and Professor I. D. Ștefănescu. From among the artists Șirato and Tonitza were in general favor as art critics, as were also such men of letters as O. W. Cisek, P. Comarnescu, and M. Simionescu-Rîmniceanu.

It was in the early years of the twentieth century that the first generation of composers with a high sound training emerged from the magic circle of the eminent symphonist and teacher Alfonso Castaldi (1874-1942). Evolving along several decades, the new composers played an important part in the world of music. On no account should such names as Dimitrie Cuclin (1885), Alfred Alessandrescu (1893-1959), Ion Nonna Ottescu (1888-1940), and Constantin C. Nottara (1890-1951) be omitted. Symphonic music thus made new strides, going beyond the limits of a certain "provincialism" that was typical of the early efforts and showing the highest exigency.

However, it was George Enescu (1881-1955), who laid the foundations of the modern Romanian musical school. As a composer, violonist, conductor, and teacher, this brilliant musician achieved a synthesis of specific national features and the universal. Borrowing and assimilating elements from the national *melos* — modalism, intervallics, rhythmicity, and heterophony — as well as from the German symphony and from the French musical school, Enescu succeeded in rendering a climate that was genuinely Romanian in forms of perfect originality. His works, from the *Romanian Poem* (1898) and the two *Romanian Rhapsodies* (1901) to *Oedypus*, first played in Paris in 1936, and his *Chamber Symphony* (1954), integrate Romanian spirituality with its most characteristic features into Europe's musical culture. They are a perfect synthesis of Romanian music and of the musical language of our century.

# CHAPTER III

# Romania during World War II (1939—1945)

THE Second World War had a number of profound consequences on Romania's situation. During the first part of the war the Romanian leaders adopted a neutral policy. Faithful to the traditional orientation toward France and Britain, they sought to ward off the danger of the country being isolated, to keep the country out of the military operations that were unfolding in the immediate neighborhood, and to protect their territorial integrity. Developments in Europe, and in particular the defeat of France, shattered the hopes Romania had pinned on this line of orientation.

Without any foreign support, Romania saw her territory reduced in the summer of 1940 and was compelled to submit to Nazi Germany. A fascist military dictatorship was installed and German forces marched into the country. Finally Romania was drawn into the anti-Soviet War.

The Romanian people showed almost unanimous hostility to Nazism, and the resistance movement developed unceasingly from 1940 to 1944, assuming various forms according to the specific conditions prevailing in the country. The movement culminated in the anti-fascist insurrection of August, 1944, organized on the basis of a wide coalition of the anti-Nazi patriotic forces, from the most consistent and most determined of them — the Romanian Communist Party — to the king and the entourage of the royal palace. Overthrowing the fascist military dictatorship on August 23, 1944, and taking up arms against the Nazis, the Romanian people made an important contribution to the war waged by the anti-fascist coalition, until the capitulation of Nazi Germany.

## 1. Romania's Neutrality

AFTER the outbreak of World War II, with the armies of Nazi Germany at the country's borders, the Romanian ruling circles made it their aim to see that Romania should not be isolated and to defend her territorial integrity, which was threatened by Germany and the countries which wanted the peace treaties reviewed. In the hope that the economic and military potentialities of Britain and France would ultimately make up for their insufficient forces in the first stage of the war, Romania's rulers sought to keep the country out of war. A communiqué was issued by the Council of Ministers on September 4, 1939, stating that Romania would carry on a neutral policy and follow a "line of balance". Practice showed that the balance was most precarious and that the right-wing circles were to gain ground as the influence of Germany increased in Southeast Europe.

Eager to secure the integrity of her frontiers, Romania sought to improve her relations with Hungary and proposed that the two countries should conclude a non-aggression pact. The Hungarian government rejected this proposal.

In the autumn of 1939 the Romanian government approached the Soviet Union with a view to reaching an understanding.

Concurrently, circumstances being unfavorable to the small States, Romania strove for the formation of a "block of neutral countries" in Southeast Europe. Germany undertook vast activities to halt this initiative. Despite the risks she incurred, Romania supported the Poles who were undergoing great trials. She permitted war materials designed for the Polish army to cross Romanian territory; received some 50,000 Polish refugees, both civilian and military, into the country; allowed the President of the Polish Republic and the Government members to settle in Romania as private people; and saved and dispatched to the West the Polish treasury.

Germany protested vehemently against these measures.

Prime Minister Armand Călinescu, spokesman of the bourgeois circles which opposed the expansion of Nazi Germany and which were intent on preserving Romania's integrity and independence, was assassinated on September 21, 1939, by the Iron Guard, a Nazi agency.

Every effort made by Romania to improve her relations with the neighboring countries, to bring them back to normal came up against the opposition of the revisionist states.

Romania strove to develop her economic relations with all countries — Britain and France, as well as Germany and Italy — but the consequences were not such as had been expected by the Romanian Government. For Nazi Germany economic relations were mere levers helping her to achieve Romania's economic and political subordination.

Romania's isolation and her complete abandonment to the hands of Berlin caused serious prejudices to Germany's opponents, for many resources, in particular Romanian oil, were thus placed at the disposal of the Germans. France's capitulation and Britain's defeat on the continent, no less than the threatened Nazi invasion of Britain, further aggravated Romania's situation.

On June 26, 1940, Bessarabia and Northern Bucovina were incorporated within the U.S.S.R.

Foreign developments and the ever more brutal interference of Nazi Germany in Romania's internal affairs favored the rise of pro-German groups in political life. On July 4, 1940, a cabinet was formed with I. Gigurtu as premier and many representatives of the fascist groups holding important positions.

The new cabinet took stern repressive measures against the democratic forces, sending the Communists and antifascists to concentration camps. Such measures weakened the Romanian people's capacity to resist at one of the most serious moments in their history.

On July 15, 1940, Hitler asked King Carol II to accept the policy of the Nazis and consent to territorial changes, threatening that non-acceptance "sooner or later, the sooner more likely, would mean Romania's annihilation".

These were difficult moments for the destinies of the country. Alone, without any outside support, a prey to Nazi Germany and her allies, Romania had to submit to the onerous conditions of the Vienna Fascist Diktat at the end of August, 1940. Northern Transylvania, with over 2,500,000 inhabitants, most of them Romanian, went to Horthy's Hungary.

The whole of Romania protested against the Vienna Diktat; every social section, all the political groups and figures of note expressed their revolt and anger at seeing the country's territory mutilated. Great demonstrations against the Vienna decision took place throughout the country with citizens, often the local authorities, and military units protesting. International public opinion attacked the Vienna Diktat, and Great Britain issued an official statement showing that she did not recognize the arbitrary Ribbentrop-Ciano sentence.

Faced with such an impressive demonstration of revolt on the part of the Romanian people, the Nazi Reich encouraged the Iron Guard and the Nazi Party of the Germans in Romania, intensified the activities of the German Legation and of the Gestapo, and made preparations to invade the country in the event of an armed resistance.

Such were the prevailing internal and external conditions under which a fascist-military dictatorship was installed in Romania with the direct participation of Hitler's emissaries. The dictatorship was followed by the penetration of German forces into the country.

On September 4, 1940, the Gigurtu cabinet resigned and General Ion Antonescu was designated prime minister by royal decree. Two days later Carol II, whom the Reich did not trust, was forced to abdicate in favor of his son Michael. General Antonescu then became "Leader of the State" with dictatorial powers.

According to the plan worked out jointly with the German Legation, and at the latter's express demand, General Antonescu formed a military-legionary cabinet with Legionaires, as Nazi agents, holding key positions. The military-fascist regime was the most reactionary, most anti-popular, and most anti-national form of government in the history of the country, enforced by the fascist and pro-Nazi circles in Romania

## 2. *The Military-Fascist Dictatorship in Romania*

THE military fascist dictatorship was based politically on the Iron Guard until January, 1941, with the mighty support of the Nazi Wehrmacht whose units filtered into the country from October, 1940, to rise to half a million men by January, 1941. Actually Romania had been occupied by Nazi Germany and this was confirmed both by the activities of the Nazi forces and officials and by the appreciations to be found in the documents of the time. In one such document it is stated: "The United States consider Romania as an occupied country for although the German forces entered the country with the assent of the Romanian government, the Romanian people would never have freely admitted it except under duress".

The fascist rulers installed a regime of terror and fierce repression. The laws issued at the time provided for stern sanctions, which included the death penalty, for any act showing resistance to the military-fascist regime and the Nazi war. New concentration camps and prisons were created for thousands of anti-fascists.

Legionaires closely cooperating with the Gestapo killed many opponents of fascism, including outstanding militants, Communists (Constantin David), and prominent scientists and men of letters (the world-famous historian Nicolae Iorga and the university professor Virgil Madgearu).

With the military-fascist regime installed, the representatives of the main parties which had held the reins of government before 1938 adopted a stand which suited their class interests and tried to save their positions now threatened by the new internal situation and by the development of the war. Maniu, D. Brătianu, and other politicians were generally for a bourgeois, constitutional form of government. As a result of their ties with the West, they were still partisans of France and Britain and believed that the western powers would be victorious. However, the international situation from the political and military points of view, the isolation of Romania in this corner of Europe, Germany's brutal pressure, and sharp internal contradictions convinced these political leaders that some concessions should be made to German pressure and to the pro-Nazi internal circles. Considering Germany's domination as temporary, they felt that the only acceptable solution to Romania's problem was the formation of a cabinet enjoying the confidence of Nazi Germany.

Counting on General Antonescu's pro-British feelings — he had been military attaché in London — and on the General's aversion to King Carol II, while at the same time fearing that a dictatorial Legionary government might be set up, the leaders of the National Peasant and of the National Liberal Parties agreed that the government should be headed by a person acceptable to Hitler who might to a certain extent defend their interests. But beyond the calculations of those politicians there was a most cruel reality: Romania's utter subordination to the interests of the Nazi Reich.

The presence of the Nazi forces in Romania and the country's political subservience created conditions that enabled the German monopolies systematically to get hold of the Romanian economy.

According to the plans of Nazi Germany, Romania's economic subordination was gradually to result in the seizing of her national industry, the country being thus turned into an outlet for the products of German industry and into a source of raw materials and foodstuffs. "Romania had better give up the idea of having an industry of her own", Hitler declared at the time. "She should direct the wealth of her soil, primarily wheat, towards the German market.... Romania's proletariat, which is infected with Bolshevism, would thus disappear and our country would never lack for anything".

Under the agreement of December 4, 1940, the government of the Third Reich obliged Romania to adapt her economy to the requirements of Nazi Germany, to have her various branches of activity controlled by German "experts", and to make payments under the "Central Clearing House in Berlin".

By consenting to this agreement, General Antonescu won the goodwill and support of Hitler to the detriment of the Iron Guard. The dissensions between the majority of the military forces and the pro-Nazi Legionaires assumed violent forms.

On January 21-23, 1941, the Legionaires' rebellion broke out, its aim being to remove General Antonescu from office and to install an Iron Guard administration for good and all. The Romanian army, hostile to the Legionaires — Nazi agents and a hotbed of anarchy and terror — put down the rebellion. The Iron Guard had received no support whatever from any internal political or social groups.

Germany, who was preparing for the anti-Soviet war and needed peace and order behind the front-to-be, supported General Antonescu, though on the other hand she gave asylum to Horia Sima and other Legionary leaders and used them as a political reserve and to blackmail Antonescu.

After the rebellion of January, 1941, a cabinet of officers and technicians was formed. Though the Nazis insisted, Antonescu opposed the plan to rebuild the Iron Guard. However, Antonescu's military dictatorship continued its profoundly antipopular internal policy and the enslavement of the country to Nazi Germany and drew the country into the war of the Reich without the approval of the Romanian general staff, government, or king.

*

When the German forces marched into Romania in the autumn of 1940, they were given a hostile reception by the people who considered them as so many bayonets supporting a fascist dictatorship and as a main instrument in ensuring the Reich's domination over the country. The terrorist methods instituted by the Iron Guard in the autumn of 1940 were continued with the support of the Nazi divisions. All this induced the Romanian people to speed up the organization of a resistance movement against the fascist dictatorship of the Nazi invaders.

Faced with disaster, the patriotic forces of the country organized a resistance movement which developed under new conditions into the anti-fascist and anti-Nazi struggle of the Romanian people.

The resistance movement involved the most different social strata and classes. The working class, being the most combative, best organized and keenest in fighting fascism, rallied round it the great patriotic forces of the peasantry, the progressive intelligentsia, and the patriotic elements in the army and drew them into an ever more active struggle.

Many scientists opposed the offensive of fascist ideology, defending the traditions of the national culture and making their contribution to the struggle of the people for removing the fascist yoke. Outstanding Romanian intellectuals repudiated Antonescu's dictatorship and the alliance with the Nazi Reich. They declared for the defense of Romania's national interest and her extrication from the anti-Soviet war.

The same spirit that prevailed among the masses was also to be found in the army, who were almost wholly against the Nazi war and regarded with hatred the Nazi armies which had violated the country's sovereignty. Clashes took place at the front between Romanian and Nazi soldiers. The German commanders sent in reports stating that they were profoundly dissatisfied with the lack of enthusiasm of the Romanian units and the difficulties made by the Romanian officers in carrying out operations under German command. The anti-Nazi feelings of the Romanian army increased as a result of the plundering carried out by Nazi Germany in Romania, of the heavy casualties at the front, and of the behavior of the Nazi troops, who, not infrequently, struck down the Romanian soldiers in their retreat, crushed the wounded under their tanks, and bullied, humbled, and attacked the Romanian soldiers. As a consequence, many Romanians refused to leave for the front or deserted and went over to the Soviet or the partisan army, or engaged in armed clashes with the German soldiers. Romanian and Nazi officers could not come to an understanding, the reasons being those which had determined the anti-Nazi feelings of the soldiers.

A number of army commanders, generals, and chiefs of staff opposed the anti-Soviet war. The anti-Nazi Romanians in France, the U.S.S.R., Czechoslovakia, Belgium, and elsewhere joined in the struggle of the patriotic forces of those countries, thus making their contribution to the common cause of the peoples of the world. Alongside the brave French resistance fighters, many Romanians fought and died for the liberation of France from Nazi occupation. In the Soviet Union tens of thousands of prisoners formed divisions to fight the Nazi armies.

Voicing the aspirations of the overwhelming majority of the country, the anti-fascist democratic forces headed the popular resistance which aimed to overthrow the military-fascist dictatorship, extricate the country from the Nazi war, and join the anti-fascist coalition. It was the Communist Party which took the initiative of rallying all the forces to a common front.

A stimulus was given to the anti-fascist resistance when in 1943 an anti-Nazi patriotic front was formed, uniting the Communist Party, the Ploughmen's Front, MADOSZ, the Socialist Peasant Party, the Patriots' Union, and the local organizations of the Social-Democratic Party.

Wide circles, which included members of the bourgeois parties and of the Royal Palace, opposed Antonescu's dictatorship and Nazi Germany, showing their hostility to the German occupants and their revolt to see the country plundered by them. They demanded that the economic treaties concluded with the Reich be revised and German interference in the country's internal affairs be restricted.

The defeats suffered by Nazi Germany at the hands of the anti-fascist coalition, in particular on the Soviet Front, the increased dissatisfaction of the masses, and the upsurge of the people's anti-fascist struggle struck the dominant classes with panic, aggravating the political crisis of the military dictatorship. Nor was the army very eager to support Antonescu's government, and this led to the disorganization of the fascist state machinery.

In 1943 and 1944 sabotage intensified among the workers in industrial enterprises and in the transport services, as did also the opposition of the peasantry to requisitioning and conscription. There were protests from the intelligentsia, and the soldiers refused to go to the front, all of which showed the people's hatred for the Nazi war and their desire to shake off the fascist yoke.

There were partisans in the Banat mountains as well as in the Bucegi and Vrancea Mountains, in Maramureş, in the Suceava county, in the Danube Delta, and in Oltenia.

The difficulties that Antonescu's dictatorship labored under and the victories of the Soviet armies, who bore the brunt of the war in Europe, as well as the victories of the British and American armies, led the leaders of the National Peasant and National Liberal Parties to renew their contacts and negotiations with the Western diplomats, the aim being to conclude a secret peace and thus extricate Romania from the war.

Talks took place to this effect in Cairo in March and May, 1944, and hopes were placed on the "Balkan version" of the Second Front in Europe as advocated by Winston Churchill.

When military operations began on Romanian territory in Northern Moldavia, the Nazi command turned the country into a devastating theater of war.

With the turn of events, the entire nation made it its aim to save the country from a disastrous total war. All sections of society, all classes, political parties, and persons of note opposed the dictatorship and the Nazi war, rallied to the cause, but definite measures had to be taken for the overthrow of Antonescu's government and the turning of the country's arms against Nazi Germany.

The National Peasant and National Liberal Parties sought to extricate Romania from the war by carrying on negotiations with the anti-fascist coalition powers, though they gave a wide berth to the Soviet Union. Their approaches overlooked the fact that the United States, Britain and the U.S.S.R. acted in unison in the war, nor did they take into account the prospects that might open up at the conclusion of the war. Hoping that an Anglo-American front would be made in the Balkan Peninsula, or that airborne Anglo-American forces would land in Romania, the politicians who represented these circles opposed for a long time the unification of all anti-fascist patriotic forces in the country. Subsequent developments showed the weakness of their orientation.

The king and the leaders of the National Peasant and National Liberal Parties had finally to submit to factual evidence and admit that the only political group able to switch over to definite action was the Communist Party. Consequently the circles in the royal palace, and a number of generals and party leaders, agreed to co-operate in one form or another with the Communists, despite their anti-Communist feelings.

The Communist Party, having considered the situation in the country and abroad, worked out a plan for unifying all the forces hostile to dictatorship and to the Nazi war, from the Communists to the royal palace, from the workers to the generals, and drew them all into a carefully prepared, well-coordinated plan which was to end in the anti-fascist insurrection of August, 1944.

In April, 1944, an understanding was reached between the Communist Party and the Social Democratic Party for the creation of a Workers' Single-Front, for building up a united action of the working class in wartime and under a military dictatorship. This was of considerable importance in speeding up the coalition of all democratic and patriotic forces with a view to overthrowing the fascist regime.

In May, 1944, an agreement was reached between the Communist Party and the Liberal group headed by Gheorghe Tătărăscu.

On June 20, 1944, the leaders of the National Peasant and National Liberal Parties subscribed to the creation of the National Democratic Bloc made up of the Communist Party, the Social-Democratic Party, the National Peasant Party, and the National Liberal Party.

Intensive activities were simultaneously being carried on in the ranks of the army, as patriotic officers and generals were induced to make military preparations for the insurrection. The military committee which was formed after the conference held by the representatives of the Romanian Communist Party, the royal palace and the army in the night of June 13, 1944, was assigned the task of preparing the military units for their participation in the insurrection.

## 3. Armed Insurrection

IN the summer of 1944 a comprehensive coalition of forces had been formed in Romania which included the working class and its parties, the bourgeois parties, and the royal palace entourage. This alliance was an essential factor of success in the overthrow of Antonescu's military dictatorship and in Romania's joining the anti-fascist coalition.

The creation of armed working class detachments designed to fight in the patriotic struggle was of great importance in the success of the insurrection. Organized in the factories of Bucharest and in certain districts of the country (Prahova Valley, Oltenia, Banat), armed and well-trained, these detachments were to rally all the patriots determined to fight against the fascist regime and the Nazi forces.

The plan for the overthrow of the fascist dictatorship was carefully worked out from the military standpoint as well as from the political. The insurrection was to begin in Bucharest in the latter half of August and at the same time in Ploiești and in the Prahova Valley oilfields.

Bucharest was a fitting place to start the insurrection for it could bring in the support of the masses. A surprise attack would cripple, from the start, the German command and the fascist repression bodies, for it was in Bucharest that the government of the military dictatorship had its headquarters; it was there that the central state institutions and the main Nazi military command for Romania were to be found.

While these measures were to be taken inside the country, certain units of the Romanian army, under the command of generals who had enthusiastically consented to help overthrow the dictatorship, were to check the penetration of Nazi forces from Northern Transylvania and over the western and southern frontiers of the country. The Romanian forces on the

Moldavian front were to separate from the Nazi units and join the forces fighting against Nazi Germany.

Military developments during the last ten days of August, 1944, created favorable conditions for the insurrection. Along the Jassy-Kishinev front a strong offensive of the Soviet Army began on August 20, 1944. The bulk of the Nazi forces were putting up a hard fight, suffering heavy casualties. Romanian regiments and divisions withdrawing from the front produced gaps in the defense line. However, the Nazi forces were far from being defeated, and the German command had prepared their withdrawal over a long period.

In the fortified area of Focşani-Nămoloasa-Galatz and along the Danube up to its confluence with the Black Sea, the Nazi command and Antonescu's government had taken special defense measures for a strong resistance line. The area between the bend of the Carpathians and the bend of the Danube at Galatz, some sixty miles long, was the only place where the Soviet armies could penetrate to make their way to the Danube plain, Bulgaria, and Yugoslavia. But the area which was fortified 40 miles deep was considered to be impregnable. The Nazi command banked on prolonged resistance in that area. Other successive lines of resistance along the larger rivers and the mountains were to have been built up within the country in order to delay the advance of the Soviet armies.

However, the armed insurrection was to overthrow all those plans. In accordance with the plan worked out by common agreement by the Communists and the representatives of the royal palace, it began on August 23, 1944. On orders from the king, the heads of the military fascist government, Ion and Mihai Antonescu, were arrested by members of the royal guard. A group of patriotic fighters headed by Communist leader Emil Bodnăraş removed them from the palace and imprisoned them in one of the secret houses of the Communist Party. Other ministers, including the Home and the War Ministers, were summoned to the palace to participate in a Crown Council and were arrested the same evening.

During the night of August 23, 1944, a government was formed. It was made up of officers and technicians, with General Sănătescu as premier and representatives of all the parties of the National Democratic Bloc (the Romanian

Communist Party, the Social Democratic Party, the National Peasant Party and the National Liberal Party), as ministers without portfolio.

During the night the army and the patriotic forces disarmed the German military units. The insurrection quickly swept over the country, from Moldavia and the Black Sea coast to Banat and Central Transylvania.

The fiercest fighting took place in Bucharest and along the Prahova Valley, where strong Nazi military units and commands were to be found.

The order Hitler sent General Friessner, commander of the Southern Ukraine armies, on August 24, 1944, to resist at any cost, "to destroy the capital and install a new pro-German government" resulted in violent attacks by German air and motorized units. Though an understanding had been reached between the king and the German general Gerstenberg, according to which the German army was to be allowed to withdraw from the country provided it abstained from destructive action, the Romanian patriotic fighters and the army had begun to clear the towns of Nazi units. When the Germans launched their air attack on Bucharest, the fighting became general wherever Nazi units were to be found.

Apart from the mortality figures during the fighting, over 50,000 of the Nazi army were made prisoners, including fourteen generals, and immense quantities of war materials were taken.

The armistice convention signed in Moscow between the governments of the Soviet Union, the United Kingdom, and the United States of America, on the one hand, and the Romanian government on the other, stated:

"At 4.00 a.m. on August 24, 1944, Romania ceased entirely her military operations against the Union of Soviet Socialist Republics in all theaters of war, ceased to make war against the United Nations, severed relations with Germany and her satellites, joined in the war on the side of the Allied Powers and fought against Germany and Hungary with the aim of restoring Romania's independence and sovereignty . . ."

By August 26, Bucharest was cleared of German troops. On August 30 and 31, 1944, the first Soviet units reached the outskirts of Bucharest, which had been liberated by the insurrection, and were welcomed by the population. By August

31, in barely eight days, the Romanian insurrectional forces had defeated the Nazi troops over most of the country's territory.

As a result of the collapse of the government of military-fascist dictatorship and of the German Command in Romania, the country did not become a ravaged territory, hundreds of thousands of lives were saved, and many towns and villages were left untouched. Industrial enterprises and particularly the installations in the Prahova Valley oilfields, were also saved. Since the Nazis had planned to destroy these installations in their withdrawal, their survival was of great importance because fuel could be supplied to the anti-Nazi front.

During the night of August 24, 1944, Soviet troops encircled the bulk of the South-Ukraine Nazi armies in the center of Moldavia and Bessarabia and by the end of August had thoroughly routed them, and even succeeded in taking some of the passes in the Moldavian Carpathians. Other important Soviet units proceded at a swift pace, making their way toward Bulgaria, Yugoslavia, and Northern Transylvania, without having to fight on Romanian soil.

The insurrection had an anti-fascist character for the forces that had achieved it had anti-Nazi aims. Antonescu's military dictatorship was overthrown, and Romania joined the anti-fascist coalition, fighting against Germany and her fascist allies with a view to the liberation of the homeland and to ensuring full national independence. Vast numbers from all sections of society took part in the overthrow of the military fascist dictatorship and in pushing the Nazis beyond the country's frontiers, for the liberation of the homeland from the fascist yoke was an aim that rallied all the forces of the nation.

At the same time, the insurrection and Romania's joining the anti-Nazi coalition were of the utmost importance in international affairs. The way was thus opened to the Soviet army toward the Danube Valley, a strategic area, as well as through the passes of the Eastern Carpathians, and a contribution was thus made to the collapse of the Nazi forces in the Balkans. The military and economic potentialities of the Allies were increased by Romania joining the anti-fascist coalition, and the war in Europe was thus shortened. The character and role of the insurrection in the anti-fascist struggle and the contribution of the Romanian people to the common cause are brought out by numerous documents originating in a large number of countries.

Before the end of the day on August 23, 1944, developments in Romania were already commented upon. That evening the BBC pointed out that "Romania's move would have marked effects. . ." and the United States radio station in Europe stated that "henceforth Romania was a new ally in the United Nations' camp for she had asserted her will to join in the struggle against the common enemy".

The following day and for many days thereafter the Soviet, French, English, American, Turkish, Swedish, and Swiss radio stations and daily papers gave special attention to Romania's move on August 23, and to her joining the anti-fascist coalition.

The foreign press described the spirit of the population which was definitely hostile to Nazism. The Swedish paper *Svenska Morgenbladet* recorded that in Romania there had always been a great feeling of sympathy with the United Nations in all sections of society.

In accounting for this state of spirit and attitude, a number of papers spoke of the consequences of Romania's dismemberment in the summer of 1940, of the dissatisfaction and great hatred of the people for the Vienna Diktat whereby the Axis Powers had ceded Northern Transylvania to Hungary.

*Le Figaro* wrote that Romania had been the only one of Germany's satellites which had "not received any territories in exchange for its alliance, but on the contrary had been compelled to cede to Hungary one of its most fertile provinces — Northern Transylvania".

Tha Nazi press, in its turn, pointed out that this was no putsch of the royal palace circles, nor a mere change of government, but a revolt that meant to change the line followed thus far.

With reference to the character and significance of the move of August 23, 1944, and to the part played by the Romanian Communist Party in preparing for and organizing that move, *L'humanité* noted: "The Romanian people are setting an example. After Antonescu's removal from power, they immediately turned against the Germans. In Romania, as well as in France and Yugoslavia, the Communist Party, though working underground, was one of the main factors in this change of allies".

Pointing to the decisive significance in the country of the move of August 23, the Swedish paper *Ny Dag* wrote: "The Romanian people are now taking their destinies in their own hands and proclaiming a democratic order".

The *New York Herald Tribune* of August 24, 1944, showed that what was left of the sixth and eighth German armies had been trapped between the Russians and the Romanians, the latter attacking the Germans from behind according to orders received from Bucharest, adding that it was the second time that the Wehrmacht had had its sixth army trapped.

The civilian and military insurrectional forces prevented the Nazis from organizing resistance along the narrow and strongly fortified line between the Eastern Carpathians, Focşani, and the Danube — one of the strongest strategic points, a gate toward the heart of the Balkans, the key to the Balkan plains, as it was described in the documents of those days.

The success of the insurrection also prevented the Nazis from resisting along the Southern Carpathians. The Romanian forces organized the defense and repelled the German-Hungarian attacks from the Transylvanian plateau, and this was of considerable importance for the subsequent development of the war. This operation of the Romanian army was widely commented on abroad. In its broadcast of August 28, 1944, a New York radio station declared that Romania had enabled the Allied forces to crush the German resistance along the Carpathians, thus making a decisive contribution to the victory of the Allied Powers.

The withdrawal of German forces from favorable positions held in Romania had serious consequences for Nazi Germany.

Moscow Radio pointed out: "Nowhere on Romanian territory did the Germans succeed in repeating the events which took place in Northern Italy in the summer of 1943. They did not succeed in disarming the Romanian army or occupying the main strategic positions".

The documents of those days also brought out the influence which the victory of the anti-fascist insurrection in Romania had on other countries and on the general progress of the war. They laid stress on the consequences abroad of Romania joining the anti-fascist coalition: military, strategic, economic, and moral-political consequences.

With reference to the effects achieved by Romania's joining the United Nations, the BBC stated in its broadcasts of August 24, 1944, that Romania's move was an act of great courage which should speed up the end of the war and that Germany's situation in the Balkans would soon be a fearful catastrophe.

The American newspaper *The Evening Star* pointed out that Romania's joining the Allies was jeopardizing all the German forces in Greece, Yugoslavia, Bulgaria, Hungary, Czechoslovakia, and southern Poland, while the French paper *Front National* claimed with reference to developments in Romania that the Reich had been dealt a terrible blow and that the Soviet divisions on the Romanian front would now be available for new offensives which would strike at the very heart of the enemy.

Indeed, according to the directions given on August 29, 1944, 27 divisions of the second and third Ukrainian fronts were placed at the disposal of Soviet headquarters, which was thus in a position to increase the pressure on the enemy along other fronts.

Moscow Radio pointed out that Romania leaving the Axis was of overwhelming importance not only for her but also for the whole Balkan Peninsula for it was a blow that caused the entire German domination system in South-East Europe to collapse. The significance of this move should not be underestimated, it was remarked. On August 27, 1944, the British paper *Sunday Times* pointed out that Romania breaking away from the Axis to go over to her traditional allies might be a deadly blow to Germany, for the latter thus lost her last important oil reserves and, at the same time, three ways were being opened for the Russians' advance: towards Bulgaria, whose position would probably be modified the moment the first Russian soldier appeared on her frontier; toward Yugoslavia and the Adriatic, where the population was sure to rise everywhere against what was left of the German army; and toward the Hungarian plain, Budapest, and Vienna, which would cause the pro-Nazi Magyar regime to collapse and bring about a revolt in Czechoslovakia. The *Sunday Times* concluded that Romania could be described as a keystone.

A communique of the Allied Headquarters in the Mediterranean stated that the Germans' withdrawal from the Peloponnesus had been considerably speeded up by Romania's defection and by the consequences of that move on the Germans' position throughout South-East Europe.

The United Nations more than once expressed their gratitude for the contribution made by the Romanian people to the general cause of the anti-fascist, anti-Nazi struggle.

A commentary of a New York radio station stated that after Romania had gone over to the Allies, Germany was threatened from the South-East, and Hungary was on the verge of collapse. The way to Budapest, Prague, and Vienna from the South-West was open, it was stated, for the Germans had no new forces in these directions. The commentator considered that the Romanian people might well feel satisfied for Romania had made an outstanding contribution toward speeding up the end of the war.

The developments in Romania also called forth a wide response in the neutral countries, as shown by diplomatic documents, and press and radio comments in Sweden, Turkey, and Switzerland.

The documents of those days also spoke of Germany's losses in Romania as disastrous and catastrophic, and also of the collapse of the South-Eastern front. The events that took place in Romania in August, 1944, have gone down in history and their consequences for the Nazis have always been described as shown above.

The Nazi High Command was compelled to admit that the developments in Romania had serious consequences on the position of Germany and her associates. In a report to Hitler drawn up by Keitel and Guderian, it was pointed out that these events, apart from their immediate military consequences, at the same time brought about a reversal of fronts which was extremely dangerous, and would lead not only to the loss of Romania but also of Bulgaria, Yugoslavia, and Greece, and jeopardize the position of the whole German army in the Balkans.

The authors of the report suggested "that every measure should be taken to wipe Romania off the map of Europe and to annihilate her people as a nation".

The August insurrection is a landmark in the history of
the Romanian people, a national and social turning point, the
beginning of a new age, the result of the people's struggle
for freedom, of their will to freedom, with roots going deep
into their history. It is a link with the other turning points
in the life of the Romanian people.

## 4. Romania's Participation in the Anti-Nazi War

DURING the first days of September, 1944, most of the
Romanian units which had taken part in the insurrection
were sent northwest of the Southern Carpathians to strengthen the positions of the Romanian forces along the western
frontier of the country. Two enemy offensives were thus
repelled: one on the Transylvanian plateau between September 5 and September 8, and another in Crişana and Banat
on September 18. Furthermore, the Romanian army ruined
the plan of the Nazi command to establish the front line on
favorable defensive positions from Slovakia's mountains, along
the Eastern and Southern Carpathians, and along the Balkans
down to Greece. The mountain passes and routes in the Banat
plain and across the Transylvanian plateau were now accessible
so that a link could be established with the rest of the country,
and Soviet and Romanian tank divisions and motorized and
infantry forces could be grouped unhindered with a view to
operations in the plain towards Debreczen, Budapest, and
Vienna.

The advance of the Soviet forces across the Eastern Carpathian passes toward the front held by the Romanian army
changed the ratio of forces to the detriment of the enemy,
conditions being thus created for a new large-scale offensive.
By early October, 1944, the joint action of the Soviet and
Romanian forces advanced the front to the upper reaches of
the river Mureş, while in Crişana and Banat the enemy was
repelled to the Romanian-Bulgarian and Romanian-Yugoslav
frontiers.

On October 6, 1944, the Romanian and Soviet armies, in
order to liberate Northwest Transylvania and the Hungarian
territory up to the river Tisza, engaged in a powerful offensive

known as the Debreczen operation. The Romanian units taking part in that operation totalled 260,000 men.

On October 25, 1944, enemy resistance was crushed in the Satu Mare and Carei areas and Romania was completely freed from the fascist yoke. Northern Transylvania, which had been seized from Romania by the Vienna Diktat, was again incorporated within the country. The news was welcomed by the entire Romanian people. Meetings and demonstrations were held, the masses showing their gratitude for the heroism and sacrifices of the soldiers at the front and pledging to increase their efforts in the war until the capitulation of Nazi Germany.

Cooperating with the Soviet forces beyond the country's frontiers, the Romanian troops took part in the liberation of Hungary and Czechoslovakia until the final defeat of Nazi Germany and the victorious conclusion of the war in Europe.

The Romanian forces fighting on Hungarian territory included seventeen infantry and cavalry divisions, an aircraft detachment, two anti-aircraft artillery brigades, a railway brigade and other units, totalling over 210,000 men. The Romanian forces had their share in the liberation of Budapest, Debreczen, Miskolcz, and other towns.

On December 18, 1944, Soviet and Romanian units crossed the Hungarian-Czechoslovak frontier. On Czechoslovak territory Romanian troops, as part of the great operative units of the Soviet army, fought bravely in the Javorina, Lower Tatra, the Slovak Metallic, and Higher Tatra Mountains. The winter was severe and the terrain unfavorable for action. Nevertheless, the resistance of the enemy was gradually broken down and many towns were liberated, among them key centers such as Lucenec, Zvollen, and Banska Bistrica.

The Romanian units taking part in operations in Czechoslovakia totalled more than 248,000 men. They were made up of sixteen infantry and cavalry divisions, an aircraft detachment, an anti-aircraft artillery division, a railway brigade, a tank regiment, and other units.

By the end of the Second World War in Europe Romania's entire military and economic potential was engaged alongside the anti-Nazi coalition.

The Romanian military units fighting in the anti-Nazi war from August 23, 1944, to the capitulation of Nazi Germany amounted to nearly 540,000 men. Some 170,000 Romanian officers and men were killed or injured in the battles waged against the fascist invaders. From August 23, 1944, to May 12, 1945, the Romanian army defeated over fourteen Nazi and Hungarian divisions.

Many orders of the day of the Romanian Ministry of War and General Staff showed the gallantry in the field of the Romanian troops, as did also seven orders of the day of the Soviet High Command and twenty-one Soviet war communiqués. Over 300,000 soldiers, non-commissioned officers, and officers were awarded Romanian, Soviet, and Czechoslovak orders and medals.

Romania's entire national economy worked for the front. Although the Romanian people made every effort and sacrifice to support the anti-Nazi war, yet the economy suffered in the extreme as a result of the Nazi plunder, the destruction caused by bombing and military operations, the blocking of Romanian foreign currency in the western countries, and the expenditure on the support of the anti-Nazi front and the war reparations. All this amounted to more than 3.5 times Romania's national revenue of 1938.

Official representatives in various countries, political and military figures as well as the foreign press often pointed to the important contributions made by Romania toward the defeat of Nazi Germany. On September 29, 1944, Anthony Eden, the British foreign secretary, pointed out that Romania had substantially helped the Allied cause.

V. M. Molotov, Minister of Foreign Affairs of the Soviet Union and head of the Soviet delegation to the Paris Peace Conference, said on October 10, 1944: "We all know that Romania, by a decisive move, shook off Antonescu's fascist regime and joined the Allies ... Together with ourselves and with the Allied troops, the new democratic Romania engaged in the fight for Hitler's defeat and made considerable sacrifices in that fight. We all recognize the services the Romanian people have made for the cause ..."

On January 7, 1945, the BBC reported that among the nations fighting against Nazi Germany Romania had the fourth largest number of men fighting for the destruction of Nazism.

In an article headed "Romania Alongside the United Nations", French General Cochet and Lieutenant Colonel Paquier pointed out that the Romanian forces fighting side by side with Soviet forces had advanced more than 800 miles through enemy positions along the river Mureş and up to Bohemia, liberating 5,830 towns and villages and taking 100,000 prisoners. They concluded: "The French who fought together with the Romanians during the 1914-1918 war were able to appreciate their power of resistance, moral unity and fervent patriotism.

Romania has given her best to the cause of the Allies."

Because of her contribution to the anti-Nazi war, it was proposed to give Romania the status of co-belligerent. Thus, in January, 1945, Ivor Thomas, a British M.P., said in the House of Commons that Romania having the fourth greatest number of men fighting against Germany, should be given this status.

The delegations of France, Czechoslovakia, the Ukrainian Soviet Socialist Republic, and the Byelorussian Soviet Socialist Republic submitted similar proposals to the Peace Conference in the autumn of 1946. But Romania was not given the status of co-belligerent.

# CHAPTER IV

# Creation of Socialist Romania

THE victory of the anti-fascist insurrection of August, 1944, opened up a new era in Romania's history. It was the beginning of a profound popular revolution in the course of which Romanian society underwent constant transformations which led to the installation of a higher social system: the socialist system.

## 1. The Struggle for the Installation of a Democratic Regime

THE people's revolution went through two distinct stages in Romania: a stage during which bourgeois-democratic changes were made, and a stage of socialist transformations, the two forming an uninterrupted revolutionary process.

After August 23, 1944, Romania was again a constitutional monarchy based on the Constitution of 1923.

In a statement to the country, the cabinet of General C. Sănătescu, which had been formed at the very beginning of the anti-fascist insurrection, pledged to ensure the continued struggle of the Romanian army side by side with the Allied armies and to establish a democratic regime of public liberties and civic rights. Measures were taken to abolish the fascist legislation and to reinstate the constitutional democratic institutions, and a general amnesty was granted to political prisoners.

Romania joined the anti-fascist coalition with all her forces, the Romanian army fighting side by side with the Soviet army, in the war against Hitler's and Horthy's troops. On September 12, 1944, the representatives of the Romanian government[1] signed in Moscow the armistice convention

---

[1] The signatories of the armistice convention on behalf of the Romanian government and the Romanian High Command were State Minister L. Pătrăşcanu, General D. Dămăceanu, Under-Secretary of State at the Ministry of Home Affairs, B. Ştirbey and G. Pop, while Soviet General Malinovsky signed on behalf of the U.S.S.R. and British governments.

between Romania and the United Nations, recording Romania's extrication from the anti-Soviet war and her turning against Nazi Germany. Under the armistice convention the frontier between the U.S.S.R. and Romania was re-established along the line of June 28, 1940; at the same time the Vienna Diktat of August 30, 1940, was declared to be null and void.

An Allied Control Commission, acting in accordance with the general directives and orders of the Soviet High Command on behalf of the Allied Powers, was formed for the purposes of checking on the carrying-out of the armistice convention provisions until such time as the peace treaty was to be signed.

The liberation of the country created new conditions for a political life, with all the democratic parties and organizations finding a wide scope for their activities. An important part was then played by the working class parties — the Romanian Communist Party and the Social-Democratic Party — acting within the framework of the United Working Class Front. No longer working underground, the Romanian Communist Party was reorganized, increased, and strengthened in town and village. The Party evolved a realistic political line concerning the immediate and far-reaching assignments of the revolutionary movement, correctly appreciating the favorable conditions that had been created for the implementation of its program, whereby the bourgeois-democratic revolution was to be completed and a switchover made to the socialist revolution. Immediately after August 23, 1944, the Romanian Communist Party pointed out that in order to consolidate national independence and the achievements won through the insurrection, in order to create a free and democratic Romania it was first necessary for all the forces of the nation to actively sustain the anti-Hitler war, up to the military smashing of Nazi-Germany, to abolish the fascist remnants at home and to democratize the country These were the major objectives listed in the call of the Central Committee of the Romanian Communist Party of August 28, 1944, to all the citizens of the country.

The Social-Democratic Party adopted an identical or nearly identical position in the fundamental problems raised by the democratic changes to be made in Romania.

Simultaneously, the trade union movement was reorganized. On September 1, 1944, representatives of the Central Committee of the Romanian Communist Party and of the Social-Democratic Party adopted by common agreement the principles and measures of organization of the Workers' Trade Unions. A commission for the organization of a United Trade Union movement was formed and subsequently in January, 1945, a congress took place during which the General Confederation of Labor was created.

Peasant Committees made up of the most active elements, irrespective of their political views, were formed in the countryside on the initiative of the Romanian Communist Party. The Peasant Committees purged the village administration, supported the anti-Nazi war, and strove for the implementation of the land reforms. At the same time, the Ploughmen's Front presided over by Dr. Petru Groza formed organizations all over the country.

The Patriots' Union and the Patriotic Defense Organization, which had been created in the course of the anti-fascist struggle, carried on their activities amid the middle social strata in the towns, in particular amid the intelligentsia.

After August 23, 1944, the old parties — the National Peasant and National Liberal Parties — resumed their activities under legal conditions and proceeded to reorganize their ranks. At this time these parties joined in the struggle against Hitler's and Horthy's followers for the liberation of the entire country. Having joined the National Democratic Bloc and agreed to the removal of Antonescu's dictatorship, they preserved some influence in political life.

The parties making up the National Democratic Bloc had a common aim — the liberation of the country's territory — but they had different views regarding the socio-political regime to be installed in the country. Whereas the king and the leaders of the National Peasant and the National Liberal Parties wished to reinstate the old regime, a large part of the political forces declared for the installation of a genuine democratic regime and for the implementation of socio-economic reforms.

The economic situation of the country was most precarious for industry was hardly developed, and the consequences of German domination and of the havoc wrought by war had also made their impact. In 1944 industrial output was about 40 to 50 per cent of the prewar level; railway transport had decreased to 30 per cent of the 1943 level; the grain production was less than half the 1939 figure. Moreover, the economic situation was aggravated by inflation, by the great difficulty of obtaining raw materials, and by the blocking of Romania's foreign currency in the western countries.

The country's expenditure as a result of its participation in the war alongside the states of the anti-Nazi coalition and the war reparations it had to pay starting in September, 1944, weighed heavily on the Romanian economy. There were further economic difficulties as a result of the stocking of considerable quantities of products and of speculation. Taxation was heavy primarily on the workers and peasants; during the 1944-1945 financial year income tax derived from salaries and wages accounted for nearly 50 per cent of the budget revenue, while trade and industry contributed only about 25 per cent. There was a great housing shortage on account of the destruction wrought by the war. The great number of disabled and war widows and orphans, the scarcity of medicines and the lack of medical staff to remedy the deplorable health situation which was aggravated by malnutrition all made their impact on the economic and social situation of the country and called for speedy remedies.

The spokesmen of the dominant classes refused to take efficient measures for improving the working people's living conditions and they also ignored or restricted civil liberties and checked the democratization process. However, they were unable to check the unrest and the movement of the masses for the installation of a genuinely democratic regime for the economic and socio-political progress of the country.

Under the circumstances, the Romanian Communist Party took the initiative of rallying all the democratic and patriotic forces in Romania for joint action. The program worked out by the Romanian Communist Party and published on September 26, 1944, stated that the fundamental problems of the country in that stage should be settled on the basis of a united national democratic front: a regime of genuine democracy should be installed, the anti-Nazi war should be supported by all possible means, economic recovery should be achieved, and the living conditions of all categories of working people should be improved. The main socio-economic measure included in the program was the implementation of a democratic land reform through expropriation of all landed estates greater than a hundred acres and the granting of land to landless peasants and peasants with little land.

The program was discussed at a joint meeting of the delegates of the leaders of the Romanian Communist Party and the Social Democratic Party on October 2, 1944, who put the finishing touches to it and adopted it as a program of action of the United Workers' Front. Subsequently, the program was submitted to all the other forces. It was endorsed by the organization commission of the Trade Union Movement, the Ploughmen's Front, the Patriots' Union, the Patriotic Defense, the Union of the Hungarian Working People of Romania (MADOSZ), the Society of Writers, and other democratic organizations. Relying on their endorsement, the National Council of the Democratic National Front was formed on October 12, 1944, out of representatives of the component parties and political and civic organizations. The talks carried on in order to obtain the cooperation of the National Peasant and National Liberal parties failed of their purpose. Consequently, cooperation between the working class parties and the National Peasant and National Liberal parties within the government became difficult. The two ministers representing the United Workers' Front withdrew from the government on October 18, 1944. The National Peasant Party tried to form a cabinet but failed on account of the powerful, popular demonstrations throughout the country. The refractory stand taken by the leaders of the National Peasant Party and of the National Liberal Party on the desiderata of the masses led to the gradual disruption of those parties. Whole county organizations, as for example the National Liberal Party organizations in the counties of Argeş, Vîlcea, and Romanați, joined the Democratic National Front.

The popular movement compelled the leaders of the National Peasant and National Liberal parties to agree to forming a coalition cabinet. Formed on November 4, 1944, again with General Sănătescu as Premier, the new cabinet included a larger number of representatives of the democratic forces grouped in the National Democratic Front: the Vice-Chairman of the Council of Ministers, Dr. Petru Groza, belonged to the Front as did also six ministers and three under-secretaries of state. The representatives of the dominant classes, however, were still in a majority and they soon took repressive measures against the people's masses, forbidding mass demonstrations and even making use of armed force. On December 2, 1944, the members of the National Peasant Party and National Liberal Party withdrew from the cabinet, their aim being to oust from it the representatives of the National Democratic Front and reconquer their lost political positions. But their attempt to form a government without any representatives of the National Democratic Front failed owing to the opposition of the revolutionary democratic forces and to their determination to bring in a democratic government. On December 6, 1944, a government presided over by General R. Rădescu was formed, all ministries being assigned as in the preceding cabinet.

The promises which the new prime minister made in his statement on taking office proved to be a means of offering right-wing circles a respite to stem the popular upsurge and avoid a revolution. It was with this aim in view that a "commission for the study of the land reform" was formed on December 15, 1944. The commission was made up mostly of landowners who were indefinitely postponing any settlement on pretense of "studying" the land problem.

From among all the problems of this stage of Romanian history, the land problem was of exceptional significance, showing the real stand taken by the socio-political forces on all the objective requirements of Romanian society. This was made plain in the early months of 1945 and brought about rapid changes in the ratio of socio-political forces in the country for the most influential bourgeois-landlord party, the National Peasant Party, was thus discredited and the Romanian Communist Party and the other parties and organizations belonging to the National Democratic Front saw their influence increasing. In the draft program of the National Democratic Front published in January, 1945, immediate implementation of the land reform was a fundamental point. As the government postponed carrying out the reform, the Ploughmen's Front launched the slogan early in February, 1945, of the forceful occupation of the landowners' estates by the peasants. In all the districts of the country peasant committees came into existence with wide powers in the matter of the land reform. The peasants, often facing the bullets of the gendar-

93. PEASANT DEMONSTRATION (1935)

94. ANTI-FASCIST DEMONSTRATION IN BUCHAREST (1936)

95. NICOLAE IORGA

96. NICOLAE TITULESCU

97. DEMONSTRATION AT CLUJ AGAINST THE VIENNA DIKTAT (1940)

Comuniştii *trebue să lege* popularizarea platformei cu popularizarea tradiţiilor de luptă pentru dezrobirea poporului român —
împotriva imperiului *german* din veacurile 17, 18, 19 şi din timpul
*războiului din 1916 — 1918.*

Comuniştii *trebue să lege* popularizarea platformei cu cam-
pania pentru *popularizarea Uniunii Sovietice, a popoarelor Sovietice
şi a eroicei armate roşii,* cari prin jertfe enorme duc războiul
împotriva hoardelor fasciste, nu numai pentru apărarea patriei sovietice
şi a cuceririlor grandioase ale socialismului, *ci şi pentru salvarea
libertăţii  t u t u r o r   popoarelor, a culturii şi civilizaţiei omeneşti,
de robia şi barbaria fascistă.*

Puternica *Uniune Sovietică,* ducând războiul împotriva sân-
gerosului fascism german, *duce războiul* pentru zdrobirea ocupan-
ţilor fascişti din ţară, *pentru eliberarea poporului român* de sub
jugul ocupaţiei hitleriste, *pentru libertatea şi independenţa naţională
a poporului  r o m â n.*

Comuniştii trebue să popularizeze Frontul Unic al tuturor
popoarelor *iubitoare de libertate* in **frunte** cu Uniunea Sovietică
împotriva fascismului german şi aliaţilor săi, pentru **salvarea
omenirei.**

Comuniştii, în interesul Frontului Unic Naţional, pentru
zdrobirea fascismului cotropitor, pentru cucerirea drepturilor şi
libertăţilor democratice şi cetăţeneşti, a independenţei poporului
român, **renunţă la orice lozincă, sau acţiune, care ar
putea să-i DESPARTĂ de celelalte partide** şi
grupări politice, cari sunt **pentru dezrobirea** naţională a poporului român. Însă ei **nu** renunţă la *programul* lor, la *propagarea*
programului lor şi a *lozincilor finale.* Cu distrugerea tiraniei hitleriste **nu** încetează nici *exploatarea şi asuprirea* celor ce muncesc,
nici *crizele* şi nici *războaiele.* **Sistemul** capitalismului monopolist,
imperialismul care se bazează pe asuprirea şi exploatarea maselor
ce muncesc şi a popoarelor subjugate, **renaşte** crizele şi
*războaiele.*

Partidul nostru trebue să lege popularizarea platformei cu
**propagarea** cuceririlor grandioase ale popoarelor sovietice, cu
**superioritatea sistemului socialist asupra sistemului
capitalist** — şi să arate maselor, că **singurul** drum pentru
salvarea lor **definitivă** de criză şi războaie, de orice exploa-
**tare** şi **asuprire,** e drumul muncitorilor şi ţăranilor *din Rusia.* **12**

98. PROGRAM OF
THE ROMANIAN
COMMUNIST PAR-
TY, SEPTEMBER 6,
1941

# CĂTRE POPORUL ROMÂN!

1 Mai 1944 găsește muncitorimea din România, precum și masele largi ale poporului Român, la marginea **prăpastiei**.

Războiul provocat de către clica hitleristă din România împotriva Uniunei Sovietice, Marei Britanii și Statelor Unite, seamănă **moarte, jale și distrugere** pretutindeni pe cuprinsul țării.

Muncitorimea, țărănimea, meseriașimea, intelectualitatea, laolaltă cu întreaga națiune Română suferă urmările pustiitoare ale acestui **război hitlerist**.

Trădătorii de țară, Antoneștii care au trimis la moarte sute de mii de Români, pentru interesele imperialiștilor hitleriști, au expus orașele, satele și populația civilă unor necruțătoare **bombardamente** aeriene, prin **continuarea** războiului alături de Hitler.

Muncitorimea din întreprinderile militarizate care lucrează pentru războiul hitlerist este condamnată **la moarte**. La Ploești, Turnu-Severin, Brașov, etc. peste **1500** de muncitori au fost uciși și alte sute grav răniți. La C.F.R. Grivița, peste **1500** de muncitori au fost deasemenea uciși și răniți.

Populația civilă **lăsată fără adăpost** de autoritățile și administratorii fasciști și evacuați forțat sunt lăsați în mizerie și amenințați cu înfometarea și decimarea de boli.

**Părăsiți fabricile și birourile în caz de bombardament! Salvați-vă viața!**

Împotriva intereselor vitale și a voinței poporului Român, guvernul trădător Antonescu, continuă războiul alături de Hitler, ca să-și servească stăpânii dela Berlin și interesele sale de clică.

## MUNCITORI ROMÂNI!

Din clipa când armatele sovietice au trecut hotarele Moldovei, urmărind armata germano-română în retragere, guvernul marei republici muncitorești și țărănești dela răsărit, prin glasul comisarului la externe Molotov, a afirmat **prietenia** față de **poporul Român**, asigurând **integritatea teritorială și independența politică** a României, precum și **neamestecul** în ce privește structura socială și politică a Țării. Aceste declarații au fost întărite de guvernele englez și american.

**Armata roșie** a trecut pe teritoriul nostru, ca **armată eliberatoare. Trebue deci sprijinită de întregul popor!**

**Războiul împotriva Uniunei Sovietice și a Aliaților trebue să înceteze!**

**Pacea cu Uniunea Sovietică și Aliații trebue imediat încheiată!**

## MUNCITORI ȘI MUNCITOARE! TINERI MUNCITORI! SALARIAȚI DE TOATE CATEGORIILE!

Frații, fiii, soții voștri au fost **omorâți** pe front și prin bombardamente. Alții sunt trimiși la robie în Germania. Viața voastră este **în pericol** din cauza bombardării uzinelor și birourilor în care lucrați.

**Drepturile**, pe care voi le-ați dobândit printr-o îndelungată luptă și pentru care voi ați manifestat în toate sărbătorile de 1 Mai, v-au fost **răpite** de regimul hitlerist al lui Antonescu. Organizațiile voastre, profesionale au fost desființate; orice de lucru **mărite** până cum s-a micșorează neîncetat puterea de cumpărare a salariilor voastre de mizerie. **Scumpetea** și neînfrânată speculă a...

Lipsa de alimente de încă mai resimțită, **voi** o suportați în primul rând. Pușii sub regimul militarizării fabricilor, glasul vostru este înăbușit prin **teroare**, sunteți **încarcerați și bătuți!**

## MUNCITOARE ȘI FUNCȚIONARE!

Lipsiți de sprijinul bărbaților, fraților și copiilor voștri, trimiși să fie carne de tun pentru interesele lui Hitler, sunteți silite din cauza lipsurilor și foamei să luați locul lor în uzine, fabricile și birourile expuse **bombardamentelor** aeriene. Voi munciți până la istovire cu salarii de **batjocoră!**

---

...TĂRĂNESC, Partidul COMUNIST și Partidul SOCIAL-DEMOCRAT, prin delegații lor, împuterniciți pentru Partidele: Național-Liberal și Național-Țărănesc de Președinții Partidelor respective, iar pentru Partidele: Comunist și Social-Democrat de organele lor de conducere. —

găsește în vedere situația gravă în care se găsește România astăzi, în urma înlăturării regimului politic constituțional-democratic și a guvernărilor cu caracter fascist,

au hotărât să constitue un BLOC NAȚIONAL-DEMOCRATIC, care să active ze pentru salvarea Țării, având următoarele țeluri:

1. Încheierea, fără întârziere, în baza ofertei făcute de Aliați a unui armistițiu cu Națiunile Unite (Uniunea Sovietică, Marea Britanie și Statele Unite ale Americii), căutând a obține condițiunile posibile, cele mai bune pentru interesele Țării.

2. Eșirea României din Axa, eliberarea Țării de ocupația germană, alăturarea ei de Națiunile Unite și restabilirea independenței și suveranității naționale.

3. În acest scop: înlăturarea actualului regim de dictatură și înlocuirea lui cu un regim constituțional, democratic, pe baza acordării drepturilor și libertăților civice, tuturor cetățenilor Țării.

4. Menținerea unei ordine democratice și realizarea păcii, conform cu interesele statului și poporului român.

5. Prezentul acord intră imediat în vigoare și obligă partidele contractante la organizarea și ducerea în comun, fără nici o rezervare, a acțiunii, pentru realizarea punctelor mai sus stabilite.

P. S. Se face mențiune, că în timpul discuțiunilor pentru contrairea acestui bloc, delegații partidelor Comunist și Social-Democrat au propus să participe grupările: „FRONTUL PLUGARILOR", „UNIUNEA PATRIOTICĂ" și „PARTIDUL MUNCITORESC ȘI ȚĂRĂNESC". În urma discuțiunilor și pe baza acestei propuneri, delegații partidelor Național-Țărănesc și Național-Liberal declarând, că întrucât cele patru partide democratice din acest bloc, reprezintă aproape unanimitatea de opinii a Țării și a forțelor politice, care au combătut în permanență, atât orientarea de Axă, cât și regimurile de dictatură, în interior, toți delegații au căzut de acord ca „blocul" să fie constituit numai din aceste 4 partide.

Formalitățile politice care acătuesc BLOCUL NAȚIONAL-DEMOCRATIC își păstrează întreaga independență ideologică și politică, acordul intervenit neprivind decât punctele mai sus fixate.

20 Iunie 1944

100. THE NATIONAL DEMOCRATIC BLOC IS FORMED (JUNE, 1944)

---

99. MANIFESTO OF THE UNITED WORKERS' FRONT OF MAY 1, 1944

101. FIRST LEGAL ISSUE OF THE "ROMÂNIA LIBERĂ" (FREE ROMANIA)

102. ROMANIAN ARTILLERY PARTICIPATING IN THE FIGHTING IN BUCHAREST STREETS IN AUGUST, 1944

103. NAZI OFFICERS CAPTURED IN BUCHAREST DURING THE INSURRECTION

104. ROMANIAN-SOVIET MILITARY COOPERATION IN TRANSYLVANIA

105. ROMANIAN TROOPS FORCING THE RIVER TISA

106. ROMANIAN ARMY PARADING UNDER THE TRIUMPHAL ARCH ON AUGUST 23, 1944

107. GHEORGHE **G**HEORGHIU-DEJ

108. DR. PETRU GROZA

109. LAND REFORM BEING CARRIED OUT

110. MEETING IN BUCHAREST ON MARCH 6, 1945

111. DR. CONSTANTIN I. PARHON

112. PALACE SQUARE, DECEMBER 30, 1947

mes, divided the estates with the support of workers' teams, without waiting for the law which refractory ministers continually put off. In a matter of weeks the drive for the division of estates became a general phenomenon throughout the country. It was at the height of the struggle for land that the alliance between the working class and the peasantry was forged, an immense socio-political force being thus built up — a force which proved of decisive importance in the subsequent development of events.

Concurrently, the remnants of the administration dating from Antonescu's dictatorship were ousted from power as were also other anti-democratic elements heading the local bodies of state power. The prefectures in 52 out of the 58 existing counties came under the control of the National Democratic Front. Occasionally, this took place after violent clashes between the masses and the forces of repression acting on orders from General Rădescu, as for example at Craiova, Constantza, and Caracal.

As the enthusiastic struggle of the masses swept over the country, the old reactionary parties gradually weakened and broke up. A considerable number of members of the National Peasant Party joined the ranks of the Ploughmen's Front. On February 23, 1945, a whole group of National Peasant Party members led by Anton Alexandrescu joined the National Democratic Front. At the same time a cooperation agreement was reached between the National Democratic Front and the Liberal Bourgeois group headed by Gh. Tătărăscu, whose program diverged from the stand of the landowners and big financiers and had points in common with the National Democratic Front program. All this widened the gap in the camp of the forces opposing the democratic and progressive development of the country.

Under the circumstances thus created, the right-wing majority in the government tried to save their positions by forceful action even at the risk of drawing the country into civil war. No longer finding any substantial support in the people and being definitely outdated, the reactionary parties, in particular the National Peasant Party, resorted to what was left of the fascist elements in order to fight the people's demonstrations, to attack the headquarters of left-wing organizations, and to implement other terrorist measures.

Political tension was running high at the close of February, 1945. Popular demonstrations, often ending in violent clashes with the forces of repression and the pro-fascist elements, took place throughout the country. Hundreds of thousands of people — workers, peasants, members of the intelligentsia, office clerks, and army people — took part in the demonstrations held on February 24 throughout the country. The masses resolutely demanded a democratic government. In certain localities the demonstrators were fired on. In Bucharest they were fired on from some public institutions, and there were a number of casualties, killed and wounded. However, the attempt to use military units against the demonstrators on a large scale was unsuccessful.

The rise of the masses, who rallied round the program of democratic and progressive changes advocated by the National Democratic Front, brought to nought the provocations of the reactionary forces and kept the country out of civil war. The Romanian Communist Party, the main force of the democratic coalition, was fully prepared to meet any developments. Carrying on intensive political and organizational activities among the masses to prevent any attempt of a fratricidal war or a coup d'état at the hands of the right-wing circles, the Romanian Communist Party strengthened its battle formations, kept the forces armed, and maintained relations with the army.

Coming up against the opposition of the masses, General Rădescu was compelled to resign on February 28, 1945. Ultimately the king agreed to the formation of a government proposed by the National Democratic Front. On March 6, 1945, a government of wide democratic concentration was formed, with Dr. Petru Groza as premier. The National Democratic Front held preponderant positions in the Cabinet: the Chairman of the Council of Ministers and fourteen Ministers belonged to the Front. The Liberal Party headed by Gh. Tătărăscu was represented by the Vice-Chairman of the Council of Ministers and three ministers.

The installation of the government of March 6, 1945, marked a new stage in the process of socio-economic and political transformations in Romania, inaugurated by the anti-fascist insurrection of August, 1944. The way was thus opened for carrying through all bourgeois-democratic transformations.

Developments in Romania and in other European countries were influenced by external events which, up to a point, followed the line of the decisions adopted by the Allied Powers at various international conferences, in particular at the Yalta Conference of February, 1945. But the decisive factor was bred within the country: it was the democratic and patriotic revolutionary struggle of the broad masses of the Romanian people which put the people's democratic regime on a durable and stable foundation.

## 2. The Bourgeois-Democratic Revolution Is Completed

AS soon as the democratic government was in, it proceeded to legalize and complete the main reform, namely the land reform. Under the law published on March 23, 1945, all landed estates exceeding 100 acres were expropriated as were also the estates belonging to collaborationists, war criminals, those guilty of the country's disaster, and those who had not themselves tilled their land during the previous 7 years, an exception being made for estates of less than 20 acres.

The law stipulated that special village committees were to draw up a list of those who were to receive land. The list was to include only landless peasants or peasants owning less than 10 acres. The order in the lists was as follows: soldiers — those mobilized and those who had fought against Nazi Germany; landless peasants, agricultural laborers, and crop sharers who had worked on the estates being expropriated, irrespective of the village they lived in; and peasants owning less than 10 acres.

An important provision of the law showed that land was to be given free of any debts and obligations (Art. 21.) The text of the law included the principle that the peasants had to pay for the land, but this did not affect the social revolutionary nature of the reform for no compensation was to be given to the landowners. The peasants were to make payment to the People's Democratic State and not to the landowners. Moreover, the price was symbolic: the average annual crop to the hectare spaced out in installments over a ten-year period for peasants who had owned little land and over a twenty years period for landless peasants.

Over 900,000 peasant families, accounting for about one-third of the total population of the country, received land by virtue of the Land Reform Law.

The land reform which was carried out through a sharp socio-political struggle resulted in the sweeping away of the big landed estates, a semi-feudal vestige which had been checking the country's economic development and its entire public life. It was a capital reform in the given historical stage, and it brought about important changes in village class relations. The proportion of poor peasants was considerably reduced and the number of middle peasants increased. Over 400,000 families of landless peasants now had their own homesteads and another 500,000 improved their economic position. The material support given by the state created conditions which favored the economic and cultural rise of the villages and drew the peasantry into the drive for the country's economic recovery and development. With the semi-feudal vestiges being swept away in the field of agriculture, conditions became favorable for the progress of production forces throughout the national economy. The land reform solved the fundamental problem in the process of bourgeois-democratic changes in Romania — a process which had been left incomplete in the stage of the revolution of 1848 and during the subsequent period. An age-old dream of the Romanian peasantry, for which they had waged unceasing battles, had come true.

A decisive contribution to the alliance between workers and peasants — the fulcrum of the new democratic regime — was made by the fact that it was the working class headed by the Romanian Communist Party which had promoted the implementation of the land reform; that the peasants had enjoyed the workers' active, multilateral support in their struggle for land.

The landowners as a class disappeared and this undermined the very foundations of the old socio-political regime and narrowed down the sphere of action of the reactionary forces. Enjoying wide popular support, the democratic government, while implementing and completing the land reform, took a number of measures designed to instill a democratic spirit into state machinery, public administration, justice, the gendarmery, and the army. Such measures together with the drive for the reorganization or the creation of institutions were part of a comprehensive process whereby the old state machinery was being transformed and a new state machinery, able to meet the requirements of Romanian society in process of renewal, was being built.

The democratic regime consistently promoted a state policy that aimed at sweeping away national discrimination and variances, and ensuring equality of rights and friendship between the Romanian people and the co-inhabiting nationalities.

The Romanian people's national independence and their democratic gains were closely bound up with the final victory against Nazi Germany. On the battlefield, Romanian soldiers were inspired by the noble goals of the anti-Nazi war and by the progress of the people's revolution which laid its seal on their minds. "Everything for the front, everything for victory!" was one of the slogans of the drives initiated and organized by the Romanian Communist Party and by the other political parties and organizations.

As soon as it had been installed, the democratic government took a number of measures designed to step up the war effort of the country. The general revolutionary process of that period included participation in the war against Nazi Germany with all the country's forces. The measures taken to carry out social reforms increased the enthusiasm of the men fighting at the front while their victories on the battlefield made possible the revolutionary gains and helped to consolidate the new system.

Having suffered a decisive political defeat, the camp of the reactionary forces changed their field of activities in the economy. A systematic drive was undertaken for sabotaging production and worsening the living conditions of the working people of town and country. Speculation and inflation were at their heights, and economic difficulties were aggravated by the consequences of a two years' drought. Incited and supported by the western imperialists outside the country, the king and the leaders of the National Peasant Party (Maniu) and of the National Liberal Party (Brătianu) started a virulent campaign against the government.

Beginning in August, 1945, the king severed all contact with the Groza cabinet and refused to sign the decrees, thereby

hoping to induce him to resign. In this climate, the provocations and attacks of the right-wing forces continued unceasingly, reaching their height on November 8, 1945. "The
royal strike", begun under the impulse of foreign forces,
ceased on account of lack of mass support and of the compromise reached in Moscow in December, 1945, at the Conference
of the Foreign Ministers of the United States, Britain, and
the U.S.S.R. [2]

Holding its ground and well supported by the masses, the
government of wide democratic concentration continued its
program of reforms and of progressive socio-economic
measures.

The greatest attention was given to the economic recovery
of the country and the improvement of the living conditions
of the masses. On June 19, 1945, a decree was issued under
which the war industry was henceforward to work for peace.
Measures were taken concerning pricing and wages, and the
repression of speculation and economic sabotage. Moreover,
trade agreements were concluded with a number of countries,
among them the U.S.S.R., Bulgaria, Yugoslavia, Hungary,
Poland, and France. The economic and socio-political changes
made in the country after March 6, 1945, no less than the new
international situation created as a consequence of the termination of World War II, called for a multilateral analysis and
for suitable measures to be taken. A fundamental part in this
respect was played by the national conference of the Romanian
Communist Party of October 16-22, 1945, the first to be
held by the Party after its underground existence. On that
occasion the acuity with which the complex problems raised
by Romania's development were defined, the advanced socio-
political ideas and concepts, the clear-sighted, far-reaching
orientation based on Romanian realities proved the Romanian
Communist Party to be the most advanced political force of
Romanian society.

Focussing its debates on the problems raised by economic
recovery and the prospective development of the country,

---

[2] In answer to the request of the United States and British representatives, this
conference demanded that the Romanian government include a representative of
the "historical" parties. The Groza cabinet agreed to this request, and Emil Haţieganu and Mihai Romniceanu thus became ministers without portfolio to represent the National Peasant Party and the National Liberal Party, respectively.

the national conference of the Romanian Communist Party showed the inconsistency of the retrograde view according to which it was impossible to develop a powerful national industry, and Romania was doomed to remain "an essentially agricultural State".

The comprehensive political report submitted to the conference and the discussions that followed it pointed out that the progress of the country was closely bound up with the progress of industrialization and that industrial expansion depended to a large extent on the independence of the state.

Following an analysis of the situation in the various branches of material production and of the natural resources of the country, it was established that the rebuilding of the national economy must be founded on the rehabilitation and expansion of industry, with priority given to heavy industry as a basis of the general economic progress. Electrification of the entire country was a far-reaching assignment set with a view to Romania's economic expansion.

Agriculture held an important place in the program for the rehabilitation and development of the national economy. In this respect the following assignments were set: to complete the land reform, to organize centers where the peasants might borrow tractors and agricultural machinery, and to help the peasantry by allowing them credit and giving them seed so that agricultural production might be kept up and turned to better account.

Furthermore, a number of measures were designed to strengthen the state-controlled economic sector; to intensify state control over private enterprises so that they might be guided toward producing goods which would help the country's economic recovery and development, with their profits fixed at equitable levels; to reorganize the credit system; and to make fiscal and monetary reforms.

The conference also advocated a number of measures of a socio-cultural character, such as the struggle against illiteracy and the reorganization of public education on democratic bases, the training of the staff needed for the rehabilitation and development of the national economy, and the improvement of public health especially in the countryside.

The realistic policy promoted by the Romanian Communist Party, which considered the recovery and rebuilding of the country as a problem of national interest and called upon "everyone who is honest and patriotic" in the country to do his bit, played a decisive part in rallying the majority of the population around the people's democratic power and moving the country along the road of progress.

Before concluding its proceedings, the national conference of the Romanian Communist Party elected the Party leaders. Gheorghe Gheorghiu-Dej was elected Secretary-General of the Central Committee.

In the following stage, Romanian socio-political life was dominated by the necessity of carrying out the important assignments set with a view to rebuilding and developing the economy of the country, consolidating the democratic regime, and preparing for the first parliamentary election to be held after Romania's liberation from the fascist yoke.

These were problems which exerted mutual influences. They were also a touchstone of the positions of the various parties and organizations and consequently determined a new distribution in the political forces of the country.

The democratic forces gave every attention to the election for they realized that they would confirm the progressive gains made by the Romanian people and would be a guarantee of the consolidation and development of those gains in the future. At the same time the election was of great international significance as it was bound up with the recognition and consolidation of the position of democratic Romania in the postwar world.

Continuing along their anti-democratic and anti-popular line, the right-wing political forces grouped around the National Peasant Party (Maniu) and the National Liberal Party (Brătianu) and expected to defeat the democratic government in the electoral struggle and to reinstate the old pseudo-democracy with its social injustices. Those parties further enjoyed the encouragement and support of the leading circles in Britain and the United States, who declared that they would not agree to the conclusion of a peace treaty with the government presided over by Dr. Petru Groza. The agreement reached in Moscow at the Conference of the Foreign Ministers of the United States, Britain, and the U.S.S.R. did not end foreign pressure and interference; in certain respects it increased them, and this was facilitated by the presence of the representatives of the reactionary parties in the Romanian cabinet. As a result of such pressure and interference, the right-wing leaders of the Social Democratic Party, headed by Titel Petrescu, diverged from the line of the United Workers' Front and proved hostile to the co-operation in the election of all the political forces that made up the government of a wide democratic concentration. Repudiating such an orientation, the extraordinary congress of the Social-Democratic Party of March, 1946, decided to co-operate with the Romanian Communist Party and with other progressive parties [3].

On the other hand, a new group headed by Dr. Nicolae Lupu made up the Democratic Peasant Party, after seceding from the main opposition party, the National Peasant Party.

The developments bound up with the electoral campaign took place in a most complex and contradictory climate. The Peace Conference was held in Paris from July 29 to October 15, 1947. Showing the position of the Romanian government, the declaration headed *Romania's attitude towards the Peace Conference*, published on August 12, 1946, pointed out that Romania, on the basis of her overall contribution to the anti-Nazi war, was entitled to demand and obtain: recognition of her status of co-belligerent, the removal from the treaty of the economic clauses which affected the situation of the country and her economic policy, and limitation of the restrictions concerning armament and the armed forces necessary for the country's defense.

Moreover, the Romanian government proposed that the problems of Danube administration, which were to be debated by the conference, should be settled by a special convention concluded by the countries bordering upon the river.

The Romanian delegation at the Peace Conference carried on a sustained activity to see the just demands of the Romanian people accepted [4]. The Romanian representatives had to

---

[3] The Congress decided with 232 votes in favor, 29 votes against, and 60 abstentions that the Social-Democratic Party should have the same lists as the other forces of the government coalition. Continuing its right-wing orientation, Titel Petrescu's group seceded from the Social-Democratic Party and formed the Independent Social-Democratic Party, thus going with the National Peasant Party and the National Liberal Party (Maniu and Brătianu).

[4] The delegation consisted of Gheorghe Tătărăscu, Vice-Chairman of the Council of Ministers and Minister of Foreign Affairs, as head of the delegation, Gh. Gheorghiu-Dej, Minister of Communications and Public Works,

fight against numberless difficulties raised not only by the contradictory interests of the Great Powers but also by the attempts made by certain states to recover the positions they had lost as a result of the defeat of fascism and of the postwar socio-political transformations. Although the great powers unanimously appreciated the multilateral effort made by the Romanian people in the fight for the defeat of Nazi Germany, and the human sacrifices they had made for the victory of the United Nations, the Peace Conference did not give Romania the status of co-belligerent. At the same time, the peace treaty included onerous clauses of war reparations to be paid for the damages caused by Antonescu's dictatorial regime which had drawn the country into the anti-Soviet war.

Despite the many difficulties, the Romanian delegation at the Peace Conference obtained recognition of Romania's "having taken an active part in the war against Germany"; the cancellation of the Vienna Diktat, and engagement on the part of the Allied and Associated Powers to back Romania's application for membership in the United Nations Organization. These were outstanding successes for the government in its foreign policy and at the same time important factors in the struggle against internal reaction.

Nearly 7,000,000 citizens took part in the parliamentary election of November 19, 1946, the greatest figure of votes ever in the history of the country.

Election returns were an indisputable victory for the bloc of democratic parties which obtained 79.86 per cent of the votes. Voicing the will of the nation, the election was proof that the democratic regime had been built up by the Romanian people themselves, who showed their determination to defend their important gains and to carry them forward, to enable

Lucrețiu Pătrășcanu, Minister of Justice, Ștefan Voitec, Minister of National Education, Lothar Rădăceanu, Minister of Labor, Ion Gheorghe Maurer, Under-Secretary of State, Florica Bagdasar, Elena Văcărescu, Șerban Voinea, General D. Dămăceanu, and the Romanian diplomatic representatives in the United States, Britain, France, and The Netherlands.

The representatives of the Romanian Communist Party — Gh. Gheorghiu-Dej, Lucrețiu Pătrășcanu, and Ion Gheorghe Maurer — distinguished themselves by their intensive and consistent activities in support of Romania's national interests.

Romania to proceed along the road of the new democracy and of social progress.

The government coalition held 376 of the 414 mandates in the Assembly of Deputies.

Parliament issued a number of laws designed to strengthen the democratic regime and Romania's independence and national sovereignty, while other laws substantially contributed to the recovery and expansion of the national economy and to the promotion of the interests and aspirations of the broad masses.

Thus on December 20, 1946, Parliament passed the law for the nationalization of the National Bank of Romania, the most important financial and money-issuing institution of the country. The state now had control over credit and money issues, and over all credit and banking institutions, whether public or private. This enabled the state to improve the financing of industry, agriculture, and transport and to step up commodity circulation in the general interest of the country.

In 1947 many coordinated measures were taken in order to bring economic life back to normal and to strengthen the democratic regime.

At the same time, the signing on February 10, 1947, of the peace treaty between Romania and the Allied and Associated Powers ended the state of truce and opened up new possibilities for the country asserting itself in the international arena [5]. That year Romania applied for membership in the United Nations, but her application was not then granted. The Romania government, however, made a point of extending its political, economic, and cultural cooperation with each and every country.

In May, 1947, Parliament passed a law for the setting up of industrial offices, whose task it was to guide, supervise, and control economic activities of both State and private capitalist concerns. The offices were joint bodies of coordination of economic activities in certain branches of industry; they

[5] On behalf of the Allied and Associated Powers, the peace treaty with Romania was signed by the representatives of the following states: the U.S.S.R., Britain, Australia, the Byelorussian Soviet Socialist Republic, Canada, Czechoslovakia, India, New Zealand, the Ukrainian Soviet Socialist Republic and the Union of South Africa (*Peace Treaty between Romania and the Allied and Associated Powers*, Bucharest, 1947, Ministry of Foreign Affairs).

were made up of representatives of the Ministry of Industry and Trade, of Trade Unions, and employers. The state, through the agency of its representatives in the management of industrial offices, was able to intervene in the activity of enterprises, to indicate a production program, establish the quotas of raw materials required and their distribution, and fix the profit percentages, the distribution and circulation of products, and wage and salary levels.

The democratic state did its best to solve some of the economic and political problems of the peasantry [6].

Favorable conditions were thus created for a switch over to a new stage in the recovery and the expansion of the national economy, as shown by "the proposals of the Romanian Communist Party for the improvement of the economic and financial situation of the country", submitted to the Council of Ministers on June 14, 1947. One of the main provisions was the currency reform, which took place on August 15, 1947, and which was a hard blow struck at speculative capital and ensured a new distribution of the national revenue in favor of the working masses. The reform put an end to economic chaos and inflation and created the prerequisites for a rapid recovery of the economy. Carried out on the basis of internal resources, without any foreign loans, the currency reform made a substantial contribution to the strengthening of national independence.

In the light of these facts and with prospects of subsequent developments, the discrepancy was made plain between the interests and goals of the political forces at grips.

While the Romanian Communist Party continued to call upon patriots and all honest people to make their contribution to "the strengthening of the country's economic position by increasing industrial production capacities through rational

---

[6] On June 5, 1947, a law was passed under which the land reform was stated to be "a Government Act" and which subsequently did away with the suits brought against the peasants who had been given land by the former landowners, as well as with the rumors spread by reactionary circles that the land reform would not be final. On June 6, 1947, another law was passed for the control of the sale of landed estates and the establishment of a juridical regime of such estates, whereby the "kulaks" were compelled to return without payment the land bought from the poor peasants by speculation and the state was given a pre-emption right where landed estates were concerned.

use of material resources", with a view to improving the deplorable economic situation and to enable Romania to advance along the road of civilization and well-being — "a country with a prosperous population from the material and cultural standpoints", the reactionary parties denied the necessity of industrialization and primarily of the development of heavy industry, which they considered "synonymous with the overthrow of the prerequisites of our very existence". This was "a belief totally opposed to Romania's socio-economic structure". History has shown the fallacy of such concepts upheld by the retrograde forces.

The correct political line of the Romanian Communist Party and of the other progressive forces was enthusiastically adopted by the broad masses who implemented the program for the recovery and flourishing of the country. In the second half of 1947, overall industrial production amounted to 75 per cent of 1938 production. Successes were also obtained in agricultural production. The state sector in industry, trade, transport, and agriculture was strengthened, and exercised ever greater influence on economic life.

The measures and achievements which showed that the changes of a bourgeois-democratic nature were being completed were accompanied by embryonic changes bearing the anti-capitalist seal and having a dialectical influence on the others. They ran in one single revolutionary stream marking the transition to a new social system.

This was also the time when considerable changes took place in the ratio of forces of society: the positions of the working class and of working class organizations in political and social life were consolidated, the alliance between the working class and the peasantry became closer, and the union of the democratic and progressive forces was strengthened. Defeated in the election and compromised by their anachronistic political views, the "historical" parties were isolated from the masses. They found no place in the arena of legal activities and were increasingly engaged in clandestine plots whereby they wrought their own destruction. On November 6, 1947, the representatives of the National Liberal Party of Gh. Tătărăscu within the government were repudiated by the Assembly of Deputies for having diverged from the political line of the government, and had to resign.

By now it had become necessary, and objectively possible, to abolish the outdated institution of the monarchy. In the morning of December 30, 1947, King Michael signed the act of abdication in the presence of Dr. Petru Groza, Chairman of the Council of Ministers, and of Gh. Gheorghiu-Dej, Secretary-General of the Romanian Communist Party. In the afternoon of the same day, the king's abdication was made known to the Council of Ministers and a proclamation to the country was issued [7]. In the evening the Assembly of Deputies met to pass the law whereby Romania became a People's Republic and to elect the Presidium of the Romanian People's Republic. The Presidium was made up of C. I. Parhon, Mihail Sadoveanu, Ştefan Voitec, Gheorghe Stere and Ion Niculi.

The republican aspirations of the most advanced forces in Romania's modern and contemporary history, vividly expressed as early as the days of the revolution of 1848, thus came true and the logical requirements of the advance of Romanian society were satisfied.

The historic act of the proclamation of the Romanian People's Republic marked the transition to a new historical stage in Romania's development — a stage of economic and socio-political changes of a socialist nature.


## 3. Building Up Socialism in Romania

THE Romanian people were faced with a number of fundamental objectives, primarily with outstripping the stage of economic development of those days and of turning Romania into a country with a well-developed industry and a mo-

[7] Speaking at the meeting of the Council of Ministers of December 30, 1947, Dr. Petru Groza, prime-minister of the country, pointed out that the abolition of the monarchy "had been achieved by agreement with the King who was aware that monarchy was a serious obstacle in the path of the people's development. History will record a friendly abolition of the monarchy without any convulsions, much against the wishes of our enemies. To use the phrase of the Queen Mother, the people achieved today a decent and elegant divorce from the monarchy". (Shorthand Notes on the Meeting of the Council of Ministers, 15 h : 30', December 30, 1947, *Archives of the Central Committee of the Romanian Communist Party*, Volume 103, File 9082, pages 1—6).

dern agriculture. The prerequisites of the rise of the people's living standards and the prosperity of the homeland along the path chosen by the new system were achieved by means of economic progress, the creation of an advanced technical basis, and the rise in labor productivity.

Organizational and political unification of the working class played a most important role in the building up of a Romanian socialist society. Unification was the consequence of an evolutionary process whereby closer relations were forged between the parties and organizations working within the working class movement — a remarkable experience of internal as well as of international significance. In February, 1948, a congress took place for the unification on Marxist-Leninist principles of the Romanian Communist Party and the Social Democratic Party. A single working class party — the Romanian Workers' Party — was thus created. The party was thus named until the Ninth Congress of the Romanian Communist Party in July, 1965. The 1948 Congress gave the main lines of the program of socialist, economic, and political construction.

The economic policy of the people's democratic state was focussed on the country's industrialization, which was considered as the most efficient method of moving the country toward progress and civilization. In June, 1948, the main industrial, mining, banking, transport, and insurance companies were nationalized, the foundations being thus laid for a powerful socialist sector in the economy. This made it possible to switch over to planned development of the national economy — a decisive step in the furtherance of the general progress of the country.

Well aware that electrification was an essential factor in the industrialization process and in raising the welfare and the degree of civilization of a country, the Romanian Communist Party and the people's democratic state worked out the directives of a Ten-Year Electrification Plan (1951-1960). The plan, which was drawn up with the contribution of numerous specialists and was debated by the Academy, established the guiding lines for rational capitalization of the power resources of the country.

During the period that followed, socialism was built up at a steady rate: industrialization was consistently carried out on the basis of new techniques; all the districts of the country were turned into important economic and cultural centers; agriculture was organized on the co-operative system and underwent a multilateral and intensive process of development; and culture and science were constantly promoted. All this made up a process of structural changes which called for the concentration of creative and constructive forces and energy — a process that came up against certain difficulties and in the course of which a number of mistakes were made and remedied. The main feature of Romania's evolution during the more than two decades that have gone by was the country's swift advance along the road of socialism, with continuous quests and solutions to keep peace with the requirements and realities of every stage.

Industrialization called for maximum capitalization of natural resources, and for the rational use of the forces of the country. Special attention was given to priority development of heavy industry, which had to make an ever-increasing contribution to the equipment of enterprises with tools and installations, to the mechanization and chemicalization of agriculture, to the country's transport facilities, and to the expansion of the consumer goods industry.

During the years of socialist construction new industrial combines and complexes were built and many of the existing enterprises were expanded, retooled, and modernized. Furthermore, a large number of socio-cultural edifices were put up. Industrial production was greatly stepped up and new branches were created, among them oilfield equipment plants, shipyards, and factories producing motor trucks, busses and trolleybusses, tractors and agricultural machinery, machine tools, and equipment for the mining, chemical, food, light, and other industries. Moreover, new sub-branches of the chemical industry were created, including plants producing plastics, synthetic yarns, chemical fertilizers, chemicals, and pharmaceuticals.

In locating the new projects, the state was guided by the principle of a rational distribution of the productive forces over the whole country with the aim of raising the industrial potentialities of every district and achieving the complex advance of the economy as a whole.

Districts such as Moldavia, Oltenia, and Dobrudja, which had lagged behind in the past, were drawn into an active

113. NICOLAE CEAUŞESCU, SECRETARY GENERAL OF THE ROMANIAN COMMUNIST PARTY, PRESIDENT OF THE SOCIALIST REPUBLIC OF ROMANIA

114. THE MOTOR CAR PLANT AT PITEŞTI

115. OPENING OF THE BUCHAREST-BRAŞOV ELECTRIC RAILWAY LINE

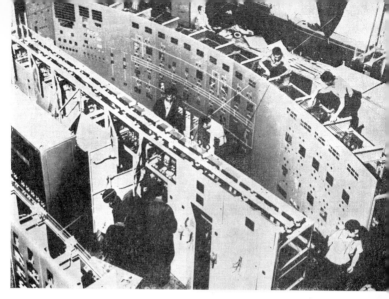

116. AUTOMATICA, SECTION ASSEMBLING AUTOMATION PANELS

117. A NEW TYPE OF ROMANIAN TRACTOR

119. IRRIGATION AT THE MĂNĂSTIREA AGRICULTURAL PRODUCTION COOPERATIVE ILFOV COUNTY

118. A VILLAGE IN SOCIALIST ROMANIA

120. COMBINES ON A STATE FARM

121. NEW BUILDINGS AT SUCEAVA

122. DEVA, PAST AND PRESENT

**PCR**

## Scînteia

*PROLETARI DIN TOATE ȚĂRILE, UNIȚI-VĂ!*

ORGAN AL COMITETULUI CENTRAL AL P.C.R.

Anul XXXV Nr. 6717    Sâmbătă 21 august 1965    6 PAGINI — 30 BANI

**Ieri s-a deschis sesiune Marii Adunări Național consacrată adoptăr noii Constituții a țăr**

# Raportul cu privire la proiectul de Constituți a Republicii Socialiste România prezentat de tovarășul Nicolae Ceaușescu, secretar general al C. C. al Partidului Comunist Rom

123. THE GRAND NATIONAL ASSEMBLY ADOPTING THE CONSTITUTION OF R. S. OF ROMANIA

**PCR**

## Scînteia

*PROLETARI DIN TOATE ȚĂRILE, UNIȚI-VĂ!*

ORGAN AL COMITETULUI CENTRAL AL P.C.R.

Anul XXXV Nr. 6718    Duminică 22 august 1965    8 PAGINI — 30 BANI

**Într-o atmosfer de puter entuzias**

# Marea Adunare Națională a adoptat
# CONSTITUȚIA REPUBLICII SOCIALISTE ROMÂN

### Consiliul de Stat al Republicii Socialiste România

economic life through judicious use of the prevailing economic and natural conditions, the creation of an industrial background in the towns, and a rational use of the labor forces in
all the districts of the country.

As a result of the industrialization policy, industry, a decisive branch of the national economy, was given a remarkable
impetus during the years of socialist construction: from 1950
to 1972 industrial production developed by 13 per cent
on an average. Industry became the leading branch of the
economy, its contribution to the national revenue increasing
from 30.8 per cent in 1938 to some 57.1 per cent in 1972. In
1972 Romania's overall industrial production was more than
21 times greater than the highest prewar level reached in 1938.

The highest growth rates in industrial production were
obtained in the branches of key importance for the expansion
of all the other branches of the national economy. A number
of thermal power and hydro-power stations of great value
to the national economy were built in the course of the implementation of the ten-year electrification plan. From 1961
to 1972 the electrification drive continued at a rate of over
20 per cent per annum. The construction of the hydro-power
system in the Iron Gates area of the Danube jointly with the
Federal Socialist Republic of Yugoslavia greatly increased
the quantum of electric power in the country. Great successes
have also been achieved in the machine building, petroleum,
chemical and agricultural-machinery industries. For example,
from 1950 to 1972, the average annual growth rate in machine
building was nearly 18.6 per cent, in the generating of
electric and thermal power nearly 17 per cent. Pig iron
production increased in 1972 more than thirty-six fold compared with 1938, and steel output more than twenty-six fold.
The machine-building industry has greatly helped to endow
agriculture with modern techniques to mechanize farming.
Also the machines produced are increasingly exported abroad,
especially tractors, oilfield equipment, and machine tools.
Romania is giving technical assistance and supplying complete
installations for industrial enterprises to countries bent on
creating an industry of their own, among them India, Iran,
and Afghanistan.

The industrialization process also accounts for the progress
made in the consumer goods industry, whose growth rates

are far above the peak levels of the prewar period. In 1972 the textile industry output was more than fourteen fold the 1938 figure; ready-to-wear clothing output was up 32 times, leather, fur and footwear output 13 times, and food industry output nearly 6 times.

In working out its agrarian policy, the state started from an analysis of the particularities of Romanian farming whose main feature was the existence of a large number of small peasant homesteads of poor productivity. Romania's experience, as also the whole contemporary history, shows that small goods production is unable to secure the development of productive forces in agriculture in pace with the evolution of science and technique, and with the constantly growing requirements of the economy and of popular consumption.

The peasantry, which accounted for two-thirds of Romania's population, was one of the main problems of the age of socialist construction. The switch-over from millions of small, poorly-equipped rural homesteads to the organization of big cooperative farms using modern agricultural machinery was tantamount to a revolution. It was no easy matter and the results of the switch over were only gradually felt for there were many deficiencies to overcome. The expansion of industry was one of the basic conditions for the socialist reorganization of agriculture. While all natural resources available in the country were used to develop industry, attention was also given to the intensive and multilateral development of agriculture, to the rise in plant and animal production.

The reorganization of Romanian agriculture was based on a program worked out in 1949 in accordance with which agricultural production cooperatives were created. The peasantry was thus guided along the path of cooperatives and gradually passed from lower to higher forms of cooperation. Material incentives, which were insufficient during the first years, played an ever more important part during the last decade. A policy was evolved for the gradual economic restriction of the well-to-do peasants, who were deprived of the possibility of exploiting the other peasants and were subsequently induced to join the cooperatives.

In Romania the building up of the cooperative system in agriculture has resulted in a gradual but appreciable rise in farming output. This increase is due to the fact that agriculture has been equipped with modern machines, chemical fertilizers and advanced technical methods have been used, and the number of skilled cadres has been increased. Furthermore, a correct proportion has been established between the various branches of agriculture, the cooperatives have been allowed credit, and material incentive has been given to the peasantry, who are paid stimulating prices for their produce.

By 1962 the cooperative system had been established throughout the country's agriculture. The results obtained in the socialist transformation of agriculture are also to be accounted for by the support given by the state, which has allocated considerable material and financial means to this sector. From 1966 to 1972 alone, the Romanian state invested nearly 55,000 million lei in agriculture. In 1972 there were more than 115,000 conventional tractors available, as well as 50,000 mechanical seeders, nearly 35,000 grain combines as also other modern farming machines. The 743 machine and tractor stations of the country ensured the mechanization of the main agricultural work.

At present there are in Romania 4,549 agricultural production cooperatives enrolling 3,452,500 peasant families tilling an agricultural area of 22,231,235 acres, as well as 364 state farms covering 5,112,653 acres.

The Romanian state has taken a number of measures with a view to developing the technical and material background of agriculture, in order to make plain the advantages of the new production relations and use all reserves for the stepping up of farming output. Management and planning in agriculture have been improved and so have the state bodies working in this sector, their attributions being carefully specified. In 1966 the National Union of Agricultural Production Cooperatives and Inter-Cooperative Unions were set up, the masses of peasants being thus drawn into the management of agriculture and the general affairs of the country.

The deep-going transformations made in the agricultural sector have fundamentally changed socio-economic relations in the villages. When the cooperative system was established throughout the country's agriculture, socialist production relations became general in the entire economy, and socialism was victorious in Romania.

The radical transformations wrought in economic life have been accompanied by large-scale changes in the socio-cultural sector. Measures have been taken for a more rational organization of the educational system to enable it to meet the requirements of modern science and technique, cultural life is being guided, and the living standards of the people are being constantly raised.

During the years of socialist construction Romanian science of long-standing tradition has progressed along an ascending line.

The National Council of Science and Technology, attached to the Council of Ministers, is assigned the task of guiding scientific research within the framework of the Academy of the Socialist Republic of Romania, of the higher educational establishments, and of the ministries and other central bodies. This is a state body called upon to coordinate scientific activities and the training of cadres and to work out directives and thus promote progress in research throughout the country along the same lines.

The spread of education in the ranks of the masses is an important activity of the Romanian state.

The Romanian state makes the best use of the traditions of national science and culture and of the treasure-store of spiritual values transmitted by our forefathers. At the same time it is considered as most important to know and master the results of the advanced contemporary scientific concepts and artistic creation of other peoples and to achieve a pooling of cultural values.

The achievements obtained in the economic and socio-cultural sectors have resulted in a rise in living standards and in increased social wealth. While the national revenue increased by barely 9.6 per cent from 1929 to 1938, which means by about 1 per cent annually, during the 1950-1972 span it rose 7.5 times or by about 10 per cent annually. The growth rate of the national revenue and its judicious distribution have made it possible to allocate the funds necessary for the ascending development of the national economy and to provide material resources for a constant rise in the material and spiritual level of the population.

The state spent over 200,000 million lei for socio-cultural requirements in the course of a decade and a half, with appropriations to this purpose amounting in 1972 to nearly seven times the 1955 figure. A comprehensive program of socio-cultural buildings has been implemented, thousands of schools, cultural establishments, and public health institutions have been built, and housing construction in town and village has been given a great impetus.

The state system of the Socialist Republic of Romania relies on the common interests and goals of all social classes and categories: workers, peasants, the intelligentsia, and the other working people. The joint economic interests and a common socialist culture have strengthened the unity of the people and the socialist nation and state. In a comparatively short space of time the new system has enhanced the development and flourishing of the Romanian nation to an extent never before known in its evolution.

Defining the aim of the state's activity, article 13 of the Constitution of the Socialist Republic of Romania passed in 1965, pointed out: "The entire activity of the State makes it its aim to develop the socialist nation and make it flourish, constantly to raise the material and cultural welfare of the people and enable the human personality to assert itself in many ways".

The Constitution of the Socialist Republic of Romania has created favorable conditions for the sovereignty and independence of the Romanian people. The transformations wrought in the national economy and in the class pattern of society make it possible to raise the Romanian nation to a higher rung of development.

All forms of inequality and of national discrimination have been abolished so that all citizens, irrespective of nationality, can freely assert themselves in social life. This is an outstanding victory of the socialist system in Romania.

The organization of state power in the Socialist Republic of Romania relies on the principle of representation, state power being exercised by elected bodies. Laying down this principle, the Constitution establishes that the people, sovereign holder of power, exercises it through the agency of the Grand National Assembly and the People's Councils, bodies elected by universal, equal, and direct suffrage and secret ballot. The citizens thus take part in state management through the agency of their representatives in the Grand

National Assembly and in the People's Commissions, and by direct participation in the activities of the county, town, and village People's Councils, and in the discussions and the settlement of the important problems of public life, such as the plans for the development of the national economy, the organization of production, and the administration of towns and villages.

The part played by the People's Councils, local bodies of state power, in socialist construction has increased. The People's Councils control economic, administrative, and sociocultural activities, and act as guides to the institutions and enterprises of local importance. In their work, the nearly 150,000 deputies to the People's Councils are assisted by the Citizens' Committees whereby millions of people make their contribution to the administration and prosperity of the towns and villages.

Actual participation of the citizens in government activities is the result of the rights and liberties conferred on them. The fundamental rights and liberties laid down in the Constitution of the Socialist Republic of Romania imply respect for man's dignity and the possibility for him to assert his personality in many ways. The Constitution provides for equal rights for all citizens, irrespective of nationality, race, sex, and religion, the state guaranteeing equality in all fields of economic, political, juridical, social, and cultural life. A person's position in society is determined by his capacities and the work he does, by his contribution to the common cause.

The Ninth Congress of the Romanian Communist Party of July, 1965, debated and elucidated problems of the utmost theoretical and practical importance for the advance of the country in building up a multilaterally developed socialist society. From among those problems we will cite: the economic, social, and political consequences of Romania's industrialization; the ways and means of achieving socialist industrialization and harmonious expansion of the national economy under the conditions created by the contemporary technical and scientific revolution; and the role of the state and of the nation in the stage of socialist construction. The Congress worked out a comprehensive program for the development of the homeland. With a view to the implementation of the program, a large number of measures were taken in the following years in order to raise all economic and social activities in Romania to a new and higher stage. Those measures made it their aim to improve the management and planning of the national economy, the administrative-territorial organization of the country and the systematization of villages, as well as all methods of organization and management of social and state life.

At present Romania has a population of 20.6 million, about 87.5 per cent are Romanians and the rest are Hungarians, Germans, Serbians, and other nationalities. The unity and cohesion of the Romanian socialist nation, the relations of fraternity and cooperation between the Romanian people and the national minorities are most important factors of progress in Romania, which is among the countries showing the most dynamic socio-economic development rate.

In external affairs, socialist Romania, a member of the United Nations since December, 1955, is an active participant of that international community, promoting a policy of peace and increasing cooperation between the peoples. At present she maintains diplomatic relations with over 100 states and carries on economic cooperation with 110 states. The international activities of the Romanian state are based on the observance of the right of all peoples to decide their own destinies without any foreign interference in internal affairs, on the principles of observance of national sovereignty and independence, and of equality in rights. The foreign policy of the Socialist Republic of Romania centers on close friendship and cooperation with all socialist countries on the basis of the principles of Marxism-Leninism and of socialist internationalism. Consequently, the country makes its full contribution to the constant development of its relations of friendship, alliance, and fruitful cooperation with the states she is organically linked to by a common social system.

At the same time the Socialist Republic of Romania, acting in the spirit of the principles of peaceful coexistence with states having different social systems, is carrying on an active foreign policy of increasing economic, political, technical, scientific, and cultural cooperation with all the states of the world. Romania, being a European state, is greatly concerned with the problem of peace and security in Europe and makes her contribution to turn those burning desiderata into realities. The

Romanian government declares for strict observance of the principles which ought to guide the relations between states, for the liquidation of military blocs and of military bases on the territories of other states, and for the creation of a climate of relaxation, confidence, and multilateral cooperation between the peoples.

The changes wrought in Romanian society in the postwar period and the building up of socialist Romania are the result of an objective historical process and constitute a higher stage and an apotheosis of many centuries of struggles and strivings of the Romanian people to make their noble and lofty ideals come true.

Along the way many difficulties of various kinds, both internal and foreign, had to be overcome; not infrequently the difficulties have seemed insuperable and have jeopardized the very existence of the Romanian state and nation. But the Romanian people have always found the strength and resources to rise above the trials and dangers. Rallying round the most advanced forces of the contemporary world and devoting her ability and power to the building up of the new system, Romania at the same time makes her contribution, alongside all the socialist countries and the progressive forces of the world, to the common cause of freedom, independence, peace, and progress.

The Tenth Congress of the Romanian Communist Party, held from August 6-12, 1969, made a comprehensive analysis of the stage reached in the process of socialist construction in the country. The directives concerning the 1971-1975 Five-Year Plan, and the guiding lines of the expansion of the national economy over the 1976-1980 span, adopted by the Congress, assigned as fundamental objectives the constant widening and improvement of the technical and material background of the country, a steady bettering of production relations, and the building up of a multilaterally developed socialist society. The Congress laid stress on the necessity of stepping up the growth rate of productive forces, of developing industry and agriculture on the basis of modern techniques, and of improving the educational and scientific research system.

Furthermore, the Congress underlined the importance of creating all the conditions necessary for raising the material

VII *Attack on Smirdan, by Nicolae Grigorescu*

VIII *New district at Galatz*

IX *New district at Pitești*

X Barrage of the hydropower station on the river Argeş
XI The Piteşti petrochemical combine

and spiritual welfare of the people, a fundamental prerequisite in the formation of the man of the new, socialist type. A democratic social life creates the organizational framework whereby every citizen can participate in the management of public life.

In the light of the program worked out by the Tenth Congress of the Romanian Communist Party, it is specified that the Party is assigned the task of building up stage by stage a society where the productive forces are ever on the ascendancy and socialist relations are being steadily improved. As production relations develop and the unity and socialist cohesion of the people are strengthened, the creative power and the initiative of the working people prove to be important factors in turning to account the advantages of the new system. The dynamic presence of the masses in the political arena at all stages of leadership and social organization is proof of the durability of the socialist system within which the people are really the subject of history.

The documents of the Congress reaffirm the fundamental principles of the foreign policy of socialist Romania: national sovereignty and independence, equal rights, non-interference in internal affairs, mutual benefits, and observance of the right of each people to decide its own destiny in accordance with their vital interests and aspirations. These are principles which have gradually gained recognition in international life, an increasing number of states considering them as a safe and lasting basis for cooperation, security, and peace.

Voicing the deepest aspirations of the Romanian people, the program mapped out by the Tenth Congress of the Romanian Communist Party and by the National Conference of the R.C.P. of July 1972 was endorsed by the entire people rallying closely around the Party and the State.

Continuing the struggles waged by the Romanian people for national and social liberation along the centuries, the Romanian Communist Party has traversed an heroic and glorious path of struggle, creditably playing its part as a revolutionary vanguard of the working class and of the broad masses. With vigorous roots in the working class movement, which during the latter half of the past century became the most advanced socio-political force of Romanian society, the Communist Party has been built up as part of the very body of the people, being organically integrated in Romania's social realities.

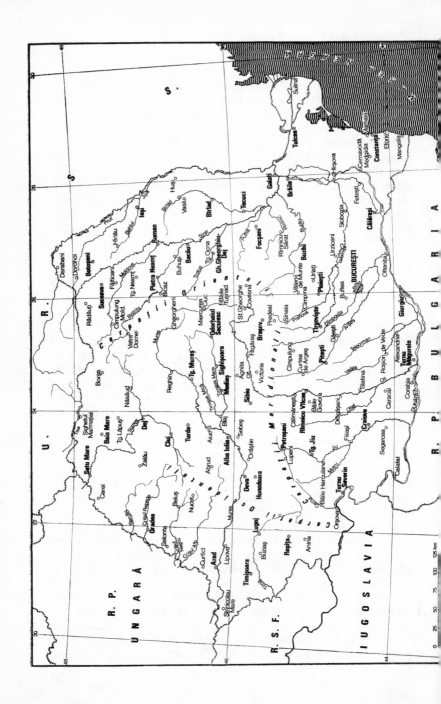

As the leader of the destinies of the people, the Romanian Communist Party has taken upon itself the lofty mission of making the highest aspirations of the best sons of the people along the centuries — the most enlightened patriots — come true: the mission of installing a new and higher system where justice reigns supreme in the homeland.

The patriotic enthusiasm of the Romanian people in the implementation of the multilateral and harmonious development of the country is inspired by the experience and teachings of old days, by the vicissitudes and hard struggle for independence, for the building up of a nation, of a single united state, for speeding up social progress and advancing along the path of civilization. The people's enthusiasm is based on the experience of the years of socialist construction, on the belief that the general orientation in the evolution of contemporary Romania is correct.

# CHAPTER V

# Development of Culture in the Age of Socialist Construction

THE radical transformations in the country's economy went hand in hand with profound changes in the field of culture. The educational system was organized on a sounder basis, a curriculum was decided upon to meet the requirements of modern science and technique, cultural life was judiciously guided, and the cultural level of the people was constantly raised. Under the guidance of the Romanian Communist Party, culture became essentially socialist and accessible to the masses, at the same time being one of the important factors in socialist construction.

## 1. Education

IN socialist Romania the educational system is the state's concern. Everyone enjoys the right of education. Ten-year elementary education is general and compulsory, education of every grade is free of charge, school textbooks are provided also free of charge, and state scholarships are given to schoolchildren and undergraduates. Illiteracy, the scourge of Romanian society in a not too distant past, has been done away with.

The number of pupils attending general-education schools is twice as great as in 1938-1939, and the number of pupils in secondary schools has increased more than twelvefold.

Higher education has also made great strides. Some 150,000 students attend the 47 higher educational establishments with their 187 faculties and a staff of more than 14,000. Two-thirds of the students have state scholarships and the more meritorious are also awarded Republican scholarships or scholarships of the Writers' or Artists' Union. Polytechnic and technical-industrial higher education, whereby specialists are trained to meet the complex requirements of the production process and of its organization and management, has also been greatly developed.

Apart from day courses, there are evening and extra-mural courses so that all citizens, irrespective of age or profession, can attend secondary general education schools and higher education establishments.

## 2. Science

IN order to build up the economic background of socialist society, the state has been carrying on a policy of industrialization and agricultural mechanization the success of which largely depends on science. With the contemporary scientific and technical revolution under way, science has itself become a productive force developing at a swift rate and undergoing a pronounced differentiation process. The new conditions in the development of science call for the active support of the state, which establishes the main directions of scientific investigation and provides suitable financial means through the agency of its planning bodies. The educational system having been reorganized and improved, the research institutions have, at the same time, been provided with a highly trained scientific staff.

At present there are in the country 264 scientific research institutes, among which are 53 Academy institutes, 163 departmental research units, and 48 big plant laboratories.

Scientific research has developed along two main lines: basic research promoting the progress of the respective science, and practical research solving production problems.

Mathematics continues to be distinguished by scholars of world renown whose reputation was already established during the interwar period, D. Pompei and S. Stoilov among them. Important results have been obtained in the theory of ideals (D. Barbilian), in the theory of probabilities and mathematical statistics (Gh. Mihoc and O. Onicescu), in the logic and algebraic study of the schemes of automatic relay mechanisms (Gr. Moisil), in the study of polyharmonic and polycolonic functions (M. Nicolescu), of equations with partial derivatives (N. Teodorescu), of non-holonomic spaces (Gh. Vrînceanu), and in the mathematical analysis and mechanics of fluids (C. Iacob). The construction in 1955 of an electronic computer for the first time in Romania is a remarkable success in the field of mathematics.

Research in physics has been given a great impetus, especially after the Physics and Atomic-Physics Institutes were set up, the Atomic-Physics Institute being endowed with an experimental reactor and a betatron. Researchers here have studied in particular elementary particle physics and nuclear physics (Șerban Țițeica), radioactive isotopes and their application (H. Hulubei), and gas discharge physics (E. Bădărău and Th. V. Ionescu). The first laser which was built in 1962 under the guidance of I. Agârbiceanu gave credit to Romania as one of the first countries to have created such a device.

The outstanding results scored in chemistry are due to a considerable extent to the Chemical Research Institute. I. Murgulescu and his disciples have concentrated on molecular structure, kinetics, and chemical thermodynamics. Organic chemistry has developed under the leadership of C. D. Nenițescu, who has invented a number of chemical procedures with wide applications in industry. E. Angelescu has studied colloidal chemistry and chemical kinetics. Inorganic chemistry has registered valuable results owing to the research carried out by R. Ripan and R. Cernătescu. C. Simionescu has undertaken research in macro-molecular chemistry and in the chemistry of timber and wood pulp. Among the achievements of Romanian chemists of great importance to the economy should be mentioned those in the field of plastics.

In biology fundamental works have been published, among them *The Romanian Flora and Fauna*, a geo-botanical survey of the country. Furthermore, Tr. Săvulescu brought out two comprehensive monographs on the Uredinales and the Ustilaginales, and Gh. Ionescu-Sisești continuing his research for a longer time, obtained valuable results in the development of new species of plants. Experimental stations have been of great help as a means of improving and spreading scientific agro-technical methods and of creating species of plants of high productivity.

Geological research, being called upon to discover underground resources and help to turn them to account, have revealed new oil deposits and considerable coal reserves. The

*Geological Map of the Romanian Socialist Republic,* a work of wide scope begun before World War II and concluded only in the years of the people's power, is a grand achievement — a crowning of all the studies on the structure of the country's soil. Gh. Macovei, Al. Codarcea, Gr. Răileanu, P. S. Ştefănescu, and N. Filipescu have gained credit in promoting the progress of geological research.

Continuing their research in medicine, an old tradition in the country, a number of scholars of note with their collaborators and disciples have enhanced the prestige of the Romanian medical school. The main fields in which Romanians have made their mark in furthering medical knowledge and advocating efficient treatments are: endocrinology (C. I. Parhon, St. Milcu, A. Aslan), infra-micro-biology (St. S. Nicolau), neurology (A. Kreindler and O. Sager), internal medicine (N. Gh. Lupu), bacteriology (M. Ciucă), physiology (Gr. Al. Benetato, D. Danielopolu), and surgery (D. Bagdasar, I. Haţieganu, N. Hortolomeiu).

The technical sciences have developed in close connection with practical life, helping to solve important problems of the national economy. From among the many branches of study which have been tackled should be quoted: aerodynamics, structure and thermodynamics of the reactions of metal slag, the theory of the internal laws of electro-magnetism, resistance and testing of metals, general theory, construction and functioning of electric machines, calculation of foundations, welding and metalworking (R. Răduleţ, I. S. Gheorghiu, St. Nădăşan, C. Micloşi). The *Romanian Technical Lexicon* in eighteen volumes, brought out under the guidance of R. Răduleţ, is a colossal informative work in the field of technical sciences.

The progress of science and technique is also reflected in the inventions and innovations of many Romanian scientists. Not a few Romanian inventions have gained world recognition: in 1968-1969, 19 Romanian inventions were shown at 6 international fairs, 16 of which were awarded prizes — 12 gold medals, 1 silver medal and 3 bronze medals. Romanian inventions include a procedure of static testing by means of sampling and a device whereby the resistance of pure shearing steel is determined; a procedure, apparatus, and installation separating the components of a gas mixture by means of absorbants in a fixed layer; a procedure of partial replacement of metallurgical coke by liquid or solid fuels in furnaces; and finally the well-known Gerovital used against ageing.

The social sciences have been given a great impetus; it is in these sciences that the profound change in the Romanian people's social consciousness on the basis of Marxist-Leninist concepts relies. Scientific investigation in the field of social sciences has made rapid progress as a result of the founding of the Academy of Social and Political Sciences (February 19-20, 1970), with Nicolae Ceauşescu, Secretary General of the Romanian Communist Party, as honorary President.

Philosophy has made important contributions to dialectical and historical materialism, defining certain concepts and aspects. Remarkable results have been obtained in the study of the forms of social consciousness, of the methodology of science, dialectical logic, and the history of philosophy.

Marxist historical science has given scientific foundations to the study of Romanian history and has answered the fundamental problems of the national history. Unlike the older historiography, which was mainly concerned with political history, present-day history gives priority to economic and social relations using the results of previous research in a critical spirit. An Institute of Historical and Socio-political Sciences has been attached to the Central Committee of the Romanian Communist Party, and the N. Iorga History Institute of the Academy has been founded. Historical research has thus assumed a planned and well-organized development which has raised historiographic inquiries to a higher level and has led to remarkable results. Thus A. Oţetea gave a new outlook on the revolution of 1821 and analyzed the evolution of agrarian relations in the period of transition from feudalism to capitalism. C. Daicoviciu excavated a number of Dacian settlements in the Orăştia Mountains and studied the Dacian's material and spiritual cultures. P. Constantinescu-Iaşi has made valuable contributions to the history of the Communist and Workers' movements in particular by revealing the activities of the legal organizations guided by the Romanian Communist Party. D. Prodan has analyzed the social and the emancipation movement of the Transylvanian Romanians. E.Condurachi has made a survey of the history of the Greek colonies on the Dobrudjan shore of the Black Sea, especially

124. MIHAI EMINESCU

125. ION HELIADE RĂDULESCU

126. DIMITRIE BOLINTINEANU

127. ION LUCA CARAGIALE

128. ION CREANGĂ

129. THEODOR AMAN: THE ARTIST'S STUDIO

130. NICOLAE GRIGORESCU: OVER HILLS AND DALES

131. ION ANDREESCU: WINTER AT BARBIZON

132. DIMITRIE PACIUREA: THE GIANT

133. STEFAN LUCHIAN: SHARING THE MAIZE

134. CAMIL RESSU: MOWERS AT REST

135. DIMITRIE GHIAŢĂ: MOUNTAIN FLOWERS

136. GHEORGHE PETRAȘCU: AT HOME

137. CONSTANTIN BRÂNCUȘI: GATE OF THE KISS

138. NICOLAE TONITZA: DECEMBER 13, 1918

139. GHEORGHE ȚUCULESCU: WOMEN HARVESTING

140. VIDA GEZA: MONUMENT TO SOLDIERS   AT CAREII MARI

141. CORNELIU BABA: PEASANTS IN THE FIELD

142. CAMIL PETRESCU        143. MIHAIL SADOVEANU

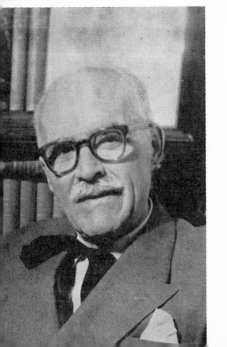

144. TUDOR ARGHEZI

studying the relations between the Greek colonists and the autochthonous populations. M. Berza has made a systematic inquiry into the obligations to the Ottoman Porte of the two Romanian countries and has studied aspects of medieval culture. I. Nestor's research has given a new outlook on the neolithic cultures of the bronze age and of the migration period. D. M. Pippidi's Greek-Latin epigraphy has revealed new aspects of the history of the Greek colonists and of the Roman rule in Dacia, while Gh. Ştefan's excavations at Garvăn — Old-time Dinogetia — have furthered our knowledge of the country's history in the tenth and twelfth centuries. St. Pascu has studied certain aspects of medieval society in Transylvania and has initiated historical demography research. Certain fundamental aspects of modern Romanian history have been revealed by V. Maciu in his surveys. In the years of the people's power, Romanian historiography boasts a new generation of young historians who have probed into the basic problems of Romania's history, have revealed new sources, and have made valuable contributions to the study of national and world history.

Older historians have also contributed their share toward the development of Romanian historiography. P. P. Panaitescu has studied the economic and social structures of feudal society as well as early medieval culture in the Romanian countries. C. C. Giurescu is the author of an ample monograph on Al. I. Cuza, and R. Vulpe has made a noteworthy study of the Geto-Dacians' history and culture and of the ancient history of Dobrudja. Emil Lăzărescu is a well-informed researcher who has concentrated on the formative period of the Romanian feudal states.

Much attention has been given to the documentary background which has been enlarged through systematic research in the country's archives and through publication of diplomatic and narrative sources. Based on the studies undertaken during the last two decades, the first vast synthesis of Romanian national history has been drawn up: this is *A History of Romania*, four volumes of which have been published so far.

A *Dictionary of Modern Romanian* and a *Romanian Grammar* are among the outstanding works achieved in the field of philology and linguistics. Important results have also been obtained in phonology and dialectology (Al. Rosetti), in onomastics and toponymy (I. Iordan), and in general linguistics (Al. Graur).

## 3. Literature

AFTER World War II the literary forces of the country grouped around such publications as *Viaţa Românească*, which reappeared in 1944, *Contemporanul*, 1946, *Revista Literară (Literary Review)*, 1947, *Flacăra (The Flame)*, 1948, *Gazeta Literară (Literary Gazette)*, 1954, renamed *România Literară (Literary Romania)* after 1968, *Luceafărul (Evening Star)*, 1968, *Utunk, Korunk, Igaz Szo, Neue Literatur*, and *Novi Jivot*. Among the writers of the older generations, were G. Călinescu, who published his novels *Poor Ioanid* and *The Black Chest*, and T. Arghezi who was at the zenith of his artistic power. But the younger generation also began scoring achievements in all spheres of literature. Zaharia Stancu published a novel, *Barefoot*, that touchingly evokes how the peasantry lived through the eventful days culminating in the uprising of 1907. In the novel *Moromeţii (In a Village)*, Marin Preda reveals unknown recesses of peasant psychology. In *The Pit* Eugen Barbu gives a picturesque image of the outskirts of Bucharest and of the underworld. The generation of prose writers which emerged after 1950 includes Titus Popovici, Fănuş Neagu, D. R. Popescu, and Ştefan Bănulescu, all responsible for novels and short stories. Besides poets who started their poetic career in the forties — Emil Botta, M. Beniuc, Miron Radu Paraschivescu, Eugen Jebeleanu, Maria Banuş, Geo Dumitrescu, and St. August. Doinaş—numerous gifted young people have asserted themselves, including A. E. Baconsky, Nicolae Labiş, Nichita Stănescu, Ana Blandiana, Marin Sorescu, Ion Alexandru, and Adrian Păunescu. Outstanding among playwrights are Horia Lovinescu, Aurel Baranga, and Paul Everac. From among the critics coming to the fore we will cite Al. Piru, Ov. S. Crohmălniceanu, Ion Dodu Bălan, Paul Georgescu, Nicolae Balotă, Ion Negoiţescu, Cornel Regman, Adrian Marino, Lucian Raicu, Matei Călinescu, Eugen Simion, and Nicolae Manolescu. Among the writers publishing in the languages of the co-inhabiting nationalities are Nagy Istvan, Meliusz Joszef, Süto Andras, Oscar Walter Cisek, Erwin

Wittstock, and Alfred Margul Sperber. Socialist construction has given a new artistic and ideological orientation to Romanian literature. The concepts of the working class — the leading force of Romanian society — have determined the outlook on the subjects taken up by writers, whether inspired by contemporary or past events and provided new solutions to the dramatic conflict. Literature has thus become for the masses a factor of education, of socialist consciousness, while contributing to the people's effort to build up a new social system.

## 4. Art

ROMANIA'S liberation and the process of building up a socialist society opened up new prospects for the development of art. Artists who gained recognition during the interwar period — Ressu, Iser, Catargi, Ghiață, Bunescu, Ciupe, and Maxy — now portray subjects reflecting the creative effort of people building socialism. But an impressive number of new artists are becoming known, among them Corneliu Baba, portraitist and painter of compositions of great expressive force (*Mihail Sadoveanu's portrait*, *Resting in the Field*, *The Evening Meal*); Al. Ciucurencu, still painting landscapes and still lifes but who now also engages enthusiastically in historical compositions (*Ana Ipătescu*, *The First Free May Day*); Ion Țuculescu, who used folklore motifs in his highly expressive paintings; Ion Musceleanu, a sensitive and subtle landscape and portrait painter; St. Szönyi (1919-1966), a painter of vast compositions illustrating the people's revolutionary struggle (*We Will Not Forget*), Micaela Eleutheriade, Lucia Dem. Bălăcescu, Ion Sima, Kovacs Zoltan, Vanda Sachelarie, Eugen Popa, Brăduț Covaliu, Gh. Șaru, Ion Pacea, V. Almășanu, Ion Gheorghiu, Ion Nicodim, Sabin Bălașa, Ion Bițan, Ion Sălișteanu, Gh. Iacob, C. Piliuță, Ilie Pavel, V. L. Șetran, and V. Mărgineanu.

Over the last decades the sculptor Ion Jalea has made remarkable expressive heads as well as reliefs on historical or contemporary themes (*Emperor and Proletarian*) and monuments (*Mircea the Old*); Cornel Medrea has added new busts of intellectuals and artists to his works (*Corneliu Baba, Mihail Jora*) and is moreover the sculptor responsible for the monument raised in memory of the 1907 uprising in the town of Buzău. Oscar Han has carved monumental busts of the old princes and also has Michael the Brave's equestrian statue at Alba Iulia to his credit. Gh. D. Anghel, at the zenith of his artistic form, has given works that show the balance of a classic and the enthusiasm of a romantic (*Eminescu, Bălcescu*). Romulus Ladea has done busts and monumental sculptures, all of which show a serene, warm beauty. Constantin Baraschi has modelled all types of sculptures showing manifold technical possibilities throughout. Ion Irimescu is master of the art of portraiture in his sculptures (*Ion Jalea, G. Oprescu*), as well as of composition *(Lupeni 1929);* Boris Caragea evokes glorious moments of Romanian contemporary history with great mastery (*Victory*) and moreover has a monumental statue of Lenin to his credit. Mac Constantinescu does decorative sculpture, especially reliefs for exterior decoration. Ion Vlasiu draws inspiration from folk art and has also produced a monument dedicated to Horia, Cloşca and Crişan.

Geza Vida, mostly a woodcarver (*Ouaş Dance*), shows concentrated expressiveness in his characters. He is also the sculptor of the monument to the *Romanian soldier* at Careii Mari and of the monument at Moisei. Other important representatives of Romanian contemporary sculpture include: Jenö Szervatiusz, I. Fekete, Z. Băicoianu, I. Oniţă, O. Maitec, P. Vasilescu, P. Balogh, Gh. Apostu, and Gh. Iliescu-Călineşti.

The achievements of Romanian draftsmanship have been no less remarkable since August 23, 1944. A galaxy of gifted artists have outstanding works to their credit in the field of posters, political cartoons, illustration, and easel drawings. V. Dobrian is noteworthy for his most suggestive color engravings. Ligia Macovei, is a painter and designer of great subtlety, and Gy. Szabo Bela is a fine woodcarver. Mariana Petraşcu is an exhuberant water colorist and engraver whose subjects illustrate folklore and industry. V. Kazar gives a faithful picture of contemporary life in a most compact style, and Paul Erdös is remarkable for his expressive portraits and his fine sense of decoration. Other talented artists include G. Ivancenco, Fred Mikos, Octav Grigorescu (a young draftsman and engraver of rare sensitivity), Marcel Chirnoagă, and Benedict Gănescu. In poster painting, I. Molnar and Petre Grant, one of the pioneers in this type of art, have made their mark. In book illustration Ligia Macovei, Florica Cordescu (1914-1965), and Val. Munteanu have also done well.

The construction of great architectural and urban ensembles has favored the development of monumental art. The paintings and mosaics that decorate many buildings — those for which St. Constantinescu and Gh. Popescu are responsible — are achievements to be followed by others. Valuable artists such as Aurelia Ghiață, P. Mateescu, M. Podeanu, and Gr. Stoichiță work in the field of decorative and applied art.

The study of the history of arts has also made good progress in the last decades. Alongside G. Oprescu, Member of the Academy, and Professor V. Vătășianu, other writers who have contributed creditably to the history of arts and to art criticism are Eugen Schileru, Petru Comarnescu, Ion Frunzetti, Mircea Popescu, Dan Hăulică, Remus Niculescu, and Radu Bogdan.

Culture is also promoted among the people, by extensive artistic and educational activities offered by cultural establishments — cultural clubs, town and country libraries, and museums — with many means of imparting a multilateral education and of satisfying the spiritual requirements of the masses. In Romania in 1972 there were 240 houses of culture and 7,800 cultural clubs, which organized over 600,000 artistic events for audiences totalling up over 55,500,000. Such events consisted of lectures and talks on political and scientific subjects, encounters with scientists, and temporary exhibitions which enable the working people to keep abreast of the basic problems of contemporary society and of the development of science and art.

Science and culture are also spread by the people's universities, of which there are 64 in the country, with 45,000 people attending them. The people's universities organize cycles of lectures delivered by highly qualified people. The subjects taken up are the latest investigations in the various fields of science, as well as the great achievements of world culture.

Publishing activities have assumed proportions without precedent, reflecting the upsurge of socialist culture and its mass character. In 1972 some 72,229,000 books and pamphlets were published so that the widest sections of the Romanian people and of the co-inhabiting nationalities should be informed of the scientific concepts of the world and society and on the achievements in science, literature, and art.

The movement of amateur artists, proving beyond doubt the talent of Romanian people, is also an efficient means of spreading culture and education among the masses. Nearly 75,000 shows were given annually by amateur musical and dance groups. Musical and choreographic performances, promenade and other entertainments amounted to 25,400, and there were 32,800 concerts, with vocalists, instrumentalists, and dancers. The fourth folk-art exhibition was also well attended, 23,000 amateur artists exhibiting 55,000 objects amid general appreciation. In order to train the many gifted young people, 26 folk-art schools have been opened, and these are attended by 11,800 pupils. The Party and the state pay every attention to mass cultural and artistic activities and provide generously for their betterment.

The Romanian cinema, which had some valuable achievements to its credit during the interwar period, has only really asserted itself during the years of the socialist system. In 1972 the Romanian cinema studios with their modern installations produced 19 feature films and 163 documentaries, some of which were awarded prizes at international competitions.

Romanian musical creation after World War II has been greatly diversified especially after 1960. This is due to the deep-going changes undergone by Romania's cultural life as well as by contemporary culture and art in general. A new generation of musicians has emerged alongside the composers of the interwar period — M. Jora, M. Andricu, M. Negrea, T. Brediceanu, P. Constantinescu, and S. Drăgoi — and those who reached maturity in the years after liberation, Gh. Dumitrescu, I. Dumitrescu, T. Ciortea, L. Feldman, S. Toduță, A. Mendelsohn, and Zeno Vancea. A salient trait of the latter composers, as also of the younger generation, is their creative use of traditional methods, especially of folk particularities and values. The younger generation of musicians includes: T. Olah, A. Stroe, A. Vieru, Th. Grigoriu, D. Popovici, Șt. Niculescu, W. Berger, P. Bentoiu, M. Istrate, M. Marbé, A. Rațiu, C. Țăranu, G. Costinescu, A. Hrisanide, and L. Glodeanu.

The latest trends are followed by musicians such as L. Mețianu, C. Miereanu, C. Cezar, M. Mitrea-Celarianu, O. Nemescu, and

M. Moldovan, and also by composers already mentioned to whom they owe contacts with the main trends in world contemporary music. These composers have reconsidered the aesthetic and technical basis of music. Starting from the necessity of establishing essential relations between the universe of the work and the outside world, they have used various musical materials, mostly new, offering vast possibilities to musical thought, revealing as they do new properties and meanings when tonality is abolished and the primary elements emerge. The rigorous determination of the musical pattern or, on the contrary, the full freedom given to the interpreter, the categories of time and space considered in relation with perception conditions, the best use of the resources offered by electro-acoustics in producing and transforming sounds, and the "complex show" forms — with sublimated folk "models" often underlying them — all endow Romanian contemporary music with artistic originality coupled to great professional exigency. These are qualities that might ensure durable results.

# Conclusion

THIS history of the Romanian people has made it its aim to show the eventful life of this people in a single process of historical development from the first men living on the present-day territory of the Romanian state to the age of all-round development of socialist construction.

The guiding principles have been the continuity of human society in the areas along the Carpathians and the Danube, the Roman origin of the people, their ethnical unity irrespective of the artificial frontiers forced upon them by historical vicissitudes, and the struggle for social freedom and political independence.

From the first record of human life on Romania's territory down to this day, there has been uninterrupted habitation. The great migrations of the peoples never made a desert of this land, and the newcomers were assimilated by the autochthonous population.

Descendants of the Daco-Romans, the Romanians have always preserved a spiritual connection with the remainder of the Roman world even when direct contact with that world was interrupted through adverse circumstances. The Romanian people's Roman origin has always been an essential element of the people's national consciousness. "We have continued to be Romanians because we could not shed the memory of Rôme", said N. Iorga, the great historian.

The consciousness of a common Roman origin has been a factor of unity for all Romanians when they lived in separate states or under foreign rule. And however much oppressed by transient foreign domination, the Romanians kept their dignity and belief in their Roman origin.

Throughout their history, the Romanian people fought for independence and later, when the great neighboring empires in their drive for expansion imposed their domination, for the recovery of independence. It is in the course of the struggle for independence that the greatest figures of our people achieved fame: Mircea the Old, Iancu of Hunedoara, Stephen the Great, and Michael the Brave.

While fighting for independence, the Romanian people, together with the co-inhabiting nationalities, also fought for democratic *rights and freedom, for safeguarding the material and spiritual values forged by joint efforts. By their struggle the masses have written glorious pages against oppression: at Bobâlna in 1437, in the Western Mountains in 1784, in Oltenia in 1821, during the revolutionary year 1848, and also throughout Romania's territory in 1907 as well as at Lupeni in 1929, and in the Prahova Valley and in Bucharest in 1933.*

*All these forms of social and national struggle whose crowning glory was the insurrection of August 23, 1944, were raised to a higher stage in our days by the Romanian Communist Party which serves the noblest causes of our people. The Romanian people consider the Party as the safest guarantee of their centuries-old aspirations after justice and independence.*

# Bibliography

## GENERAL WORK

CONSTANTINESCU, M., C. DAICOVICIU et ST. PASCU, *Histoire de la Roumanie*, Paris, 1970.

IORGA, N., *Geschichte des rumänischen Volkes im Rahmen seiner Staatsbildungen*, vol. I—II, Gotha, 1905.

IORGA, NICOLAE, *Histoire des Roumains et de la Romanité orientale*, vol. I—X, Bucarest, 1937-1944.

IORGA, N., *La place des Roumains dans l'histoire universelle*, vol. I—III, Bucureşti, 1935-1936.

*Istoria României* (A History of Romania), I—IV, Bucureşti, 1960-1964.

*Istoria României în date* (A History of Romania in Dates), Bucureşti, 1971.

SETON-WATSON, R. W., *A History of the Roumanians from Roman Times to the Completion of Unity*, Cambridge, 1934.

XENOPOL, A. D., *Istoria Românilor din Dacia Traiană* (A History of the Romanians in Trajan's Dacia), ed. a 3-a, vol. I—XIV.

*

CĂLINESCU, G., *Istoria literaturii române de la origini pînă în prezent* (A History of Romanian Literature from its Origin to Date), Bucureşti, 1941.

*Din istoria Dobrogei* (About the History of Dobrudja), vol. I—III, Bucureşti, 1965—1972.

IORGA, N., *Istoria armatei româneşti* (The History of the Romanian Army), vol. I—III, 2nd ed., Bucureşti, 1929-1930.

IORGA, N., *Istoria bisericii româneşti şi a vieţii religioase a românilor* (The History of the Romanian Church and the Religious Life of the Romanians), 2nd ed., vol. I—II, Bucureşti, 1929-1932.

IORGA, N., *Istoria comerţului românesc* (A History of Romanian Trade), 2nd ed., vol. I—II, Bucureşti, 1937.

IORGA, N., *Istoria învăţămîntului românesc* (A History of Romanian Education), Bucureşti, 1928.

IORGA, N., *Istoria presei româneşti de la primele începuturi pînă la 1916* (A History of the Romanian Press from its Early Beginnings to 1916), Bucureşti, 1922.

*Istoria artelor plastice în România* (The History of Fine Arts in Romania) vol. I—II, Bucureşti, 1968-1970.

KIRIŢESCU, COSTIN, *Sistemul bănesc al leului şi precursorii lui* (The Monetary System of the Leu and its Predecessors), vol. I—II, Bucureşti, 1964-1967.

LUPAŞ, I., *Istoria Unirii Românilor* (The History of the Romanians Unification), 1937, Bucureşti.

PASCU ŞTEFAN, I. IONAŞCU, C. CIHODARU, GH. GEORGESCU-BUZĂU, *Istoria medie a României*, I (sec. X — sfîrşitul sec. XVI), (Romanian Mediaeval History), Bucureşti, 1966.

VĂTĂŞIANU, V., *Istoria artei feudale în ţările române*, vol. I (A History of Feudal Arts in the Romanian Countries), Bucureşti, 1959.

## ANCIENT HISTORY

BERCIU, D., *Contribuţii la problema neoliticului în România în lumina ultimelor cercetări* (Contributions to the neolithic Problem in Romania in the Light of Recent Research), Bucureşti, 1961.

DAICOVICIU, C., *La Transylvanie dans l'Antiquité*, Bucarest, 1945.

MACREA, M., *Viaţa în Dacia romană* (Life in Roman Dacia), Bucureşti, 1969.

PÂRVAN, V., *Dacia. An Outline of the Early Civilizations of the Carpatho-Danubian Countries*, Cambridge, 1928.

PĂUNESCU, A., *Evoluţia armelor şi uneltelor de piatră cioplită pe teritoriul României* (Evolution of Chipped Stone Weapons and Tools on Romania's Territory), Bucureşti, 1970.

PÂRVAN, V., *Getica, O protoistorie a Daciei* (Getica — An Early History of Dacia), Bucureşti, 1926.

PIPPIDI, D. M., *Contribuţii la istoria veche a României* (Contributions to Ancient Romanian History), 2nd ed., Bucureşti, 1969.

PIPPIDI, D. M., *I Greci nel Basso Medio dall'éta arcaica alla conquista romana*, Milano, 1971.

PROTASE, D., *Problema continuităţii în Dacia în lumina arheologiei şi numismaticei* (The Problem of Continuity in Dacia in the Light of Archeology and Numismatics), Bucureşti, 1966.

PROTASE, D., *Riturile funerare la Daci şi la Daco-romani* (Funeral Rites Among Dacians and Daco-Romans), Bucureşti, 1971.

RUSU, I. I., *Ilirii* (The Illyrians), Bucureşti, 1969.

RUSU, I. I., *Limba traco-dacilor* (The Language of the Thraco-Dacians), Bucureşti, 1967.

TUDOR, D., *Oltenia romană* (Oltenia in Roman Times), 3rd ed., București, 1968.

TUDOR, D., *Orașe, tîrguri și sate în Dacia romană* (Towns, Boroughs and Villages in Roman Dacia), București, 1968.

ZAHARIA, E., *Săpăturile de la Dridu. Contribuție la arheologia și istoria perioadei de formare a poporului român* (The Excavations at Dridu. A Contribution to the Archeology and History of the Period when the Romanian People was Formed), București, 1967.

## MEDIEVAL HISTORY

BRĂTIANU, GH. I., *Une énigme et un miracle historique; le peuple Roumain*, Bucarest, 1937.

CONSTANTINIU, FLORIN, *Relațiile agrare din Țara Românească în secolul al XVIII-lea* (Agrarian Relations in Wallachia in the 18th Century), București, 1972.

CORFUS, I., *Agricultura Țării Românești în prima jumătate a secolului al XIX-lea*, (Agriculture in Wallachia in the First Half of the 19th Century), București, 1969.

*Cultura moldovenească în epoca lui Ștefan cel Mare* (Moldavian Culture in the Age of Stephen the Great), București, 1964.

GIURESCU, C., *Studii de istorie socială* (Studies of Social History), București, 1943.

IORGA, N., *Byzance après Byzance*, Bucarest, 1971.

MIHORDEA, V., *Relațiile agrare din secolul al XVIII-lea în Moldova* (Agrarian Relations in Moldavia in the 18th Century), București, 1968.

NISTOR, I. I., *Handel und Wandel in der Moldau bis zum Ende des XVI. Jahrhunderts, nach den Quellen dargestellt*, Cernăuți, 1917.

NISTOR, I. I., *Die Auswärtigen Handelsbeziehungen der Moldau im XIV, XV und XVI Jahrhundert, nach Quellen dargestellt*, Gotha, 1911.

ONCIUL, D., *Scrieri istorice* (Historical Essays), vol. I—II, București, 1968.

PANAITESCU, P. P., *Introducere la istoria culturii românești* (An Introduction to the History of Romanian Culture), București, 1969.

PANAITESCU, P. P., *Mircea cel Bătrîn* (Mircea the Old), București, 1944.

PANAITESCU, P. P., *Mihai Viteazul* (Michael the Brave), București, 1936.

PAPACOSTEA, Ș., *Oltenia sub stăpînirea austriacă* (1718-1739). (Oltenia under Austrian Rule), București, 1971.

PASCU, ST., *Voievodatul Transilvaniei* (The Principality of Transylvania), vol. I, Cluj, 1971.

POPA, R., *Ţara Maramureşului în veacul al XIV-lea* (The Maramureş Country in the 14th Century), Bucureşti, 1970.

PRODAN, D., *Iobăgia în Transilvania în sec. al XVI-lea* (Serfdom in Transylvania in the 16th Century), vol. I—III, 1967-1968.

PRODAN, D., *Supplex Libellus Valachorum*, Bucureşti, 1967.

STAHL, H. H., *Les anciennes communautés villageoises roumaines. Asservissement et pénétration capitaliste*, Bucarest, 1969.

STOICESCU, N., *Sfatul domnesc şi marii dregători din Ţara Românească şi Moldova* (The Prince's Council and the Great Dignitaires in Wallachia and Moldavia), Bucureşti, 1968.

ŞTEFĂNESCU, ŞT., *Bănia în Ţara Românească* (The Title of Ban [Governor] in Wallachia), Bucureşti, 1965.

VIRTOSU, E., *Titulatura domnilor şi asocierea la domnie în Ţara Românească şi Moldova* (The Titles of the Ruling Princes and Association to the Ruling of the Country in Wallachia and Moldavia), Bucureşti, 1960.

## MODERN HISTORY

ADANILOAIE N. şi D. BERINDEI, *Reforma agrară din 1864* (The 1864 Land Reform), Bucureşti, 1967.

BODEA, C., *The Roumanian Struggle for Unification 1834-1849*, Bucureşti, 1970.

COPOIU, N., *Refacerea Partidului Social-Democrat din România (1910-1911)*, (Reinstatement of the Social Democratic Party in Romania (1910-1911), Bucureşti, 1966.

DEAC, A., *Internaţionala I şi România* (The First International and Romania), Bucureşti, 1964.

EAST, W. S., *The Union of Moldavia and Wallachia, 1859*, Cambridge, 1929.

GEORGESCU, TITU, *De la revoluţionarii democraţi la făurarii P.C.R.* (From the Democratic Revolutionaries to the Creators of the Romanian Communist Party), Bucureşti, 1971.

HITCHINS, K., *The Rumanian National Movement in Transylvania* (1780-1849), Cambridge, 1969.

KIRIŢESCU, C., *Istoria războiului pentru întregirea României, 1916-1919* (The History of the War for Romania's Unification, 1916-1919), 2nd ed., vols I—III, Bucureşti.

LIVEANU, V., M. RUSENESCU, TR. LUNGU, I. KOVÁCS, V. BOGZA *Relații agrare și mișcări țărănești în România între 1908-1921* (Agrarian Relations and Peasant Uprisings in Romania between 1908 and 1921), București, 1967.

LUNGU, Tr., *Viața politică în România la sfîrșitul secolului al XIX-lea (1888-1899)* (Political Life in Romania at the Close of the 19th Century (1888-1899), București, 1967.

OȚETEA, A., *Tudor Vladimirescu și revoluția din 1821* (Tudor Vladimirescu and the Revolution of 1821), București, 1971.

OȚETEA, A. și I. POPESCU-PUȚURI, *Marea răscoală a țăranilor din 1907* (The Great Peasant Uprising of 1907), București, 1967.

POPESCU-PUȚURI, I. (Redactor responsabil), N. GOLDBERGHER, A. DEAC, D. HUREZEANU, *Mișcarea muncitorească din România 1893-1900* (The Working Class Movement in Romania), București, 1965.

RIKER, W., *The Making of Roumania*, Oxford, 1931.

STAN, A., *Le problème agraire pendant la révolution du 1848 en Valachie*, București, 1971.

*Studii privind Unirea Principatelor* (Essays on the Union of the Romanian Principalities), București, 1960.

ZANE, G., *Le mouvement révolutionnaire de 1840. Prélude de la révolution roumaine de 1848*, Bucarest, 1964.

ION POPESCU-PUȚURI, AUGUSTIN DEAC, *Unirea Transilvaniei cu România. 1918* (The Union of Transylvania and Romania. 1918), București, 1972 2nd ed.

## CONTEMPORARY HISTORY

ANESCU, V., *Efortul economic al poporului român în războiul antihitlerist*, (The Economic Effort of the Romanian People in the Anti-Nazi War), București 1964.

CEAUȘESCU, ILIE, *P.C.R., stegarul luptelor revoluționare din anii 1929-1933* (The Romanian Communist Party, the Standard-Bearer of the Revolutionary struggle of 1929-1933), București, 1971.

CAMPUS, ELIZA, *Mica înțelegere* (The Little Entente), București, 1968.

CONSTANTINESCU, M., E. CIMPONERIU, V. LIVEANU, M. RUSENESCU, I. CHIPER, *Études d'histoire contemporaine de la Roumanie*, Bucarest, 1970.

FĂTU, M., *Din istoria politică a României contemporane* (On the Political History of Contemporary Romania), București, 1968.

IONIȚĂ, GH., *Pentru un front popular antifascist în România* (For an Anti-Fascist People's Front in Romania), București, 1971.

MATEI, GHEORGHE, *La Roumanie et les problèmes du désarmement, 1919-1934*, București, 1970.

OPREA, ION, *Nicolae Titulescu*, București, 1967.

*P.C.R. în viața social-politică a României. 1921-1944* (The Romanian Communist Party in Romania's Socio-Political Life. 1921-1944), București, 1971.

PETRIC, A., GH. ȚUȚUI, *L'instauration et la consolidation du régime démocratique populaire en Roumanie*, Bucarest, 1964.

POPESCU-PUȚURI, I. și A. DEAC (redactori), *Crearea Partidului Comunist Român, mai 1921* (The Creation of the Romanian Communist Party, May 1921), București, 1971.

POPIȘTEANU, C., *România și Antanta Balcanică* (Romania and the Balkan Entente), București, 1968.

*România în războiul antihitlerist. 23 august 1944 — 9 mai 1945* (Romania in the Anti-Nazi War. 23 August 1944-9 May 1945), București, 1966.

SAVU, AL., *Dictatura regală (1938-1940)* (The Royal Dictatorship), București, 1970.

STĂNESCU, M., *Mișcarea muncitorească din România în anii 1921-1924* (The Working Class Movement in Romania over 1921-1924), București, 1971.

*Studii privind politica externă a României (1919-1939)* [Studies on Romania's Foreign Policy (1919-1939)], București, 1969.

ȚUȚUI, GH. și A. PETRIC, *Frontul unic muncitoresc în România* (The United Worker's Front in Romania), București, 1971.

ZAHARIA, GH.(coordonator), I. ALEXANDRESCU, M. FĂTU, P. NICHITA, C. OLTEANU, GH. ȚUȚUI, V. ZAHARESCU, *România în anii revoluției democrat-populare, 1944-1947* (Romania in the Years of the Democratic Popular Revolution, 1944-1947), București, 1971.

# List of Illustrations

## COLOR

## BLACK AND WHITE

31 *The Battle of Tîrgovişte (1595)*

32 *Sinan Pasha withdrawing across the Danube at Giurgiu after his defeat at Tîrgovişte (October, 1595).* Copperplate from *Pannoniae historia chronologica* by Theodore De Bry, Frankfurt am Main, 1596

33 *The Battle of Goräsläu with the trophies taken during the battle (1601). In the lower register, the delegations sent by Michael the Brave and Giorgio Basta to Prague with the 110 banners that had been conquered.* Copperplate from *Annales Ferdinandi* by Khevenhiller, vol. V, Leipzig, 1722, p. 2419

34 *Assassination of Michael the Brave (August 19, 1601).* Copperplate from *Historische Chronica* by Johann Gottfried, Frankfurt am Main, 1642, p. 946

35 *Matei Basarab. Contemporary copperplate by Marco Boschini, Venice* (Library of the Academy of the S. R. of Romania. Print Cabinet)

36 *Vasile Lupu. Copperplate by Willan Hondius after Abraham van Westereldt, 1651* (Library of the Academy of the S. R. of Romania. Print Cabinet)

37 *High Steward Constantine Cantacuzino.* Detail from votive painting at Hurez Monastery

38 *The Princely Church at Curtea de Argeş*

39 *The Three Hierarchs' Church at Jassy*

40 *Brâncoveanu's Palace at Mogoşoaia*

41 *George Rakoczy II. Contemporary engraving, anonymous* (Library of the Academy of the S. R. of Romania. Print Cabinet)

42 *Mihnea III. Copperplate by Elias Widemann, 1651* (Library of the Academy of the S. R. of Romania. Print Cabinet)

43 *Constantine Brâncoveanu and his four sons.* Copperplate by Alessandro dalla Via in Anton Maria Del Chiaro, *Istoria delle Moderne rivoluzioni della Vallahia,* Venice, 1718

44 *Demetrius Cantemir. Copperplate by Christian Fritsch 1745* (Library of the Academy of the S. R. of Romania. Print Cabinet)

45 *Nicholas Mavrocordat.* Engraving by Johann Georg Wolfgang, published as frontispiece to the second edition of Nicholas Mavrocordat's Work: *On Debts* (Liber de officiis), Leipzig, 1722 (Library of the Academy of the S.R. of Romania)

46 *Alexander Ypsilanti. Contemporary engraving, anonymous* (Library of the Academy of the S. R. of Romania. Print Cabinet)

47 *Constantine Mavrocordat.* Copperplate by Georg Friedrich Schmidt after Jean Etienne Liotard

48 *Horea, Cloşca and Crişan. Portraits painted by Johann Martin Stock in the Alba Iulia prison, 1784* (Bruckenthal Museum, Sibiu)

61 *The Battle of Dealul Spirei (September 13-25, 1848)*. Made after the information provided by Major Pavel Zăgănescu, commander of the firebridge. Lithograph (Library of the Academy of the S. R. of Romania)

62 *Eftimie Murgu*

63 *Avram Iancu. Painting by Barbu Iscovescu* (Fine Arts Museum of the S. R. of Romania)

64 *Revolutionary leaders of the Transylvanian Romanians (1848-1849)*. Lithograph made on the initiative of the Revolutionary Committee who took refuge in Paris, after drawings by Barbu Iscovescu. (Bruckenthal Museum, Sibiu)

65 *The Règlement Organique and the Almanac of the Nobility are hanged*. Cartoon lithographed in Paris by François Grenier at the request of the Romanian Revolutionary Committee in France, who had taken refuge there after the defeat of the revolution. (Library of the Academy of the S. R. of Romania. Print Cabinet)

66 *General Gheorghe Magheru*. Lithograph by Petru Mateescu. (Library of the Academy of the S. R. of Romania. Print Cabinet)

67 *Simion Bărnuțiu*. Lithograph made in E. Sieger's shop in Vienna and published as a frontispiece to S. Bărnuțiu's *The Romanians' Public Law*, Jassy, 1867.

68 *Revolutionary Romania*. Allegorical painting by Constantin Daniel Rosenthal (Fine Arts Museum of the S. R. of Romania)

69 *Deputies to the Ad-hoc Assembly in Moldavia opened on September 22/30, 1857. Photograph*. (Library of the Academy of the S. R. of Romania. Print Cabinet)

70 *Solemn opening of Ad-hoc Assembly in Wallachia. September 30-October 12, 1857*. Lithograph by Carol Popp de Szathmari. (Library of the Academy of the S. R. of Romania. Print Cabinet)

71 *Alexandru Ioan Cuza*. Lithograph made in Paris after Carol Popp de Szathmari, 1863. (Library of the Academy of the S. R. of Romania. Print Cabinet)

72 *Prince Cuza opening the Assembly of Deputies (February 29/March 12, 1860)*. Lithograph by K. Danielis (Library of the Academy of the S. R. of Romania. Print Cabinet)

73 *Cuza's Proclamation to crop-sharers on the publication of the land law (August 14/26, 1864)*. Contemporary lithograph (Library of the Academy of the S.R. of Romania. Print Cabinet)

74 *Bucharest University founded by Prince Alexandru Ioan Cuza's Decree of July 4-16, 1864*. Detail from lithograph showing Bucharest, 1866. (Library of the Academy of the S. R. of Romania. Print Cabinet)

75 *Inauguration of the Romanian Academic Society (August 1/13, 1867)* Lithograph by Kaiser published by Iosif Vulcan as a supplement to the review *Familia (1868).* (Library of the Academy of the S. R. of Romania. Print Cabinet)

76 *Romanian deputies to the Hungarian Diet (1861): Vincenţiu Babeş, Vincenţiu Bogdan, Vasile Guteanu, Aurel Maniu, Gabriel Mihali de Apşa, F. Pascu, Giorgiu Popa de Teiuş, Ioan Popovici Deseanu, S. Popovici, Aloisiu Vlad de Sălişte.* Lithograph by Kollartz after Nicolae Popescu, published in Vienna under the heading "Romanian front-rank fighters for national equality". (Library of the S. R. of Romania. Print Cabinet)

77 *Conquest of the Griviţa Redoubt (August 30 / September 11, 1877).* Chromo-lithograph published as a supplement to the Calendar for All Romanians (1881) (Library of the Academy of the S. R. of Romania. Print Cabinet)

78 *The indicted in the Memorial Trial of 1893. In the middle Ioan Raţiu and Vasile Lucaciu.* (Library of the S.R.R. Academy. Print Cabinet)

79 *Demonstration of the Bucharest students for the signatories of the Transylvanian Memorials (1892).* Photograph. (Library of the S.R.R. Academy. Print Cabinet)

80 *Tantalus: The Workers Are Set Free (1895).* Allegorical composition published in *The New World, Scientific and Literary*

81 *Nicolae Vermont: "Ion, Ion! Why did you ask for land?"* Drawing recalling the peasant uprising of 1907, published in *Viaţa Socială (Social Life)* 1910. (Fine Arts Museum of the S.R. of Romania)

82 *Corneliu Medrea: 1907*

83 *The Mărăşeşti Mausoleum erected to the memory of the Romanian heroes fallen in battle*

84 *Transylvanian volunteers in Union Square in Jassy, June 9, 1917.* (Photograph Library of the S.R.R. Academy. Print Cabinet)

85 *The National Assembly of Alba Iulia (December, 1918).* (Photograph Library of the S.R.R. Academy. Print Cabinet)

86 *A group of worker participants in the general strike of October, 1920* (Photograph Library of I.S.I.S.P., attached to the Central Committee of the Romanian Communist Party)

87 *Creation of the Romanian Communist Party.* Facsimile from *Socialismul* on the debats of the first Congress (Photograph Library of I.S.I.S.P., Central Committee of the Romanian Communist Party)

88 *Oilfield at Moreni.* (Photograph Library of I.S.I.S.P., Central Committee of the Romanian Communist Party)

89 *The Malaxa Works.* (Photograph Library of I.S.I.S.P., Central Committee of the Romanian Communist Party)

90 *The Reşiţa Works.* (Photograph Library of I.S.I.S.P., Central Committee of the Romanian Communist Party)

91 *Workers in the courtyard of the Griviţa shops during the strike of February 15-16, 1933.* (Photograph Library of I.S.I.S.P., Central Committee of the Romanian Communist Party)

92 *Postcard published in France by the French section of the International Red Aid and widely distributed in many countries of the world by workers' organizations in sympathy with the struggle of the Romanian Proletariat.* (Instead of Dumitru Gh. Petrescu, the printed text has Gheorghe Petrescu and instead of Gheorghe Vasilichi, Ghitaal Vasilighiei)

93 *Peasant Demonstration (1935).* (Photograph Library of I.S.I.S.P., Central Committee of the Romanian Communist Party)

94 *Anti-fascist demonstration in Bucharest (1936).* (Photograph Library of I.S.I.S.P., Central Committee of the Romanian Communist Party)

95 *Nicolae Iorga*

96 *Nicolae Titulescu*

97 *Demonstration at Cluj against the Vienna Diktat (1940).* (Photograph Library of I.S.I.S.P., Central Committee of the Romanian Communist Party)

98 *Program of the Romanian Communist Party, September 6, 1941.* (Photograph Library of I.S.I.S.P., Central Committee of the Romanian Communist Party)

99 *Manifesto of the United Workers' Front of May 1, 1944.* (Photograph Library of I.S.I.S.P., Central Committee of the Romanian Communist Party)

100 *The National Democratic Bloc is formed (June, 1944).* (Photograph Library of I.S.I.S.P., Central Committee of the Romanian Communist Party)

101 *First legal issue of the România Liberă (Free Romania), Facsimile, August 24, 1944.* (Photograph Library of I.S.I.S.P., Central Committee of the Romanian Communist Party)

102 *Romanian artillery participating in the fighting in Bucharest streets in August, 1944* (Photograph Library of I.S.I.S.P., Central Committee of the Romanian Communist Party)

103 *Nazi officers captured in Bucharest during the Insurrection* (Photograph Library of I.S.I.S.P., Central Committee of the Romanian Communist Party)

104 *Romanian-Soviet military cooperation in Transylvania*

131 *Ion Andreescu: Winter at Barbizon* (The Art Museum of the S. R. of Romania)

132 *Dimitrie Paciurea: The Giant* (Bucharest, Liberty Park)

133 *Ştefan Luchian: Sharing the Maize* (The Art Museum of the S. R. of Romania)

134 *Camil Ressu: Mowers at Rest* (The Art Museum of the S.R. of Romania)

135 *Dimitrie Ghiaţă: Mountain Flowers* (The Art Museum of the S.R. of Romania)

136 *Gheorghe Petraşcu: At Home* (Fine Arts Museum of the S.R. of Romania)

137 *Constantin Brâncuşi: Gate of the Kiss* (Tîrgu Jiu)

138 *Nicolae Tonitza: December 13, 1918*

139 *Gheorghe Ţuculescu: Women Harvesting* (Fine Arts Museum of the S.R. of Romania)

140 *Vida Geza: Monument to soldiers at Careii Mari*

141 *Corneliu Baba: Peasants in the Field* (Fine Arts Museum of the S.R. of Romania)

142 *Camil Petrescu* (Library of the S.R.R. Academy. Print Cabinet)

143 *Mihail Sadoveanu* (Library of the S.R.R. Academy. Print Cabinet)

144 *Tudor Arghezi* (Library of the S.R.R. Academy. Print Cabinet)

ILLUSTRATIONS BY E. NICULESCU AND TH. POPESCU

# Brief Biographies
## of the Major Contributors

ANDREI OȚETEA. Born in 1894. Graduated from a secondary school in Brașov. B. A. and D. Litt. of the University of Paris (Sorbonne). Professor at University of Iași (Jassy) and at University of Bucharest, 1927-64. Rector of University of Iași, 1945-47. Vice-Rector of University of Bucharest, 1947-48. Director of the Nicolae Iorga Institute of History, 1948 and 1956-71. Vice President of the Academy of the Latin World since 1967. Chairman of the UNESCO National Council, 1966-71. Publications: *François Guichardin — La vie publique et sa pensée politique*, Ed. Picart, Paris, 1926; *Francesco Guicciardini à Bartolomeo l'Anfrédini*, Aquilla, 1927; *Contribution à la question d'Orient, 1746-1821*, 1930; *The Renaissance and the Reformation*, Fundația Regală pentru Literatură și Artă, Bucharest, 1941; *Tudor Vladimirescu and the Haeteria Movement in Wallachia in 1821*, Institut d'Etudes et Recherches Balkaniques, série historique, Bucharest, 1945, nr. 5; *Karl-Marx — Observations on the Romanians*, Editura Academiei R.P.R., Bucharest, 1964; *The Renaissance*, Editura Științifică, Bucharest, 1964. *Tudor Vladimirescu and the Revolution of 1821*, Editura Științifică, 1971.

ION POPESCU-PUȚURI. Born in 1906. Director of the Institute of Historical and Socio-Political Studies since 1966. Member of the Academy of Social and Political Sciences of the Socialist Republic of Romania since 1970. Publications: *Documents on the History of the Working Class and the Socialist Movement in Romania* (5 vols.); *Creation of the Romanian Communist Party*, Editura Științifică, Bucharest 1971; *Revolutionary Standard-Bearers*, Editura Științifică, Bucharest, 1971; *The Strikes of February 1933*; *The Paris Commune*, Editura Politică, Bucharest, 1971 etc.

ION NESTOR. Born in 1905. B.A., in classical philology, University of Bucharest (1926). Studied archaeology at the Universities of Berlin and Marburg (1927-32). Doctor of Archaeology, University of Marburg (1932). Curator of the National Antiquities Museum (1932-45). Professor of Archaeology and Prehistory, Department of History, University of Bucharest (1945—). Head of Department of the Institute of Archaeology of the Academy S.R.R. since 1956. Corresponding member of the Academy S.R.R. since 1955. Member of the Academy of Social and Political Sciences since 1970. Publications: *Nachtrag zu Cerna-Vodă*, in "Prähistorische Zeitschrift", Berlin, 1928; *Zur*

*Chronologie der Rumänischen Steinkupferzeit*, in "Prähistorische Zeitschrift", Berlin, 1928; *Fouilles de Glina*, in "Dacia", Recherches et Découvertes archéologiques en Roumanie, Bucharest, 1932; *Der Stand der Vorgeschichts-Forschung in Rumänien*, in 22. Bericht der römisch-germanischen Kommission, Frankfurt am Main, 1932; *New Problems concerning the Neolithic Age in the People's Republic of Romania*, in "Studii şi Cercetări de Istorie veche", Bucharest, 1950; *The Culture of Linear Ceramics in Moldavia*, in "Studii şi Cercetări de Istorie veche", Bucharest, 1951; *The Slavs on the Territory of the People's Republic of Romania according to Archaeological Documents*, in "Studii şi Cercetări de Istorie veche", 1959; *Contributions archéologiques au problème des Proto-Roumains. La civilisation de Dridu*, in "Dacia", Revue d'archéologie et d'histoire ancienne, nouvelle série, Bucharest, 1958; *Die Menschliche Gesellschaft an der Untern-Donau in Vor-und Nach-Römischer Zeit*, in "Actes du XI-e Congrès International des Sciences Historiques", Stockholm, 1960; *The People's Migration*, in "Istoria României", vol. I, Editura Academiei R.P.R., Bucharest, 1960; *La pénétration des slaves dans la péninsule balkanique et la Grèce continentale*, in "Revue des Etudes Sud-Est-Européennes", Bucharest, 1963; *Les données archéologiques et le problème de la formation du peuple roumain*, in "Revue Roumaine d'Histoire", Bucharest, 1964; *Sur la période de transition du néolithique à l'age du bronze dans l'aire des civilisations de Cucuteni et de Gumelniţa*, in "Dacia", Revue d'archéologie et d'histoire ancienne, nouvelle série, Bucharest, 1968, XII; *La fin du monde ancien et les "barbares"*, in "Documents du XIII-e Congrès International des Sciences Historiques", Moscou, 1970.

MIHAI BERZA. Born in 1907. Graduate of the Department of Arts and Philosophy, University of Iaşi (Jassy), concentrating in History (1926-29). Member of the Romanian School in Rome (1931-33). Librarian of the same school (1933-34) and Secretary of the school (1936-38). Audit student at École pratique des Hautes Études in Paris (1933-36). D. Lit., University of Iaşi (1935). Professor and chairman, Department of History, University of Bucharest. Director of the Institute of South-East European Studies in Bucharest. Corresponding member of the Academy of the Socialist Republic of Romania. Member of the Academy of Social and Political Sciences. Chairman of the International Commission for the History of Ideas attached to A.I.E.S.E.E. Member of the Bureau of the International Committee of Historical Sciences Vice Chairman of the International Association of Byzantine Studies. Publications: *The Tribute Paid by Wallachia and Moldavia to the Porte in the 15th to 19th Centuries*, in "Studii şi Materiale de Istorie Medie" 1957; *Peasant Uprisings in the Middle Ages*, în "Revue roumaine d'histoire", 1958; *Wallachia's Material Obligations to the Porte*, in "Studii", 1958; presently Editor of "Revue des Etudes Sud-Est Européennes" (Bucharest).

VASILE MACIU. Born in 1904. Graduate, Department of Philosophy and Arts, University of Bucharest (1927). Professor of History, University of Bucharest. Corresponding member of the Academy S.R.R. Member of the Academy of Social and Political Sciences of the S.R.R. Awarded the State Prize of the People's Republic of Romania, 2nd Class (1954). Contributor to 9 volumes of documents on the War for Romania's Independence in 1877-78, and to the volumes in *History of Romania* (1964). Other publications include *Mouvement nationaux et sociaux roumains au 19ème siècle*, Editura Academiei R.S.R., Bibliotheca Historica Romaniae, 1971.

RADU VULPE. Born in 1899. B.A. in History (1924) and D. Lit. (1927), University of Bucharest. Professor of Archaeology, University of Iaşi. Head of Department at Institute of Archaeology of the Academy S.R.R., Scientific consultant at the same Institute. Member of the Honorary Committee of the International Union of Prehistoric and Proto-Historic Sciences. Corresponding member of the German Archaeological Institute. Member of the Academy of Social and Political Sciences of the S.R.R. Publications: *Gli Illiri dell' Italia Imperiale Romana*, in "Ephemeris Dacoromana", vol. III, 1925, Roma; *L'age du fer dans les régions thraces*, in "Mélanges de l'École Roumaine en France", Editions Gamber, Paris, 1929; *Piroboridava*, in "Revue Archéologique", Paris, 1931, II; *La succession des rois Odryses*, in "Histros", Bucharest, 1934, I, 2; *Histoire ancienne de la Dobroudja*, in Academia Româna, Series "Connaissance de la terre et de la pensée roumaine", "Cultura Naţională" publ., Bucharest, 1938; *Excavations at Poieneşti*, în "Materialele şi studiile arheologice", Editura Academiei R.P.R., Bucharest, 1953; *Izvoare — An Archaeological Monograph*, Editura Academiei R.P.R., Bucharest, 1957; *Le vallum de la Moldavie inférieure et le mur d'Athanarique*, Mouton Publishers, The Hague, 1957; *Les Buresalliés de Décébal*, in "Studii clasice", 1963, vol. V; *The Romans on the Lover Danube*, Editura Academiei R.S.R., 1968.

IOAN CHIPER. Born in 1936. Graduate, Department of History, University of Bucharest (1960). Chief Researcher, Nicolae Iorga Institute of History. Author of works on Romania's internal and external policies, international politics, and Romanian and foreign historiography during the 20th Century.

FLORIN CONSTANTINIU. Born in 1933. Doctor of History, University of Bucharest (1968). Chief Researcher, Nicolae Iorga Institute of History. Publications: *Agrarian Relations in Wallachia in the 18th Century*, Editura Academiei R.S.R., Bucharest, 1972 etc.

AUGUSTIN DEAC. Born in 1928. B.A. in History, University of Cluj (1954), Doctor of History, University of Cluj (1959). Professor, "Ştefan Gheorghiu" Academy. Corresponding member of the Academy of Social and Political Sciences of the S.R.R. (1970). Publications: *The Working Class Movement in Transylvania, 1890-1895*, Editura Ştiinţifică, Bucharest, 1962; *The First International and Romania*, Editura Politică, Bucharest, 1964; *The Year 1907 as Seen Abroad*, Editura Ştiinţifică, Bucharest, 1967; *Friedrich Engels and Romania*, Editura Politică, Bucharest, 1970; *Creation of the Romanian Communist Party*, Editura Ştiinţifică, Bucharest, 1971; *The Working Class and the Socialist Press in Romania, 1865-1921*, Editura Politică, Bucharest etc.

TITU GEORGESCU. Born in 1929. Graduate, Department of History, University of Bucharest. Doctor of History. Corresponding member of the Academy of Social and Political Sciences of the S.R.R. Publications; *Nicolae Iorga against Nazism*, Editura Ştiinţifică, Bucharest, 1966; *Anti-Nazi Intellectuals in Romanian Literature*, Editura Ştiinţifică, Bucharest, 1967; *French Testimonies to the 1848 Revolution in the Romanian Lands*, Editura Ştiinţifică, Bucharest, 1968; articles in various reviews in France, Austria, Poland, and the U.S.S.R.

GHEORGHE MATEI. Born in 1919. B.A., Department of Arts and Philosophy, University of Bucharest (1946); Doctor of History, University of Bucharest (1971). Associate Professor, Institute of International Relations (1948-50). Associate Professor, Department of History, University of Bucharest (1950-51). Chief Researcher, Institute of Historical and Socio-Political Studies (1955-71). Editor-in chief, *Analele de Istorie* (1971—  ). Publications: *The 1848 Revolution and the Peasantry*, Editura Ministerului Artelor şi Informaţiilor, 1948; *The Crisis of the Colonial System after World War II*, Editura de Stat pentru Literatură Politică, Bucharest, 1949; *International Response to the Great Peasant Uprising of 1907*, Editura de Stat, Bucharest, 1957; *Socialist Clubs in the Countryside in 1898-99*, Editura Ştiinţifică, Bucharest, 1968; *Disarmament as Viewed as Part of International Problems and Romania's Attitude, 1918-34*, Editura Academiei R.S.R., Bucharest, 1971; *La Roumanie et les problèmes du désarmement, 1919-34*, Editura Academiei R.S.R., Bucharest, 1971 etc.

REMUS NICULESCU. Born in 1927. Graduate, University of Bucharest. Art historian. Keeper of the Prints Collection of the Romanian Academy (1951-1959). Head, European Art Department of the Institute of the History of Arts, Bucharest. Publications: *G. Asachi and the Beginnings of Lithography in Moldavia*, in "Studii şi Cercetări de Bibliologie", I, 1955; *N. Grigorescu* (in collab. with G. Oprescu), 2 vols, Editura Meridiane, 1961-1962; *Eustatie Altini*, în "Studii şi Cercetări de istoria Artei", XII, 1965, 1; *Bourdelle et Anastase Simu*, in "Revue Roumaine d'Histoire de l'Art", III, 1966; *Georges de Bellio, l'ami des impressionistes*, in "Paragone", Florence, 1970; *Romanian Writers and French Caricaturists between 1835 and 1860*, în "Studii şi Cercetări de istoria artei", XVIII, 1971, 2; *Daumier's Contemporaries*, 1971 etc.

ŞERBAN PAPACOSTEA. Born in 1928. Doctor of History, University of Bucharest (1968). Head, World History Department, Nicolae Iorga Institute of History. Publications: *Oltenia under Austrian Rule*, Editura Academiei R.S.R. Bucarest, 1971; *Contributions to the Problem of Agrarian Relations in the First Half of the 18th Century in Wallachia*, in "Studii şi materiale de istoria medie", vol. I, 1959 etc.

ŞTEFAN ŞTEFĂNESCU. Born in 1929. Doctor of History, University of Bucharest (1957). Researcher, Nicolae Iorga Institute of History (1952-60). Head of Mediaeval History Department of Institute (1960-66), Deputy Director of the Institute (1966-70), Director (1970-). Member of the Academy of Social and Political Sciences of the S.R.R.; Chairman of the Department of History and Archaeology of the Academy (1970). Professor of Ancient and Mediaeval History, University of Bucharest (1970-). Publications: *Evolution of Feudal Property in Wallachia to the 17th Century*, in "Studii", XI, 1 1958; Vol. II of *History of Romania*, Editura Academiei R.P.R., 1962; *Byzanz und die Dobrudscha in der Zweiten Helfte des 14. Jahrhunderts*, in "Byzantinische Beiträge", Akademie-Verlag Berlin, 1964; *Oltenian Governors in Wallachia*, Editura Ştiinţifică, Bucharest, 1965; *Michel le Brave-Restitutor Daciae*, în "Revue roumaine d'histoire", 1968; *Wallachia from Basarab I to Michael the Brave*, Editura Academiei R.S.R., Bucharest, 1970; *From the History of Dobrudja*, Editura Academiei R.S.R., Bucharest, vol. III, 1971; *Documenta Romaniae Historica*, vol. II, Editura Academiei R.S.R., Bucharest, 1972 etc. Member of La commission nternationale pour l'histoire des Assemblées d'Etat. Awarded the Nicolae iBălcescu Prize of the Academy S.R.R.

PRINITED IN ROMANIA